Challenging the Gifted

SERVING SPECIAL POPULATIONS SERIES

Challenging the Gifted

Curriculum Enrichment and Acceleration Models

Corinne P. Clendening
and
Ruth Ann Davies

R. R. BOWKER COMPANY
New York and London, 1983

Corinne P. Clendening and Ruth Ann Davies bring to the
writing of this book a total of 47 years of experience in
developing curricular programs for the gifted and in
teaching the gifted. Their experience covers the whole
spectrum—elementary, secondary, and graduate levels.
Since the beginning of the 1970s, Clendening has been
directly involved in gifted education, first working with
teachers and students in advanced placement and secondary
honors courses in each academic area, and then serving as
coordinator of and teacher in the North Hills School
District Elementary Gifted Program in Pittsburgh.
For 35 years Davies has designed and supervised
enrichment-acceleration programs for the gifted, grades
K–12. She has taught graduate level courses for teachers of
the gifted at the University of Pittsburgh. Clendening and
Davies have conducted workshops and served as
consultants and speakers on gifted education in the United
States and Canada. Both authors have written and
published in the field of education.

Published by R. R. Bowker Company
1180 Avenue of the Americas, New York, NY 10036
Copyright © 1983 by Xerox Corporation
All rights reserved
Printed and bound in the United States of America

Library of Congress Cataloging in Publication Data

Clendening, Corinne P.
  Challenging the gifted.

  (Serving special populations series)
  Bibliography: p.
  Includes index.
  1. Gifted Children—Education—Curriculum—
Handbooks, manuals, etc. 2. Curriculum enrichment—
Handbooks, manuals, etc. 3. Educational acceleration—
Handbooks, manuals, etc. I. Davies, Ruth Ann,
1915–   . II. Title. III. Series.
LC3993.C558   1983   371.95′3   82-20777
ISBN 0-8352-1682-9

To Our Families
with Appreciation and Affection

Contents

EXAMPLES

HANDOUTS

LEARNING GUIDES

STUDY CENTER BIBLIOGRAPHIES

Preface

With the publication of *Creating Programs for the Gifted* (Bowker, 1980), the authors designed a guide to give practical, workable answers for teachers, librarians, administrators, school board members, and parents involved either in initiating new programs or in strengthening existing programs for the gifted and talented. It was an ambitious undertaking that concerned itself with providing answers to such basic and persistent questions as: Who are the gifted? Why should we be particularly concerned about them? It also offered model programs to provide appropriate learning experiences for gifted students.

With the publication of *Challenging the Gifted*, the authors have assumed an even more ambitious—and challenging—undertaking, for here is a comprehensive source book that offers a wide selection of alternative methods of programming for the gifted. The model programs included in this guide translate the theory of excellence in gifted education into actuality.

Part I of *Challenging the Gifted* covers the basics of program design and program implementation and contains a bibliography. Part II, the heart of this source book, contains 15 model programs, grades K–12. Concluding the book are a Publisher/Producer/Distributor Directory and an Index.

Each of the model programs selected for inclusion in *Challenging the Gifted* has been carefully designed to provide information coverage far *beyond* that required by any *one* school, by any *one* teacher, or by any *one* class. Each model contains comprehensive content coverage, depth and breadth of skill integration, diversity of creative activities, variety of approaches, and a wealth of support media; so much so that all who are involved in educating the gifted—administrators, supervisors, teachers—can readily find viable program elements uniquely appropriate for and adaptable to their own program design and implementation needs.

Winnowed from a vast reservoir of fine instructional materials, more than 7,400 items of print and nonprint media—books, documents, programmed instructional guides, periodicals, art prints, audio modules, cassette and disc recordings, charts and graphs, computer programs, filmstrips, maps, microfiche and microfilm, motion pictures, posters, promotional materials, resource kits, study prints, transparencies—are highlighted in Parts I and II. Care has been taken to select for inclusion *only* the very best of the best. Each item recommended in this book represents a sound investment in instructional support.

Consultants will bring an added dimension to this book. Jean Gatling Farr and John Grossi will explore with the reader questions pertaining to program development, implementation, staffing, in-service, funding, resources, facilities, and evaluations. Farr may be contacted at 580 Newtown Road, Warminster, PA 18974 (215-675-7136). Grossi may be contacted at the Council for Exceptional Children, 1920 Association Drive, Reston, VA 22091 (800-336-3728). The authors, Corinne P. Clendening and Ruth Ann Davies, can be contacted at 156 McIntyre Road, Pittsburgh, PA 15237 (412-364-4585).

Part I

Program Design and Implementation

Chapter 1

Basics of Program Design

Gifted and talented children are those identified by professionally qualified persons who, by virtue of outstanding abilities, are capable of high performance. These are children who require differentiated educational programs and/or services beyond those normally provided by the regular school program in order to realize their contribution to self and society.

*Sidney P. Marland, U.S. Commissioner of Education**

To be dynamically effective, a *differentiated* educational program for the gifted must be scientifically designed and humanely and creatively implemented. Educational excellence is never the result of chance or whim. A scientifically designed program synthesizes philosophy and theory of program excellence, research recommendations, and educational standards into (1) viable program goals, (2) curriculum content, (3) teaching strategies, and (4) learning projects. The hallmarks of excellence—continuity, unity, balance, and harmony—are the structural framework supporting and unifying a differentiated program for the gifted, kindergarten through high school.[†]

PROGRAM GOALS

In the design of any program, there are certain goals to be met, or ideals to be achieved.[1] They are:

1. *Superior achievement.* Gifted and talented youngsters should have ample opportunities to realize their potential to the fullest extent possible.

---

*Sidney P. Marland, Jr., *Education of the Gifted and Talented,* vol. 1, Report to the Congress of the United States by the U.S. Commissioner of Education (Washington, D.C.: Government Printing Office, 1972), p. 25.

[†]For expanded and detailed development of philosophy, theory, research, standards, and learning projects pertaining to differentiated programs for the gifted, see Corinne P. Clendening and Ruth Ann Davies, *Creating Programs for the Gifted: A Guide for Teachers, Librarians, and Students,* Serving Special Populations series (New York: R. R. Bowker, 1980).

Note: A Bibliography for Part I is on pp. 19–20.

3

2. *Self-directedness.* The freedom, responsibility, and capability to manage one's time is an important ingredient of self-fulfillment and productivity.
3. *Acceptance and responsibility.* The leadership capabilities of gifted and talented pupils imply increased responsibilities to self, home, and society.
4. *Creative thinking and expression.* This goal seeks the development of creativity in a rich variety of constructive ways.
5. *Aesthetic awareness.* This goal focuses on the development of positive feelings toward things of beauty and consequence.
6. *Acceptance of divergent views.* This goal views tolerance for divergent thought as an aid to learning.
7. *Pursuit of alternative solutions.* This focus is on development of patterns of thinking that seek alternate solutions to problems prior to action. It seeks the development of a capacity for reasoning and effective decision making.
8. *Commitment to inquiry.* Stress is placed on the development of a pattern of thinking that continually questions, probes, tests, and investigates.
9. *Preparation for satisfying life-style and career.* The need for a gifted and talented person to enter into a career that is commensurate with his or her abilities, interests, and spiritual satisfaction is understood.

CURRICULUM ALTERNATIVES AND CONTENT

What is to be learned? What processes facilitate learning?

1. *Enrichment of content*—any learning experience that replaces, supplements, or extends instruction beyond the restrictive bonds and boundaries of course content, textbook, and classroom and that includes *depth* of understanding, *breadth* of understanding, and *relevance* to the student and to the world in which he or she lives.
2. *Acceleration*—curricular offerings, courses of study, and challenging learning experiences beyond regular grade level. Typical accelerated programs include:

> Honors courses
> Mini-courses
> Special courses, projects, or seminars
> Advanced placement
> Independent study
> Tutorials
> Continuous-progress and/or levels programs
> Subject acceleration
> Collegiate courses
> Correspondence courses
> Early college admission

3. *Grouping*—provisions that facilitate the student's access to special learning opportunities, such as:[2]

> Cluster grouping within the regular class
> Special regular or "pull-out" classes
> Part-time groups before, during, after school

Alternative schools
Resource rooms
Itinerant or resource teachers
Field learning experiences
Special summer programs

4. *Variations and adjustments to meet individual differences* (see Checklists 1 and 2 at the end of this chapter):

Individual study
Individualized Educational Program (IEP)
Special projects
Scholars' programs
Leadership experiences

5. *Difference between "provisions" and "programs":*[3]

Provisions are offered as part of the regular educational program when the gifted student is mainstreamed rather than a participant in a separate differentiated program; enrichment, acceleration, and individualization are the major provisions offered the gifted student in the regular classroom.

Programs are separate from the regular instructional program and are scientifically planned and directed toward the systematic development of long-range goals designed to develop the abilities and competencies of gifted students from the time of their identification through their graduation.

6. *Program guidelines for planning curriculum:*

Provide academically sound, open-ended, seamless curriculum responsive to individual student achievement level, capabilities, talents, concerns, interests, and aspirations.

Provide content broad enough and rich enough to match the divergently-faceted spectrum of gifted student abilities.

Provide content of significance, satisfaction, and challenge—the antithesis of "busy work" and "fun and games."[*]

Provide learning experiences at the higher levels of the cognitive domain: knowledge, comprehension, application, analysis, synthesis, and evaluation.[4]

Provide learning experiences that translate the affective domain into thought and action: receiving, responding, valuing, organization, and characterization by a value or value complex.[5]

Provide learning experiences that both evoke and nurture creativity, and also encourage the risk-taking of adventurous thinking.

Provide learning experiences that introduce, reinforce, and extend thinking-learning-communicating skills as integral components of the

---

[*]"In conducting evaluation studies, I have witnessed far too many programs for the gifted that are essentially fun-and-games activities; such activities lack continuity and show little evidence of developing in a systematic fashion the mental processes that led these children to be identified as gifted" (Joseph S. Renzulli, *The Enrichment Triad Model: A Guide for Developing Defensible Programs for the Gifted and Talented* [Mansfield Center, Conn.: Creative Learning Press, 1977], p. 6).

total teaching-learning program (see Checklist 3 at the end of this chapter).

7. *Major themes* recurring throughout the program encourage students to become:

Alive to architecture and the arts
Alive to beauty in nature
Alive to the power and beauty of language and literature
Alive to the promise of the future
Alive to the power of positive thought and action
Alive to the promise of personal excellence
Alive to the challenge of probing beyond the threshold of knowledge
Atune to the challenge and responsibility of self-actualization
Atune to the needs of fellow human beings
Atune to the global view of events, concerns, and societal needs
Aware of the inevitability of change
Aware of the tides of justice
Aware of what it really means to be an American
Aware that freedom is never secure
Aware that the past is prologue to the future
Aware that each person is answerable for his or her own actions
Aware that people do make a difference
Aware of the impact of science and technology
Aware that life on this planet is imperiled by destructive actions of human beings

STRATEGY OF STRATEGIES FROM A TO Z

"Strategies are those *carefully conceived and executed plans and methods* designed to provide differentiated programming to meet the unique needs of the gifted and in so doing maximize human development and obtain the greatest benefits from the creative, intellectual, and leadership resources of the young."[*]

What are the strategies to be followed in designing programs for the gifted?

1. Providing *orientation* experiences designed to initiate a preview and/or overview of: an instructional program, K-12; a year's program of study; a unit of study or a learning project; or an activity or field learning experience (see Checklist 4 at the end of this chapter).

2. Seizing the "teachable moment" by timing and planning activities calculated to:

Heighten anticipation and *initiate* the desire or need to know *before* a new unit or learning project is undertaken.

Motivate students to dig deeper, question vigorously differing viewpoints, pursue pertinent problems in depth, and link spin-off ideas

[*]Paul D. Plowman, *Teaching the Gifted and Talented in the Social Studies Classroom,* Teaching the Gifted and Talented in the Content Area series (Washington, D.C.: National Education Association, 1980), p. 15. Emphasis added.

into new patterns of understanding *during* the course of a unit or learning project.

Prolong and *reinvigorate* interest beyond the immediate learning experience.*

3. Planning for, recognizing, and seizing at all times the teachable moment to demonstrate the beneficence (pragmatic as well as idealistic) to be derived from employing *brainstorming,* nurturing *synergistic* cooperation, and reaping the bounty of *serendipity!*

4. Sparking, reinforcing, and nurturing creativity by enthusiastically welcoming its various facets of *imaginative, divergent,* and *adventurous* thinking.

5. Providing learning experiences that encourage the students to discover their own potential as creative human beings.

6. Providing learning experiences that give the students opportunity to share their *ideas, concerns,* and *dreams* without fear of ridicule.

7. Providing ample time for the students to *incubate* ideas.

8. Organizing classroom study centers to bring depth, breadth, relevance, and challenge as well as freshness, variety, and delight to the classroom instructional program (see Checklist 5 at the end of this chapter).

9. Bringing *depth* to the instructional program by providing learning experiences calling for: *extensive* and *intensive reading, viewing,* and *listening;* the *probing* of facts and events; the *exploration* of cause-and-effect relationships; and the *quest* for answers to provocative questions such as "then what happened?" "why did it happen?" and "what were the consequences, implications, and results?"

10. Bringing *breadth* to the instructional program by providing extensive and intensive reading, viewing, and listening experiences to extend learning beyond the usual; beyond the commonplace; and beyond the prescribed to encompass discovery of that which is significant, vital, but unsuspected.

11. Bringing *relevance* to the instructional program by providing extensive and intensive reading, viewing, and listening experiences to match abilities, needs, interests, concerns, and aspirations of the individual student as well as reflecting the contemporary world in which the student lives.

12. Promoting the school library's role and function as a *learning laboratory* rich in all types and kinds of media essential for optimum support of the educational program, and affording each student the opportunity to work intelligently, intensively, and extensively with the ideas in an environment conducive to maximum learning.

13. Recognizing, utilizing, and promoting the school librarian's role and function as a team teacher uniquely qualified and eager to facilitate any/all learning enterprise in programming for the gifted.

14. Promoting the free-flow access to and loan of *all* library resources—print, nonprint, microform, or computerized information—when, where, and as needed to facilitate learning, that is, a school district-

*Reflective of the recommendations made by E. Paul Torrance in *Creativity in the Classroom,* What Research Says to the Teacher series (Washington, D.C.: National Education Association, 1977), pp. 28–29.

wide, fully functioning, interlibrary loan system encompassing networking and data base search where possible.

15. Utilizing *professional* wisdom and expertise in designing learning programs and experiences that:*

Implement the recommendations advanced in *Education of the Gifted and Talented,* vol. 1.

Implement the recommendations advanced in the publications of the Council for Exceptional Children.

Implement the recommendations advanced in the National Education Association's series *Teaching the Gifted and Talented in the Content Areas* and *What Research Says to the Teacher.*

Implement the recommendations advanced in *Curriculum Change Toward the 21st Century* by Harold G. Shane (Washington, D.C.: National Education Association, 1977).

Implement the recommendations advanced by experts in the field of gifted education: Carolyn M. Callahan, Marsha M. Correll, James J. Gallagher, John C. Gowan, J. P. Guilford, Sandra N. Kaplan, Ruth A. Martinson, Abraham Maslow, Sidney J. Parnes, Joseph S. Renzulli, Calvin W. Taylor, E. Paul Torrance, and Frank E. Williams.[6]

16. Facilitating the learning task at hand by providing appropriate models, guides, checklists, and other forms.

17. Designing assignments that are reasonable, stimulating, and meaningful—the antithesis of tedious, boring, punitive busy work (see Checklist 6 at the end of this chapter).

18. Requesting parental permission in writing for students to study content and literature of an adult nature *prior* to student admission to an adult-level program.

19. Weaving into the very fabric of the program safeguards against depersonalizing instruction.

20. Providing continuous opportunity for each student to discover the joy of learning and the satisfaction of academic achievement.

21. Encouraging each student to perceive of self as a *humane* person, responsive to the dreams, aspirations, and needs of others.

22. Designing units, projects, and activities that humanize and enjoyably enhance learning by personalizing the history and development of each discipline or area of study.

23. Designing carefully and employing skillfully techniques to nurture leadership qualities.

24. Providing continuing emphasis on student self-awareness, self-direction, and self-discipline—all building toward self-actualization.

25. Providing learning experiences reflective of the truth that gifted children and youth differ one from the other not only in terms of physical, emotional, social, and intellectual development, but in drive, commitment, caring, and valuing as well.

---

*For in-depth coverage of professional recommendations concerning the development of gifted and talented programs, see Clendening and Davies, *Creating Programs for the Gifted.*

NOTES

1. Marsha M. Correll, *Teaching the Gifted and the Talented.* © 1978 Phi Delta Kappa Educational Foundation (Bloomington, Ind.: Phi Delta Kappa Educational Foundation, 1978), pp. 23–24.
2. Adapted from ibid, p. 25.
3. Adapted from ibid, pp. 23–24.
4. Benjamin S. Bloom et al, eds., *Taxonomy of Educational Objectives: The Classification of Educational Goals,* Handbook I: *Cognitive Domain* (New York: Longman, 1956).
5. David R. Krathwohl et al, *Taxonomy of Educational Objectives: The Classification of Educational Goals,* Handbook II: *Affective Domain* (New York: Longman, 1964).
6. Carolyn M. Callahan, *Developing Creativity in the Gifted and Talented* (Reston, Va.: Council for Exceptional Children, 1978); Correll, *Teaching the Gifted and the Talented;* James J. Gallagher, *Teaching the Gifted Child,* 2nd ed. (Boston: Allyn and Bacon, 1975); John C. Gowan et al, *The Guidance of Exceptional Children,* 2nd ed. (New York: Longman, 1972); J. P. Guilford, *The Nature of Human Intelligence* (New York: McGraw-Hill, 1967); Sandra N. Kaplan, *Providing Programs for the Gifted and Talented: A Handbook* (Reston, Va.: Council for Exceptional Children, 1975); Ruth A. Martinson, *The Identification of the Gifted and Talented* (Reston, Va.: Council for Exceptional Children, 1975); Abraham Maslow, ed., *Motivation and Personality,* 2nd ed. (New York: Harper, 1970); Sidney J. Parnes, *Creativity: Unlocking Human Potential* (Buffalo, N.Y.: D.O.K., 1972); Joseph S. Renzulli, *The Enrichment Triad Model: A Guide for Developing Defensible Programs for the Gifted and Talented* (Mansfield Center, Conn.: Creative Learning Press, 1977); Calvin W. Taylor, ed., *Creativity across Education* (Ogden: University of Utah Press, 1968); E. Paul Torrance, *Creativity in the Classroom,* What Research Says to the Teacher series (Washington, D.C.: National Education Association, 1977); Frank E. Williams, *Classroom Ideas for Encouraging Thinking and Feeling,* 2nd ed. (Buffalo, N.Y.: D.O.K., 1970).

CHECKLIST 1 VARIATIONS AND ADJUSTMENTS TO MEET INDIVIDUAL DIFFERENCES*

DIAGNOSIS

Has information been collected on individual differences?

_____interests	_____capabilities	_____language skills
_____problems	_____reading level	_____achievement
_____other: _____		

INDIVIDUAL STUDY

What variations and adjustments can be made in individual research activities?

_____topics to investigate	_____depth and breadth	_____type of report
_____sources of data	_____people to interview	_____use of library
_____assistance from others	_____use of free time	_____form of presentation
_____other: _____		

*John U. Michaelis, *Social Studies for Children in a Democracy: Recent Trends & Developments,* 6th ed. Copyright © 1976, pp. 129–130. Reprinted by permission of Prentice-Hall, Inc., Englewood Cliffs, N.J.

CHECKLIST 1 (cont.)

INDIVIDUAL TUTORIAL

_____ by the teacher   _____ by another pupil   _____ by programmed material

_____ by a parent   _____ by a teacher aide   _____ by computer

_____ other: _____

SUBGROUPS

What subgroups might be formed within the class?

_____ interest groups   _____ groups needing special instruction

_____ reading groups   _____ groups to make maps, murals, and the like

_____ committees   _____ groups of two or three for team learning

_____ work centers   _____ groups for interviewing, finding materials, and the like

_____ other: _____

METHODS AND ACTIVITIES

_____ individual   _____ small group   _____ whole group

_____ discovery lessons   _____ expository lessons   _____ home study

_____ different questions for subgroups   _____ different explanations for subgroups   _____ varied directions for subgroups

_____ different standards for individuals   _____ varied assignments for individuals or groups   _____ varied assessment of outcomes

_____ other: _____

MATERIALS

What variations or adjustments can be made in instructional materials?

_____ reading materials on various levels   _____ audiovisual materials for group and individual use   _____ community resources for group and individual use

_____ rewritten material   _____ library resources   _____ work centers

_____ study guides   _____ practice materials   _____ taped material

_____ reading lists   _____ use of material in kits   _____ picture sets

_____ other: _____

TIME

What variations in time should be made for individuals and groups?

_____ building readiness for use of materials   _____ introducing a topic or problem   _____ carrying out basic activities

_____ assimilation of new ideas   _____ accommodation of new ideas   _____ expressing one's own ideas

CHECKLIST 1 (cont.)

_____making maps   _____preparing oral   _____home study
and other   and written   and use of
items   reports   community
                                                       resources

_____other: _____

STANDARDS AND EVALUATION

What variations and adjustments should be made in expectations and assessment of outcomes?

_____quantitative   _____qualitative   _____vocabulary
_____concepts   _____information   _____main ideas
_____use of inquiry   _____use of map   _____expression of
processes   reading and   feelings
                          other skills

_____self-evaluation   _____evaluative   _____testing
                          charts

_____other: _____

CHECKLIST 2   VARIATIONS AND ADJUSTMENTS FOR GIFTED STUDENTS*

_____ Provision of a variety of challenging reading materials, maps, and other sources to optimize development of inquiry skills

_____ Provision of a balanced program of activities to promote well-rounded development of intellectual, social, physical, and emotional growth

_____ Extension of learning by means of additional opportunities to formulate hypotheses, draw inferences, state generalizations, synthesize main ideas, and contrast points of view

_____ Provision of many opportunities for independent inquiry, use of library and community resources, and synthesis of data from several sources

_____ Emphasis on self-direction and self-evaluation and individual growth and achievement through practice activities and group work that meet individual needs

_____ Encouragement of individual initiative and planning, leadership, concern for others, sharing, teamwork, and regard for different types of contributions

_____ Provision of direct instruction and guidance to develop basic skills, concepts, inquiry processes, and emotional stability and to avoid gaps or deficiencies in essential learning

_____ Extension of learning through wide reading of materials that take students far beyond basic and supplementary texts

_____ Emphasis on positive traits and attitudes such as individualism without being overbearing, self-criticism without being overly critical of others, and respect for intellectual attainment without lack of regard for other accomplishments

_____ Provision of opportunities for creative expression in individual and group work, oral and written reports, map making, construction, and other activities

_____ Avoidance of activities that may be needed by other students but are boring or irrelevant to the needs and pace of learning of students, such as reteaching of selected material, reviews of concepts taught earlier in the week, drill on terms that may be useful for less able students, and other items already mastered by students

*John U. Michaelis, *Social Studies for Children in a Democracy: Recent Trends & Developments,* 6th ed. Copyright © 1976, pp. 141–142. Reprinted by permission of Prentice-Hall, Inc., Englewood Cliffs, N.J.

CHECKLIST 2 (cont.)

_____ Provision of home study with planned home cooperation to extend and enrich reading, construct models and other objects, use library resources, visit places, and interview experts to gather data on topics under study

CHECKLIST 3   BASIC THINKING, LEARNING, COMMUNICATING SKILLS*

THINKING SKILLS

Thinking processes

_____ Making effective use of perceptive thinking

_____ Making effective use of associative thinking

_____ Making effective use of conceptual thinking

_____ Making effective use of problem solving

_____ Making effective use of critical thinking

_____ Making effective use of creative thinking

_____ Making effective use of adventurous thinking

Thinking in the cognitive area

_____ Making effective use of knowledge-building skills

_____ Making effective use of comprehension skills

_____ Making effective use of application skills

_____ Making effective use of analysis skills

_____ Making effective use of synthesis skills

_____ Making effective use of evaluation skills

Thinking in the affective area

_____ Making effective use of receiving (attending) skills

_____ Making effective use of responding skills

_____ Making effective use of valuing skills

_____ Making effective use of organizing skills

_____ Making effective use of characterizing/valuing skills

LEARNING SKILLS

Locating information

_____ Making effective use of libraries

_____ Making effective use of books

_____ Making effective use of dictionaries

_____ Making effective use of encyclopedias

_____ Making effective use of other basic reference tools

_____ Making effective use of periodicals and periodical indexes

_____ Making effective use of newspapers and newspaper indexes

_____ Making effective use of U.S. government documents, publications, and indexes

_____ Making effective use of pamphlets

_____ Making effective use of primary source materials

_____ Making effective use of print, nonprint, and computerized materials

*For the complete 37-page "Thinking-Learning-Communicating Continuum, K–12," from which the skills in this checklist have been abstracted, see Corinne P. Clendening and Ruth Ann Davies, *Creating Programs for the Gifted* (New York: R. R. Bowker, 1980), pp. 486–523.

CHECKLIST 3 (cont.)

Acquiring information through purposeful and appreciative reading
_____ Developing reading competence
_____ Adjusting rate of reading to purpose
_____ Reading to form relationships
_____ Reading literature with perception and appreciation

Acquiring information through purposeful and appreciative listening
_____ Developing listening competence
_____ Making effective use of critical listening
_____ Making effective use of appreciative listening

Acquiring information through purposeful viewing and observing
_____ Recognizing that viewing is visual inspection
_____ Recognizing that observing goes beyond viewing and stresses adherence to criteria or following a scientific model
_____ Recognizing that viewing is purposeful looking and that observing is carefully and scientifically studying and interpreting what is seen
_____ Applying critical thinking skills when "reading" visual media
_____ "Reading" visual media and employing the inquiry processes
_____ Studying teacher-constructed and/or commercially prepared learning guides
_____ Organizing and consolidating the ideas gained from viewing and observing with ideas gained from other media as well as from past experience
_____ Exploring the artistic, technical, psychological, biographical, and historical components of the fine arts
_____ Becoming acquainted with the great artists, past and present, and their works
_____ "Reading," viewing, and observing the record of the historical past

Constructing and interpreting surveys and opinion polls
_____ Recognizing that a survey is an investigation of things as existing or of events past
_____ Recognizing that a poll is a sampling or collection of opinions
_____ Recognizing that an opinion is an answer that is given to a question in a given situation
_____ Recognizing the basic steps employed in conducting an opinion poll
_____ Recognizing various data-collecting techniques
_____ Analyzing and interpreting nationally recognized surveys and opinion polls
_____ Designing and field-testing surveys and opinion polls

Learning through group and social interaction
_____ Recognizing that excellence in interpersonal relationships is based on psychological maturity
_____ Perceiving the characteristics of a psychologically mature person
_____ Perceiving the characteristics of an effective group member
_____ Recognizing the purpose and function of a committee
_____ Recognizing the purpose and function of a panel
_____ Recognizing the purpose and function of a buzz group
_____ Appreciating the value and function of parliamentary procedure

Organizing information
_____ Making effective use of outlining techniques
_____ Recognizing the distinguishing characteristics and mechanics of the basic outlining systems
_____ Making effective use of note-taking techniques
_____ Making effective use of information storage and retrieval systems

CHECKLIST 3 (cont.)

COMMUNICATING SKILLS

Writing as a communication tool

_____ Perceiving the significance of writing

_____ Perceiving the significance of functional literacy

_____ Perceiving the hallmarks of excellence in written communication

Writing the essay

_____ Perceiving the distinguishing characteristics of the essay form

_____ Becoming conversant with the techniques employed in planning and writing the essay

Writing the research paper

_____ Recognizing the purpose, value, and form of the research paper

_____ Applying the procedures and rules of research as outlined in basic style manuals and guides

Speaking as a communication tool

_____ Perceiving that speech is a vehicle for conveying thought and emotion

_____ Perceiving that effective speaking requires training and practice

_____ Perceiving the requirements for a speech of quality and effectiveness

_____ Perceiving the distinguishing characteristics of a speech designed to entertain or amuse

_____ Perceiving the distinguishing characteristics of a speech designed to inform or instruct

_____ Perceiving the distinguishing characteristics of a speech designed to stimulate emotion

_____ Perceiving the distinguishing characteristics of a speech designed to convince or move to action

_____ Perceiving the distinguishing characteristics of debate

CHECKLIST 4   ORIENTATION PLANNING GUIDE FOR UNIT OR LEARNING PROJECT

Orientation to a unit or learning project should provide an introduction and overview of a new learning experience. By highlighting the purpose, dimension, and options of the unit or project, anticipation is heightened and interest is motivated.

BASICS TO COVER

_____ Unit or project goals

_____ Unit or project objectives

_____ Scope and dimension

_____ Basic terminology

_____ Overall design

_____ Tie-in with previous learning experiences

_____ Time schedule: target dates

_____ Procedural outline

_____ Options and alternatives

_____ Bibliography of required reading, viewing, listening, and data search sources

_____ Learning guides

_____ Field learning experiences

CHECKLIST 4 (cont.)

_____ Consultants and/or mentors
_____ Culminating and/or closure activities
_____ Evaluation procedures and instruments

CHECKLIST 5 GIFTED CLASSROOM STUDY CENTERS: CHARACTERISTICS AND REQUIREMENTS

1. *Definition.* A study center is a special area of the classroom, where students as individuals or as members of a group work at enrichment-acceleration tasks at their own rate and level of achievement

2. *Purpose.* The purpose of the classroom study center is to provide resource-based learning experiences that will bring to the gifted program greater depth, breadth, relevance, vitality, and challenge

3. *Organization.* Organization is the key to the instructional impact and value of the study center; therefore, all aspects of the study center must be carefully planned and set up so that the students can readily perceive:

    The purpose, the focus, the value of this particular classroom center project

    The separate components of this program and their interrelationships

    The requirements, the options, and the alternatives of this project

    The time limitations of this project

    The procedures to be followed in this project

    The print and nonprint media identified, annotated, and classified under main categories or topics in a handout bibliography

    The learning guides, summary checklists, report forms, and the reaction/evaluation forms to be employed in this project

    The follow-up activities, the field experiences, and the further opportunities for individual and/or group exploration and extension

4. *Orientation.* The students are oriented to each new classroom study center project and given ample opportunity:

    To ask questions

    To study the bibliography, learning guides, checklists, and forms

    To suggest additional topics, activities, and experiences

    To examine media listed in the project bibliography and to learn to use unfamiliar equipment

    To consider participation in group or committee activities or working alone

    To select those learning experiences of special interest

5. *Study Center Maintenance.* The bibliography for the study center project serves as an organizational, availability, and maintenance control guide:

    A volunteer student committee is responsible for the orderly maintenance of both the media and the equipment in the study center

    Individual student responsibility for the care and maintenance of media and equipment is stressed

6. *Teacher's Role.* After orientation by the teacher, students work at their own pace, at their own special tasks, and are free to experiment with different ways of investigating, interpreting, and communicating information; the teacher is available for consultation, suggestions, and guidance when and as requested by the students

7. *Closure.* Activities/experiences signifying pattern completion and/or goal realization; those activities/experiences culminating at the conclusion of a study center project that call for student employment of the behaviors at the higher register of both the cognitive and affective domains, i.e., application, evaluation, synthesis, appreciation, and valuing

CHECKLIST 6   CRITERIA FOR DETERMINING FEASIBILITY OF ASSIGNMENTS

_____ Is this assignment worthy of the gifted program?

_____ Is this assignment supportive of unit or learning project theme, goals, or objectives?

_____ Is this assignment so structured that the students will quickly perceive its significance and value?

_____ Is this assignment stated clearly so the students can readily translate what is required?

_____ Is this assignment defensible in the light of availability/accessibility of appropriate support media?

_____ Is this assignment reasonable and justifiable in the light of both time and effort required?

_____ Is this assignment differentiated to meet the varying interests, capabilities, talents, experiences, and aspirations of individual students in the group or class?

_____ Is this assignment designed to encourage original thinking, independent learning, self-initiated projects, and/or creative interpretation?

_____ Is this assignment designed so the students have the opportunity to synthesize what they are currently learning with previous learning experiences?

_____ Is this assignment designed to bring zest, satisfaction, and/or delight to learning?

_____ Is this assignment designed to guard against frustration and boredom?

_____ Is this assignment designed to generate interest in further learning?

Chapter 2

Basics of
Program Implementation

Implementation in this context means to facilitate and expedite attainment of goals and objectives by translating courses of study, learning projects, and other instructional programs into actual teaching-learning experiences.* Implementing a program for the gifted involves certain priorities:

1. Administrative staff that endorses, supports, and

    Appoints a planning-steering committee to formulate a quality differentiated program for the district that complies with state regulations.

    Appoints a coordinator or supervisor to provide leadership in initiating and directing the program for the gifted.

    Initiates faculty in-service workshops.

    Initiates community program to inform the public about the purpose and the value of differentiated programs for gifted and talented students.

    Selects for the gifted program those teachers who have the competencies, attitudes, and personality requisite for successful teaching of gifted children and youth.

    Provides adequate budget to support a successful program.

    Provides adequate staff, facilities, equipment, and learning resources to support a successful program.

    Establishes regularly scheduled time for teachers of the gifted to meet and plan together on a continuing basis.

*For detailed information concerning the procedure for initiating a district program for the gifted, see Corinne P. Clendening and Ruth Ann Davies, *Creating Programs for the Gifted* (New York: R. R. Bowker, 1980), pp. 42–69, 97–152.

Note: A Bibliography for Part I is on pp. 19–20.

2. Teachers who demonstrate the personal and professional characteristics requisite for working with the gifted:*

> Are highly intelligent with broad academic background and interests; exhibit a genuine love of learning.
>
> Show an ardent interest in and dedication to teaching itself, and an enthusiastic preference for and a sincere desire to work with the gifted.
>
> Are committed to the cause and philosophy of gifted education although cognizant of the political vicissitudes and absence of federal funding for the program.
>
> Possess emotional maturity, flexibility, and professional self-confidence, such that (1) they are neither intimidated by gifted students themselves nor by inherently unique problems associated with teaching the gifted; (2) they welcome the opportunity to work cooperatively as team teachers pooling energy, expertise, experiences, observations, and resources willingly; and (3) they view themselves as guides, listeners, questioners, reactors, and facilitators of learning.
>
> Are skilled in using those techniques advocated by recognized experts in the field of gifted education to provoke, nurture, and reinforce creativity and adventurous thinking (see Checklists 7 and 8 at the end of this model).
>
> Exhibit the ability to teach at the level of inspiration; warm, caring persons who consistently demonstrate zest for scholarship and learning.
>
> The role of the teacher in the gifted program cannot be overemphasized. The finest program can be readily scuttled by a less than able, unenthusiastic, or insensitive teacher. Likewise, even the most limping program can be stirred to a gallop by a teacher who not only brings professional expertise, but also demonstrates infectious vivacity and genuine commitment to the cause of gifted education.

3. An adequate media support program appropriate for a gifted program of excellence; one that:

> Incorporates in the instructional support program *all* authentic carriers of information regardless of format.
>
> Utilizes the multimedia, cross-media approach to knowledge building.
>
> Values and utilizes the school library as a learning laboratory where the students—as members of a class or group or as individuals—work intensively, extensively, and creatively with ideas in an environment conducive to optimum learning.
>
> Recognizes that the school librarian is a teacher whose subject is learning itself; a teacher who works and plans with the teachers of the gifted, as a cooperative participant on the gifted teaching team, as well as with individual teachers, to bring depth, breadth, relevance, vitality, and challenge to the gifted program (see Checklist 9 at the end of this chapter).
>
> Field-tests media, whenever possible, before purchase to determine both instructional value and student appeal.

*C. June Maker, *Training Teachers for the Gifted and Talented: A Comparison of Models* (Reston, Va.: Council for Exceptional Children, 1975).

Provides for the free flow of media resources among all the schools and libraries in the school district.

Provides for direct communication between the public library staff and the school librarians and faculty members, alerting the public library staff to special projects; curricular areas of emphasis; class, group, or individual student interests; and special activities requiring public library support.

Values classroom study centers as an effective means of bringing enrichment, acceleration, and individualization to the classroom instructional program and provides appropriate study center support media* (see Checklist 5 in the preceding chapter).

4. School district policy statements articulating:

District gifted program entrance and withdrawal requirements and procedures.

Confidentiality of student records.

Flexibility of scheduling to accommodate student and faculty participation in the gifted program and supportive field learning experiences.

Provision of preparation time and regularly scheduled in-service meetings for teachers of the gifted program.

Fiscal arrangements for student and faculty admission fees, transportation costs, speakers' fees, and such, required for special gifted program activities.

Insurance liability coverage for gifted students, faculty, and/or parents taking part in special gifted program learning activities involving transportation or other risks.

BIBLIOGRAPHY

Bloom, Benjamin S., ed. *Taxonomy of Educational Objectives: The Classification of Educational Goals, Handbook I, Cognitive Domain.* New York: David McKay, 1956.

Callahan, Carolyn M. *Developing Creativity in the Gifted and Talented.* Reston, Va.: Council for Exceptional Children, 1978.

Clendening, Corinne P., and Ruth Ann Davies. *Creating Programs for the Gifted: A Guide for Teachers, Librarians, and Students.* Serving Special Populations series. New York: R. R. Bowker, 1980.

Correll, Marsha M. *Teaching the Gifted and Talented.* Bloomington, Ind.: Phi Delta Kappa Educational Foundation, 1978.

Davies, Ruth Ann. *The School Library Media Program: Instructional Force for Excellence,* 3rd ed. New York: R. R. Bowker, 1979.

Gallagher, James J. *Teaching the Gifted,* 2nd ed. Boston: Allyn and Bacon, 1975.

Gowan, John C. et al. *The Guidance of Exceptional Children,* 2nd ed. New York: Longmans, 1972.

Guilford, J. P. *The Nature of Human Intelligence.* New York: McGraw-Hill, 1967.

Kaplan, Sandra N. *Providing Programs for the Gifted and Talented: A Handbook.* Reston, Va.: Council for Exceptional Children, 1975.

Krathwohl, David R. et al. *Taxonomy of Educational Objectives: The Classification of Educational Goals, Handbook II: Affective Domain.* New York: David McKay, n.d.

*For a general discussion of classroom study centers, see *Learning Centers in the Classroom,* ed. by Jimmy E. Nations (Washington, D.C.: National Education Association, 1976).

Maker, June C. *Training Teachers for the Gifted and Talented: A Comparison of Models.* Reston, Va.: Council for Exceptional Children, 1975.

Marland, Sidney P., Jr. *Education of the Gifted and Talented, Report to the Congress of the United States by the U.S. Commissioner of Education,* 2 vols. Washington, D.C.: U.S. Government Printing Office, 1972.

Martison, Ruth A. *The Identification of the Gifted and Talented.* Reston, Va.: Council for Exceptional Children, 1975.

Maslow, Abraham, ed. *Motivation and Personality,* 2nd ed. New York: Harper, 1970.

Michaelis, John U. *Social Studies for Children in a Democracy: Recent Trends and Developments,* 6th ed. Englewood Cliffs, N.J.: Prentice-Hall, 1976.

Nations, Jimmy E., ed. *Learning Centers in the Classroom.* Washington, D.C.: National Education Association, 1976.

Parnes, Sidney J. *Creativity: Unlocking Human Potential.* Buffalo, N.Y.: D.O.K., 1972.

Plowman, Paul D. *Teaching the Gifted and Talented in the Social Studies Classroom.* Teaching the Gifted and the Talented in the Content Area series. Washington, D.C.: National Education Association, 1980.

Renzulli, Joseph S. *The Enrichment Triad Model: A Guide for Developing Defensible Programs for the Gifted and Talented.* Mansfield Center, Conn.: Creative Learning Press, 1977.

Shane, Harold G. *Curriculum Change Toward the 21st Century.* Curriculum series. Washington, D.C.: National Education Association, 1977.

Taylor, Calvin W., ed. *Creativity Across Education.* Ogden: University of Utah Press, 1968.

Torrance, E. Paul. *Creativity in the Classroom.* What Research Says to the Teacher series. Washington, D.C.: National Education Association, 1977.

Williams, Frank E. *Classroom Ideas for Encouraging Thinking and Feeling,* 2nd ed. Buffalo, N.Y.: D.O.K., 1970.

CHECKLIST 7   CREATIVE WAYS OF TEACHING*

What can teachers do to provide the conditions in which creative thinking abilities have a predominate role?

1. Provide opportunities for creative behavior

    Make assignments that call for original work, independent learning, self-initiated projects, and experimentation

    Ask questions that call for productive thinking

    Use curricular materials which provide progressive warm-up exercises, which permit one thing to lead to another, and activities which make creative thinking both legitimate and rewarding

    Use curricular materials which familiarize children with the nature of the creative-thinking process through the lives of eminent creative people

    Develop skills in the use of analogy

2. Develop skills for creative teaching

    Stress the skills and strategies of inquiry, creative research, and problem solving

3. Reward creative achievements

    Be respectful of the unusual questions children ask

    Be respectful of the unusual ideas and solutions of children

    Show children that their ideas have value

*E. Paul Torrance, *Creativity in the Classroom,* What Research Says to the Teacher series (Washington, D.C.: National Education Association, 1977), pp. 23–27.

CHECKLIST 7 (cont.)

Provide opportunities for and give credit for self-initiated learning

Provide chances for children to learn, think, and discover without threats of immediate evaluation

4. Establish creative relationships with children

Permit one thing to lead to another, to embark with the child on an unknown adventure

Be ready to accept and respond to student inventiveness

Create an environment which is definitely a responsive one in which the child finds encouragement, respect, and guidance

5. Facilitate creative behavior

Give purpose to creative writing

Provide experiences which make children more sensitive to environmental stimuli

Develop a constructive attitude toward the information taught

Provide adequate warm-up for creative activities

In warming up pupils for creative thinking, avoid giving examples or illustrations which will freeze or unduly shape their thinking

Provide unevaluated (off-the-record) practice

To evoke originality in thinking, make it clear that such thinking is expected and will be rewarded

CHECKLIST 8 DEVELOPING CREATIVITY IN THE GIFTED AND TALENTED: PRACTICAL IMPLICATIONS FOR THE TEACHER*

Research leads to some general considerations about what a teacher might do to encourage creative production by students in the classroom.

1. Provide a nonthreatening atmosphere. The classroom environment should be structured in such a way that students' ideas and opinions are respected, ridicule of new ideas is eliminated, questioning is encouraged, and questions are asked that allow students to be open and uninhibited in response.

2. Refrain from becoming the judge of the worth of all products in the classroom. An open, nonjudgmental attitude on the part of the teacher will allow more freedom for divergent production as well as the evaluative skills necessary for the complete creative process. Encourage students to develop criteria to judge both the work of peers and themselves.

3. Model creative thinking and/or introduce other individuals who are able to illustrate the creative thinking process to the students. The teacher should take care to model creative problem solving procedures on as many occasions as possible, not simply during "creativity time."

4. Attempt to integrate activities and questions that encourage divergent production and evaluation into as many content areas as possible. The necessity of illustrating transfer of these skills to all areas of thinking cannot be overestimated.

5. Make a conscious effort to remind students to be creative, to be original, to try to think of new ways to solve a problem, etc.

6. Systematically reward novel production. The use of operant conditioning to reinforce specific types of novel behavior can lead to an overall increase in creative production. For example, the reinforcement of the use of a variety of sentence structures in an essay has been shown to influence overall creative writing skill. Care should be taken

*Carolyn M. Callahan, *Developing Creativity in the Gifted and Talented* (Reston, Va.: Council for Exceptional Children, 1978), pp. 71–72.

CHECKLIST 8 (cont.)

to choose appropriate reinforcement. Gifted children can be expected to value rewards that are somewhat unique.

7. Provide stimuli for as many of the senses as possible. A variety of stimuli encourage the student to view the problem from a variety of perspectives and also seem to enhance the sense of openness and psychological freedom.

8. Make use of warm-up activities when moving from highly structured convergent or memory type activities into activities requiring students to engage in creative production. Such brief activities should be used to reaffirm the nonthreatening environment and are most effective if they relate to the task to be accomplished.

9. Incorporate activities into the classroom instruction that require students to generate a large number of correct responses. That is, provide open-ended questions that have no single, right answer.

10. Instruct students in the principles of brainstorming, but incorporate strategies for self evaluation of the quality of ideas. Furthermore, brainstorming activities will be most productive if tied to "real problems" or "meaningful production" rather than simple games.

11. Be a participant in the actions. Do not merely pose problems, but be an active problem solver.

12. Encourage students to express positive self statements about their creativity and avoid negative self evaluations. Provide them with guiding statements of attitudes, approaches to problems, and orientations to the process.

13. Attempts to incorporate published material into the curriculum are dependent on the understanding and commitment of the teachers who are using the curriculum. No packaged materials are independent of the teacher's use of those materials, and the effectiveness of creativity training materials seems to be particularly influenced by the teacher's attitude and the environment of the classroom.

14. Whichever strategies are adopted for classroom use must be evaluated within the particular classroom with your particular students and teaching style. What works in one situation will not always work in others. Continual assessment of the objectives of instruction is crucial.

CHECKLIST 9   PLANNING GUIDE FOR COOPERATIVE INSTRUCTIONAL SUPPORT BY THE TEACHER OF THE GIFTED AND THE SCHOOL LIBRARIAN*

Cooperation of teacher(s) and the school librarian is the keystone of an effective media support program for the gifted. Since curriculum is the *planned interaction* of students with content, resources, and instructional processes, face-to-face communication between the teacher or teaching team and the librarian is absolutely essential. The following guide outlines a step-by-step procedure to facilitate cooperative planning.

1. The teacher(s) and the school librarian in a scheduled planning conference determine the developmental support needs of the unit or learning project by identifying:

   _____ Unit or learning project goals

   _____ Behavioral objectives

   _____ Special class, group, and/or individual student needs, interests, goals, abilities, progress rate, or concerns

   _____ Specific topics, concepts, skills, and attitudes to be introduced, reinforced, and/or extended

*Adapted from Ruth Ann Davies, *The School Library Media Program: Instructional Force for Excellence,* 3rd ed. (New York: R. R. Bowker, 1979), pp. 89–91.

CHECKLIST 9 (cont.)

2. The teacher(s) and the school librarian analyze the basic components of the unit or learning project requiring instructional media support:

   Identifying specific topics in the *cognitive domain* under the following headings:

   _____ What persons?   _____What events?

   _____ What places?   _____What concepts?

   _____ What things?   _____What fundamentals?

   Identifying specific topics in the *affective domain* under the following headings:

   _____ What attitudes?   _____What value judgments?

   _____ What appreciations?   _____What self-perceptions?

   Identifying specific thinking-learning-communicating skills under the following headings:

   _____ Reading   _____Making assumptions

   _____ Listening   _____Analyzing

   _____ Recalling   _____Criticizing

   _____ Observing   _____Problem solving

   _____ Outlining   _____Interpreting

   _____ Comparing   _____Reporting

   _____ Summarizing   _____Evaluating

   _____Classifying   _____Synthesizing

   _____ Generalizing   _____Communicating

   _____ Categorizing   _____Other

   Identifying specific orientation strategies (see Checklist 4 in the preceding chapter).

3. The teacher(s) and the school librarian determine those:

   _____ Experiences required of the class

   _____ Experiences required of special groups

   _____ Experiences required of individual students

4. The teacher(s) and the school librarian design strategies for:

   _____ Orientation to the unit or learning project

   _____ Linking ideas

   _____ Stimulating creativity

   _____ Encouraging group interaction

   _____ Introducing, reinforcing, or extending skills

   _____ Stimulating divergent thinking

   _____ Stimulating creativity

   _____ Encouraging group interaction

   _____ Sustaining interest

   _____ Encouraging student self-appraisal of progress

5. The teacher(s) and the school librarian design:

   _____ Appropriate learning guides

   _____ Optional and/or branching experience and/or activities

6. The teacher(s) and the school librarian carefully consider the following:

   _____ How can understanding be facilitated?

   _____ How can learning be developed logically?

   _____ How can learning be individualized?

   _____ How can failure be avoided?

   _____ How can boredom and frustration be minimized?

   _____ How can interest be motivated, directed, and rewarded?

   _____ How can previous learning be reinforced and extended?

CHECKLIST 9 (cont.)

_____ How can depth, breadth, and relevancy be provided?

_____ How can open-ended learning be encouraged?

_____ How can learning be extended into other curricular and/or co-curricular areas?

_____ How can alternative enrichment-acceleration experiences be provided in the classroom study center?

Part II
Model Programs, Grades K–12

Model Programs

The teacher is the key to the success of each of the model programs presented in Part II. It is the teacher who breathes life into unit or course plan; who imbues words with meaning; who shapes thought into insight; who infuses the spirit of challenge and adventure into the day-to-day business of learning itself. It is the teacher who seizes the teachable moment, sparks interest, changes pace and emphasis to accommodate individual, group, and class reactions, and, above all, brings that special excitement to learning that reflects the true artistry of creative teaching.

Each model in this book has been designed to provide myriad topics that the students "might like to explore at greater depths and higher levels of involvement."[*] The content of each model is of greater scope than any class, group, or individual student could possibly master.[†] The design is intentional—*individualization begins with informed choices among significant options.*

Questions concerning any of these models should be directed to the authors, Corinne P. Clendening or Ruth Ann Davies, who can be contacted at their office, 156 McIntyre Road, Pittsburgh, PA 15237 (412-364-4585).

[*]Joseph S. Renzulli, *The Enrichment Triad: A Guide for Developing Defensible Programs for the Gifted and Talented* (Mansfield Center, Conn.: Creative Learning Press, 1977), p. 17.

[†]One source in particular, *The New York Times* Microfilm/Microfiche Programs (Microfilming Corporation of America), is highlighted and recommended in Part II on the secondary level. In the authors' judgment, *The New York Times'* unique approach in providing microfiche and/or microfilm in specialized curriculum support packages is truly a most exciting innovation available to educators today. These superlative program guides and their accompanying specialized collections of microfiche and/or microfilm offer greater curriculum support and impetus to true scholarship than is currently offered by any other individual source. It is recommended that the combination microfiche reader/projector and the microfilm reader/projector be purchased so that the microform articles, editorials, documents, etc., can be projected for group and/or class use. Questions about any phase of *The New York Times* Microfilm/Microfiche Programs, as well as types and sources of microform equipment, should be directed to the attention of Howard F. McGinn, Jr., Microfilming Corporation of America, 1620 Hawkins Avenue, Box 10, Sanford, NC 27330. Telephone: 800-334-7501.

Model 1

Experiencing Literature: A Continuous-Progress Literature Study Program, K–6

The concept of *literacy** in today's society includes knowledge of literature as well as the ability to read and the ability to write. The study of literature, therefore, must be a vital component of both the elementary and the secondary curricula. Traditionally, the teaching of literature has been assigned on the elementary level to two separate curricular areas—the language arts program and the reading program. Such duality of coverage *should* assure a literature study program of excellence, a planned and articulated program of balance and harmony throughout the primary and middle grades. Unfortunately, such is not the case; traditionally, the literature component of the language arts program is completely separate from and unrelated to the literature component of the reading program. Rather than building strength and unity, this typical example of compartmentalization often results in a fragmented literature program rather than an articulated program of excellence.

Paradoxically, even though literature is considered basic to both the language arts and reading programs, much that is fine in children's literature is too often omitted due to the limitations of language arts and reading textbook selections. Regrettable as this circumstance is for all students, it is particularly lamentable for the gifted student, who more often than not is an accelerated, compulsive reader. The gifted student's delight in reading is consequently shortchanged, and basic quality literary experiences all too frequently are ignored, forgotten, or just overlooked. Too much of literary merit is just waiting to be discovered to permit or excuse inadvertent omission or needless duplica-

*Literate—having or showing knowledge of literature, writing . . . well-read . . . characterized by skill, lucidity . . . a person who can read and write (*The Random House Dictionary of the English Language* [New York: Random House, 1967]).

tion due to lack of articulation in the elementary literature study program. A literature study program should, therefore, be carefully planned and meticulously articulated as a basic component of any differentiated program for the gifted on the elementary level.* Such an articulated program should:

1. Provide teachers with a basic checklist of quality literary experiences to be integrated into the gifted program (see Checklists 1-1, 1-2, 1-3, and 1-4 at the end of this model).
2. Serve as a high-speed vehicle to realms far beyond those the student would ever discover on his or her own.
3. Promote continuous progress and smooth transition from grade to grade and from reading experience to reading experience.
4. Promote aesthetic appreciation of the power and beauty of language and literature.
5. Encourage student exploration and selection reflective of individual interest and preference.

Designing a continuous-progress literature program should be a team endeavor involving the teachers and supervisor of the gifted program, the elementary librarians, and, ultimately, the language arts and reading teachers. The initial team enterprise for the teachers and supervisor of the gifted program, in cooperation with the elementary librarians, is to:

1. Define program goals and objectives.
2. Determine basic authors and titles to be highlighted.
3. Identify literary award winners to be highlighted.
4. Determine literary genres to be studied in depth.
5. Design and develop basic checklists, guides, forms, and such.
6. Design and develop enrichment-acceleration experiences and activities.
7. Identify basic print and nonprint support media.

After determining the above, the teachers and supervisor of the gifted program work with the teachers of the language arts and reading programs to identify the authors and the titles highlighted in their respective programs by using Checklist 1-1, Delightful Literary Fare; Checklist 1-2, Caldecott Award Books; Checklist 1-3, Newbery Award Books; and Checklist 1-4, Master List of Authors and Illustrators (all at the end of this model) as comprehensive author/title identification tools. Through the use of these checklists as objective identification tools, the pattern of which authors and which titles are the special province of the language arts program and which are the special province of the reading program quickly emerges. Likewise, it is immediately discernible which authors and which titles are *not* being highlighted by either program and, therefore, should logically be the special enrichment-acceleration province of the gifted program.

Model 1, Experiencing Literature, applies certain guidelines in design, as indicated below.

GOAL

The program goal is to provide an enrichment-acceleration literature study program that affords the gifted student myriad opportunity to "experience" the

---

*Barrett J. Mandel, ed., *Three Language-Arts Curriculum Models: Pre-Kindergarten through College* (Urbana, Ill.: National Council of Teachers of English, 1980), pp. 35–46.

best of the literary greats—past and present—with perception, appreciation, challenge, and delight.

OBJECTIVES

The purpose of this literature study program is to enable gifted students to:

Build an in-depth knowledge of literature by sampling widely from and savoring deeply the best in the world of quality literature.

Form a wide acquaintanceship and build lasting friendship with authors and illustrators who have won literary acclaim.

Perceive the messages of literature as well as its themes, styles, and patterns of character, setting, and plot.

Explore with openness of mind all types and kinds of quality literature, including fiction, fantasy, myth, legend, tall tale, folktale, biography, auto-biography, poetry, drama, history, essay, diaries, journals, and letters.

Realize that insight into human nature is a valued dividend accrued from reading.

Appreciate that the appeal of quality literature is timeless and universal.

View and value school and public libraries as one's own literary treasure trove.

Develop a lifelong, insatiable desire to read for information, recreation, and pleasure.

Appreciate that reading is both thought and emotion evoking, and, as such, can be the springboard for adventurous thinking.

Use the reading of literature as an impetus for personal experimentation with creative writing.

Become alive to the power and beauty of language and literature.

SUBJECT CONTENT

1. Determine basic authors and titles to be highlighted, using the following selection tools:

    Adventuring with Books: A Booklist for Preschool–Grade 6 ed. by Mary Lou White, rev. ed. (Urbana, Ill.: National Council of Teachers of English, 1981). This edition features 2,500 children's books selected from 10,000 titles published between the beginning of 1977 and the end of 1980. All books listed are recommended for their literary merit and their high potential interest for children. A multicategorized table of contents organizes books by genre, subject, and theme. "Classics" are cited under each category.

    Best Books for Children, Preschool through the Middle Grades ed. by John T. Gillespie and Christine B. Gilbert, 2nd ed. (New York: R. R. Bowker, 1981). This edition provides an annotated, subject-arranged, curriculum-oriented listing of 9,000 recommended titles, nearly three times as many as any other book-selection guide. An excellent re-source for identifying the best in children's literature.

    Children and Books by Zena Sutherland and May Hill Arbuthnot, 6th ed. (Glenview, Ill.: Scott, Foresman, 1981). A popular textbook for courses in children's literature, which provides a comprehensive survey of children's literature past and present. Highlights current trends in writing, illustrating, and reading interests, as well as how to bring children and books together.

Children's Literature, a *World Book Encyclopedia* reprint (Chicago: World Book–Childcraft, 1978). An excellent survey of children's literature including history, kinds, the best of children's literature, and books about children's literature. This reprint, which costs 25¢, is one of the most effective tools for identifying the "best" in children's literature.

Fantasy for Children: An Annotated Checklist by Ruth Nadelman Lynn (New York: R. R. Bowker, 1979). A comprehensive checklist of fantasy books for children in grades 3 to 8, divided into 13 categories. Annotations provide a brief description of the book and a list of sequels or related works by the same author; also notations of major awards won. Books of outstanding quality are indicated by an asterisk.

Learning to Love Literature: Preschool through Grade 3 ed. by Linda Leonard Lamme (Urbana, Ill.: National Council of Teachers of English, 1981). The purpose of this book is to bring the best of children's literature into the mainstream of the curriculum. It is a storehouse of literature-related information including goals of a literature program, teaching techniques, examples of literature units, and listings of books with "magnet appeal."

2. Identify literary award winners to be highlighted using:

   Children's Books: Awards and Prizes, latest ed. (New York: Children's Book Council, biennial). A listing of awards given exclusively to children's books and their creators in the United States and internationally. A brief description of each award, including criteria, is provided along with a listing of all award recipients. All awards are arranged alphabetically within the book's three major sections: U.S. Awards, British Commonwealth Awards, and International Awards. The book also includes person and title indexes.

3. Assemble the following checklists (all at the end of this model):

   Delightful Literary Fare (see Checklist 1-1).

   Caldecott Award Books (see Checklist 1-2).

   Newbery Award Books (see Checklist 1-3).

   Master List of Authors and Illustrators (see Checklist 1-4).

4. Using Checklists 1-1 to 1-4, determine which authors and/or illustrators and which titles are the special province of the language arts program, which are the special province of the reading program, and which are the special province of the gifted program.

5. Determine literary components to be studied in depth.

   There are two basic literary forms:

   Fiction—novels, short stories, and other prose writings that tell about imaginary people and events.

Nonfiction—factual information about persons, places, things, events, and ideas.

The basic elements of fiction are:*

Character(s)—whom the story is about: protagonist, the main character; antagonist, one who contends with another, a foe.

Theme—the main idea of the story, the center of interest, what the story is about.

Plot—what happens, the action.

Style—the manner of telling the story, the use of language, the setting of a mood, the ability to hold the reader's interest.

Climax—the highest peak of the action, the highpoint of suspense.

Conclusion—the end of the story, which quickly follows the climax.

Setting—the place and time of a story.

Types of fiction to be studied in depth are:

Adventure stories: orientation presented by Pied Piper Productions sound filmstrip Literature for Children, Series 3: *Adventure.*[†]

Animal stories: orientation presented by Pied Piper Productions sound filmstrip Literature for Children, Series 2: *Animals.*

Fantasy:[‡] orientation presented by Pied Piper Productions sound filmstrip Literature for Children, Series 1: *Fantasy.*

Historical fiction: orientation presented by Pied Piper Productions sound filmstrip Literature for Children, Series 3: *Historical Fiction.*

Mysteries: orientation presented by Pied Piper Productions sound filmstrip Literature for Children, Series 6: *Mysteries.*

Realistic fiction: orientation presented by Pied Piper Productions sound filmstrip Literature for Children, Series 6: *Realistic Fiction* (see Teaching Guide 1-1 at the end of this model).

Science fiction: orientation presented by Pied Piper Productions sound filmstrip Literature for Children, Series 6: *Science Fiction* (see Teaching Guide 1-2 at the end of this model).

Folktales to be studied in depth are:

Epics and legends: orientation presented by Pied Piper Productions sound filmstrip Literature for Children, Series 6: *Epics and Legends* (see Teaching Guide 1-3 at the end of this model).

Fairy Tales: orientation presented by Study Center Program 1-1 (end of this model).

Myths: orientation presented by Pied Piper Productions sound filmstrip Literature for Children, Series 3: *Myths.*

---

*Pied Piper Productions (Verdugo City, Calif. 91046) offers an excellent teaching tool, Series 5: *Narrative Writing* (four sound filmstrips and learning guides), which includes Elements of a Story, Creating a Beginning, Building a Conflict, and Developing a Character.

[†]The quality of the Pied Piper Productions (Verdugo City, Calif. 91046) Literature for Children Series is uniformly excellent. They are especially useful in classroom study centers.

[‡]Upstart Library Promotionals (Box 889, Hagerstown, Md. 21740) offers for sale an attractive series of posters, bookmarks, bulletin board displays, and mobiles on the theme "Fantasy-Read."

Tall Tales: orientation presented by Pied Piper Productions sound filmstrip Literature for Children, Series 1: *Tall Tales.*

Two main kinds of nonfiction are:

Exposition—explains something, conveys information in order to develop understanding.

Argument—attempts to persuade or convince the reader to believe, accept, or endorse something.

Types of nonfiction to be studied in depth are:

Biography and *autobiography:* orientation presented by Pied Piper Productions sound filmstrip Literature for Children, Series 1: *Biography.*

History: orientation presented by Pied Piper Productions sound filmstrip Literature for Children, Series 5: *History* (see Teaching Guide 1-4 at the end of this model).

Poetry: orientation presented by Study Center Program 1-2 (end of this model).

Science: orientation presented by. Pied Piper Productions sound filmstrip Literature for Children, Series 5: *Science* (see Teaching Guide 1-5 at the end of this model).

Sport and hobby: orientation presented by Pied Piper Productions sound filmstrip Literature for Children, Series 5: *Sport and Hobby.*

6. Design and develop basic checklists, guides, and forms, for example:

Checklist 1-5, Best of the Literary Greats (end of this model).

Checklist 1-6, My Favorite Literary Characters (end of this model).

Checklist 1-7, Fiction Book Evaluation Form (end of this model).

Checklist 1-8, Nonfiction Book Evaluation Form (end of this model).

7. Design and develop enrichment-acceleration experiences and activities, for example:

Teaching Guide 1-1, Realistic Fiction (Filmstrip).

Teaching Guide 1-2, Science Fiction (Filmstrip).

Teaching Guide 1-3, Epics and Legends (Filmstrip).

Teaching Guide 1-4, History Books (Filmstrip).

Teaching Guide 1-5, Science Books (Filmstrip).

Study Center Program 1-1, Folk Literature.

Study Center Program 1-2, Exploring Poetry.

8. Identify basic print and nonprint media to support the literature study program.

Basic tools for identifying quality printed media:

Adventuring with Books: A Booklist for Preschool–Grade 6 (see annotation earlier under "Subject Content").

Best Books for Children, Preschool through the Middle Grades (see annotation earlier under "Subject Content").

Books for the Gifted Child by Barbara H. Baskin and Karen H.

Harris, Serving Special Populations series (New York: R. R. Bowker, 1980). Here is a concise, annotated bibliography of some 150 intellectually challenging books—ranging from picture books to contemporary novels—for the gifted prereader and reader up to age 12. Each book is analyzed with a concentration on those qualities that promote cognitive challenge and add a pleasurable dimension to the act of reading.

Children's Books in Print (New York: R. R. Bowker, annual). This is a current one-volume source of authoritative data on virtually all in-print children's books—from preschool through grade 12. More than 42,300 hardcover and paperback titles are listed alphabetically by author, title, and illustrator.

Children's Catalog (New York: H. W. Wilson, new edition published at five-year intervals with four annual supplements). This is a selected catalog of fiction and nonfiction books suitable for children from preschool to sixth-grade level, divided into three parts: Part I, entries arranged according to Dewey Decimal Classification; Part II, author, title, subject index; Part 3, directory of publishers and distributors.

Fantasy for Children: An Annotated Checklist (see annotation earlier under "Subject Content").

Paperbound Books for Young People from Kindergarten through Grade 12, 2nd ed. (New York: R. R. Bowker, 1980). This bibliography contains finding and ordering information on nearly 15,000 paperbound titles. Full information on each title is given in four separate indexes—subject, author, title, illustrator.

Subject Guide to Children's Books in Print (New York: R. R. Bowker, 1970–   ). This annual volume classifies the more than 42,000 juvenile fiction and nonfiction titles listed in *Children's Books in Print* under 7,500 subject headings.

Basic tools for identifying quality nonprint media:

American Folklore Films and Videotapes: An Index, vol. I (Memphis, Tenn.: Center for Southern Folklore, 1976). Paper. This comprehensive catalog indexes more than 1,800 films and videotapes by title and subject.

American Folklore Films and Videotapes: A Catalog, vol. II (New York: R. R. Bowker, 1982). Paper. Indexes more than 2,000 films and videotapes by title and subject.

Core Media Collection for Elementary Schools by Lucy Gregor Brown, 2nd ed. (New York: R. R. Bowker, 1978). This comprehensive guide lists more than 3,000 nonprint titles of all kinds, including 16mm films, for grades K–8. The annotated titles are grouped by subject. This basic tool also provides a list of recommended sources, title and media indexes, and a producer/distributor directory.

Educational Film Locator of the Consortium of University Film Centers and R. R. Bowker, 2nd ed. (New York: R. R. Bowker, 1980). This tool catalogs some 40,000 films available for sale or rental from the 50-member Consortium of University Film Centers

(CUFC). Films are listed alphabetically and are fully annotated. Includes bibliographic data such as title, running time, format, subject, audience level, color or black and white.

Feature Films on 8mm, 16mm, and Videotape: A Directory of Feature Films Available for Rental, Sale, and Lease in the United States and Canada ed. by James L. Limbacher, 7th ed. (New York: R. R. Bowker, 1982). This comprehensive bibliography gives information on where to buy and how to rent 8mm and 16mm movies and videocassettes. It indexes 95 percent of all films available in the United Sates and Canada; includes 23,000 film and videocassette entries, a section on film reference books, and contact data on film companies and distributors.

A Multimedia Approach to Children's Literature: A Selective List of Films, Filmstrips, and Recordings Based on Children's Books by Ellin Greene and Madalynne Schoenfeld, 2nd ed. (Chicago: American Library Association, 1977). This tool lists 500 children's books and identifies 225 16mm films, 300 filmstrips, and 375 sound recordings adapted from or based on the printed originals.

PBS Video Catalog (Washington, D.C.: Public Broadcasting Service, annual). This catalog lists 2,800 programs produced by television stations and independent producers on videocassettes and available for classroom use.

Recommended sources of "first-choice," quality literary audiovisual support media are:*

Pied Piper Productions, which produces literary study and appreciation sets such as:

Favorite Fiction (4 filmstrips, 4 cassettes, 4 teaching guides, 12 paperbacks, 1 hardback)

First Choice: Authors and Books, units including: (each 1 filmstrip, 2 cassettes, 1 teaching guide and includes author interview unless otherwise noted):

The Mouse and the Motorcycle by Beverly Cleary
White Bird by Clyde Bulla
Brighty of the Grand Canyon by Marguerite Henry
Jack and the Robbers by Richard Chase
The Cay by Theodore Taylor
The Cat and Mrs. Cary by Doris Gates
By the Great Horn Spoon! by Sid Fleischman
Black and Blue Magic by Zilpha Snyder
Ramona the Pest by Beverly Cleary
House of Dries Drear by Virginia Hamilton
Henry and the Clubhouse by Beverly Cleary (1 filmstrip, 1 cassette, 1 teaching guide)
Ribsy by Beverly Cleary (1 filmstrip, 1 cassette, 1 teaching guide)
From the Mixed-Up Files of Mrs. Basil E. Frankweiler by E. L. Konigsburg (2 filmstrips, 2 cassettes, 1 teaching guide [includes author interview])

---

*Each of the three recommended first-choice sources issues media catalogs on request; they also provide preview service to teachers.

The Headless Cupid by Zilpha Snyder (1 filmstrip, 1 cassette, 1 teaching guide)

Tales of a Fourth Grade Nothing by Judy Blume

The Great Brain Reforms by John D. Fitzgerald

Otherwise Known as Sheila the Great by Judy Blume (1 filmstrip, 1 cassette, 1 teaching guide)

The Pied Piper of Hamelin by Robert Browning (1 filmstrip, 1 cassette, 1 teaching guide)

Story of a Book, 2nd ed. with Marguerite Henry (1 double-length filmstrip, 1 cassette, 1 teaching guide; or 1 motion picture, color, 16mm)

First Choice: Poets and Poetry (5 filmstrips, 5 cassettes, 5 teaching guides) (see Study Center Program 1-2, end of this model)

Literature for Children is a program of eight series of sound filmstrips for elementary grades 4–6. These programs are especially useful for study centers. (Pied Piper Productions):

Series 1: Story of a Book; Biography; Tall Tales; Fantasy

Series 2: Animals; Distant Lands: Fairy Tales; Humor

Series 3: Enjoying Illustrations; Historical Fiction; Myths; Adventure

Series 4: Haiku; Descriptive Words . . . ; Sounds of Poetry; Humorous Verse

Series 5: History; Art and Music; Science; Sport and Hobby

Series 6: Mysteries; Epics and Legends; Realistic Fiction; Science Fiction

Series 7A: Imagine That!; Just Like Me; Books About Real Things; Stories Without Words

Series 7B: Animal Stories; What's So Funny?; Exploring New Places; Stories About Friends

Series 8: Storytelling Then and Now; Talking Beasts; Witches, Giants and Elves; Noodlehead Stories; Folktale Themes; Tales of Enchantment

Random House/Miller-Brody produces the following literature media support programs:

Newbery Award Media—the largest collection of sound filmstrips based on the Newbery Award Books ever assembled (see Checklist 1-3 at the end of this model). *Note:* These filmstrips and cassettes come in a package that looks like a book and fits on bookshelves right next to the books themselves; a slot on the inside of the container holds a Media-Gram, which contains background information about the book and the author (see Example 1-1).

Caldecott Award Media—selected sound filmstrips introduce primary students to a number of award-winning picture books (see Checklist 1-2 at the end of this model).

Children's Literature—a veritable treasure trove of 246 sound filmstrips introducing elementary students to the literary best—past and present.

Weston Woods pioneered in producing sound filmstrips and motion pictures to recreate for children and young people the best in children's literature, including:

EXAMPLE 1-1   A WRINKLE IN TIME,
BY MADELEINE L'ENGLE (NEWBERY SERIES)* (MEDIA-GRAM)

BACKGROUND

THE AUTHOR

Her life as an actress, country storekeeper, wife, and mother has provided Madeleine L'Engle with an excellent variety of source material for her writing, which she considers "an essential function," like sleeping and breathing. Ms. L'Engle wrote her first book, *The Small Rain,* while working in theater after graduating from Smith College. She met her husband, actor Hugh Franklin, when they both appeared in *The Cherry Orchard.* Upon becoming Mrs. Franklin, she gave up the stage in favor of her career as an author. While her children—Josephine, Maria, and Bion—were asleep, she wrote *A Wrinkle in Time* and many other fine books for young people.

THE BOOK

Story: When Mr. Murry, an atomic physicist, disappears on a secret mission, his daughter Meg, her brother Charles Wallace, and their teenage friend Calvin set out on a bizarre search for him. Led by three wonderfully whimsical characters—Mrs. Whatsit, Mrs. Who, and Mrs. Which—the trio are taken on an interplanetary journey in which they manage to span time and space by *tessering.* They reach the planet Camazotz where they find Mr. Murry, but they lose Charles Wallace to the omnipotent brain that has robotized everyone.

Characters:

Mr. and Mrs. Murry

Meg, their 12-year-old daughter

Charles Wallace, her five-year-old brother

Calvin O'Keefe, a teenage friend

Mrs. Whatsit, a mysterious friend of Charles Wallace

Mrs. Who, her friend who speaks in quotations

Mrs. Which, her friend who never completely materializes

IT, the computerized brain that rules Camazotz

The Black Thing (or the Dark Thing), the symbol of evil

Aunt Beast, an inhabitant of the planet Ixchel

Setting: This science fiction fantasy takes place on Earth and on three imaginary planets: Uriel, Camazotz, and Ixchel. Madeleine L'Engle has said that Uriel is named for one of the four archangels, Camazotz for an evil South American god, and Ixchel for a good South American god.

In the story, the characters are able to travel from planet to planet, through time and space, due to a phenomenon called a *tesseract.* The *tesseract* is author Madeleine L'Engle's concept of the fifth dimension, and *tessering* is the wrinkling away of time between two separate points—as one would gather a piece of material—to bring the points together. As described in the book, people can travel across time in the same way as a very small insect travels across a piece of material. The trip from one edge of the material to the other would be very long unless someone brought the edges together, by wrinkling the material in between. Then the insect would be at the other edge without a long trip. So, Mrs. Which, Mrs. Who, and Mrs. Whatsit take the three children across a wrinkle in time.

WORDS AND MEANINGS

frenzied. During the hurricanelike weather, Meg Murry watched the trees tossing in the *frenzied*—wildly excited—lashings of the wind.

* © 1981 Random House, Inc., Miller-Brody Productions, a division of Random House, Inc., listening cassette unit.

EXAMPLE 1-1 (cont.)

physicist. Mr. Murry was a famous *physicist*—an expert in the science of matter and energy.

bacteriologist. Mrs. Murry was a *bacteriologist*—a scientist who deals with bacteria, or organisms that can be seen only through a microscope.

deters. When Mrs. Who said, "Nothing *deters* a good man from doing what is honorable," she meant that nothing, not even fears or doubts, would keep Mr. Murry from doing what was right.

materialize. "I don't think I'll *materialize* completely," said Mrs. Which. She meant that she would not take a form, such as a human body.

hovered. Instead, Mrs. Which *hovered*—stayed suspended above ground in one spot—only as a vague, pulsing glow in the dark air.

fragrant. The large, green field where Meg, Calvin, and Charles Wallace landed was filled with *fragrant*—sweet-smelling —flowers and grass.

spiral nebula. Uriel was the third planet of the star Malak in the *spiral nebula* Messier 101—a misty, cloudlike patch in the sky, formed like a curlicue.

frantic. Meg said that when they didn't come in at bedtime, their mother would be *frantic,* or greatly excited by worry.

transformed. The children watched as Mrs. Whatsit *transformed*—changed—into a new creature.

centaur. It was very much like a *centaur,* a mythical creature that was half horse, half man.

unaltered. In the fading light of day, as stars began appearing in the sky, the shadow remained *unaltered*—unchanged.

clammy. When Meg was swept into nothingness for the second time, the nothingness was interrupted by a feeling of *clammy*—moist and clinging—coldness.

identical. Each of the houses on Camazotz had the *identical*—exactly the same—square of lawn in front.

simultaneously. On Camazotz, the doors of the houses opened *simultaneously*—all at the same time—and out came women like a row of paper dolls.

oriented. When the newsboy on Uriel called his city the most *oriented* on the planet, he meant that everyone and everthing was geared for a certain purpose.

reprocessing. A man on Camazotz stated that he didn't want to risk *reprocessing*—going through a certain procedure or course of events again.

opaque. Charles Wallace focused his eyes until the pupils became smaller and smaller, and his eyes were nothing but *opaque* blue—a deep blue that doesn't let any light show through it.

transparent. Meg and Charles Wallace looked into a room containing a column that was large, round, and *transparent*—that you could see through.

corridors. In their trip through time and space, the children passed through a blur of streets and *corridors,* or long hallways or passageways.

vaulted and *disembodied.* In a *vaulted* room—a room having many arches—Meg met a *disembodied* brain—one that floats free from the body, by itself.

tentacles. Meg was cared for by a great beast with long, waving *tentacles*—slender, leglike parts which some animals have and use to feel, grasp, or move forward.

indentations. The beast has soft *indentations*—small dents or hollows—for eyes, nose, and mouth.

solar system. Mr. Murry said that he didn't intend to leave our *solar sytem*—all the planets, stars, moons, and heavenly bodies that revolve around our sun, plus the sun itself.

SPIN-OFF

In the story, the children leave our galaxy and go to Uriel, a planet in another galaxy. What are the special properties of Uriel? In addition to Earth, what other planets are in our galaxy? What are their properties? Make up a planet of your own—one that has no sound, or has extreme heat, or muddy ground, or whatever unusual characteristics you want. Then create characters to inhabit it, and write a science fiction story about them.

Create an "IT." Try using different types of materials: clay, boxes, paints, wires, etc.

Caldecott Medal and Honor Books (see Checklist 1-2 at the end of this model).

Theme Libraries offer sound filmstrips, books, and media packages under the following categories: Fables and Folktales, Stories from Many Lands and Cultures, Self-Awareness, Early Childhood, Musical Stories, Poetry, Stories for Seasons and Special Occasions, Our American Heritage.

A wide variety of media numbering well over 300 separate items, including sound filmstrips with text booklets, sound filmstrip and book package, book and cassette package, storytelling records, and motion pictures.

Recommended sources of first-choice promotional aids to support a literature study and appreciation program are:

Children's Book Council, Inc. (CBC), a nonprofit trade association of children's book publishers, which offers the following:

The Calendar—official CBC newsletter is published at eight-month intervals. Its "Materials Available" section is filled with tips on where to write for free or inexpensive materials. (A one-time-only charge of $5 places you on *The Calendar* mailing list. Recipients receive CBC materials brochures automatically.)

Bookmarks, such as:
Caldecott Bookmark
Care for Books Bookmark
Curious George Dewey Decimal Bookmark
How a Book Is Made Bookmark
Music Illustrated Bookmark
Music Photographic Bookmark
Newbery Bookmark
Spring Reading Bookmark
Summer Reading Bookmark

Posters, such as:
Book Week Poster
Humor Poster
Music Poster
Seasonal Reading Poster
Sports Poster

Kits, such as:
Book Week Kit
Music Kit
Seasonal Reading Kit

Pinetree Media, Ltd., produces a variety of quality promotional aids:

Bookmarks, such as:
Bookfeast Bookmark
Caring & Sharing Bookmark
Set Your Mind Free Bookmark
You've Always Got a Friend Bookmark

Balloons, such as:
  Bookfeast Balloon

Buttons, such as:
  Hooked on Books Button
  I Read Button
  Purrrfect Reading Button
  Student Library Aide Button
  You've Always Got a Friend Button

Posters, such as:
  Bookfeast Poster
  Caring & Sharing Poster
  Set Your Mind Free Poster
  You've Always Got a Friend Poster

Reading Certificates, such as:
  Purrrfect Reader Certificate
  Reading Adventure Certificate

Kits, such as:
  Bookfeast Kit
  Early Bird Special Kit

Reading Logs, such as:
  Adventures Reading Log

Upstart Library Promotionals produces a variety of quality promotional aids, including:

Book Bags (plastic), such as:
  Let the Book Bug Bite Book Bag
  Libraries Are #1 Book Bag
  Love My Library Book Bag
  Pass the Word—Read Book Bag

Bookmarks, such as:
  Big Foot Bookmark
  Book Bugs Bookmark
  Books Are Big Fun Bookmark
  Butterfly Bookmark
  Hare and Tortoise Bookmark

Buttons, such as:
  Book Lover Button
  Books Are Big Fun Button
  Eager Reader Button
  Find Your Fantasy, Read Button
  I Read Button
  Libraries Are Full of Wonder Button
  Member USA Reading Team Button
  Read On Button

Posters, such as:
  Book Bugs Poster
  Find Your Fantasy, Read Poster
  Read On Poster

Kits, such as:
Book Bugs Kit
Book Week Kit
Holiday Kit
Pass the Word Kit

Bulletin Board Display, such as:
Biography Bulletin Board Display

Recommended single-ordering source for books produced by the major publishing houses is the Follett Library Book Company, which:

Offers a basic list of 36,000 titles listed in their *Guide to Good Reading,* the most comprehensive school catalog available; free on request to teachers.

Supplies all the Caldecott and Newbery Award and Honor Books currently in print.

Offers teachers printouts of award-winning and/or notable books, including the following:

American Book Awards
ALA Best Books for Young Adults
Best of Cover to Cover 1/Public Television
The Book Bird/Public Television
Boston Globe–Horn Book Awards
Children's Books
Children's Choices
Children's Reviewers' Choice
Horn Book's Honor List
Junior High School Library Catalog
ALA Notable Books
ALA Notable Children's Books
Notable Children's Books in the Field of Social Studies
Outstanding Science Books for Children
School Library Journal Best Books
School Library Journal Best Books for Young Adults
Young Adult Reviewers' Choice
Young Adult Reviewers of Southern California
University Press Books

**CHECKLIST 1-1 DELIGHTFUL LITERARY FARE:
BASIC LITERARY EXPERIENCES***

Determine the grade level within which program—language arts, reading, or gifted—each title is introduced. Then note that grade level on the blank line provided in the appropriate column.

Language Arts	Reading	Gifted	
			KINDERGARTEN–SECOND GRADE
——	——	——	*A Is for Annabelle* by Tasha Tudor (Walck, 1954; paper, Rand)
——	——	——	*Angus and the Ducks* by Marjorie Flack (Doubleday, n.d. [entire series]; sound filmstrip, Weston Woods)
——	——	——	*Baseball Mouse* by Syd Hoff (Putnam, 1969; paper)
——	——	——	*Bears in the Night* by Stan Berenstain and Jan Berenstain (Random, 1960 [entire series]; sound filmstrip, Miller-Brody)
——	——	——	*Big Fraid, Little Fraid* by Ellis Credle (Elsevier-Nelson, 1964)
——	——	——	*Billy and Blaze* by C. W. Anderson (Macmillan, 1962)
——	——	——	*C Is for Cupcake* by Carolyn Haywood (Morrow, 1974)
——	——	——	*Caleb and Kate* by William Steig (Farrar, 1977)
——	——	——	*The Camel Who Took a Walk* by Jack Tworkov (Dutton, 1974; paper; sound filmstrip, Weston Woods)
——	——	——	*Caps for Sale* by Esphyr Slobodkina (Whitman, 1947; paper, Scholastic; sound filmstrip, Weston Woods)
——	——	——	*The Cat in the Hat* by Dr. Seuss (Random, 1957; sound filmstrip, Random)
——	——	——	*Charlie the Tramp* by Russell Hoban and Lillian Hoban (Scholastic, 1970; paper)
——	——	——	*The Country Bunny and the Little Gold Shoes* by Dubose Heyward (Houghton, 1974; paper)
——	——	——	*Curious George* by H. A. Rey (Houghton, 1941; paper [entire series]; sound filmstrips, Random)
——	——	——	*Dandelion* by Don Freeman (Viking, 1964; paper, Penguin; sound filmstrip, Random)
——	——	——	*The Duchess Bakes a Cake* by Virginia Kahl (Scribner, n.d.; paper; sound filmstrip, Miller-Brody)
——	——	——	*First Poems of Childhood* by Tasha Tudor (Platt, 1967; paper)
——	——	——	*Frederick* by Leo Lionni (Pantheon, 1966; paper)
——	——	——	*Frog and Toad Together* by Arnold Lobel (Harper, 1972; paper [entire series]; sound filmstrip, Random)

*This list highlights the children's perennial favorites, their acclamation of the "best of the best."

CHECKLIST 1-1 (cont.)

Language Arts	Reading	Gifted	
—	—	—	*Georgie* by Robert Bright (Doubleday, 1959; paper [entire series]; motion picture, Weston Woods; sound filmstrip, Weston Woods)
—	—	—	*Gingerbread Boy* illus. by Paul Galdone (Seabury, 1975)
—	—	—	*Going Barefoot* by Aileen Fisher (Crowell, 1960)
—	—	—	*The Golden Egg Book* by Margaret Brown (Simon & Schuster, 1947)
—	—	—	*The Hare and the Tortoise* illus. by Paul Galdone (McGraw, 1962)
—	—	—	*Harry the Dirty Dog* by Gene Zion (Harper, 1956; paper [entire series]; sound filmstrip, Random)
—	—	—	*Henny Penny* illus. by Paul Galdone (Seabury, 1968)
—	—	—	*The House That Jack Built* illus. by Paul Galdone (McGraw, 1961; sound filmstrip, Weston Woods)
—	—	—	*In a Pumpkin Shell* by Joan Walsh Anglund (Harcourt, 1960; paper)
—	—	—	*Ira Sleeps Over* by Bernard Waber (Houghton, 1972; paper)
—	—	—	*Jack and the Wonder Beans* by James Still, rev. ed. (Putnam, 1977)
—	—	—	*John Henry* by Ezra Jack Keats (Pantheon, 1965)
—	—	—	*Katy and the Big Snow* by Virginia Lee Burton (Houghton, 1943; paper)
—	—	—	*Katy-No Pocket* by Emmy Payne (Houghton, 1969; paper)
—	—	—	*Lentil* by Robert McCloskey (Viking, 1940; paper, Penguin; motion picture, Weston Woods; sound filmstrip, Weston Woods)
—	—	—	*Little Bear's Sunday Breakfast* by Janice. (Lothrop, 1959 [entire series])
—	—	—	*Little Brute Family* by Russell Hoban (Macmillan, 1966; paper)
—	—	—	*The Little Engine That Could* by Watty Piper, rev. ed. (Platt, 1976; paper, Scholastic)
—	—	—	*The Little Red Hen* illus. by Paul Galdone (McGraw, 1973; paper, Scholastic; sound filmstrip, Weston Woods)
—	—	—	*Little Toot* by Hardie Gramatky, rev. ed. (Putnam, 1978; paper; sound filmstrip, Weston Woods)
—	—	—	*Mike Mulligan and His Steamshovel* by Virginia Lee Burton (Houghton, 1939; motion picture, Weston Woods; sound filmstrip, Weston Woods)
—	—	—	*Mike's House* by Julia L. Sauer (Viking, 1954)
—	—	—	*Milton the Early Riser* by Robert Kraus (Dutton, 1972; paper)
—	—	—	*The Mitten* by Alvin R. Tresselt (Lothrop, 1964)
—	—	—	*The Mother Goose Treasury* by Raymond Briggs (Prentice-Hall, 1965; paper; sound filmstrip, Weston Woods)

CHECKLIST 1-1 (cont.)

Language Arts	Reading	Gifted	
—	—	—	*Old Mother Hubbard and Her Dog* illus. by Paul Galdone (McGraw, 1960; sound filmstrip, Weston Woods)
—	—	—	*The Old Woman and Her Pig* illus. by Paul Galdone (McGraw, 1961; sound filmstrip, Weston Woods)
—	—	—	*The Old Woman and Her Pig and 10 Other Stories* by Anne Rockwell (Crowell, 1979)
—	—	—	*Over in the Meadow* by John Langstaff (Harcourt, 1967; paper; motion picture, Weston Woods; sound filmstrip, Weston Woods)
—	—	—	*Petunia Takes a Trip* by Roger Duvoisin (Knopf, 1953; paper, Pantheon [entire series]; sound filmstrip, Random)
—	—	—	*The Plant Sitter* by Gene Zion (Harper, 1959; paper)
—	—	—	*The Rice Bowl Pet* by Patricia Miles Martin (Crowell, 1962)
—	—	—	*Richard Scarry's Animal Nursery Tales* by Richard Scarry (Western, 1975; sound filmstrip, Random)
—	—	—	*The Shoemaker and the Elves* illus. by Adrienne Adams (Scribner, 1960; paper; sound filmstrip, Miller-Brody)
—	—	—	*Snow White and Rose Red* illus. by Adrienne Adams (Scribner, 1964)
—	—	—	*The Story about Ping* by Marjorie Flack (Viking, 1933; paper, Penguin)
—	—	—	*The Tale of Peter Rabbit* by Beatrix Potter (Warne, 1902; paper, Troll [entire series]; sound filmstrip, Random)
—	—	—	*The Three Bears* illus. by Paul Galdone (Seabury, 1972; paper, Scholastic)
—	—	—	*The Three Billy Goats Gruff* illus. by Marcia Brown (Harcourt, 1957; paper; sound filmstrip, Weston Woods)
—	—	—	*The Three Little Pigs* illus. by Eric Blegvad (Atheneum, n.d.)
—	—	—	*Tikki Tikki Tembo* by Arlene Mosel (Harper, 1968; motion picture, Weston Woods; sound filmstrip, Weston Woods)
—	—	—	*Tom, Tom the Piper's Son* illus. by Paul Galdone (McGraw, n.d.)
—	—	—	*The Ugly Duckling* illus. by Adrienne Adams (Scribner, 1965; paper; sound filmstrip, Random)
—	—	—	*Wait Till the Moon Is Full* by Margaret Brown (Harper, 1948)
—	—	—	*The Year at Maple Hill Farm* by Alice Provensen and Martin Provensen (Atheneum, 1978)

THIRD–FOURTH GRADE

—	—	—	*All-of-a-Kind Family* by Sydney Taylor (Follett, 1951; paper, Dell [entire series])

CHECKLIST 1-1 (cont.)

Language Arts	Reading	Gifted	
—	—	—	*Amelia Bedelia* by Peggy Parish (Harper, 1963; paper, Scholastic [entire series]; sound filmstrip, Random)
—	—	—	*And to Think That I Saw It on Mulberry Street* by Dr. Suess (Vanguard, 1937)
—	—	—	*An Anteater Named Arthur* by Bernard Waber (Houghton, 1967; paper)
—	—	—	*A Bear Called Paddington* by Michael Bond (Houghton, 1960; paper, Dell [entire series])
—	—	—	*The Best New Thing* by Isaac Asimov (World, 1971)
—	—	—	*The Best of Grimm's Fairy Tales* by Jacob Grimm and Wilhelm Grimm. (Larousse, 1979)
—	—	—	*The Blind Men and the Elephant* illus. by Janice Holland (Scribner, 1959; paper; sound filmstrip, Random)
—	—	—	*Bread and Butter Indian* by Anne Colver (Harper, 1964)
—	—	—	*Brer Rabbit: Stories from Uncle Remus* adapted by Margaret W. Brown (Harper, 1941)
—	—	—	*Brer Rabbit and Brer Fox* by Joel Chandler Harris (Collins, 1970)
—	—	—	*The Cabin Faced West* by Jean Fritz (Coward, 1958)
—	—	—	*Carolina's Courage* by Elizabeth Yates (Dutton, 1964)
—	—	—	*A Child's Garden of Verses* by Robert Louis Stevenson (Western, 1951)
—	—	—	*The Day the Spaceship Landed* by Beman Lord (Walck, 1967)
—	—	—	*A Dog and a Half* by Barbara Willard (Elsevier-Nelson, 1971)
—	—	—	*East of the Sun and West of the Moon* by Kay Nielsen (Doubleday, 1977)
—	—	—	*The Emperor's New Clothes* illus. by Monika Laimgruber (Addison, 1973)
—	—	—	*Encyclopedia Brown: Boy Detective* by Donald J. Sobol (Elsevier-Nelson, 1963; paper, Bantam [entire series]; sound filmstrips, Random)
—	—	—	*Everyone Is Good for Something* by Beatrice Schenk de Regniers (Clarion, 1980)
—	—	—	*Fables* by Jean de La Fontaine, trans. by Marianne Moore (Viking, 1954)
—	—	—	*The Fantastic Mister Fox* by Roald Dahl (Knopf, 1970; paper, Bantam)
—	—	—	*The 500 Hats of Bartholomew Cubbins* by Dr. Seuss (Vanguard, n.d.)
—	—	—	*Ghost in a Four-Room Apartment* by Ellen Raskin (Atheneum, 1969; paper)
—	—	—	*The Ghost on a Saturday Night* by Sid Fleischman (Little, 1974)

CHECKLIST 1-1 (cont.)

Language Arts	Reading	Gifted	
—	—	—	*The Goose Girl* illus. by Marguerite de Angeli (Doubleday, n.d.)
—	—	—	*Heidi* by Johanna Spyri (Grosset, n.d.)
—	—	—	*Henry Huggins* by Beverly Cleary (Morrow, 1950; paper, Dell [entire series]; sound filmstrip, Random)
—	—	—	*How the Moolah Was Taught a Lesson* trans. and adapted by Estelle Titiev and Lila Pargment (Dial, 1976)
—	—	—	*Just So Stories* by Rudyard Kipling (Doubleday, 1973; paper, Airmont; sound filmstrips, Random)
—	—	—	*Kermit the Hermit* by Bill Peet (Houghton, 1965)
—	—	—	*The Lion and the Mouse* illus. by Ed Young (Doubleday, 1979)
—	—	—	*Listen Rabbit* by Aileen Fisher (Crowell, 1964)
—	—	—	*The Little House in the Big Woods* by Laura Ingalls Wilder (Harper, 1953; paper [entire series])
—	—	—	*McBroom Tells a Lie* by Sid Fleischman (Little, 1976)
—	—	—	*Macaroon* by Julia Cunningham (Pantheon, 1962; paper, Dell)
—	—	—	*Mousekin's Golden House* by Edna Miller (Prentice-Hall, 1964; paper [entire series]; sound filmstrips, Random)
—	—	—	*Old Mother West Wind* by Thornton Burgess (Little, 1960)
—	—	—	*Once in a Wood: Ten Tales from Aesop* adapted and illus. by Eve Rice (Greenwillow, 1979)
—	—	—	*A Puppy Named Gih* by Sara Machetanz (Scribner, 1957; paper only)
—	—	—	*Puss in Boots* illus. by Paul Galdone (Seabury, 1976)
—	—	—	*The Rainbow Fairy Book: A Selection of Outstanding Fairy Tales from the Color Fairy Books by Andrew Lang* ed. by Kathleen Lines (Schocken, 1977)
—	—	—	*The Rich Man and the Shoemaker* illus. by Brian Wildsmith (Oxford, 1979; paper; sound filmstrip, Weston Woods)
—	—	—	*Six Chinese Brothers: An Ancient Tale* by Chen Hou-tien (Holt, 1979)
—	—	—	*Stuart Little* by E. B. White (Harper, 1945; paper)
—	—	—	*Tales of a Fourth Grade Nothing* by Judy Blume (Dutton, 1972; paper, Dell)
—	—	—	*Teeny-Tiny and the Witch-Woman* retold by Barbara K. Walker (Pantheon, 1975; motion picture, Weston Woods)
—	—	—	*The Tomten* adapted by Astrid Lindgren, illus. by Harold Wiberg (Coward, 1961; motion picture, Weston Woods; sound filmstrip, Weston Woods)

CHECKLIST 1-1 (cont.)

Language Arts	Reading	Gifted	
—	—	—	*The Town Mouse and the Country Mouse* illus. by Paul Galdone (McGraw, 1971)
—	—	—	*Tucker's Countryside* by George Selden (Farrar, 1969; sound filmstrip, Random)
—	—	—	*Twelve Clever Brothers and Other Fools* comp. by Myra Ginsburg (Lippincott, 1979)
—	—	—	*The Velveteen Rabbit* by Margery Williams (Doubleday, 1958; paper, Avon; motion picture, LSB Productions)
—	—	—	*Why the Chimes Rang* by Raymond Alden (Bobbs, 1954; paper)
—	—	—	*Winnie-The-Pooh* by A. A. Milne (Dutton, 1962)
—	—	—	*Yonie Wondernose* by Marguerite de Angeli (Doubleday, 1944)

FIFTH–SIXTH GRADE

Language Arts	Reading	Gifted	
—	—	—	*Adventures of Pinocchio* by Carlo Collodi (Macmillan, 1963)
—	—	—	*The Adventures of Tom Sawyer* by Mark Twain (Dodd, 1979; paper, Dell)
—	—	—	*Akavak: An Eskimo Journey* by James Houston (Harcourt, 1968)
—	—	—	*Alice's Adventures in Wonderland* by Lewis Carroll (Macmillan, 1963; paper)
—	—	—	*Alvin's Secret Code* by Clifford Hicks (Harper, 1963; paper, Scholastic)
—	—	—	*And Then What Happened, Paul Revere?* by Jean Fritz (Coward, 1973 [entire series])
—	—	—	*Ben and Me* by Robert Lawson (Little, 1939; paper, Dell)
—	—	—	*The Big Joke Game* by Scott Corbett (Dutton, 1972; paper)
—	—	—	*Big Red* by Jim Kjelgaard (Holiday, n.d.; paper, Bantam)
—	—	—	*Black Beauty* by Anna Sewell (Macmillan, 1962; paper, Airmont; sound filmstrip, Films, Inc.)
—	—	—	*Black Stallion* by Walter Farley (Random, 1944; paper [entire series])
—	—	—	*Blackbeard's Ghost* by Ben Stahl (Houghton, 1965; paper, Scholastic)
—	—	—	*The Borrowers* by Mary Norton (Harcourt, 1953; paper [entire series])
—	—	—	*Bright April* by Marguerite de Angeli (Doubleday, 1946)
—	—	—	*By Crumbs! It's Mine* by Patricia Beatty (Morrow, 1976)
—	—	—	*By the Great Horn Spoon* by Sid Fleischman (Little, n.d.)
—	—	—	*The Case of the Baker Street Irregulars* by Robert Newman (Atheneum, 1978)

CHECKLIST 1-1 (cont.)

Language Arts	Reading	Gifted	
—	—	—	*Casey at the Bat* by Ernest Thayer (Prentice 1964; paper, Dover)
—	—	—	*The Cay* by Theodore Taylor (Doubleday, 1969; paper, Avon)
—	—	—	*A Christmas Carol* by Charles Dickens, illus. by Arthur Rackham (Lippincott, 1966)
—	—	—	*The Chronicles of Narnia* by C. S. Lewis (Macmillan, 1950–1956)
—	—	—	*Clown of God* by Tomie de Paola (Harcourt, 1978; paper; motion picture, Weston Woods; sound filmstrip, Weston Woods)
—	—	—	*Danny Dunn and the Homework Machine* by Jay Williams and Raymond Abrashkin (McGraw, 1958; paper, Archway [entire series])
—	—	—	*The Dog on Barkham Street* by Mary Stolz (Harper, 1960; paper, Dell)
—	—	—	*The Eighteenth Emergency* by Betsy Byars (Viking, 1973; paper, Avon)
—	—	—	*Ellen Grae* by Vera Cleaver and Bill Cleaver (Lippincott, 1967; paper, NAL)
—	—	—	*Ellen Tebbits* by Beverly Cleary (Morrow, 1951; paper, Dell)
—	—	—	*Escape to Witch Mountain* by Alexander Key (Westminster, 1968; paper, Archway)
—	—	—	*Fog Magic* by Julia Sauer (Viking, 1943; paper, Archway)
—	—	—	*Gertrude Kloppenberg, Private* by Ruth Hooker (Archway, n.d.; paper)
—	—	—	*Getting Something on Maggie Marmelstein* by Marjorie Sharmat (Harper, 1971; paper)
—	—	—	*The Ghost Belonged to Me* by Richard Peck (Viking, 1975)
—	—	—	*The Great Brain* by John Fitzgerald (Dial, 1967; paper, Dell)
—	—	—	*Greenhorn on the Frontier* by Ann Finlayson (Warne, 1974)
—	—	—	*Henry Reed, Inc.* by Keith Robertson (Viking, 1958; paper, Dell [entire series])
—	—	—	*Heroes in American Folklore* by Irwin Shapiro (Messner, 1962)
—	—	—	*The Hobbit* by J. R. Tolkien (Houghton, 1937)
—	—	—	*Homer Price* by Robert McCloskey (Viking, 1943; paper, Penguin; motion picture, Weston Woods)
—	—	—	*How Many Miles to Sundown* by Patricia Beatty (Morrow, 1974)
—	—	—	*The Incredible Journey* by Sheila Burnford (Little, 1961; paper, Bantam)
—	—	—	*Jack Tales* by Richard Chase (Houghton, 1943)
—	—	—	*Lassie-Come-Home* by Eric Knight (Harper, 1978; paper, Dell; sound filmstrip, Films, Inc.)

CHECKLIST 1-1 (cont.)

Language Arts	Reading	Gifted	
—	—	—	*The Lion, the Witch, and the Wardrobe* by C. S. Lewis (Macmillan, 1951; paper)
—	—	—	*The Little Princess* by Frances H. Burnett (Lippincott, 1963; paper, Grosset)
—	—	—	*Little Women* by Louisa May Alcott, illus. by Tasha Tudor (Collins, 1969)
—	—	—	*Me and the Terrible Two* by Ellen Conford (Little, 1974; paper, Archway)
—	—	—	*Merry Adventures of Robin Hood . . .* by Howard Pyle (Scribner, 1946)
—	—	—	*Mustang, Wild Spirit of the West* by Marguerite Henry (Rand, 1966; paper)
—	—	—	*The Nightingale* by Hans Christian Andersen (Harper, 1965)
—	—	—	*Otherwise Known as Sheila the Great* by Judy Blume (Dutton, 1972; paper, Dell)
—	—	—	*The Pinballs* by Betsy Byars (Harper, 1977)
—	—	—	*The Prince and the Pauper* by Mark Twain (Harper, n.d.; paper, Airmont)
—	—	—	*The Pushcart War* by Jan Merrill (Whitman, 1964; paper, Dell)
—	—	—	*The Rain Forest* by Armstrong Sperry (Macmillan, 1947)
—	—	—	*Rebecca's War* by Ann Finlayson (Warne, 1972)
—	—	—	*A Secret Friend* by Marilyn Sachs (Doubleday, 1978)
—	—	—	*The Secret Garden* by Frances Burnett, illus. by Tasha Tudor (Lippincott, 1962; paper, Dell)
—	—	—	*The Story of King Arthur and His Knights* by Howard Pyle (Scribner, 1903)
—	—	—	*A Swiftly Tilting Planet* by Madeleine L'Engle (Farrar, 1978; paper, Dell)
—	—	—	*Tasha Tudor's Favorite Stories* by Tasha Tudor (Lippincott, 1965)
—	—	—	*Toliver's Secret* by Esther Brady (Crown, 1976; paper, Avon)
—	—	—	*Trail through Danger* by William Steele (Harcourt, 1965)
—	—	—	*Treasure Island* by Robert Louis Stevenson (McKay, 1977; paper, Schocken; sound filmstrip, Films, Inc.)
—	—	—	*Trial Valley* by Vera Cleaver and Bill Cleaver (Lippincott, 1965; paper)
—	—	—	*Two on an Island* by Bianca Bradbury (Houghton, 1965)
—	—	—	*The Unmaking of Rabbit* by Constance C. Greene (Viking, 1972)
—	—	—	*The Velvet Room* by Zilpha Snyder (Atheneum, 1965; paper)
—	—	—	*Where the Lilies Bloom* by Vera Cleaver and Bill Cleaver (Lippincott, 1969; paper, NAL)

CHECKLIST 1-1 (cont.)

Language Arts	Reading	Gifted	
—	—	—	*Where the Sidewalk Ends* by Shel Silverstein (Harper, 1974)
—	—	—	*A Wind in the Door* by Madeleine L'Engle (Farrar, 1973; paper, Dell)
—	—	—	*Wind in the Willows* by Kenneth Grahame (Scribner, 1933; paper; sound filmstrips, Random)
—	—	—	*Wings from the Wind: An Anthology of Poetry* by Tasha Tudor (Lippincott, 1964)
—	—	—	*Wolf Brother* by Jim Kjelgaard (Holiday, 1957)
—	—	—	*The Wolves of Willoughby Chase* by Joan Aiken (Doubleday, 1963; paper, Dell)
—	—	—	*The Wonderful Wizard of Oz* by L. Frank Baum (Western, 1977; paper)
—	—	—	*Yankee Doodle's Cousins* by Anne Malcolmson (Houghton, n.d.)
—	—	—	*The Young Unicorns* by Madeleine L'Engle (Farrar, 1968; paper, Dell)
—	—	—	*Zenas and the Shaving Mill* by Ferdinand Monjo (Coward, 1976)
—	—	—	*Zia* by Scott O'Dell (Houghton, 1976; paper, Dell)

CHECKLIST 1-2 CALDECOTT AWARD BOOKS*

Determine the grade level within which program—language arts, reading, or gifted—each title is introduced. Then note that grade level on the blank line provided in the appropriate column.

Language Arts	Reading	Gifted	
			1938 MEDAL
—	—	—	*Animals of the Bible* by Helen Dean Fish, illus. by Dorothy P. Lathrop (Lippincott)
			1938 HONOR BOOKS
—	—	—	*Seven Simeons* by Boris Artzybasheff (Viking)
—	—	—	*Four and Twenty Blackbirds* by Helen Dean Fish, illus. by Robert Lawson (Stokes)
			1939 MEDAL
—	—	—	*Mei Li* by Thomas Handforth (Doubleday)
			1939 HONOR BOOKS
—	—	—	*The Forest Pool* by Laura Adams Armer (Longman)

*In 1938, the first Caldecott Medal, donated by Frederic G. Melcher, was awarded to the artist of the most distinguished American picture book for children published in the United States during the preceding year. The name of Randolph Caldecott, the famous illustrator of books for children, was chosen for the medal because his work best represented "joyousness of picture books as well as their beauty." Awarded annually by The Association for Library Service to Children, The American Library Association.

CHECKLIST 1-2 (cont.)

Language Arts	Reading	Gifted	
—	—	—	*Wee Gillis* by Munro Leaf, illus. by Robert Lawson (Viking)
—	—	—	*Snow White and the Seven Dwarfs* by Wanda Gág (Coward)
—	—	—	*Barkis* by Clare Newberry (Harper)
—	—	—	*Andy and the Lion* by James Daugherty (Viking; motion picture, Weston Woods; sound filmstrip, Weston Woods)

1940 MEDAL

Language Arts	Reading	Gifted	
—	—	—	*Abraham Lincoln* by Ingri d'Aulaire and Edgar d'Aulaire (Doubleday)

1940 HONOR BOOKS

Language Arts	Reading	Gifted	
—	—	—	*Cook-a-Doodle Doo* by Berta Hader and Elmer Hader (Macmillan)
—	—	—	*Madeline* by Ludwig Bemelmans (Viking)
—	—	—	*The Ageless Story* illus. by Lauren Ford (Dodd)

1941 MEDAL

Language Arts	Reading	Gifted	
—	—	—	*They Were Strong and Good* by Robert Lawson (Viking; sound filmstrip, Weston Woods)

1941 HONOR BOOK

Language Arts	Reading	Gifted	
—	—	—	*April's Kittens* by Clare Newberry (Harper)

1942 MEDAL

Language Arts	Reading	Gifted	
—	—	—	*Make Way for Ducklings* by Robert McCloskey (Viking; motion picture, Weston Woods; sound filmstrip, Weston Woods)

1942 HONOR BOOKS

Language Arts	Reading	Gifted	
—	—	—	*An American ABC* by Maud Petersham and Miska Petersham (Macmillan)
—	—	—	*In My Mother's House* by Ann Nolan Clark, illus. by Velino Herrera (Viking)
—	—	—	*Paddle-to-the Sea* by Holling C. Holling (Houghton)
—	—	—	*Nothing At All* by Wanda Gág (Coward)

1943 MEDAL

Language Arts	Reading	Gifted	
—	—	—	*The Little House* by Virginia Lee Burton (Houghton; sound filmstrip, Weston Woods)

1943 HONOR BOOKS

Language Arts	Reading	Gifted	
—	—	—	*Dash and Dart* by Mary Buff and Conrad Buff (Viking)
—	—	—	*Marshmallow* by Clare Newberry (Harper)

1944 MEDAL

Language Arts	Reading	Gifted	
—	—	—	*Many Moons* by James Thurber, illus. by Louis Slobodkin (Harcourt)

1944 HONOR BOOKS

Language Arts	Reading	Gifted	
—	—	—	*Small Rain: Verses from the Bible* selected by Jessie Orton Jones, illus. by Elizabeth Orton Jones (Viking)

CHECKLIST 1-2 (cont.)

Language Arts	Reading	Gifted	
—	—	—	*Pierre Pigeon* by Lee Kingman, illus. by Arnold E. Bare (Houghton)
—	—	—	*The Mighty Hunter* by Berta Hader and Elmer Hader (Macmillan)
—	—	—	*A Child's Good Night Book* by Margaret Wise Brown, illus. by Jean Charlot (Scott, Foresman)
—	—	—	*Good Luck Horse* by Chin-Yi Chan, illus. by Plao Chan (Whittlesey)

1945 MEDAL

—	—	—	*Prayer for a Child* by Rachel Field, illus. by Elizabeth Orton Jones (Macmillan)

1945 HONOR BOOKS

—	—	—	*Mother Goose* illus. by Tasha Tudor (Walck)
—	—	—	*In the Forest* by Marie Hall Ets (Viking)
—	—	—	*Yonie Wondernose* by Marguerite de Angeli (Doubleday)
—	—	—	*The Christmas Anna Angel* by Ruth Sawyer, illus. by Kate Seredy (Viking)

1946 MEDAL

—	—	—	*The Rooster Crows* illus. by Maud Petersham and Miska Petersham (Macmillan)

1946 HONOR BOOKS

—	—	—	*Little Lost Lamb* by Golden MacDonald, illus. by Leonard Weisgard (Doubleday)
—	—	—	*Sing Mother Goose* by Opal Wheeler, illus. by Marjorie Torrey (Dutton)
—	—	—	*My Mother Is the Most Beautiful Woman in the World* by Becky Reyher, illus. by Ruth C. Gannett (Lothrop)
—	—	—	*You Can Write Chinese* by Kurt Wiese (Viking)

1947 MEDAL

—	—	—	*The Little Island* by Golden MacDonald, illus. by Leonard Weisgard (Doubleday; sound filmstrip, Weston Woods)

1947 HONOR BOOKS

—	—	—	*Rain Drop Splash* by Alvin Tresselt, illus. by Leonard Weisgard (Lothrop)
—	—	—	*Boats on the River* by Marjorie Flack, illus. by Jay Hyde Barnum (Viking)
—	—	—	*Timothy Turtle* by Al Graham, illus. by Tony Palazzo
—	—	—	*Pedro, the Angel of Olvera Street* by Leo Politi (Scribner)
—	—	—	*Sing in Praise: A Collection of the Best Loved Hymns* by Opal Wheeler, illus. by Marjorie Torrey

1948 MEDAL

—	—	—	*White Snow, Bright Snow* by Alvin Tresselt, illus. by Roger Duvoisin (Lothrop; sound filmstrip, Weston Woods)

CHECKLIST 1-2 (cont.)

Language Arts	Reading	Gifted	
			1948 HONOR BOOKS
—	—	—	*Stone Soup* by Marcia Brown (Scribner; motion picture, Weston Woods; sound filmstrip, Weston Woods)
—	—	—	*McElligot's Pool* by Dr. Seuss (Random; sound filmstrip, Miller-Brody)
—	—	—	*Bambino the Clown* by George Schreiber (Viking)
—	—	—	*Roger and the Fox* by Lavinia Davis, illus. by Hildegard Woodward (Doubleday)
—	—	—	*Song of Robin Hood* ed. by Anne Malcolmson, illus. by Virginia Lee Burton
			1949 MEDAL
—	—	—	*The Big Snow* by Berta Hader and Elmer Hader (Macmillan; sound filmstrip, Weston Woods)
			1949 HONOR BOOKS
—	—	—	*Blueberries for Sal* by Robert McCloskey (Viking; motion picture, Weston Woods; sound filmstrip, Weston Woods)
—	—	—	*All Around the Town* by Phyllis McGinley, illus. by Helen Stone (Lippincott)
—	—	—	*Juanita* by Leo Politi (Scribner)
—	—	—	*Fish in the Air* by Kurt Wiese (Viking; sound filmstrip, Weston Woods)
			1950 MEDAL
—	—	—	*Song of the Swallows* by Leo Politi (Scribner; sound filmstrip, Miller-Brody)
			1950 HONOR BOOKS
—	—	—	*America's Ethan Allen* by Stewart Holbrook, illus. by Lynd Ward (Houghton)
—	—	—	*The Wild Birthday Cake* by Lavinia Davis, illus. by Hildegard Woodward (Doubleday)
—	—	—	*The Happy Day* by Ruth Krauss, illus. by Marc Simont (Harper; sound filmstrip, Weston Woods)
—	—	—	*Bartholomew and the Oobleck* by Dr. Seuss (Random; sound filmstrip, Miller-Brody)
—	—	—	*Henry Fisherman* by Marcia Brown (Scribner)
			1951 MEDAL
—	—	—	*The Egg Tree* by Katherine Milhous (Scribner)
			1951 HONOR BOOKS
—	—	—	*Dick Whittington and His Cat* by Marcia Brown (Scribner)
—	—	—	*The Two Reds* by Will, illus. by Nicolas (Harcourt)
—	—	—	*If I Ran the Zoo* by Dr. Seuss (Random; sound filmstrip, Miller-Brody)
—	—		*The Most Wonderful Doll in the World* by Phillis McGinley, illus. by Helen Stone (Lippincott)
—	—	—	*T-Bone, The Baby Sitter* by Clare Newberry (Harper)

CHECKLIST 1-2 (cont.)

Language Arts	Reading	Gifted	

1952 MEDAL

— — — *Finders Keepers* by Will, illus. by Nicolas (Harcourt; sound filmstrip, Weston Woods)

1952 HONOR BOOKS

— — — *Mr. T. W. Anthony Woo* by Marie Hall Ets (Viking)

— — — *Skipper John's Cook* by Marcia Brown (Scribner)

— — — *All Falling Down* by Gene Zion, illus. by Margaret Bloy Graham (Harper)

— — — *Bear Party* by William Pène du Bois (Viking; sound filmstrip, Miller-Brody)

— — — *Feather Mountain* by Elizabeth Olds (Houghton)

1953 MEDAL

— — — *The Biggest Bear* by Lynd Ward (Houghton; sound filmstrip, Weston Woods)

1953 HONOR BOOKS

— — — *Puss in Boots* by Charles Perrault, trans. and illus. by Marcia Brown (Scribner; sound filmstrip, Miller-Brody)

— — — *One Morning in Maine* by Robert McCloskey (Viking; sound filmstrip, Miller-Brody)

— — — *Ape in a Cape* by Fritz Eichenberg (Harcourt)

— — — *The Storm Book* by Charlotte Zolotow, illus. by Margaret Bloy Graham (Harper)

— — — *Five Little Monkeys* by Juliet Kepes (Houghton)

1954 MEDAL

— — — *Madeline's Rescue* by Ludwig Bemelmans (Viking; sound filmstrip, Weston Woods)

1954 HONOR BOOKS

— — — *Journey Cake, Ho!* by Ruth Sawyer, illus. by Robert McCloskey (Viking; sound filmstrip, Weston Woods)

— — — *When Will the World Be Mine?* by Miriam Schlein, illus. by Jean Charlot (Scott, Foresman)

— — — *The Steadfast Tin Soldier* by Hans Christian Andersen, illus. by Marcia Brown (Scribner; sound filmstrip, Miller-Brody)

— — — *A Very Special House* by Ruth Krauss, illus. by Maurice Sendak (Harper)

— — — *Green Eyes* by A. Birnbaum (Capitol)

1955 MEDAL

— — — *Cinderella, Or the Little Glass Slipper* by Charles Perrault, trans. and illus. by Marcia Brown (Scribner; sound filmstrip, Miller-Brody)

1955 HONOR BOOKS

— — — *Book of Nursery and Mother Goose Rhymes* illus. by Marguerite de Angeli (Doubleday)

— — — *Wheel on the Chimney* by Margaret Wise Brown, illus. by Tibor Gergely (Lippincott; motion picture, Weston Woods; sound filmstrip, Weston Woods)

CHECKLIST 1-2 (cont.)

Language Arts	Reading	Gifted	
—	—	—	*The Thanksgiving Story* by Alice Dalgliesh, illus. by Helen Sewell (Scribner)
			1956 MEDAL
—	—	—	*Frog Went A-Courtin'* by John Langstaff, illus. by Feodor Rojankovsky (Harcourt; motion picture, Weston Woods; sound filmstrip, Weston Woods)
			1956 HONOR BOOKS
—	—	—	*Play with Me* by Marie Hall Ets (Viking; sound filmstrip, Weston Woods)
—	—	—	*Crow Boy* by Taro Yashima (Viking; motion picture, Weston Woods; sound filmstrip, Weston Woods)
			1957 MEDAL
—	—	—	*A Tree Is Nice* by Janice May Udry, illus. by Marc Simont (Harper; sound filmstrip, Weston Woods)
			1957 HONOR BOOKS
—	—	—	*Mr. Penny's Race Horse* by Marie Hall Ets (Viking)
—	—	—	*1 Is One* by Tasha Tudor (Walck)
—	—	—	*Anatole* by Eve Titus, illus. by Paul Galdone (McGraw)
—	—	—	*Gillespie and the Guards* by Benjamin Elkin, illus. by James Daugherty (Viking)
—	—	—	*Lion* by William Pène du Bois (Viking)
			1958 MEDAL
—	—	—	*Time of Wonder* by Robert McCloskey (Viking; motion picture, Weston Woods; sound filmstrip, Weston Woods)
			1958 HONOR BOOKS
—	—	—	*Fly High, Fly Low* by Don Freeman (Viking)
—	—	—	*Anatole and the Cat* by Eve Titus, illus. by Paul Galdone (McGraw)
			1959 MEDAL
—	—	—	*Chanticleer and the Fox* adapted from Chaucer and illus. by Barbara Cooney (Crowell; sound filmstrip, Weston Woods)
			1959 HONOR BOOKS
—	—	—	*The House That Jack Built* by Antonio Frasconi (Harcourt)
—	—	—	*What Do You Say, Dear?* by Sesyle Joslin, illus. by Maurice Sendak (Scott, Foresman; sound filmstrip, Weston Woods)
—	—	—	*Umbrella* by Taro Yashima (Viking; sound filmstrip, Weston Woods)
			1960 MEDAL
—	—	—	*Nine Days to Christmas* by Marie Hall Ets and Aurora Labastida, illus. by Marie Hall Ets (Viking)

CHECKLIST 1-2 (cont.)

Language Arts	Reading	Gifted	
			1960 HONOR BOOKS
—	—	—	*Houses from the Sea* by Alice E. Goudey, illus. by Adrienne Adams (Scribner; sound filmstrip, Miller-Brody)
—	—	—	*The Moon Jumpers* by Janice May Udry, illus. by Maurice Sendak (Harper)
			1961 MEDAL
—	—	—	*Baboushka and the Three Kings* by Ruth Robbins, illus. by Nicholas Sidjakov (Parnassus)
			1961 HONOR BOOK
—	—	—	*Inch by Inch* by Leo Lionni (Astor-Honor)
			1962 MEDAL
—	—	—	*Once a Mouse . . .* by Marcia Brown (Scribner)
			1962 HONOR BOOKS
—	—	—	*The Fox Went Out on a Chilly Night* illus. by Peter Spier (Doubleday; motion picture, Weston Woods; sound filmstrip, Weston Woods)
—	—	—	*Little Bear's Visit* by Else Holmelund Minarik, illus. by Maurice Sendak (Harper; sound filmstrip, Weston Woods)
—	—	—	*The Day We Saw the Sun Come Up* by Alice E. Goudey, illus. by Adrienne Adams (Scribner)
			1963 MEDAL
—	—	—	*The Snowy Day* by Ezra Jack Keats (Viking; motion picture, Weston Woods; sound filmstrip, Weston Woods)
			1963 HONOR BOOKS
—	—	—	*The Sun Is a Golden Earring* by Natilia M. Belting, illus. by Bernarda Bryson (Holt)
—	—	—	*Mr. Rabbit and the Lovely Present* by Charlotte Zolotow, illus. by Maurice Sendak (Harper; sound filmstrip, Weston Woods)
			1964 MEDAL
—	—	—	*Where the Wild Things Are* by Maurice Sendak (Harper; motion picture, Weston Woods; sound filmstrip, Weston Woods)
			1964 HONOR BOOKS
—	—	—	*Swimmy* by Leo Lionni (Pantheon; sound filmstrip, Miller-Brody)
—	—	—	*All in the Morning Early* by Sorche Nic Leodhas, illus. by Evelyn Ness (Holt)
—	—	—	*Mother Goose and Nursery Rhymes* illus. by Philip Reed (Atheneum)
			1965 MEDAL
—	—	—	*May I Bring a Friend* by Beatrice Schenk de Regniers, illus. by Beni Montresor (Atheneum; sound filmstrip, Weston Woods)
			1965 HONOR BOOKS
—	—	—	*Rain Makes Applesauce* by Julian Scheer, illus. by Marvin Bileck (Holiday)

CHECKLIST 1-2 (cont.)

Language Arts	Reading	Gifted	
—	—	—	*The Wave* by Margaret Hodges, illus. by Blair Lent (Houghton)
—	—	—	*A Pocketful of Cricket* by Rebecca Caudill, illus. by Evelyn Ness (Holt; sound filmstrip, Miller-Brody)
			1966 MEDAL
—	—	—	*Always Room for One More* by Sorche Nic Leodhas, illus. by Nonny Hogrogian (Holt)
			1966 HONOR BOOKS
—	—	—	*Hide and Seek Fog* by Alvin Tresselt, illus. by Roger Duvoisin (Lothrop)
—	—	—	*Just Me* by Marie Hall Ets (Viking; sound filmstrip, Weston Woods)
—	—	—	*Tom Tit Tot* by Evelyn Ness (Scribner)
			1967 MEDAL
—	—	—	*Sam, Bangs and Moonshine* by Evelyn Ness (Holt; sound filmstrip, Miller-Brody)
			1967 HONOR BOOK
—	—	—	*One Wide River to Cross* by Barbara Emberley, illus. by Ed Emberley (Prentice-Hall)
			1968 MEDAL
—	—	—	*Drummer Hoff* by Barbara Emberley, illus. by Ed Emberley (Prentice-Hall; motion picture, Weston Woods; sound filmstrip, Weston Woods)
			1968 HONOR BOOKS
—	—	—	*Frederick* by Leo Lionni (Pantheon; sound filmstrip, Miller-Brody)
—	—	—	*Seashore Story* by Taro Yashima (Viking)
—	—	—	*The Emperor and the Kite* by Jane Yolen, illus. by Ed Young (Philomel; sound filmstrip, Miller-Brody)
			1969 MEDAL
—	—	—	*The Fool of the World and the Flying Ship* by Arthur Ransome, illus. by Uri Shulevitz (Farrar; sound filmstrip, Weston Woods)
			1969 HONOR BOOK
—	—	—	*Why the Sun and the Moon Live in the Sky* by Elphinstone Dayrell, illus. by Blair Lent (Houghton)
			1970 MEDAL
—	—	—	*Sylvester and the Magic Pebble* by William Steig (Windmill/Simon & Schuster)
			1970 HONOR BOOKS
—	—	—	*Goggles* by Ezra Jack Keats (Macmillan; motion picture, Weston Woods; sound filmstrip, Weston Woods)

CHECKLIST 1-2 (cont.)

Language Arts	Reading	Gifted	
—	—	—	*Alexander and the Wind-Up Mouse* by Leo Lionni (Pantheon; sound filmstrip, Miller-Brody)
—	—	—	*Pop Corn & Ma Goodness* by Edna Mitchell Preston, illus. by Robert Andrew Parker (Viking)
—	—	—	*Thy Friend, Obadiah* by Brinton Turkle (Viking; sound filmstrip, Miller-Brody)
—	—	—	*The Judge* by Harve Zemach, illus. by Margot Zemach (Farrar; sound filmstrip, Miller-Brody)

1971 MEDAL

—	—	—	*A Story—A Story* by Gail E. Haley (Atheneum, motion picture, Weston Woods; sound filmstrip, Weston Woods)

1971 HONOR BOOKS

—	—	—	*The Angry Moon* by William Sleator, illus. by Blair Lent (Atlantic-Little)
—	—	—	*Frog and Toad Are Friends* by Arnold Lobel (Harper; sound filmstrip, Miller-Brody)
—	—	—	*In the Night Kitchen* by Maurice Sendak (Harper)

1972 MEDAL

—	—	—	*One Fine Day* by Nonny Hogrogian (Macmillan; sound filmstrip, Weston Woods)

1972 HONOR BOOKS

—	—	—	*Hildilid's Night* by Cheli Duran Ryan, illus. by Arnold Lobel (Macmillan)
—	—	—	*If All the Seas Were One Sea* by Janina Domanska (Macmillan)
—	—	—	*Moja Means One* by Muriel Feelings, illus. by Tom Feelings (Dial)

1973 MEDAL

—	—	—	*The Funny Little Woman* retold by Arlene Mosel, illus. by Blair Lent, (Dutton)

1973 HONOR BOOKS

—	—	—	*Anansi the Spider* adapted and illus. by Gerald McDermott (Holt; sound filmstrip, Weston Woods)
—	—		*Hosie's Alphabet* by Hosea Baskin, Tobias Baskin, and Lisa Baskin, illus. by Leonard Baskin (Viking)
—	—	—	*Snow-White and the Seven Dwarfs* trans. by Randall Jarrell, illus. by Nancy Ekholm Burkert (Farrar)
—	—	—	*When Clay Sings* by Byrd Baylor, illus. by Tom Bahti (Scribner)

1974 MEDAL

—	—	—	*Duffy and the Devil* by Harve Zemach, illus. by Margot Zemach (Farrar; sound filmstrips, Miller-Brody)

1974 HONOR BOOKS

—	—	—	*Three Jovial Huntsmen* by Susan Jeffers (Bradbury)

CHECKLIST 1-2 (cont.)

Language Arts	Reading	Gifted	
—	—	—	*Cathedral* by David Macaulay (Houghton)

1975 MEDAL

—	—	—	*Arrow to the Sun* by Gerald McDermott (Viking; sound filmstrip, Weston Woods)

1975 HONOR BOOK

—	—	—	*Jambo Means Hello* by Muriel Feelings, illus. by Tom Feelings (Dial)

1976 MEDAL

—	—	—	*Why Mosquitoes Buzz in People's Ears* by Verna Aardema, illus. by Leo Dillon and Diane Dillon (Dial; sound filmstrip, Weston Woods)

1976 HONOR BOOKS

—	—	—	*The Desert Is Theirs* by Byrd Baylor, illus. by Peter Parnall (Scribner)
—	—	—	*Strega Nona* retold and illus. by Tomie de Paola (Prentice-Hall; motion picture, Weston Woods; sound filmstrip, Weston Woods)

1977 MEDAL

—	—	—	*Ashanti to Zulu: African Traditions* by Margaret Musgrove, illus. by Leo Dillon and Diane Dillon (Dial; sound filmstrip, Weston Woods)

1977 HONOR BOOKS

—	—	—	*The Amazing Bone* by William Steig (Farrar; sound filmstrip, Miller-Brody)
—	—	—	*The Contest* retold and illus. by Nonny Hogrogian (Greenwillow)
—	—	—	*Fish for Supper* by M. B. Goffstein (Dial)
—	—	—	*The Golem* by Beverly Broadsky McDermott (Lippincott; sound filmstrip, Weston Woods)
—	—	—	*Hawk, I'm Your Brother* by Byrd Baylor, illus. by Peter Parnall (Scribner)

1978 MEDAL

—	—	—	*Noah's Ark* illus. by Peter Spier (Doubleday; sound filmstrip, Weston Woods)

1978 HONOR BOOKS

—	—	—	*Castle* by David Macaulay (Houghton)
—	—	—	*It Could Always Be Worse* retold and illus. by Margot Zemach (Farrar; sound filmstrip, Miller-Brody)

1979 MEDAL

—	—	—	*The Girl Who Loved Wild Horses* by Paul Goble (Bradbury; sound filmstrip, Miller-Brody)

1979 HONOR BOOKS

—	—	—	*Freight Train* by Donald Crews (Greenwillow; sound filmstrip, Miller-Brody)
—	—	—	*The Way to Start a Day* by Byrd Baylor, illus. by Peter Parnall (Scribner)

CHECKLIST 1-2 (cont.)

Language Arts	Reading	Gifted	
			1980 MEDAL
—	—	—	*Ox-Cart Man* by Donald Hall, illus. by Barbara Cooney (Viking; sound filmstrip, Miller-Brody)
			1980 HONOR BOOKS
—	—	—	*Ben's Trumpet* by Rachel Isadora (Greenwillow; sound filmstrip, Miller-Brody)
—	—	—	*The Garden of Abdul Gasazi* by Chris Van Allsburg (Houghton)
—	—	—	*The Treasure* by Uri Shulevitz (Farrar)
			1981 MEDAL
—	—	—	*Fables* by Arnold Lobel (Harper; sound filmstrip, Miller-Brody)
			1981 HONOR BOOKS
—	—	—	*The Bremen-Town Musicians* retold and illus. by Ilse Plume (Doubleday; sound filmstrip, Miller-Brody)
—	—	—	*The Grey Lady and the Strawberry Snatcher* by Molly Bang (Four Winds/Scholastic Books; sound filmstrip, Miller-Brody)
—	—		*Mice Twice* by Joseph Low (McElderry/Atheneum; sound filmstrip, Miller-Brody)
—	—	—	*Truck* by Donald Crews (Greenwillow; sound filmstrip, Miller-Brody)
			1982 MEDAL
—	—	—	*Jumanji* written and illus. by Chris Van Allsburg (Houghton)
			1982 HONOR BOOKS
—	—	—	*On Market Street* by Arnold Lobel, illus. by Anita Lobel (Warne)
—	—	—	*Outside Over There* written and illus. by Maurice Sendak (Harper)
—	—	—	*A Visit to William Blake's Inn* written by Nancy Willard, illus. by Alice Provensen and Martin Provensen (Harcourt)

CHECKLIST 1-3   NEWBERY AWARD BOOKS*

Determine the grade level within which program—language arts, reading, or gifted—each title is introduced. Then note that grade level on the blank line provided in the appropriate column.

Language Arts	Reading	Gifted	
			1922 MEDAL
—	—	—	*The Story of Mankind* by Hendrik Willem van Loon (Liveright)
			1922 HONOR BOOKS
—	—	—	*The Great Quest* by Charles Hawes (Little)
—	—	—	*Cedric the Forester* by Bernard Marshall (Appleton)
—	—	—	*The Old Tobacco Shop* by William Bowen (Macmillan)
—	—	—	*The Golden Fleece and the Heroes Who Lived before Achilles* by Padraic Colum (Macmillan)
—	—	—	*Windy Hill* by Cornelia Meigs (Macmillan)
			1923 MEDAL
—	—	—	The *Voyages of Doctor Doolittle* by Hugh Lofting (Lippincott; sound filmstrips, Miller-Brody)
			1923 HONOR BOOK
			No Record
			1924 MEDAL
—	—	—	*The Dark Frigate* by Charles Hawes (Atlantic-Little; sound filmstrip, Miller-Brody)
			1924 HONOR BOOK
			No Record
			1925 MEDAL
—	—	—	*Tales from Silver Lands* by Charles Finger (Doubleday; sound fimstrips, Miller-Brody)
			1925 HONOR BOOKS
—	—	—	*Nicholas* by Anne Carroll Moore (Putnam)
—	—	—	*Dream Coach* by Anne Parrish (Macmillan)
			1926 MEDAL
—	—	—	*Shen of the Sea* by Arthur Bowie Crisman (Dutton; sound filmstrips, Miller-Brody)
			1926 HONOR BOOK
—	—	—	*Voyagers* by Padraic Colum (Macmillan)
			1927 MEDAL
—	—	—	*Smoky, the Cowhorse* by Will James (Scribner)
			1927 HONOR BOOK
			No Record

*The Newbery Medal was first offered in 1921 by Frederic G. Melcher as an incentive for better quality in children's books. Named after John Newbery, the famous eighteenth-century publisher and seller of children's books, it is awarded annually to the author of the most distinguished contribution to American literature for children published during the preceding year. Awarded annually by The Association for Library Service to Children, The American Library Association.

CHECKLIST 1-3 (cont.)

Language Arts	Reading	Gifted	
			1928 MEDAL
—	—	—	*Gayneck, the Story of a Pigeon* by Dhan Gopal Mukerji (Dutton, sound filmstrips, Miller-Brody)
			1928 HONOR BOOKS
—	—	—	*The Wonder Smith and His Son* by Ella Young (Longman)
—	—	—	*Downright Dencey* by Caroline Snedeker (Doubleday)
			1929 MEDAL
—	—	—	*The Trumpeter of Krakow* by Eric P. Kelly (Macmillan; sound filmstrips, Miller-Brody)
			1929 HONOR BOOKS
—	—	—	*Pigtail of Ah Lee Ben Loo* by John Bennett (Longman)
—	—	—	*Millions of Cats* by Wanda Gág (Coward; motion picture, Weston Woods; sound filmstrip, Weston Woods)
—	—	—	*The Boy Who Was* by Grace Hallock (Dutton)
—	—	—	*Clearing Weather* by Cornelia Meigs (Little)
—	—	—	*Runaway Papoose* by Grace Moon (Doubleday)
—	—	—	*Tod of the Fens* by Elinor Whitney (Macmillan)
			1930 MEDAL
—	—	—	*Hitty, Her First Hundred Years* by Rachel Field (Macmillan)
			1930 HONOR BOOKS
—	—	—	*Daughter of the Seine* by Jeanette Eaton (Harper)
—	—	—	*Pran of Albania* by Elizabeth Miller (Doubleday)
—	—	—	*Jumping-Off Place* by Marian Hurd McNeely (Longman)
—	—	—	*Tangled-Coated Horse and Other Tales* by Ella Young (Longman)
—	—	—	*Vaino* by Julia Davis Adams (Dutton)
—	—	—	*Little Blacknose* by Hildegarde Swift (Harcourt)
			1931 MEDAL
—	—	—	*The Cat Who Went to Heaven* by Elizabeth Coatsworth (Macmillan; sound filmstrips, Miller-Brody)
			1931 HONOR BOOKS
—	—	—	*Floating Island* by Anne Parrish (Harper)
—	—	—	*The Dark Star of Itza* by Alida Malkus (Harcourt)
—	—	—	*Queer Person* by Ralph Hubbard (Doubleday)
—	—	—	*Mountains Are Free* by Julia Davis Adams (Dutton)
—	—	—	*Spice and the Devil's Cave* by A. Hewes (Knopf)
—	—	—	*Meggy Macintosh* by Elizabeth Janet Gray (Doubleday)
—	—	—	*Garram the Hunter* by Herbert Best (Doubleday)
—	—	—	*Ood-Le-Uk the Wanderer* by Alice Lide and Margaret Johansen (Little)

CHECKLIST 1-3 (cont.)

Language Arts	Reading	Gifted	
			1932 MEDAL
—	—	—	*Waterless Mountain* by Laura Adams Armer (Longman)
			1932 HONOR BOOKS
—	—	—	*The Fairy Circus* by Dorothy P. Lathrop (Macmillan)
—	—	—	*Calico Bush* by Rachel Field (Macmillan)
—	—	—	*Boy of the South Seas* by Eunice Tietjens (Coward)
—	—	—	*Out of the Flame* by Eloise Lownsbery (Longman)
—	—	—	*Jane's Island* by Marjorie Allee (Houghton)
—	—	—	*Truce of the Wolf and Other Tales of Old Italy* by Mary Gould Davis (Harcourt)
			1933 MEDAL
—	—	—	*Young Fu of the Upper Yangtze* by Elizabeth Lewis (Winston; sound filmstrips, Miller-Brody)
			1933 HONOR BOOKS
—	—	—	*Swift Rivers* by Cornelia Meigs (Little)
—	—	—	*The Railroad to Freedom* by Hildegarde Swift (Harcourt)
—	—	—	*Children of the Soil* by Nora Burglon (Doubleday)
			1934 MEDAL
—	—	—	*Invincible Louisa* by Cornelia Meigs (Little)
			1934 HONOR BOOKS
—	—	—	*The Forgotten Daughter* by Caroline Snedeker (Doubleday)
—	—	—	*Swords of Steel* by Elsie Singmaster (Houghton)
—	—	—	*ABC Bunny* by Wanda Gág (Coward)
—	—	—	*Winged Girl of Knossos* by Erik Berry (Appleton)
—	—	—	*New Land* by Sarah Schmidt (McBride)
—	—	—	*Big Tree of Bunlahy* by Padraic Colum (Macmillan)
—	—	—	*Glory of the Seas* by Agnes Hewes (Knopf)
—	—	—	*Apprentice of Florence* by Anne Kyle (Houghton)
			1935 MEDAL
—	—	—	*Dobry* by Monica Shannon (Viking)
			1935 HONOR BOOKS
—	—	—	*Pageant of Chinese History* by Elizabeth Seeger (Longman)
—	—	—	*Davy Crockett* by Constance Rourke (Harcourt)
—	—	—	*Day on Skates* by Hilda Van Stockum (Harper)
			1936 MEDAL
—	—	—	*Caddie Woodlawn* by Carol Ryrie Brink (Macmillan; sound filmstrips, Miller-Brody)
			1936 HONOR BOOKS
—	—	—	*Honk, the Moose* by Phil Strong (Dodd)
—	—	—	*The Good Master* by Kate Seredy (Viking)
—	—	—	*Young Walter Scott* by E. J. Gray (Viking)

CHECKLIST 1-3 (cont.)

Language Arts	Reading	Gifted	
—	—	—	*All Sail Set* by Armstrong Sperry (Winston)

1937 MEDAL

—	—	—	*Roller Skates* by Ruth Sawyer (Viking)

1937 HONOR BOOKS

—	—	—	*Phebe Fairchild: Her Book* by Lois Lenski (Stokes)
—	—	—	*Whistler's Van* by Idwal Jones (Viking)
—	—	—	*Golden Basket* by Ludwig Bemelmans (Viking)
—	—	—	*Winterbound* by Margery Bianco (Viking)
—	—	—	*Audubon* by Constance Rourke (Harcourt)
—	—	—	*The Codfish Musket* by Agnes Hewes (Doubleday)

1938 MEDAL

—	—	—	*The White Stag* by Kate Seredy (Viking)

1938 HONOR BOOKS

—	—	—	*Pecos Bill* by James Cloyd Bowman (Little)
—	—	—	*Bright Island* by Mabel Robinson (Random)
—	—	—	*On the Banks of Plum Creek* by Laura Ingalls Wilder (Harper)

1939 MEDAL

—	—	—	*Thimble Summer* by Elizabeth Enright (Rinehart; sound filmstrips, Miller-Brody)

1939 HONOR BOOKS

—	—	—	*Nino* by Valenti Angelo (Viking)
—	—	—	*Mr. Popper's Penguins* by Richard Atwater and Florence Atwater (Little; sound filmstrips, Miller-Brody)
—	—	—	*Hello! The Boat* by Phyllis Crawford (Holt)
—	—	—	*Leader by Destiny: George Washington, Man and Patriot* by Jeanette Eaton (Harcourt)
—	—	—	*Penn* by Elizabeth Janet Gray (Viking)

1940 MEDAL

—	—	—	*Daniel Boone* by James Daugherty (Viking)

1940 HONOR BOOKS

—	—	—	*The Singing Tree* by Kate Seredy (Viking)
—	—	—	*The Runner of the Mountain Tops* by Mabel Robinson (Random)
—	—	—	*By the Shores of Silver Lake* by Laura Ingalls Wilder (Harper)
—	—	—	*Boy with a Pack* by Stephen W. Meader (Harcourt)

1941 MEDAL

—	—	—	*Call It Courage* by Armstrong Sperry (Macmillan; sound filmstrips, Miller-Brody)

1941 HONOR BOOKS

—	—	—	*Blue Willow* by Doris Gates (Viking)
—	—	—	*Young Mac of Fort Vancouver* by Mary Jane Carr (Crowell)

CHECKLIST 1-3 (cont.)

Language Arts	Reading	Gifted	
—	—	—	*The Long Winter* by Laura Ingalls Wilder (Harper)
—	—	—	*Nansen* by Anne Gertrude Hall (Viking)

1942 MEDAL

Language Arts	Reading	Gifted	
—	—	—	*The Matchlock Gun* by Walter D. Edmonds (Dodd; sound filmstrips, Miller-Brody)

1942 HONOR BOOKS

Language Arts	Reading	Gifted	
—	—	—	*Little Town on the Prairie* by Laura Ingalls Wilder (Harper)
—	—	—	*George Washington's World* by Genevieve Foster (Scribner)
—	—	—	*Indian Captive: The Story of Mary Jemison* (Lippincott)
—	—	—	*Down Ryton Water* by Eva Roe Gaggin (Viking)

1943 MEDAL

Language Arts	Reading	Gifted	
—	—	—	*Adam of the Road* by Elizabeth Janet Gray (Viking)

1943 HONOR BOOKS

Language Arts	Reading	Gifted	
—	—	—	*The Middle Moffat* by Eleanor Estes (Harcourt)
—	—	—	*Have You Seen Tom Thumb?* by Mabel Leigh Hunt (Lippincott)

1944 MEDAL

Language Arts	Reading	Gifted	
—	—	—	*Johnny Tremain* by Esther Forbes (Houghton)

1944 HONOR BOOKS

Language Arts	Reading	Gifted	
—	—	—	*These Happy Golden Years* by Laura Ingalls Wilder (Harper)
—	—	—	*Fog Magic* by Julia Sauer (Viking)
—	—	—	*Rufus M* by Eleanor Estes (Harcourt)
—	—	—	*Mountain Born* by Elizabeth Yates (Coward)

1945 MEDAL

Language Arts	Reading	Gifted	
—	—	—	*Rabbit Hill* by Robert Lawson (Viking)

1945 HONOR BOOKS

Language Arts	Reading	Gifted	
—	—	—	*The Hundred Dresses* by Eleanor Estes (Harcourt; sound filmstrips, Miller-Brody)
—	—	—	*The Silver Pencil* by Alice Dalgliesh (Scribner)
—	—	—	*Abraham Lincoln's World* by Genevieve Foster (Scribner)
—	—	—	*Lone Journey: The Life of Roger Williams* by Jeanette Eaton (Harcourt)

1946 MEDAL

Language Arts	Reading	Gifted	
—	—	—	*Strawberry Girl* by Lois Lenski (Lippincott; sound filmstrips, Miller-Brody)

1946 HONOR BOOKS

Language Arts	Reading	Gifted	
—	—	—	*Justin Morgan Had a Horse* by Marguerite Henry (Rand; sound filmstrips, Miller-Brody)
—	—	—	*The Moved-Outers* by Florence Crannell Means (Houghton)

CHECKLIST 1-3 (cont.)

Language Arts	Reading	Gifted	
—	—	—	*Bhimsa, the Dancing Bear* by Christine Weston (Scribner)
—	—	—	*New Found World* by Katherine Shippen (Viking)
			1947 MEDAL
—	—	—	*Miss Hickory* by Carolyn Sherwin Bailey (Viking)
			1947 HONOR BOOKS
—	—	—	*Wonderful Year* by Nancy Barnes (Messner)
—	—	—	*Big Tree* by Mary Buff and Conrad Buff (Viking)
—	—	—	*The Heavenly Tenants* by William Maxwell (Harper)
—	—	—	*The Avion My Uncle Flew* by Cyrus Fisher (Appleton)
—	—	—	*The Hidden Treasure of Glaston* by Eleanor Jewett (Viking)
			1948 MEDAL
—	—	—	*The Twenty-One Balloons* by William Pène du Bois (Viking)
			1948 HONOR BOOKS
—	—	—	*Pancakes—Paris* by Claire Huchet Bishop (Viking)
—	—	—	*Li Lun, Lad of Courage* by Carolyn Treffinger (Abingdon)
—	—	—	*The Quaint and Curious Quest of Johnny Longfoot* by Catherine Besterman (Bobbs)
—	—	—	*The Cow-Tail Switch and Other West African Stories* by Harold Courlander (Holt)
—	—	—	*Misty of Chincoteague* by Marguerite Henry (Rand; sound filmstrips, Miller-Brody)
			1949 MEDAL
—	—	—	*King of the Wind* by Marguerite Henry (Rand; sound filmstrips, Miller-Brody)
			1949 HONOR BOOKS
—	—	—	*Seabird* by Holling C. Holling (Houghton)
—	—	—	*My Father's Dragon* by Ruth S. Gannett (Random)
—	—	—	*The Story of the Negro* by Arna Bontemps (Knopf)
			1950 MEDAL
—	—	—	*The Door in the Wall* by Marguerite de Angeli (Doubleday; sound filmstrips, Miller-Brody)
			1950 HONOR BOOKS
—	—	—	*Tree of Freedom* by Rebecca Caudill (Viking)
—	—	—	*The Blue Cat of Castle Town* by Catherine Coblentz (Longman)
—	—	—	*Kildee House* by Rutherford Montgomery (Doubleday)
—	—	—	*George Washington* by Genevieve Foster (Scribner)

CHECKLIST 1-3 (cont.)

Language Arts	Reading	Gifted	
—	—	—	*Song of the Pines* by Walter Havighurst and Marion Havighurst (Winston)
			1951 MEDAL
—	—	—	*Amos Fortune, Free Man* by Elizabeth Yates (Dutton; sound filmstrips, Miller-Brody)
			1951 HONOR BOOKS
—	—	—	*Better Known as Johnny Appleseed* by Mabel Leigh Hunt (Lippincott)
—	—	—	*Gandhi, Fighter without a Sword* by Jeanette Eaton (Morrow)
—	—	—	*Abraham Lincoln, Friend of the People* by Clara Ingram Judson (Follett)
—	—	—	*The Story of Appleby Capple* by Anne Parrish (Harper)
			1952 MEDAL
—	—	—	*Ginger Pye* by Eleanor Estes (Harcourt; sound filmstrips, Miller-Brody)
			1952 HONOR BOOKS
—	—	—	*Americans before Columbus* by Elizabeth Baity (Viking)
—	—	—	*Minn of the Mississippi* by Holling C. Holling (Houghton)
—	—	—	*The Defender* by Nicholas Kalashnikoff (Scribner)
—	—	—	*The Light at Tern Rocks* by Julia Sauer (Viking)
—	—	—	*The Apple and the Arrow* by Mary Buff and Conrad Buff (Houghton)
			1953 MEDAL
—	—	—	*Secret of the Andes* by Ann Nolan Clark (Viking)
			1953 HONOR BOOKS
—	—	—	*Moccasin Trail* by Eloise McGraw (Coward)
—	—	—	*Red Sails to Capri* by Ann Weil (Viking)
—	—	—	*The Bears on Hemlock Mountain* by Alice Dalgliesh (Scribner)
—	—	—	*The Birthdays of Freedom,* vol. 1, by Genevieve Foster (Scribner)
			1954 MEDAL
—	—	—	*. . . And Now Miguel* by Joseph Krumgold (Crowell; sound filmstrips, Miller-Brody)
			1954 HONOR BOOKS
—	—	—	*All Alone* by Claire Huchet Bishop (Viking)
—	—	—	*Shadrach* by Meindert DeJong (Harper)
—	—	—	*Hurry Home Candy* by Meindert DeJong (Harper; sound filmstrips, Miller-Brody)
—	—	—	*Theodore Roosevelt, Fighting Patriot* by Clara Ingram Judson (Follett)
—	—		*Magic Maize* by Mary Buff and Conrad Buff (Houghton)

CHECKLIST 1-3 (cont.)

Language Arts	Reading	Gifted	
			1955 MEDAL
—	—	—	*The Wheel on the School* by Meindert DeJong (Harper; sound filmstrips, Miller-Brody)
			1955 HONOR BOOKS
—	—	—	*Courage of Sarah Noble* by Alice Dalgliesh (Scribner; sound filmstrips, Miller-Brody)
—	—	—	*Banner in the Sky* by James Ullman (Lippincott)
			1956 MEDAL
—	—	—	*Carry On, Mr. Bowditch* by Jean Lee Latham (Houghton; sound filmstrips, Miller-Brody)
			1956 HONOR BOOKS
—	—	—	*The Secret River* by Marjorie Kinnan Rawlings (Scribner)
—	—	—	*The Golden Name Day* by Jennie Lindquist (Harper)
—	—	—	*Men, Microscopes, and Living Things* by Katherine Shippen (Viking)
			1957 MEDAL:
—	—	—	*Miracles on Maple Hill* by Virginia Sorensen (Harcourt; sound filmstrips, Miller-Brody)
			1957 HONOR BOOKS
—	—	—	*Old Yeller* by Fred Gipson (Harper)
—	—	—	*The House of Sixty Fathers* by Meindert DeJong (Harper; sound filmstrips, Miller-Brody)
—	—	—	*Mr. Justice Holmes* by Clara May Judson (Follett)
—	—	—	*The Corn Grows Ripe* by Dorothy Rhoads (Viking)
—	—	—	*Black Fox of Lorne* by Marguerite de Angeli (Doubleday)
			1958 MEDAL
—	—	—	*Rifles for Watie* by Harold Keith (Crowell; sound filmstrips, Miller-Brody)
			1958 HONOR BOOKS
—	—	—	*The Horsecatcher* by Mari Sandoz (Westminster; sound filmstrips, Miller-Brody)
—	—	—	*Gone-Away Lake* by Elizabeth Enright (Harcourt)
—	—	—	*The Great Wheel* by Robert Lawson (Viking)
—	—	—	*Tom Paine, Freedom's Apostle* by Leo Gurko (Crowell)
			1959 MEDAL
—	—	—	*The Witch of Blackbird Pond* by Elizabeth George Speare (Houghton)
			1959 HONOR BOOKS
—	—	—	*The Family under the Bridge* by Natalie Savage Carlson (Harper; sound filmstrips, Miller-Brody)
—	—	—	*Along Came a Dog* by Meindert DeJong (Harper)

CHECKLIST 1-3 (cont.)

Language Arts	Reading	Gifted	
—	—	—	*Chucaro: Wild Pony of the Pampa* by Francis Kalnay (Harcourt; sound filmstrips, Miller-Brody)
—	—	—	*The Perilous Road* by William O. Steele (Harcourt; sound filmstrips, Miller-Brody)

1960 MEDAL

Language Arts	Reading	Gifted	
—	—	—	*Onion John* by Joseph Krumgold (Crowell; sound filmstrips, Miller-Brody)

1960 HONOR BOOKS

Language Arts	Reading	Gifted	
—	—	—	*My Side of the Mountain* by Jean Craighead George (Dutton; sound filmstrips, Films, Inc.)
—	—	—	*America Is Born* by Gerald W. Johnson (Morrow)
—	—	—	*The Gammage Cup* by Carol Kendall (Harcourt; sound filmstrips, Miller-Brody)

1961 MEDAL

Language Arts	Reading	Gifted	
—	—	—	*Island of the Blue Dolphins* by Scott O'Dell (Houghton; sound filmstrips, Films, Inc.)

1961 HONOR BOOKS

Language Arts	Reading	Gifted	
—	—	—	*America Moves Forward* by Gerald W. Johnson (Morrow)
—	—	—	*Old Ramon* by Jack Schaefer (Houghton; sound filmstrips, Miller-Brody)
—	—	—	*The Cricket in Times Square* by George Selden (Farrar; sound filmstrips, Miller-Brody)

1962 MEDAL

Language Arts	Reading	Gifted	
—	—	—	*The Bronze Bow* by Elizabeth George Speare (Houghton; sound filmstrips, Miller-Brody)

1962 HONOR BOOKS

Language Arts	Reading	Gifted	
—	—	—	*Frontier Living* by Edwin Tunis (Philomel)
—	—	—	*The Golden Goblet* by Eloise McGraw (Coward; sound filmstrips, Miller-Brody)
—	—	—	*Belling the Tiger* by Mary Stolz (Harper)

1963 MEDAL

Language Arts	Reading	Gifted	
—	—	—	*A Wrinkle in Time* by Madeleine L'Engle (Farrar; sound filmstrips, Miller-Brody)

1963 HONOR BOOKS

Language Arts	Reading	Gifted	
—	—	—	*Thistle and Thyme* by Sorche Nic Leodhas (Holt)
—	—	—	*Men of Athens* by Olivia Coolidge (Houghton)

1964 MEDAL

Language Arts	Reading	Gifted	
—	—	—	*It's Like This, Cat* by Emily Cheney Neville (Harper; sound filmstrips, Miller-Brody)

1964 HONOR BOOKS

Language Arts	Reading	Gifted	
—	—	—	*Rascal* by Sterling North (Dutton)
—	—	—	*The Loner* by Ester Wier (McKay; sound filmstrips, Miller-Brody)

1965 MEDAL

Language Arts	Reading	Gifted	
—	—	—	*Shadow of a Bull* by Maja Wojciechowska (Atheneum; sound filmstrips, Miller-Brody)

CHECKLIST 1-3 (cont.)

Language Arts	Reading	Gifted	
			1965 HONOR BOOK
—	—	—	*Across Five Aprils* by Irene Hunt (Follett; sound filmstrips, Miller-Brody)
			1966 MEDAL
—	—	—	*I, Juan de Pareja* by Elizabeth Borton de Trevino (sound filmstrips, Miller-Brody)
			1966 HONOR BOOKS
—	—	—	*The Black Cauldron* by Lloyd Alexander (Holt)
—	—	—	*The Animal Family* by Randall Jarrell (Pantheon)
—	—	—	*The Noonday Friends* by Mary Stolz (Harper)
			1967 MEDAL
—	—	—	*Up a Road Slowly* by Irene Hunt (Follett; sound filmstrips, Miller-Brody)
			1967 HONOR BOOKS
—	—	—	*The King's Fifth* by Scott O'Dell (Houghton; sound filmstrips, Miller-Brody)
—	—	—	*Zlateh the Goat and Other Stories* by Isaac Bashevis Singer (Harper; sound filmstrips, Miller-Brody)
—	—	—	*The Jazz Man* by Mary H. Weik (Atheneum)
			1968 MEDAL
—	—	—	*From the Mixed-Up Files of Mrs. Basil E. Frankweiler* by E. L. Konigsburg (Atheneum)
			1968 HONOR BOOKS
—	—	—	*Jennifer, Hecate, Macbeth, William McKinley, and Me, Elizabeth* by E. L. Konigsburg (Atheneum)
—	—	—	*The Black Pearl* by Scott O'Dell (Houghton; sound filmstrips, Miller-Brody)
—	—	—	*The Fearsome Inn* by Isaac Beshevis Singer (Scribner)
—	—	—	*The Egypt Game* by Zilpha Keatley Snyder (Atheneum)
			1969 MEDAL
—	—	—	*The High King* by Lloyd Alexander (Holt; sound filmstrips, Miller-Brody)
			1969 HONOR BOOKS
—	—	—	*To Be a Slave* by Julius Lester (Dial)
—	—	—	*When Shlemiel Went to Warsaw and Other Stories* by Isaac Bashevis Singer (Farrar; sound filmstrips, Miller-Brody)
			1970 MEDAL
—	—	—	*Sounder* by William H. Armstrong (Harper; sound filmstrips, Miller-Brody)
			1970 HONOR BOOKS
—	—	—	*Our Eddie* by Sulamith Moore (Pantheon)

CHECKLIST 1-3 (cont.)

Language Arts	Reading	Gifted	
—	—	—	*The Many Ways of Seeing: An Introduction to the Pleasures of Art* by Janet Gaylord Moore (Philomel)
—	—	—	*Journey Outside* by Mary Q. Steele (Viking)
			1971 MEDAL
—	—	—	*Summer of the Swans* by Betsy Byars (Viking)
			1971 HONOR BOOKS
—	—	—	*Knee-Knock Rise* by Natalie Babbit (Farrar; sound filmstrips, Miller-Brody)
—	—	—	*Enchantress from the Stars* by Sylvia Louise Engdahl (Atheneum)
—	—	—	*Sing Down the Moon* by Scott O'Dell (Houghton; sound filmstrips, Miller-Brody)
			1972 MEDAL
—	—	—	*Mrs. Frisby and the Rats of Nimh* by Robert C. O'Brien (Atheneum; sound filmstrips, Miller-Brody)
			1972 HONOR BOOKS
—	—	—	*Annie and the Old One* by Miska Miles (Atlantic-Little; sound filmstrips, Miller-Brody)
—	—	—	*The Headless Cupid* by Silpha Keatly Snyder (Atheneum)
—	—	—	*The Incident at Hawk's Hill* by Allan W. Eckert (Little)
—	—	—	*The Planet of Junior Brown* by Virginia Hamilton (Macmillan; sound filmstrips, Miller-Brody)
—	—	—	*The Tombs of Atuan* by Ursula K. Le Guin (Atheneum; sound filmstrips, Miller-Brody)
			1973 MEDAL
—	—	—	*Julie of the Wolves* by Jean Craighead George (Harper; sound filmstrips, Miller-Brody)
			1973 HONOR BOOKS
—	—	—	*Frog and Toad Together* by Arnold Lobel (Harper; sound filmstrips, Miller-Brody)
—	—		*The Upstairs Room* by Johanna Reiss (Crowell; sound filmstrips, Miller-Brody)
—	—	—	*The Witches of Worm* by Zilpha Keatley Snyder (Atheneum; sound filmstrips; Miller-Brody)
			1974 MEDAL
—	—	—	*The Slave Dancer* by Paula Fox (Bradbury)
			1974 HONOR BOOK
—	—	—	*The Dark Is Rising* by Susan Cooper (McElderry/ Atheneum)
			1975 MEDAL
—	—	—	*M. C. Higgins, the Great* by Virginia Hamilton (Macmillan; sound filmstrips, Miller-Brody)

CHECKLIST 1-3 (cont.)

Language Arts	Reading	Gifted	
			1975 HONOR BOOKS
—	—	—	*Figgs and Phantoms* by Ellen Raskin (Dutton)
—	—	—	*My Brother Sam Is Dead* by James Lincoln Collier and Christopher Collier (Four Winds; sound filmstrips, Miller-Brody)
—	—	—	*The Perilous Gard* by Elizabeth Marie Pope (Houghton)
—	—	—	*Phillip Hall Likes Me, I Reckon Maybe* by Bette Green (Dial; sound filmstrips, Miller-Brody)
			1976 MEDAL
—	—	—	*The Grey King* by Susan Cooper (McElderry/ Atheneum)
			1976 HONOR BOOKS
—	—	—	*Dragonwings* by Laurence Yep (Harper; sound filmstrips, Miller-Brody)
—	—	—	*The Hundred Penny Box* by Sharon Bell Mathis (Viking; sound filmstrips, Miller-Brody)
			1977 MEDAL
—	—	—	*Roll of Thunder, Hear My Cry* by Mildred D. Taylor (Dial; sound filmstrips, Miller-Brody)
			1977 HONOR BOOKS
—	—	—	*Abel's Island* by William Steig (Farrar)
—	—	—	*A String in the Harp* by Nancy Bond (McElderry/ Atheneum)
			1978 MEDAL
—	—	—	*Bridge to Terabithia* by Katherine Paterson (Crowell; sound filmstrips, Miller-Brody)
			1978 HONOR BOOKS
—	—	—	*Anpao: An American Indian Odyssey* by Jamake Highwater (Lippincott; sound filmstrips, Miller-Brody)
—	—	—	*Ramona and Her Father* by Beverly Cleary (Morrow; sound filmstrips, Miller-Brody)
			1979 MEDAL
—	—	—	*The Westing Game* by Ellen Raskin (Dutton)
			1979 HONOR BOOK
—	—	—	*The Great Gilly Hopkins* by Katherine Paterson (Crowell; sound filmstrips, Miller-Brody)
			1980 MEDAL
—	—	—	*A Gathering of Days* by Joan W. Blos (Scribner)
			1980 HONOR BOOK
—	—	—	*The Road from Home: The Story of an Armenian Girl* by David Kherdian (Greenwillow)
			1981 MEDAL
—	—	—	*Jacob Have I Loved* by Katherine Paterson (Crowell)

CHECKLIST 1-3 (cont.)

Language Arts	Reading	Gifted	
			1981 HONOR BOOKS
—	—	—	*The Fledgling* by Jane Langton (Harper)
—	—	—	*A Ring of Endless Light* by Madeleine L'Engle (Farrar)
			1982 MEDAL
—	—	—	*A Visit to William Blake's Inn* by Nancy Willard (Harcourt)
			1982 HONOR BOOKS
—	—	—	*Ramona Quimby, Age 8* by Beverly Cleary (Morrow)
—	—	—	*Upon the Head of the Goat* by Aranka Siegal (Farrar)

CHECKLIST 1-4   MASTER LIST OF AUTHORS AND ILLUSTRATORS*

Determine the grade level within which program—language arts, reading, or gifted—each title is introduced. Then note that grade level on the blank line provided in the appropriate column.

Language Arts	Reading	Gifted	
—	—	—	Verna Aardema (C)
—	—	—	Raymond Abrashkin
—	—	—	Adrienne Adams (C)
—	—	—	Julia Davis Adams (N)
—	—	—	Aesop
—	—	—	Joan Aiken
—	—	—	Louisa May Alcott
—	—	—	Raymond Alden
—	—	—	Lloyd Alexander (N)
—	—	—	Marjorie Allee (N)
—	—	—	Hans Christian Andersen
—	—	—	C. W. Anderson
—	—	—	Valenti Angelo (N)
—	—	—	Joan Walsh Anglund
—	—	—	Laura Adams Armer (C) (N)
—	—	—	William H. Armstrong (N)
—	—	—	Boris Artzybasheff (C)
—	—	—	Isaac Asimov
—	—	—	Florence Atwater (N)
—	—	—	Richard Atwater (N)
—	—	—	Natalie Babbit (N)
—	—	—	Tom Bahti (C)
—	—	—	Carolyn Sherwin Bailey (N)
—	—	—	Elizabeth Baity (N)
—	—	—	Molly Bang (C)
—	—	—	Arnold E. Bare (C)
—	—	—	Nancy Barnes (N)
—	—	—	Jay Hyde Barnum (C)

*This master list is a composite of the authors and/or illustrators highlighted in Checklist 1-1, Delightful Literary Fare; Checklist 1-2, Caldecott Award Books; and Checklist 1-3, Newbery Award Books. N and/or C following name indicate Newbery and/or Caldecott winners.

CHECKLIST 1-4 (cont.)

Language Arts	Reading	Gifted	
—	—	—	Leonard Baskin (C)
—	—	—	L. Frank Baum
—	—	—	Byrd Baylor (C)
—	—	—	Patricia Beatty
—	—	—	Natalia M. Belting (C)
—	—	—	Ludwig Bemelmans (C) (N)
—	—	—	John Bennett (N)
—	—	—	Jan Berenstain
—	—	—	Stan Berenstain
—	—	—	Erik Berry (N)
—	—	—	Herbert Best (N)
—	—	—	Catherine Besterman (N)
—	—	—	Margery Bianco (N)
—	—	—	Marvin Bileck (C)
—	—	—	A. Birnbaum (C)
—	—	—	Claire Huchet Bishop (N)
—	—	—	Eric Blegvad
—	—	—	Judy Blume
—	—	—	Michael Bond
—	—	—	Nancy Bond (N)
—	—	—	Arna Bontemps (N)
—	—	—	William Bowen (N)
—	—	—	James Cloyd Bowman (N)
—	—	—	Bianca Bradbury
—	—	—	Esther Brady
—	—	—	Raymond Briggs
—	—	—	Robert Bright
—	—	—	Carol Ryrie Brink (N)
—	—	—	Marcia Brown (C)
—	—	—	Margaret Wise Brown (C)
—	—	—	Bernarda Bryson (C)
—	—	—	Conrad Buff (C) (N)
—	—	—	Mary Buff (C) (N)
—	—	—	Thornton Burgess
—	—	—	Nora Burglon (N)
—	—	—	Nancy Ekholm Burkert (C)
—	—	—	Frances H. Burnett
—	—	—	Sheila Burnford
—	—	—	Virginia Lee Burton (C)
—	—	—	Betsy Byars (N)
—	—	—	Natalie Savage Carlson (N)
—	—	—	Mary Jane Carr (N)
—	—	—	Lewis Carroll
—	—	—	Rebecca Caudill (C) (N)
—	—	—	Chin-Yi Chan (C)
—	—	—	Plao Chan (C)
—	—	—	Jean Charlot (C)
—	—	—	Richard Chase
—	—	—	Geoffrey Chaucer (C)
—	—	—	Ann Nolan Clark (N)
—	—	—	Beverly Cleary (N)
—	—	—	Bill Cleaver
—	—	—	Vera Cleaver
—	—	—	Elizabeth Coatsworth (N)
—	—	—	Catherine Coblentz (N)
—	—	—	Christopher Collier (N)

CHECKLIST 1-4 (cont.)

Language Arts	Reading	Gifted	
—	—	—	James Lincoln Collier (N)
—	—	—	Carlo Collodi
—	—	—	Padraic Colum (N)
—	—	—	Anne Colver
—	—	—	Ellen Conford
—	—	—	Olivia Coolidge (N)
—	—	—	Barbara Cooney (C)
—	—	—	Susan Cooper (N)
—	—	—	Scott Corbett
—	—	—	Harold Courlander (N)
—	—	—	Phyllis Crawford (N)
—	—	—	Ellis Crews (C)
—	—	—	Arthur Bowie Crisman (N)
—	—	—	Julia Cunningham
—	—	—	Roald Dahl
—	—	—	Alice Dalgliesh (C) (N)
—	—	—	James Daugherty (C) (N)
—	—	—	Edgar Parin d'Aulaire (C)
—	—	—	Ingri d'Aulaire (C)
—	—	—	Lavinia Davis (C)
—	—	—	Mary Gould Davis (N)
—	—	—	Elphinstone Dayrell (C)
—	—	—	Marguerite de Angeli (C) (N)
—	—	—	Meindert De Jong (N)
—	—	—	Tomie de Paola (C)
—	—	—	Beatrice de Regniers (C)
—	—	—	Elizabeth Borton de Trevino (N)
—	—	—	Charles Dickens
—	—	—	Diane Dillon (C)
—	—	—	Leo Dillon (C)
—	—	—	Janina Domanska (C)
—	—	—	William Pène du Bois (C) (N)
—	—	—	Roger Duvoisin (C)
—	—	—	Jeanette Eaton (N)
—	—	—	Allan W. Eckert (N)
—	—	—	Walter D. Edmonds (N)
—	—	—	Fritz Eichenberg (C)
—	—	—	Benjamin Elkin (C)
—	—	—	Barbara Emberley (C)
—	—	—	Ed Emberley (C)
—	—	—	Sylvia Louise Engdahl (N)
—	—	—	Elizabeth Enright (N)
—	—	—	Eleanor Estes (N)
—	—	—	Marie Hall Ets (C)
—	—	—	Walter Farley
—	—	—	Muriel Feelings (C)
—	—	—	Tom Feelings (C)
—	—	—	Rachel Field (C) (N)
—	—	—	Charles Finger (N)
—	—	—	Ann Finlayson
—	—	—	Helen Dean Fish (C)
—	—	—	Aileen Fisher
—	—	—	Cyrus Fisher
—	—	—	John Fitzgerald
—	—	—	Marjorie Flack (C)
—	—	—	Sid Fleischman

CHECKLIST 1-4 (cont.)

Language Arts	Reading	Gifted	
—	—	—	Esther Forbes (N)
—	—	—	Lauren Ford (C)
—	—	—	Genevieve Foster (N)
—	—	—	Paula Fox (N)
—	—	—	Antonio Frasconi (C)
—	—	—	Don Freeman (C)
—	—	—	Jean Fritz
—	—	—	Wanda Gág (C) (N)
—	—	—	Eva Roe Gaggin (N)
—	—	—	Paul Galdone (C)
—	—	—	Ruth S. Gannett (C) (N)
—	—	—	Doris Gates (N)
—	—	—	Jean Craighead George (N)
—	—	—	Tibor Gergely (C)
—	—	—	Myra Ginsburg
—	—	—	Fred Gipson (N)
—	—	—	Paul Goble (C)
—	—	—	M. B. Goffstein (C)
—	—	—	Alice E. Goudey (C)
—	—	—	Al Graham (C)
—	—	—	Margaret Bloy Graham (C)
—	—	—	Kenneth Graham
—	—	—	Hardie Gramatky
—	—	—	Elizabeth Janet Gray (N)
—	—	—	Bette Green (N)
—	—	—	Jacob Grimm
—	—	—	Wilhelm Grimm
—	—	—	Leo Gurko (N)
—	—	—	Berta Hader (C)
—	—	—	Elmer Hader (C)
—	—	—	Gail E. Haley (C)
—	—	—	Anne Gertrude Hall (N)
—	—	—	Donald Hall (C)
—	—	—	Grace Hallock (N)
—	—	—	Virginia Hamilton (N)
—	—	—	Thomas Handforth (C)
—	—	—	Joel Chandler Harris
—	—	—	Marion Havighurst (N)
—	—	—	Walter Havighurst (N)
—	—	—	Charles Hawes (N)
—	—	—	Carolyn Haywood
—	—	—	Marguerite Henry (N)
—	—	—	Velino Herrera (C)
—	—	—	Agnes Hewes (N)
—	—	—	Du Bose Heyward
—	—	—	Clifford Hicks
—	—	—	Jamake Highwater (N)
—	—	—	Lillian Hoban
—	—	—	Russell Hoban
—	—	—	Margaret Hodges (C)
—	—	—	Syd Hoff
—	—	—	Nonny Hogrogian (C)
—	—	—	Stewart Holbrook (C)
—	—	—	Janice Holland
—	—	—	Holling C. Holling (C) (N)
—	—	—	Ruth Hooker

CHECKLIST 1-4 (cont.)

Language Arts	Reading	Gifted	
—	—	—	James Houston
—	—	—	Chen Hou-Tien
—	—	—	Ralph Hubbard (N)
—	—	—	Irene Hunt (N)
—	—	—	Mabel Leigh Hunt (N)
—	—	—	Rachek Isadora (C)
—	—	—	Will James (N)
—	—	—	Janice
—	—	—	Randall Jarrell (C) (N)
—	—	—	Susan Jeffers (C)
—	—	—	Eleanore Jewett (N)
—	—	—	Margaret Johansen (N)
—	—	—	Gerald W. Johnson (N)
—	—	—	Elizabeth Orton Jones (C)
—	—	—	Idwal Jones (N)
—	—	—	Jesse Orton Jones (C)
—	—	—	Sesyle Joslin (C)
—	—	—	Clara Ingram Judson (N)
—	—	—	Virginia Kahl
—	—	—	Nicholas Kalashnikoff (N)
—	—	—	Francis Kalnay (N)
—	—	—	Ezra Jack Keats (C)
—	—	—	Harold Keith (N)
—	—	—	Eric P. Kelly (N)
—	—	—	Carol Kendall (N)
—	—	—	Juliet Kepes (C)
—	—	—	Alexander Key
—	—	—	Lee Kingman
—	—	—	Rudyard Kipling
—	—	—	Jim Kjelgaard
—	—	—	Eric Knight
—	—	—	E. L. Konigsburg (N)
—	—	—	Robert Kraus
—	—	—	Ruth Krauss (C)
—	—	—	Joseph Krumgold (N)
—	—	—	Anne Kyle (N)
—	—	—	Aurora Labastida (C)
—	—	—	Jean de La Fontaine
—	—	—	Monika Laimgruber
—	—	—	Andrew Lang
—	—	—	John Langstaff (C)
—	—	—	Jane Langton (N)
—	—	—	Jean Lee Latham (N)
—	—	—	Dorothy P. Lathrop (C) (N)
—	—	—	Robert Lawson (C) (N)
—	—	—	Munro Leaf (C)
—	—	—	Ursula K. Le Guin (N)
—	—	—	Madeleine L'Engle (N)
—	—	—	Lois Lenski (N)
—	—	—	Blair Lent (C)
—	—	—	Sorche Nic Leodhas (C) (N)
—	—	—	Julius Lester (N)
—	—	—	C. S. Lewis
—	—	—	Elizabeth Lewis (N)
—	—	—	Alice Lide (N)
—	—	—	Jennie Lindquist (N)

CHECKLIST 1-4 (cont.)

Language Arts	Reading	Gifted	
—	—	—	Kathleen Lines
—	—	—	Leo Lionni (C)
—	—	—	William Lipkind (C)
—	—	—	Arnold Lobel (C) (N)
—	—	—	Hugh Lofting (N)
—	—	—	Beman Lord
—	—	—	Joseph Low
—	—	—	Eloise Lownsbery (N)
—	—	—	David Macauley (C)
—	—	—	Robert McCloskey (C)
—	—	—	Beverly Broadsky McDermott (C)
—	—	—	Gerald McDermott (C)
—	—	—	Golden MacDonald (C)
—	—	—	Phyllis McGinley (C)
—	—	—	Eloise McGraw (N)
—	—	—	Sara Machetanz
—	—	—	Marian Hurd McNeeley (N)
—	—	—	Anne Malcolmson (C)
—	—	—	Alida Malkus (N)
—	—	—	Bernard Marshall (N)
—	—	—	Patricia Miles Martin
—	—	—	Sharon Bell Mathis (N)
—	—	—	William Maxwell (N)
—	—	—	Stephen W. Meader (N)
—	—	—	Florence Crannell Means (N)
—	—	—	Cornelia Meigs (N)
—	—	—	Jan Merrill
—	—	—	Miska Miles (N)
—	—	—	Katherine Milhous (C)
—	—	—	Edna Miller
—	—	—	Elizabeth Miller (N)
—	—	—	A. A. Milne
—	—	—	Else Holmelund Minarik (C)
—	—	—	Ferdinand Monjo
—	—	—	Rutherford Montgomery (N)
—	—	—	Beni Montresor (C)
—	—	—	Grace Moon (N)
—	—	—	Carol Moore (N)
—	—	—	Janet Gaylord Moore (N)
—	—	—	Marianne Moore (N)
—	—	—	Sulamith Moore (N)
—	—	—	Nicolas Mordvinoff (C)
—	—	—	Arlene Mosel (C)
—	—	—	Dhan Gopal Mukerji (N)
—	—	—	Margaret Musgrove (C)
—	—	—	Evelyn Ness (C)
—	—	—	Emily Cheney Neville (N)
—	—	—	Clare Newberry (C)
—	—	—	Robert Newman
—	—	—	Nicolas. *See* Nicholas Mordvinoff
—	—	—	Kay Nielson
—	—	—	Sterling North (N)
—	—	—	Mary Norton
—	—	—	Robert C. O'Brien (N)
—	—	—	Scott O'Dell (N)
—	—	—	Elizabeth Olds (C)

CHECKLIST 1-4 (cont.)

Language Arts	Reading	Gifted	
—	—	—	Tony Palazzo (C)
—	—	—	Lila Pargment
—	—	—	Peggy Parish
—	—	—	Robert Andrew Parker (C)
—	—	—	Peter Parnall (C)
—	—	—	Anne Parrish (N)
—	—	—	Katherine Paterson (N)
—	—	—	Emmy Payne
—	—	—	Richard Peck
—	—	—	Bill Peet
—	—	—	Charles Perrault
—	—	—	Maud Petersham (C)
—	—	—	Miska Petersham (C)
—	—	—	Watty Piper
—	—	—	Ilse Plume (C)
—	—	—	Leo Politi (C)
—	—	—	Elizabeth Marie Pope (N)
—	—	—	Beatrix Potter
—	—	—	Edna Mitchell Preston (C)
—	—	—	Alice Provensen
—	—	—	Howard Pyle
—	—	—	Robert Quackenbush
—	—	—	Arthur Ransome (C)
—	—	—	Ellen Raskin (N)
—	—	—	Marjorie Kinnan Rawlings (N)
—	—	—	Philip Reed (C)
—	—	—	Johanna Reiss (N)
—	—	—	H. A. Rey
—	—	—	Becky Reyher (C)
—	—	—	Dorothy Rhoads (N)
—	—	—	Eve Rice
—	—	—	Ruth Robbins (C)
—	—	—	Keith Robertson
—	—	—	Mabel Robinson (N)
—	—	—	Anne Rockwell
—	—	—	Feodor Rojankovsky (C)
—	—	—	Constance Rourke (N)
—	—	—	Cheli Duran Ryan (C)
—	—	—	Marilyn Sachs
—	—	—	Mari Sandoz (N)
—	—	—	Julia Sauer (N)
—	—	—	Ruth Sawyer (C) (N)
—	—	—	Richard Scarry
—	—	—	Jack Schaefer (N)
—	—	—	Julian Scheer (C)
—	—	—	Miriam Schlein (C)
—	—	—	Sarah Schmidt (N)
—	—	—	George Schreiber (C)
—	—	—	Elizabeth Seeger (N)
—	—	—	George Selden (N)
—	—	—	Maurice Sendak (C)
—	—	—	Kate Seredy (C) (N)
—	—	—	Dr. Seuss (C)
—	—	—	Anna Sewell
—	—	—	Helen Sewell (C)
—	—	—	Monica Shannon (N)

CHECKLIST 1-4 (cont.)

Language Arts	Reading	Gifted	
—	—	—	Irwin Shapiro
—	—	—	Marjorie Sharmat
—	—	—	Katherine Shippen (N)
—	—	—	Uri Shulevitz (C)
—	—	—	Nicholas Sidjakov (C)
—	—	—	Shel Silverstein
—	—	—	Marc Simont (C)
—	—	—	Isaac Bashevis Singer (N)
—	—	—	Elsie Singmaster (N)
—	—	—	William Sleator (C)
—	—	—	Esphyr Slobodkina
—	—	—	Louis Slobodkin (C)
—	—	—	Carol Dale Snedeker (N)
—	—	—	Zelpha Keatley Snyder (N)
—	—	—	Donald J. Sobol
—	—	—	Virginia Sorensen (N)
—	—	—	Elizabeth George Speare (N)
—	—	—	Armstrong Sperry (N)
—	—	—	Peter Spier (C)
—	—	—	Johanna Spyri
—	—	—	Ben Stahl
—	—	—	William O. Steele (N)
—	—	—	William Steig (C) (N)
—	—	—	James Still
—	—	—	Mary Stolz (N)
—	—	—	Helen Stone (C)
—	—	—	Phil Stong (N)
—	—	—	Hildegarde Swift (N)
—	—	—	Mildred Taylor
—	—	—	Sydney Taylor
—	—	—	Theodore Taylor
—	—	—	Ernest Thayer
—	—	—	Eunice Tietjens (N)
—	—	—	Estelle Titiev
—	———		Eve Titus (C)
—	—	—	J. R. Tolkein
—	—	—	Marjorie Torrey (C)
—	—	—	Carolyn Treffinger (N)
—	—	—	Alvin R. Tresselt (C)
—	—	—	Tasha Tudor (C)
—	—	—	Edwin Tunis
—	—	—	Brinton Turkle (C)
—	—	—	Mark Twain
—	—	—	Jack Tworkov
—	—	—	Janice May Udry
—	—	—	James Ullman (N)
—	—	—	Chris Van Allsburg (C)
—	—	—	Hendrik Willem van Loon (N)
—	—	—	Hilda Van Stockum (N)
—	—	—	Bernard Waber
—	—	—	Barbara K. Walker
—	—	—	Lynd Ward (C)
—	—	—	Mary H. Weik (N)
—	—	—	Ann Weil (N)
—	—	—	Leonard Weisgard (C)
—	—	—	Christine Weston (N)

CHECKLIST 1-4 (cont.)

Language Arts	Reading	Gifted	
—	—	—	Opal Wheeler (C)
—	—	—	E. B. White
—	—	—	Elunor Whitney (N)
—	—	—	Harold Wiberg
—	—	—	Ester Wier (N)
—	—	—	Kurt Wiese (C)
—	—	—	Laura Ingalls Wilder (N)
—	—	—	Brian Wildsmith
—	—	—	Will. *See* William Lipkind
—	—	—	Barbara Willard
—	—	—	Jay Williams
—	—	—	Margery Williams
—	—	—	Maja Wojciechowska
—	—	—	Hildegard Woodward (C)
—	—	—	Taro Yashima (C)
—	—	—	Elizabeth Yates (N)
—	—	—	Laurence Yep (N)
—	—	—	Jane Yolen (C)
—	—	—	Ed Young
—	—	—	Ella Young (N)
—	—	—	Harve Zemach (C)
—	—	—	Margot Zemach (C)
—	—	—	Gene Zion (C)
—	—	—	Charlotte Zolotow (C)

CHECKLIST 1-5   BEST OF THE LITERARY GREATS

Student _____ Date _____

My nomination for the best of the fiction greats is:

Adventure—
  Title:
  Author:
Animal—
  Title:
  Author:
Fantasy—
  Title:
  Author:
Historical—
  Title:
  Author:
Mystery—
  Title:
  Author:
Newbery Award—
  Title:
  Author:
Realistic—
  Title:
  Author:
Science—
  Title:
  Author:

CHECKLIST 1-6   MY FAVORITE LITERARY CHARACTERS

Student _____ Date _____

Please list your favorite literary character(s) and then identify the title and author of the book in which you discovered the character(s) in the following manner:

— Dorothy and Toto in *The Wizard of Oz* by Frank Baum

— Ramon Salazar in *The Black Pearl* by Scott O'Dell

—

—

—

—

—

—

—

CHECKLIST 1-7   FICTION BOOK EVALUATION FORM

Student _____ Date _____

Novels, short stories, and other prose writings that tell about imaginary people, places, and events.

Criteria for Evaluation   *Evaluation*

1. Is the theme of this book significant?   Yes ___   No ___
   Comment _____
   _____

2. Does the plot have action, suspense, and a logical conclusion?   Yes ___   No ___
   Comment _____
   _____

3. Are the characters well drawn and convincing?   Yes ___   No ___
   Comment _____
   _____

4. Is the style compelling?   Yes ___   No ___
   Comment _____
   _____

5. Is the format of this book attractive?   Yes ___   No ___
   Comment _____
   _____

6. Does this book generate interest and stimulate the desire for further reading?   Yes ___   No ___
   Comment _____
   _____

7. Would you recommend this book to someone else?   Yes ___   No ___
   If so, to whom? _____
   _____

CHECKLIST **1-8**   NONFICTION BOOK EVALUATION FORM

Student_____ Date _____

Factual books that tell about actual people, places, things, events, and ideas.

Criteria for Evaluation   *Evaluation*

1. Is the information accurate and
   current?   Yes __   No __
   Comment _____
   _____
   _____

2. Is the information presented in a
   readable style?   Yes __   No __
   Comment _____
   _____
   _____

3. Are sufficient details provided?   Yes __   No __
   Comment _____
   _____
   _____

4. Is the format attractive?   Yes __   No __
   Comment _____
   _____
   _____

5. Is the table of contents an ade-
   quate informational key?   Yes __   No __
   Comment _____
   _____
   _____

6. Is there an index?   Yes __   No __
   Comment _____
   _____
   _____

7. Does this book generate interest
   and stimulate the desire for fur-
   ther reading on this topic?   Yes __   No __
   Comment _____
   _____
   _____

CHECKLIST 1-9   ACCOUNTING FOR TIME IN FOLKTALES

Student _____ Date _____

Time is accounted for or indicated in the following manner in these folktales:

Title:
Author:
Reference to time:

Title:
Author:
Reference to time

Title:
Author:
Reference to time:

Title:
Author:
Reference to time

Title:
Author:
Reference to time:

Title:
Author:
Reference to time:

STUDY CENTER PROGRAM 1-1   FOLK LITERATURE:
TALES FROM OTHER TIMES AND PLACES

Inclusive Dates: From _____ To _____

Teaching Goal: To provide an in-depth study of fairy tales as an old and ever popular form of folk literature about adults and children in many lands and in times both past and present.

Teaching Objectives:

To introduce students to the study of folktales.

To acquaint students with the universality of folk literature—that it is a form of literature found in all parts of the world.

To encourage students to explore fairy tales from "far and near."

To encourage students to experiment with telling fairy tales.

To introduce students to the art of puppetry.

Orientation Strategies:

  I. The class is introduced to the study of fairy tales via the sound filmstrip, *Fairy Tales* from the Pied Piper Productions Literature for Children, Series 2.

    A. The origin and "special magic" of fairy tales are explored.

    B. Puppets are used to present a dramatization of the fairy tale *Hansel and Gretel*.

    C. One of the most enchanting fairy tales of Japan, *Issun Boshi, the Inchling*, is presented.

  II. The class compiles a list of favorite fairy tales.

    A. Each student takes a copy of the list to his or her family, relations, neighbors, and school friends.

      1. The student submits the list and asks that the friend check each title with which he or she is familiar.

    B. The class makes a composite list of fairy tale titles that have been identified as favorites.

    C. Based on the number of titles identified as favorites, the students make several observations, such as:

STUDY CENTER PROGRAM 1-1 (cont.)

---

    1. Why so many titles that were originally listed by this class turned out to be favorites of parents, grandparents, aunts and uncles, and neighbors.

    2. Folktales are frequently passed from one generation to the next via story-telling.

    3. When people from Europe migrated to America, they brought their store-house of fairy tales in their minds and then told these stories to their children and to their children's children.

  D. The class defines fairy tales, drawing on their own experiences with hearing and reading these folktales; next they check their definition with that found in an unabridged dictionary. The students then decide which definition is better and, if they decide to expand either, do so; a typical definition is: *Fairy Tales* are folktales that tell about fairies, elves, pixies, and other imaginary beings who possess magical powers.

III. The class extends its understanding of folk literature.

  A. The class views and discusses the Pied Piper Productions filmstrip set *All about Folktales* (6 filmstrips, 6 cassettes).

    1. Storytelling Then and Now: Explores the oral tradition and the days of story-tellers. The fascinating ways in which stories such as "Jack and the Bean-stalk" and "Cinderella" change to reflect each culture are depicted.

    2. Talking Beasts: Animals are favorite folktale characters, as in "The Blue Jackal," retold and illustrated by Marcia Brown.

    3. Witches, Giants and Elves: A most appealing element of many folktales is the character with supernatural powers, found in stories from all cultures. Jacqueline Ayer's "Rumpelstiltskin" represents the wee folk: elves, gnomes, and leprechauns. Outstanding tales populated with witches and giants are introduced.

    4. Noodlehead Stories: Paul Galdone's "Obedient Jack" typifies the simpleton characters and broad comedy action that were popular centuries ago and are still present in television comedy today. The attributes of humor in folk-tales are reinforced with Hoffman's "Hans in Luck."

    5. Folktale Themes: Mercer Mayer's captivating "Beauty and the Beast" repre-sents the kind of tale that has meaning for young and old. What is the story saying to us? introduces an exploration of "theme" in folktales. Also features "The Fisherman and His Wife" as well as other classic tales.

    6. Tales of Enchantment: The illuminating illustrations of Trina Schart Hyman's "Sleeping Beauty" are used to reflect the basic conventions of the "once upon a time" stories. Explores the royal characters, palatial settings, and unique motifs that lend these stories their special magic.

  B. The students discuss the information presented in the filmstrip set *All About Folktales* (Pied Piper Productions); they summarize their learning under the fol-lowing topics:

    1. Taking the definition for fairy tales that was decided on at the beginning of this project, are all folktales fairy tales? *Definition:* Fairy tales are folktales that tell about fairies, elves, pixies, and other imaginary beings who possess magical powers.

    2. Are noodlehead stories fairy tales since there are no "fairies, elves, pixies, and other imaginary beings who possess magical powers" portrayed in these stories?

    3. What conclusion can you draw from the fact that fairy tales are folktales and noodlehead stories are folktales but not fairy tales?

    4. What is the meaning of the term *motif* as used in the filmstrip *Tales of Enchantment? Definition:* Motif is the principal or main idea or theme in a work of art, music, or literature.

IV. The class is introduced to the study center program Folk Literature: Tales from Other Times and Places.

  A. An overview of the goals and objectives of this program is presented by the teacher.

STUDY CENTER PROGRAM 1-1 (cont.)

1. Students are reminded that the print and nonprint media in the study center are but a sample of the wealth of media awaiting their consideration in the school and public libraries.
    2. Students are encouraged to explore any or all types of folk literature.
B. Possible culminating activities are discussed.
    1. This is an open-ended discussion; all suggestions are welcomed.
    2. A suggestion box is placed on the study center table so additional suggestions may be offered as the students progress through the program.
C. The three main types of folktales are discussed:
    1. Talking Beast Tales.
    2. Noodlehead Tales: Drolls, Sillies, and Dimwits.
    3. Enchantment Tales: Paranatural and Magic Tales.
D. The concept of the illustrator's also being a "teller of stories" is explored.
    1. The Randolph Caldecott Award for the most distinguished picture book for children published each year in the United States is a memorial to Randolph Caldecott, the British illustrator of children's books who lived from 1846–1886. For a biography of Randolph Caldecott, see *Something about the Author: Facts and Pictures about Authors and Illustrators of Books for Young People,* ed. by Anne Commire (Detroit: Gale, 1971 to date), vol. 17, 31.
    2. Books illustrated by the following artists are included in this center collection:

Adrienne Adams	Michael Foreman
Edward Adrizzone	Gyo Fujikawa
Joan Anglund	Paul Galdone
Sheila Beckett	Imero Gobbato
Fred Brenner	Janusz Grabianski
Marcia Brown	Yoshitaro Isaka
Anthony Browne	Erroll Le Cain
Nancy Elkholm Burkett	Gerald McDermott
Eric Carle	Kay Nielsen
Barbara Cooney	Arthur Rackham
George Cruikshank	Josef Scharl
Edgar d'Aulaire and Ingri d'Aulaire	Yasuo Segawa
Marguerite De Angeli	Otto S. Svend
Donna Diamond	Tasha Tudor
Disney Studios	Ryo Hei Yauagrihara

E. A bibliography of materials available in the study center is distributed and the students are introduced to the major headings under which the material is grouped.
    1. Beings with Magical Power
        Book of Dragons by Ruth Manning-Sanders (Dutton, 1965)
        Book of Enchantments and Curses by Ruth Manning-Sanders (Dutton, 1977)
        Book of Magic Animals by Ruth Manning-Sanders (Dutton, 1975)
        Book of Ogres and Trolls by Ruth Manning-Sanders (Dutton, 1973)
        Book of Witches by Ruth Manning-Sanders (Dutton, 1966)
        Come Follow Me . . . to the Secret World of Elves and Fairies and Gnomes and Trolls illus. by Gyo Fujikawa (Grosset, 1979)
        An Encyclopedia of Fairies: Hobgoblins, Brownies, Bogies, and Other Supernatural Creatures by Katherine Briggs (Pantheon, 1978; paper)
        Trolls by Edgar d'Aulaire and Ingri d'Aulaire (Doubleday, 1972; paper)
    2. Fairy Tale Collections from Here, There, and Everywhere
        The Fairy Tale Treasury ed. by Virginia Haviland, illus. by Raymond Briggs (Coward, 1972; paper, Dell)

STUDY CENTER PROGRAM 1-1 (cont.)

Fairy Tales from Many Lands illus. by Arthur Rackham (Puffin Books, 1978; paper)

Favorite Fairy Tales Told in Denmark by Virginia Haviland (Little, 1971)

Favorite Fairy Tales Told in England by Virginia Haviland (Little, 1959)

Favorite Fairy Tales Told in France by Virginia Haviland (Little, 1959)

Favorite Fairy Tales Told in Greece by Virginia Haviland (Little, 1973)

Favorite Fairy Tales Told in India by Virginia Haviland (Little, 1973)

Favorite Fairy Tales Told in Ireland by Virginia Haviland (Little, 1961)

Favorite Fairy Tales Told In Italy by Virginia Haviland (Little, 1965)

Favorite Fairy Tales Told in Japan by Virginia Haviland (Little, 1967)

Favorite Fairy Tales Told in Norway by Virginia Haviland (Little, 1961)

Favorite Fairy Tales Told in Russia by Virginia Haviland (Little, 1961)

Favorite Fairy Tales Told in Scotland by Virginia Haviland (Little, 1963)

Favorite Fairy Tales Told in Spain by Virginia Haviland (Little, 1963)

Favorite Fairy Tales Told in Sweden by Virginia Haviland (Little, 1966)

Japanese Children's Favorite Stories by Florence Sakade (Tuttle, 1958)

Little One-Inch and Other Chinese Stories by Florence Sakade (Tuttle n.d.)

The Little Swineherd and Other Tales by Paula Fox (Dutton, 1978)

The Magic Boat and Other Chinese Folk Tales by Moritz Jagendorf and Virginia Weng (Vanguard, 1980)

Peach Boy and Other Stories by Florence Sakade (Tuttle, n.d.; paper)

Tasha Tudor's Favorite Stories comp. and illus. by Tasha Tudor (Lippincott, 1965)

Urashima Taro and Other Stories by Florence Sakade (Tuttle, n.d.)

FILMSTRIPS:

Best Loved Fairy Tales from Asia (Educational Enrichment Materials—4 filmstrips, 4 cassettes, or 4 records)

> *The Dragons of Peking,* (China)
>
> *Five Wise Sayings* (India)
>
> *The Magic Kettle* (Japan)
>
> *Ali Baba* (Arabia)

Best Loved Fairy Tales from Europe (Educational Enrichment Materials—4 filmstrips, 4 cassettes, or 4 records)

> *The Colony of Cats* (Italy)
>
> *The Musicians of Bremen* (Germany)
>
> *Sleeping Beauty* (France)
>
> *Why the Sea Is Salty* (Norway)

Folk and Fairy Tales from Distant Lands (Spoken Arts—4 filmstrips, 4 cassettes)

> *Ekun and Opolo Go Looking for Wives* (Africa)
>
> *The Frog Tsarevna* (Russia)
>
> *Goldilocks and the Three Bears* (England)
>
> *The Story of Kintaro* (Japan)

Folktales from the Ancient East (Educational Enrichment Materials—4 filmstrips, 4 cassettes)

> *Foolish Friends* (Turkey)
>
> *The Rajah's Garden* (India)
>
> *The Wishing Bowl* (China)

STUDY CENTER PROGRAM 1-1 (cont.)

  The Lost Wisdom (Israel)
 Folktales from the Old World (Educational Enrichment Materials—4 filmstrips, 4 cassettes)
  The Little House (Ukraine)
  Seven with One Blow (Italy)
  The Foxy Wisdom (Greece)
  Unselfish Prisoners of the Sea (Portugal)
 Tales from Africa (Random—4 filmstrips, 4 cassettes)
  Old Man and Deer
  The Origin of the Animals
  The Law of Mapaki
  Musar and His Parents
 Tales from Asia (Random—4 filmstrips, 4 cassettes)
  Hok Lee and the Dwarf (China)
  The Rajah's Sons and the Princess (India)
  The Jellyfish and the Monkey (Japan)
  The Nightingale (China)
 Tales from Europe (Random—4 filmstrips, 4 cassettes)
  The Ugly Duckling (Denmark)
  The Good Woman (Norway)
  The Glass Ax (Hungary)
  The Hobyahs (England)
 Tales from Our Parents' Lands (Spoken Arts—4 filmstrips, 4 cassettes)
  Hudden and Dudden O'Leary
  Catherine and Her Destiny
  The King's Drum
  Tepozton and Giant
 Treasury of Chinese Fairy Tales (Spoken Arts—4 filmstrips, 4 cassettes, 4 scripts)
  The Little Sisters of the Grasslands
  The Battle of the Giant Sturgeon
  The Great Hunt
  Monkey Subdues the White-Bone Demon
 Urashima Taro: A Japanese Folktale (Guidance Associates—1 filmstrip, 1 cassette)

3. Collectors' Editions of Fairy Tales from the Metropolitan Museum of Art
 Fairy Tales by Hans Christian Anderson, illus. by Kay Nielsen (Viking, 1981)
 The Tale of the Shining Princess by Sally Fisher (Viking, 1980)

4. Classical Fairy Tales Set to Classical Music
 Popular Stories with Classical Music Filmstrips (Random—4 filmstrips, 4 cassettes, or 4 records)
  Cinderella (ballet music composed by Serge Prokofieff, narrated by Anne Jackson)
  Peter and the Wolf (music composed by Serge Prokofieff, narrated by Eli Wallach)
  Sleeping Beauty (ballet music composed by Peter Ilyich Tchaikovsky, narrated by Robert Dryden)

STUDY CENTER PROGRAM **1-1** (cont.)

The Firebird (ballet music composed by Igor Stravinsky, narrated by Theodore Bikel)

5. Names to Remember in Folk Literature

Hans Christian Andersen (1805–1875) (Denmark); for biographical information, see *Yesterday's Authors of Books for Children: Facts and Pictures about Authors and Illustrators of Books for Young People, from Early Times to 1960,* ed. by Anne Commire (Detroit: Gale, 1977–1979), vol. 1, p. 23.

BOOKS:

Ardizzone's Hans Andersen: Fourteen Classic Tales trans. by Stephen Corrin, illus. by Edward Ardizzone (Atheneum, 1979)

The Complete Fairy Tales and Stories by Hans Christian Andersen (Doubleday, 1974)

Fairy Tales by Hans Christian Andersen, illus. by Kay Nielsen (Viking, 1981)

Hans Andersen: His Classic Fairy Tales illus. by Michael Foreman (Doubleday, 1978)

It's Perfectly True: And Other Stories trans. by Paul Leyssac (Harcourt, 1938)

Seven Stories by Hans Christian Andersen illus. by Eric Carle (Watts, 1978)

The Snow Queen adapted by Naomi Lewis, illus. by Errol Le Cain (Viking, 1979)

The Steadfast Tin Soldier illus. by Marcia Brown (Scribner, 1952); illus. by Paul Galdone (Houghton, 1979)

Thumbelina illus. by Adrienne Adams (Scribner, 1961)

The Ugly Duckling illus. by Adrienne Adams (Scribner, 1975; paper)

FILMSTRIPS:

Hans Christian Andersen Fairy Tales (Educational Enrichment Materials—4 filmstrips, 4 cassettes, or 4 records)

> *The Nightingale*
>
> *The Tinderbox*
>
> *The Emperor's New Clothes*
>
> *The Steadfast Tin Soldier*
>
> *The Snow Queen,* Parts I and II
>
> *Thumbelina,* Parts I and II
>
> *The Little Mermaid,* Parts I and II

The Swineherd illus. by Bjorn Winiblad (Weston Woods—1 filmstrip, 1 cassette)

The Ugly Duckling illus. by Adrienne Adams (Miller-Brody—1 filmstrip, 1 cassette)

RECORDING:

Hans Christian Andersen in Central Park: Stories told by Diane Wolkstein (Weston Woods—1 record)

Jacob Ludwig Grimm (1785–1863) and Wilhelm Grimm (1786–1859) (Germany); for biographical information, see *Something about the Author: Facts and Pictures about Authors and Illustrators of Books for Young People* ed. by Anne Commire (Detroit: Gale, 1971 to date), vol. 22, p. 126.

BOOKS:

The Best of Grimm's Fairy Tales illus. by Otto S. Svend (Larousse, 1980)

The Brave Little Tailor illus. by Otto S. Svend (Larousse, 1980)

The Brothers Grimm: Popular Folk Tales by Jacob Grimm and Wilhelm Grimm (Doubleday, 1978)

Grimm's Fairy Tales illus. by George Cruikshank (Puffin Books, n.d.; paper)

Grimm's Fairy Tales: Twenty Stories illus. by Arthur Rackham (Puffin Books, n.d.; paper)

Hansel and Gretel illus. by Adrienne Adams (Scribner, 1975; paper)

Hansel and Gretel illus. by Anthony Browne (Julia Macrae Books, Watts, 1982)

Jorinda and Joringel trans. by Elizabeth Shub, illus. by Adrienne Adams (Scribner, 1968)

The Juniper Tree and Other Tales from Grimm selected and translated by Lore Segal, illus. by Maurice Sendak, 2 vols. (Farrar, 1973; paper)

King Grisly-Beard illus. by Maurice Sendak (Farrar, 1973)

Little Red Riding Hood illus. by Paul Galdone (McGraw, 1974)

Nibble Nibble Mousekin: A Tale of Hansel and Gretel by Joan Anglund (Harcourt, 1962; paper)

Rumpelstiltskin ed. and illus. by Jacqueline Ayer (Harcourt, 1967)

The Seven Ravens: A Grimm's Fairy Tale illus. by Donna Diamond (Viking, 1979)

The Shoemaker and the Elves illus. by Adrienne Adams (Scribner, 1960; paper)

The Sleeping Beauty illus. by Warwick Hutton (Atheneum, 1979)

Snow White (Larousse, 1975)

Snow White trans. by Paul Heim, illus. by Trina Schart Hyman (Little, 1974)

Snow White and Rose Red illus. by Adrienne Adams (Scribner, 1964)

Snow White and Rose Red illus. by Barbara Cooney (Delacorte, 1966)

Snow White and the Seven Dwarfs trans. by Randall Jarrell, illus. by Nancy Ekholm Burkert (Farrar, 1972)

Thorn Rose or the Sleeping Beauty illus. by Errol LeCain (Bradbury, 1977)

Tom Thumb illus. by Felix Hoffmann (Atheneum, 1973)

The Twelve Dancing Princesses, illus. by Errol LeCain (Viking, 1978; paper)

The Wolf and the Seven Little Kids trans. by Anne Rogers, illus. by Otto S. Svend (Larousse, 1977)

FILMSTRIPS:

Brothers Grimm Fairy Tales (Miller-Brody—8 filmstrips, 8 cassettes, or 8 records)

Snow White and Rose Red

The Frog Prince

The Golden Goose

The Sorcerer's Apprentice

Rapunzel

Rumpelstiltskin

STUDY CENTER PROGRAM 1-1 (cont.)

Hansel and Gretel

The Hedgehog and the Rabbit

Tales from the Brothers Grimm (Charles Clark—6 filmstrips, 6 cassettes)

The Elves and the Shoemaker

The Golden Goose

Rumpelstiltskin

Clever Grethel

The Musicians of Bremen

Hansel and Gretel

Treasury of Grimm's Fairy Tales (Spoken Arts—6 filmstrips, 6 cassettes)

Hansel and Gretel, Parts I and II

The Fisherman and His Wife

Tom Thumb

The Juniper Tree, Parts I and II

MOTION PICTURE:

The Sorcerer's Apprentice (Weston Woods)

Joseph Jacobs (1854–1916) (England); for biographical information, see *Something about the Author: Facts and Pictures about Authors and Illustrators of Books for Young People* ed. by Anne Commire (Detroit: Gale, 1971 to date), vol. 25, p. 159.

BOOKS:

Henry Penny illus. by Paul Galdone (Seabury, 1968)

Henny Penny illus. by William Stobbs (Follett, 1970)

Jack the Giant Killer (Walck, 1971)

Johnny Cake illus. by William Stobbs (Viking, 1973)

Mr. Miacca: An English Folk Tale illus. by Evaline Ness (Holt. 1967)

The Old Woman and Her Pig illus. by Paul Galdone (McGraw-Hill, 1960)

Pied Piper and Other Fairy Tales (Macmillan, 1968)

The Story of the Three Bears illus. by William Stobbs (McGraw, 1965)

The Three Bears illus. by Paul Galdone (Seabury, 1972)

The Three Little Pigs illus. by Walt Disney Studios (Western, n.d.)

The Three Little Pigs illus. by William Pène DuBois (Viking, 1962)

The Three Little Pigs illus. by Paul Galdone (Seabury, 1972)

The Three Little Pigs illus. by William Stobbs (McGraw, 1965)

Tom Tit Tot illus. by Evaline Ness (Scribner, 1965)

FILMSTRIPS:

The Old Woman and Her Pig (Weston Woods—1 filmstrip, 1 cassette, or 1 record)

The Three Little Pigs (Walt Disney—1 filmstrip, 1 cassette)

Andrew Lang (1844–1912) (England); for biographical information, see *Something about the Author: Facts and Pictures about Authors and Illustrators of Books for Young People* ed. by Anne Commire (Detroit: Gale, 1971 to date), vol. 16, p. 178.

BOOKS (all published by Viking):

Blue Fairy Book (1978)

Green Fairy Book (1978)

Red Fairy Book (1978)

Charles Perrault (1628–1703) (France); for biographical information, see *Something about the Author: Facts and Pictures about Authors and Illustrators of Books for Young People* ed. by Anne Commire (Detroit: Gale, 1971 to date), vol. 25, p. 192.

BOOKS:

Beauty: A Retelling of the Story of Beauty and the Beast by Robin McKinley (Harper, 1978)

Beauty and the Beast retold by Rosemary Harris, illus. by Errol LeCain (Doubleday, 1980)

Beauty and the Beast retold by Marianna Mayer, illus. by Mercer Mayer (Four Winds, 1978)

Cinderella illus. by Paul Galdone (McGraw, 1978)

Cinderella from the opera by Gioacchino Rossini, illus. by Beni Montresor (Knopf, 1965; opera libretto)

Cinderella illus. by Otto S. Svend (Larousse, 1978)

Cinderella, or, The Little Glass Slipper illus. by Marcia Brown (Scribner, 1954; Caldecott Award 1975)

The Girl Who Sat by the Ashes by Padraic Colum, illus. by Imero Gobbato (Macmillan, 1968)

Perrault's Complete Fairy Tales illus. by Heath Robinson (Dodd, 1971)

Puss in Boots illus. by Marcia Brown (Scribner, 1952)

Puss in Boots illus. by Paul Galdone (Seabury, 1976)

FILMSTRIPS (both illus. by Marcia Brown; both Miller-Brody):

Cinderella (2 filmstrips, 2 cassettes)

Puss in Boots (1 filmstrip, 1 cassette)

6. Making and Using Puppets for Storytelling

The Complete Book of Puppetry by David Currell (Plays, 1975)

Easy to Make Puppets by Joyce Luckin (Plays, 1975; paper)

Eight Plays for Hand Puppets by A. R. Philpott (Plays, 1980)

Folk Tale Plays for Puppets by Lewis Mahlmann (Plays, 1980)

Hand Puppets: How to Make and Use Them by Laura Ross (Lothrop, 1969)

Puppet Plays from Favorite Stories by Lewis Mahlmann (Plays, 1977)

7. Dramatizing Folk Tales

Dramatized Folk Tales of the World by Sylvia Kamerman (Plays, 1972)

Plays from African Folktales (Scribner, 1975)

Plays from Famous Stories and Fairy Tales by Adele Thane (Plays, 1967)

Plays from Folktales of Africa and Asia by Barbara Winther (Plays, 1976)

F. The students are alerted to:

Information found on the title page, such as, Compiled by, Edited by, Illustrated by, Retold by, Translated by.

How time is indicated in folktales (see Checklist 1-9 in this model), for example

In olden times when wishing still helped one . . .

Long ago and far away . . .

Once upon a time . . .

Once upon a time, and a very good time too . . .

STUDY CENTER PROGRAM 1-1 (cont.)

A thousand years ago tomorrow . . .

The term *ellipsis* is used to indicate omission of a word or words; asterisks may be used instead of three periods.

The Dewey Decimal Classification numbers

398   Folklore

398.2 Tales and legends

The procedure to follow in obtaining a printout of the holdings of the public library via the school district computer network center, including:

Searching under the headings, such as:

Fairy Tales

Fairy Tales—England (name of the country)

Folklore

Folklore—Germany (name of the country)

Joseph Jacobs (name of the author, compiler, etc.)

Sharing the printouts with the class; placing them in a special folder that is kept on the study center table.

V. Students work independently.

1. Selecting from the various media groups those resources of personal interest.
2. Maintaining a careful record of both the print and nonprint media utilized.

VI. Students share reading, viewing, and listening experiences as well as personal reactions to folk literature.

1. Using the Study Center Bibliography as a checklist, the students indicate which topics, Groups 1–7, are of major interest.
2. Volunteer committees, one for each of the seven groups—Beings with Magical Power; Fairy Tale Collections from Here, There, and Everywhere; Collectors' Editions of Fairy Tales from the Metropolitan Museum of Art; Classical Fairy Tales Set to Classical Music; Names to Remember in Folk Literature; Making and Using Puppets for Storytelling; and Dramatizing Folk Tales—take the responsibility for developing and carrying out appropriate summarizing activities.
3. The students at the completion of the culminating activities decide which of the following class or group learning experiences to elect:
   a. The Learning Project: Book Illustrators and Their Art*
   b. The Learning Project: Noodlehead Stories of Drolls, Sillies, and Dimwits.

*The Learning Project: Book Illustrators and Their Art is fully developed in *Creating Programs for the Gifted: A Guide for Teachers, Librarians, and Students* by Corinne P. Clendening and Ruth Ann Davies (New York: R. R. Bowker, 1980), pp. 238–247.

STUDY CENTER PROGRAM 1-2   EXPLORING POETRY

Grades: 5–6

Inclusive Dates: From _____ To _____

Teaching Goal: To encourage the student to become aware of and atune to poetry—its melody, its form, its beauty, and its power.

Teaching Objectives:

To provide opportunity for the student as an individual or as a member of a group to extend his or her understanding of poets and poetry.

To provide opportunity for the student to experience the delight of enjoying poetry discussed by a contemporary distinguished poet.

STUDY CENTER PROGRAM 1-2 (cont.)

To provide opportunity for the student to become acquainted with all types and kinds of poetry, ranging from nonsense verse to the epic.

To provide opportunity for the student to experiment with reading poetry aloud.

To provide opportunity for the student to compile an anthology of poems he or she particularly enjoys.

To provide opportunity for the student to experiment with creating poems.

To provide opportunity for the student to explore poetry to his or heart's content.

Orientation Strategies:
  I. The class is introduced to the study of poetry via the book *How to Read and Write Poetry* by Anna Cosman (Watts, 1979).
   A. Students read this book on their own.
   B. Students, in a series of discussions, pool their understanding of
     1. What a poem is.
     2. How a poem develops.
     3. Why poetry has persisted as a favorite literary form down through history.
     4. Typical examples of poetry that are part of our American heritage.
 II. The class is introduced to the study center program Exploring Poetry.
   A. An overview of the goals and the objectives of this program is presented by the teacher.
     1. Students are assured that they will not be required to memorize poetry nor will they be required to write poetry. ·
     2. Students are encouraged to explore any or all of the media.
   B. Possible culminating activities are discussed.
     1. This is an open-ended discussion; all suggestions are welcomed.
     2. A suggestion box is placed on the study center table so additional suggestions may be offered as the students progress through the program.
   C. The main themes of the program are discussed and the supporting media examined.
     1. Theme 1: There Is Rhyme and Reason to Poetry.

     First Choice Poets and Poetry (Pied Piper Productions—5 double-length filmstrips, 5 cassettes, and 1 teacher's guide) provides an in-depth study of the following contemporary poets and their poetry: Eve Merriam, Karla Kuskin, Nikki Giovanni, Myra Cohn Livingston, and David McCord.
     2. Theme 2: Songs Are Poems to Be Sung.

     A bibliography of books, filmstrips, and motion pictures is provided to facilitate students' locating titles of interest.
     3. Theme 3: Poems to Read, to Hear, to Sing, to Write, and to Enjoy.

     A bibliography of books, filmstrips, and motion pictures is provided to facilitate students' locating titles of special interest.
   D. The class is reminded that there are additional books of poetry available in the school library and several approaches to locating these resources are discussed..
     1. The card catalog is the key to retrieving print and nonprint media. Students suggest subject headings, such as:

Poetry	Russian Poetry
Poetry—Collections	Cats—Poetry
American Poetry	Dogs—Poetry
American Poetry—Collections	Nature in Poetry
English Poetry	Sea Poetry
English Poetry—Collections	Poets, American
Chinese Poetry	Poets, English
Japanese Poetry	

     2. A committee is formed to explore the school library's card catalog, to discover the Dewey decimal numbers for each category listed above and to

STUDY CENTER PROGRAM 1-2 (cont.)

compile a mimeographed checklist of subject headings with corresponding Dewey classification numbers.

3. Students who discover books, filmstrips, posters, and study prints of special appeal are invited to place the pertinent information on 3"-by-5" cards in the card file labeled "Poetry Sources Too Good to Miss."

A Student volunteers to maintain the card file and to design sample catalog cards to be used as models for print and nonprint media.

A compilation of these recommended titles will be prepared and distributed to the class at the close of the program.

III. The students as individuals or as memebers of groups work with the material in the study center and in the school library.

IV. Closure activities following termination of this program might include:

A. Individual students share with a group or with the class their favorite poems in any manner they choose, for example:

Reading the poem(s) aloud to the group or class.

Making a tape recording of the poem(s) and making the tape available to other students by placing it in the classroom study center or the school library.

Designing a poster highlighting the poem(s) and displaying it in the classroom or the school library.

Preparing mimeographed handouts for the students in the class or other areas of the school.

Submitting the poem(s) for inclusion in the school paper.

B. Individual students share with the group or with the class poetry they have written in any manner they choose; see examples above.

C. The class summarizes its impressions of poetry in today's world following the viewing and discussion of the sound filmstrip set *Poetry Is Alive and Well and Living in America* (Random—6 filmstrips, 6 cassettes).

THEME 1: THERE IS RHYME AND REASON TO POETRY
Introduction: This theme is developed by the sound filmstrip set *First Choice Poets and Poetry* (Pied Piper Productions—5 double-length filmstrips, 5 cassettes, and teacher's guide).

Overview of the Program As Outlined in the Teaching Guide:

With all the modern curriculum demands, why take time for poetry in the classroom? A child finds in poetry what an adult finds—an exhilaration that comes from the compatibility of ideas and form, from the melody and movement of lines, from the shivers of delight that good poems produce. More than any other type of literature, poetry has the power of arousing strong emotional responses and vivid sensory images.

First Choice Poets and Poetry offers students a variety of enjoyable experiences with poetry. Famous poets present their own favorite poems to viewers, showing how and where they find ideas, and how they turn them into poems. Perhaps, best of all, a little of their love of poetry may be left with students.

At the end of each filmstrip, a Workshop Lesson presents an opportunity for viewers to create their own poems. It should be remembered that for some students, the act of creating or just enjoying the poems of others is satisfaction enough. Overemphasis on rhyme, rhythm, and poetic form can be counterproductive.

Enjoyment and appreciation of poetry are the main goals.

These filmstrips may be used as part of an instructional unit or for enrichment. They may be used in any order, shown to an entire class, or viewed by one or more individuals at a study center.

Each filmstrip is organized into two parts: a visit with a well known contemporary poet and a workshop lesson. The workshop lesson focuses on a particular aspect of writing

STUDY CENTER PROGRAM 1-2 (cont.)

poetry, such as couplets, comparisons, or rhythm. Many ideas for creating original poems are presented.

FILMSTRIP: EVE MERRIAM

Objectives

1. Students will experience the sheer enjoyment of outstanding poetry presented by a distinguished author.
2. Learners will gain a greater appreciation of poetry through experiencing a personal visit with a poet and through taking part in the suggested activities.
3. Viewers will create a poem using nonsense words and a poem using a comparison.

Content

Eve Merriam shows students how to enjoy having fun with words—"Words can chime like bells or taste as sour as pickles." Her workshop lesson shows how to use nonsense words and comparisons to create word pictures.

Suggested activities

1. Before the filmstrip
2. After the filmstrip
3. The workshop lesson

About the author

Thoughts about poetry

Bibliography (all by Eve Merriam)

1. *There Is No Rhyme for Silver* (Atheneum, 1962)
2. *It Doesn't Always Have to Rhyme* (Atheneum, 1964)
3. *Catch a Little Rhyme* (Atheneum, 1966)
4. *Out Loud* (Atheneum, 1970)
5. *Rainbow Writing* (Atheneum, 1976)
6. *The Birthday Cow* (Knopf, 1978)

FILMSTRIP: KARLA KUSKIN

Objectives

1. Students will experience the sheer enjoyment of outstanding poetry presented by a distinguished author.
2. Learners will gain a greater appreciation of poetry through experiencing a personal visit with a poet and through taking part in the suggested activities.
3. Viewers will create a rhythmic poem about an object or an animal.

Content

Karla Kuskin says, "Imagining is what I love about writing poems. . . . With imagination I can be anything I want, live in any time or place." Her workshop lesson is full of ideas for using imagination to create poems.

Suggested activities

1. Before showing the filmstrip
2. After showing the filmstrip
3. The workshop session

About the author

Thoughts about poetry

Bibliography (abridged) (all by Karla Kuskin; published, by Harper)

1. *A Boy Had a Mother Who Brought Him a Hat* (1976)
2. *Any Me I Want to Be* (1972)
3. *Near the Window Tree* (1975)
4. *A Space Story* (1978)
5. *What Did You Bring Me?* (1973)

STUDY CENTER PROGRAM 1-2 (cont.)

FILMSTRIP: NIKKI GIOVANNI

Objectives

1. Students will experience the sheer enjoyment of outstanding poetry presented by a distinguished author.
2. Learners will gain a greater appreciation of poetry through experiencing a personal visit with a poet and through taking part in the suggested activities.
3. Viewers will create a poem about rain or a picnic using sensory description.

Content

Nikki Giovanni shows us that the colors, sounds, and rhythms of sidewalk musicians, vendors, and children's games can be turned into poetry. In her workshop lesson, she helps young writers make discoveries for themselves.

Suggested activities

1. Before the filmstrip
2. After the filmstrip
3. The workshop lesson

About the author

Thoughts about poetry

Bibliography (all by Nikki Giovanni)

1. *Spin a Soft Black Song* (Farrar, 1971)
2. *Ego Tripping and Other Poems for Young Readers* (Larry Hill, 1973)
3. *The Reason I Like Chocolate* (Folkways Records, 1976)

FILMSTRIP: MYRA COHN LIVINGSTON

Objectives

1. Students will experience the sheer enjoyment of outstanding poetry presented by a distinguished author.
2. Learners will gain a greater appreciation of poetry through experiencing a personal visit with a poet and through taking part in the suggested activities.
3. Viewers will create a poem about feelings, using the couplet form.

Content

Myra Cohn Livingston says that "feelings are the heart of poetry." She makes the students aware of their own varied feelings and how their feelings can be used as a starting point for writing. In her workshop lesson, she helps young writers use the couplet to create a poem based on feelings.

Suggested activities

1. Before the filmstrip
2. After the filmstrip
3. The workshop lesson

About the author

Thoughts about poetry

Bibliography (abridged) (all by Myra Cohn Livingston)

1. *A Crazy Flight and Other Poems* (Harcourt, 1971)
2. *A Lollygag of Limericks* (Atheneum, 1978)
3. *Speak Roughly to Your Little Boy* (Harcourt, 1971)
4. *O Frabjous Day* (Atheneum, 1977)
5. *Callooh! Callay!* (Atheneum, 1978)

FILMSTRIP: DAVID McCORD

Objectives

1. Students will experience the sheer enjoyment of outstanding poetry presented by a distinguished author.
2. Learners will gain a greater appreciation of poetry through experiencing a personal visit with a poet and through taking part in the suggested activities.

3. Viewers will create a rhythmic poem about an object, a seagull, or an eagle.

Content

David McCord shows how rhythm is the very essence of poetry. The poet shares intriguing anecdotes, including some about his childhood, some "serious" advice on "how to talk to frogs." Emphasis in the workshop lesson is on helping students improve the rhythm of their original verses.

Suggested activities

1. Before the filmstrip
2. After the filmstrip
3. The workshop lesson

About the author

Thoughts about poetry

Bibliography (all by David McCord; published by Little)

1. *All Day Long* (1966)
2. *Away and Ago* (1975)
3. *Every Time I Climb a Tree* (1967)
4. *Far and Few* (1952)
5. *For Me to Say* (1970)
6. *One at a Time* (1977)
7. *The Star in the Pail* (1977)

THEME 2: SONGS ARE POEMS TO BE SUNG

BOOKS

America the Beautiful: Stories of Patriotic Songs by Robert Kraske (Garrard, 1972)

Boy Scout Songbook (Boy Scouts of America, 1972; paper)

Brownies Own Songbook (Girl Scouts of the U.S.A., 1968; paper)

Fireside Book of Children's Songs by Marie Winn and Allan Miller (Simon & Schuster, 1966)

Fireside Book of Favorite American Songs by Margaret Boni and Norman Lloyd (Simon & Schuster, 1975; paper)

Fireside Book of Folk Songs (Margaret Boni and Norman Lloyd (Simon & Schuster, 1966)

The Fox Went Out on a Chilly Night illus. by Peter Spier (Doubleday, 1961)

Go Tell Aunt Rhody by Robert Quackenbush (Lippincott, 1973)

The Great Song Book ed. by Timothy John and Peter Hankey (Doubleday, 1978)

Hot Cross Buns and Other Street Cries comp. by John Langstaff (Atheneum, 1978)

The Laura Ingalls Wilder Song Book ed. by Eugenia Garson and Herbert Haufrecht (Harper, 1968)

The Man on the Flying Trapeze by Robert Quackenbush (Lippincott, 1975)

The Moon on the One Hand: Poetry in Song by William Crofut (Atheneum, 1975)

Over the River and Through the Wood by Lydia M. Child (Coward, 1974; paper, Scholastic)

Pop! Goes the Weasel and Yankee Doodle: New York in 1776 and Today with Songs and Pictures by Robert Quackenbush (Lippincott, 1976)

She'll Be Comin' 'round the Mountain by Robert Quackenbush (Lippincott, 1973)

The Silly Songbook by Esther L. Nelson (Sterling, 1981; paper)

Skip to My Lou by Robert Quackenbush (Lippincott, 1975)

The Star Spangled Banner illus. by Peter Spier (Doubleday, 1973)

Stories of Our American Patriotic Songs by John H. Lyons (Vanguard, n.d.)

Story of Our National Ballads by C. A. Browne, rev. ed. (Harper, 1960)

STUDY CENTER PROGRAM 1-2 (cont.)

Sweetly Sings the Donkey: Animal Rounds for Children to Sing or Play on Recorders ed. by John Langstaff (Atheneum, 1976)

There'll Be a Hot Time in the Old Town Tonight by Robert Quackenbush (Lippincott, 1974)

Turnabout adapted by Elaine Raphael and Don Bolognese (Viking, 1980)

Yankee Doodle by Edward Bangs (Scholastic, 1976; paper)

SOUND FILMSTRIPS (all Weston Woods)

Clementine by Robert Quackenbush (1 filmstrip, 1 cassette)

The Erie Canal by Peter Spier (1 filmstrip, 1 cassette, 1 motion picture)

The Foolish Frog by Pete Seeger and Charles Seeger (1 filmstrip, 1 cassette, 1 motion picture)

The Fox Went Out on a Chilly Night by Peter Spier (1 filmstrip, 1 cassette, 1 motion picture)

Frog Went A-Courtin by John Langstaff (1 filmstrip, 1 cassette, 1 motion picture)

Hush, Little Baby by Aliki (1 filmstrip, 1 cassette, 1 motion picture)

The Little Drummer Boy by Katherine Davis, Henry Onorati, and Harry Simeone (1 filmstrip, 1 cassette, 1 motion picture)

London Bridge Is Falling Down by Peter Spier (1 filmstrip, 1 cassette)

Noisy Nora by Rosemary Wells (1 filmstrip, 1 cassette)

Over in the Meadow by John Langstaff (1 filmstrip, 1 cassette, 1 motion picture)

She'll Be Comin' Round the Mountain by Robert Quackenbush (1 filmstrip, 1 cassette)

The Star-Spangled Banner by Peter Spier (1 filmstrip, 1 cassette, 1 motion picture)

The Twelve Days of Christmas by Robert Broomfield (1 filmstrip, 1 cassette, 1 motion picture)

Waltzing Matilda by A. B. Paterson (1 filmstrip, 1 cassette)

Yankee Doodle by Edward Bangs (1 filmstrip, 1 cassette, 1 motion picture)

THEME 3: POEMS TO READ, TO HEAR, TO SING, TO WRITE, AND TO ENJOY

BOOKS

Animal Stories in Limerick Land ed. by Leland Jacobs (Garrard, 1971)

Away and Ago by David McCord (Little, 1975)

The Bad Child's Book of Beasts by Hilaire Belloc (Knopf, 1965)

Beastly Boys and Ghastly Girls ed. by William Cole (Philomel, 1964)

Birds and the Beasts Were There ed. by William Cole (Philomel, 1963)

Casey at the Bat by Ernest L. Thayer (Prentice-Hall, 1962; hardback and paper)

A Child's Garden of Verses by Robert Louis Stevenson, illus. by Tasha Tudor (Rand, 1981)

Dinosaurs and Other Beasts of Yore ed. by William Cole (Philomel, 1979)

Ego Tripping and Other Poems for Young Readers by Nikki Giovanni (Lawrence Hill, 1974; hardback and paper)

Four-Way Stop and Other Poems by Myra Cohn Livingston (Atheneum, 1976)

Funny Bone Ticklers in Verse and Rhyme ed. by Leland Jacobs (Garrard, 1972)

Funny Folks in Limerick Land ed. by Leland Jacobs (Garrard, 1971)

Good Dog Poems ed. by William Cole (Scribner, 1981)

Holiday Happenings in Limerick Land ed. by Leland Jacobs (Garrard, 1972)

The Malibu and Other Poems by Myra Cohn Livingston (Atheneum, 1972)

More Cricket Songs: Japanese Haiku trans. by Harry Behn (Harper, 1971)

Poem Stew ed. by William Cole (Harper, 1981)

STUDY CENTER PROGRAM 1-2 (cont.)

Poems of Magic and Spells ed. by William Cole (Collins, 1971)

The Poetry of Horses ed. by William Cole (Scribner, 1979)

Poetry of Witches, Elves and Goblins ed. by Leland Jacobs (Garrard, 1970)

Shrieks at Midnight: Macabre Poems, Eerie and Humorous ed. by Sara Brewton and John Brewton (Harper, 1969)

A Visit to William Blake's Inn by Nancy Willard (Harcourt, 1981)

What a Wonderful Bird the Frog Are: An Assortment of Humorous Poetry-Verse ed. by Myra Livingston (Harcourt, 1973)

Wings from the Wind: An Anthology of Poetry ed. and illus. by Tasha Tudor (Lippincott, 1964)

The Yak, The Python, The Frog: Three Beast Poems by Hilaire Belloc (Parents, 1975)

You Read to Me, I'll Read to You by John Ciardi (Lippincott, 1961)

SOUND FILMSTRIPS AND MOTION PICTURES

Humorous Poetry (Miller-Brody—4 filmstrips, 4 cassettes, or 4 records)

The Pobble Who Has No Toes and *The Duck and the Kangaroo* by Edward Lear

You Are Old Father William by Lewis Carroll

Story of the Wild Huntsman by Heinrich Hoffman

Old Mother Hubbard (Anonymous)

Pick a Peck o'Poems comp. by Lee Bennett Hopkins (Miller-Brody—6 filmstrips, 6 cassettes, or 6 records)

What Is Poetry?

Animals, Animals, Animals

When It's Cold, When It's Hot, and When It's Not

Sing a Song of Cities

Our Earth to Keep

A Poem Belongs to You

Attic of the Wind and *In a Spring Garden* by Doris Lund (Weston Woods—1 filmstrip, 1 cassette)

Casey at the Bat by Ernest Thayer (Weston Woods—1 filmstrip, 1 cassette)

Chicken Soup with Rice by Maurice Sendak (Weston Woods—1 filmstrip, 1 cassette, 1 motion picture)

Custard the Dragon by Ogden Nash (Weston Woods—1 filmstrip, 1 cassette)

The House That Jack Built illus. by Paul Galdone (Weston Woods—1 filmstrip, 1 cassette)

The Mother Goose Treasury, illus. by Raymond Briggs (Weston Woods—1 filmstrip, 1 cassette)

Old Mother Hubbard and Her Dog illus by Paul Galdone (Weston Woods—1 filmstrip, 1 cassette)

The Owl and the Pussy-Cat by Edward Lear (Weston Woods—1 filmstrip, 1 cassette, 1 motion picture)

The Pied Piper of Hamelin by Robert Browning, narrated by Orson Welles. (Pied Piper Productions—1 filmstrip, 1 cassette, 1 teacher's guide)

Waltzing Matilda by A. B. Paterson (Weston Woods—1 filmstrip, 1 cassette)

Wynken, Blynken and Nod by Eugene Field (Weston Woods—1 filmstrip, 1 cassette, 1 motion picture)

TEACHING GUIDE 1-1   REALISTIC FICTION* (FILMSTRIP)

CONTENT

Robert Burch's *Queenie Peavy* introduces Realistic Fiction—stories which didn't really happen, but which seem so real that they might have happened. Viewers learn that characters are not all "good" or all "bad," and that settings and dialogue are similar to real life. Excerpts from *The TV Kid* and *Harriet the Spy* illustrate themes such as facing problems and getting along with peers. Additional examples leave young people with the idea that Realistic Fiction tells about other people just like themselves.

OBJECTIVES

1. Students will be motivated to read one or more realistic fiction books.
2. Students will name two or more attributes of realistic fiction books.
3. Students will discuss the plot, setting, and characters of *Queenie Peavy*.
4. Students will be motivated to write a realistic story about a "real" problem.

SUGGESTED DISCUSSION AND ACTIVITIES

Before the filmstrip

Ask students to look at the person next to them. What would it be like to live in that person's skin for a day? Exchange a few ideas: Do you like spinach? Do you have your own room or do you share one? How many brothers and sisters do you have?

Realistic fiction books give the reader a chance to get into someone else's head for awhile. Hang on to your hats as we find out more about Realistic Fiction.

After the filmstrip (These activities appear on the screen.)

1. Discussing realistic fiction
   a. Leading characters are often likeable, but not perfect. How does Queenie fit this idea?
   b. In realistic fiction, settings seem quite real. What was the setting for *The TV Kid*?
   c. Stories of realistic fiction often deal with growing up and facing problems. What was Harriet the Spy's problem?
2. Thinking about the characters
   a. Would you like to have someone like Queenie for a friend? Explain.
   b. Lennie tried to escape from his troubles by watching TV. If you were his friend, what advice would you give him?
3. Creative writing. Write a story about a person with a "real" problem such as the following: an important promise is broken . . . a bully is making life miserable . . . a person not good at sports tries to make friends.

EXTENDING LEARNING

After students have read a realistic fiction book, reinforce the basic concepts of the filmstrip. In what ways are the main characters individuals (as opposed to stereotypes)? Which events seem most realistic, which most imagined? Did the characters change their ideas about life? Beyond telling a good story, is there a message from the author? List the various author themes, such as getting along with others, facing reality, death, divorce, acceptance of physical impairment.

Some students may wish to collect news articles which could provide the basis for episodes in writing Realistic Fiction. People and events in the community may spark additional story ideas.

Write a letter to the main character of your book. Ask him or her questions. Tell your main character how he or she could have stayed out of trouble. Offer your help.

Advanced students might discuss how the author reveals the main character to the reader (directly and indirectly). Is the story told in first person? Is there a narrator. How do the other characters relate to the main character?

*Literature for Children, Series 6, Pied Piper Productions, Verdugo City, Calif. 91046.
Copyright © 1980 Pied Piper Productions.

TEACHING GUIDE 1-1 (cont.)

Bulletin board—have students find and copy the author's introductory description of the main character. Or have them write their own description. Add an original illustration. Put the two together on a bulletin board entitled "New Friends."

RECOMMENDED BOOKS

Blume, Judy. *Are You There God? It's Me Margaret* (Bradbury, 1970). Physical maturation; religion.

Brooks, Jerome. *Uncle Mike's Boy* (Harper, 1973). Divorce; uncle/nephew relationship.

Byars, Betsy. *Summer of the Swans* (Viking, 1970). Brother/sister relationship; mental retardation.

Carlson, Natalie. *Ann Aurelia and Dorothy* (Harper, 1968). Foster home; black/white friendship.

Cleaver, Vera, and Cleaver, Bill. *Where the Lilies Bloom* (Lippincott, 1969). Family relationship.

Clymer, Eleanor. *Luke Was There* (Holt, 1973). Foster home; runaway.

Cohen, Barbara. *Thank You, Jackie Robinson* (Lothrop, 1974). Fatherless boy; adult/child relationship.

Confurd, Ellen. *The Luck of Pokey Bloom* (Little, 1975). Growing up; parent/child relationship.

Corcoran, Barbara. *A Dance to Still Music* (Atheneum, 1974). Coping with handicap; deafness.

Farley, Carol. *The Garden Is Doing Fine* (Atheneum, 1975). Death.

Fenton, Edward. *Duffy's Rocks* (Dutton, 1974). Depression era; male maturation.

Fitzhugh, Louise. *Harriet the Spy* (Harper, 1964). Parent/friend/child relationship.

Fox, Paula. *How Many Miles to Babylon?* (White, 1967). Coping with gang activities.

George, Jean. *Julie of the Wolves* (Harper, 1971). Survival; girl/wolves.

Greene, Bette. *Philip Hall Likes Me. I Reckon, Maybe* (Dial, 1974). School story; girl maturing.

Greene, Constance. *A Girl Called Al* (Viking, 1969). Coping with death; overweight problems.

Hamilton, Virginia. *The Planet of Junior Brown* (Macmillan, 1971). Friendship of loners.

Hentoff, Nat. *This School Is Driving Me Crazy* (Delacorte, 1975). School story; father/son relationship.

Hinton, Susan. *Rumble Fish* (Delacorte, 1975). Older/younger brother relationship.

Holman, Felice. *Slake's Limbo* (Scribner, 1974). Survival-urban.

Ish-Kishor, Sulamith. *Our Eddie* (Pantheon, 1969). Family relationships.

Klein, Norma. *Confessions of an Only Child* (Pantheon, 1974). Birth of sibling.

Konigsburg, Elaine. *About the B'nai Bagels* (Atheneum, 1969). Sports; maturation; prejudice.

Lampman, Evelyn. *The Year of Small Shadow* (Harcourt, 1971). Prejudice.

Little, Jean. *Look through My Window* (Harper, 1970). Family relationships.

Miles, Betty. *The Real Me* (Knopf, 1974). Feminist.

Murray, Michele. *Nellie Cameron* (Seabury, 1971). Rejection; reading clinic provides confidence.

Paterson, Katherine. *Bridge to Teriabithia* (Crowell, 1977). Death.

———. *The Great Gilly Hopkins* (Crowell, 1978). Foster homes.

Sachs, Marilyn. *The Bear's House* (Doubleday, 1971). Broken home; mother unable to cope.

Smith, Doris. *A Taste of Blackberries* (Crowell, 1973). Death.

Sorensen, Virginia. *Around the Corner* (Harcourt, 1971). Prejudice.

Sowthall, Ivan. *Let the Balloon Go* (St. Martin's, 1967). Physical handicap; cerebral palsy.

Stolz, Mary. *The Noonday Friends* (Harper, 1965). Racial understanding; family survival.

Ter Haar, Jaar. *Boris* (Delacorte, 1970). Survival; World War II.

Weik, Mary. *The Jazz Man* (Atheneum, 1968). Parental neglect.

Wrightson, Patricia. *A Race Course for Andy* (Harcourt, 1968). Mental retardation.

TEACHING GUIDE 1-1 (cont.)

STUDENT FOLLOW-UP

Name _____ Date _____

REALISTIC FICTION

I. About Realistic Fiction
   Directions: Answer the questions below in complete sentences.
   A. Leading characters are often likeable but not perfect. How does Queenie Peavy fit this idea? _____
   _____
   _____

   B. In realistic fiction, settings seem quite real. What was the setting for *The TV Kid*? _
   _____
   _____

   C. Stories of realistic fiction often deal with growing up and facing problems. What was Harriet the Spy's problem? _____
   _____
   _____

II. Thinking about Characters
   Directions: Answer the questions below in complete sentences.
   A. Explain why you would (or would not) want to have someone like Queenie for your friend. _____
   _____
   _____

   B. Lennie tried to escape from his troubles by watching TV. If you were his friend, what advice would you give him? _____
   _____
   _____

III. Creative Writing
   Write a story about a person with a "real" problem, such as:
   An important promise is broken.
   A bully is making life miserable.
   A person who is not good in sports tries to make friends.

   _____
   _____
   _____
   _____

TEACHING GUIDE 1-2   SCIENCE FICTION* (FILMSTRIP)

CONTENT

City of Gold and Lead by John Christopher and glimpses of *A Wrinkle in Time* by Madeleine L'Engle [see Example 1-1 earlier in this model] illustrate the marvelous way science and fiction can be combined. How science fiction writers get ideas by examining scientific developments and social problems and projecting them into the future is also exemplified.

OBJECTIVES

1. Students will be motivated to read one or more realistic science fiction books.
2. Students will name two or more attributes of science fiction books.
3. Students will discuss the plot, setting, and characters of *City of Gold and Lead*.
4. Students will be motivated to write a science fiction story about a pet robot.

*Literature for Children, Series 6, Pied Piper Productions, Verdugo City, Calif. 91046.
Copyright © 1980 Pied Piper Productions.

TEACHING GUIDE 1-2 (cont.)

SUGGESTED DISCUSSION AND ACTIVITIES

Before the filmstrip
Share a few science fiction stories students may have read or seen on TV or film. Watch the filmstrip to see how writers of science fiction view the future and what subjects they enjoy writing about.

After the filmstrip (These activities appear on the screen.)

1. About science fiction: Three multiple choice questions reinforce literary attributes of science fiction. (Questions appear on student follow-up.)
2. Future problems: Tell how a problem, such as the population explosion, might be used in a science fiction story.
3. Recognizing science fiction: Given four sentences, three of which are factual and one of which is fictional, students are asked to rewrite the three factual sentences as science fiction. (Sentences appear on student follow-up.)
4. Creative writing: Viewers are invited to create their pet robot. What special inventions will it have? With "a wrinkle in time," what adventures?

EXTENDING LEARNING

After students have read a science fiction book (see recommended books list), discuss a few main ideas the filmstrip presented. Share examples of how science and fiction have been combined. What current new inventions or social problems has the writer projected into the future?

Do research on one of the planets in our solar system. Draw a space creature and include four ways in which it would look different from you or me because of conditions on that planet. What adventures could it have?

Make a science fiction learning center in the classroom. Include a list of words to define such as *robot, orbit, asteroid;* creative writing ideas such as rewriting a comic strip story as science fiction; and a bulletin board where students can put into orbit titles of books they have read.

Make a time line showing a certain car or other invention as it was in the 1900s, how it looks today, and how it might look in the future. Choose airplanes, houses, toys, schools, clothing or ships. Make a tape recording to explain your time line.

Advanced students might do research in an area of science—space travel, disease prevention, robots and computers, psychic phenomena, cryogenics. They could write a story about the future using the scientific facts they find.

Note: This filmstrip could launch an entire unit on futurism. Many resources are available on the subject.

RECOMMENDED BOOKS

Beatty, Jerome. *Matthew Looney in the Outback* (Addison, 1969).
Bova, Ben. *City of Darkness* (Scribner, 1976).
———. *End of Exile* (Dutton, 1975). Trilogy.
———. *Exiled from Earth* (Dutton, 1971).
Brink, Carol. *Andy Buckram's Tin Men* (Viking, 1966).
Cameron, Eleanor. *Stowaway to the Mushroom Planet* (Little, 1956).
Christopher, John. *Beyond the Burning Lands* (Macmillan, 1971).
———. *Dom and Va* (Macmillan, 1973).
———. *The Pool of Fire* (Macmillan, 1968).
———. *The Prince in Waiting* (Macmillan, 1970).
———. *White Mountain* (Macmillan, 1967).
Clarke, Arthur. *Dolphin Island* (Holt, 1963).
Dickinson, Peter. *The Devil's Children* (Little, 1970).
———. *The Gift Atlantic* (Little, 1974).
Engdahl, Sylvia. *Beyond the Tomorrow Mountains* (Atheneum, 1973).
———. *The Far Side of Evil* (Atheneum, 1971).
Heinlein, Robert. *Have Space Suit—Will Travel* (Scribner, 1958).

TEACHING GUIDE 1-2 (cont.)

——. *Podkayne of Mars: Her Life & Times* (Putnam, 1963).
Karl, Jean. *The Turning Place: Stories of a Future Past* (Dutton, 1976).
L'Engle, Madeleine. *A Swiftly Tilting Planet* (Farrar, 1979).
——. *Wind in the Door* (Farrar, 1973).
Lightner, Alice. *Doctor to the Galaxy* (Norton, 1965).
McHargue, Georgess. *Hot and Cold Running Cities* (Holt, 1974).
Norton, Andre. *Moon of Three Rings* (Viking, 1966).
——. *The Zero Stone* (Viking, 1968).
O'Brien, Robert. *Z for Zachariah* (Atheneum, 1975).
Snyder, Zilpha. *And All Between* (Atheneum, 1976).
——. *Below the Root* (Atheneum, 1975).
Steele, Mary. *Journey Outside* (Viking, 1969).
Williams, Jay. *Danny Dunn and the Antigravity Planet* (McGraw, 1956).

STUDENT FOLLOW-UP

Name ————————————————— Date —————————————

SCIENCE FICTION

I. About Science Fiction
Directions: Circle the best answer. Explain your choice.
A. Science fiction combines imagination with
   (1) fantasy   (2) facts   (3) fiction

   —————————————————————————————————————

B. Most science fiction stories take place in the
   (1) past   (2) present   (3) future

   —————————————————————————————————————

C. In science fiction you are most likely to find struggles between
   (1) good and evil   (2) rich and poor   (3) young and old

   —————————————————————————————————————

II. Recognizing Science Fiction
Directions: One of the ideas below is fictional. Three are factual. Restate the factual ideas as science fiction.
A. Flying machines are driven only by human thought. ————————————
B. At the beach, a boy and girl discover a cave.
   (Example: A boy and girl discover a domed city.)

   —————————————————————————————————————

C. A clown rides a tiger.

   —————————————————————————————————————

D. A pen is used to write a message.

   —————————————————————————————————————

III. Future Problems
Science fiction writers are often concerned with growing social problems such as the population explosion, the crime rate, and loss of freedom. Tell how one of these ideas could become a science fiction story.

   —————————————————————————————————————
   —————————————————————————————————————
   —————————————————————————————————————

IV. Creative Writing
On a separate piece of paper, design your own robot. Decide all the things you want it to do. Tell what special inventions it will have. Explain how it can change your life. Perhaps (with "a wrinkle in time") you and your robot could journey to the moon.

TEACHING GUIDE 1-3 EPICS AND LEGENDS* (FILMSTRIP)

CONTENT

A young storyteller presents episodes from *Robin Hood, King Arthur* and *The Trojan Horse*. Viewers are introduced to the origin of these tales and to the attributes of the heroic character. That epics and legends come from many lands is a point of emphasis.

OBJECTIVES

1. Students will be motivated to read one or more epics or legends about Robin Hood, King Arthur or other heroic characters of their choice.
2. Students will recall that epics and legends come from many lands.
3. Students will give an example of how epics and legends reflect the values of the time in which they were written.
4. Students will be motivated to write an adventure about an ancient hero or heroine in a modern setting.

SUGGESTED DISCUSSION AND ACTIVITIES

Before the filmstrip
Have students discuss a few superheroes of today. What kinds of stories are told about them? Explain that even in the most ancient of times, people loved to create stories about superheroes, only their names were King Arthur, Ulysses and Robin Hood. Watch the filmstrip to learn about some "superheroes" of long ago.

After the filmstrip (These activities appear on the screen.)

1. About Epics and Legends:
   Directions: Answer true or false. Restate the false statements so they are true.
   a. Legends are tales about heroes we can admire.
   b. Though legends have changed with retelling, most of them are based partly on fact.
   c. Legends come from only one or two countries.
   d. Through legends we can learn about the values of people who lived long ago.
2. Future legends: Tell about a person who could become a future legend: a sports figure, a great scientist, or another leader.
3. Creative writing: Choose an ancient hero or heroine and describe his or her adventures in modern times. What might happen if Robin Hood landed at Los Angeles Airport? What evil would he find to outwit? Include ideas such as *bold, courageous, fair, honest, honorable, loyal, noble, trustworthy*.

EXTENDING LEARNING

After the students have read an epic or legend (see recommended books list), compare examples of the hero's character. How does the story reflect the values, the time, and the place in which it was written?

To sample the poetic language and unique style of epics, tape excerpts from Howard Pyle's *King Arthur* or Anne Malcolmson's *Song of Robin Hood*.

To illustrate that epics and legends come from many lands, place the names or caricatures of legendary heroes on a world map and display on a bulletin board.

Write some news headlines about the deeds of legendary heroes.

After students have shared information, conduct a quiz show modeled after What's My Line or 20 Questions.

Discuss why almost all epics and legends are about male heroes as opposed to female heroines. What was the stereotyped role of women in those times? How have roles changed?

A study of early legendary heroes leads quite naturally into North American Legendary Heroes and a language arts unit on Tall Tales. Many rich resources exist.

*Literature for Children, Series 6, Pied Piper Productions, Verdugo City, Calif. 91046. Copyright © 1980 Pied Piper Productions.

TEACHING GUIDE 1-3 (cont.)

RECOMMENDED BOOKS

ENGLISH

Hieatt, Constance. *Sir Gawain and the Green Knight* (Crowell, 1967).
Hosford, Dorothy. *By His Own Might; The Battles of Beowulf* (Holt, 1947).
Lanier, Sidney. *The Boy's King Arthur* (Scribner, 1942).
McSpadden, J. Walker. *Robin Hood and His Merry Outlaws* (World, 1946).
Malcolmson, Anne, ed. *Song of Robin Hood* (Houghton, 1947).
Nye, Robert. *Beowulf: A New Telling* (Hill, 1968).
Picard, Barbara. *Stories of King Arthur and His Knights* (Walck, 1955).
Robbins, Ruth. *Taliesin and King Arthur* (Parnassus, 1970).
Schiller, Barbara. *Eric and Enid* (Dutton, 1970).
———. *The Kitchen Knight* (Holt, 1965).
———. *The Wandering Knight* (Dutton, 1971).
Sutcliff, Rosemary. *Beowulf* (Dutton, 1962).
———. *Tristan and Iseult* (Dutton, 1971).

GREEK

Church, Alfred. *The Aeneid* (Macmillan, 1962).
———. *The Iliad and the Odyssey of Homer* (Macmillan, 1964).
———. *The Odyssey of Homer* (Macmillan, 1951).
Colum, Padraic. *The Children's Homer* (Macmillan, 1962).
———. *The Golden Fleece* (Macmillan, 1962).
DeSelincourt, Aubrey. *Odysseus the Wanderer* (Criterion, 1956).
Lang, Andrew. *The Adventures of Odysseus* (Dutton, 1962).
Picard, Barbara. *The Iliad of Homer* (Walck, 1960).
———. *The Odyssey of Homer* (Walck, 1952).
Reeves, James. *The Trojan Horse* (Watts, 1969).
Watson, Jane. *The Iliad and the Odyssey* (Golden Press, 1964).

NORSE

Coolidge, Olivia. *Legends of the North* (Houghton, 1961).
Hosford, Dorothy. *Sons of the Volsungs* (Holt, 1949).
Schiller, Barbara. *Hrafkel's Saga: An Icelandic Story* (Seabury, 1972).
Sellew, Catherine. *Adventures with the Heroes* (Little, 1954).

OTHER

Almedingen, E. M. *The Story of Gudrun* (Norton, 1967). German.
Bosley, Kenneth. *The Devil's Horse, Tales from the Kalevala* (Pantheon, 1971). Finnish.
Brown, Marcia. *Backbone of the King* (Scribner, 1966). Hawaii.
Bryson, Bernarda. *Gilgamesh* (Holt, 1967). Babylonia.
Carlson, Dale. *Warlord of the Gengi* (Atheneum, 1970). Japan.
Deutsch, Babette. *Heroes of the Kalevala* (Messner, 1940). Finnish.
Euslin, Bernard. *The Green Hero: Early Adventures of Finn McCool* (Four Winds, 1975). Irish.
Feayles, Anita. *He Who Saw Everything; The Epic of Gilgamesh* (Scott/Addison, 1966). Babylonia.
Gaer, Joseph. *The Adventures of Rama* (Little, 1954). India.
Goldston, Robert. *The Legend of the Cid* (Bobbs, 1963). Spanish.
Hazeltine, Alice. *Hero Tales from Many Lands* (Abingdon, 1961).
Hodges, Elizabeth. *A Song for Gilgamesh* (Atheneum, 1971). Babylonia.
Picard, Barbara. *Tales of Ancient Persia* (Walck, 1973). Persia.
Seeger, Elizabeth. *The Five Sons of King Pandu* (Scott/Addison, 1969).
———. *The Ramayana* (Scott/Addison, 1969). India.
Sutcliff, Rosemary. *The High Deeds of Finn McCool* (Dutton, 1967).
———. *The Hound of Ulster* (Dutton, 1964). Irish.
Young, Ella. *The Tangle-coated Horse and Other Tales: Episodes from the Fionn Saga* (McKay, 1968). Irish.

TEACHING GUIDE 1-3 (cont.)

STUDENT FOLLOW-UP

Name _____ Date _____

EPICS AND LEGENDS

I. About Epics and Legends
   Directions: Answer true or false. Restate any false statements so that they are true.
   A. Legends are tales about heroes whom we can admire.
   B. Although legends have changed with retelling, most of them are based partly on fact.
   C. Legends come from only one or two different countries.
   D. Through legends we can learn about the values of people who lived long ago.

   _____
   _____
   _____

II. Future Legends
    Tell about a person who could become a future legend, a sports figure, a great scientist, or another great leader.

   _____
   _____
   _____

III. Creative Writing
     Choose an ancient hero or heroine and describe his or her adventures in modern times. What might happen if Robin Hood landed at Los Angeles Airport? What evil might he find to outwit? Include such ideas as *bold, courageous, fair, honest, honorable, loyal, noble, trustworthy.*

TEACHING GUIDE 1-4   HISTORY BOOKS:
NONFICTION TOO GOOD TO MISS* (FILMSTRIP)

CONTENT

The extraordinary illustrations of David Maccaulay's *Pyramid* launch viewers into the world of history books. Exciting works by Edwin Tunis and M. Sasek are introduced, and an overview for using the Dewey Decimal Systerm is offered.

OBJECTIVES

1. Students will become aware of the wide variety of well-written history books and will be motivated to read at least one of them.
2. Students will select books using subject cards in the card catalog. They will recognize that nonfiction books on the same subject usually have the same Dewey decimal classification number.
3. Students will participate in an activity designed to increase their knowledge and appreciation of books about history.

SUGGESTED DISCUSSION AND ACTIVITIES

Before the filmstrip
Briefly discuss the idea of time machines. Ask students if they would like to have their own time machine that could take them into the past.

*Literature for Children, Series 5, Pied Piper Productions, Verdugo City, Calif. 91046.
Copyright © 1980 Pied Piper Productions.

TEACHING GUIDE 1-4 (cont.)

Conclude by saying, "Let's watch the filmstrip to find out how history books are like time machines."

After the filmstrip (These activities appear on the screen.)

1. Talk about a time and place from the past which you would like to know more about, such as ancient Egypt, King Arthur's court, the early West, or World War II.
2. Here is a card from a card catalog. Tell which parts you would copy so that you could find the book.
3. During your next library time, select a book about a past time and place. Or read about a person from history such as Cleopatra or Martin Luther King. To find a book you want, look in the card catalog under the subject you are interested in, or go directly to the library shelves. Most history books are in the 900s. Biographies are in the biography section. (See recommended books list.)
4. After you have read your book, you might like to share a few ideas. Perhaps you could pretend you are the host of a talk show and interview a famous person, or perhaps you are a witness to a historical event. Here is another idea: pretend you are a reporter for a newspaper. Write up the event from history as if it just happened. (See History—What Interests You Most?, below.)

EXTENDING LEARNING

Discuss the kinds of research that often go into writing a book of history, the difference between firsthand and secondhand research. It may be of interest to know that Mr. Macaulay traveled to Egypt where his investigations necessitated taking his first ride on a camel, scaling the Great Pyramid, and shooting 18 rolls of film.

Compare historical fiction and nonfiction. Share a well-written historical fiction book such as *Sarah Noble* by Alice Dalgliesh with the class. Discuss the historical background and its authenticity. Then introduce one or more nonfiction books related to the same subject, such as *Colonial America* by Edwin Tunis. Compare characteristics such as purpose, writing style, and organization.

Dramatize history. Offer students an opportunity to dramatize a scene representing life at some period in the past. They will need to use nonfiction books to verify historical details, such as patterns for making clothing.

Make a time line. Have students identify the period and/or locale of each book of historical nonfiction they read. Then write the title on a blank time line and/or map of the world posted on a bulletin board.

Travel to the past via posters. After reading a book of historical nonfiction, students can create travel posters designed to lure travelers to a place in the past.

HISTORY—WHAT INTERESTS YOU MOST?

Would you like to read about a famous person, an event, a distant time or place? Below are a few ideas.

PEOPLE

1. Susan B. Anthony
2. Sir Francis Bacon
3. John Brown
4. Pearl S. Buck
5. Buffalo Bill
6. Ralph J. Bunche
7. Kit Carson
8. George Washington Carver
9. Charlemagne
10. César Chávez
11. Cleopatra
12. Crazy Horse
13. Davy Crockett
14. Marie Curie
15. Dwight D. Eisenhower
16. Anne Frank
17. Benjamin Franklin
18. John C. Fremont
19. Mohandas Gandhi
20. Helen of Troy
21. Chief Joseph
22. Helen Keller
23. Martin Luther King, Jr.
24. Lawrence of Arabia
25. Jenny Lind
26. Golda Meir
27. John Muir
28. Sir Isaac Newton
29. Sacagawea
30. Sitting Bull
31. Socrates
32. Henry David Thoreau
33. King Tutankhamen
34. Mark Twain

TEACHING GUIDE 1-4 (cont.)

EVENTS

1. The Alamo
2. Civil War
3. Discovery of the New World
4. French Revolution
5. Gold Rush
6. The Great Depression (U.S.)
7. Harpers Ferry
8. Lewis and Clark Explorations
9. Louisiana Purchase
10. The Magna Carta
11. The Mexican War
12. Pearl Harbor
13. The Renaissance
14. Vietnam War

TIMES AND PLACES

1. African Kingdoms
2. American Indians Before Columbus
3. Ancient China
4. Arctic Exploration
5. Castles and Knights in Armor
6. Classical Ages of Greece
7. Cowboys and Cattle Country
8. Early Jerusalem
9. Egyptian Pharaohs
10. Exploring South America
11. Festivals of Japan
12. Frontier Days in America
13. Hawaiian Islands and Captain Cook
14. The Klondike During the Gold Rush
15. Medieval Europe
16. The Norsemen
17. Prehistoric Man
18. Pyramids of the New World
19. The Roman Empire
20. Russia During Time of Czar Nicholas II
21. Steamboats on the Mississippi
22. Trappers and Mountain Men

RECOMMENDED BOOKS

(Many of these books are mentioned within the filmstrip.)

Behrens, June, and Brower, Pauline. *Colonial Farm* (Childrens, 1976).

———. *Pilgrims Plantation* (Childrens, 1977).

Boase, Wendy. *Ancient Egypt* (Watts, 1978).

Coerr, Eleanor B. *Sadako and the Thousand Paper Cranes* (Putnam, 1977).

Dalgliesh, Alice. *Sarah Noble* (Scribner, 1954).

Felton, Harold. *Nancy Ward, Cherokee* (Dodd, 1975).

Fritz, Jean. *Who's That Stepping on Plymouth Rock* (Coward, 1975).

Fukuda, Hanako. *Wind in My Hand* (Golden Gate, 1970).

Grant, Clara Louise, and Watson, Jane Werner. *Mexico: Land of the Plumed Serpent* (Garrard, 1968).

Gridley, Marion E. *American Indian Women* (Hawthorn, 1974).

Hilton, Suzanne. *Who Do You Think You Are? Digging for Your Family Roots* (Westminster, 1976).

Hofsinde, Robert. *Indian Sign Language* (Morrow, 1956).

Macaulay, David. *Castle* (Houghton, 1977).

———. *Cathedral* (Houghton, 1973).

———. *City* (Houghton, 1974).

———. *Pyramid* (Houghton, 1975).

———. *Underground* (Houghton, 1976).

Meltzer, Milton. *Never to Forget: The Jews of the Holocaust* (Harper, 1976).

Musgrove, Margaret. *Ashanti to Zulu: African Traditions* (Dial, 1976).

Ortiz, Victoria. *Sojourner Truth* (Lippincott, 1974).

Perl, Lila. *Mexico, Crucible of the Americas* (Morrow, 1978).

Price, Christine. *Made in Ancient Egypt* (Dutton, 1970).

Rau, Margaret. *The People of New China* (Messner, 1978).

Sasek, M. *This Is Historic Britain* (Macmillan, 1974).

———. *This Is Hong Kong* (Macmillan, 1965).

———. *This Is Paris* (Macmillan, 1959).

———. *This Is San Francisco* (Macmillan, 1962).

Tunis, Edwin. *Colonial Craftsmen* (Crowell, 1976).

———. *Colonial Living* (Crowell, 1976).

———. *Frontier Living* (Crowell, 1976).

———. *Shaw's Fortune* (Crowell, 1976).

TEACHING GUIDE 1-4 (cont.)

————. *The Young United States* (Crowell, 1976).
Unstead, R. J. *See Inside an Egyptian Town* (Watts, 1978).
White, Anne Terry. *All about Archaeology* (Random, 1959).

TEACHING GUIDE 1-5 SCIENCE BOOKS: NONFICTION TOO GOOD TO MISS* (FILMSTRIP)

CONTENT

The undersea world of *Octopus* created by Carol and Donald Carrick introduces viewers to a wide range of outstanding science books. Interest is piqued in the curiosities of nature and the wonders of the universe. Viewers meet two well-known science authors, Isaac Asimov and Millicent Selsam. Techniques for using the various parts of a book to find information are reviewed.

OBJECTIVES

1. Students will become aware of the variety of nonfiction books related to science. They will be motivated to read at least one science book on a subject they would like to know more about.
2. Students will briefly state the purpose of each of these parts of a book: title page, table of contents, glossary, and index. Students will use the copyright date to determine if information in a book is current.
3. Students will participate in an activity designed to increase their knowledge and appreciation of science books.

SUGGESTED DISCUSSION AND ACTIVITIES

Before the filmstrip
Pose some of the following questions:
Why does the earth quake? Where do shooting stars fall? Do insects sleep? Briefly discuss other kinds of science questions students may have wondered about.

Conclude by saying, "Science tries to find answers to puzzling questions. Watch the filmstrip to discover at least two science subjects you'd like to know more about."

After the filmstrip (These activities appear on the screen.)

1. When you read about certain science subjects, you want up-to-date facts. Why? Give examples.
2. Briefly tell the purpose of each of these parts of a book: title page, table of contents, glossary, index.
3. Talk about one or two science subjects you might like to know more about, such as living things, the earth, energy and matter, or outer space.
4. During your next library time, select a book of science. Try the card catalog or go directly to the library shelves and browse around. Science books are in the 500 section. (See recommended books list.)
5. After you've read a book of science, you might like to make up some questions to ask others. Write one or two questions about something you've learned such as, "How do ants communicate?" or, "How far is the nearest star?" Questions and answers, together with illustrations, may be combined into a class booklet such as "Mysteries of the Universe." (See list of starter questions.)

EXTENDING LEARNING

Share a simple science fiction book such as *Miss Pickerell Goes to Mars*. Then present a related nonfiction book about planets and have students compare. How are the books

*Literature for Children, Series 5, Pied Piper Productions, Verdugo City, Calif. 91046. Copyright © 1980 Pied Piper Productions.

TEACHING GUIDE 1-5 (cont.)

alike/different? What is the purpose of each book? What kinds of research were needed for each book?

Meet the author. Have groups of students "present" science authors to the class. (Isaac Asimov, Franklyn Branley, or Millicent Selsam would be good choices.) They will want to gather many of the author's books and information about them before making their presentations. (The card catalog and the reference book *More Junior Authors* will be helpful.)

Motivate research and writing. Refer to the book *Octopus* (as shown in the filmstrip) to remind students that both research and imagination are needed to create this kind of nonfiction book. Invite them to create their own exciting nonfiction accounts of animals. Suggest a plan for students: (1) Choose an animal, (2) Do some research to gather facts about this animal, (3) Plan an interesting way of putting these facts together, (4) Write a nonfiction account. (Remember to make facts the basis for descriptions and events.)

SCIENCE STARTER QUESTIONS

Look over the questions below. What are you most curious about? Answers to the questions may be found in the recommended books.

MATTER AND ENERGY

1. Why is the sun like a power plant?
2. Its diameter is less than a hundred millionth of an inch. It takes a million of them, edge to edge, to match the thickness of this page; yet everything is made up of them. What are they? (Atoms)
3. Are metals mixable?
4. Can you name the elements in the air we breathe?
5. What does a cloud's shape tell you about the weather?
6. What causes a tornado?
7. Can you explain how running water in a dam makes electricity?
8. How do plants make food for themselves?
9. Our bodies are like machines because we use energy. What kind of fuel do we use?
10. What makes the wind move?
11. Can you think of an example of a natural underground furnace?
12. What turns iron into steel?

EARTH

1. Can you explain what gravity is?
2. What makes it rain?
3. How are lightning and thunder related?
4. Can you describe a hurricane's eye?
5. What makes ocean waves?
6. Do continents drift? Why?
7. What makes a glacier grow?
8. Have you ever found a fossil? What secret did it tell you?
9. What makes a volcano erupt?
10. Do mountains ever shrink?
11. Can you describe a magnetic storm?
12. What is a tidepool?

UNIVERSE

1. How is a star born?
2. Have you ever seen a sunspot? What is it?
3. What is a moon? Does every planet have one?
4. What is a star made of?
5. Can you describe a comet? What is a comet's tail like?
6. Which planet in our solar system has a mysterious red spot?
7. Who lives on a giant ball spinning in space?
8. What planet has a super-hot desert with a sky full of constant thunder and lightning?
9. What would a house on the moon be like?
10. Can you read a star map?
11. What is a solar eclipse?
12. What planet has ice rings around it?

TEACHING GUIDE 1-5 (cont.)

LIVING THINGS

1. How does a cricket sing?
2. Where do germs come from?
3. How does a seed grow?
4. What's inside a root?
5. Why is a worm like a plow?
6. How do dolphins communicate with each other?
7. Why does a whale need eyelids?
8. Can you name the oldest living trees?
9. Why do birds sing?
10. How do ants give themselves baths?
11. What kind of parent does an alligator make?
12. Why do we dream?

RECOMMENDED BOOKS

(Many of these books are mentioned within the filmstrip.)

Arnold, Lois, and Arnold, Ned. *Great Science Magic Show* (Watts, 1979).
Asimov, Isaac. *ABC's of the Ocean* (Walker, 1970).
———. *Galaxies* (Follett, 1968).
———. *How Did We Find Out about Outer Space?* (Walker, 1977).
———. *What Makes the Sun Shine?* (Little, 1971).
Branley, Franklyn M. *The Earth* (Crowell, 1966).
———. *Eclipse: Darkness in Daytime* (Crowell, 1973).
Carrick, Carol. *Octopus* (Seabury, 1978).
———. *Sand Tiger Shark* (Seabury, 1977).
Dowden, Anne. *Wild Green Things in the City* (Crowell, 1972).
Farb, Peter, ed. *The Forest* (Silver, 1969).
Fodor, R. V. *What Does a Geologist Do?* (Dodd, 1978).
Gallant, Roy A. *Exploring Mars* (Doubleday, 1968).
George, Jean C. *All upon a Stone* (Crowell, 1971).
Golden, Frederic. *Colonies in Space: The Next Giant Step* (Harcourt, 1977).
Goudey, Alice E. *Here Come the Dolphins* (Scribner, 1961).
Harris, Susan. *Volcanoes* (Watts, 1979).
Hirsch, Carl. *The Living Community* (Viking, 1966).
Hoke, John. *Ecology* (Watts, 1977).
Lauber, Patricia. *Earthquakes* (Random, 1972).
———. *Friendly Dolphins* (Random, 1963).
McClung, Robert. *How Animals Hide* (National Geographic, n.d.).
———. *Thor, Last of the Sperm Whales* (Morrow, 1971).
McGowan, Thomas E. *Album of Astronomy* (Rand, 1979).
McNulty, Faith. *Whales: Their Life in the Sea* (Harper, 1975).
Moffett, Martha, and Moffett, Robert. *Dolphins* (Watts, 1971).
Olney, Pat, and Olney, Ross. *Keeping Insects as Pets* (Watts, 1978).
Patent, Dorothy H. *How Insects Communicate* (Holiday, 1975).
Ravielli, Anthony. *The World Is Round* (Viking, 1970).
Riedman, Sarah R. *Sharks* (Watts, 1977).
Rosenfeld, Sam. *Ask Me a Question about the Atom* (Harvey, 1969).
Scheffer, Victor B. *Little Calf* (Scribner, 1970).
Selsam, Millicent. *Animals as Parents* (Morrow, 1965).
———. *Questions & Answers about Ants* (Scholastic, 1970).
Silverstein, Alvin, and Silverstein, Virginia. *Exploring the Brain* (Lippincott, 1973).
———. *Sleep and Dreams* (Lippincott, 1974).
Simon, Hilda. *Living Lanterns* (Viking, 1971).
Simon, Seymour. *Look to the Night Sky* (Viking, 1977).
———. *Science at Work: Projects in Space Science* (Watts, 1971).
Smith, Norman. *Moonhopping: Through Our Solar System* (Coward, 1977).
Vevers, Gwynne. *Octopus, Cuttlefish and Squid* (McGraw, 1978).
Watson, Jane W. *Whales: Friendly Dolphins and Mighty Giants of the Sea* (Western, 1975).

Model 2

Reading Enrichment and Acceleration Program

GRADES: 1–6

GOAL: The program goal is to bring depth, breadth, relevance, challenge—and above all, delight—to the reading program.

Objectives

1. To stimulated student development of an ever-broadening outreach in reading.
2. To reinforce, extend, and refine student informational reading, viewing, listening, and communicating skills.
3. To implement a challenging, rewarding literature study program reflective of individual student abilities, interests, and preferences.

Basic Terms

1. *Enrichment*—learning experiences that replace, supplement, or extend instruction beyond the restrictive boundaries of course content, textbook, and classroom.
2. *Acceleration*—challenging learning experiences above and beyond regular grade level.
3. *Differentiated*—course content that denotes higher cognitive concepts and processes, instructional strategies that accommodate the learning styles of the gifted, and grouping arrangements that facilitate student performance.
4. *Grouping*—provisions that provide student access to special, differentiated learning experiences.
5. *Basic reading series*—planned reading program presented in a series of books issued by a single publisher; each reading series, while containing

much that is basic and similar, will differ in method and content from others.

6. *Developmental reading*—that part of any basic reading series devoted to developing basic reading skills, such as decoding skills and comprehension skills.
7. *Informational reading*—that part of any basic reading series devoted to the development of thinking-learning-communicating skills, with special emphasis on reference skills.
8. *Recreational reading*—that part of any reading series devoted to student self-selection of reading and providing opportunities for students to develop lifelong reading interests and habits.
9. *Literature study*—that part of any reading series devoted to developing specific understandings about literature: its origins; its various forms; its purposes; the people who create it; and the personal pleasure and delight to be derived from experiencing literature. (For a detailed elementary literature study program, see Model 1, Experiencing Literature, preceding chapter.)

TYPES OF READING PROGRAMS

BASIC READING PROGRAM—GRADE BY GRADE

A *heterogeneous* program includes all students in a given grade or classroom regardless of reading competence level.

Since this program embraces the spectrum of student ability from the lowest level of reading achievement to the highest, it is common practice for the reading teacher to group students of like ability into separate reading groups and to accommodate the potential of the gifted reader by *planned* enrichment and/or accelerated experiences.

The broad spread from high to low achiever in a heterogeneous class steadily increases as students reach the middle grades—"the spread from high to low achiever frequently is one and one-half to twice the number of the grade level. Hence, in the fifth grade, there frequently is an eight-year spread in reading achievement between the best and poorest readers."[*]

BASIC READING PROGRAM—PERFORMANCE LEVELS

For a *homogeneous* program designed to provide students with basic reading reflective of the individual student level of reading competence, the levels program provides for the wide diversity of student performance.

Typically there are three divergent kinds of readers: the accelered reader, the "on-grade-level" reader, and the "below-grade" reader. "Accelerated readers are excellent readers, competent with materials designed for students in grades higher than their own."[†]

Opinion differs as to whether the accelerated reader on the elementary level should be assigned to a basic reading program; some few have advocated releasing the accelerated student from a formal reading program altogether. Most experts in the field of reading share the conclusions reached by Maryann and Gary Manning: "Teachers must challenge . . . accelerated readers and be

[*]John I. Goodlad quoted in Maryann Murphy Manning and Gary L. Manning, *Reading Instruction in the Middle School* (Washington, D.C.: National Education Association, 1979), p. 15.
[†]Ibid.

challenged by them. Teachers need to take the ceiling off and let students progress at their own rate. But teachers cannot remove the floor. In other words, there is a continuing need for reading instruction if students are to make progress and become better and better readers."*

READING ENRICHMENT AND ACCELERATION PROGRAMS

An enrichment-acceleration reading program brings depth, breadth, relevance, and challenge to the informational, recreational, and literature study phases of the traditional grade-by-grade reading program as well as to the innovative reading levels program.

Enrichment and acceleration experiences are provided mainly by two separate media support approaches: classroom study centers and the integration of the services, resources, and guidance of the school library as a reading support laboratory.

TEACHING STRATEGIES

What is a classroom study center (see Checklist 5, Gifted Classroom Study Centers: Characteristics and Requirements, Part I, Chapter 1)?

Definition—a special area of the classroom where students as individuals or as members of a group work at enrichment-acceleration tasks at their own rate and level of achievement.

Purpose—to provide learning outreach experiences that will bring to the reading program greater depth, breadth, relevance, and challenge.

The classroom study center can be organized in any number of ways; possible approaches are limited only by the ingenuity, imagination, and creativity of the reading teacher and the availability of appropriate support media.

Following are titles of typical study center programs designed to acquaint students with authors and illustrators of merit (see Study Center Bibliography 2-1 through Study Center Bibliography 2-15 at the end of this model).

Meet My Friend Adrienne Adams
Meet My Friend Joan Walsh Anglund
Meet My Friends Stan and Jan Berenstain
Meet My Friend Marcia Brown
Meet My Friend Walt Disney
Meet My Friend Don Freeman
Meet My Friend Paul Galdone
Meet My Friend Astrid Lindgren
Meet My Friend Arnold Lobel
Meet My Friend Edna Miller
Meet My Friend A. A. Milne
Meet My Friend Peggy Parish
Meet My Friend Beatrix Potter
Meet the Author Lloyd Alexander
Meet the Author Robert Burch

Incorporated in a planned and integrated library enrichment and acceleration support program is the major basic reading series—American Book; Ginn;

*Ibid.

Harcourt Brace; Houghton Mifflin; Lippincott; Macmillan; Singer–Random House—stressing the necessity for a scientifically planned and systematically implemented school library support program to bring depth, breadth, relevance, challenge, and delight to the reading program. Harcourt Brace, for example, specifically recommends a planned and integrated program of library support:

> Teachers and children must have access to a good collection of children's books.
>
> In a good program of literature study, the textbook and the library complement each other. . . . Boys and girls must be introduced as individuals to the riches of the library. Through a variety of planned experiences, they should be encouraged to follow their own interests, to read and to share a variety of books and periodicals, and to learn for themselves the delight, the practical aid, and the inspiration that reading can bring.
>
> School librarians have specific responsibilities related to the teaching of literature. . . . As they help to guide children in reading, librarians, too, must continuously study group and individual characteristics of children. Obviously, in good schools, teachers and librarians share their planning, their experiences with children, and their evaluation of children's learning about literature.*

Because library resources are vital to the success of the reading program, their use should be as carefully planned as the use of the basic reader itself. The following guides will enable the teacher and the librarian to provide media support activities of significance and challenge:

1. Provide print and nonprint resources to bring depth, breadth, relevance, and challenge to the reading textbook unit, and to match the spectrum of individual student ability, interest, and preference.
2. Provide the *complete* literary work—novel, short story, biography, autobiography, play, poem, essay, journal, diary, legend, myth, fairy tale, tall tale, fable—if that work is abridged or condensed in the basal reader. EXAMPLE: When the students read in the fourth-grade Houghton Mifflin Basic Reader *Keystone* excerpts from *Jennifer, Hecate, Macbeth, William McKinley, and Me, Elizabeth* by Elaine Konigsburg (Atheneum, 1967); from *The Cat Who Went to Heaven* by Elizabeth Coatsworth (Macmillan, 1930); from *Call It Courage* by Armstrong Sperry (Macmillan, 1940); from *Ben and Me* by Robert Lawson (Little, 1939); from *Henry Reed, Inc.* by Keith Robertson (Viking, 1958); and from *Wind in the Willows* by Kenneth Grahame (Scribner, 1933), the students should have available to them the complete book from which each excerpt has been taken.
3. Provide biographical information that will enable the student to visualize the writer as a human being. EXAMPLE: When the students read in the fifth-grade Houghton Mifflin Basic Reader *Medley* the selection "The Wolf Pack" from *The Little House on the Prairie* by Laura Ingalls Wilder (Harper, 1953), they should have available *Something about the Author: Facts and Pictures about Authors and Illustrators of Books for Young People,* ed. by Anne Commire (Gale, 1971 to date), vol. 15, p. 300; the sound filmstrip *Meet the Newbery Author: Laura Ingals Wilder* (Miller-Brody); and "Never Too Late—The Little House in the Big

---

Much Majesty, ed. by Margaret Early, Teacher's Ed. (New York: Harcourt Brace Jovanovich, Inc., 1968).

Woods" in *The Story behind Modern Books* by Elizabeth Rider Montgomery (Dodd, 1949).

4. Provide sequels to the basic reader selection, if sequels exist; if the selection is part of a series, acquaint the students with the remaining titles in the series. EXAMPLE: When the students read in the fourth-grade Houghton Mifflin Basic Reader *Keystone* the excerpt from *Henry Reed, Inc.* by Keith Robertson (Viking, 1958), they should have the opportunity to read the other Viking titles in this series: *Henry Reed's Baby-Sitting Service* (1966); *Henry Reed's Big Show* (1970); and *Henry Reed's Journey* (1963); and when the students read in the sixth-grade Harcourt, Brace Literature Reader *First Splendor* the excerpt from *Island of the Blue Dolphins* by Scott O'Dell (Houghton, 1960), they should have the opportunity to read the sequel, *Zia* by Scott O'Dell (Houghton, 1976).

5. Provide various illustrated editions of the literary work highlighted in the basic reader. EXAMPLE: When the students read in the fourth-grade Houghton Mifflin Basic Reader *Keystone* the excerpt from *Wind in the Willows* by Kenneth Grahame (Scribner, 1933), they should have available to them the editions of that work illustrated by: Adrienne Adams (*The River Bank,* Scribner, 1978); Arthur Rackham (Heritage, 1940); Ernest Shepard (Scribner, 1933); and Tasha Tudor (World, 1966).

6. Provide other works by the author of the selection in the basic reader. EXAMPLE: When the students read in the fifth-grade Houghton Mifflin Basic Reader *Medley* "Paul Revere's Big Ride" by Jean Fritz, taken from her book *And Then What Happened, Paul Revere?* (Coward, 1973), the students should have the opportunity to explore other books written by Jean Fritz (all published by Coward), such as: *The Animal of Doctor Schweitzer* (1958), *Brady* (1960), *The Cabin Faced West* (1958), *Can't You Make Them Behave, King George?* (1977), *Early Thunder* (1967), *What's the Big Idea, Ben Franklin?* (1976), *Where Was Patrick Henry on the 29th of May?* (1975), *Who's That Stepping on Plymouth Rock?* (1975), *Why Don't You Get a Horse, Sam Adams?* (1974), and *Will You Sign Here, John Hancock?* (1976).

7. Provide print and nonprint resources to reinforce and extend understanding of informational articles found in the basic reader. EXAMPLE: When the students read in the fourth-grade Houghton Mifflin Basic Reader *Medley* the informational article "New Hope for the Whooping Crane," they should have the opportunity to extend their understanding of ways people can protect threatened species by reading such books as: *America's Endangered Wildlife on the Comeback Trail* by Olive W. Burt (Messner, 1980); *Animal Rescue: Saving Our Endangered Wildlife* by William Wise (Putnam, 1978); *Lost Wild Worlds, The Story of Extinct and Vanishing Wildlife* by Robert McClung (Morrow, 1976); . . . *The Fairest One of All* by the U.S. Department of Agriculture, Forest Service (Superintendent of Documents, n.d.); *In Defense of Animals* by J. J. McCoy (Houghton, 1978); *Park Rangers and Game Wardens the World Over* by Floyd J. Torbert (Hastings, 1968); *Ranger Rick's Answer Book* ed. by Howard F. Robinson (National Wildlife, 1981); *Rescue from Extinction* by Joseph E. Brown (Dodd, 1981); and *Wildlife Alert* by Gene S. Stuart (National Geographic, 1980); and by viewing sound filmstrips such as: National Audubon Environmental Series, Set 1: *Con-*

serving Our Wildlife (1 filmstrip, 1 cassette, or 1 record); and Set 2: *Conserving our Birds, Conserving Our Wildlife Refuges, Conserving Our Vanishing Species,* and *How You Can Help* (4 filmstrips, 4 cassettes, or 4 records (Random).

8. Provide print and nonprint resources to reinforce and extend understanding of reading skill lessons included in the basic reader. EXAMPLE: When the students are introduced in the sixth-grade Houghton Mifflin Basic Reader *Impressions* to the Reading Skill Lesson "Reading Graphs," they should have the opportunity to reinforce and apply that information by using appropriate instructional media such as the books *Elements of Graphics: How to Prepare Charts and Graphs . . .* by Robert Lefferts (Harper, 1981) and *Graphs* by Dino Lowenstein, and the Math Minisystem 100, Level G: *Graphing,* an accelerated self-study program (Coronet).

9. Provide the students with other literary works that parallel the theme, plot, setting, or characterization of the selection in the basic reader. EXAMPLE: When the students read in the sixth-grade Houghton Mifflin Basic Reader *Galaxies* the excerpts from *Island of the Blue Dolphins* by Scott O'Dell (Houghton, 1960), they should have the opportunity to explore via print and nonprint media the classic theme of fighting to survive against incredible odds. Typical of the wealth of reading, viewing, and listening materials supporting this theme are the following books: *Akavak: An Eskimo Journey* by James Houston (Harcourt, 1968); *Firestorm* by Maurine Gee (Morrow, 1968); *Julie of the Wolves* by Jean George (Harper, 1972); *The Loner* by Ester Wier (McKay, 1963); *My Journals and Sketch Books* by Robinson Crusoe (Harcourt, 1974); *Swiss Family Robinson* by Johann Wyss (Grosset, n.d.); and *Zia* by Scott O'Dell (Houghton, 1976). Useful sound filmstrips are (both Miller-Brody—2 filmstrips, 2 cassettes, or 2 records): *Julie of the Wolves* and *The Loner*. The motion pictures for viewing are: *Island of the Blue Dolphins* (Teaching Films Custodians) and *Swiss Family Robinson* (Disney).

10. Provide the students with other examples of the same literary type or genre as that of the reading selection in the basic reader: If the selection in the reader is from a historical novel, the students should have the opportunity to explore other historical novels; if the selection is from a biography or autobiography, the students should have the opportunity to explore other biographies and autobiographies; if the selection is from a narrative poem, the students should have the opportunity to explore other narrative poems; if the selection is a myth, a legend, or a folktale, the students should have the opportunity to explore other myths, legends, and folktales, and so on.

USING THE MICROCOMPUTER TO TEACH READING

The microcomputer is a teaching tool offering the reading teacher new and exciting approaches to individualizing the teaching of basic reading and reference skills. Scott, Foresman has developed a reading skills courseware series, kindergarten through grade six, that combines educational expertise in the field of elementary reading with advanced microcomputer technology. This series of 12 modules features:

High Quality Content: The stories at each level reflect literary variety, children's interests, and appropriate readability. Each is imaginatively adapted to microcomputer presentation through color graphics and animation. Speech capacity helps young learners with limited reading skills.

Major Skill Strands: Each module can be used at grade level for supplementing basal textbook instruction in major areas of the reading curriculum: word identification, comprehension, study and research, literary understanding and appreciation. The modules can be used at other levels for remediation and enrichment.

Vocabulary Instruction: Vocabulary used in early-grade modules is based on words found on recognized high-frequency word lists. A "talking glossary" that precedes each teaching story introduces new words in context and in isolation. Students can also refer to the glossary while they are reading stories.

Consistent Pattern of Skill Instruction: Each lesson in the Reading Skills Courseware Series follows a consistent teach/practice/apply/assess format. Skills are *taught* through stories, *practiced* through gamelike activities, and *applied/assessed* through wrap-up stories in which the students use the skills they have learned.

Finding excellent Reading Skills Courseware was almost impossible prior to 1981. Scott, Foresman pioneered in developing sound, curriculum-related programs. Accompanying each module they distribute is a *Teacher's Guide,* which helps the teacher with everything from operating the computer to fitting each module's activities into his or her own reading curriculum and teaching program (see Checklist 2-1). Gifted students find using microcomputer modules an innovation that makes mastering vocabulary, comprehension, study and reference skills, and literature understanding not a bore or a chore, but a delight.

To promote independent reading and safeguard interest among gifted children, Houghton Mifflin specifies two main goals for its basal reading program: (1) sequential development of reading skills, and (2) deliberate development of interest in reading.

To encourage teachers to provide a delightfully challenging independent reading program unfettered by the restrictive bonds of the traditional book report, Houghton Mifflin distributes a service bulletin, *50 Ways to Raise Bookworms, Or Using Independent Reading* by Robert L. Hillerich. Following are the ideas suggested by Hillerich.*

PROMOTING GOOD BOOKS

1. *A Library Corner,* complete with bulletin board display, is essential to good book promotion. Responsibility for orderliness and timeliness may be rotated around the class. Themes for the displays might be related to topics (horse stories, baseball, science), popular authors (Dr. Seuss, Corbett, Wilder), or types of books (fairy tales, mysteries, poetry).

2. *New Books* in the classroom library deserve some fanfare. Just a few well-chosen words about each new book will go far toward keeping it circulating. Some children may enjoy helping the teacher by assuming responsibility for presenting brief previews of new books to their classmates.

3. *Selling a Book* to the class is a novel way of presenting an oral report. The reader-seller must convince the rest of the class that the book he or she read is the best book of its kind. Two pupils may compete in trying to sell two different books on the same topic or theme.

*Robert L. Hillerich, *50 Ways to Raise Bookworms, Or Using Independent Reading* (Boston: Houghton Mifflin, 1981).

CHECKLIST 2-1   MICROCOMPUTER MODULES: READING SKILLS COURSEWARE*

WORD IDENTIFICATION

Early Reading (1A)	Picture clues
	Meaning and syntax clues
Reading Cheers (2B)	Root words with spelling changes before endings and suffixes
	Contractions
	Compounds

COMPREHENSION

Reading Rainbows (1B)	Class relationships
	Part-whole relationships
	Size relationships
Reading Fun (2A)	Story problem and solution
	Cause-effect relationships
	Feelings of characters
Reading Adventures (3B)	Main idea and supporting details
	Conclusions
	Sequence relationships
Reading Roundup (4A)	Figures of speech
	Appropriate word meaning/Unfamiliar words
	Idioms
Reading Rally (5A)	Fact and opinion
	Author's purpose
	Bias/connotations of words

STUDY AND RESEARCH

Reading On (3A)	Maps
	Graphs
	Schedules
Reading Power (5B)	Dictionary/glossary
	Card catalog
	Encyclopedia
Reading Flight (6A)	Classifies information
	Summarizes information
	Outlines

LITERARY UNDERSTANDING AND APPRECIATION

Reading Trail (4B)	Characters
	Settings
	Point of view
Reading Wonders (6B)	Historical fiction
	Modern realistic fiction
	Science fiction
	Biography
	Autobiography
	Informational articles

*Learning modules for use with the Texas Instruments computer. Electronic Publishing, Scott, Foresman and Company, 1981.

4. *Holding a Book Fair* is an ideal device for getting middle-grade children involved in book reviewing with a purpose. A class or classes may assume responsibility for reviewing important books prior to the exhibit. Representatives then travel to other classes to review some of the books to be exhibited.

In one school, fourth graders took the responsibility for reviewing Caldecott Award winners for the primary graders. Even the most reluctant readers became enthusiastic as a result of this purposeful reading.

5. *Oral Reading by the Teacher* will often stimulate re-reading by children. Oral reading of part of a book—up to a crucial point—is an excellent motivating device. For example, what fifth grader could resist *Groundhog's Horse* when a Cherokee boy set out into the Appalachian wilderness to recapture his stolen horse, or what sixth grader *A Wrinkle in Time* after Meg and Charles Wallace become lost in the fifth dimension?

6. *Oral Reading by the Children* can include such activities as reading the "most interesting" or "most exciting" parts of a story. For high drama, a sixth grader could read to the class from *Call It Courage* of a South Sea Islands boy's life-or-death struggle with an octopus. A particularly vivid description of a character or setting also makes good read-aloud material.

7. *Favorite Poems* brought to class and read or recited by pupils (after adequate preparation) stimulate further reading of poetry by the group.

8. *Informal Conferences* with children about their books do much to stimulate continued reading. In fact, the teacher should circulate among children during their independent reading time to encourage, guide, or just listen to a child talk about a book.

9. *A Visit to the Public Library,* with plenty of time to browse among the shelves, serves to awaken many children to the lively world of books. If prior arrangements are made, most librarians are happy to present a story time during the visit.

KEEPING READING RECORDS

10. *Individual Book Shelves* can be made of construction paper. For each book read, the child makes a miniature by covering a piece of corrugated cardboard (about the size of a matchbook) with plain paper, then writes the book title and author on it. Children enjoy seeing their "personal-size libraries" grow.

11. *A Bookworm* of constuction paper may be put on the bulletin board by the teacher. When the children read a book, they write the title and author on a segment to be added to the bookworm. The whole class will enjoy watching the bookworm grow and helping it to make several complete turns around the room.

12. *The Book Tree* is a variation of the bookworm idea. In this case, leaves are added to a construction paper tree for each book read.

13. *File Cards* (3″ × 5″) with children's brief summaries and reactions to books read independently can be a valuable asset to the class. Children should understand that they are building a file to be used by classmates who want to get ideas for future reading.

14. *A Class Book* may be developed in which each child has one page to review a favorite book. The review should include a brief statement of what the book is about and the reasons it is a favorite. Children should be encouraged to replace their pages when new favorites are discovered. In the first grade the child may contribute a full-page illustration of a favorite part, along with the title and author of the book.

15. *Cumulative Book Reports,* collected in a folder, offer children an opportunity to compare reactions. For any given title, each child who reads the book adds his or her reaction to those previously recorded. Use separate folders for each book reviewed.

16. *A Class List* of favorite books, in chart form offers kindergarten and first-grade groups an opportunity to express their interests and preferences. Such a list can be revised periodically as the children's tastes and interests broaden.

SHARING READING THROUGH ART

17. *Original Book Jackets, Illustrations, or Advertising Posters* can be made by children to illustrate a book read. These make interest-evoking bulletin board displays.

18. *Illustrated Maps,* showing a character's travels or the area encompassed by a story, offer a novel way of sharing a book. Examples of this kind of work may range from a map of Mafatu's travels to one of Boston in Johnny Tremain's day.

19. *Murals or Montages* make excellent group activities. Children may depict as many events from books as their imaginations and the available materials allow.

20. *Cut-Outs* of favorite characters, which have been copied from the original illustrations, will provide a constantly changing population for a section of the bulletin board that might be called "Friends from Books."

21. *Mobiles* may be constructed of major characters from a story. Some children may choose the animals from *George and Martha, The Cat Who Went to Heaven, Little Red Hen,* or *Rabbit Hill,* while others may select the characters from *The Bushbabies, A Wrinkle in Time,* or *The Jack Tales.*

22. *Dioramas and Shadow Boxes* offer opportunities to express creativity in interpreting a scene from a book. Young children may like to reconstruct the Boy being transformed into an arrow or Anatole's cheese factory, while older pupils may want to interpret Bright Morning and her people marching to a new home, or Julie living as a wolf, or the tidal wave striking Ojiisan's village.

23. *Life-sized Figures or Favorite Characters* may be drawn on mural paper. As a display for a book exhibit, this activity provides a chance for others to try to identify the characters. Primary graders usually prefer to draw the animals they know: Frances, Horton, Lyle, and Curious George, while the older children enjoy doing such favorites as Henry Reed, Karana, Homer Price, and Laura.

24. *A Movie or TV Show* can be made of a story by drawing and pasting together scenes from a book. The series of scenes, rolled on a broom handle, may be passed through a frame cut from a packing carton. Or an opaque projector may be used to project separate scenes.

25. *Bookmarks,* illustrated by the children with "the part I liked best" or "my favorite character," make lasting mementos of enjoyable reading experiences.

26. *Felt Board* characters provide an excellent vehicle for storytelling. Also, some children might like to give a "chalk-talk" about the books they have read.

27. *Dolls or Clay Figures* may be dressed to represent favorite characters. Materials for the costumes need not be more elaborate than construction paper or crepe paper, but some ambitious children may want to use scrap pieces of cloth, lace, or anything else that will help add authenticity to the outfit.

SHARING READING THROUGH WRITING

28. *Book Characters May Exchange Letters* in the middle grades. Have pupils write to one another as the characters might. For example, Ramona might ask Homer Price all about the doughnut machine, and Madeline might be interested in discussing French customs with Anatole.

29. *New Endings* might be written by children for their favorite books, or original episodes written for particular story characters. What, for example, might happen if Geraldine and Curious George met? What might Queenie Peavy or Henry Reed do if either one accompanied Mr. Bass to the Mushroom Planet? Children may also be eager to write their own solution to mysteries such as that presented in *The House of Dies Drear.*

30. *A Diary or Log* may be written by children to represent the experiences of the main character of a book. While keeping the diary, the children pretend they really are Mrs. Frisby, Bilbo, Charlotte, or Kerby.

31. *Analogous Stories or Poems,* written in the manner of old favorites, offer a challenge to middle graders. Lear's nonsense can lead to original limericks and

the *Just So Stories* to other how-it-happened reports. The poems on color in *Hailstones and Halibut Bones* could lead to a collection of original poems about sounds, smells, and so on.

32. *Coded Book Reports* are fun for children who have read *The First Book of Codes and Ciphers*.

33. *Samples of Particularly Good Writing* selected by individual children may be read to their classmates and discussed in terms of the qualities exhibited. Such a discussion will help set effective standards for writing projects.

34. *Writing Headlines* is a fascinating activity. A provocative headline such as "Twelve-year-old Makes a Million" might be posted on the bulletin board and children encouraged to guess what book is represented. Popular primary books may lead to such headlines as "Dinosaur Missing from Museum," "City of Geoppolis Rescued by Tractor," or "Johnny Orchard Gives Pet to Zoo." Older children can develop their own headlines to stump classmates, such as "Trio Takes Trip Through Time," or "Musical Cricket Wows Broadway."

35. *Booklets About Favorite Authors,* complete with cover illustrations, might be "published" by the class. Such booklets provide an opportunity for middle-grade children to do some research on the backgrounds of both the authors and their works.

36. *Every School Newspaper or Magazine* should include a good feature section devoted to children's books. The section might have a different theme for each issue, such as Children in Other Lands, Science Fiction, Fantasy, Biography, Life in the City, etc. The class or classes responsible for this section ought to concentrate on novel ways of stimulating interest in the books presented.

DRAMATIZING AND DISCUSSING

37. *Pantomime* is an interesting means of sharing an event or a characterization from a story that has proved especially popular with the class as a whole. One or more children can put on the pantomime while the rest of the class tries to guess who or what the performers represent.

38. *Puppets* are as much fun to make as they are to operate. A large packing box or a table turned on its side can serve as the stage. Kindergartners enjoy making small drawings of characters introduced in picture books or storytelling sessions and pasting them on pencils or sticks to use as puppets. More elaborate puppets can be made by sticking a ball of clay on the end of a finger and using a handkerchief around the rest of the hand to form the puppet's body.

39. *Radio Shows* may be presented with a tin-can "microphone" or with a tape recorder. The older the children are, the more likely it is that they will be able to write a dramatization of a favorite story as well as to perform it.

40. *Newspaper and Magazine Articles* about chilren's books, authors, or illustrators stimulate an awareness of the importance of children's literature. Have students bring these articles to class for discussion.

41. *Comparisons* are always interesting. For example, middle graders might like to compare *Child of the Silent Night* and *From Anna,* or *Charlotte's Web* and *Rabbit Hill.* More capable students may want to compare the fairy tales of Andersen with those of the Grimm brothers, or compare the ways of life observed in stories about different cultures.

42. *Panel Discussions* of various kinds are possible even though no two members of the panel have read the same book. As early as fourth grade, children can discuss stories in terms of the problems faced by the main characters. They can compare stories with one another and react in terms of the kind of solution presented in each story; did it involve magic, accident, or effort on the part of the particular character who is being discussed? Would the panel members have handled the problem in a different way if they had been there? Why or why not? How is each solution different from (or the same as) solutions mentioned by other members of the panel? The panel may also want to discuss favorite characters,

how they are similar or different, and why individual pupils either like or dislike certain ones.

43. *Authors* are important. Especially by the middle grades, children should begin to be aware of prominent authors. This awareness can lead to discussions of various authors and comparisons of their works.

→ 44. *"Homework"* can be fun. Suggest that the children might enjoy reading a book to a younger child at home and reporting her or his reactions to the class.

45. *Small-Group Reporting* offers a pleasant variation from the more formal book report. Three or four groups may be exchanging information in different corners of the room at the same time.

46. *Quiz Shows,* patterned after "Twenty Questions," offer an opportunity for middle graders to become acquainted in depth with book characters. The quiz might be kept to a simple guessing game in which children take turns being a secret book character and answer only "yes" or "no" to questions from the class about their identity.

47. *Questions in Envelope Pockets* on the bulletin board present a continuous challenge and stimulus for children to add to the envelopes or to read and find out more about a particular story. An envelope labeled "Who am I?" might present clues about popular characters, such as "I am an elephant who is faithful one hundred percent." Or "I am a cat who had my kittens in a very strange place." Another, labeled "Where did it happen?" might include clues about events in various books, such as "An elephant has his nose stretched" or "A rice field was burned to save a village."

48. *A First-Grade Buddy System* is an effective way to encourage those first faltering steps toward the selection of library books. Try pairing the children and letting each pair find a nook where they can read to each other from books especially written for independent reading.

49. *Acting as Evaluators* for first- and second-grade books helps less capable middle graders become interested in independent reading. Sometimes a group of evaluators will become so enthusiastic about their work that they will inspire the rest of the class to want to join in their discussions.

50. *Children's Magazines* afford a wealth of varied material that can serve as a springboard for lively class discussions and motivate further reading by individuals. Have children bring in their favorite magazines to discuss and evaluate the contents.

STUDY CENTER BIBLIOGRAPHY 2-1   **MEET MY FRIEND ADRIENNE ADAMS**

Grades: 1–3

Printed Resources (all illus. by Adrienne Adams)

Arion and the Dophins: Based on an Ancient Greek Legend by Lonzo Anderson (Scribner, 1978)

The Day We Saw the Sun Come Up by Alice E. Goudey (Scribner, 1961)

The Easter Egg Artists by Adrienne Adams (Scribner, 1976)

Going Barefoot by Aileen Fisher (Crowell, 1960)

The Halloween Party by Lonzo Anderson (Scribner, 1974)

Hansel and Gretel by the Brothers Grimm (Morrow, 1980)

Izard by Lonzo Anderson (Scribner, 1973)

Jorinda and Joringel by the Brothers Grimm (Scribner, 1968)

The Littlest Witch by Jeanne Massey (Knopf, 1959)

The Shoemaker and the Elves by the Brothers Grimm (Scribner, 1960)

Snow White and Rose Red by the Brothers Grimm (Scribner, 1964)

Thumbelina by Hans Christian Andersen (Scribner, 1961)

STUDY CENTER BIBLIOGRAPHY 2-1 (cont.)

Two Hundred Rabbits by Lonzo Anderson (Penguin, 1968; paper)
The Ugly Duckling by Hans Christian Andersen (Scribner, 1965; also paper)
A Waggle of Witches by Adrienne Adams (Scribner, 1971)

Nonprint Resources

Easter Egg Artists (Random—1 filmstrip, 1 cassette)
Houses from the Sea (Miller-Brody—1 filmstrip, 1 cassette, or 1 record)
Shoemaker and the Elves (Random—1 filmstrip, 1 cassette)
The Ugly Duckling (Random—2 filmstrips, 2 cassettes, or 2 records)
A Waggle of Witches (Random—1 filmstrip, 1 cassette, or 1 record)

STUDY CENTER BIBLIOGRAPHY 2-2   MEET MY FRIEND JOAN WALSH ANGLUND

Grades: 1–3
Printed Resources (all by Joan Walsh Anglund)

The Brave Cowboy (Harcourt, 1959; also paper)
A Child's Book of Old Nursery Rhymes (Atheneum, 1971)
Christmas Is a Time of Giving (Harcourt, 1961)
Cowboy and His Friend (Harcourt, 1961; also paper)
The Cowboy's Christmas (Atheneum, 1972)
Cowboy's Secret Life (Harcourt, 1963; also paper)
Cup of Sun: A Book of Poems (Harcourt, 1967)
A Friend Is Someone Who Likes You (Harcourt, 1958; also paper)
In a Pumpkin Shell: A Mother Goose ABC (Harcourt, 1960; also paper)
Joan Walsh Anglund Sampler (Harcourt, 1963)
Joan Walsh Anglund Storybook (Random, 1978)
Look Out the Window (Harcourt, 1959)
Love Is a Special Way of Feeling (Harcourt, 1960)
Nibble Nibble Mousekin: A Tale of Hansel and Gretel (Harcourt, 1962; also paper)
Pocketful of Proverbs (Harcourt, 1964)
Spring Is a New Beginning (Harcourt, 1963)
What Color Is Love (Harcourt, 1966)
A Year Is Round (Harcourt, n.d.)

Art Prints

Packet of Pictures (Harcourt, 1970)

STUDY CENTER BIBLIOGRAPHY 2-3   MEET MY FRIENDS STAN AND JAN BERENSTAIN

Grades: 1–3
Printed Resources (all by Stan and Jan Berenstain)

BEAR FACTS LIBRARY (all published by Random)
The Bears' Almanac (1973)
The Bears' Nature Guide (1975)
The Berenstain Bears' Science Fair (1977)

BEGINNER BOOKS (all published by Random)
The Bear Detectives (1975)

STUDY CENTER BIBLIOGRAPHY 2-3 (cont.)

The Bear Scouts (1967)
The Bears' Christmas (1970)
The Bears' Picnic (1966)
The Bears' Vacation (1968)
The Berenstain Bears and the Missing Dinosaur Bone (n.d.)
The Big Honey Hunt (1962)
The Bike Lesson (1964)

BRIGHT AND EARLY BOOKS (all published by Random)
Bears in the Night (1971)
Bears on Wheels (1969)
The Berenstain Bears and the Spooky Old Tree (1978)
He Bear, She Bear (1974)
Inside, Outside, Upside Down (1968)
Old Hat, New Hat (1970)

Sound Filmstrips (all by Random; each 1 filmstrip, 1 cassette, or 1 record unless otherwise indicated)

The Bear Detectives
The Bear Scouts
The Bears' Almanac (2 filmstrips, 2 cassettes, or 2 records)
The Bears' Christmas
Bears in the Night
Bears' Nature Guide (2 filmstrips, 2 cassettes, or 2 records)
Bears on Wheels
Bears' Picnic
Bears' Vacation
Berenstain Bears and the Spooky Old Tree
The Berenstain Bears' Science Fair
The Big Honey Hunt
The Bike Lesson
He Bear, She Bear
Meet Stan and Jan Berenstain (1 filmstrip, 1 cassette)
Old Hat, New Hat

STUDY CENTER BIBLIOGRAPHY 2-4   MEET MY FRIEND MARCIA BROWN

Grades: 1–3
Printed Resources (all written or retold and illus. by Marcia Brown)

All Butterflies: An ABC (Scribner, 1972)
The Blue Jackal (Scribner, 1977)
The Bun: A Tale from Russia (Harcourt, 1972)
Cinderella (Scribner, 1954; also paper; Caldecott Medal 1955)
Dick Whittington and His Car (Scribner, 1950; Caldecott Honor Book 1951)
Felice (Scribner, 1958)
How, Hippo! (Scribner, 1969; also paper)
Listen to a Shape (Watts, 1979)
Once a Mouse . . . (Scribner, 1961; Caldecott Medal 1962)

STUDY CENTER BIBLIOGRAPHY 2-4 (cont.)

Puss in Boots (Scribner, 1952; Caldecott Honor Book 1953)
Steadfast Tin Soldier (Scribner, 1953)
Stone Soup (Scribner, 1974)
Three Billy Goats Gruff (Harcourt, 1972; paper only)
Touch Will Tell (Watts, 1979)
Walk with Your Eyes (Watts, 1979)

Nonprint Resources: Sound Filmstrips

Cinderella (Miller-Brody—2 filmstrips, 2 cassettes, or 2 records)
How, Hippo! (Miller-Brody—1 filmstrip, 1 cassette, or 1 record)
Once a Mouse . . . (Miller-Brody—1 filmstrip, 1 cassette)
Puss in Boots (Miller-Brody—1 filmstrip. 1 cassette)
Stone Soup (Weston Woods—1 filmstrip, 1 cassette, or 1 record)
The Three Billy Goats Gruff (Weston Woods—1 filmstrip, 1 cassette, or 1 record)

Nonprint Resources: Motion Picture

Stone Soup (Weston Woods)

Nonprint Resources: Poster

The Caldecott Medal: A Pictorial Record of The Caldecott Medal Awarded Each Year for the Most Distinguished American Picture Book (rev. annually; dist. free to schools on request by Follett Library Book Company)

Nonprint Resources: Stickers

The Caldecott Medal (offered for sale by the Children's Book Center)

STUDY CENTER BIBLIOGRAPHY 2-5   MEET MY FRIEND WALT DISNEY

Grades: 1–3

Printed Resources (all produced by Walt Disney Studios; published by Western)

Alice in Wonderland (1978)
Cinderella (1978)
Hansel and Gretel (1976)
Snow White and the Seven Dwarfs (1948)

Nonprint Resources: Sound Filmstrips (all Disney Educational Media)

Alice in Wonderland (Fantasy Classics, Set 10) (4 filmstrips, 4 cassettes, or 4 records)
Bambi (Fantasy Classics, Set 1B) (2 filmstrips, 2 cassettes, or 2 records)
Bednobs and Broomsticks (Fantasy Classics, Set 8) (2 filmstrips, 2 cassettes, or 2 records)
Ben and Me (Fantasy Classics, Set 2A) (1 filmstrip, 1 cassette, or 1 record)
Dumbo (Fantasy Classics, Set 3A) (2 filmstrips, 2 cassettes, or 2 records)
Mary Poppins, (Fantasy Classics, Set 11) (4 filmstrips, 4 cassettes, or 4 records)
Peter Pan (Fantasy Classics, Set 4B) (2 filmstrips, 2 cassettes, or 2 records)
Pinocchio (Fantasy Classics, Set 4A) (2 filmstrips, 2 cassettes, or 2 records)
Sleeping Beauty (Fantasy Classics, Set 6) (2 filmstrips, 2 cassettes, or 2 records)
Snow White and the Seven Dwarfs (Fantasy Classics, Set 1A) (2 filmstrips, 2 cassettes, or 2 records)
The Three Little Pigs (Fantasy Classics, Set 4A) (1 filmstrip, 1 cassette, or 1 record)
Toby Tyler Joins the Circus (Adventure Classics, Set 1B) (2 filmstrips, 2 cassettes, or 2 records)
The Ugly Duckling (Fantasy Classics, Set 1A) (1 filmstrip, 1 cassette, or 1 record)

STUDY CENTER BIBLIOGRAPHY 2-6   MEET MY FRIEND DON FREEMAN

Grades: 1–3
Printed Resources (all by Don Freeman; published by Viking)

Beady Bear (1977; also paper)
Corduroy (1968; also paper)
Dandelion (1964; also paper)
Guard Mouse (1967; also paper)
Hattie, the Backstage Bat (1970; also paper)
Mop Top (1955; also paper)
Norman the Doorman (1959; also paper)
A Pocket for Corduroy (1978)
A Rainbow of My Own (1966; also paper)
Space Witch (1959)
Tilly Witch (1969)
Will's Quill (1977; also paper)

Nonprint Resources: Doll

Corduroy (13 inches high; sold by Live Oak Media)

Nonprint Resources: Sound Filmstrips (all Live Oak Media—1 filmstrip, 1 cassette unless otherwise indicated)

Corduroy
Dandelion
Hattie, the Backstage Bat
Mop Top
Norman the Doorman (Weston Woods—1 filmstrip, 1 cassette)
A Pocket for Corduroy
A Rainbow of My Own

Nonprint Resources: Motion Picture

Norman the Doorman (Weston Woods)

STUDY CENTER BIBLIOGRAPHY 2-7   MEET MY FRIEND PAUL GALDONE

Grades: 1–3
Printed Resources (all retold and illus. by Paul Galdone)

Cinderella, (McGraw, 1978)
The Frog Prince (McGraw, 1974)
The Hare and the Tortoise (McGraw, 1962)
Henny Penny (Seabury, 1968)
Hereafterthis (McGraw, n.d.)
The Horse, the Fox and the Lion (Seabury, 1968)
The House That Jack Built (McGraw, 1961)
The Life of Jack Sprat, His Wife and His Cat (McGraw, 1969)
The Little Red Hen (Seabury, 1973; paper, Scholastic)
Little Tuppen (Seabury, 1967)
The Magic Porridge Pot (Seabury, 1976)
The Monkey and the Crocodile (Seabury, 1969)
Obedient Jack (Watts, 1971)
Old Mother Hubbard and Her Dog (McGraw, 1960)

STUDY CENTER BIBLIOGRAPHY 2-7 (cont.)

Old Woman and Her Pig (McGraw, 1961)
Puss in Boots (Seabury, 1976)
Three Aesop Fox Fables, (Seabury, 1971)
The Three Bears (Scholastic, 1970; paper)
The Three Little Pigs (Seabury, 1970)
Three Wishes (McGraw, 1961)
The Town Mouse and the Country Mouse (McGraw, 1971)

Nonprint Resources: Sound Filmstrips (Weston Woods—each 1 filmstrip and 1 cassette)

The House That Jack Built
The Little Red Hen
Old Mother Hubbard and Her Dog
The Old Woman and Her Pig

STUDY CENTER BIBLIOGRAPHY 2-8   MEET MY FRIEND ASTRID LINDGREN

Grades: 1–3
Printed Resources (all by Astrid Lindgren)

The Brothers Lionheart (Viking, 1975)
Children of Noisy Village (Viking, 1962)
Children on Troublemaker Street (Macmillan, 1964)
Christmas in Noisy Village (Viking, 1964)
Emil and the Piggy Beast (Follett, 1973)
Emil in the Soup Tureen (Follett, 1970)
Emil's Pranks (Follett, n.d.)
Pippi Goes on Board (Viking, 1957)
Pippi in the South Seas (Viking, 1959)
Pippi Longstocking (Viking, 1950)
Pippi on the Run (Viking, 1976)
The Tomten (Coward, 1961)
The Tomten and the Fox (Coward, 1965)

Nonprint Resources: Sound Filmstrips

Christmas in Noisy Village (Live Oak Media—1 filmstrip, 1 cassette)
Pipi Longstocking (Films, Inc.—2 filmstrips, 2 cassettes, 1 guide, 1 paperback book)

STUDY CENTER BIBLIOGRAPHY 2-9   MEET MY FRIEND ARNOLD LOBEL

Grades: 1–2
Printed Resources (all written and illus. by Arnold Lobel)

Days with Frog and Toad (Harper, 1979)
Fables (Harper, 1980; Caldecott Medal 1981)
Frog and Toad All Year (Harper, 1976)
Frog and Toad Are Friends (Harper, 1970; Caldecott Honor Book 1971)
Frog and Toad Together (Harper, 1972)
Gregory Griggs and the Nursery Rhyme People (Greenwillow, 1978)
Holiday for Mister Mouse (Harper, 1963)

STUDY CENTER BIBLIOGRAPHY 2-9 (cont.)

Mouse Soup (Harper, 1977)
Mouse Tales (Harper, 1972)

Nonprint Resources: Sound Filmstrips (all Miller-Brody)

Fables (1 filmstrip, 1 cassette)
Frog and Toad Are Friends series (5 filmstrips, 5 cassettes, or 5 records)
Frog and Toad Together series (5 filmstrips, 5 cassettes, or 5 records)
Meet the Newbery Author, Arnold Lobel (1 filmstrip, 1 cassette, or 1 record)

STUDY CENTER BIBLIOGRAPHY 2-10 MEET MY FRIEND EDNA MILLER

Grades: 2–3
Printed Resources (all written and illus. by Edna Miller; published by Prentice-Hall)

Mousekin Finds a Friend (1967; also paper)
Mousekin Takes a Trip (1977)
Mousekin's ABC's (1972; also paper)
Mousekin's Christmas Eve (1965; also paper)
Mousekin's Close Call (1978)
Mousekin's Family (1969; also paper)
Mousekin's Golden House (1964; also paper)
Mousekin's Woodland Birthday (1974)
Mousekin's Woodland Sleepers (n.d.—each 1 filmstrip and 1 cassette)

Nonprint Resources: Sound Filmstrips (Educational Enrichment Materials)

Mousekin Finds a Friend
Mousekin Takes a Trip
Mousekin's Christmas Eve
Mousekin's Close Call
Mousekin's Family
Mousekin's Golden House
Mousekin's Woodland Sleepers

STUDY CENTER BIBLIOGRAPHY 2-11 MEET MY FRIEND A. A. MILNE

Grades: 2–4
Printed Resources (all by A. A. Milne unless otherwise indicated)

Christopher Robin Story Book (Dutton, 1966)
House at Pooh Corner rev. ed. (Dutton, 1961; also paper)
Now We Are Six rev. ed. (Dutton, 1961; also paper)
Pooh Song Book (Dutton, 1961)
Pooh Story Book (Dutton, 1965)
Pooh's Pot of Honey (Dutton, 1968)
Pooh's Quiz Book (Dutton, 1977)
Walt Disney's Winnie the Pooh: A Tight Squeeze by Walt Disney Studios (Western, 1962)
Walt Disney's Winnie the Pooh and Eeyore's Birthday by Walt Disney Studios (Western, 1964)

STUDY CENTER BIBLIOGRAPHY 2-11 (cont.)

When We Were Very Young (Dutton, 1961)

Winnie-the-Pooh (Dutton, n.d.)

World of Christopher Robin (Dutton, 1958)

Nonprint Resources: Art Prints

Pooh: His Art Gallery pictures by Ernest H. Shepard (Dutton)

Nonprint Resources: Sound Filmstrips (Walt Disney Studios—each 2 filmstrips and 2 cassettes)

Winnie the Pooh and the Blustery Day

Winnie the Pooh and the Honey Tree

Winnie the Pooh and Tigger

Nonprint Resources: Game

Winnie-The Pooh Game (Child Craft)

Nonprint Resources: Motion Picture

The Many Adventures of Winnie the Pooh (Disney Educational Media)

Nonprint Resources: Posters

Christmas in Other Lands with Winnie-the-Pooh (dist. by Association Sterling Films—set of 12 posters and 12 booklets)

Nonprint Resources: Realia

Stuffed Animals: Eeyore, Kanga, Owl, Piglet, Rabbitt, Winie-the-Pooh (Sears, Roebuck)

STUDY CENTER BIBLIOGRAPHY 2-12   MEET MY FRIEND PEGGY PARISH

Grades: 2–4

Printed Resources (all by Peggy Parish)

AMELIA BEDELIA SERIES

Amelia Bedelia (Harper, 1963; also paper)

Amelia Bedelia and the Surprise Shower (Harper, 1966)

Come Back, Amelia Bedelia (Harper, 1970; also paper)

Good Work, Amelia Bedelia (Greenwillow, 1976)

Play Ball, Amelia Bedelia (Harper, 1978; also paper)

Teach Us, Amelia Bedelia (Greenwillow, 1977)

Thank You, Amelia Bedelia (Harper, 1964)

GRANNY SERIES (all published by Macmillan)

Granny and the Desperadoes (1973; also paper)

Granny and the Indians (1969; also paper)

Granny, the Baby, and the Big Gray Thing (1972)

Nonfiction

Costumes to Make (Macmilan, 1970)

Let's Be Early Settlers with Daniel Boone (Harper, 1967)

Let's Be Indians (Harper, 1962)

Let's Celebrate: Holiday Decorations You Can Make (Greenwillow, 1976)

Sheet Magic: Games, Toys and Gifts from Old Sheets (Macmillan, 1971)

Nonprint Resources: Sound Filmstrips (all Educational Enrichment Materials)

Amelia Bedelia

Amelia Bedelia and the Surprise Shower
Come Back, Amelia Bedelia
Good Work, Amelia Bedelia
Play Ball, Amelia Bedelia
Teach Us, Amelia Bedelia
Thank You, Amelia Bedelia

STUDY CENTER BIBLIOGRAPHY 2-13   MEET MY FRIEND BEATRIX POTTER

Grades: 1–3
Printed Resources: Peter Rabbit Books, 23 vols. (all written and illus. by Beatrix Potter; published by Warne)

1. *The Tale of Peter Rabbit* (1902)
2. *The Tale of Squirrel Nutkin* (1903)
3. *The Tailor of Gloucester* (1903)
4. *The Tale of Benjamin Bunny* (1904)
5. *The Tale of Two Bad Mice* (1904)
6. *The Tale of Mrs. Tiggy-Winkle* (1905)
7. *The Tale of Jeremy Fisher* (1906)
8. *The Tale of Tom Kitten* (1907)
9. *The Tale of Jemima Puddle-Duck* (1908)
10. *The Tale of the Flopsy Bunnies* (1909)
11. *The Tale of Mrs. Tittlemouse* (1910)
12. *The Tale of Timmy Tiptoes* (1911)
13. *The Tale of Mr. Tod* (1912)
14. *The Tale of Pigling Bland* (1913)
15. *The Tale of Johnny-Town-Mouse* (1918)
16. *The Roly Poly Pudding* (1908)
17. *The Pie and the Patty Pan* (1905)
18. *Ginger and Pickles* (1909)
19. *The Tale of Little Pig Robinson* (1930)
20. *The Story of a Fierce Bad Rabbit* (1906)
21. *The Story of Miss Moppet* (1906)
22. *Appley Dapply's Nursery Rhymes* (1917)
23. *Cecily Parsley's Nursery Rhymes* (1922)

Nonprint Resources: Art Prints (Warne)

   Portfolio of Beatrix Potter Pictures (8 art prints, 14″ by 17″)

   Potter Wallpaper Nursery Frieze (3 friezes, 39″ by 10″)

Nonprint Resources: Sound Filmstrips (Spoken Arts—each 1 filmstrip, 1 cassette, 1 script)

Treasury of Animal Stories, Set 1

   The Tale of Peter Rabbit

   The Tale of Benjamin Bunny

   The Tale of Squirrel Nutkin

   The Tale of Jeremy Fisher

Treasury of Animal Stories, Set 2

   The Tale of Two Bad Mice

   The Tale of Mrs. Tiggy-Winkle

   The Tailor of Gloucester, Parts 1 and 2

Note: This is the *teachable moment* for introducing other stories about animals that talk and act as human beings. The following stories on an advanced reading level should delight the gifted reader.

STUDY CENTER BIBLIOGRAPHY 2-13 (cont.)

AUTHOR—MICHAEL BOND

A Bear Called Paddington (Houghton, 1960)
Paddington Helps Out (Houghton, 1961)
More about Paddington (Houghton, 1962)
Paddington at Large (Houghton 1963)
Paddington Marches On (Houghton, 1965)
Paddington at Work (Houghton, 1967)
Paddington Goes to Town (Houghton, 1968)
Paddington Takes the Air (Houghton, 1971)
Paddington Abroad (Houghton, 1972)
Paddington's Garden (Random, 1973)
Paddington at the Circus (Random, 1974)
Paddington's Lucky Day (Houghton, 1974)
Paddington Takes to TV (Houghton, 1974)
Paddington on Top (Houghton, 1974)
Paddington on Stage (Houghton, 1977)
Paddington at the Seaside (Random, 1978)
Paddington at the Tower (Random, 1978)

AUTHOR—THORNTON BURGESS (both published by Little)

Old Mother West Wind (1960)
Mother West Wind's Children (1962)

AUTHOR—RUMER GODDEN (both published by Viking)

The Mouse House, illus. by Adrienne Adams (1957)
The Mousewife illus. by Heidi Holder (1982)

AUTHOR—KENNETH GRAHAME

The Wind in the Willows illus. by Ernest Shepard (Scribner, 1954)
The Wind in the Willows, sound filmstrips (Educational Enrichment Materials—each part 4 filmstrips, 4 cassettes, 1 paperback book). Part I: *The River Bank, The Wild Wood and Mr. Badger, The Open Road, Mr. Toad.* Part II: *Toad's Adventures, The Further Adventures of Toad, Like Summer Tempests Came His Tears, The Return of Ulysses.*

AUTHOR—ROBERT LAWSON, (all illus. by the author)

Rabbit Hill, (Viking, 1944; also paper, Newbery Medal 1945)
Ben and Me: A New and Astonishing Life of Benjamin Franklin as Written by His Good Mouse, Amos . . . (Little, 1951)
Mr. Revere and I: Being an Account of Certain Episodes in the Career of Paul Revere, Esq., as Recently Revealed by His Horse, Scheherazade . . . (Little, 1953)
Tough Winter (Viking, 1954; also paper)
Captain Kidd's Cat: Being the True and Dolorous Chronicle of Wm. Kidd, Gentleman and Merchant of New York . . . (Little, 1956)
I Discover Columbus: A True Chronicle of the Great Admiral and His Finding of the New World, Narrated by the Venerable Parrot Aurelio . . . (Little, 1971)

AUTHOR—HUGH LOFTING

The Voyages of Dr. Dolittle (Lippincott, 1922; Newbery Medal 1922)
Doctor Dolittle, sound filmstrips (Films, Inc.—2 filmstrips, 2 cassettes, 1 guide, 1 paperback book)

AUTHOR—E. B. WHITE (both published by Harper)

Charlotte's Web (1945)

STUDY CENTER BIBLIOGRAPHY 2-13 (cont.)

Stuart Little (1945)

Charlotte's Web, multimedia kit (Films, Inc.—2 filmstrips, 2 cassettes, 1 guide, 1 paperback book, 5 copies of the Activity Book)

TELEVISION PPROGRAM—THE MUPPETS

The Great Muppet Caper by Jocelyn Stevenson (Random, 1981)

Muppet Magic by Patricia D. Frevert (Creative Education, 1980)

STUDY CENTER BIBLIOGRAPHY 2-14   MEET THE AUTHOR LLOYD ALEXANDER

Grades: 4–7
Printed Resources (all by Lloyd Alexander; published by Holt)

THE CHRONICLES OF PRYDAIN

The Book of Three (1964)

The Black Cauldron (1965)

The Castle of Llyr (1966)

Taran Wanderer (1967)

The High King (1968; Newbery Medal 1969)

OTHER TALES SET IN PRYDAIN

Coll and His White Pig (1965)

The Truthful Harp (1967)

Nonprint Resources: Sound Filmstrips (both Miller-Brody)

The High King (4 filmstrips, 4 cassettes, or 4 records)

Meet the Newbery Author: Lloyd Alexander (1 filmstrip, 1 cassette, or 1 record)

Note: This is the *teachable moment* to introduce an in-depth study of fantasy.

Introduction: "In fantasy, the impossible takes place; animals talk, magical events occur, the barriers of time dissolve, mythical creatures exist, and inanimate objects come to life."*

Basic Teaching Tool: *Fantasy Literature for Children,* Series 1 (Pied Piper Productions—1 filmstrip, 1 cassette, 1 teacher's guide). Highlights fantasies by George Selden, C. S. Lewis, and Hugh Lofting

AUTHOR—SUSAN COOPER

Over Sea, Under Stone (Harcourt, 1966)

The Dark Is Rising (Atheneum, 1973)

Greenwitch (Atheneum, 1974)

The Grey King (Atheneum, 1975; Newbery Medal 1976)

Silver on the Tree (Atheneum, 1977)

Meet the Newbery Author: Susan Cooper, sound filmstrips (Miller-Brody—1 filmstrip, 1 cassette, or 1 record)

AUTHOR—C. S. LEWIS; NARNIA SERIES (all published by Macmillan)

The Lion, the Witch and the Wardrobe (1951)

Prince Caspian (1951)

The Voyage of the Dawn Treader (1952)

The Silver Chair (1953)

The Horse and His Boy (1954)

*Ruth Nadelman Lynn, *Fantasy for Children: An Annotated Checklist* (New York: R. R. Bowker, 1979), p. vii.

STUDY CENTER BIBLIOGRAPHY 2-14 (cont.)

The Magician's Nephew (1955)

The Last Battle (1956)

AUTHOR—J. R. R. TOLKIEN

The Hobbit; or There and Back Again rev. ed. (Houghton, 1966)

The Lord of the Rings Trilogy (all rev. ed., published by Houghton)

The Fellowship of the Ring (1967)

The Two Towers (1967)

The Return of the King (1966)

The Hobbit, sound filmstrips (Guidance Associates—NBC TV Classic)—6 filmstrips, 6 casettes, 1 guide, 2 posters)

The Lord of the Rings, sound filmstrips (Media Basics, dist. by Charles Clark—4 filmstrips, 4 cassettes)

The Shadow of the Past

A Knife in the Dark

The Breaking of the Fellowship

The Riders of Rohan

Promotional Materials

Posters, bookmarks, bulletin board displays, and mobiles highlighting the theme *"Fantasy"* are available from Upstart Library Promotionals.

STUDY CENTER BIBLIOGRAPHY 2-15 MEET THE AUTHOR ROBERT BURCH

Grades: 5–7

Printed Resources (all by Robert Burch; published by Viking)

D. J.'s Worst Enemy (1965)

Queenie Peavy (1966)

Skinny (1964; also paper)

Note: This is the *teachable moment* to introduce an in-depth study of realistic fiction.

Introduction

Robert Burch's *Queenie Peavy* is highlighted in the Pied Piper Productions' *Literature for Children*, Series 6: *Realistic Fiction* sound filmstrip set (See Teaching Guide 1-1, *Realistic Fiction*, in Model 1, Experiencing Literature)

In the Pied Piper Teaching Guide, Realistic Fiction is presented as "stories which didn't really happen, but seem so real that they might have happened. . . . Characters are not all 'good' or all 'bad' and the settings and dialogue are similar to real life."

AUTHORS—VERA AND BILL CLEAVER (all published by Lippincott)

Dust of the Earth (1975; also paper)

Ellen Grae (1967)

Trial Valley (1977)

Where the Lillies Bloom (1969)

AUTHOR—JEAN GEORGE (both published by Dutton)

My Side of the Mountain (1959)

River Rats, Inc. (1979)

My Side of the Mountain, sound filmstrips (Films, Inc.—2 filmstrips, 2 cassettes, 1 guide, 1 paperback book)

AUTHOR—ELAINE KONIGSBURG (all published by Atheneum)

About the B'nai Bagels (1969; also paper)

Altogether, One at a Time (1971; also paper)

From the Mixed-up Files of Mrs. Basil E. Frankweiler (1967; also paper; Newbery Medal 1968)

Jennifer, Hecate, Macbeth, William McKinley and Me, Elizabeth (1967; also paper)

From the Mixed-Up Files of Mrs. Basil E. Frankweiler, sound filmstrips (Films, Inc.—2 filmstrips, 2 cassettes, 1 guide, 1 paperback book)

AUTHOR—WALT MOREY

Deep Trouble (Dutton, 1971)

AUTHOR—SCOTT O'DELL

The Black Pearl (Houghton, 1967; Newbery Honor Book 1968)

The Black Pearl, sound filmstrips (Miller-Brody—2 filmstrips, 2 cassettes, 10 student activity booklets)

AUTHOR—KATHERINE PATERSON (both published by Crowell)

Bridge to Terabithia (1977; Newbery Medal 1978)

The Great Gilly Hopkins (1978; Newbery Honor Book 1979)

Bridge to Terabithia and *The Great Gily Hopkins,* sound filmstrips (Miller-Brody—each 2 filmstrips and 2 cassettes).

AUTHOR—ARTHUR ROTH

Two for Survival (Scribner, 1976)

AUTHOR—A. RUTGERS VAN DER LOEF

Avalanche (Morrow, 1968)

AUTHOR—ROBB WHITE

Fire Storm (Doubleday, 1979)

AUTHOR—ESTER WIER

The Loner (McKay, 1963; Newbery Honor Book 1964)

The Loner, sound filmstrips (Miller-Brody—2 filmstrips, 2 cassettes, or 2 records)

Model 3

Communication: Past, Present, and Future—A Differentiated Program for the Gifted

GRADES: 4–6

GOAL: The program goal is to provide learning experiences that will enable the student to understand, appreciate, and value the historical, social, economic, scientific, artistic, and personal significance of communication in today's world and that of the future.

OBJECTIVES

This project has been designed and structured to provide these basic *cognitive* concepts:

Reading, writing, speaking, and listening skills are not only basic learning skills but also basic life skills.

Human beings need to think, communicate, and cooperate in order to survive.

At least 1,000 different languages are spoken in the world today.

The invention of the alphabet was one of the greatest civilizing events in human history.

It is difficult to communicate exactly what one feels or thinks.

Media are information carriers.

Organization of information is the key to retrieval.

Creating clear images in speaking and writing begins with clear mental images organized into meaningful patterns.

This project has been designed and structured to foster these basic *affective* attitudes and appreciations:

Communication is both a science and an art.

Communication is a mirror of one's own thinking competence.

Writing transcends time and place and makes it possible for those living today to communicate with those no longer living or those not yet born.

Creative use of language can bring power and beauty to both the spoken and the written word.

Literature is a creative form of communication.

Honesty in communcation requires intellectual discipline and integrity.

In interpersonal communication, emotion must not be substituted for reason.

Mutual respect between parents and children and between teachers and students bridges the generation gap when they communicate.

STRATEGIES AND METHODS

No time limits are imposed on this project. The number of students in the group coupled with student interest are the factors determining the duration of the project, two weeks, two months, or longer.

A basic part of group orientation to the project is to provide opportunities for the student to explore the synergistic effect of sharing knowledge with others.

Each student will be encouraged to explore areas of personal interest, challenge, and satisfaction.

PROCEDURAL OUTLINE

    I. Group orientation to the project.

       A. Definition of basic terms serves as an introduction.

          1. *Communication*—sharing information; exchanging information.

          2. *Language*—human speech, spoken or written.

          3. *Medium, media*—carrier of information; carriers of information.

       B. Students discuss the following concepts:

          1. Words are but symbols for things or objects, for actions or events, and for ideas or feelings.

             a. Spoken words are sound symbols; written words are sight symbols.

             b. When you hear or see a word, you mentally translate it into an image of the thing, object, action, event, idea, or feeling.

          2. You cannot think without the help of language; thinking is carrying on a conversation in your mind and involves seven steps:

             a. Remembering—recalling or recognizing information.

             b. Translating—changing information from one form into a different form, such as words into pictures.

             c. Interpreting—discovering relationships among facts, ideas, objects, or experiences.

             d. Applying—using previously acquired knowledge and skills in solving a new problem.

             e. Analyzing—separating complicated material into its basic parts in order to see and understand their relationship.

      f. Synthesizing—putting ideas together in a form that is meaningful, new, and original.

      g. Evaluating—appraising the adequacy of the ideas, methods, materials, and resolution appropriate to any given task or problem.

II. Group exploration of the various ways humans communicate.

  A. Gestures and signals.

    1. Gesture—movement of the hands, arms, or any part of the body to convey a message. Examples: Quiet, come, go, stop.

    2. Signal—sign, object, light, sound, or the like, giving notice of something. Examples: Telephone bell signals a phone call; traffic signals.

  B. Pictures and symbols.

    1. Picture—drawing, painting, illustration, portrait, cartoon, or photograph used to impart information. Examples: Study prints, newspaper cartoons, pictographs, TV commercials.

    2. Symbol—something that stands for or represents an idea, quality, condition, government, organization, association, institution, holiday, and so on. Examples: Santa Claus, Uncle Sam, bald eagle, Russian bear.

  C. Language and writing.

    1. Language—systematic way of using words so that people can share information. Examples: Language has two basic elements: a group of words whose meanings are understood by the members of the society, and an accepted way of linking words; an established usage or grammar pattern.

    2. Writing—established method of recording words. Examples: Syntax is the arrangement and interrelationship of words in phrases and sentences; grammar determines standards of correctness for both speech and writing.

  D. Mass media—sharing information with many people in many places with the help of machines. Examples: Machine-produced books, magazines, newspapers, television programs, and motion pictures are media, or means, of mass communication.

III. Group exploration of the history of communication.

  A. The group views and discusses the motion picture *Discovering Language: The Alphabet* (Coronet).

    1. This motion picture is the first in the series Discovering Language. The other titles in the Coronet film series are:

      a. *Discovering Language: How English Borrowed Words*

      b. *Discovering Language: How English Changes in America*

      c. *Discovering Language: How Words Are Made*

      d. *Discovering Language: How Words Get New Meanings*

      e. *Discovering Language: Varieties of English*

    2. If students are interested, they may elect to view the other motion pictures in the Discovering Language series.

  B. The history of the alphabet as presented in the motion picture *The Alphabet* is summarized by the group. The following events are highlighted:

1. In the caves of prehistoric peoples, drawings on the walls depict everyday activities; these drawing date back 50 thousand years.
2. About 3300 B.C., the ancient Egyptians developed a picture language called hieroglyphics:
   a. The Egyptians used several hundred different symbols in writing the words of their language.
   b. The Rosetta stone (now housed in the British Museum, London) is a slab of black basalt found in 1799 near the mouth of the Nile River. A decree was carved on this slab in two kinds of ancient Egyptian writing and also in Greek.
   c. Jean Francois Champollion, French Egyptologist, studied the inscription on the Rosetta stone and discovered the key to translating the hieroglyphics.
   d. The Metropolitan Museum of Art (New York City) has published a self-instructional device called the "Hieroglyphic Computer," which introduces the original hieroglyphic "alphabet" of 25 signs. It gives the English pronunciation of each sign and shows what that sign represents and also indicates numbers in powers of 10, from one to one million.
3. About 1000 B.C., the Phoenicians developed the first true alphabet.
4. About 600 B.C., the ancient Greeks borrowed from the Phoenicians the idea of using letters to represent sounds.
5. About A.D. 100, the ancient Romans modified the Greek alphabet and developed the alphabet that was adopted by Western civilization.

C. The group prepares charts and/or transparencies for overhead projection, illustrating the historical development of each of the letters of the alphabet.
1. The historical evolution begins with the Egyptians and extends to the Semites, the Phoenicians, the Greeks, and the Romans.
2. Graphic illustration of the individual letters of the alphabet can be found in two readily available reference tools, *The World Book Encyclopedia* and *The World Book Encyclopedia Dictionary*.

D. The group builds a chronology of red-letter dates in the history of communication.
1. The concept of building and interpreting chronologies is introduced.
   a. The section in *The World Almanac and Book of Facts* entitled "Memorable Dates" is used as a model.
      (1) Attention is called to the use of B.C.E. as well as B.C. in this chronology: B.C. means Before Christ; B.C.E. means before Common Era.
      (2) Attention is called to the use of c. (the abbreviation of the Latin word *circa*) to indicate that the exact date is not known.
   b. The *Information Please Almanac* section "A Chronology from 2300 B.C. to 1982" (updated each year) is examined and compared with the chronology in *The World Almanac*.

c. The chronology "Red-Letter Days in Communication," found in the article "Communication" in *The World Book Encyclopedia,* is used as a capsule review of noteworthy people and events in the history of communications.

Students are encouraged to research the following dates:

c. 1000 B.C.   Egyptians used papyrus sheets for written records.

c. 800 B.C.   Assyrians and Babylonians established libraries.

c. 300 B.C.   Hindus invented numerals.

c. 200 B.C.   Use of parchment was introduced in Western Asia.

c. 105 A.D.   Chinese used paper and ink.

c. 450   Block printing was practiced in Asia.

c. 800   Arabs adopted our present number system from India.

c. 1440   Johannes Gutenberg invented movable type.

1755   Samuel Johnson published one of the first English dictionaries.

1783   First daily newspaper in America, the *Pensylvania Evening Post and Daily Advertiser,* was founded in Pennsylvania.

c. 1803   In England, the Fourdrinier brothers perfected a machine for making paper.

1814   Cylinder press was invented.

1828   Noah Webster published the first comprehensive American dictionary.

1822–1839   Louis Daguerre and Joseph Niepce of France invented a method of photography.

1833   First public library in the United States was established in Peterborough, New Hampshire.

1837   Massachusetts legislature established free public education under state supervision.

1844   Samuel Morse sent the first telegraph message.

1858   First transatlantic cable was laid.

1867   Christopher Sholes, Carlos Glidden, and S. W. Soule made the first practical typewriter.

1876   Alexander Graham Bell invented the telephone.

1877   Thomas Edison invented the phonograph.

1889   George Eastman developed photographic film.

1894   Motion pictures were perfected and shown to the public.

1895   Guglielmo Marconi invented the wireless telegraph.

1918   World's first airmail service was established between New York City, Philadelphia, and Washington, D.C.

1920   Radio station KDKA, Pittsburgh, Pennsylvania, began the world's first regularly scheduled radio broadcast.

1923	Pictures were televised between New York City and Philadelphia.
1941	Commercial television began in the United States.
1957	First artificial satellite sent back information from beyond the moon.

2. The concept of building and interpreting time lines is introduced.
   a. A variety of time lines are examined as a basis for students' discovering types and kinds of time lines as well as how time lines highlight the interplay of people and events. The following sources are examined.
      (1) *Arrow Book Club Time Lines* (Scholastic)
      (2) *Highlights of American History* (*World Book Encyclopedia,* vol. 20)
      (3) . . . *If You Lived with the Sioux Indians* by Ann McGovern (Scholastic), p. 7
      (4) *Man's Cultural Heritage: A World History* by Paul Thomas Welty (Lippincott), pp. 142–143, 224–225, 330–331, 444–445, 504–505, 584–585, 624–625
      (5) *Time Line of Ancient Egypt* (Metropolitan Museum of Art, 1980)
   b. The group is introduced to *Communication: A Time Line Story* (Child's World—a set of 16 picture cards). Students construct a time line using the picture cards; they expand this time line to include those events and people they have discovered through their individual research projects.

IV. Group builds its knowledge of labels as communication agents.
   A. Each student receives Kit A: Labels with a Message.
      1. Using the labels included in the kit, the students are instructed to see if they can discover the one identification mark that is common to each label.
         a. The kit contains the following labels:*

Eskimo Pie	Myoflex
Kroger Instant Rice	Purina Fit and Trim
Milk-Bone	Zesta Saltine Crackers
Milk Duds	

         b. Students discover that common to each label is a capital R enclosed in a circle following the trade name and the trademark on each label, as ®.
         c. Attention is called to the explanation found on the Eskimo Pie label: Eskimo Pie and the associated pictorial representation are the *registered* trademarks of Eskimo Pie Corporation for products made by it or under its authority and direction.
         d. Attention is called to the statement found on the Milk-Bone label: Milk-Bone and bone design are *registered* trademarks of Nabisco, Inc.
         e. Students discover that the ® used on the labels indicates that

---

*Labels included in the kit are suggestions only; availability and teacher preference should determine label inclusion.

the trade name and trademark were registered with the Patent and Trademark Office, Washington, D.C. 20231.

2. Students search for all types and kinds of labels—food, clothes, household furnishings, pharmaceuticals, cosmetics, stationery, greeting cards, toys, and so on—that indicate a registered trademark. A student committee takes the responsibility for organizing, categorizing, and listing the various labels.

V. Group builds its knowledge of logos as communication agents.

A. *Logos* are defined as identification symbols used by businesses, industries, societies, associations, organizations, schools, colleges, universities, and so on.

1. Each student receives Kit B containing the following logos:*

Atari	Michelin
CBS	Nabisco
Calvin Klein	Ocean Spray
Ford	Pac-Man
General Electric	Pillsbury
Gloria Vanderbilt	Seiko
Heinz	Wearever
Jordache	Westinghouse
Levi's	Wrangler

2. Students list as many logos as they can recall; they decide which of the logos, such as McDonald's Golden Arches, are the most commonly known.

B. *Colophons* are defined as logos used by publishers to identify their company or to identify a series of books the company publishes.

1. Students work independently in the library to discover as many different colophons as possible.

2. Students design a collage illustrating their findings.

C. Students prepare to teach their classmates what logos are and why they are effective communication agents.

1. This is a practical problem in communication.

2. Basic rules for communicating information effectively are formulated by the group:

a. Draw up a plan for communicating the message.

b. Use specific detail, which gives *exact* information such as who, where, when, what, and why.

c. Define your topic and all basic terms.

d. Strive to create *clear* images.

e. Give only one idea at a time.

f. Go from the simple to the complex.

g. Remember that an appropriate illustration—chart, graph, picture, transparency, filmstrip, slide, poster—is more effective than a thousand words.

h. Use concrete details to make images more vivid and more interesting; where possible, use realia.

i. Remind your listeners of what they know or have experienced.

*Logos included in the kit are suggestions only; availability and teacher preference should determine logo inclusion.

      j. Link what you are saying now with previous learnings and experiences.

   3. The group organizes a committee to prepare and present information about logos to the class. Basic rules for committee function are formulated:

      a. Members of a committee must work together congenially.

      b. Chairperson must demonstrate leadership and must focus attention of the committee members on the purpose of the undertaking; solicit ideas from the group; have the group reach a consensus on the goals of the committee and the procedure to be followed; establish target dates and keep the group on schedule; be a facilitator, not a dictator.

      c. To be effective, a committee member must: welcome suggestions from other members of the committee; enjoy sharing responsibilities, ideas, time, and materials; learn how to compliment the efforts of others; fulfill commitments once they have been accepted.

      d. Each committee member has an individual assignment, such as: introducing the concept of logos and colophons to the class; preparing posters or transparencies of exemplary logos or colophons; demonstrating various types and kinds of logos and colophons; preparing summarizing activities such as logos- and colophon-identifying contest.

   4. The group presents the information to the class.

VI. Group exploration of charts as communication agents.

   A. *Charts* are defined as sheets of information arranged in pictures, tables, or diagrams.

     1. Charts organize information for rapid retrieval.

     2. Three common types of charts are:

      a. Picture chart—presents a visual representation of an object or scene on a flat surface.

      b. Table chart—presents information in a list or other brief form.

      c. Diagram—presents drawings or sketches showing important parts of an object; a diagram may be an outline, a plan, a figure, or a combination of these, made to show clearly what an object is and how it works.

     3. The 25-page *World Book Encyclopedia* reprint *Insects* serves as the basic teaching tool for introducing and/or reinforcing student understanding of charts as communication agents. This reprint contains the following charts:

      a. "Familiar Insects of North America"—picture chart

      b. "Some Common Insect Pests"—picture chart

      c. "The External Anatomy of an Insect"—diagram

      d. "Insect Mouth Parts"—diagram

      e. "Insect Legs and Feet"—diagram

      f. "The Internal Anatomy of an Insect"—diagram

      g. "The Three Patterns of Insect Growth and Development"— table

        h. "Major Groups of Insects: Order and Common Name, Cha-racteristics of Adults and Type of Metamorphosis"—table

  B. Students search in the school library's print and nonprint resources to discover charts of exceptional significance:

    1. Each student shares with the group those charts he or she finds.

    2. Group selects those charts judged worthy of serving as model examples.

VII. Group exploration of graphs as communication agents.

  A. *Graphs* are defined as lines or diagrams showing how one quantity depends on or changes with another; graphs are used to give simpler and clearer messages than long tables of statistics.

    1. Statistics are the raw materials used in a graph.

    2. Making graphs involves two basic steps:

      a. The technique of plotting statistics.

      b. Understanding statistics and their interrelationships.

    3. There are four main types of graphs:

      a. Line graph—successive points connected by a line.

      b. Bar graph—successive points indicated by rectangles.

      c. Pie graph—circle divided into wedges.

      d. Pictograph—horizontal bar graphs in which the bars are broken up into symbol units.

    4. The book *Graphs: A First Book* by Dyno Lowenstein (Watts, 1976) serves as a basic guide for introducing and/or reinforcing the concept of graphs as communication agents.

    5. Current issues of periodicals such as *Newsweek, Time,* and *U.S. News and World Report* are searched to discover how these news magazines use graphs and other charts to convey information.

    6. *The E.Q. Index,* a reprint on environmental quality from the magazine *National Wildlife,* serves as a case study of how graphs and other charts are effective in conveying statistical information.

  B. In the school library, students are introduced to the following basic statistical reference sources by the school librarian:

    1. Almanacs, fact books, statistical yearbooks

        Information Please Almanac
        Reader's Digest Almanac
        Statistical Abstract of the United States
        World Almanac and Book of Facts
        Yearbook of the United Nations

    2. Economic atlas

        Oxford Economic Atlas of the World

    3. Encyclopedia yearbooks

        Americana Annual
        Britannica Book of the Year
        Collier's Encyclopedia Yearbook
        World Book Year Book

VIII. Group exploration of interpersonal communication.

  A. *Interpersonal communication* is defined as communication between people.

1. Communication with spoken and written words makes cooperation easier.
2. Words help people to express their feelings and ideas.
3. Human beings need to think, communicate, and cooperate in order to survive.
4. Conversation, an informal or friendly talk, should be an *exchange* of ideas—dialogue rather than monologue.
   a. A good conversationalist has something of significance to say, says it with candor and directness, does not monopolize the conversation but engages in a lively give and take.
   b. A good conversationalist is also a good listener.
5. Letter writing is a written form of conversation.
   a. A well-written personal letter sounds as though the writer is speaking directly to you.
   b. *The First Book of Letter Writing* by Helen Jacobson and Florence Mischel (Watts, 1957) provides guidelines and models for effective letter writing.

B. *Intrafamily communication* is defined as communication within or inside the family.
   1. Respect for parents by children and respect for children by parents bridges the generation gap in communication.
      a. Mutual respect between teachers and students likewise bridges the generation gap when they communicate.
   2. Family discussion should be an honest exchange of ideas.
      a. Viewpoints of each family member should be respected.
      b. Decisions affecting the family should be looked at from *all* viewpoints.
   3. The group role plays a typical family discussion about whether to get a dog.
      a. Each student in the group assumes the role of a particular family member, mother, father, sister, brother, and so on.
      b. Advantages and disadvantages of having a family dog are identified and honestly weighed. Responsibility of each family member should be identified including who will be responsible for:

> Buying the dog
> Paying for visits to the veterinarian
> Buying the food
> Feeding the dog
> Grooming the dog
> Walking the dog
> Training the dog

   c. Voting to get the dog is a contractual agreement. A contract is equally binding on all persons entering into the agreement.
   4. The observation is made that you can disagree without being disagreeable.

C. The concept that excellence in interpersonal communication requires that the participants be psychologically mature is discussed.
   1. A psychologically mature person is judged not by age but by behavior.

2. A psychologically mature person is one who:
   a. Is secure within him or herself.
   b. Has the capacity to give more of him or herself than he or she expects of others.
   c. Has the ability to sympathize with others and see things from their point of view.
   d. Is objective about him or herself, recognizing his or her own limitations.
   e. Is comparatively unselfish; willingly shares time, energy, responsibility, and ideas with others.
   f. Is self-reliant and independent in thinking, but cooperative in acting.
   g. Takes the objective view in solving problems.
   h. Makes intelligent and sensitive choices.
   i. Is sufficiently flexible to adjust to or cope with all types and kinds of situations.
   j. Appreciates that it is just and right to march to a different drumbeat just so long as one keeps in tune with one's fellow humans and in step with one's own best self.

IX. Group exploration of the school intercom system as a communication agent.
   A. Guidelines for intercom communication are developed as follows:
      1. Preplan the use of the intercom so as to minimize class disruption; use the intercom at regularly scheduled times.
      2. Never break into scheduled class time except for an emergency.
      3. All announcements must be written.
      4. The announcer must sequence the announcements—"first things first" is the basic rule; i.e., today—A.M. and P.M.; tomorrow—A.M. and P.M., and so on.
      5. The announcer must read the announcements in a clear, well-modulated voice.
      6. The announcer must pause between announcements, leaving no doubt in the mind of the listener that this is a separate announcement.
      7. The announcer must sign off by identifying him or herself and must thank the listeners for their attention.
   B. Techniques for governing the use of the microphone are formulated:
      1. Do not hold the microphone too close to the mouth.
      2. Do not breathe into the microphone.
      3. Do not shout into the microphone; speak distinctly in a conversational tone of voice.
   C. The group practices using the microphone.
      1. Performance using the public address system is critiqued by the group. This is a "dry run" with the public addres system limited only to the classroom.
      2. When the group decides that each member can perform well, arrangements are made with the principal for the students to take part in daily broadcasts via the system.

CHECKLIST 3-1　ASSEMBLY PLANNING GUIDE*

School:
Date:
Time:
Grades:
Topic or Theme:
Length of Program:
Participants:
    Students—

    Teachers—

    Principal—

    Guests—

    Stage Crew/Projectionists/Technicians—

    Ushers—

Publicity:
    In-School—
        Bulletin announcements
        Public address announcements
        Homeroom announcements
        Posters
        School newspaper
        Others
    Community—
        Parent Teachers' Organizations and Mothers' Clubs
        Community Action Committee
        Kiwanis
        Rotary
        American Legion
        Veterans of Foreign Wars
        Chamber of Commerce
        Cable TV
        Newspapers
        Others
Program Introduction:
    By Whom—

    Length of Introduction—

    What Is to Be Said?
        Explain the purpose of the assembly
        Establish rapport with the audience
        Stimulate interest

    Introducing a Speaker
        Briefly sketch speaker's background
        Welcome the speaker on behalf of the students, faculty, principal
    Thanking the Speaker
        Briefly indicate appreciation
Equipment Needed:

( )	Filmstrip Projector	( )	Record Player
( )	Motion Picture Projector	( )	Slide Projector
( )	Projection Screen	( )	Videotape-Television Camera
( )	Public Address System	( )	Other Equipment

*Corinne P. Clendening and Ruth Ann Davies, *Creating Programs for the Gifted: A Guide for Teachers, Librarians, and Students* (New York: R.R. Bowker, 1980), pp. 210–211.

X. Group exploration of planning and presenting assemblies as an effective means of intergroup communication.
  A. The group discusses the purposes of having assemblies and decides the following:
    1. The main purpose is not entertainment but communication of significant educational information and activities.
    2. The theme or topic of the assembly must be appropriate to the comprehension level of the audience and well within the ability range of the performers.
    3. All aspects of the assembly must be carefully preplanned and appropriately rehearsed.
    4. A checklist, Assembly Planning Guide, is developed (see Checklist 3-1).
  B. The group plans and produces an assembly program.

XI. Group exploration of communication shortcuts and time savers.
  A. The group builds its knowledge of abbreviations and acronyms.
    1. *Abbreviation* is defined as a part of a word or phrase standing for the whole, such as the initial letter of a word, or the first and last letters of a word, or the first part of a word. Examples:

A.D.—in the year of [our] Lord	int.—interest
adj.—adjective	isl.—island
adv.—adverb	M.D.—doctor of medicine
ant.—antonym	mfg.—manufacturing
B.C.—before Christ	Mr.—mister
c.—circa	Ms.—miss, mistress
def.—definition	mt.—mountain
est.—estimate	n.d.—no date
ft.—foot	oz.—ounce
gal.—gallon	p.—page
govt.—government	pop.—population
grad.—graduate	qt.—quart
hr.—hour	rev.—revised
ht.—height	sec.—second
in.—inch	wk.—week

    2. *Acronym* is defined as a word formed from the first letters or syllables of other words. Examples:

    AAA—American Automobile Association
    ABC—American Broadcasting Company
    BYU—Brigham Young University
    CPA—certified public accountant
    ETV—educational television
    GOP—Grand Old Party (Republican party)
    IQ—intelligence quotient
    JP—justice of the peace
    MS—multiple sclerosis
    NASA—National Aeronautics and Space Administration
    NFL—National Football League
    TM—trademark
    UFO—unidentified flying object
    UN—United Nations
    US—United States

    3. Abbreviations and acronyms can stand for a variety of meanings. Examples:

c. is an abbreviation for the following: about, approximately, circa; cent or cents; center; centimeter; copy; copyright; cubic.

AAA is an abbreviation for the following: Agricultural Adjustment Administration; American Automobile Association; antiaircraft artillery; highest rank in financial rating; third in a series of narrow shoe widths.

Context determines the precise meaning of an abbreviation or an acronym.

4. The group explores the reference collection of the school library to find specific tools listing abbreviations and acronyms. They discover that:

a. Many standard dictionaries include within their alphabetical arrangement both abbreviations and acronyms, for example:

   (1) *Thorndike-Barnhart Advanced Junior Dictionary* (Doubleday)

   (2) *Thorndike-Barnhart High School Dictionary* (Doubleday)

   (3) *World Book Encyclopedia Dictionary* (Field Enterprises)

b. Some dictionaries devote a special section to abbreviations, for example:

   (1) *Funk & and Wagnalls Standard Dictionary of the English Language* (Funk & Wagnalls)

   (2) *Webster's New Twentieth Century Dictionary Unabridged,* 2nd ed. (Simon & Schuster)

   (3) *Webster's Seventh New Collegiate Dictionary* (Merriam)

c. Some few dictionaries are devoted entirely to abbreviations and/or acronyms, for example:

   (1) *Acronyms Dictionary: A Guide to Alphabetical Designations* (Gale)

   (2) *A Concise Dictionary of Abbreviations* (Tudor)

   (3) *Dictionary of Initials: A Comprehensive Guide Listing Thousands of Initials and Acronyms and Their Meanings* (Citadel)

B. The group builds its knowledge of codes.

1. *Code* is defined as a system of colors, words, letters, figures, and so on, used to keep a message short.

2. *Color* coding is used to convey information.

a. Traffic is controlled by color signals:

   Red   = stop
   Yellow = caution
   Green = go

b. Individual telephone cable wires are color coded for quick identification to facilitate cable installation and repair.

c. Multilevel parking garages designate separate floors by color:

   1st floor—blue
   2nd floor—green
   3rd floor—orange
   4th floor—red

d. Highways bypassing a city are color coded to indicate roads to follow around the city, for example:

Blue Belt
Green Belt
Orange Belt
Red Belt
Yellow Belt

   e. Color-banded catalog cards identify nonprint media in the school library card catalog.

3. Many products are designated by a code *number.*
   a. Paint is ordered by a code number.
   b. Recordings are ordered by a code number.
   c. Mail order companies assign a product-order number to each item listed in their catalogs.
   d. The *International Standard Book Numbering* System (ISBN) assigns an identity number to each book published in the United States and other English-speaking countries.
   e. U.S. and foreign postage stamps are designated by number in commercial and government stamp catalogs such as:
      (1) *Scott Stamp Catalogue: United States, United Nations, and Canada* (Scott)
      (2) *United States Stamps and Stories* (U.S. Postal Service)
   f. The *Universal Product Code* number (UPC) is a computer code number assigned to and appearing on the label of each product manufactured and/or distributed in the United States.

4. Telephone area codes are three-digit numbers designating localities.
   a. Area codes for local and long-distance calling are located in the preliminary pages of the white section of the telephone book.
   b. Placing international telephone calls involves
      (1) First, dialing the international access code: 011.
      (2) Next, the country code (a two-or-three digit number).
      (3) Then, the city code (a one-to five-digit number).
      (4) Then, the local number.

5. The *Zoning Improvement Plan*—better known as ZIP code—has been devised by the U.S. Postal Service to increase postal efficiency.
   a. ZIP codes for an area are listed in the local telephone book.
   b. ZIP codes for all post offices in the United States are listed in *The United States Postal Office National ZIP Code and Post Office Directory* (U.S. Postal Service).
   c. *The World Almanac and Book of Facts* includes a table identifying the ZIP code and telephone area codes for all U.S. places of 5,000 or more population.

6. The Morse code is an arbitrary set of signals used to send messages via telegraph; the unit of the code is the *dot,* representing a very brief depression of the telegraph key; the *dash* represents a depression lasting three times as long as the dot.
   a. The International Morse Code is as follows (all but the starred letters are the same in the American Morse Code):

```
A · -          N - ·
B - · · ·       *O - - -
*C - · - ·      *P · - - ·
D - · ·        *Q - - · -
E ·            *R · - ·
*F · · - ·      S · · ·
G - - ·        T -
H · · · ·       U · · -
I · ·          V · · · -
*J · - - -      W · - -
K - · -        *X - · · -
*L · - · ·      *Y - · - -
M - -          *Z - - · ·
```

b. The American Morse Code differs from the International Morse Code as follows:

```
C · ·  ·       Q · · - ·
F · - ·        R · · ·  ·
J - · - ·      X · - · ·
L · · · · ·    Y · ·  · ·
O ·  ·        Z · · ·  ·
P · · · · ·
```

7. The Dewey decimal system of classification is a library media location code.

   a. Nonfiction is assigned a classification number that indicates the subject matter of the book.

   b. The 10 major classes of the Dewey decimal classification system are:

000	General Works	500	Pure Sciences
100	Philosophy	600	Technology
200	Religion	700	The Arts
300	Social Sciences	800	Literature
400	Language	900	Geography and History

   c. A handy portable guide to the Dewey decimal classification system is the *Library Flipper* (Christopher Lee). This convenient guide lists 540 major classes, divisions, sections, and subsections.

XII. Group exploration of the concept of the school library as a communications laboratory.

   A. The group discusses the following:

   1. The library is much more than a materials storehouse; it is a laboratory where students and teachers work with ideas latent in library media.

      a. A laboratory is a facility for research, for testing, for experimenting.

      b. Library media are not things but are carriers of knowledge.

         (1) Printed resources—books, newspapers, periodicals, and the like—are the traditional library media.

         (2) Nonprint resources—art prints, study prints, filmstrips, slides, motion pictures, disc and tape recordings, overhead projection transparencies, models, realia, multimedia kits, and the like—are contemporary library carriers of knowledge of proven effectiveness and worth.

      c. Open-ended learning utilizes all types and kinds of media appropriate to the topic being researched.

  2. The school librarian is a teacher whose subject is learning itself.

      a. The school librarian gives guidance not only in locating information but especially in how to work with ideas and communicate information gained.

      b. The school librarian welcomes opportunities to guide students in searching for answers to personal quests as well as to academic quests for information.

  3. Using the resources of the library intelligently and creatively can widen, deepen, and intensify learning.

B. The group identifies the basic skills involved in using the library and its resources intelligently, such as:

  1. Using the card catalog as a key to locating materials.

  2. Using the title page to identify:

Author(s)	Edition
Editor(s)	Translation
Compiler(s)	Publisher
Illustrator(s)	Place of publication
Abridgement	Imprint date

  3. Using the verso of the title page to identify:

Date of first and subsequent copyrights
Owner(s) of copyright
Place of copyright registration

  4. Using the table of contents to identify:

Titles of chapters
Sequence of chapters
Pages of chapters, appendixes, lists of maps, lists of illustrations, glossary, bibliography, and index

  5. Using preliminary information:

End papers	Preface
Frontispiece	Foreword
Dedication	Introduction

  6. Using the index to discover:

Subjects or topics
Cross references to key topics

  7. Going about the task of knowledge building in a logical, systematic way.

      a. Preparing an outline of what needs to be learned, such as: who, what, where, when, and why important.

      b. Reading, thinking, questioning, and summarizing.

      c. Asking oneself the questions, Have I completed my search? Do I need to do more?

XIII. Group exploration of the concept of the museum as a communications agent.

A. Students view and then discuss the sound filmstrip set *A Museum Is a Place to Learn* (Random—each 1 filmstrip and 1 cassette)

  1. *Introducing Museums*

  2. *Learning about Science in Museums*

      3. *Learning about History in Museums*

      4. *Learning about Geography in Museums*

      5. *Learning about Art in Museums*

      6. *Small Museums*

B. Students explore the Smithsonian Institution as the prototype of a museum as a place to learn.

    1. Using the handbook *Official Guide to the Smithsonian* (Smithsonian, 1981) as a guide, students discover that:

      a. The Smithsonian Institution is the largest complex of museums in the world with holdings in every area of human interest totaling more than 75 million objects and specimens.

      b. The National Air and Space Museum highlights:

> Milestones of Flight: Kitty Hawk Flyer, *Spirit of St. Louis,* Friendship 7, Explorer I, Goddard Rockets, Pioneer 10, Apollo 11, and Lunar Exploration Vehicles
>
> Sea-air operations
> World War I aviation
> World War II aviation
> Flight technology

      c. The National Museum of Natural History highlights:

> Fossils: The History of Life
> African, Asian, and Pacific Cultures
> Splendors of Nature
> Dynamics of Evolution
> Eskimo and Indian Cultures
> Birds
> Sea Life
> Mammals
> Minerals and Gems
> Western Civilization: Origins and Traditions
> Prehistoric North American Cultures
> South America: Continent and Culture

      d. The National Museum of American History highlights:

> The Star-Spangled Banner
> First Ladies' Gowns
> Whitney's Cotton Gin
> Edison's Light Bulb
> Ford's Model T
> Foucault Pendulum
> Hall of Electricity
> Folk Art
> Computers
> Medical Science
> Iron and Steel
> Textiles
> Atom Smashers
> Everyday Life in America's Past

    2. The National Gallery of Art provides (at no cost) extension programs for schools. These programs* include:

      a. Color slide programs such as: *700 Years of Art, Survey of American Painting; Paintings of the Great Spanish Masters;*

---

*Contact the Extension Service, National Gallery of Art, Washington, D.C. 20565 for the descriptive catalog *National Gallery of Art Extension Programs.*

> *Famous Men and Women in Portraits, African Art; Treasures of Tutankhamun; Color and Light in Painting; The Far North: 2000 Years of American Eskimo and Indian Art;* and *Thomas Jefferson and the Arts*

    b. Motion pictures such as: *The National Gallery of Art; Leonardo: To Know How to See; Treasures of Tutankhamun; Mobile, by Alexander Calder;* and *Adventures in Art*

XIV. Group exploration of the concept of the computer as a communications agent.

  A. Students use the 1982 *World Book* reprint *Computer** to build background knowledge of the computer, including the following topics:

    1. Uses of the computer in

> Business and industry
> Government and law enforcement
> The military
> Engineering
> The sciences
> Fine arts
> Education
> The home

    2. Kinds of computers

> Digital
> Analog
> Hybrid

    3. Parts of a digital computer

> Input equipment
> Main memory
> Control unit
> Arithmetic/logic unit
> Output equipment

    4. Programming a digital computer

> Preparing a program
> Using programming languages

    5. The computer industry

> Research and development
> Manufacturing
> Sales
> Service and repair

    6. Development of the computer

    7. Careers

> Computer engineering
> Computer science
> Computer operations

  B. Students extend their knowledge of computers by viewing and discussing the sound filmstrip set *All about Computers* (dist. by Charles Clark—4 filmstrips, 4 cassettes)

---

*Available from Childcraft, Inc., Chicago at 25 cents each, up to 19 copies; 20 cents each for 20 copies and above.

Part 1—What Are Computers?
Part 2—How Do They Work?
Part 3—Communicating with Computers
Part 4—All Kinds of Output

C. Students, using the Texas Instrument computer program LOGO, build their knowledge of computer language and have the hands-on experience of discovering how computers work and what computers can do.

XV. Group exploration of creative communication.
A. Students define creative communication as producing, fashioning, inventing, or expressing messages that are characterized by originality of thought and execution.
1. Jacolyn A. Mott, in *Creativity and Imagination: A Creative Understanding Book* (Creative Education, 1973), provides insight into creative communication in the chapter entitled, "Magic of the Mind."
a. The power of creativity is to form new ideas, to invent, to discover.
b. Psychologists believe that creativity occurs in four steps:
(1) Preparation—a time of gathering facts.
(2) Incubation—a time of organizing the ideas gathered during preparation and then of comparing and combining this material with facts and ideas previously known.
(3) Inspiration—a sudden solution to a problem or insight into new patterns of thought and action.
(4) Verification—a time of testing, evaluating, and critical appraisal.
c. No matter how sincere the desire to create, creativity can never happen without *imagination*.
(1) Imagination is the ability to form in the mind new ideas or pictures or plans.
(2) New ideas, pictures, and plans are like the images in a kaleidoscope—they constantly change, blend, emerge, and evolve.
d. Imagination needs information before it can create ideas; all learning prepares us for creativity; experience is one of the most important sources of raw material for creativity. Imagination makes all learning more effective; it is the magic ingredient of creative thinking.
2. The magic of creativity is the power both to form new ideas and to *communicate* them effectively.
B. Communicating creative ideas effectively is the major thrust of those productively engaged in many fields of endeavor, such as:

Advertising	Music
Architecture	Painting
Book illustration	Radio
Commercial art	Sculpture
Dance	Teaching
Fashion design	Television
Interior design	Textiles
Journalism	Theater
Literature	

C. As a group and/or individually, students search for examples of creative communication they judge to be noteworthy.

D. As a group and/or individually, students experiment with various modes of communication: producing, fashioning, inventing, or expressing ideas creatively.

XVI. Group exploration of literature as a form of creative communication.

   A. Students discuss and react to the following statements:

     1. "Literature is the direct communication between author-writer and reader; it is a very *private* conversation. . . . All the miracles of technology cannot surpass the miracle of this private pursuit. The imagination creates its own setting, the mind its own interpretation. The words are there to be read over and over, if one chooses, at any hour of the day or night" (Frances Clarke Sayers).

     2. "When you sell a man a book, you don't sell him just twelve ounces of paper and ink and glue—you sell him a whole new life" (Christopher Morley).

     3. "Tis the good reader that makes the good book" (Ralph Waldo Emerson).

   B. Students discuss what makes a book have lasting appeal.

     1. They define a *literary classic* as follows: a literary work of acknowledged worth that has lasting merit.

       a. A classic has certain hallmarks, such as:*

         (1) It is multidimensional in its appeal, capturing the reader's interest and imagination.

         (2) It is uncluttered, clean in its execution, and direct in telling a story.

         (3) It deals with issues and emotions that are timeless; it does not become dated.

         (4) The characters are "real" people; the writers are often both masters of human psychology and master artists with the written word.

         (5) It is well written, has a compelling style, and a beauty of language.

       b. Classics provide a common link between generations.

     2. They compile a list of titles recommended by parents, grandparents, neighbors, teachers, and other friends as classics too good to be passed by. Typical titles are:

       a. *The Adventures of Huckleberry Finn* by Mark Twain

       b. *The Adventures of Tom Sawyer* by Mark Twain

       c. *Alice's Adventures in Wonderland* by Lewis Carroll

       d. *Hans Brinker, or the Silver Skates* by Mary M. Dodge

       e. *Heidi* by Johanna Spyri

       f. *The Life and Strange Surprising Adventures of Robinson Crusoe* by Daniel Defoe

       g. *Little Women* by Louisa May Alcott

       h. *The Merry Adventures of Robin Hood* by Howard Pyle

       i. *Peter Pan* by James Barrie

*Adapted from Dewey W. Chambers, *Children's Literature in the Curriculum* (Chicago: Rand McNally, 1971), pp. 200–204.

        j. *The Secret Garden* by Frances H. Burnett

        k. *The Story of King Arthur and His Knights* by Howard Pyle

        l. *Swiss Family Robinson* by Johann R. Wyss

        m. *Twenty Thousand Leagues under the Sea* by Jules Verne.

    3. They explore together the possibility of sharing with their classmates the classics they have read. They discuss possible approaches to follow in "selling" their classmates on reading the *best* in literature; they consider:

        a. Using the public address system to highlight television shows such as "Once Upon a Classic."

        b. Planning and carrying out assembly programs to highlight Book Week and Library Week.

        c. Organizing a Great Books Club.

  C. Students experiment with creative writing.

    1. They examine copies of the magazine *Chart Your Course* (a quarterly by and for gifted and talented children).

    2. They share with the group the poems, short stories, myths, legends, biographies, plays, and so on, they have written.

  D. They discuss the possibility of electing to devote their next learning project to the exploration of creative writing. An overview of the Learning Project: Creative Writing is presented by the teacher.

XVII. Group exploration of the U.S. Postal Service: its history, its services, its stamps.

  A. The latest issue of the U.S. Postal Service publication *Stamps and Stories: The Encyclopedia of U.S. Stamps* serves as the basic resource for building students' background knowledge.

  B. *Stamps and Stories* highlights the following:

    1. *Philately* is the collecting or study of stamps. There are over 20,000,000 philatelists in the United States.

    2. Introduction to stamp collecting.

How to begin.	Stamp color guide.
Types of stamps.	Stamp collector terms.
Equipment and tools.	Definition of catalog prices.
Stamp conditions.	

    3. Price trends of selected stamp issues.

    4. How to use *Stamps and Stories*.

    5. Commemorative and definitive postage stamps.

    6. Air mail postage stamps, special delivery postage stamps.

    7. Registration, certified mail stamps, postage due stamps.

    8. Official postage stamps.

    9. Newspaper stamps, parcel post stamps.

   10. Confederate States of America.

   11. Major U.S. philatelic publications and societies.

   12. Specialty collecting.

   13. Plate number block, sheet and first day cover prices.

   14. Postal stationary.

   15. Important dates in U.S. postal history.

   16. Souvenir cards.

   17. Commemorative panels.

   18. Stamp clubs.

19. U.S. Postmasters General.
20. Souvenir pages.
21. U.S. stamp production.
22. Commemorative stamps—quantities issued.
C. Students discuss the possibility of forming a stamp club.
1. The Benjamin Franklin Stamp Club program is explored.
   a. This stamp club is sponsored by the U.S. Postal Service. By 1980 more than 1.1 million students were members of this club.
   b. The purpose of the club is to:
      (1) Study about stamps.
      (2) Collect stamps.
      (3) Share information about stamps with others.
2. A stamp collector from the community is invited to share with the group his or her knowledge of stamp collecting as a hobby and as an investment.

XVIII. Group exploration of communications careers.
A. Students compile a list of communications careers with which they are familiar. Typical careers included are:

> Advertising: copy writer, illustrator, salesperson
> Author, writer, editor, publisher
> Cartoonist
> Cinematographer
> Commercial artist
> Commercial photographer
> Communications engineer
> Computer programmer
> Disc jockey
> Journalist
> Minister, priest, rabbi
> Museum docent
> Printer
> Teacher
> Telephone operator
> Television or radio announcer, script writer,
>   program director
> Travel agent

B. Students peruse the *Dictionary of Occupational Titles* (U.S. Department of Labor) to discover other careers in communications.
1. Individual students research careers of interest. After building background knowledge, individual students are scheduled to interview persons involved in careers of special interest.
2. Students as a group formulate questions to be asked during an interview.
3. Students spell out the basic rules of interviewing:
   a. Preschedule all interviews.
   b. Specify: the purpose of the interview, when you will begin and terminate the interview, basic questions to be asked.
   c. If a tape recorder is to be used, ask permission before the interview.
   d. When the interview is completed, courteously thank the resource person.
   e. Send a written note of appreciation indicating not only your

appreciation of the time spent but especially the value of the information received.

C. If the classroom teacher wishes, students share with their classmates information about communications careers.

XIX. Group exploration of the challenge of the future.
  A. The students read and discuss the book *Future Communication*.
    1. The statement that follows is used as a point of orientation:

    > In the past, predicting the future was an intellectual game. Sometimes the predictions came true. More often they didn't.

    > Today there is a new branch of science developing throughout the world. The people working in this field are called "Futurists." They are recognized as top experts in their fields. No one can say positively what the world will be like in the twenty-first century. But the Futurists are making some exciting predictions.*

    2. A statement attributed to George Bernard Shaw is discussed:

    > You see things; and you say, "Why?" But I dream things that never were; and I say, "Why not?"

    3. The following topics are explored in the light of future improvements and possibilities:
      a. Tomorrow's newspapers and magazines.
      b. Future libraries.
      c. Electronic meetings: state, national, international.
      d. People to people: telephone, videotape, television.
      e. Television, computers, and education.
      f. Space communication.
  B. The National Aeronautics and Space Administration (NASA) publication *Space Settlements: A Design Study* (NASA, 1977) is employed as a case study of how futurists in the field of space act and react when predicting the future.
  C. The recording *A Report on the Kurzweil Reading Machine for the Blind* (Kurzweil) is played for the group.
    1. The Kurzweil Reading Machine is a recent breakthrough in enabling the blind to "read."
    2. Students experiment with reading Braille—a system of printing for the blind in which the characters consist of raised dots to be read by the fingers.
    3. Students compare the two systems—Kurzweil Reading Machine and Braille—to have a basis for judging the real value of the reading machine over the Braille system.
  D. Students share their predictions about communications improvements and innovations in the future.

XX. Group exploration of the concept of self-communication.
  A. Students define the term *introspection* as looking into one's own mind, feelings, beliefs, actions, reactions, values, and goals.
    1. They discuss the implications of Shakespeare's admonition: "To thine own self be true, and it must follow, as the night the day, thou canst not then be false to any man." (*Hamlet,* Act I).
    2. They extend their understanding of introspection by discussing Cervantes' recommendation: "Make it thy business to know

*Harriette S. Abel, *Future Communication* (Mankato, Minn: Crestwood House, 1980), p. 5.

thyself, which is the most difficult lesson in the world." (*Don Quixote,* Chap. 42).

    3. They consider the statement made by Diogenes, the Greek philosopher who lived circa A.D. 200: "When Thales was asked what was difficult, he said, 'To know one's self.' And what was easy, 'To advise another.' " (Bohn Classical Library, *The Lives and Opinions of Eminent Philosophers, Thales,* 9).

B. Students explore the relationship between maturity and self-knowledge. The following concepts are explored:
    1. Self-discipline demands a high level of maturity.
    2. Objectivity in judging oneself is extremely difficult to attain.
    3. Maturity substitutes foresight for hindsight, selflessness for selfishness, and self-discipline for self-indulgence.

C. Students discuss the value of recording one's thoughts and feelings in a journal.
    1. Keeping a journal where one records not only one's thoughts and feelings but also the contemporary scene has been commonplace in history, for example:
        a. Samuel Pepys, 1633–1703, meticulously recorded his observations, feelings, and reactions to people and events. Pepys wrote for himself alone; therefore, he was completely frank and honest in his *Diary.*
        b. Anne Frank recorded her thoughts and experiences during World War II in Nazi-occupied Holland. Anne hid with her family and others for two years until the Gestapo discovered them. Her diary, *Anne Frank: The Diary of a Young Girl* (Doubleday) is a classic.
    2. Students discuss the value to be accrued from honestly recording in a journal one's reactions to everyday happenings, as well as one's goals, achievements, defeats, and feelings.

D. Students explore the concept of taking a test as a means of self-communication. They discuss the following:
    1. What is the purpose of taking a test?
    2. Why do so many people become tense and nervous when under pressure?
    3. If self-evaluation were the purpose of taking a test, the following questions would be uppermost in the student's mind:
        a. What have I learned?
        b. How am I doing?
        c. Do I still need to spend more time on this topic or unit?

E. Students discuss the value of using a self-appraisal form such as Checklist 3-2: A Student Looks at Himself/Herself.
    1. Students complete the self-appraisal form (see Checklist 3-2 at the end of this model).
    2. Students share their reaction to self-evaluation as a means of self-communication.

XXI. Group consideration of possible culminating activities.
  A. Research topics for individual or group selection.
    1. Organizing a communications service club. Club activities could include:

    a. Planning, scheduling, publicizing, and carrying out assembly programs.

    b. Reading announcements over the school's intercom.

    c. Preparing a weekly or monthly calendar of school and community events.

2. Photographing examples of communicated messages found in the community. Typical examples are:

Church bulletin boards	Store displays
Outdoor advertising billboards	Political posters
Bumper stickers	

3. Compiling a reference file of logos such as:

Colophons
Emblems
Trademarks

4. Compiling a list of brand or product names that are excellent examples of the commercial use of descriptive language. Examples might include:

Children's Palace	Miracle Fabrics
Dairy Queen	Tastee Freeze
Eveready Batteries	Taster's Choice Coffee
Fit and Trim Dog Food	Wearever Cooking Utensils

5. Designing a pictorial dictionary for a special field of interest such as:

Baseball	Hockey
CB Radio	Mathematics
Football	Mythology
History	Space

6. Compiling a quick-reference directory of telephone numbers frequently needed in the home:

Ambulance service	Hospitals
Bakery	Library
Church	Minister, priest, rabbi
Department stores	Poison center
Doctors, dentists, veterinarians	Police
Drug stores	School district hotline, schools
Family/friends	Sports hotline
Fire company	Temperature
Garage	Theaters
Grocery stores	Time
Hardware stores	Weather

7. Designing a chart or series of charts conveying information graphically. Topics might include:

History of transportation
Metric signs and symbols
Steps to follow in critical thinking
Water-safety rules and procedures
Weather-predicting guidelines

8. Developing and taping a disc jockey program including narration and music.

9. Designing a poster or series of posters advertising events such as:

> Book Week/Library Week
> Careers workshop
> Charity fund-raising drive
> Health-arama
> Scouting jamboree
> Water sports exhibition

10. Setting up a dial-access information retrieval system. Possibilities include:

> Books by author, title, and subject
> Guide to birds, flowers, insects, trees, and so on
> Sport events
> Travel information

11. Preparing instructional programs for use with the Cyclo-teacher. (The Cyclo-teacher is a self-instructional teaching machine with programmed cycles for each of the disciplines on the elementary and junior high school levels. This machine and accompanying cycles are sold only by Field Educational Publications, Inc., 609 Mission St., San Francisco, Calif. 94105.) Suggested program topics include:

Acronyms	Insignia
Chemistry symbols and formulas	Logos
Codes	Russian alphabet
Colophons	Signs and symbols
Dewey decimal classification system	Time lines
Egyptian heiroglyphs	Trademarks
Elements of graph making	

12. Preparing a series of transparencies for use with the overhead projector. Possible kinds of transparencies are:

> Story illustrations
> Transvision maps, charts, graphs, or tables
> Solar schematics

13. Conducting interviews with experts in the field of communications to discover future trends; taping or videotaping the interviews; preparing a synopsis of the findings and reporting them in the school or community newspaper.

14. Preparing a commercial paint, fabric, or yarn catalog; originating descriptive names for the paint chips and fabric and yarn swatches.

15. Exploring and experimenting with the fundamentals of calligraphy.

16. Preparing a videotaped program explaining hand talk; highlighting finger spelling and sign language.

B. Field learning experiences for individual or group selection.

1. Senior high school complex

> Computer center
> Library: references collection, microfilms, slides, filmstrips, recordings, periodicals, multimedia kits
> OCLC networking center
> Television studio

2. Community resources

Airport communication center
Art gallery and/or museum
Commercial computer center
Newspaper electronic communication center
Public and/or university libraries
Radio and/or television studio
School for the blind and/or the deaf
Weather bureau

CHECKLIST 3-2   A STUDENT LOOKS AT HIMSELF/HERSELF

Show whether you agree or disagree with the statements by marking one of the spaces.

	Strongly Agree	Agree	Disagree	Strongly Disagree
1. I am a good athlete.	—	—	—	—
2. I am a good student.	—	—	—	—
3. I am popular with other students.	—	—	—	—
4. I am one who understands and accepts other people.	—	—	—	—
5. I am very sociable and know how to get along with people.	—	—	—	—
6. Other people recognize that I am an intelligent person.	—	—	—	—
7. I am warm and understanding.	—	—	—	—
8. I am easy to get along with.	—	—	—	—
9. I enjoy working with scientific and mechanical things.	—	—	—	—
10. I enjoy abstract or mathematical problems.	—	—	—	—
11. I am one who likes to work independently on special projects.	—	—	—	—
12. I enjoy debating/discussing ideas.	—	—	—	—
13. I enjoy "losing myself" in a good book or in imagination.	—	—	—	—
14. I have a good sense of humor.	—	—	—	—
15. My work is often quite original.	—	—	—	—
16. I am able to come up with a large number of ideas or solutions to problems.	—	—	—	—
17. I am able to take charge of planning a project.	—	—	—	—
18. I don't mind being different from other students.	—	—	—	—
19. I like to study subjects that are challenging or difficult.	—	—	—	—
20. I often use music, art, or drama to express my feelings.	—	—	—	—
21. I don't like to accept what someone else says without challenging it.	—	—	—	—

CHECKLIST 3-2 (cont.)

Show whether you agree or disagree with the statements by marking one of the spaces.

	Strongly Agree	Agree	Disagree	Strongly Disagree
22. I feel strongly about things and often express my feelings even if I think others will disagree.	—	—	—	—
23. I spend more time than I would need to on assignments because I enjoy the learning.	—	—	—	—

24. Here are six areas of talent. In which area do you see yourself as being most talented? Rank them as you see them applying to your abilities. (1) First talent area, (2) Second talent area, etc.

_____General intellectual ability

_____Specific academic aptitude (in one subject area, such as science, math)

_____Creative thinking

_____Leadership ability

_____Visual and performing arts.

_____Psychomotor ability (such as mechanical skills or athletic ability)

Model 4

Exploring the United States: Its History, Geography, Peoples and Culture—An Enrichment Acceleration Program

GRADES: 5–6

GOALS: The program goals are to provide continuing opportunity for the gifted student mainstreamed in a heterogeneous social studies program to work at a higher cognitive level: to delve deeply, to explore widely, to interpret creatively, and to communicate effectively; and to undertake a leadership role in sharing with his or her classmates the understandings gained.

OBJECTIVES

To implement the program goals:

Provide ample opportunity for the gifted student to realize his or her potential to the fullest.

Provide the freedom, responsibility, and guidance basic for the gifted student to manage his or her time wisely.

Encourage the gifted student to accept leadership responsibilities.

Encourage the gifted student to develop creative thinking and expression.

Encourage the gifted student to develop positive feelings toward things of beauty and consequence.

Encourage the gifted student to respect divergent views and to disagree without being disagreeable.

Encourage the gifted student to seek alternate solutions to problems prior to action.

Encourage the gifted student to master and practice the inquiry method of thinking.

Encourage the gifted student to explore career opportunities commensurate with his or her abilities, interests, and aspirations.

To provide learning experiences that will enable the gifted student to become:

Alive to architecture and the arts.

Alive to beauty in nature.

Alive to the power and beauty of language and literature.

Alive to the promise of the future.

Alive to the power of positive thought and action.

Alive to the promise of personal excellence.

Alive to the challenge of probing beyond the threshold of knowledge.

Atune to the challenge and responsibility of self-actualization.

Atune to the needs of fellow human beings.

Atune to the global view of events, concerns, and societal needs.

Aware of the inevitability of change.

Aware of the tides of justice.

Aware of what it really means to be an American.

Aware that freedom is never secure.

Aware that the past is prologue to the future.

Aware that each person is answerable for his or her own actions.

Aware that people do make a difference.

Aware of the impact on society of science and technology.

Aware that life on this planet is imperiled by destructive actions of human beings.

INTRODUCTION

This course, Exploring the United States: Its History, Geography, Peoples, and Culture, is designed as a year's work totaling 180 days. The time allotment will vary from school to school and from teacher to teacher. A typical unit and time sequence might be:

Semester 1:   5 days, Orientation to Exploring the United States: Its History, Geography, Peoples, and Culture
25 days, Unit I, Colonial America and the War for Independence
30 days, Unit II, The Northeast
30 days, Unit III, The South and the Civil War

Semester 2:   20 days, Unit IV, The Midwest and the Great Plains
30 days, Unit V, When Roads Led West
30 days, Unit VI, The West
10 days, Unit VII, This Land Is Ours: Its Past Is Prologue to the Future

The textbook used as prototype for this program is *The United States* by Jerry E. Jennings, Marion H. Smith, and Walter Havighurst (Grand Rapids, Mich.: Fideler, 1982). The text is divided into eight major sections.

I. The Northeast
Part 1—Land and Climate: (1) A Global View, (2) Land, (3) Climate

Part 2—People: (4) People, (5) Cities, (6) Citizenship and Government, (7) The Arts

Part 3—Earning a Living: (8) Farming, (9) Natural Resources and Energy, (10) Industry

Index

II. The South

Part 1—Land and Climate: (1) A Global View, (2) Land, (3) Climate

Part 2—People: (4) People, (5) Cities, (6) Citizenship and Government, (7) The Arts

Part 3—Earning a Living: (8) Farming, (9) Natural Resources and Energy, (10) Industry

Index

III. The Midwest and the Great Plains

Part 1—Land and Climate: (1) A Global View, (2) Land, (3) Climate

Part 2—People: (4) People, (5) Cities, (6) Citizenship and Government, (7) The Arts

Part 3—Earning a Living: (8) Farming, (9) Natural Resources and Energy, (10) Industry

Index

IV. The West

Part 1—Land and Climate: (1) A Global View, (2) Land, (3) Climate

Part 2—People: (4) People, (5) Cities, (6) Citizenship and Government, (7) The Arts

Part 3—Earning a Living: (8) Farming, (9) Natural Resources and Energy, (10) Industry

Index

V. Pictorial Story of Our Country

Our Country

1. People Build Communities in America

Who were the first Americans?

How did Europeans learn about America?

What part did the Spanish play in settling America?

Which lands were settled by the French, Dutch, and Swedish?

Why did the English decide to start settlements in America?

What was life like in the British colonies?

2. The American Communities Form a Nation

How did Britain win control of France's lands in North America?

Why were the American colonists unhappy under British rule?

How did the colonists gain their independence?

What kind of government was established in the new nation?

3. The Nation Grows

How did life in America change during the early 1800s?

How did the United States gain land west of the Mississippi?

Why did many people come to the western part of our country?

4. The Union Is Saved

How did the United States become a divided country?

How did the Civil War affect our country?

5. Our Country Becomes a World Leader

How did the United States become a great manufacturing nation?

How did great cities grow up in the United States?

How did the United States become involved in world problems?

6. Years of Amazing Change

How have science and industry changed American life?

How has concern for human needs changed American life?

VI. Skills Manual

1. Thinking—seven kinds

Remembering	Analysis
Translation	Synthesis
Interpretation	Evaluation
Application	

2. Solving problems
    Choose an important, interesting problem.
    Think about all possible solutions.
    Test your hypotheses.
    Summarize what you have learned.
3. Learning social studies skills

What is a skill?	Making reports
Why are skills important?	Holding a group discussion
Developing a skill	Working with others
Written sources of information	Building your vocabulary
Other ways of getting information	Learning map skills
Evaluating information	

VII. Needs of People
 1. Physical needs
    Air
    Water
    Food
    Protection from heat and cold
    Sleep and rest
    Exercise
 2. Social needs
    Belonging to a group
    Goals
    A chance to think and learn
    A feeling of accomplishment
 3. The need for faith
    Faith in yourself
    Faith in other people
    Faith in nature's laws
    Religious faith
 4. Meeting needs in communities
VIII. Great Ideas That Built Our Nation
    1. Cooperation
    2. Loyalty
    3. Freedom
    4. Rules and government
    5. Using natural resources
    6. Using tools
    7. Division of labor
    8. Exchange
    9. Language
    10. Education

ORIENTATION

I. Students are introduced to the theme of this year's social studies program: Exploring the United States: Its History, Geography, Peoples, and Culture.
 A. Defining terms:
    1. *History*—a systematic, chronological account of important events connected with a country, people, individual, and so on, usually with an explanation of causes and effects.
    2. *Geography*—the study of the earth's surface, climates, physical features, countries, peoples, products, industries, and resources.
    3. *People*—a body of persons composing a community, tribe, or nation; emphasizes cultural and social unity, applying to a group

united by a common culture, common ideals, and a feeling of unity arising from common interests.

    4. *Ethnic group*—coming from or belonging to a distinctive cultural or national group.

    5. *Culture*—the civilization of a given race or nation; its customs, arts, aesthetic and intellectual achievements, and ideals.

  B. The basic textbook, *The United States,* is distributed, examined, and discussed.

    1. The qualifications of the three authors are read and evaluated.

    2. The Contents is examined and discussed; the term *conterminous* United States is defined in the Glossary.*

    3. The sequence and time allotted each unit are explained.

    4. The "Skills Manual" is studied with special attention being directed to: (a) holding a group discussion, and (b) working with others.

II. Students organize their loose-leaf notebooks for this course and include:

  A. *Title page*—name, homeroom, period assigned to social studies, room where class is held, name of the teacher.

  B. *Section dividers*—bristol board dividers with tabs labeled:

    Assignments
    Unit I—*Colonial America and the War for Independence*
    Unit II—*The Northeast*
    Unit III—*The South and the Civil War*
    Unit IV—*The Midwest and the Great Plains*
    Unit V—*When Roads Led West*
    Unit VI—*The West*
    Unit VII—*This Land Is Ours*
    Learning Guides
    Terminology
    Reference Tools
    Self-Evaluation Records

  C. The following mimeographed learning guides are distributed, discussed, and filed in the loose-leaf notebook in the section labeled "Learning Guides." (See Learning Guides 4-1, 4-2, and 4-3 at the end of this model.)

    Learning Guide 4-1—Guidelines for Holding a Group Discussion
    Learning Guide 4-2—Ways to Build and Share Information
    Learning Guide 4-3—Good Study Habits

III. Students are introduced to the concept of taking responsibility for their own learning and for sharing what they have learned with their classmates.

  A. The textbook is but the beginning of understanding.

  B. Each student should have the opportunity to read, view, listen, and explore far beyond the textbook.

  C. The concept of a student's choosing an area of specialization for continuous study throughout the entire course is discussed.

    1. The possible areas of specialization for this course are presented in checklist form (see Checklist 4-1 at the end of this model).

    2. The advantages and the disadvantages of concentrating on one area are discussed.

Conterminous—the 48 states of the United States that are enclosed in an unbroken boundary. The word *conterminous* means "having the same boundary."

3. Personal interest should be considered when choosing any topic for serious study.
4. Specialized study requires the ready availability of both print and nonprint resources.
   a. Basic tools will be available in the classroom in the study center (see Bibliography at end of this model).
   b. The school library will serve as a learning laboratory where the students will have a special research collection available for each of the units.
5. Students electing to pursue independent research study will be scheduled into the library to work. Freedom to work independently is granted those who use their time wisely.

UNIT I: COLONIAL AMERICA AND THE WAR FOR INDEPENDENCE

I. Information will be built by:
  A. Reading the textbook *The United States,* and answering and/or discussing the questions listed under the section heading "Discover Our Country's Story," pp. 19, 29.
    1. Why did the first people who lived in America become known as Indians?
    2. Why did people in Europe want to find an all-water route to Asia?
    3. How did Christopher Columbus hope to reach Asia? Was he successful? Explain your answer.
    4. What parts of the United States were settled by people from Spain?
    5. What happened to the Dutch and Swedish settlements in America?
    6. Why was Jamestown important in American history?
    7. Why did the Pilgrims decide to come to America?
    8. Why were there fewer farmers in New England than in the other colonies?
    9. Why were the Southern Colonies so well suited to farming?
    10. In colonial days, most people did not think it was wrong to own slaves. Why do you suppose they felt this way?
    11. Why were the English able to win the French and Indian War?
    12. Why did the colonists feel that the British Parliament had no right to tax them?
    13. How did the Revolution begin?
    14. What caused the British government to decide that it had lost the war in America?
    15. Why was a constitution needed for the United States? Is the Constitution still being used today? How can you find out?
    16. Why were some people against the new Constitution? Why were other people in favor of it? Which side won?
  B. Working in the school library to build understanding in these significant areas not introduced in the textbook:
    1. Colonial Americans at work

Architects	Potters
Blacksmiths	Printers
Cabinetmakers	Schoolmasters
Doctors	Shipbuilders
Farmers	Shoemakers
Glassmakers	Silversmiths
Hatters	Slaves
Indentured servants	Tanners
Papermakers	Weavers
Peddlers	Wigmakers

2. Colonial Americans at home

Homes	Favorite Recipes
Household tasks	Furniture
Kitchen	Children's Work
Heating the home	Women's work
Lighting the home	Men's work
Preparing and serving meals	Flower gardens

3. Colonial Americans at church

Sermons	Religious beliefs
Sunday restrictions	Power of the church

4. Colonial Americans at school

Dame schools	Curriculum
Hornbooks	Discipline

5. Colonial Americans at play

Husking bees
Spelling bees
Quilting bees

6. Colonial travel, transportation, and taverns

Boats, canoes, dugouts, ferries	Saddle horses
Toll roads	Work horses
Milestones	Coaches
Covered bridges	Wagons
Packhorses	Taverns

7. Colonial laws, courts, and punishments

Laws passed at town meetings
Ducking stools
Whipping posts
Stocks
Hangings
Salem Witch Trials
Trial of Peter Zenger
Trial of the British soldiers following the Boston Massacre

8. The American Revolution

Causes	Memorable events
Leaders	Outcomes
Campaigns	

II. Students explore the value of reading biography to gain historical background information.

A. The colonial biographies by Jean Fritz are researched as examples of the rich historical background found in well-written biography.

B. A bibliography of colonial biographies written by Jean Fritz (all published by Coward unless otherwise indicated) is distributed to the class. It highlights the following titles:

> *And Then What Happened, Paul Revere?* (1973)
>
> *Can't You Make Them Behave, King George?* (1977)
>
> *Cast for a Revolution: Some American Friends and Enemies, 1728–1814* (Houghton, 1972)
>
> *What Was Patrick Henry Doing on the 29th of May?* (1975)
>
> *What's the Big Idea, Ben Franklin?* (1976)
>
> *Why Don't You Get a Horse, Sam Adams?* (1974)
>
> *Will You Sign Here, John Hancock?* (1976)

C. The value of using a biography analysis form is discussed (see Learning Guide 4-4 at the end of this model).

III. Students explore the Colonial Americans series written and illustrated by Leonard Fisher. Titles in the series are (all published by Watts):

> *The Architects* (1970) *The Printers* (1965)
>
> *The Blacksmiths* (1976) *The Schoolmasters* (1967)
>
> *The Cabinet Makers* (1966) *The Shipbuilders* (1971)
>
> *The Doctors* (1968) *The Shoemakers* (1967)
>
> *The Glassmakers* (1964) *The Silversmiths* (1965)
>
> *The Hatters* (1965) *The Tanners* (1966)
>
> *The Homemakers* (1973) *The Weavers* (1966)
>
> *The Papermakers* (1965) *The Wigmakers* (1965)
>
> *The Peddlers* (1968)

IV. Students compare the Colonial Americans series with the books written and illustrated by Edwin Tunis that portray colonial history. Titles examined and discussed are (all published by Crowell):

> *Colonial Craftsmen: The Beginnings of American Industry* (1976)
>
> *Shaw's Fortune: The Picture Story of a Colonial Plantation* (1976)
>
> *The Young United States, 1783–1830* (1976)

V. Students explore the value of reading historical fiction to gain historical background knowledge.
   A. The following authors and novels are highlighted:
      1. James Collier and Christopher Collier (all published by Four Winds)

> *The Bloody Country* (1976)
>
> *My Brother Sam Is Dead* (1974), Newbery Award 1975
>
> *The Winter Hero* (1978)

FILMSTRIPS (both Miller-Brody)

Meet the Newbery Authors: James Lincoln Collier and Christopher Collier (1 filmstrip, 1 cassette)

My Brother Sam Is Dead (3 filmstrips, 3 cassettes)

2. Ann Finlayson (all published by Warne)

Greenhorn on the Frontier (1974)

Rebecca's War (1972)

Redcoats in Boston (1971)

3. Esther Forbes

Johnny Tremain: A Novel for Old and Young (Houghton, 1943; Newbery Award 1944)

FILMSTRIPS

Johnny Tremain (Disney—2 filmstrips, 2 cassettes or 2 records)

4. Jean Fritz (both published by Coward)

The Cabin Faced West (1958)

Early Thunder (1967)

5. Conrad Richter

The Light in the Forest (Knopf, 1966; paper, Bantam)

6. Elizabeth Speare (both published by Houghton)

The Calico Captive (1957)

The Witch of Blackbird Pond (1958; Newbery Award 1959)

FILMSTRIPS

The Witch of Blackbird Pond (Miller-Brody—1 cassette or 1 record)

B. The value of using a historical novel analysis form is discussed (see Learning Guide 4-5 at the end of this model).

VI. Culminating Activities.

A. The Media Committee presents nonprint media to summarize and underscore basic concepts presented in the unit. (Note: This is a coveted committee assignment of special delight to the nonreaders in the class. The committee members are responsible for obtaining and setting up the necessary equipment and for introducing each filmstrip, motion picture, study print, and so on.)

1. The following filmstrips are presented and discussed:

   a. *America: Colonization to Constitution* (National Geographic—5 filmstrips, 5 cassettes, or 5 records)

   Penetrating the Wilderness
   The Colonies Mature
   Road to Independence
   Years of War: Lexington to Valley Forge
   Victory and Constitution

          b. *Life in Colonial America* (National Geographic—2 filmstrips, 2 cassettes)

            New England and the Middle Colonies
            The South

    2. The following motion pictures are presented and discussed (all Coronet)
        a. *Plymouth Colony*
        b. *Puritan Family of Early New England*
        c. *William Penn and the Quakers*

B. Individual students share their research findings with the class.
    1. Any student who wishes to present information places his or her name and special research topic on a mimeographed schedule form (see Checklist 4-2 at the end of this model). The students are encouraged to present information in a well-organized, effective, and, if possible, creative manner.
    2. The class enters into the discussion following the individual student's presentation.

C. The class compiles lists of recommended titles of biographies, histories, and novels for inclusion in the class journal "Exploring Our Nation."

D. Students are invited to write their reactions, impressions, and/or observations for inclusion in the class journal "Exploring Our Nation—Colonial America."

Unit II: The Northeast

I. Students identify the 12 states and 1 district comprising the Northeast and the abbreviation for each state.

    Connecticut—CT
    Delaware—DE
    District of Columbia—DC
    Maine—ME
    Maryland—MD
    Massachusetts—MA
    New Hampshire—NH
    New Jersey—NJ
    New York—NY
    Pennsylvania—PA
    Rhode Island—RI
    Vermont—VT
    West Virginia—WV

II. Students are introduced to the American Automobile Association (AAA) TourBooks, which should be kept readily available in the classroom study center.

A. AAA TourBooks are revised annually.

B. The following five TourBooks pertain to the Northeast:
    1. *Maine, New Hampshire, Vermont TourBook*
    2. *Connecticut, Massachusetts, Rhode Island TourBook*
    3. *New York TourBook*
    4. *New Jersey, Pennsylvania TourBook*
    5. *Mid-Atlantic States: Delaware, District of Columbia, Maryland, Vir-*

ginia, West Virginia (Note: Virginia is included in the unit The South)

C. Information under each state includes:
1. History
2. Geography
3. Things to know

Population	Highest point
Area	Time zone
Capital	Minimum age for drivers
Nickname	Holidays
Flower	Recreation information
Motto	State information centers

4. Economy
5. Major annual events
6. Recreation
7. What to see. Each major city is listed; identifies museums, libraries, universities, historic landmarks, monuments, and so on

D. Maps of major areas are included.

III. Students are introduced to the Enchantment of America series, rev. ed. (Chicago: Childrens, 1978).
A. This series is edited by Allan Carpenter, who has written 135 books.
B. This is a basic set of books; a book for each state in the Northeast will be available in the classroom study center.
C. The information in each book is grouped under the following section headings:
1. A True Story to Set the Scene
2. Lay of the Land
3. Footsteps on the Land
4. Yesterday and Today
5. Natural Treasures
6. People Use Their Treasures
7. Human Treasures
8. Teaching and Learning
9. Enchantment of the State
10. Handy Reference Section

IV. Students read the textbook and answer the questions or solve the problems posed by the textbook authors. For example:
A. Learn to Read Maps: Answer the following questions:
1. What is the "scale" of a map?
2. What does a map legend, or key, show?
3. What do the terms longitude and latitude mean?
4. What do the terms parallel and meridian mean?
5. What is a topographic map?
B. The Land—Imagine you are a geographer who has been asked to write a magazine article about a trip through the Northeast. Choose one of the following trips, or plan your own.
1. An automobile trip from New York City to the Adirondeck Mountains.

    2. A boat trip on the New York Barge Canal from Lake Champlain to Lake Erie.

    3. A helicopter trip from Philadelphia to Pittsburgh, Pennsylvania.

C. The Climate—Explore the climate of the Northeast:

    1. What facts help to explain why many areas of the Northeast receive heavy snowfall?

    2. How does the long growing season along the Atlantic coast help farmers here?

    3. Why is the climate along Lake Ontario and Lake Erie good for growing fruit?

    4. What is the climate like where you live? How does it affect your everyday life?

D. The People—People of many different races and nationalities have influenced life in our country. Eight of those people are listed below. Make a chart for your classroom that shows the national origin of each person and how he or she has influenced American life.

    1. John James Audubon

    2. Marian Anderson

    3. Arturo Toscanini

    4. Wernher von Braun

    5. Lin Yutang

    6. Maria Tallchief

    7. Knute Rockne

    8. Michael Pupin

E. Cities—New York City is an interesting place to visit. Do research in other sources about one or more of the following:

    1. The arts of New York City

    2. The United Nations

    3. The Statue of Liberty

    4. The Empire State Building

F. Citizenship and Government

    1. Seven important beliefs in a democracy:

        a. Every person is important.

        b. People have the right to govern themselves.

        c. Decisions should be made by majority vote.

        d. All citizens should have a chance to get a good education.

        e. Laws should be the same for all citizens.

        f. All people have certain rights that no one can take away.

        g. Citizens have responsibilities as well as rights.

    2. When you go home, read your daily newspaper. Or listen to a news report on radio or television. Take notes about some of the news stories of the day. Bring your notes to class, and be prepared to answer the following questions about each story:

        a. How does this news story relate to the seven beliefs that make democracy possible?

        b. Are the people in the news stories being loyal to the seven beliefs? Or are they acting against these beliefs? Explain your answer.

        c. Are the actions of these people making life better or worse for other citizens of our country? Give facts to support your answer.

G. The Arts—How do the arts of the Northeast help us to understand our country's history?

H. Earning a Living—Imagine you are a truck farmer in the Northeast and have been asked to write a story about your farm for a leading farm magazine. Before you write your story, you will need to do research. Take careful notes and then make an outline before you begin to write. Some of the things your readers will be interested in are:
1. Where your truck farm is located.
2. Why this is a good location.
3. What crops you grow.
4. How your farm products are sent to market and who buys them.
5. What kinds of work you do on the farm.

I. Natural Resources and Energy—All of us can help save energy in a number of different ways. Prepare to discuss the following questions with the other members of your class:
1. What things do you and your family use that need energy?
2. What are some of the ways you can help to save energy?

J. Industry—The Northeast is one of the most important regions in the United States and also of the world. Why is this true? In order to solve this problem you need to know how the growth of industry in the Northeast has been affected by:
1. Its location.
2. Its history.
3. The raw materials available.
4. The markets for manufactured goods.
5. Transportation routes.
6. The sources of power available.
7. The skills of the people.

V. Students elect to work in the school library to build understanding in these significant areas:
A. If the state in which the students reside is located in the Northeast, a depth study of that state should receive top priority.
B. Biographies of artists and sculptors such as:
1. George Catlin
2. Chester Daniel French
3. Winslow Homer
4. Norman Rockwell
5. Andrew Wyeth
6. N. C. Wyeth
C. Biographies of immigrants such as:
1. Irving Berlin
2. Andrew Carnegie
3. George Gershwin
4. Emma Lazarus
5. Pierre Charles L'Enfant
6. Joseph Pulitzer
D. Biographies of presidents:
1. John Adams—MA

    2. John Quincy Adams—MA
    3. Martin Van Buren—NY
    4. Millard Fillmore—NY
    5. Franklin Pierce—NH
    6. James Buchanan—PA
    7. Chester A. Arthur—VT
    8. Grover Cleveland—NY
    9. Theodore Roosevelt—NY
   10. Calvin Coolidge—VT
   11. Franklin Delano Roosevelt—NY
   12. John Fitzgerald Kennedy—MA
E. Biographies of first ladies:
    1. Abigail Smith Adams—MA
    2. Louise Catherine Johnson Adams—MD
    3. Hannah Hoes Van Buren—NY
    4. Anna Symmes Harrison—NJ
    5. Julia Gardner Tyler—NY
    6. Margaret Smith Taylor—MD
    7. Abigail Powers Fillmore—NY
    8. Caroline Carmichael McIntosh Fillmore—NJ
    9. Jane Means Appleton Pierce—NH
   10. Frances Folsome Cleveland—NY
   11. Mary Scott Harrison—PA
   12. Alice Hathaway Roosevelt—MA
   13. Edith Kermit Carow Roosevelt—CT
   14. Anna Eleanor Roosevelt Roosevelt—NY
   15. Jacqueline Lee Bouvier Kennedy—NY
   16. "Nancy" Robbins Davis Reagan—NY
F. Biographies of inventors and scientists:
    1. Alexander Graham Bell
    2. George Eastman
    3. Thomas A. Edison
    4. Robert Fulton
    5. Crawford Long
    6. George Pullman
    7. Isaac Singer
    8. Charles Steinmetz
    9. George Westinghouse
G. Biographies of literary greats:
    1. Louisa May Alcott
    2. Marguerite De Angeli
    3. Jean Fritz
    4. Robert Lawson
    5. Henry Wadsworth Longfellow
    6. Robert McCloskey
H. Biographies of musicians:
    1. Arthur Fiedler
    2. Stephen Collins Foster
    3. Henry Mancini
    4. Beverly Sills
    5. John Philip Sousa

VI. Culminating Activities.
    A. The Media Committee presents nonprint media to summarize and underscore basic concepts presented in the unit.
        1. The following filmstrips are presented and discussed (each Educational Enrichment Materials unless otherwise indicated):
            a. *Indians of the Northeast* (1 filmstrip, 1 cassette)
            b. *The New England States* (4 filmstrips, 4 cassettes)

> *Land and Climate*
> *Food from Land and Sea*
> *Economy and Industry*
> *History and People*

            c. *The Middle Atlantic States* (6 filmstrips, 6 cassettes)

> *Land and Climate*
> *Natural Resources*
> *Agriculture and Fishing*
> *Industry*
> *Transportation and Commerce*
> *History and People*

            d. **New York: The Nation's Largest City* (1 filmstrip, 1 cassette, 1 guide)
            e. **The Statue of Liberty* (1 filmstrip, 1 cassette)
            f. *The Liberty Bell* (1 filmstrip, 1 cassette)
            g. *Philadelphia: City of Brotherly Love* (1 filmstrip, 1 cassette)
            h. **Monuments of America* (Washington, D.C.) (4 filmstrips, 4 cassettes, 1 guide)

> *The Capitol*   *The White House*
> *The Lincoln Memorial*   *The Supreme Court*

            i. **National Gallery of Art* (Encyclopaedia Britannica—10 captioned filmstrips)
            j. **Washington: Our Nation's Capital—A Sound Filmstrip Tour* (2 filmstrips, 2 cassettes, 1 wall map, 6 spirit duplicating masters)
            k. **Washington, D.C.* (National Geographic—2 filmstrips, 2 cassettes)

> *Visiting Our Government Buildings*
> *Monuments and Museums*

        2. The following motion pictures are presented and discussed:
            a. *Ben Franklin—Portrait of a Family* (National Park Service)
            b. *Cape Cod* (National Park Service)
            c. *Portrait of a Coal Miner* (West Virginia) (National Geographic)
            d. *Portrait of a Fisherman* (Massachusetts) (National Geographic)
            e. *Portrait of a Steelworker* (Pennsylvania) (National Geographic)
            f. **Washington, D.C., Fancy Free* (National Park Service)
        3. The following recording of John Philip Sousa's marches is introduced: *On Parade: The Music of John Philip Sousa* (National Geographic—1 cassette or 1 record).
    B. Individual students share their research findings with the class.
        1. Any student who wishes to present information places his or her name and special research topic on a mimeographed schedule form (see Checklist 4-2). Students are encouraged to present information in a well-organized, effective, and, if possible, creative manner.

---

*Titles preceded by asterisks are presented as part of individual or committee reports when appropriate to the topic.

2. The class enters into the discussion following the individual student's presentation.

C. The "Let's Visit New York City" Committee shares with the class its impressions of the "Big Apple." The following are highlighted:

1. The Statue of Liberty National Monument, Upper New York Bay, on Liberty Island.

 a. The Statue of Liberty was given to the people of the United States by the people of France.

 b. The statue weighs 450,000 pounds, or 225 tons; the copper sheeting weighs 200,000 pounds.

 c. There are 167 steps from the land level to the top of the pedestal, 168 steps inside the statue to the head, and 54 rungs on the ladder leading to the arm that holds the torch.

 d. It is the tallest statue of modern times.

 e. A poem by Emma Lazarus, "The New Colossus," is graven on a tablet within the pedestal on which the statue stands.

 f. The American Museum of Immigration, at the base of the statue, traces the history of immigration into the United States.

 g. Nearby Ellis Island, gateway to America for more than 12 million immigrants from 1892 to 1954, was proclaimed part of the Statue of Liberty National Monument by President Johnson in 1965.

 h. The Statue of Liberty is a symbol of freedom to the peoples of the world; it is America's shrine of freedom.

2. The United Nations headquarters is located between First Avenue and Roosevelt Drive and East 42 Street and East 48 Street.

 a. The General Assembly Building, the Secretariat, and the Conference and Library buildings are all interconnected.

 b. There are 154 members of the United Nations; the list of the member nations is given in *The World Almanac and Book of Facts*.

 c. The General Assembly meets for about 14 weeks starting in mid-September; tickets to the visitors' gallery are available just before the meeting of the General Assembly.

 d. The leaflet *What Is the United Nations* (provided free of charge by the United Nations, Office of Public Information, Public Inquiries Unit), is distributed to the class, read, and discussed.

3. The theater district is known the world over as Broadway.

 a. It is centered in the Times Square area, between 41 and 55 streets from Eighth Avenue to the Avenue of the Americas (Sixth Avenue).

 b. Students present a skit based on the Broadway show *Annie;* the recordings from the Broadway production are available in the school library and may be borrowed for home use.

D. The "Let's Visit Washington, D.C." Committee shares with the class its impressions of the nation's capital.

1. Using the filmstrip sets *Monuments of America, National Gallery of Art, Washington: Our Nation's Capital,* and *Washington, D.C.* and the motion picture *Washington, D.C., Fancy Free,* the committee takes the class on a guided tour of Washington.

a. The committee organizes the tour; introduces each landmark; selects just those filmstrip frames germane to a specific landmark; indicates the location of each landmark on a wall map of Washington.

b. The committee extends the tour beyond the Lincoln Memorial, across the Potomac River to the Arlington National Cemetery, and highlights the following:

> The Tomb of the Unknown Soldier
> Arlington House, the home of Robert E. Lee
> The Confederate Memorial
> The grave of President John F. Kennedy
> The grave of Robert Kennedy
> Marine Corps War Memorial: Iwo Jima
> Mast of the Battleship *Maine*
> The grave of Pierre L'Enfant
> The grave of President William Howard Taft
> The grave of General John J. Pershing
> The grave of Rear Admiral Robert E. Peary
> The grave of Rear Admiral Richard E. Byrd

E. Students, using Learning Guide 4-6 (at end of model), Places I Would Like to Visit, indicate their choice of places to visit in the Northeast.

F. Students are invited to write their reactions, impressions, and/or observations for inclusion in the class journal, "Exploring Our Nation—The Northeast."

UNIT III: THE SOUTH AND THE CIVIL WAR

I. Students identify the 11 states that comprise the South and the abbreviation for each state:

Alabama—AL
Arkansas—AR
Florida—FL
Georgia—GA
Kentucky—KY
Louisiana—LA
Mississippi—MS
North Carolina—NC
South Carolina—SC
Tennessee—TN
Virginia—VA

II. Students are introduced to the American Automobile Association (AAA) TourBooks, which should be kept readily available in the classroom study center.

A. AAA TourBooks are revised annually.

B. The following six TourBooks pertain to the South:

1. *Mid-Atlantic States: Delaware, District of Columbia, Maryland, Virginia, West Virginia TourBook*

2. *Georgia, North Carolina, South Carolina TourBook*

3. *Alabama, Louisiana, Mississippi TourBook*

4. *Kentucky, Tennessee TourBook*

5. *Florida TourBook*

6. *Arkansas, Kansas, Missouri, Oklahoma TourBook*

    C. Information under each state includes:
        1. History
        2. Geography
        3. Things to know

            Population
            Area
            Capital
            Nickname
            Flower
            Motto
            Highest point
            Time zone
            Minimum age for drivers
            Holidays
            Recreation information
            State information centers

        4. Economy
        5. Major annual events
        6. Recreation
        7. What to see. Each major city is listed; identifies museums, libra-
            ries, universities, historic landmarks, monuments, and so on
    D. Maps of major areas are included.

III. Students are introduced to the Enchantment of America series, ed. by
      Allan Carpenter (Chicago: Childrens, 1978), which have been placed in
      the classroom study center.

IV. Students read the textbook and answer the questions or solve the prob-
     lems posed by the textbook authors. For example:
     A. The Land—Imagine that you have a pen pal in another country and
         that you want to tell your friend about the main land regions of the
         South. Do research in this book to discover the most important land
         and water features of each of the South's regions. Then write your pen
         pal a letter. Describe what you might see if you were to take a trip
         through these regions. Be sure to use words that will create pictures in
         your friend's mind.
     B. The Climate—Some parts of the Coastal Plain of the South receive
         more than 70 thunderstorms each year. Why do so many of these
         storms take place here? The following questions suggest hypotheses
         you will need to think about:
         1. How do the high temperatures in these parts of the Coastal Plain
             affect the forming of thunderstorms?
         2. How does warm moist air from the Gulf of Mexico and the Atlantic
             Ocean affect the formation of thunderstorms?
     C. The People—Explore population:
         1. About how many people live in the South?
         2. Which state of the South is one of the fastest-growing states in our
             country?
         3. Over the years, people from many countries have made their
             homes in the South. Name several of the countries from which
             these people have come.
     D. The Cities—Discover new cities: Choose a city in the South where you

would like to spend your summer vacation. What are some of the interesting places you would like to visit?

E. Citizenship and Government—In our country today, most people have a chance to get a good education. With the other members of your class, discuss the following question: Why is it important for people in a democracy to get a good education?

F. The Arts—A Problem to Solve: How do the arts of the South help us understand the people of the region? In forming hypotheses to solve this problem, you will need to think about the following:
    1. Southern painting and architecture.
    2. Literature of the South.
    3. Music of the South.
    4. Southern crafts.

G. Farming—Do research to find out what main crops are raised in the South. Also find out where these crops are grown. Then do the following:
    1. Trace an outline map of the South.
    2. Choose a symbol for each crop you want to show on your map.
    3. Draw the symbol for each crop in the right place on the map. The symbols should show where in the South each crop is grown.
    4. Include a key with your map.

H. Natural Resources and Engery—The South has valuable energy fuels and many other mineral sources. Do research about them, then make a mineral resource chart. In the first column of your chart, list the energy fuels and other mineral resources of the South. In the second column, list the states in the South in which each resource is found. In the third column, list some of the ways in which each resource is used.

I. Industry—An important forest-products industry in the South is the making of paper. How important is paper in your life? To answer this question, you may do the following:
    1. List some of the ways in which you and your family use paper and things made of paper, such as cups and envelopes.
    2. From old newspapers and magazines, cut out pictures that show the uses you have listed. Arrange the pictures in a display to share with your class.
    3. You and the other members of your class may wish to discuss what your lives might be like without paper and things made of paper.

V. Students elect to work in the school library to build understanding in these significant areas:
    A. If the state in which the students reside is located in the South, a depth study of that state should receive top priority.
    B. Slavery from 1619 to 1865.
        1. The following books are on reserve in the school library:
            a. *All Times, All Peoples: A World History of Slavery* by Milton Meltzer, illus. by Leonard Fisher (Harper, 1980)
            b. *Amos Fortune: Free Man* by Elizabeth Yates (Dutton, 1950; Newbery Award 1951)
            c. *Black Bondage: The Life of the Slaves in the South* by Walter Goodman (Farrar, 1969; firsthand reports)

    d. *Exploring Black America: A History and Guide* by Marcella Thum (Atheneum, 1975)

    e. *Flight to Freedom: The Story of the Underground Railroad* by Henrietta Buckmaster (Harper, 1958)

    f. *Harriet Tubman: Guide to Freedom* by Sam Epstein and Beryl Epstein (Garrard, 1968)

    g. *Human Cargo: The Story of the Atlantic Slave Trade* by Anne T. White (Garrard, n.d.)

    h. *In Their Own Words: A History of the American Negro* ed. by Milton Meltzer, 3 vols. (Crowell, 1964–1967; firsthand reports)

    i. *The Long Bondage* by James McCague (Garrard, 1972)

    j. *The Man Who Bought Himself: Peter Still* by Peggy Mann and Vivian Siegal (Macmillan, 1975)

    k. *The Road to Freedom* by James McCague (Garrard, 1972)

    l. *Slavery in the United States* by William Hine (Viking, 1976)

    m. *Slavery in the United States* by Leonard Ingraham (Watts, 1968)

    n. *To Be a Slave* by Julius Lester (Dial, 1968; paper, Dell; Newbery Honor Book 1969)

FICTION

    o. *Bimby* by Peter Burchard (Coward, 1968)

    p. *Dark Venture* by Audrey W. Beyer (Knopf, 1968)

    q. *Jump Ship to Freedom* by James Collier and Christopher Collier (Delacorte, 1981)

    r. *Slave Dancer* by Paula Fox (Bradbury, 1973; Newbery Award 1974)

    s. *Uncle Tom's Cabin* by Harriet Beecher Stowe (Houghton, n.d.)

2. The students are reminded to discover rich historical background information in both biography and historical fiction.

C. The Civil War.

  1. The following books are on reserve in the school library:

    a. *Abraham Lincoln in Peace and War* by Earl S. Miers and Paul M. Angle (American Heritage, 1964)

    b. *Across Five Aprils* by Irene Hunt (Follett, n.d.)

    c. *An Album of the Civil War* by William Katz (Watts, 1974)

    d. *The Blue and the Gray: The Story of the Civil War as Told by Participants* ed. by Henry S. Commager (Mentor, NAL, n.d.; paper)

    e. *Fifty Basic Civil War Documents* ed. by Henry S. Commager (Van Nostrand, 1965; paper)

    f. *The First Book of the Civil War* by Dorothy Levenson, rev. ed. (Watts, 1977)

    g. *Marching toward Freedom* by James McPherson (Knopf, 1968)

    h. *Military History of the Civil War Land Battles* by Trevor N. Dupuy, illus. by Leonard Fisher (Watts, 1960)

    i. *Military History of the Civil War Naval Action* by Trevor N. Dupuy, illus. by Leonard Fisher (Watts, 1960)

    j. *The Negro in American History* ed. by Mortimer J. Adler, 3 vols. (Encyclopaedia Britannica, 1972)

    k. *The Perilous Road* by William O. Steele (Harcourt, 1965; paper; Newbery Honor Award 1966)

      l. *Rifles for Watie* by Harold Keith (Crowell, 1957; Newbery Award 1958)

      m. *The Road to Fort Sumter* by LeRoy Hayman (Harper, 1972)

      n. *Runaway Balloon: The Last Flight of Confederate Air Force One* by Burke Davis (Coward, 1976)

  2. The following filmstrips (all Miller-Brody) are available:

      a. *Across Five Aprils* (2 filmstrips, 2 cassettes or 2 records)

      b. *The Perilous Road* (2 filmstrips, 2 cassettes)

      c. *Rifles for Watie* (2 filmstrips, 2 cassettes or 2 records)

D. Martin Luther King, Jr., and the civil rights movement.

  1. The following books are on reserve in the school library:

      a. *The Life and Death of Martin Luther King, Jr.* by James Haskins (Lothrop, 1977)

      b. *Martin Luther King: Fighter for Freedom* by Edward Preston (Doubleday, 1970)

      c. *Martin Luther King: The Peaceful Warrior* by Ed Clayton, 3rd ed. (Prentice-Hall, 1968)

      d. *Meet Martin Luther King* by James T. DeKay (Random, 1969)

  2. The biography of Martin Luther King, Jr., as reported in the *New York Times* is available on microfiche in the school library as part of the microfiche program *The New York Times Great Personalities,* pp. 50–51 (see Example 4-1 at the end of this model).

E. Biographies of presidents:

  1. George Washington—VA

  2. Thomas Jefferson—VA

  3. James Madison—VA

  4. James Monroe—VA

  5. Andrew Jackson—SC

  6. William Henry Harrison—VA

  7. John Tyler—VA

  8. James Knox Polk—NC

  9. Zachary Taylor—VA

  10. Abraham Lincoln—KY

  11. Andrew Johnson—NC

  12. Woodrow Wilson—VA

  13. Jimmy Carter—GA

F. Biographies of first ladies:

  1. Martha Dandridge Custis Washington—VA

  2. Martha Wayles Skelton Jefferson—VA

  3. Dolley Payne Todd Madison—NC

  4. Rachel Donelson Robards Jackson—VA

  5. Letitia Christian Tyler—VA

  6. Sarah Childress Polk—TN

  7. Mary Todd Lincoln—KY

  8. Eliza McCardie Johnson—TN

  9. Ellen Lewis Herndon Arthur—VA

  10. Ellen Louise Axson Wilson—GA

  11. Rosalynn Smith Carter—GA

G. Jazz, ragtime, and country music.

  1. The following books are on reserve in the school library:

      a. *Cutting a Record in Nashville* by Lani van Ryzin (Watts, 1980)

    b. *The Illustrated Encyclopedia of Country Music* by Fred Dellar, Roy Thompson, and Douglas B. Green (Harmony/Crown, 1977; also paper)

    c. *The Illustrated Encyclopedia of Jazz* by Brian Case and Stan Britt (Harmony/Crown, 1978; also paper)

    d. *Jazz* by Langston Hughes, rev. ed. (Watts, 1982)

    e. *Let's Hear It for America! Symbols, Songs, and Celebrations* ed. by Bennett Wayne (Garrard, 1969)

2. The following recording is available in the school library: *Dixieland Jazz* (National Geographic—1 cassette or 1 record).

VI. Culminating Activities.

  A. The Media Committee presents nonprint media to summarize and underscore basic concepts presented in the unit.

    1. The following filmstrips are presented and discussed (each Educational Enrichment Materials—1 filmstrip, 1 cassette, unless otherwise indicated):

      a. *The Everglades,* Small Worlds of Life series (National Geographic—1 filmstrip, 1 cassette)

      b. *Indians of the Southeast*

      c. *Miami/Atlanta: The New South*

      d. *Monticello*

      e. *Mount Vernon*

      f. *New Orleans/St. Louis: Mississippi River Cities*

      g. *The South* (National Geographic—2 filmstrips, 2 cassettes)

      h. *The South* (Society for Visual Education—6 filmstrips, 3 cassettes, 6 guides)

        Southern Appalachia: An Area Left Behind
        The TVA: Conservation in the Tennessee Valley
        Atlanta, Georgia: Progress and Problems
        Black People in the New South
        The Cajuns: A Fading Culture
        The Mississippi River: A Major Resource in a Changing Economy

    2. The following motion pictures are presented and discussed (each National Park Service unless otherwise noted):

      a. *The Everglades: Conserving a Balanced Community* (Encyclopaedia Britannica)

      b. *Lincoln: The Kentucky Years*

      c. *Living Waters of the Big Cypress* (The Big Cypress National Preserve, Florida)

      d. *Pa-Hay-Okee-Grassy Waters* (Everglades, Florida)

      e. *Sanctuary—The Great Smokey Mountains*

      f. *What's a Heaven For?* (Booker T. Washington)

  B. Individual students share their research findings with the class:

    1. Any student who wishes to present information places his or her name and special research topic on a mimeographed schedule form (see Checklist 4-2). Students are encouraged to present information in a well-organized, effective, and, if possible, creative manner.

    2. The class enters into the discussion following the individual student's presentation.

C. The "Slavery from 1619 to 1865" Committee shares with the class its findings and highlights the following biographies:
1. Mary McLeod Bethune
2. Frederick Douglass
3. Robert Smalls
4. Peter Still
5. Harriet Tubman

FILMSTRIPS
1. *Folk Songs and Frederick Douglass* (Schloat—6 filmstrips, 6 cassettes or 6 records, 1 guide)
2. *Leading American Negroes* (Society for Visual Education—6 filmstrips, 6 cassettes or 6 records, 6 guides)

D. The "Civil War" Committee shares with the class its findings and highlights the following biographies:
1. Jefferson Davis
2. Ulysses S. Grant
3. Robert E. Lee
4. Abraham Lincoln

FILMSTRIPS
1. *The Civil War* (Educational Enrichment Materials—5 filmstrips, 5 cassettes or 5 records, 1 guide)

> *A Nation Divided*
> *The Clash of Amateur Armies*
> *The Iron Vise Is Forged*
> *Gettysburg*
> *An Ending and a Beginning*

2. *The Divided House—The Second American Revolution* (Random—4 filmstrips, 4 cassettes)

The committee shares with the class its enjoyment of several historical fiction titles and filmstrips, such as:

3. *Across Five Aprils* by Irene Hunt (Follett, 1964; Newbery Award 1965) and *Across Five Aprils* (Miller-Brody—2 filmstrips, 2 cassettes, or 2 records)
4. *The Perilous Road* by William O. Steele (Harcourt, 1965; also paper; Newbery Honor Award 1966) and *The Perilous Road* (Miller-Brody—2 filmstrips, 2 cassettes)
5. *Rifles for Watie* by Harold Keith (Crowell, 1957; Newbery Award 1958) and *Rifles for Watie* (Miller-Brody—2 filmstrips, 2 cassettes, or 2 records)

E. The "Martin Luther King, Jr., and the Civil Rights Movement" Committee, using the following filmstrips, shares with the class its appreciation of Martin Luther King, Jr., as a spokesman for the civil rights movement:
1. *Martin Luther King, Jr.: I'd Give My Life for the Cause* (Educational Enrichment Materials—1 filmstrip, 1 cassette)
2. *Dr. Martin Luther King, Jr.* (Society for Visual Education—1 filmstrip, 1 cassette, 1 guide)

The committee introduces to the class the use of microfiche as a source of information on current events. The value of using the articles in the *New York Times* to gain understanding of Martin Luther King, Jr., and the civil rights movement (see Example 4-1) is shared with the class.

F. The "Jazz, Ragtime, and Country Music" Committee shares its findings with the class and highlights the following:
1. *Jazz: The Music of Black Americans* (Educational Dimensions—4 filmstrips, 4 cassettes, or 4 records)
2. *Scott Joplin: King of Ragtime* (Spoken Arts—4 filmstrips, 4 cassettes, 1 guide, 8 duplicating masters)

Members of the class are invited to bring their favorite jazz, ragtime, or country music recordings from home and share with the class.

The committee introduces the three separate *Schwann Record and Tape Guides* (all Schwann):

Schwann-1 Record and Tape Guide (rev. monthly)
Schwann-2 Record and Tape Guide (Fall and Winter supplement to *Schwann-1*)
Schwann Artist Issue (annual)

G. The "Let's Visit Williamsburg and Busch Gardens" Committee shares with the class its impressions. The following filmstrips are presented and discussed (Educational Enrichment Materials—2 filmstrips, 2 cassettes):
1. *Williamsburg: A New Capital*
2. *Williamsburg: Life in Colonial Virginia*

H. Students, using Learning Guide 4-6, Places I Would Like to Visit, indicate their choice of places to visit in the South.

I. Students are invited to share their reactions, impressions, and/or observations for inclusion in the class journal "Exploring Our Nation—The South."

UNIT IV: THE MIDWEST AND THE GREAT PLAINS

I. Students identify the 14 states that comprise the Midwest and the Great Plains and the abbreviation for each state.

Illinois—IL
Indiana—IN
Iowa—IA
Kansas—KS
Michigan—MI
Minnesota—MN
Missouri—MO
Nebraska—NE
North Dakota—ND
Ohio—OH
Oklahoma—OK
South Dakota—SD
Texas—TX
Wisconsin—WI

II. Students are introduced to the American Automobile Association (AAA) TourBooks, which should be kept readily available in the classroom study center.

A. AAA TourBooks are revised annually.

B. The following five TourBooks pertain to the Midwest and the Great
   Plains:
   1. *Illinois, Indiana, Ohio*
   2. *North Central: Iowa, Minnesota, Nebraska, North Dakota, South
      Dakota*
   3. *Michigan, Wisconsin*
   4. *Kansas, Missouri, Oklahoma*
   5. *Texas*
C. Information under each state includes:
   1. History
   2. Geography
   3. Things to know

Population	Highest point
Area	Time zone
Capital	Minimum age for drivers
Nickname	Holidays
Flower	Recreation information
Motto	State information centers

   4. Economy
   5. Major annual events
   6. Recreation
   7. What to see. Each major city is listed; identifies museums, libra-
      ries, universities, historic landmarks, monuments, and so on
D. Maps of major areas are included.

III. Students are introduced to the Enchantment of America series, ed. by
     Allan Carpenter (Chicago: Childrens, 1978), which have been placed in
     the classroom study center.

IV. Students read the textbook and answer the questions or solve the prob-
    lems posed by the textbook authors. For example:
    A. The Land—The Mississippi River and its tributaries form one of the
       largest river systems in the world. Do research about this great river
       system. Then, with a group of your classmates, draw pictures to make
       a wall mural. Show ways in which people have used the Mississippi
       River and its tributaries over the past 300 years. Books such as *Life on
       the Mississippi* by Mark Twain and *The Upper Mississippi* by Walter
       Havighurst will provide useful information. You might also like to
       make a map of the Mississippi River and its tributaries. On your map,
       show the states through which these rivers flow and the states they
       border. Print the names of these states on your map. You may also
       wish to show the names and locations of important port cities along
       these rivers.
    B. The Climate—A problem to solve: How does the climate of the Mid-
       west and Great Plains affect the people who live there? In forming
       hypotheses to solve this problem, you will need to think about the
       ways in which climate affects each of the following:
       1. The clothing people wear.
       2. The kinds of homes people live in.
       3. Transportation.
       4. Sports and recreation.

C. The People—Imagine you have taken a trip through parts of the Midwest and Great Plains. You began your trip in Milwaukee, Wisconsin, and went to Chicago, Illinois. Then, from Chicago you went to Sioux City, Iowa. Write a letter to a friend and tell what you saw. In your letter, you should tell about the following:
   1. A densely populated area.
   2. A thinly populated area.
   3. Some of the different people you saw.

D. The Cities—Make Discoveries about Cities:
   1. Which city in the Midwest and Great Plains is the most important transportation center in the United States?
   2. Which city is the largest city in the Great Plains states?
   3. Name two important cities in the Midwest and Great Plains that were founded by the French.
   4. Which city in the Midwest is famous for the manufacture of automobiles?
   5. Which states in the Midwest and Great Plains have cities with populations of 500,000 or more?
   6. Two cities in the Midwest and Great Plains have populations of 500,000 or more, and are also the state capitals. Which cities are these?
   7. Two states in the Great Plains have no cities with populations of 100,000 or more. Name these states. Why do you think these states have no large cities?

E. Citizenship and Government—Exploring Citizenship: Try to think of different situations in which people *are* or *are not* doing their part as citizens.
   Make a list with two columns. In the first column, give examples of citizens who are meeting their responsibilities. In the second column, give examples of citizens who are not meeting their responsibilities. Use newspapers, magazines, radio, and television to get the facts you need. For each example on your list, do the following:
   1. Give the facts about the situation. Also, tell where you got these facts.
   2. Tell how you feel about this situation. Are the people helping the community or are they hurting it? Explain.
   3. If the people are not meeting their responsibilities, tell what you think should be done about it. How can we get more people to do their part as citizens?
   When you have finished your research, share your findings with others in your class. Find out how they feel about the examples you have described. You may also want to present your findings in a written report.

F. The Arts—Mark Twain was a great American writer of the 1800s. Perhaps you have read *The Adventures of Tom Sawyer* and *The Prince and the Pauper*. In his works, Mark Twain expressed his ideas about people and the ways in which they live. Could he have shared his ideas without the use of language? Explain your answer. Do you think it is important for people to write books? To read books? Why? Why not?

G. Farming—Use Your Reasoning Ability: Choose a state in the Midwest and Great Plains that you, as a farmer, would find well suited to raising each of the following:

1. Spring wheat
2. Beef cattle
3. Corn
4. Cotton
5. Dairy cows
6. Winter wheat

Give reasons for each choice.

H. Natural Resources and Energy—Making a Minerals Chart: The Midwest and the Great Plains have many valuable minerals. Do research about them and make a chart. Your chart should have two columns. In the first column, name the minerals found in the Midwest and Great Plains. In the second column, tell some of the ways in which these minerals are used. Share your chart with your class.

I. Industry—Choose a Place to Build: Imagine that you are a businessperson who would like to build a manufacturing plant in the Midwest and Great Plains. Choose one of the following plants and decide the best location for it.

1. Automobile plant
2. Farm machinery plant
3. Steel mill
4. Oil refinery

In choosing the place to build your plant, you will have to think about:

1. Location of raw materials
2. Supply of workers
3. Transportation routes

V. Students elect to work in the school library to build understanding in these significant areas:

A. If the state in which the students reside is located in either the Midwest or the Great Plains region, a depth study of that state should receive top priority.

B. The automobile industry in the United States.

1. The following books are on reserve in the school library:

a. *Antique Car Models* by Frank Ross, Jr. (Lothrop, 1978)
b. *Antique Cars* by Robert B. Jackson (Walck, 1976)
c. *Automobile Factory* by Melvin Berger (Watts, 1977)
d. *Car Facts and Feats* ed. by Anthony Harding (Sterling, 1977)
e. *Classic Sports Cars* by Richard L. Knudson (Lerner, 1979)
f. *Electric Cars* by E. John DeWaard and Aaron E. Klein (Doubleday, n.d.)
g. *Fabulous Cars of the 1920's and 1930's* (Lerner, 1978)
h. *Famous Custom and Show Cars* by George Barris and Jack Scagnetti (Dutton, 1973)
i. *First Book of Automobiles* by Jeanne Bendick, 2nd rev ed. (Watts, 1978)
j. *Henry Ford: Automotive Pioneer* by Elizabeth R. Montgomery (Garrard, 1969)

    k. *Historic Racing Car Models: Their Stories and How to Make Them* by Frank Ross, Jr. (Lothrop, 1976)

    l. *How Will We Move All the People? Transportation for Tomorrow's World* by Sterling McLeod and the Editors of Science Book Associates (Messner, 1971)

    m. *Model Cars* by Richard L. Knudson (Lerner, 1981)

    n. *New Automobiles of the Future* by Irwin Stambler (Putnam, 1978)

    o. *The Roads We Travel: An Amusing History of the Automobile* by Douglas Waitley (Messner, 1979)

    p. *Supercars* by John Navarra (Doubleday, 1975)

    q. *The Tin Lizzie: A Model-Making Book* by Frank Ross, Jr. (Lothrop, 1980)

    r. *Transportation in the World of the Future* by Hal Hellman (Evans/Dutton, 1974)

    s. *Unusual Automobiles of Today and Tomorrow* by Irwin Stambler (Putnam, 1972)

    t. *Yesterday's Cars* by Paul R. Dexler (Lerner, 1979)

2. The following books on American invention and technology are introduced at this time:

    a. *How to Be an Inventor* by Harvey Weiss (Harper, 1980)

    b. *The Invention of Ordinary Things* by Don L. Wuffson (Lothrop, 1981)

    c. *Man with a Million Ideas: Fred Jones, Genius Inventor* by Virginia Ott and Gloria Swanson (Lerner, 1976)

    d. *New Trail Blazers of Technology* by Harland Manchester (Scribner, 1976)

    e. *Shortchanged by History: America's Neglected Inventors* by Vernon Pizer (Putnam, 1979)

    f. *Why Didn't I Think of That: From Alarm Clocks to Zippers* by Webb Garrison (Prentice-Hall, 1977)

FILMSTRIP

    g. *Yankee Inventiveness and Test Tube Miracles* (Educational Enrichment Materials—1 filmstrip, 1 cassette)

C. Cowboys and cattle drives.

1. *The Cowboy Trade* by Glen Rounds (Holiday, 1972)

2. *Cowboys and Cattle Country* by Don Ward and J. C. Dykes (American Heritage, 1961)

3. *Cowboys and Cattle Drives* by Edith McCall (Childrens, 1980)

4. *Famous American Cowboys* by Bern Keating (Rand, 1977)

5. *Greatest Cattle Drive* by Paul I. Wellman (Houghton, 1964)

D. The history and importance of the buffalo.

1. *Buffalo Harvest* by Glen Rounds (Holiday, 1952)

2. *The Indian and the Buffalo* by Robert Hofsinde (Morrow, 1961)

3. *Indian Hunting* by Robert Hofsinde (Morrow, 1962)

4. *The Wildlife of North America* by George F. Mason (Hastings, 1966)

FILMSTRIP

5. *The North American Buffalo* (McGraw—1 filmstrip)

STUDY PRINT

6. *"The Bison"* ("Large Animals of North America" set) (Society for Visual Education)

E. Three Midwestern authors and their work:

1. Marguerita Henry and her books (Rand unless otherwise indicated).
   a. *Album of Dogs* (1970)
   b. *Album of Horses* (1951)
   c. *Benjamin West and His Cat Grimalkin* (Bobbs, 1947)
   d. *Black Gold* (1957; also paper)
   e. *Born to Trot* (1950; also paper)
   f. *Brighty of the Grand Canyon* (1953; also paper)
   g. *Dear Marguerite Henry* (1978; paper)
   h. *Five O'Clock Charlie* (1962; also paper)
   i. *Justin Morgan Had a Horse* (n.d.; also paper)
   j. *King of the Wind* (1948; also paper; Newbery Award 1949)
   k. *The Little Fellow* (1975)
   l. *Misty of Chincoteague* (1947; also paper; Newbery Honor Book 1948)
   m. *Mustang: Wild Spirit of the West* (1966; also paper)
   n. *One Man's Horse* (1977; also paper)
   o. *San Domingo: The Medicine Hat Stallion* (1972; also paper)
   p. *Sea Star: Orphan of Chincoteague* (1949; also paper)
   q. *Stormy: Misty's Foal* (1963; also paper)
   r. *White Stallion of Lipizza* (1964; also paper)
   s. *Wildest Horse Race in the World* (1960; also paper)

   FILMSTRIPS
   t. *Brighty of the Grand Canyon* (Pied Piper Productions—1 filmstrip, 1 cassette, 1 guide)
   u. *Justin Morgan Had a Horse* (Miller-Brody—2 filmstrips, 2 cassettes or 2 records)
   v. *King of the Wind* (Miller-Brody—2 filmstrips, 2 cassettes, 2 records)
   w. *Meet the Newbery Author: Marguerite Henry* (Miller-Brody—1 filmstrip, 1 cassette)
   x. *Story of a Book,* 2nd ed. (Pied Piper Productions—1 double-length filmstrip, 1 cassette)

   MOTION PICTURES
   y. *Brighty of Grand Canyon*
   z. *Story of a Book,* 2nd ed. (Pied Piper Productions)

2. Mark Twain and his books.
   a. *Adventures of Huckleberry Finn* (Macmillan, 1962).
   b. *Adventures of Tom Sawyer* (Macmillan, 1962)
   c. *The Complete Adventures of Tom Sawyer and Huckleberry Finn* (Harper, 1979)
   d. *The Prince and the Pauper* (Pendulum, 1978; paper)

   FILMSTRIPS
   e. *Huckleberry Finn* (Pendulum—1 filmstrip, 1 cassette, 1 paperback book, 1 poster)

f. *The Prince and the Pauper* (Disney—2 filmstrips, 2 cassettes or 2 records)

g. *Tom Sawyer* (Pendulum—1 filmstrip, 1 cassette, 1 paperback book, 1 poster)

h. *Tom Sawyer The Glorious Whitewasher* (Random—1 filmstrip, 1 cassette)

3. Laura Ingalls Wilder and her books (all Harper).

   a. *By the Shores of Silver Lake*, rev. ed. (1953)

   b. *Farmer Boy*, rev. ed. (1953)

   c. *Little House in the Big Woods*, rev. ed. (1953)

   d. *Little House on the Prairie*, rev. ed. (1953)

   e. *Little Town on the Prairie*, rev. ed. (1953)

   f. *The Long Winter*, rev. ed. (1953)

   g. *On the Banks of Plum Creek*, rev. ed. (1953; also paper; Newbery Honor Book 1938)

   h. *On the Way Home* ed. by Rose Wilder Lane (1962; also paper)

   i. *These Happy Golden Years*, rev. ed. (1953; also paper)

   j. *West from Home: Letters of Laura Ingalls Wilder, San Francisco, 1915* (1974)

   FILMSTRIPS

   k. *Laura: Little House, Big Prairie* (Perfection Form—1 filmstrip, 1 cassette or 1 record, script)

   l. *Meet the Newbery Author: Laura Ingalls Wilder* (Miller-Brody—1 filmstrip, 1 cassette)

F. Biographies of the presidents born in the Midwest or Great Plains:

   1. Ulysses S. Grant—OH
   2. Rutherford B. Hayes—OH
   3. James A. Garfield—OH
   4. Benjamin Harrison—OH
   5. William McKinley—OH
   6. William Howard Taft—OH
   7. Warren G. Harding—OH
   8. Herbert Hoover—IA
   9. Harry S. Truman—MO
   10. Dwight D. Eisenhower—TX
   11. Lyndon B. Johnson—TX
   12. Gerald R. Ford—NE
   13. Ronald W. Reagan—IL

G. Biographies of first ladies born in the Midwest and Great Plains:

   1. Julia Dent Grant—MO
   2. Lucy Ware Bebb Hayes—OH
   3. Lucretia Rudolph Garfield—OH
   4. Caroline Lavinia Scott Harrison—OH
   5. Ida Saxton McKinley—OH
   6. Helen Herron Taft—OH
   7. Florence King DeWolfe Harding—OH
   8. Lou Henry Hoover—IA
   9. Bess Wallace Truman—MO

      10. Mamie Geneva Doud Eisenhower—IA
      11. Alta Taylor "Lady Bird" Johnson—TX
      12. Elizabeth Bloomer Warren Ford—IL

VI. Culminating Activities.
  A. The Media Committee presents nonprint media to summarize and underscore basic concepts presented in the unit.
    1. The following filmstrips are presented and discussed (each Educational Enrichment Materials—1 filmstrip, 1 cassette, 1 guide unless otherwise indicated):
      a. *Chicago: Central Market Place*
      b. *Cleveland: Midwest Culture Center*
      c. *Indians of the Plains* (1 filmstrip, 1 cassette)
      d. *Minneapolis/St. Paul: The Twin Cities*
      e. *New Orleans/St. Louis: Mississippi River Towns*
      f. *The Scandanavians* (BFA—1 filmstrip, 1 cassette)
      g. *Seeing the Great Lakes States* (6 filmstrilps, 6 cassettes)
      h. *Seeing the Plains States* (4 filmstrips, 4 cassettes)
    2. The following motion pictures are presented and discussed (each National Park Service unless otherwise indicated):
      a. *Earthshapers* (Effigy Mounds National Monument)
      b. *The Fishermen of Isle Royale* (Michigan)
      c. *Mr. Lincoln's Springfield*
      d. *Pace of the Seasons* (Voyageurs National Park)
      e. *Portrait of a Wheat Farmer* (Kansas) (National Geographic)
  B. Individual students share their research findings with the class:
    1. Any student who wishes to present information places his or her name and special research topic on a mimeographed schedule form (see Checklist 4-2). Students are encouraged to present information in a well-organized, effective, and, if possible, creative manner.
    2. The class enters into the discussion following individual student's presentation.
  C. The "Automobile Industry and Its Wonderful Cars" Committee shares with the class its findings:
    1. A chart, *Car Facts and Feats,* is introduced and discussed.
    2. The filmstrip *Detroit: Major Industrial City* (Educational Enrichment Materials—1 filmstrip, 1 cassette) is presented and discussed.
    3. The following topics are introduced and discussed:
      a. Antique cars.
      b. Electric cars.
      c. Fabulous cars of the 1920s and 1930s.
      d. Foreign car competition.
      e. The future of the automotive industry in the United States.
  D. The "Inventions in America" Committee shares with the class its findings:
    1. The filmstrip *Yankee Inventiveness and Test Tube Miracles* (Educational Enrichment Materials—1 filmstrip, 1 cassette) is presented and discussed.
    2. The book *These Inventive Americans* by the Editors of the National

Geographic (Washington: National Geographic, 1971) is introduced to the class and recommended for independent study. It is then placed in the classroom study center.

E. The "Cowboys and Cattle Drives" Committee shares with the class its findings:

1. The filmstrip *Cowboys* (National Geographic—1 filmstrip, 1 cassette) is presented and discussed.

2. The book *The American Cowboy in Life and Legend* by Bart McDowell (Washington: National Geographic, 1972) is introduced and discussed. It is then placed in the classroom study center.

F. The "History and Importance of the Buffalo" Committee shares with the class its findings:

1. The following background statistics are presented:

   a. When the first explorers came to North America, there were approximately 60 million buffalo roaming free in what is now the United States.

   b. It has been estimated that the buffalo population had been reduced to 40 million by 1800.

   c. By 1900 the buffalo population had been reduced to fewer than 800 animals.

2. Dr. Hungerford, in his book *Ecology, the Circle of Life* (Chicago: Childrens, 1971), devotes an entire chapter to the wanton destruction of the buffalo. The class discusses the following:

   a. How did the Plains Indians safeguard the buffalo?

   b. Why did the Indians call the buffalo "the giver of life"?

   c. Did the disappearance of the buffalo contribute to the Plains Indians' giving up their struggle for independence and their finally accepting the federal government's placing them on reservations?

   d. Why did so-called civilized men kill hundreds of buffalo not for need but for "sport"?

3. The description of how "gentlemen" travelers shot buffalo from slowly moving railroad cars, as found in Chapter 4 of *When the Rails Ran West* by James McCague (Chicago: Childrens, 1967), is read and discussed.

G. The "Literary" Committee introduces the following writers and their books:

1. Marguerite Henry is presented to the class via the following filmstrips:

   a. *Meet the Newbery Author: Marguerite Henry* (Miller-Brody—1 filmstrip, 1 cassette)

   b. *Story of a Book* (Pied Piper Productions—1 double-length filmstrip, 1 cassette)

2. Mark Twain classics are presented to the class via the following filmstrips:

   a. *Huckleberry Finn* (Pendulum—1 filmstrip, 1 cassette, 1 paperback book, 1 poster)

   b. *The Prince and the Pauper* (Disney—2 filmstrips, 2 cassettes or 2 records)

      c. *Tom Sawyer* (Pendulum—1 filmstrip, 1 cassette, 1 paperback book, 1 poster)

   3. Laura Ingalls Wilder is presented to the class via the following filmstrips:

      a. *Laura: Little House, Big Prairie* (Perfection Form—1 filmstrip, 1 cassette or 1 record, script)

      b. *Meet the Newbery Author: Laura Ingalls Wilder* (Miller-Brody—1 filmstrip, 1 cassette)

H. Stressing that the action takes place during a tornado in Kansas, the "Literary" Committee introduces the ever-popular book and motion picture classic *The Wizard of Oz* to the class via the following filmstrips: *The Wizard of Oz* (Films, Inc.—2 filmstrips, 2 cassettes, 1 paperback book, 1 guide).

I. The "Let's Take a Trip to Texas" Committee shares its findings with the class using the following filmstrips (Educational Enrichment Materials—each 1 filmstrip and 1 cassette):

   1. *The Alamo*

   2. *Dallas/Fort Worth*

   3. *Houston: Inland Port City*

J. The "Presidents of the United States" Committee acquaints the class with the following presidential libraries and museums located in the Midwest and Great Plains:

   1. Dwight D. Eisenhower Library, Abilene, KS 67410

   2. Gerald R. Ford Library, 1000 Beal Ave., Ann Arbor, MI 48109; Gerald R. Ford Museum, 303 Pearl St. NW, Grand Rapids, MI 49504

   3. Herbert Hoover Presidential Library and Museum, West Branch IA 52358

   4. Lyndon B. Johnson Library and Museum, 2313 Red River, Austin, TX 78705

   5. Harry S Truman Library, Independence, MO 64050

   Note: These libraries and museums supply pamphlet materials on request.

K. Students, using Learning Guide 4-6, Places I Would Like to Visit, indicate their choice of places to visit in the Midwest and Great Plains.

L. Students are invited to share their reactions, impressions, and/or observations for inclusion in the class journal "Exploring Our Nation—The Midwest and the Great Plains."

Unit V: When Roads Led West*

GOALS: To provide learning experiences that will enable students to perceive and value American history in general, and the Westward Movement in particular, as an ongoing heroic drama with the happenings of the past setting the stage for the happenings of the present and the future and, to introduce students to the inquiry method and to the mysteries of adventurous, creative thinking.

*Adapted from *Creating Programs for the Gifted: A Guide for Teachers, Librarians, and Students* by Corinne P. Clendening and Ruth Ann Davies (New York: R. R. Bowker, 1980), pp. 220–230.

OBJECTIVES

This project has been designed and structured to provide these basic understandings:

The Westard Movement in American History is more than recorded events: It is men and women and young people doing things—making choices; deciding what is important and what is not; taking a stand for what they believe; venturing into the unknown; being courageous despite overwhelming odds; facing trouble and uncertainty; often succeeding but sometimes failing.

Life, liberty, and the pursuit of happiness—and all other basic human rights—have been painfully and slowly won at the cost of great human suffering and sacrifice.

Reading biographies is an exciting way to relive the historic happenings of the past, for people are the shapers of history.

All societies and all human beings are interdependent; no society and no human being can long survive as an island unto itself.

This project has been designed and structured to foster and develop these attitudes and appreciations.

Appreciation of the rich heritage each American inherits from the past; the perception that contemporary humans stand on the shoulders of those who have gone before.

Appreciation of the fact that America has been shaped by many kinds of people from many walks of life; perception that destiny is no respecter of race, color, or creed.

Appreciation of the fact that, while many great and famous people helped build America, countless others—pioneer men, women, and young people whose names go unrecorded, unnoted, and unsung—were the means and the force that carried a new civilization from the Atlantic to the Pacific.

Appreciation of the continuity and interrelatedness of history; the perception that history is an unrolling tapestry of human events.

Appreciation of the human attributes of greatness; perception of the necessity of critically and objectively evaluating the personal quality of those seeking leadership positions in the school, the community, the state, and the nation.

Appreciation of biography as a rich source of insight into the past; perception of the human dimension of history as expressed by Thomas Carlyle. "The history of the world is but the biography of great men."

Appreciation that "legend" makes history larger than life; perception that in legend the line between fact and fiction is all too often obliterated.

Appreciation of historical novels as an effective means of vicariously experiencing the happenings of the past.

Appreciation of the necessity and the value of reading between and beyond the lines.

Appreciation of the value to be accrued from successful group endeavors.

Appreciation of the high degree of satisfaction to be attained by completing a challenging assignment.

TEACHING STRATEGIES AND METHODS

No time limitations are imposed on this project. Number of students involved coupled with student interest is the factor that determines the duration of each project whether it be two weeks, two months, or longer.

A basic part of group orientation to this project is to provide opportunities for the students to explore the synergistic effect to be derived from sharing knowledge.

Each student, after orientation to the purpose, scope, and dimension of this project, will draw up and sign a performance contract specifying the special area of knowledge-building for which he or she will be responsible.

PROCEDURAL OUTLINE

I. Group orientation to and overview of this project.
   A. Definition of basic terms.
      1. *Adventurous thinking*—daring to think bold, new thoughts; projecting beyond the facts to fashion creative, yet plausible, answers to tantalizing questions such as "What if . . . ?" "What would happen if . . . ?" "Do you suppose . . . ?" "Is there a possibility . . . ?"
      2. *Creativity*—the power to develop to the fullest all abilities, those that are known and those that are hidden; to be all that one can be. The magic of creativity is to form new ideas, to invent, to discover.
      3. *Frontier*—the farthest part of a settled country; where the wilds begin.
      4. *Pioneer*—a person who settles in a part of the country that has not been occupied before except by primitive tribes.
   B. Discussion of the value of learning about America's past.
      1. William Jay Jacobs, American historian, in his book *Search for Freedom; America and Its People* (Encino, Calif.: Benziger Bruce & Glencoe, 1973, pp. 9–10, 18–19), explains the value of the past in the light of the present and the future as follows:

         "What is the past?

            "The past is what happened yesterday. And it is what happened all the yesterdays before that . . .

            "The past is things that men have built . . .

            "The past is the different tools and machines that men have used to make all those buildings . . .

            "The past is art . . .

            "The past is music . . .

            "The past is everything that has ever interested human beings . . .

            "The past is feelings . . .

            "The past is ideas . . .

"The past is events . . .

"The past is all these things, and many more. But most of all, the past is people.

"Who built America? Certainly, great men built the American nation. . . . But they were not alone. They are only part of the story.

"Many men and women whose names nobody remembers also built the American nation: the pioneer woman tending her fire in a wilderness cabin; the storm-tossed New England fisherman; the Negro slave, his back bent with work in a Southern cotton field.

"Who built America? The Pony Express riders—most of them teenagers . . . ; the farmer harvesting his crop alone in a Kansas wheat field; the Mississippi River steamboat pilot guiding his sternwheeler through treacherous currents.

"Who built America? The steelworker feeding coal to a fiery furnace in Pittsburgh for pennies a day . . . ; the country doctor faithfully making calls . . . ; the immigrant peddler wandering through the West. . . .

"America was built by many people. Most of them were ordinary people—carpenters and mechanics and lawyers and truck-drivers and housewives and students and railroad workers. Ordinary people.

"And you? What about you?

"Someday America will be yours. You will inherit it. And the decisions about what kind of country it will be—those choices will be yours.

"America is forever new. It is always being built. And you are its future builders."

2. The purpose of this project is to help you answer the question "Who built America in the past, and what will I be able to contribute to America's present and America's future?"
3. People make the difference.
   During this project, each student will compile a list of people who have influenced American history in either a positive or a negative way.

C. Exploration of the process of adventurous, creative thinking.
   1. What is creativity?

      Latin root word *creare* meaning to make.
      Greek root word *krainen* meaning to fulfill—a promise, a prophecy, or oneself.
      The magic of creativity is to form new ideas, to invent, to discover.
      Creativity includes the ability to wonder, to be surprised and puzzled, to see what others have seen and to respond differently.

   2. Four steps in creative thought:

      Preparation—gathering facts and seeking answers.
      Facts are the raw materials from which creative thought is fashioned.
      Incubation—the mind works with the facts and ideas.

Inspiration—a sudden solution or a unique idea.
Verification—testing the solution or idea.

3. Imagination is the mind's eye.

Imagination is the ability to form in the mind a picture or idea of something that is not present.
Such pictures are like the images in a kaleidoscope.
We use imagination to recreate the past, to wonder about unfamiliar people or places, and to toy with ideas about the future.

4. Creative power is a hidden treasure.

Margaret Mead, the anthropologist, estimated that man uses but 6 percent of his creative potential.
Can you develop creativity? Psychologists say yes.
Practice improves creativity.
Highly creative people invent new responses when solving problems—they experiment with what might have been.
Creative thinking looks for a number of ideas, for variety and originality.

D. At the conclusion of this project, the student will be given the challenge of creatively imagining what his or her life could have been if he or she had been a pioneer trailblazer.

II. The group begins to build its knowledge of westward migration in American history.
A. The students read the *World Book* reprint "Pioneer Life."
1. Attention is called to the fact that the article was critically reviewed by Robert G. Athearn, professor of history at the University of Colorado.
The significance of a "signed article" is discussed.
2. The necessity of following through on the two cross-references—"Western Frontier Life" and "Westward Movement"—is stressed.
3. The transvision map reprint from the *World Book* is used throughout the reading of the reprint "Pioneer Life in America" and of reprints "Western Frontier Life" and "Westward Movement."
Maps are invaluable in visualizing both time and place.
4. Using the main and subheadings of the reprint "Pioneer Life," the following outline is developed:
a. Pioneer life in America
(1) Conquering the wilderness
(2) Establishing the frontier
b. Moving westward
(1) Crossing the Appalachians
(2) How people traveled
(3) Trails of the pioneers
c. A pioneer settlement
(1) A pioneer home
(2) Education and religion
(3) Law and order
(4) Social activities
(5) Indian attacks
d. Crossing the Plains
(1) The wagon train
(2) Life on the trail

B. The group views and then discusses the motion picture *Daniel Boone* (Coronet).
1. The value of using a motion picture is explored.
2. The significance of the term *film literacy* is introduced and discussed.
3. Professor John Michaelis, University of California, believes that motion pictures are very important when studying history because:

> "Processes, people, the world of nature, various types of activities, and significant events can be seen in action in a realistic setting.

> "Contemporary affairs, past events, and faraway places can be brought into the classroom.

> "Processes that cannot be visualized in any other way can be seen in action on the screen.

> "A broad sweep of events may be seen with various relationships highlighted, as in films showing the development of inventions, the growth of institutions, or the contributions of great men and women."[*]

4. The group reacts to Michaelis's appraisal of the value of motion pictures.
C. The group views, discusses, and then evaluates the educational effectiveness of the following motion pictures (all Coronet):
1. *Folksongs of the Western Movement, 1787–1853*
2. *Pioneer Journey across the Appalachians*
3. *Pioneer Living: Education and Recreation*
4. *Pioneer Living: The Home*
5. *Pioneer Living: Preparing Foods*
6. *Travel in America in the 1840s*
D. Each student reads the historical novel *Young Pioneers* by Rose Wilder Lane (Bantam Books).
1. Students discover that the author of this novel is the daughter of Laura Ingalls Wilder.
2. Students read other novels portraying the Westward Movement.
3. Students discuss the value of historical novels as an effective means of vicariously reliving the past.
E. Students read the reprint "Western Frontier Life" and develop the following outline:
1. Life on the frontier
   a. People
   b. Food
   c. Clothing
   d. Amusements
   e. Religion
   f. Frontier towns
   g. Life in the country
2. Transportation and communication
3. Law and order
   a. Crime
   b. Law enforcement
   c. Indian fighting

[*]John U. Michaelis, *Social Studies for Children in a Democracy: Recent Trends and Developments,* 5th ed. (Englewood Cliffs, N.J.: Prentice-Hall, 1972), p. 481.

4. An American tradition
   a. Literature
   b. Music
   c. Art
   d. Entertainment

III. Each student selects a topic or topics from the above outline to research.
   A. The concept of "film literacy" is reintroduced and the students select appropriate sound filmstrips from the following bibliography:
      1. *The Cowboy: Tough Man on a Mustang* (American Pageant)
      2. *Gold and Dreams of Gold* (Society for Visual Education)

         Gold Towns of the Old West
         Ghost Towns—What Happened
         How Gold is Mined
         A Modern-Day Prospector Named George

      3. *The Gunslingers* (American Pageant)
      4. *Pathfinders Westward* (Society for Visual Education)

         Daniel Boone's Wilderness Trail
         Rivers and Roads to the Mississippi
         Lewis and Clark Expedition, parts I and II
         First Trails into the West
         The Mountain Men

      5. *Pioneer Women and Belles of the Wild West* (Teaching Resources)
      6. *Settling the West* (Society for Visual Education)

         The Trail Blazers
         The Miners
         Wagon Trains to Railroads
         The Cattlemen
         The Farmers
         Growth of Towns and Cities

      7. *Stories from the Old West* (Society for Visual Education)

         El Camino Real
         Vaquero! Vaquero!
         The Comanches: Greatest Horsemen of the West
         The Pony Express Rider
         Iron Horse, Golden Spike
         Pawnee: The Buffalo Pony

      8. *The West: The Way It Was* (American Pageant)
      9. *Westward Migration* (Society for Visual Education)

         Into the Southwest
         The Oregon Country
         The Gold Rush
         Three Routes to Eldorado

   B. The students check the U.S. Landmark series to discover titles appropriate for their topic.
      1. Attention is directed to the Landmark colophon (an emblematic or ornamental device used to identify a publishing house or a series of books).
      2. Recommendation is made that the students check the biographical note about the author that is found in the back of the book. Is the author qualified by training and experience to be recognized as an authority?

3. Attention is directed to the list of series titles found at the back of each book in the series.

IV. As a culminating activity the students as a group nominate candidates for a Hall of Fame of American Frontiersmen.
   A. A "Who's Who in the Westward Movement" serves as a summary of names highlighted in American historical annals.
   B. Students nominate their candidates and defend each candidate's claim to fame.
   C. The students, based on their observations of the Westward Movement and their appraisal of the human drama of the period, discuss the validity of the statement "truth is stranger than fiction."

V. The group views and then discusses the motion picture *Westward Ho! The Wagons* (Disney Studios)
   A. Does this motion picture give a valid picture of the times?
   B. Was this motion picture biased in its portrayal of either whites or Indians?
   C. Who was your favorite character in the motion picture?
   D. If you had been the director of *Westward Ho! The Wagons*, what changes, if any, would you have made?
   E. What insight into human nature did you gain from viewing this motion picture?
   F. If you had been a pioneer trailblazer, what adventures might you have had?

WHO'S WHO IN THE WESTWARD MOVEMENT

Teacher's Answer Key.   Please place in the parentheses ( ) before each name the number of the phrase that best describes that person.

Persons	*Descriptive Phrases*
(17) Grizzly Adams	1. Adventurer and explorer; a mountain named for him
(10) Stephen Austin	2. Apache warrior
(34) Sam Bass	3. Author of *Ox-Team Days on the Oregon Trail;* lived to be 98
(9) Charles Bent	4. Blazed the Wilderness Trail
(4) Daniel Boone	5. California mission priest
(19) Jemima Boone	6. Designed hunting knife; killed at the Battle of the Alamo
(6) Jim Bowie	7. Discovered the Great Salt Lake
(7) Jim Bridger	8. Discovered Yellowstone
(38) Kit Carson	9. Established a fort and trading post on the Santa Fe Trail
(29) George Catlin	10. Father of Texas
(22) John Chapman	11. Father of the Wild West Show
(11) Bill Cody	12. Founder of the Church of the Latter-Day Saints
(21) Sam Colt	13. Frontier doctor
(8) John Colter	14. Frontier peace officer; nicknamed "Wild Bill"
(15) Davy Crockett	15. Frontier legendary hero; killed defending the Alamo
(32) Abigail Scott Duniway	16. Gold discovered at his mill in California

Persons (cont.)	*Descriptive Phrases (cont.)*
(39) Wyatt Earp	17. Hermit in the Sierras; tamed and trained bears
(33) Escalante	18. Historian of the Sante Fe Trail
(23) Mike Fink	19. Indian captive
(31) John Charles Fremont	20. Indian guide for the Lewis and Clark Expedition
(2) Geronimo	21. Inventor of the six-shooter
(18) Josiah Gregg	22. Johnny Appleseed
(14) Bill Hickok	23. Keelboatman, marksman, fighter, teller of "tall tales"
(37) Sam Houston	24. Led first wagon train over Oregon Trail
(27) Andrew Jackson	25. Led Mormons over Oregon Trail to Great Salt Lake
(35) Mary Layola	26. Missionary to Oregon Indians
(13) Ephraim McDowell	27. "Old Hickory"
(3) Ezra Meeker	28. One-armed explorer of the Colorado River
(40) Annie Oakley	29. Painted Indian portraits now in the Smithsonian Institution
(1) Zebulon Pike	30. Painted western frontier scenes
(28) John Wesley Powell	31. "The Pathfinder"
(30) Frederic Remington	32. Pioneer suffragette
(20) Sacajawea	33. Priest explorer of Colorado, Utah, and Arizona
(5) Junipero Serra	34. Robin Hood of Texas
(36) Sitting Bull	35. Roman Catholic nun, missionary to the Oregon Indians
(12) Joseph Smith	36. Sioux warrior
(24) Jedediah Smith	37. Tallest Texan; hero of the Battle of San Jacinto
(16) John Sutter	38. Trapper and scout; explored Death Valley
(26) Narcissa Whitman	39. U.S. marshall; "Lion of Tombstone"
(25) Brigham Young	40. Woman sharpshooter

PRINTED RESOURCES

Bent's Fort: Crossroads of the Great West by Wyatt Blassingame (Garrard, 1967)

Bull Wagon by Glen Dines (Macmillan, 1963)

Cumberland Gap and Trails West by Edith McCall (Childrens, 1980)

Famous American Trails by Bruce Grant (Rand, 1971)

Famous Pioneers by Franklin Folsome (Harvey, 1964)

Flatboat Days on Frontier Rivers by James McCague (Garrard, 1968)

Forts in the Wilderness by Edith McCall (Childrens, 1980)

Frontier Living by Edwin Tunis (Crowell, 1976)

Ghost Town of the American West by Robert Silverberg (Crowell, 1968)

The Homestead Act by Ronald C. Stein (Childrens, 1978)

Homesteaders and Indians by Dorothy Levenson (Watts, 1971)

Hunters Blaze the Trails by Edith McCall (Childrens, 1980)

Into the Wilderness by Lowell Georgia (National Geographic, 1978)

The Lewis and Clark Expedition, 1804–06 by Dan Lacy (Watts, 1974)

Mail Riders by Edith McCall (Childrens, 1980)

Over the Mormon Trail by Helen Hinckley Jones (Childrens, 1980)

Overland Stage by Glen Dines (Macmillan, 1961)

Pioneering on the Plains by Edith McCall (Childrens, 1980)

Prairie Schooners by Glen Rounds (Holiday, 1968)

The Price of Free Land by Treva Adams Strait (Lippincott, 1979)

Stalwart Men of Early Texas by Edith McCall (Childrens, 1980)

Steamboats to the West by Edith McCall (Childrens, 1980)

Trails West by the Editors of National Geographic (National Geographic, 1979)

Wagons over the Mountains by Edith McCall (Childrens, 1980)

Westward Adventure: The True Story of Six Pioneers by William O. Steele (Harcourt, 1962)

When Mountain Men Trapped Beaver by Richard Glendinning (Garrard, 1967)

When Pioneers Pushed West to Oregon by Elizabeth R. Montgomery (Garrard, 1967)

When Wagon Trains Rolled to Santa Fe by Erick Berry (Garrard, 1966)

Women of the West, by Dorothy Levenson (Watts, 1973)

FILMSTRIPS

The Conestoga Wagon (Educational Enrichment Materials—1 filmstrip, 1 cassette)

Expanding Our Nation (Society for Visual Education—4 filmstrips, 4 cassettes, 28 skill sheets, 1 guide)
> *Building Nationalism*
> *Moving to the Mississippi*
> *Moving toward the Pacific*
> *Life on the Frontier*

The Gunslingers (American Pageant—1 filmstrip, 1 record, 1 script)

Heroes and Heroines of the Great West (Eye Gate—8 filmstrips, 4 cassettes)
> *The Great Indian Chiefs of the Plains*
> *The Great Indian Chiefs of the Southwest*
> *The Horseback Generals*
> *The Kings of the Mines and Railroads*
> *The Legendary Cowgirls and Civilizers*
> *The Pathfinders*
> *The Scouts, Lawmen and Outlaws*
> *The Story of Explorers*

Pathfinders Westward (Society for Visual Education—6 filmstrips, 3 cassettes)
> *Daniel Boone's Wilderness Trail*
> *First Trails into the West*
> *Lewis and Clark Expedition, Parts 1 and 2*
> *The Mountain Men*
> *Rivers and Roads to the Mississippi*

Pioneers of America (Eye Gate—10 filmstrips, 5 cassettes)

> *Life of the Settlers*
> *Miners and 49ers*
> *Pioneer Craftsmen*
> *Pioneer Folk Art*
> *Pioneer Farming*
> *Pioneer Government and Law*
> *Pioneer Transportation and Communication*
> *Tradesmen and Cattlemen*
> *Trappers—The Mountain Men*
> *Westward Expansion—A Vivid Portrayal of the Kind of Men and Women Who Conquered the Wilderness*

Settling the West (Coronet—6 filmstrips, 6 cassettes, 1 guide)

> *The Cattlemen*
> *The Farmers*
> *Growth of Towns and Cities*
> *The Miners*
> *The Trail Blazers*
> *Wagon Trains to Railroads*

Stories from the Old West (Society for Visual Education—6 filmstrips, 3 cassettes, 6 guides)

> *The Comanches: Greatest Horsemen of the West*
> *El Camino Real*
> *Iron Horse, Golden Spike*
> *Pawnee: The Buffalo Pony*
> *The Pony Express Rider*
> *Vaquero! Vaquero!*

Westward Migration (Society for Visual Education—4 filmstrips, 2 cassettes)

> *The Gold Rush*
> *Into the Southwest*
> *The Oregon Country*
> *Three Routes to El Dorado*

MAP

Westward Ho!—1803–1860 (Rand)

RECORDING

Westward Ho! (National Geographic—1 cassette or 1 record)

COMPUTER PROGRAM

Trail West: A Game of Options and Events (PET dist. by Society for Visual Education)

Unit VI: The West

I. Students identify the 11 states that comprise the West and the official abbreviation for each state:

> Arizona—AZ
> California—CA
> Colorado—CO
> Idaho—ID
> Montana—MT

    Nevada—NV
    New Mexico—NM
    Oregon—OR
    Utah—UT
    Washington—WA
    Wyoming—WY

II. Students are introduced to the American Automobile Association (AAA) TourBooks, which should be kept readily available in the classroom study center.
   A. AAA TourBooks are revised annually.
   B. The following five TourBooks pertain to the West:
      1. *Arizona, New Mexico*
      2. *Colorado, Utah*
      3. *Idaho, Montana, Wyoming*
      4. *California, Nevada*
      5. *Oregon, Washington*
   C. The information under each state includes:
      1. History
      2. Geography
      3. Things to know

            Population
            Area
            Capital
            Nickname
            Flower
            Motto
            Highest point
            Time zone
            Minimum age for drivers
            Holidays
            Recreation information
            State information centers

      4. Economy
      5. Major annual events
      6. Recreation
      7. What to see. Each major city is listed; identifies museums, libraries, universities, historic landmarks, monuments, and so on.
   D. Maps of major areas are included.

III. Students are introduced to the Enchantment of America series, ed. by Allan Carpenter (Chicago: Childrens, 1978), which have been placed in the classroom study center.

IV. Students read the textbook and answer the questions or solve the problems posed by the textbook authors. For example:
   A. The Land—Making Discoveries: Look for information about one of the subjects below:
      1. The Rocky Mountains:
         a. How were the Rocky Mountains formed?
         b. About how old are the Rockies?
         c. What kinds of plants and animals are found in these mountains?
         d. What is the Continental Divide?

    2. The Grand Canyon

       a. How was the Grand Canyon formed?

       b. What kinds of plants and animals are found in the Grand Canyon?

B. The Climate—Problems to solve:

    1. Winter weather varies from place to place in the West. Winters are cold in some areas and mild in others. Why is this so? In making hypotheses to solve this problem, you will need to consider how temperatures in different parts of the West are affected by the following:

       a. Distance from the equator.

       b. Height above sea level.

       c. Distance from large bodies of water.

    2. How does the climate in different parts of the West affect farming? To solve this problem, you will need to consider facts about each of the following:

       a. The length of the growing season in different parts of the West.

       b. The amount of rainfall in these areas.

       c. The kinds of crops that are grown.

       d. The kinds of livestock that are raised.

C. The People—A problem to solve: Why have so many people chosen to make their homes in California? In forming hypotheses to solve this problem, consider facts about:

    1. Climate.

    2. Land and water features.

    3. Natural resources, such as minerals, forests, and fertile soil.

    4. Job opportunities.

D. The Cities—Exploring Cities:

    1. Do research to discover how one of the cities described in this unit began and how it has developed. Answer the following questions in a short report:

       a. Who were the first settlers?

       b. Why did they settle here?

       c. How has the city grown in size from the time it was founded until now?

    2. Describe a visit to one of the cities described in this unit. Present a short report to your class. Include the following in your report:

       a. How you traveled to the city.

       b. The most interesting things you saw there.

       c. Your opinion of what the city's most serious problems might be.

E. Citizenship and Government—Find Out How Your Government Works: Find out how the government of your own community works. Do research to answer the following questions:

    1. Who makes the laws for your community? How are these people chosen?

    2. Who is in charge of carrying out the laws in your community? How is this person (or persons) chosen?

    3. About how many people work for your community's government? What kinds of jobs do they have?

    4. What courts do you have in your community? What kinds of cases

do they deal with? How do the judges in these courts get their jobs? How long do they serve?

5. Where does your community get the money it needs to run the government? Who decides how this money will be spent?

F. The Arts—Gain an Understanding: In order to gain a greater understanding of western painting, literature, or music, do one of the following:

1. Borrow a library book that shows paintings by an artist mentioned in this unit. Choose the painting you like best. Explain to the class why you like it.

2. Read a novel by Jack London, such as *The Call of the Wild* or *White Fang*.

3. Play a recording of the *Grand Canyon Suite.* As you listen to the music, write a few sentences describing how it makes you feel.

G. Earning a Living—In What Ways Do People in the West Earn Their Living? Discover answers to the following questions:

1. What natural resources would you find in the West? In what ways do the people of the West use these resources?

2. What is dry farming? What is the most important crop grown by dry farming in the West? What other crops are raised here?

3. What are the West's leading industrial cities? What are some of the products made in these cities?

H. Farming—Investigate an Interesting Topic:

1. Wheat is an important farm product of the West. Do research about wheat. Then write a report about it to share with your class. You may wish to use the questions below as a guide.
   a. What are the parts of the wheat plant and the wheat kernel?
   b. How is wheat planted?
   c. How is wheat harvested?
   d. What is the difference between winter wheat and spring wheat?
   e. What are some of the uses of wheat?

2. Barley is raised by using dry farming methods. Dry farming makes it possible to grow crops in areas that receive only 10 to 20 inches of rainfall a year.
   a. Besides water, what other important resource must farmers try to save?
   b. How is this resource sometimes lost?
   c. Do you think it can ever be replaced? Why? Why not?

I. Natural Resources and Energy—Use Your Creativity: Choose one of the following projects:

1. Write a report about a dam in the West that provides water both for irrigation and for making electricity. For example, you might wish to write about Shasta Dam or Hoover Dam. You may wish to illustrate your report with diagrams and pictures.

2. Write a story about the life of a salmon. Tell where the salmon was hatched and where it spent most of its life. Also tell how it made its way upstream as a full-grown fish.

J. Industry—Make Discoveries about Airplanes: Airplanes are made in several factories in the West. Do research about airplanes in other sources. Record your findings in a written report. Your report may include information about one or more of the following:

1. History and development of the airplane.
2. Different kinds of airplanes.
3. The parts of an airplane.
4. How an airplane flies.
5. How airplanes are built.

V. Students elect to work in the school library to build understanding in these significant areas:
  A. If the state in which the students reside is located in the West, a depth study of that state should receive top priority.
  B. The California Gold Rush: The following books are on reserve in the school library:
    1. *The California Gold Rush* by Ralph Andrist and Archibald Hanna (American Heritage, 1961)
    2. *The Fools of '49: The California Gold Rush, 1848–1856* by Laurence I. Seidman (Knopf, 1976)
    3. *The Forty-Niners* by William W. Johnson (Time-Life, Silver, 1974)
    4. *Gold Rush Adventures* by Edith McCall (Childrens, 1980)
    5. *The Story of Gold at Sutter's Mill* by R. C. Stein (Childrens, 1981)
    Students are reminded to discover the rich historical background information in both biography and historical fiction.
  C. Deserts of the West: The following books are on reserve in the school library:
    1. *American Deserts* by the Editors of National Geographic (National Geographic, 1972)
    2. *Death Valley* by George Laycock (Four Winds, 1976)
    3. *Deserts of the World: Future Threat or Promise?* by Jane W. Watson (Philomel, 1980)
    4. *The Great American Desert* by Donald Young (Messner, 1980)
    5. *Southwest Desert* by Norman Hammond Wakeman (Dodd, 1965)
  D. Endangered Western Plants and Animals: The following books are on reserve in the school library:
    1. *Animal Facts and Figures* by Tibor Gergely (McGraw, 1975)
    2. *Endangered Plants* by Dorothy C. Hogner (Harper, 1977)
    3. *Endangered Predators* by John Harris and Alta Pahl (Doubleday, 1976)
    4. *Endangered Species* by Sandra Hochman (Putnam, 1977)
    5. *Giant Condor of California* by Julian May (Creative Education, 1972)
    6. *Guinness Book of Amazing Animals* by Norris Whittier (Sterling, n.d.)
    7. *Our Threatened Wildlife: An Ecological Study* by William Perry (Coward, 1970)
    8. *Vanishing Wildlife of North America* by Thomas B. Allen (National Geographic, 1974)
    9. *Vanishing Wings: A Tale of Three Birds of Prey* by Griffing Bancroft (Watts, 1972)
  E. Noteworthy Westerners:
    1. History makers
      a. Grizzly Adams
      b. Luther Burbank

      c. "Wild Horse" Annie Johnson
      d. John Muir
      e. Annie Oakley
      f. John Wesley Powell
      g. Junipero Serra
      h. John Sutter
      i. Brigham Young

2. Spanish-American leaders of the twentieth century:
      a. Herman Badillo: A Man for the Cities
      b. Francesco Bravo: Doctor, Banker, Civic Leader
      c. César Chávez: Leader of the Downtrodden
      d. Luis Quero Chiesa: Culture of a Proud People
      e. Jose Feliciano: Against All Odds
      f. Henry Gonzalez: Voice of the Southwest
      g. Leopoldo Sanchez: The Judge from California
      h. Piri Thomas: Down These Mean Streets

F. National Parks and National Monuments:
1. The following books are on reserve in the school library:
      a. *Brighty of the Grand Canyon* by Marguerite Henry (Rand, 1953; also paper)
      b. *Bryce Canyon National Park* by Ruth Radlauer (Childrens, 1980)
      c. *Carlsbad Caverns National Park* by Ruth Radlauer (Childrens, 1981)
      d. *Glacier National Park* by Ruth Radlauer (Childrens, 1977)
      e. *The Grand Canyon National Park* by Ruth Radlauer (Childrens, 1977)
      f. *Grand Teton National Park* by Ruth Radlauer (Childrens, 1980)
      g. *Mesa Verde National Park* by Ruth Radlauer (Childrens, 1977)
      h. *Olympic National Park* by Ruth Radlauer (Childrens, 1978)
      i. *Rocky Mountain National Park* by Ruth Radlauer (Childrens, 1977)
      j. *Yellowstone National Park* by Ruth Radlauer (Childrens, 1975)
      k. *Yosemite National Park* by Ruth Radlauer (Childrens, 1975)
      l. *Zion National Park* by Ruth Radlauer (Childrens, 1978)
2. Students are alerted to the up-to-date statistical information about the national parks and national monuments of the United States to be found in *The World Almanac and Book of Facts.*

G. Volcanoes and Earthquakes: Agents of Disaster
1. The following books are on reserve in the school library:
      a. *Disaster: Earthquakes* by Dennis Fradin (Childrens, 1982)
      b. *Disaster: Volcanoes* by Dennis Fradin (Childrens, 1982)
      c. *Disastrous Volcanoes* by Melvin Berger (Watts, 1981)
      d. *Earth a Fire: Volcanoes and Their Activities* by R. V. Fodor (Morrow, 1981)
      e. *Earthquake* by Bryce Walker and the Editors of Time-Life Books (Time-Life, 1982)
      f. *Geological Disasters: Earthquakes and Volcanoes* by Thomas G. Aylesworth (Watts, 1979)
      g. *How Did We Find Out about Volcanoes* by Isaac Asimov (Walker, 1981)

     h. *Mt. St. Helens: A Sleeping Volcano Awakes* by Marian T. Place (Dodd, 1981)

     i. *Volcanoes: The Fiery Mountains* by Margaret Poynter (Messner, 1980)

     j. *Volcanoes* by Ruth Radlauer (Childrens, 1981)

     k. *Volcanoes* by the Editors of Time-Life Books (Time-Life, 1982)

     l. *Volcanoes and Earthquakes* by Robert Irving (Knopf, 1962)

     m. *Why St. Helens Blew Its Top* by Kathryn Goldner and Carole G. Vogel (Dillon, 1981)

  2. Students are alerted to the microfiche program *Mount St. Helens Erupts 1980* as reported in the *New York Times* (*Great Events Three,* Microfilming Corporation of America, Sanford, N.C., 1981) (see Example 4-2 at the end of this model).

H. Three Western authors and their works:

  1. Patricia Beatty (all published by Morrow)

     a. *By Crumbs, It's Mine!* (1976)

     b. *Hail Columbia* (1970)

     c. *How Many Miles to Sundown?* (1974)

     d. *I Want My Sunday, Stranger* (1977)

     e. *A Long Way to Whiskey Creek* (1971)

     f. *Me, California Perkins* (1968)

     g. *The Queen's Own Grove* (1966)

     h. *Something to Shout About* (1976)

     i. *Wait for Me, Watch for Me, Eula Bec* (1978)

  2. Jack London

     a. *The Call of the Wild* (Grosset, n.d.)

     b. *White Fang* (Macmillan, 1935)

  3. Scott O'Dell (all published by Houghton)

     a. *The Black Pearl* (1967; Newbery Honor Book 1968)

     b. *The Captive* (1979)

     c. *Island of the Blue Dolphins* (1960; Newbery Award 1961)

     d. *King's Fifth* (1966; Newbery Honor Book 1967)

     e. *Sing Down the Moon* (1970; Newbery Honor Book, 1971)

     f. *Zia* (1978)

I. Hollywood, Movie Capital of the World

  1. The following books are on reserve in the school library:

     a. *The Four Worlds of Walt Disney* by Walt Disney Studios, 4 vols. (Western, 1976)

       Walt Disney's America
       Walt Disney's Fantasy Land
       Walt Disney's Stories from Other Lands
       Walt Disney's World of Nature

     b. *Great Movie Spectaculars* by Edward Edelson (Doubleday, 1976)

     c. *The Magic Lantern: How Movies Got to Move* by Judith Thurman and Johnathan David (Atheneum, 1978)

     d. *Silents to Sound: A History of the Movies* by Juliet P. Schoen (Four Winds, 1976)

     e. *Walt Disney: Master of Make-Believe* by Elizabeth R. Montgomery (Garrard, 1971)

  2. The students are alerted to the following section in *The World*

Almanac and Book of Facts: Motion Pictures (Academy awards; Stars, producers)

VI. Culminating Activities.
   A. The Media Committee presents nonprint media to summarize and underscore basic concepts presented in the unit.
      1. The following filmstrips are presented and discussed:
         a. *Seeing the Rocky Mountain States* (Coronet—4 filmstrips, 4 cassettes)
         b. *Seeing the Pacific States* (Coronet—6 filmstrips, 6 cassettes)
         c. *Seeing the Southwestern States* (Coronet—6 filmstrips, 6 cassettes)
      2. The following motion pictures are presented and discussed:
         a. *The Great Mojave Desert* (National Geographic—TV Documentary Film)
         b. *America's Wonderlands: The National Parks* (National Geographic—TV Documentary Film)
         c. *Grizzly!* (National Geographic—TV Documentary Film)
   B. Individual students share their research findings with the class.
      1. Any student who wishes to present information places his or her name and special research topic on a mimeographed schedule form (see Checklist 4-2).
      2. The class enters into the discussion following the individual student's presentation.
   C. "The California Gold Rush" Committee shares with the class its findings using the following filmstrips as discussion starters:
      1. *Gold and Dreams of Gold* (Society for Visual Education—4 filmstrips, 4 cassettes)

      Gold Towns of the Old West
      Ghost Towns—What Happened?
      How Gold Is Mined
      Present-Day Prospector Named George

   D. The "Deserts of the West" Committee shares its research findings with the class using the following filmstrips as discussion starters:
      1. *Deserts* (National Geographic—1 filmstrip, 1 cassette)
      2. *The Ecology of a Desert: Death Valley* (Educational Development—2 filmstrips, 2 cassettes or 2 records, 1 manual)
      3. *The Wild Young Desert* (Lyceum/Mook and Blanchard—2 filmstrips, 2 cassettes or 2 records)
   E. The "Endangered Western Plants and Animals" Committee shares its research findings with the class using the following as discussion starters:
      1. Filmstrips:
         a. *The Buffalo: Caring in Time* (Encyclopaedia Britannica—1 filmstrip, 1 cassette)
         b. National Audubon Environmental series (Random—each 1 filmstrip and 1 cassette, or 1 record)

---

*Projected as part of individual or committee reports when appropriate to the topic being presented.

Set 1: *Conserving Our Wildlife*
Set 2: *Conserving Our Birds*
    Conserving Our Wildlife Refuges
    Conserving Our Vanishing Species
    How You Can Help

  c. *The Redwood: Why Save a Tree?* (Encyclopaedia Britannica)
  d. *Vanishing Animals of North America* (National Geographic—5 filmstrips, 5 cassettes)

    Tragedy of the Past
    Hunted Animals
    Damage to Ecosystems
    Protected Animals
    Prospects for the Future

2. Motion Picture: *Grizzly!* (National Geographic—TV Documentary Film).
3. The sound filmstrip *The Grizzly,* distributed by Pied Piper Productions, based on the novel *The Grizzly* by Annabel and Edgar Johnson (New York: Harper, 1964), is presented by the committee to dramatize the size and power of the grizzly.
  a. The setting of this story is California's Stanislaus National Forest.
  b. The photographs comprising many of the frames of this filmstrip provide an impressive view of the rugged forests, the beautiful rivers, and the awesome grizzly bears.
F. The "National Parks and National Monuments" Committee shares its research findings with the class.
  1. Using the motion picture *John Muir—Father of Our National Parks* (Disney) as an introduction, the committee dramatically portrays John Muir's crusade to establish national parks and preserve America's scenic beauty.
  2. The committee presents the following filmstrips as discussion starters:
    a. *Exploring Wilderness Trails* (Coronet—6 filmstrips, 6 cassettes)

      Across Desert Country
      Down the Grand Canyon
      Up the High Country
      Through the Winter Valley
      Along the Snake River
      In Yellowstone National Park

    b. *Grand Canyon* (Pied Piper Productions—1 filmstrip, 1 cassette)
    c. *Yellowstone National Park* (Pied Piper Productions—1 filmstrip, 1 cassette)
    d. *Yosemite National Park* (Pied Piper Productions—1 filmstrip, 1 cassette)
  3. The committee presents the following National Park Service films:*
    a. *The Bighorn Canyon Experience*
    b. *Challenge of Yellowstone*
    c. *Giant Sequoia*

---

*These excellent motion pictures are offered for rent or for sale by the National Audiovisual Center, Washington, D.C. Videocassettes are also available at very reasonable cost.

    d. *The Great Sand Dunes*

    e. *The Incredible Wilderness: Olympic National Park*

    f. *Lehman Caves National Monument*

    g. *Sunset Crater Arizona*

G. The "Volcanoes and Earthquakes: Agents of Disaster" Committee shares its research findings with the class using the following for discussion starters:

1. Filmstrips:

    a. *Earthquakes and Volcanoes* (National Geographic—1 filmstrip, 1 cassette)

    b. *Mount St. Helens: A Volcano Erupts* (Society for Visual Education—1 black and white Newstrip, 1 cassette, 1 guide)

    c. *Powers of Nature* (National Geographic—4 filmstrips, 4 cassettes or 4 records)

2. Motion Picture: *The San Andreas Fault* (Encyclopaedia Britannica).

H. The "Literary" Committee introduces the following authors to the class:

1. Patricia Beatty—A reading list of the novels written by Patricia Beatty, which are being held on reserve for the *Exploring the United States* class, is distributed.

2. Jack London—The classic story *The Call of the Wild* is reviewed for the class and the following filmstrips are presented (both Random):

    a. *The Call of the Wild* (2 filmstrips, 2 cassettes)

    b. *To Build a Fire* (1 filmstrip, 1 cassette)

3. Scott O'Dell—The following filmstrips introduce Scott O'Dell to the class:

    a. *The Black Pearl* (Miller-Brody—2 filmstrips, 2 cassettes; Newbery Honor Book 1968)

    b. *The Island of the Blue Dolphin* (Films, Inc.—2 filmstrips, 2 cassettes, 1 guide, 1 paperback; Newbery Award 1961)

    c. *Meet the Newbery Author: Scott O'Dell* (Miller-Brody—1 filmstrip, 1 cassette or 1 record)

    d. *Sing Down the Moon* (Miller-Brody—2 filmstrips, 2 cassettes or 2 records; Newbery Honor Book 1971)

    e. *Zia* (Miller-Brody—2 filmstrips, 2 cassettes)

I. The "Hollywood, Movie Capital of the World" Committee shares its research findings with the class; for example:

1. The World Book *Year Book,* as a regular feature, discusses the motion picture industry: its box office successes, its cinematic innovations, and motion pictures based on best-selling novels.

2. *The World Almanac and Book of Facts* offers up-to-date information such as:

    a. Entertainment personalities—where and when born.

    b. Noted entertainers—personalities of the past.

    c. Motion Picture Academy Awards (Oscars) 1927 to date.

3. Many children's classics have been made into very popular and successful motion pictures.

    a. MovieStrips, produced by Films, Inc., are filmstrips that use the sound tracks and still frames of Hollywood movies. Some of the more popular MovieStrips are:

The Adventures of Huckleberry Finn
Benji
Black Beauty
Captains Courageous
Charlotte's Web
Doctor Dolittle
From the Mixed-Up Files of Mrs. Basil E. Frankweiler
Island of the Blue Dolphins
Lassie Come Home
My Side of the Mountain
Pippi Longstocking
Treasure Island
The Wizard of Oz

4. Walt Disney perfected the art of cartoon animation.
   a. Disney's full-length feature film *Fantasia* is a classic that has never lost its charm. The following filmstrip is available in the school library:
      (1) *Music from Fantasia* (Disney—4 filmstrips, 4 cassettes, 1 guide)

      The Sorcerer's Apprentice
      Dance of the Hours
      Night on Bald Mountain
      The Rite of Spring

   b. Disney was as successful with live actors as he was with cartoon characters. The following filmstrips adapted from Walt Disney films are in the school library:
      (1) *The Great Locomotive Chase*
      (2) *Hans Brinker by the Zuider Zee*
      (3) *The Legend of Young Dick Turpin*
      (4) *Rob Roy the Highland Rogue*
      (5) *Toby Tyler Joins the Circus*
   c. For those students who would like to experiment with the art of animation and cartoon making, the following kit is in the school library: *Steps in Cartoon Making/The Art of Animation* (Disney—1 filmstrip, 2 cassettes, 10 activity books)
J. Students using Learning Guide 4-6, Places I Would Like to Visit, indicate their choice of places to visit in the West.
K. Students are invited to share their reactions, impressions, and/or observations for inclusion in the class journal "Exploring Our Nation—The West."

UNIT VII: THIS LAND IS OURS: ITS PAST IS PROLOGUE TO THE FUTURE

GOAL: To provide opportunity for students to summarize, question, relate, evaluate, and synthesize what has been learned in this year's study of U.S. history.

STUDENT ORIENTATION

 I. The purpose of this unit is:
   A. To provide opportunity for each student to summarize, evaluate, and synthesize what he or she has learned from this year's study of the United States by answering these questions:
      1. What have I learned about the *history* of my country?
      2. What have I learned about the *geography* of my country?
      3. What have I learned about the *people* of my country?
      4. What have I learned about the *culture* of my country?
   B. To provide opportunity for each student to share his or her observations, concerns, and projections with the class.
   C. To provide opportunity for each student to explore beyond what has happened in our nation's past to considering what might happen in the future. For example:
      1. How can science and technology help America solve its energy crisis?
      2. How can our generation make our country stronger?

 II. Individual student options for summarizing what they have learned; choose one of the following activities:
   A. Using Checklist 4-1 Exploring the United States: Topics for Independent Study, select two or more topics from this checklist that you wish to summarize for your class. Sign your name on the master list in the margin to the left of the topics you have selected. If several of your classmates have indicated interest in the same topics you have chosen, form a committee to share the responsibility for summarizing this topic or topics for the class. *Please keep in mind that there are but two weeks alotted for this activity.* Not more than ten minutes can be given to the presentation of any one topic. Be sure you know what you wish to say, organize your ideas, condense your information; be informative, not wordy!
   B. If you could have been a participant in America's past, which historic personage would you like to have been? In what event or events would you have chosen to participate? Explain your choice of personage and event in one or two well-thought-out paragraphs. Be specific; base your answer on research evidence.
   C. Take the responsibility for introducing to the class information presented in the sound filmstrip set *20th Century Update* (Harcourt, 2 filmstrips, 2 cassettes, 2 manuals). This set is on an advanced comprehension level and will demand careful thought and preparation. Chose but one of the following three topics to prepare and present:
      1. Television—*The Growth of the Industry,* the history of TV's technology and programming; *The Industry at Work,* behind the scenes with the people who turn ideas into broadcasts (2 filmstrips, 2 cassettes, 2 teacher's manuals)
      2. Technology—*Inventions That Have Changed the World,* the impact of the computer and other forms of modern technology on our daily lives; *Ideas Whose Time Has Come,* a look at the series of inventions that had to take place before we could realize our ancient desire for flight. (2 filmstrips, 2 cassettes, 2 teacher's manuals)

3. Energy and Resources—*Energy: The New Frontier,* traditional and alternative methods of energy production including fossil, solar, geothermal, and others; *Natural Resources: How Long Will They Last,* a discussion of the use, conservation, and management of renewable and nonrenewable natural resources (2 filmstrips, 2 cassettes, 2 teacher's manuals)

D. Take the responsibility for presenting, leading the discussion following the presentation, and then summarizing the high points of each of the filmstrips in Set I *or* Set II of the following Educational Enrichment Materials series (each 1 filmstrip and 1 cassette):
   1. *The Other American Minorities: Set I*
      a. *The American Indian*
      b. *The Mexican-American*
      c. *The Puerto Rican/The Cuban*
      d. *The Oriental-American*
   2. *The Other American Minorities: Set II*
      a. *The Irish-Americans*
      b. *The Jewish-Americans*
      c. *The Italian-Americans*
      d. *The German-Americans*

   For statistical information on each of the minorities consult:
   1. *The Ethnic Almanac* by Stephanie Bernardo (Doubleday, 1981)
   2. *The World Almanac and Book of Facts* (Newspaper Enterprise Association, annual)

E. Express your love of and/or pride in your nation by writing a verse to the music of one of the following patriotic songs: "America the Beautiful," "God Bless America," "This Is My Country."

F. Design a travel brochure advertising a city, a national park or monument, or entertainment center in the United States.

CULMINATING ACTIVITIES

I. Synthesize the geographic concepts developed in the units (the Northeast, the South, the Midwest and the Great Plains, and the West) by presenting and discussing the Walt Disney filmstrip series *Discovering Our Land: The Geography of North America.*
   A. The content of these filmstrips covers the following:
      1. "Spaceship Earth's" natural "life support" systems, how climate and erosion combine to make the land suitable for life.
      2. The physical and cultural characteristics of America's major geographic regions.
      3. How air, water, the sun, and the earth itself create weather.
      4. How the water cycle insures our survival.
      5. How soils are formed and the importance of soil conservation.
      6. Why each of America's frontier regions attracted settlers.
      7. How climate, resources, landform, and population affect land use.
      8. Factors influencing the development of American cities.
      9. How advancing technology has enabled us to alter the face of the land.
      10. Satellites as a geographic tool; conservation and the wise use of

resources; recognizing our ability to resolve environmental problems.

B. The individual titles in the series *Discovering Our Land: The Geography of North America* are presented and discussed (Walt Disney Educational Media, 1 guide; 1 filmstrip, 1 cassette, 1 spirit master each)
1. *Floor Plan for Spaceship Earth*
2. *Regions of North America*
3. *The Climate Machine*
4. *Liquid of Life*
5. *The Dirt Show*
6. *The Frontier*
7. *Using the Land*
8. *Cities*
9. *The Land and Technology*
10. *The Future: Earth in the Time Machine*

II. The two students responsible for presenting the filmstrip series *The Other American Minorities* (Educational Enrichment Materials) present the nine filmstrips and lead class discussion of the concepts presented. At the conclusion of this series, a group of students sings the Irving Berlin song "Give Me Your Tired, Your Poor," from the Broadway musical *Miss Liberty* (1949).

A. The class learns that this song is really the last five lines from the poem "The New Colossus," which is engraved on a bronze tablet and is affixed to the pedestal near the main entrance of the Statute of Liberty. The conclusion of the poem follows:

> Give me your tired, your poor,
> Your huddled masses
>   yearning to breathe free,
> The wretched refuse
>   of your teeming shore.
> Send these, the homeless,
>   tempest-tost to me,
> I lift my lamp
>   beside the golden door!
>   *Emma Lazarus*

B. The class discovers that Irving Berlin was born in Russia and came to America when he was five years old. He wrote the song "God Bless America" because he said, "I feel very deeply about this country, and I want people to know it."

C. Students in the class who have written a verse or verses telling about their appreciation of America share their songs with the class.

III. Students who have chosen to summarize topics from Checklist 4-1, Exploring the United States: Topics for Independent Study, present their topics to the class.

IV. As a summary, the students write a paragraph on the topic "Let's Hear It for America."

CLASSROOM STUDY CENTER: BIBLIOGRAPHY*

ALMANACS AND STATISTICAL HANDBOOKS

The Books of American Rankings: Social, Economic, and Political. New York: Facts on File, 1979.

The Hammond Almanac of a Million Facts, Records, Forecasts. New York: New American Library, 1979– . Annual.

Information Please Almanac. New York: Simon & Schuster, 1947– . Annual.

Statistical Abstract of the United States. Bureau of the Census. Washington, D.C.: Government Printing Office, 1878– . Annual.

The World Almanac and Book of Facts. New York: Newspaper Enterprise Association, 1868– . Annual.

ATLASES

Hammond Nature Atlas of America by Roland C. Clement, 2nd ed. Maplewood, N.J.: Hammond, 1976.

National Geographic Picture Atlas of Our Fifty States ed. by Margaret Sedeen. Washington, D.C.: National Geographic, 1978. (Note: Landsat map of the United States is slipped into a pocket affixed to the book.)

BIOGRAPHICAL DICTIONARY

Webster's American Biographies ed. by Charles Van Doren. Springfield, Mass.: Merriam, 1979). (Note: Two special indexes: alphabetically by careers and professions, and alphabetically by state or territory.)

FACTS ABOUT THE STATES

Bird and Flower Emblems of the United States by Hilda Simon. New York: Dodd, 1978.

Facts about the 50 States by Sue R. Brandt, rev. ed. New York: Watts, 1979.

Great State Seals of the United States by Annemarie Berg. New York: Dodd, 1979.

State Flowers by Anne Dowden. New York: Crowell, 1978.

The United States Book: Facts and Legends about the Fifty States by Max H. Short and Elizabeth N. Felton. Minneapolis, Minn.: Lerner, 1975.

COMPUTER PROGRAMS

Regions of the United States Apple TRS80. Dist. by Society for Visual Education.

States and Capitals Apple TRS80. Dist. by Society for Visual Education.

DIST-O-MAP

Dist-O-Map: A New Concept in Travel Planning. Chicago: Rand.

FOLKLORE AND LEGEND

American Folklore and Legend by the Editors of Reader's Digest. Pleasantville, NY: Reader's Digest, 1978.

Heroes in American Folklore by Irwin Shapiro. New York: Messner, 1962.

The Hurricane's Children by Carl Carmer. New York: McKay, 1967.

Kickle Snifters and Other Fearsome Critters Collected from American Folklore ed. by Alvin Schwartz. New York: Lippincott, 1976. Also paper.

The Life Treasury of American Folklore by the Editors of Life. New York: Life, 1961.

A Treasury of American Folklore ed. by B. A. Botkin. New York: Bantam, 1981. Paper.

*This bibliography is not a mandatory list but a recommended list of possible titles for teacher consideration.

Whoppers: Tall Tales and Other Lies Collected from American Folklore ed. by Alvin
    Schwartz. New York: Lippincott, 1975.
Yankee Doodle's Cousins by Anne Malcolmson. Boston: Houghton, n.d.

FORCES OF NATURE

Disastrous Earthquakes by Henry Gilfond. New York: Watts, 1981.
Disastrous Fires by George S. Fichter. New York: Watts, 1981.
Disastrous Floods and Tidal Waves by Melvin Berger. New York: Watts, 1981.
Disastrous Hurricanes and Tornadoes by Max Alth and Charlotte Alth. New York:
    Watts, 1981.
Disastrous Volcanoes by Melvin Berger. New York: Watts, 1981.
Earthquake by Bryce Walker and the Editors of Time-Life Books. Alexandria, Va:
    Time-Life, 1982.
Earthquakes by Dennis B. Fradin. Chicago: Childrens, 1982.
Flood by Champ Clark and the Editors of Time-Life Books. Alexandria, Va.: Time-
    Life, 1982.
Our Violent Earth by the Editors of National Geographic. Washington, D.C.: National
    Geographic, 1982.
Powers of Nature by the Editors of National Geographic. Washington, D.C.: National
    Geographic, 1978.
Tornadoes by Dennis B. Fradin. Chicago: Childrens, 1982.
Volcano by the Editors of the Time-Life Books. Alexandria, Va.: Time-Life, 1982.
Volcanoes by Dennis B. Fradin. Chicago: Childrens, 1982.

FILMSTRIPS

Powers of Nature (National Geographic—5 filmstrips, 5 cassettes). Titles: *Weather and
    Man, Floods, Forest Fires, Earthquakes, Volcanoes.*

MAP

Map of Planet Earth's Disaster Areas. Alexandria, Va.: Time-Life, 1982.

MOTION PICTURE

Day of the Killer Tornadoes (National Audiovisual Center).

MINERALS

Audubon Society Beginner Guide: Rocks and Minerals by George S. Fichter. New
    York: Random, 1982.
Gems and Minerals of America: A Guide to Rock Collecting by Jay Ransom. New York:
    Harper, 1975.
Getting Started in Mineral Collecting by Barbara J. Amlich. New York: Macmillan,
    1972.
The Rock-Hounds Book by Seymour Simon. New York: Viking, 1973.

NATIONAL PARKS

Exploring Our National Parks and Monuments ed. by Devereaux Butcher. Ipswich,
    Mass.: Gambit, 1976. Paper.
National Parks by Michael Frome. Chicago: Rand, 1979. Paper.
National Parks Guide by Michael Frome, rev. ed. Chicago: Rand, 1982.
New America's Wonderland: Our National Parks ed. by Ross Bennett. Washington,
    D.C.: National Geographic, 1975.
*Your National Parks: A Photographic Guide to the National Park System of the United
    States* ed. by George Hornby. New York: Crown, 1979.

MAP

National Parks of the United States: Guide and Map. Washington, D.C.: National Park Service, U.S. Department of the Interior. For sale by the Government Printing Office.

MOTION PICTURE

National Parks: Promise and Challenge (National Geographic).

PEOPLES OF THE UNITED STATES: ETHNIC DIVERSITY

America Immigration by Edward Hartmann. Minneapolis, Minn.: Lerner, 1979.

America's Fascinating Indian Heritage by the Editors of Reader's Digest. Pleasantville, N.Y.: Reader's Digest, 1978.

Black Americans. World Book Reprint. Chicago: World Book. (Note: This excellent resource is available from World Book at the cost of 25¢ per copy up to 20 copies; 20 or more copies cost 20¢ each.)

Famous Indians: A Collection of Short Biographies. Washington, D.C.: Bureau of Indian Affairs, U.S. Department of the Interior. For sale by the Government Printing Office. Paper.

The Negro in American History. Chicago: Encyclopaedia Britannica. 3 vols.

To America by Eleanor B. Tripp. New York: Harcourt, 1969.

FILMSTRIPS

America's Ethnic Heritage—The Beginnings (Discovery to 1800) (BFA—4 filmstrips, 4 cassettes). Titles: *The Beginnings, Indians, Blacks, Germans and Scotch-Irish.*

America's Ethnic Heritage—Growth and Expansion (1800–1880) (BFA—4 filmstrips, 4 cassettes). Titles: *Growth and Expansion, Scandinavians, Irish, Chinese and Japanese.*

Native Americans: Yesterday and Today (BFA—4 filmstrips, 4 cassettes). Titles: *The Hopi Way, An Iroquois Way of Life, Cherokee Land, White Nation, A Navajo Reservation.*

MAP

Federal and State Indian Reservations and Indian Trust Areas. Washington, D.C.: Bureau of Indian Affairs, U.S. Department of the Interior. For sale by the Government Printing Office.

PHYSICAL FEATURES

America's Magnificent Mountains. Washington, D.C.: National Geographic, 1980.

Caverns: A World of Mystery and Beauty by Geraldine Sherman. New York: Messner, 1980.

Caves by Ronal C. Kerbo. Chicago: Childrens, 1981.

PLACE NAMES

American Place Names: A Concise and Selective Dictionary of the Continental United States of America. New York: Oxford University Press, 1970.

Ink, Ark, and All That: How American Places Got Their Names by Vernon Pizer. New York: Putnam, 1976.

Webster's New Geographical Dictionary: A Dictionary of Names of Places, with Geographical and Historical Information and Pronunciations, rev. ed. Springfield, Mass.: Merriam, 1977.

POSTAGE STAMPS

United States Stamps and Stories. Washington, D.C.: U.S. Postal Service, annual.

PRESIDENTS, VICE PRESIDENTS, AND FIRST LADIES

First Ladies by Rhoda Blumberg, rev. ed. New York: Watts, 1981.
Presidents by Harold Coy, rev. ed. New York: Watts, 1981.
Vice Presidents by John D. Feerick and Emalie P. Feerick, rev. ed. New York: Watts, 1981.

RESTORED TOWNS AND VILLAGES

Restored Towns and Historic Districts of America: A Tour Guide by Alice Cromie. New York: Dutton, 1979.

SCENIC WONDERS

America's Wonderlands. Washington, D.C.: National Geographic, 1980.
Joy of Nature by Alma E. Guiness. Pleasantville, N.Y.: Reader's Digest, 1977.
Pictorial Travel Guide of Scenic America by E. L. Jordan, rev. ed. Maplewood, N.J.: Hammond, 1973.

WILDLIFE

Audubon Society Beginner Guide: Birds of North America by George S. Fichter. New York: Random, 1982. Paper.
Audubon Society Beginner Guide: Reptiles and Amphibians of North America by George S. Fichter. New York: Random, 1982. Paper.
Audubon Society Beginner Guide: Wildflowers of North America by George S. Fichter. New York: Random, 1982. Paper.
Guide to the National Wildlife Refuges: How to Get There, What to See and Do by Laura Riley and William Riley. New York: Doubleday, 1979.
North American Wildlife: An Illustrated Guide to 2,000 Plants and Animals by the Editors of Reader's Digest. Pleasantville, N.Y.: Reader's Digest, 1982.
Our Magnificent Wildlife by the Editors of Reader's Digest. Pleasantville, N.Y.: Reader's Digest, 1975.
Song and Garden Birds of North America by the Editors of National Geographic, rev. ed. Washington, D.C.: National Geographic, 1975.
Vanishing Wildlife of North America by the Editors of National Geographic. Washington, D.C.: National Geographic, 1974.
Wild Animals of North America by the Editors of National Geographic. Washington, D.C.: National Geographic, 1979.

CHECKLIST 4-1 EXPLORING THE UNITED STATES:
TOPICS FOR INDEPENDENT STUDY

Agriculture: methods, machinery, products
Archaeological evidence of America's past
Architecture: past, present, future
Artists and their art
Authors and other literary figures
Biography: doers, dreamers, leaders, rascals, and scoundrels
Cities: past, present, future
Communication: past, present, future
Ecology: human impact on the environment
Education: past, present, future
Energy: sources, problems, challenge
Ethnic groups: one nation, many people
Family living: past, present, future
Festivals
Folklore and legends
Foods: regional cookery
Forces of nature: earthquakes, fires, floods, tornadoes, volcanoes
Historic landmarks and events of note
Historical novels
Indigenous animals and plants
Industry and manufacturing
Law, courts, justice
Medicine: past, present, future
Museums and libraries
Music: band, country, folk, jazz, patriotic, opera, contemporary
National monuments and shrines
Occupations, trades, professions: past, present, future
Physical features: deserts, forests, lakes, mountains, plains, rivers
Place names: their stories
Places to visit: where to go, what to see, what to do
Postage stamps: the stories they tell
Presidents, vice presidents, and first ladies
Scenic wonders
Sports and recreation
Statistical data: exports, imports, immigrants, taxes, population, rankings
Transportation: past, present, future

CHECKLIST 4-2 SCHEDULE: RESEARCH REPORTS

Student	Topic	Date

EXAMPLE 4-1   MARTIN LUTHER KING (1929–1968)*
(Clergyman; social reformer. Fiche #25)

Martin Luther King Jr. was born in Atlanta, Georgia on Auburn Avenue—one of the nation's most widely known black sections. King went to Atlanta's black Morehouse College, the integrated Crozier Theological Seminary in Pennsylvania, and finally to Boston College for his doctorate. In 1954, Dr. King became pastor of the Dexter Avenue Baptist Church in Montgomery, Alabama.

King was still relatively unknown in the city's black community when, in December 1955, Mrs. Rosa Parks was arrested for refusing to give up her seat to a white man. The famous Montgomery bus boycott had begun. King was placed in charge, and following a year of pressure and agitation on both sides, the Supreme Court ruled in favor of the protesters. To Dr. King, however, goes the credit for dramatizing the boycott; he was the one who had determined to make it the testing ground of his belief in the nonviolent civil disobedience teachings of Henry Thoreau and Mahatma Gandhi.

Early in 1957 the Southern Christian Leadership Council was formed with King as its president. With this organization, he was able to broaden his civil rights activities to include the entire South. In 1959, King moved to Atlanta to become co-pastor of his father's church.

In the early 1960s, King continued to build up the civil rights movement and make front-page headlines through his leadership at Birmingham and Selma Alabama, Albany, Georgia, and the massive March on Washington in 1963 where he delivered his famous "I Have a Dream" speech. By 1966, he had begun to bring his campaign to Northern cities.

In the spring of 1968, King was in Memphis, Tennessee to help improve the employment conditions of city workers when he was assassinated April 4 by a sniper.

Winner of the Nobel Peace Prize in 1964, Dr. King became a symbol of racial equality. The *New York Times* account of his life contains special coverage of a libel suit against The *Times* for an advertisement criticizing Alabama, and supporting Dr. King, many feature articles, and a two-part series on the "legacy of Martin Luther King" ten years after his death.

COMPREHENSION QUESTIONS

1. Define what both the white Northerner and white Southerner mean by the "new Negro." What are the "new times"? Why did Montgomery, Alabama, become the first testing grounds for civil rights? (1957, Mr 3, VI, p11/1).
2. What facts does the advertisement provide to support its statement that the defense of Dr. King is an "integral part of the total struggle for freedom in the South"? Why is the verb "behead" used to describe how Southern violators are trying to destroy the black struggle? (1960, Mr 29, p25/2).
3. What was the main purpose of the March on Washington? Identify the main issues voiced by civil rights leaders. Which speech, and for what reason, had its original text altered? (1963, Ag 29, 1:8/3).
4. Identify the five "old American reformers" with whom the writer of the "I Have a Dream" article compares Dr. King. What three things could the politicians not ignore about the demonstration? What was Dr. King's central theme? (1963, Ag 29, 1:5/3).
5. How is the editorial written on Dr. King's death organized? Explain the statement that Dr. King had a "naive optimism in nonviolence."

DISCUSSION QUESTIONS

1. Dr. King is often called the "symbol" of the civil rights movement in the articles. Discuss how people become symbols. What are the differences among symbols, legends, and myths? What other "Great Personalities" might also be called symbols? Why?
2. Speculate on how Dr. King's career would have progressed if he had not been

*From *Great Personalities as Reported in The New York Times,* John Dooling, ed. (Sanford, N.C.: Microfilming Corporation of America, 1979), pp. 50–51.

EXAMPLE 4-1 (cont.)

assassinated. If he had lived, how would this have altered the course of the civil rights movement?

3. Mahatma Gandhi and Dr. King, both nonviolent men, met violent deaths. Compare the political and social issues which caused Gandhi's death with those that caused King's.

4. Discuss James Baldwin's article on Dr. King (1978, Ap 5, 29:1/34c). Do you agree or disagree with his statement that "the State of the Union is catastrophic"? Explain your answers.

5. Do you think James Earl Ray killed Martin Luther King? Why or why not? What should have been done to prevent the slaying?

PROJECTS AND ACTIVITIES

1. Select one of the books written by Dr. King such as *Stride Toward Freedom* or *Why We Can't Wait* and prepare a written or oral report.

2. No black leader has yet appeared who has been able to fill Dr. King's place as leader of the civil rights movement. Survey the current black leaders and write an essay stating which candidate is the best prospect to replace King. Support your choice with factual data.

3. The assassination case of Martin Luther King was reopened by Congress with James Earl Ray still proclaiming innocence. Consult *The New York Times Index* or *Reader's Guide to Periodical Literature* and give a brief report on the status of the case.

4. Imagine you were an eyewitness to one of the landmark civil rights events such as the Montgomery, Alabama bus boycott or the March on Washington. Reconstruct the events as you might have witnessed them and keep a diary account of your observation.

5. View the television drama on Martin Luther King's life entitled *King* and discuss why the show drew such a small audience and *Roots* such a large one.

FICHE INDEX (DECEMBER 6, 1955–APRIL 5, 1978)

1. Montgomery, Alabama, buses boycotted over race issues, 1955, D 6, 31:2/8a
2. King arrested for speeding in Montgomery, 1956, Ja 28, 36:3/8a
3. $1,000 reward offered for those who bombed Dr. King's home, F 1, 64:5/8c
4. Battle against traditional; personality sketch of Dr. King (illus.), Mr 21, 28:4/8d
5. Negro minister convicted of directing bus boycott (illus.), Mr 23, 1:2/9a
6. "Jim Crow, he's real tired"; feature article on Montgomery and King's role (illus.), 1957, Mr 3, VI, p11/1
7. Dr. King stabbed by woman in a store in Harlem (illus.), 1958, S 21, 1:7/10b
8. Dr. King of Montgomery plans move to Atlanta (illus.), 1959, D 1, 23:2/11b
9. Dr. King is seized in tax indictment, 1960, F 18, 14:3/11c
10. *Times* advertisement for committee to defend Martin Luther King, Mr 29, p25/2
11. Montgomery suing The *Times* over ad, Ap 20, 25:8/11d
12. *Times* loses libel case, N 4, 67:2/12a
13. Dr. King, symbol of the segregation struggle; feature article (illus.), 1961, Ja 22, VI, p10/12b
14. Federal court finds for *Times,* ending an Alabama libel case, Je 15, 22:4/14a
15. Dr. King is jailed in Albany, Georgia protest (illus.), 1962, Jl 11, 1:6/14b
16. Dr. King is jailed again at prayer rally in Georgia, Jl 28, 1:2/15a
17. Dr. King set free after conviction, Ag 11, 1:6/15b
18. Negro leaders' statements on Birmingham, Alabama accord, 1963, My 11, 8:5/15c
19. 200,000 march for civil rights in orderly Washington rally (illus.), Ag 29, 1:8/3
20. Dr. King's "I have a dream" speech, Ag 29, 1:5/3
21. Dr. King accepts Nobel Peace Prize as "trustee" (illus.), 1964, D 11, 1:2/17b
22. Dr. King leads march at Selma; 1,500 turned back (illus.), 1965, Mr 10, 1:8/4
23. The walk through Selma, Mr 10, 1:6/4
24. Dr. King and 500 jeered in 5-mile Chicago march (illus.), 1966, Ag 22, 1:6/19a

EXAMPLE 4-1 (cont.)

25. Dr. King to weigh civil disobedience if war intensifies (illus.), 1967, Ap 2, 1:3/19b
26. Martin Luther King defines "Black Power"; feature article by Dr. King (illus.), 1967, Je 11, VI, p26/20b
27. Dr. King plans mass protest in capital June 15 (illus.), 1968, Mr 20, 18:4/23b
28. Looting and violence disrupt a massive protest march in Memphis; a black is killed (illus.), Mr 29, 1:4/24a
29. Martin Luther King is slain in Memphis; National Guard called out (illus.), Ap 5, 1:8/5
30. President Johnson urges calm; the President's plea, Ap 5, 1:5/5
31. Dismay in nation over assassination, Ap 5, 1:4/5
32. Dr. King: his career reviewed (illus.), Ap 5, p25/6
33. Statement by President Johnson on death of Dr. King, Ap 6, 23:6/27a
34. A non-violent man is martyred; article on his career as civil rights leader, Ap 7, IV, 1:4/27b
35. He had a dream (edit.), Ap 7, IV, 12:2/28b
36. "A drum major for justice"; editorial cites Dr. King sermon on his eulogy, Ap 9, 46:1/28c
37. Dr. King buried in Atlanta; leaders at rites (illus.), Ap 10, 1:8/7
38. But his truth is marching on; Andrew Young article on Dr. King (illus.), 1974, Ja 15, 37:2/30a
39. Pupils at P.S. 180 wonder, "if Dr. King were alive . . .", Ja 15, 39:1/30b
40. Excerpts from Justice Department report on Dr. King assassination, 1977, F 19, 11:3/31b
41. Decade of black struggle: the legacy of Martin Luther King; first of two articles (illus.), 1978, Ap 2, 1:5/31c
42. Revolution in South: the legacy of Martin Luther King; second of two articles (illus.), Ap 3, 1:1/33
43. Without Martin Luther King (edit.), Ap 4, 32:1/34b
44. James Baldwin article on Dr. King (illus.), Ap 5, 29:1/34c

---

EXAMPLE 4-2   MOUNT ST. HELENS ERUPTS 1980*

When Mount St. Helens erupted on May 18, 1980, it sent into the atmosphere more than one ton of material for every man, woman, and child on earth. This eruption, not the first of a series of 1980 Mount St. Helens displays, but the largest to date, demonstrated the power which nature can produce in even one of its smaller volcanic areas. For example, the eruption of Krakatoa (1883) on Pulau Island, between Java and Sumatra, Indonesia, claimed 36,000 lives, and the volcanic violence of Mount Pelee (1902), in French Martinique, claimed 30,000.

Mount St. Helens had been active before. Though the volcano had been dormant for 123 years, it had been active many times in recorded history and is at least 40,000 years old. The series of 1980 eruptions, however, were the first to occur at a time when the Washington area around the volcano was inhabited by a significant number of people.

The death toll from the eruptions remains unclear, but an estimate of at least 100 between March and June 1980 is not unreasonable. In addition to deaths, usually by landslides, mudslides, or asphyxiation by ash, there were an uncounted number of injuries. The damage to the surrounding land, of course, was significant. Acres and acres of prime timber were destroyed or damaged, farmland was overrun and crops destroyed, and volcanic ash, spread for miles around, caused difficulties for communities that were otherwise out of the volcano's way. The cost of the damage, and of the cleanup, runs into billions of dollars.

There had been some warning that the volcano was near eruption. Seismographs recorded earthquakes within and around Mount St. Helens at least three days before the

---

*From *Great Events Three as Reported in The New York Times* (Sanford, N.C.: Microfilming Corporation of America, 1981), pp. 91–92.

EXAMPLE 4-2 (cont.)

first eruption on March 27, 1980. Without such warning, the damage and loss of life would undoubtedly have been much higher.

No one can be certain that the series of eruptions is over; volcanoes typically erupt periodically over a period of several years before beginning another dormant period. Once people who are threatened by the volcano are evacuated, perhaps a certain pleasure can be taken in one of nature's most magnificent spectacles, the almost spontaneous release of energy that can be measured in terms of hundreds of times the strength of the man-made atomic bomb dropped on Hiroshima, Japan, in 1945.

COMPREHENSION QUESTIONS

1. What was the last active volcano in the continental United States before Mount St. Helens? (1980, Mr 28, 1:5/15A).
2. How big was the ash cloud that came from Mount St. Helens on May 19? (1980, My 20, 1:3/4).
3. In what possible way might Mount St. Helens' eruptions prove to be an economic boon? (1980, My 25, 1:2/23C).
4. How long did geologists speculate that volcanic activity might continue at Mount St. Helens? (1980, My 27, 20:1/25A).
5. Who owns the land on top of Mount St. Helens? (1980, Je 5, IV, 1/26A).

DISCUSSION QUESTIONS

1. Why did souvenirs of Mount St. Helens' eruptions (primarily ash), and other souvenirs, such as T-shirts, become so popular both in the Pacific Northwest and throughout the United States? What might the popularity of such items tell us about ourselves and our culture?
2. What psychological and sociological conclusions, if any, might we make about people who knowingly choose to live in an area near an active volcano or a volcano which is likely to become active? Is there any relationship between people who live near sites of possible natural disruptions like volcanoes, and people who live near potential man-made disruptions such as nuclear power plants?
3. What responsibility, if any should the federal government take for the survivors of the Mount St. Helens eruptions? Under what instances, if any, ought the Federal government function as an "insurer of last resort"?
4. Do you feel that emergency and relief measures taken before, during, and after the Mount St. Helens eruptions were adequate? If not, why not? If you were a police officer or fire chief in the area, what preparations and emergency plans would be necessary to deal with an eruption?
5. What are some of the scientific questions that need to be answered before we can better understand and predict volcanic eruptions such as Mount St. Helens? What knowledge do we have today about volcanoes that we did not have 50 or 100 years ago?

PROJECTS AND ACTIVITIES

1. Define each of the following words, and use each in a sentence or paragraph: (a) magma (b) harmonic tremor (c) effusive volcano (d) explosive volcano (e) andesitic rock (f) lava (g) basaltic rock (h) nuee ardente (i) seismograph.
2. Using information available from your school and/or local library, construct a model of either a volcano or Mount St. Helens. Your model should show the forces that are constantly working in a volcano which is dormant, how an eruption occurs, or how and why a volcano signals an impending eruption.
3. Use *The New York Times Index* to help you list all the volcanoes that have erupted since 1850, their location and year of eruption. Then chart the violence of the explosions and frequency of activity. What conclusions can you draw from your statistics?
4. Indians in the Pacific Northwest had a legend to account for the existence of Mount

EXAMPLE 4-2 (cont.)

St. Helens (1980, Je 15, 18:1/28A). Identify other myths and legends people in other areas of the United States or other countries have had to account for volcanoes.

5. Locate Krakatoa on a map, and then do the research needed to help you answer these questions: (a) How many times (other than in 1883) has Krakatoa erupted? (b) How high is Krakatoa from its base to its cone? (c) How far is Krakatoa from Australia, where its explosions were heard? (d) How high in the air did Krakatoa fling ash? (e) How many square miles were covered by ash? (f) How far away were tsunamis (tidal waves) recorded? (g) How long did it take for plant and animal life to be reestablished after 1883?

FICHE INDEX (AUGUST 30, 1883–JUNE 25, 1980)

1. Events Beyond The Sea, 1883, Ag 30, 1:3/9A
2. The Devastation In Java, 1883, Ag 31, 1:4/9B
3. The Great Volcanic Eruptions, 1883, S 1, 1:4/9C
4. The Java Eruptions, 1883, S 3, 1:4/9D
5. The Calamity In Oceanica, 1883, S 5, 1:5/9E
6. The Oceanica Calamity, 1883, S 6, 5:2/9F
7. Flashes Of Light From Mount Pelee, 1902, My 17, 1:7/10A
8. Further Martinique Horrors, 1902, My 17, 1:7/10B
9. Volcanoes Of America, 1902, My 18, 2:3/10C
10. Steamer *Etona* Fled From Fiery Shower, 1902, My 19, 1:7/10D
11. Clouds Of Sand At Sea, 1902, My 19, 2:2/11B
12. Panic In Fort De France, 1902, My 21, 1:5/12A
13. Fleeing From Fort De France, 1902, My 22, 1:7/12B
14. Martinique May Be Entirely Abandoned, 1902, My 23, 1:7/13A
15. Among The Ruins Of St. Pierre (illus.), 1920, Je 8, 25:1/1
16. Story Of An Eye-Witness, 1902, Je 8, 26:4/14B
17. Pelee's Warnings To St. Pierre (illus.), 1902, Je 8, 27:1/2
18. Seismic Jolts On Coast Mountain Raise Fears of Volcanic Eruption, 1980, Mr 25, 17:2/14C
19. Volcano, Dormant For 123 Years, Spewing Ash in Washington State (map), 1980, Mr 28, 1:5/15A
20. Volcanic Steam and Ash Billow From Mountain, 1980, Mr 29, 6:1/15B
21. The Gods Are Angry In The Cascades (illus.), 1980, Mr 30, IV, 7:1/16B
22. Volcano Spurts Biggest Eruption Of Ashy Plumes, 1980, Ap 2, 16:1/16C
23. Mount St. Helens Reported 'Perking Away' On Coast, 1980, Ap 8, 12:5/17A
24. Near Mount St. Helens, Souvenirs Of Volcano Erupt (map), 1980, Ap 20, 26:2/17B
25. Quakes And Eruptions Shake Mount St. Helens, 1980, My 10, 8:5/17C
26. At Least 8 Dead As Peak Erupts: Worst Blast Yet (illus.), 1980, My 19, 1:2/3
27. Mt. St. Helens Pours Its Cloud Of Ashes Across Northwest (illus.), 1980, My 20, 1:3/4
28. 50,000 Warned Of Volcano Flood Threat (illus.), 1980, May 21, 1:2/5
29. Dust Likely To Have Little Weather Impact, 1980, My 21, 20:2/20B
30. Fears Of Flooding From Volcano Ease, 1980, My 22, 1:4/20C
31. Carter Arrives In Pacific Northwest To Assess Damage, 1980, My 22, II, 12:1/21A
32. Volcano Fallout Is Expected To Have Little Effect on Health Or Crops, 1980, My 22, II, 12:1/21B
33. Volcano's Neighbors Happy To Be Safe, 1980, My 22, II, 12:4/22A
34. Carter Tours Volcano Area and Promises Federal Aid (illus.), 1980, My 23, 1:4/6
35. U-2 Pilot Tells Of His 'Gruesome' Flight Over The Volcano, 1980, My 23, 12:2/22C
36. Cleanup Of Tons Of Volcanic Ash Begins In Nearly Closed Coast Towns, 1980, My 24, 8:2/23B
37. Damage By Volcano May Top $1.5 Billion, 1980, My 25, 1:2/23C
38. Even To Experts, St. Helens Was Powerful Surprise, 1980, My 25, 18:1/24B
39. Mount St. Helens Erupts Again, Raining Ash In Oregon (map), 1980, My 26, 1:3/7
40. Mount St. Helens Is Quiet As A New Cleanup Begins, 1980, My 27, 20:1/25A
41. Man and Dogs Evacuated At Cabin Near Volcano, 1980, Je 1, 26:1/25B
42. Search Ends For Victims Of Volcano, With Toll At 22, 1980, Je 2, 14:6/25C

EXAMPLE 4-2 (cont.)

43. Carter To Seek $860 Million In Aid For Volcano Victims, 1980, Je 5, 16:6/25D
44. After Volcano, The Logjam (illus.), 1980, Je 5, IV, 1:5/26A
45. Costs Of Coast Volcano Eruption Put At $2.7 Billion, 1980, Je 11, 17:1/26B
46. A New Eruption Hits 50,000 Feet At Mt. St. Helens, 1980, Je 13, 12:1/27A
47. Debris Expected To Move West, 1980, Je 13, 12:1/27B
48. Rain And Winds Disperse Debris Of A 3d Eruption (map), 1980, Je 14, 6:1/27C
49. Taste Of Ashes Lingering In Northwest, 1980, Je 15, 18:1/28A
50. Volcano A Woman In Indian Lore, 1980, Je 15, 18:1/28B
51. Around Mount St. Helens, Hope Sprouts From The Ash, 1980, Je 15, IV, 9:1/28C
52. Service Held for Mountain Man Who Refused To Leave Volcano (illus.), 1980, Je 16, 19:5/29B
53. Lava Dome Grows Rapidly In Mount St. Helens Crater, 1980, Je 19, 16:4/29C
54. Pet Dirt (illus.), 1980, Je 22, III, 17:2/30A
55. Hundreds Of Blazes Smolder Dangerously Under Volcano's Ash, 1980, Je 25, 22:5/30B

LEARNING GUIDE 4-1 GUIDELINES FOR HOLDING A GROUP DISCUSSION

A discussion is an important way of learning; it is an orderly way to share information. The following guidelines will help you have a successful discussion.

1. BE PREPARED

Be sure you understand the topic of discussion; ask yourself:

_____ What does this topic mean?

_____ Can I define the topic so that others will understand it?

Build your understanding of the topic by thoughtful reading, viewing, and listening:

_____ Take careful notes.

_____ Be sure of your facts.

_____ Define new terms.

_____ Identify each book, filmstrip, study print, cassette, chart, etc., from which you have taken your notes.

Organize your information:

_____ Make an outline.

_____ Group your notes under each main topic of the outline.

_____ List questions you wish to ask; comments you wish to make.

2. TAKE PART IN THE DISCUSSION

Express your ideas clearly.

_____ Use as few words as possible.

_____ Stick to the point.

_____ Be courteous.

LEARNING GUIDE 4-2 WAYS TO BUILD AND SHARE INFORMATION*

Listening: individual student and group reports, materials read by others, cassettes, records, panel discussions, radio programs.

Viewing: films, filmstrips, slides, motion pictures, videotapes, study prints, charts, graphs, exhibits, television programs.

Reading: reference materials, newspaper articles, current periodicals, biographies, autobiographies, diaries, journals, history, historical novels, plays.

Writing: reports, stories, poems, plays, skits, songs, quizzes, games.

Designing and Making: time lines, murals, charts, maps, dioramas, puppets, models, displays.

Arranging: special centers of interest, exhibits, assembly programs.

Participating in: group discussions, workshops, committee activities, assemblies.

Investigating: American history and customs, contributions of great men and women, ethnic arts and crafts, landmark events.

*Adapted from John U. Michaelis, *Social Studies for Children in a Democracy,* 6th ed. (Englewood Cliffs, N.J.: Prentice-Hall, 1976), pp. 271–272.

LEARNING GUIDE 4-3 GOOD STUDY HABITS*

AT SCHOOL
Know what to do!
Stop—stop other activities so that you can get the direction clear.
Look—watch the teacher so that you get each point.
Listen—get the exact details on what to do.
Ask—raise questions if you do not understand any part.
Proceed to do it!
Organize—arrange the needed materials and plan the steps to take.
Concentrate—stick to your job and do not be distracted.
Finish—complete the assignment before starting other activities.
Check—review your work to be sure it is complete and well done.

AT HOME
Know exactly what you are to study.
Be sure to take the necessary materials home.
Plan your study time so that you will not have to stay up late.
Study in a place where you will not be bothered.
Arrange the study materials so that they can be used effectively.
Stick to the job once you have started it.
Do your own work even though others may help you with difficult parts.
Review the main ideas after you have completed your work.
Be ready to ask questions the next day on any parts you do not understand.

*Adapted from John U. Michaelis, *Social Studies for Children in a Democracy,* 6th ed. (Englewood Cliffs, N.J.: Prentice-Hall, 1976). p. 296.

LEARNING GUIDE 4-4 BIOGRAPHY SUMMARY*

I read the following biography:

Title _____ Author _____

This is the story of _____ who lived in the colony or colonies of

_____ during the period:

‾‾‾‾ ‾‾ ‾‾ ‾‾ ‾‾ ‾‾ ‾‾ ‾‾ ‾‾‾‾ ‾‾ ‾‾ ‾‾ ‾‾ ‾‾ ‾‾ ‾‾
1620   '30 '40 '50 '60 '70 '80 '90 1700 '10 '20 '30 '40 '50 '60 '70

While reading this biography I learned these facts about colonial manners and customs:

Concerning food, I discovered
    The various kinds of foods commonly eaten. For example:

    How foods were prepared. For example:

    How foods were stored. For example:

    Other facts such as:

Concerning homes, I discovered
    What colonial houses looked like. For example:

    The number and size of rooms. For example:

    The various pieces of furniture commonly used. For example:

Concerning household chores, I discovered
    The typical chores performed by the women of the family. For example:

    The typical chores performed by the men of the family. For example:

    The typical chores performed by the children of the family. For example:

    Other facts such as:

Concerning clothing, I discovered
    The kinds of garments worn and how they were made. For example:

Concerning schools, I discovered
    How colonial schools differed from our schools today. For example:

Concerning occupations, I discovered
    The following occupations that were new to me:

    Other facts such as:

Concerning animals, I discovered
    The following mentioned:

*Corinne P. Clendening and Ruth Ann Davies, *Creating Programs for the Gifted: A Guide for Teachers, Librarians, and Students* (New York: R. R. Bowker, 1980), pp. 212–213.

LEARNING GUIDE 4-5   HISTORICAL NOVEL SUMMARY*

Student _____ Date _____

I have read the following historical novel:

Title _____ Author _____

This novel portrayed life during the period _____

The setting of this novel was _____

The plot of this novel was _____

_____

_____

In analyzing the historical significance of this novel, the following facts are noteworthy:
Concerning Food—
    Kinds of food commonly eaten:

    How foods were prepared, preserved, and stored:

    Other interesting facts about food, such as:

Concerning Family Living—
    The role of the father:

    The role of the mother:

    The role of children:

    Other interesting facts about family living, such as:

    Concerning the Manners and Customs of the People—

    Concerning Religion—

    Concerning Law and Order—

    Concerning Socioeconomic Problems—

    Concerning Occupations—

    Concerning Education—

    Concerning Games, Sports, Recreation—

    Concerning Transportation and Communication—

    Other Noteworthy Background Information—

Would you have enjoyed living in the time and place portrayed in this novel? Elaborate on your answer.

*Corinne P. Clendening and Ruth Ann Davies, *Creating Programs for the Gifted: A Guide for Teachers, Librarians, and Students* (New York: R. R. Bowker, 1980), pp. 213–214.

LEARNING GUIDE 4-6   PLACES I WOULD LIKE TO VISIT

Where to Visit	What to Do and What to See

Model 5

The Oceans: A Key to Our Future

GRADES: 6–8.

DURATION. 45 Days.

GOAL: To provide opportunity for the student to explore the many-faceted ocean world: its history, its science, its mystery, its beauty, and its place in the earth's ecosystem.

OBJECTIVES

To present key concepts relating to the ocean as a habitat, as a physical environment, and as a delicately balanced ecosystem.

To perceive the imminent threat to human existence if the oceans of the world are thrown out of balance.

To perceive that the commonly held belief that the oceans and the land masses are eternal is but an illusion.

To discover those men and women who have contributed to human knowledge of the ocean.

INTRODUCTION

This model program does not utilize a textbook. The sound filmstrip program *The Oceans: A Key to Our Future* (United Learning) is employed to build the students' background knowledge of oceanography before they undertake an in-depth study of those topics and concepts of special individual interest and concern. The *teacher's guide and lesson activities manual* from United Learning, reproduced on the following pages, provides the structure and content of the program.*

*This instructional program used with permission from United Learning, a division of MJE Corporation, Niles, Ill., is an example of commercially produced instructional programs of excellence, well worthy of use with the gifted.

After using the filmstrip program as an introduction, the teacher can then provide myriad opportunities for students to explore widely, to delve deeply, and to concentrate on an area of special interest (see Checklist 5-1 and Resource List at the end of this model).

THE OCEANS: A KEY TO OUR FUTURE*

CONTENTS

Purpose and Description of the Program
Materials in the Program
    Teacher's Guide and Lesson Activities Book
    Sound Filmstrips
Content Covered in the Program
Self-Evaluation Quizzes
Placement in the Curriculum
Instructional Notes
    Order of Presentation
    List of Resources
Suggested Instructional Procedures
    Episode 1: THE OCEANS: PAST, PRESENT AND FUTURE
    Episode 2: THE OCEANS: A STOREHOUSE OF FOOD
    Episode 3: THE OCEANS: A STOREHOUSE OF RAW MATERIALS
    Episode 4: THE OCEANS: A STOREHOUSE OF POWER
    Episode 5: CHANGING THE OCEANS

PURPOSE AND DESCRIPTION OF THE PROGRAM

This five-part series is designed for use with the intermediate and junior high general science curriculum to underscore basic earth and life science concepts pertaining to oceans. The program presents these concepts in a manner that captures the mystery and excitement of the study of marine environment.

The oceans, or, in fact, the World Ocean, is viewed as a major resource for future development. Human interdependence with the sea is discussed from a variety of perspectives—historical, geographical, ecological, economic and technological.

Students viewing the filmstrips will gain a knowledge of the ocean's size, depth, physical features, composition, life forms, life zones and relationship to land masses and waterways. Past, present and future reliance upon ocean resources is explained and visualized with a combination of diagrammatic art and marine photography. The visuals are both factual and imaginative, adding a dimension that is in keeping with the scope of the subject. Learning objectives are interwoven into effective narration and visualization in a logical and memorable fashion. The presentation, a dramatic mix of legend, fact, photographic exploration and artistic conjecture, will hold viewer interest while offering a coherent understanding of the interplay of life and forces that make up the World Ocean.

Within the context of a look at the ocean from the standpoint of its potential as a source of food, raw materials and energy, the life story of the ocean and its effects upon our lives now and in the future is presented in a progressive fashion so that the material takes on cohesiveness, excitement and relevance. Potential damage to the ocean environment through human inter-

*United Learning, 1977.

vention is discussed in a straightforward fashion, designed to elicit concern without causing undue fright, striking a sensible balance between human needs and technological progress. The program also offers a consideration of a wide range of future marine-related occupations which will arise from increased utilization of ocean resources.

Marine scientists have cooperated in the formulation of this program, which incorporates their fascination with the subject into a solid unit of basic science material that has both learning and entertainment value. The program takes advantage of the resources of the filmstrip medium—music, sound effects, color, drama, live photography and well-researched narrative content—to present a wide-ranging picture of an environment that comprises three quarters of the earth's surface.

MATERIALS IN THE PROGRAM

TEACHER'S GUIDE AND LESSON ACTIVITIES BOOK

This book contains a description of the series, its purpose and content. Also included are suggestions for teacher and student preparation, filmstrip presentation techniques, recommendations for curricular placement and specific information about each filmstrip in the program. Specific learning outcomes are stated and are further emphasized in the Lesson Activities Sections, which include discussion questions and projects based upon these learning outcomes.

SOUND FILMSTRIPS

There are five sound filmstrips in this program, each on considering the marine environment from a different perspective and containing some specific learning outcomes. Each filmstrip, however, underscores and reinforces the others, so that the basic science concepts covered in the program as a whole can be understood as interdependent and interrelated.

The audio is on cassettes with manual and automatic 50 HZ signals. The manual advance is contained on the gold label side of the cassette and will allow for individual pacing. The inaudible signal, contained on the white label side of the cassette, is for use on automatic advance projectors.

The individual episodes are:

1. The Oceans: Past, Present and Future
2. The Oceans: A Storehouse of Food
3. The Oceans: A Storehouse of Raw Materials
4. The Oceans: A Storehouse of Power
5. Changing the Oceans

CONTENT COVERED IN THE PROGRAM

Episode 1. Ocean topography, geography, exploration methods, food chains, properties of water, underwater and surface weather and its effects upon our atmosphere, and a summary of human utilization of ocean resources.

Episode 2. Food from the sea—animal and vegetable, methods of extraction, fish and seaweed farming, life zones, the food cycle and future possibilities for increasing the yield.

Episode 3. The life story of the ocean as a depository of land materials, animal and vegetable remains; uses of fossil materials; living vegetables as resources; mineral content of sea water; methods of desalinization, its feasibility and use; medicinal and chemical utilization of ocean minerals; ocean mining and a consideration of further utilization of raw materials from the sea.

Episode 4. Energy potential of the ocean—tides, currents, winds, waves, thermal properties, chemical energy potential and a discussion of future potential in the use of ocean power.

Episode 5. Fanciful and factual human-engineered changes in the ocean, the continental drift theory, oceanic activity and its effect upon land formation, civilization and technology and its impact upon the ocean, the importance of international cooperation in the use and maintenance of the ocean environment and human interdependence with the sea.

SELF-EVALUATION QUIZZES

These quizzes, one for each filmstrip in the program, incorporate the stated learning outcomes which should occur as a result of viewing each filmstrip. They contain true-false, multiple choice, completion and essay questions which are designed to test understanding of the concepts presented in the program. They can be used as pretests in advance of filmstrip viewing, as post-tests for reinforcement and review, or both before and after viewing as individual self-tests.

Pretest. The Self-Evaluation Quizzes can be used to spark interest in filmstrip content by lending additional purpose to viewing. They provide a brief summary of student understanding of the marine environment and can serve to stimulate curiosity about the material to be covered. In administering the quizzes, emphasize that they are intended for self-evaluation and instruct the students to provide answers only if they are reasonably certain of the facts. The papers can then be collected, marked and returned, but it is suggested that they not be corrected. Instead, call attention to those questions which have been answered incorrectly or not at all, and ask the students to be alert to answers which will be provided by the filmstrip. They can also be self-evaluated during a class discussion of the questions and the possible answers without being collected and graded, and the students can fill in the missing answers after viewing the filmstrip.

Post-Test. Used in combination with a pretest as suggested above, the post-test can provide immediate reinforcement and help to underscore those concepts which are least understood. The Self-Evaluation Quizzes can also serve as the basis for review discussion after viewing. Encourage the students to write the correct answers after any questions they may have missed.

PLACEMENT IN THE CURRICULUM

This program can be used specifically for a unit of study on the ocean environment which is usually a part of the general science curriculum. In addition, since it treats questions of national and international concern, the program can be used to implement or supplement social studies discussions on the influence of civilization upon the natural environment, economic dependence upon natural resources, or the development of international cooperation in the implementation of laws and treaties to protect the environment.

The "futuring" theme, which runs as a common thread throughout the program, would also make it adaptable for use as part of a careers seminar, particularly for those students interested in the scientific social studies professions.

INSTRUCTIONAL NOTES

It is suggested that you read this Teacher's Guide, preview the sound film-strips, and familiarize yourself with the Suggested Instructional Procedures before presenting the program. This will enable you to determine where it best fits into your curriculum and ways in which you can use it to reinforce other class material, and also give you an opportunity to procure related materials. Note also that the metric systems of measurements are used throughout the program.

ORDER OF PRESENTATION

The filmstrips are numbered in a sequential order that the authors feel is best suited to a cohesive presentation of the material included in the program. Episode 1 is introductory in purpose and also provides a summary of what is to follow in succeeding episodes. Episodes 2, 3 and 4, while not directly sequential to one another, have been planned so that interrelated concepts are built upon in a logical and memorable fashion from one episode to the next. Episode 5 brings all of the concepts together in a consideration of their significance to future use and development of ocean resources. The Self-Evaluation Quizzes are also geared to take advantage of this logical development of interrelated concepts.

LIST OF RESOURCES

This list is furnished as a supplement to available resources listed in library card catalogs and includes current publications, periodicals and organizations that can furnish information and materials.

Periodicals, Newsletters, and Serial Publications

AAAS Science Books & Films. American Association for Advancement of Science Publications Department (Dept. W-3), 1515 Massachusetts Ave. NW, Washington, DC 20005

AAZPA Newsletter. American Association of Zoological Parks and Aquariums, Oglebay Park, Wheeling, WV 26003

Animal Kingdom. New York Zoological Society, Membership Department, Bronx, NY 10460

Audubon. National Audubon Society, 950 Third Ave., New York, NY 10022

Booklist. American Library Association, 50 E. Huron St., Chicago, II 60611

The Economic Value of Ocean Resources to the United States. Committee on Commerce, United States Senate, National Ocean Policy Study, U.S. Government Printing Office, Washington, DC 20402

Fisheries. American Fisheries Society, Carl R. Sullivan, ed., 5410 Grosvenor Lane, Bethesda, MD 20014

Marine Mammal Chart. U.S. Department of Commerce, National Oceanic and Atmospheric Administration, Robert M. White, Administrator, National Marine Fisheries Service, U.S. Government Printing Office, Washington, DC 20402

Marine Technology Society Journal. Marine Technology Society, 1730 M St. NW, Suite 412, Washington, DC 20036

Oceans. Oceanic Society, Membership Services, Box 26, Uxbridge, MA 01569

Sea Frontiers. International Oceanographic Foundation, 3979 Rickenbacker Causeway, Virginia Key, Miami, FL 33149

Sea Grant '70s. Texas A&M University, Sea Grant College Program, College Station, TX 77843

Sea Secrets. International Oceanographic Foundation, 3979 Rickenbacker Causeway, Virginia Key, Miami, FL 33149

Selected U.S. Government Publications. Superintendent of Documents, U.S. Government Printing Office, Washington, DC 20402

SUGGESTED INSTRUCTIONAL PROCEDURES

EPISODE 1: THE OCEANS: PAST, PRESENT AND FUTURE*

I. Teacher Preparation
   1. The teacher should become familiar with the content of the filmstrip and the material in this guide so as to have a knowledge of the specific concepts presented in this filmstrip and follow-up material.
   2. This filmstrip has an introductory purpose, as it touches upon each of the aspects covered in the other four filmstrips, and should, therefore, be viewed first.

II. Student Preparation
   1. Use the Self-Evaluation Quiz as an introduction to the subject by presenting it as a survey of student knowledge about the ocean. Once administered, the answers to the questions on the quiz can provide material for class discussion about conceptions and misconceptions pertaining to the ocean's terrain, size, composition, life forms, exploration and its effect upon the land.
   2. Preface the showing of the filmstrip with viewing and discussion of a world globe with emphasis upon ocean areas. Try to elicit recognition of the absence of real boundaries between known ocean areas, and appreciation of its size in relation to land areas.
   3. In lieu of using the self-evaluation quiz prior to viewing, you might simply ascertain, and perhaps list, some student conceptions about the ocean's size, depth, topography and its importance to human life.
   4. Ask students to name some ways in which they are affected by the existence of the ocean. Try to bring out recognition of its value as a

*Viewing Time 9:00 Frames 50

source of food and raw materials, its effect upon the land, and its importance as a highway and a barrier between continents.

III. Learning Outcomes

As a result of viewing this filmstrip and participating in follow-up discussion and activities, students should be able to demonstrate a knowledge of the following facts and concepts:

1. The ocean waters serve as international avenues of trade.
2. Continental shorelines are surrounded by continental shelves and slopes.
3. The topography of the ocean floor resembles that of the surface of the land.
4. The oceans are interconnected and can be more properly considered as the World Ocean.
5. Underwater exploration has been made possible by the invention of life-support systems and through the use of depth-sounding methods.
6. Ocean life, both plant and animal, is dependent upon oxygen, and all forms of ocean life are part of a complex food chain.
7. Water is denser than air, and this density helps to account for differences between water and land creatures.
8. Surface temperatures vary, but deep seawater remains constantly just above freezing.
9. Ocean surface temperatures affect coastal weather because of the stability of these temperatures.
10. Storms occur underwater.
11. The ocean is both constructive and destructive, in that its movements build up or wear down shorelines.
12. The ocean is a catch-all, or dumping ground, for materials from the land and the atmosphere, some of which are beneficial and others which are destructive.
13. We utilize ocean resources at present, but there is potential for even greater utilization by future generations.

IV. Filmstrip Presentation

This introductory filmstrip is intended to present facts and concepts about ocean topography, geography, exploration methods, food chains, water properties, weather and resources. In addition, it presents the overall concept of human interdependence with the sea.

V. Lesson Activities

Discussion Questions. After viewing the filmstrip, some of the following questions or discussion topics might be used to underscore and reinforce filmstrip content:

1. In what ways are we dependent upon the ocean, both in terms of its resources and its historical importance as a highway or barrier?
2. How does the topography of the ocean floor compare to that of the land?
3. Is the area in which you live affected by ocean temperatures? If so, how and why? If not, why not?
4. What are some possibilities for further utilization of ocean resources?
5. Discuss the concept of a World Ocean as compared to the "seven seas"

idea. Refer to a global map to point up the validity of the interconnected oceans concept.

Projects. Following are some suggested topics for special reports or research projects:

1. What are the various methods of taking depth soundings, and how do they work?
2. Find out what areas of the North American continent, or another continent, were once covered by sea water. What characteristics do these areas have in common? How do we know that a given area was once a part of the ocean? Prepare a written or verbal report.
3. Research and report on the kinds of jobs available that pertain to marine science. Imaginative papers might be done on such subjects as "Life as a Marine Biologist," "Drilling for Oil at Sea," "What It's Like to Live in a SeaLab," "Farm Life in the Middle of the Ocean," and other such personalized approaches to ocean-related jobs.
4. Interview aquarium personnel or individuals who work in some field of marine science and prepare a report on the interview, or invite that person to speak to the class and take part in a question and answer session.
5. If possible, arrange to visit an area that shows the effects of oceanic activity, or ask the students to assemble a pictorial display of such areas.

EPISODE 2: THE OCEANS: A STOREHOUSE OF FOOD*

I. Teacher Preparation
1. The teacher should become familiar with the content of the filmstrip and the material in this guide so as to have a knowledge of the specific concepts presented in this filmstrip and follow-up material.
2. It is recommended that this filmstrip be used early in the program because it deals with an aspect of the ocean that is probably most familiar to students. It also explains the life cycle and life zones, concepts that are essential to a complete understanding of the material in the filmstrips which follow.

II. Student Preparation
1. Exhibit pictures of plankton, ask if anyone knows what they are, where they are found, and what purpose they serve. This can lead into a discussion of food chains, which can provide an introduction to the material in the filmstrip.
2. Make a list of the kinds of food students know about that are obtainable from the ocean. Retain the list for later additions after viewing.
3. Ask students to name species of ocean animals with which they are familiar. Discuss the differences in size and structure and see if the students can give some possible reasons for these differences, such as available food supplies, the areas of the ocean they inhabit, and the amount of light and air available.

*Viewing Time 10:25 Frames 52

III. Learning Outcomes

As a result of viewing this filmstrip and participating in follow-up discussion and activities, students should be able to demonstrate a knowledge of the following facts and concepts:

1. It is within the realm of possibility that ocean food resources could be depended upon to feed the majority of the world population.
2. Fish and shellfish have formed a part of the human diet since earliest times.
3. Fishing is a major industry, and it is accomplished by modern technological methods.
4. Fish and shellfish farming have been developed, and serve the same functions as land farming, i.e., regulated feeding and increased yield.
5. Seaweed has long been a part of human diets in Oriental countries.
6. Plankton are microscopic forms of plant and animal life, and serve as food for larger ocean animals. Being plentiful and rich in food value, they could be processed for human food.
7. Use of ocean food products can be increased substantially.
8. Dredging devices have been used to find out what lies on the ocean floor.
9. The ocean has been scientifically classified into zones, divided according to physical and biological features. The zones and their characteristics are:
   a. The tidal zone, marked by abundant light and oxygen and a corresponding abundance of plant and animal life.
   b. The shallow water zone on continental shelves, which also has abundant light and oxygen and much marine life.
   c. The deeper, or middle zone, has less plant life because of decreased penetration of sunlight, and a thinner animal population.
   d. The deep sea zone is perpetually dark, available food is scarce, and life forms are adapted to the darkness and scarcity of food.
   e. The sea floor—the bottom or benthic zone—contains many life forms, some of which are blind, unmoving, boneless or nearly boneless.
10. The ocean food cycle starts at the top with sun-absorbing plankton which are eaten by the swimming creatures of the sea; their droppings and dead or dying creatures provide food for middle zone animals; what is left is eaten by bottom feeders or dissolves into sediment. Upward moving ocean currents carry unused nutrients back up to surface to be absorbed by the plankton.
11. Overfishing can seriously interrupt the ocean food cycle.
12. More national and international laws are needed to protect ocean life.

IV. Filmstrip Presentation

This filmstrip explains and graphically illustrates ocean life zones and the food cycle. The marine environment is ideal for clarification of these concepts, as it is relatively uncomplicated in comparison to land zones and cycles. The effects of human intervention into the food cycle are very obvious, thus the filmstrip can serve as an excellent vehicle for enabling students to realize our inherent responsibilities toward maintaining an ecological balance. By pointing up our possible future reliance upon ocean food resources, the filmstrip makes a convincing statement for the economic value of maintaining and enhancing this balance.

V. Lesson Activities
Discussion Questions. After viewing the filmstrip, some of the following questions or discussion topics might be used in order to underscore and reinforce filmstrip content:
1. Discuss life zones both on land and in the sea in terms of adaptation of the various life forms that occupy those zones.
2. Does seafood form a regular part of your family's diet? Compare the nutritive value of fish and meat, and discuss why it would be of value to increase the ocean's yield of food.
3. Discuss and draw a parallel between the food cycles on land and in the ocean.
4. Why does the amount of sunlight that penetrates into a given zone affect the availability of food in that zone?

Projects. Following are some suggested topics for special reports or research projects:
1. Select one of the ocean zones for study, and report on the kinds of life in that zone, which of these provide food for humans, and the special characteristics of the zone's light, temperature, plant and animal life. This report could be in the form of a kind of story of what takes place during a given day in one area, or it could be a verbal report illustrated with drawings or cut-out pictures.
2. Research and report on one of the major classifications of animal life in the ocean, for example mollusks, echinoderm, chordates, or arthropods. What is their place in the food chain? Do they serve as human food? What zone do they inhabit? What characteristics do they have in common? What are some examples of individual species within the group? If possible, illustrate a verbal or written report with drawings or pictures of some of the species.
3. Using drawings or pictures from magazines, illustrate the ocean food chain. This could be a group project and take the form of a large poster for class display.
4. With parental cooperation, plan and carry out a seafood tasting. Endeavor to get as much variety as possible.

Episode 3: The Oceans:
A Storehouse of Raw Materials*

I. Teacher Preparation
1. The teacher should become familiar with the content of the filmstrip and the material in this guide so as to have a knowledge of the specific concepts presented in this filmstrip and follow-up material.
2. This filmstrip logically follows Episode 2 because it deals with the end result of ocean food chains and life cycles, and clarifies the interrelationship of land and ocean, marine life and human life.

II. Student Preparation
1. Ask students if they know the meaning of the term "fossil fuels," and

*Viewing Time 8:54 Frames 39

ask them to name those fuels. Find out also if they are aware of other fossil materials such as chalk, limestone, and diatomaceous earth and the uses to which we put them.

2. Discuss diatoms. This discussion might be started with the question, "Do you know what known form of life is most abundant on this planet?" Point out that diatoms are single-celled plants that occur in both fresh water and salt water, and that they are essential to water food chains.

3. Ask the students to name some raw materials that we get from the ocean. Refer back to the notion that ocean terrain is very similar to that of land, thereby perhaps eliciting the realization that the same raw materials available on land can probably be found in the ocean. Some of the materials which the students might know of are oil, iodine, and monosodium glutamate.

III. Learning Outcomes

As a result of viewing this filmstrip and participating in follow-up discussion and activities, students should be able to demonstrate a knowledge of the following facts and concepts:

1. Usable raw materials exist in ocean water, on the floor of the sea, and beneath the ocean floor.

2. The ocean is like a giant collecting basin and contains materials that originated on land, in volcanic eruptions from the earth's center, and in outer space.

3. Some animal remains, such as shells and skeletons, disintegrate into chalk or limestone. This process has been going on for millions of years, and is still going on.

4. The fossil fuels—oil, gas and coal—are formed of animal and vegetable remains.

5. Skeletal remains of diatoms are used for industrial purposes, including the manufacture of highway paint. This diatomaceous earth is present under ocean water or on land areas that were once covered by ocean water.

6. Fossil materials are produced by disintegration, heat and pressure.

7. Living ocean vegetables also yield raw materials for use in industrial products.

8. Water contains minerals.

9. Salt is found in ocean water.

10. Desalinization of ocean water is possible but not yet economically practical.

11. We extract minerals from sea water for medicinal and chemical purposes.

12. The ocean terrain was formed by the same processes that formed the land.

13. Metal ores and minerals are found underwater.

14. Finding and extracting raw materials from the ocean will create jobs for increasing numbers of people.

IV. Filmstrip Presentation

Within the context of an exploration of ocean resources used in technology and industry, this filmstrip explains the process of fossil formation as a part of the life story of the ocean. The composition of water is discussed, and the ocean is viewed as a vast repository of terrigenous, volcanic, organic, commercial, cosmic and human active materials. It presents another facet of the story of our interrelationship with the sea and suggests the development of an even closer relationship.

V. Lesson Activities

Discussion Questions. After viewing the filmstrip, some of the following questions or discussion topics might be used in order to underscore and reinforce filmstrip content:
1. What ocean products can you think of that are used by you, your family, or your community?
2. Discuss the processes of fossil formation, both on land and in the sea.
3. What materials found on land give a clue to the fact that an area was once covered by ocean water?
4. List all the possible occupations you can think of that would pertain to the finding and extraction of ocean resources.

Projects. Following are some suggested topics for special reports or research projects:
1. Find out and report on the kinds and number of minerals contained in sea water. How does it compare to fresh water?
2. Find out about the process of offshore drilling for oil. How much is being currently done? How does the process differ from land drilling?
3. Prepare a display of pictures or objects showing products that come from the ocean, or are partly formed of ocean materials.
4. If the equipment is available, have the students prepare slides using water from a nearby pond or stream and observe fresh water diatoms. Use a plankton net to collect organisms.
5. Appoint two groups of students to plan and present a debate about the use of ocean resources. Have one group represent the technological outlook, and the other group represent citizens concerned for the environment.

EPISODE 4: THE OCEANS: A STOREHOUSE OF POWER*

I. Teacher Preparation
1. The teacher should become familiar with the content of the filmstrip and the material in this guide so as to have a knowledge of the specific concepts presented in this filmstrip and the follow-up material.
2. This filmstrip deals with currents, waves, tides; physical, chemical and thermal energy production; and the interrelationship of sun, moon and earth. If you feel that review of some of the principles involved may be necessary, have materials such as books and charts available.

II. Student Preparation
1. Ask members of the class to explain the ways in which energy is produced, touching upon physical, chemical and thermal energy production, or elicit recognition of the different kinds of energy production by asking questions designed to bring them out. For instance: "By what

*Viewing Time 8:54 Frames 38

methods do we heat our homes?" "What is hydroelectric power?" or "How is electricity produced?"

2. What are tides and what causes them? Review the sun, moon, earth relationship.
3. Ask the students to name ways in which we have used water to produce power, and attempt to bring out the use of water wheels and dams.
4. Why are many people concerned about the use of oil, gas and coal? Touch upon the pollutive side effects, depletion of resources and dependence upon other countries for supplies.

III. Learning Outcomes

As a result of viewing this filmstrip and participating in follow-up discussion and activities, students should be able to demonstrate a knowledge of the following facts and concepts:

1. The mapping of ocean currents is important to the movement of ships.
2. Hydroelectric power is an important source of energy that is clean and nondestructive.
3. Ocean tides are a response to the gravitational pull of the moon and, to a lesser extent, the sun.
4. Tides are regular and predictable and unaffected by temperature or air movements.
5. Experiments in the use of tidal energy have been and are being conducted.
6. Ocean energy might be put to work through the use of windmills, water wheels and wave power generators.
7. The use of thermal energy, or stored heat, from the ocean has been explored and found to be too expensive for current use.
8. Ocean resources can be used for chemical energy production, one method being the conversion of seaweed into methane gas by burning.
9. Undersea earthquakes and volcanic eruptions occur, sometimes causing tsunamis—mistakenly called tidal waves.
10. Ocean waves can creat natural channels reaching far inland.
11. Use of chemical resources must be balanced against possible ecological damage.

IV. Filmstrip Presentation

A historical perspective on the power potential of the ocean introduces the idea of the tremendous motive power contained in the vast body of water that surrounds us. Tidal movements are explained and an experimental tidal energy project is pictured. The possibilities for energy production through the use of gravitational, thermal and chemical sources are all explored and viewed as alternatives to the use of fossil fuels.

V. Lesson Activities

Discussion Questions. After viewing the filmstrip, some of the following questions or discussion topics might be used in order to underscore and reinforce filmstrip content:

1. View charts of major ocean currents and discuss what they mean in terms of shipping.
2. Review the sun, moon, earth relationship and discuss what happens as the tides advance and recede.

3. What is the difference between waves and tides?
4. What sources of gravitational, thermal and chemical energy do we use on land?

Projects. Following are some suggested topics for special reports or research projects.
1. What is a dam? How is it built? How does it work to produce energy? What are the advantages of hydroelectric power over other kinds of power?
2. Read further about tidal movements and explain, with the aid of drawings, what occurs on a daily and a monthly basis.
3. Map the major ocean currents, explain what causes them, who first mapped them, what direction they move in, and how they are used to advantage by shippers.

EPISODE 5: CHANGING THE OCEANS*

I. Teacher Preparation
1. The teacher should become familiar with the content of the filmstrip and the material in this guide so as to have a knowledge of the specific concepts presented in this filmstrip and the follow-up material.
2. This filmstrip brings together all the concepts previously treated into a consideration of our past, present and future relationship with the ocean, and underlines its importance to human welfare. Thus it serves as an appropriate summing up of the entire program.

II. Student Preparation
1. Ask the students to recall and list the kinds of resources available from the ocean. Which are we using now?
2. Discuss the ocean food chain, and ask the students to speculate on what might happen if one link in the chain is destroyed. Can they think of any land disruption that has occurred and what effects it had?
3. Discuss changes in land formation that have occurred because of volcanic eruptions, earthquakes, land erosion and human intervention. What major changes have taken place over the centuries? Point to the existence of like fossils found on widely separated continents. Ask the students how they think this might have happened.
4. Discuss why the ocean is important to humans.

III. Learning Outcomes
As a result of viewing this filmstrip and participating in follow-up discussion and activities, students should be able to demonstrate a knowledge of the following facts and concepts:
1. The ocean is in constant movement and its movements cause changes on land.
2. The continental drift is a scientific theory which proposes that the continents were once part of one or more super continent(s) which separated into the major continents.
3. Identical and specific fossils found in widely separated places in the world lend support to the theory of continental drift.

*Viewing Time 10:25 Frames 48

4. Fossil, animal, vegetable and mineral deposits have helped scientists to reconstruct the earth's history.
5. Dramatic changes sometimes take place underwater as the result of volcanic action.
6. The ocean is a final dumping place for land materials including waste products and materials from the atmosphere.
7. We have the technological means to create major changes in the ocean and the responsibility of maintaining a safe ecological balance.
8. Interruption of the ocean food chain can have dramatic ongoing effects, causing disruption at points further down the line.
9. Many things threaten the biological balance of the ocean, such as pollution, overfishing and the deliberate destruction of some forms of life.
10. Full utilization of ocean resources calls for international cooperation to safeguard the environment against irreversible damage.

IV. Filmstrip Presentation
Changes in the ocean have been brought about by human intervention, but the most dramatic changes are the result of natural causes. The ocean's effect upon land is dramatically illustrated in a description of the possible reshaping of the earth that may have occurred because of volcanic activity on the ocean floor. Ancient ocean deposits are shown to be clues to what the earth looked like millions of years ago, and ocean water's role as a landshaper is illustrated. The effects of human intervention, from the time when primitive man threw cast-offs into rivers to the present day pollution caused by the side effects of technology, are considered in a straightforward manner. The filmstrip ends on a positive note, pointing out that human inventiveness can find ways to overcome ecological damage and work toward a balanced co-relationship with the ocean.

V. Lesson Activities
Discussion Questions. After viewing the filmstrip, some of the following questions or discussion topics might be used in order to underscore and reinforce filmstrip content:
1. Refer to a map of the continents and note and discuss the possibility of the continents having once been joined. Do any of the coastline features of one continent seem to correspond with another?
2. What specific places or land features can you name that were formed by oceanic activity?
3. Review the concept of food chains and discuss the reasons for concern about the effects of pollution upon the ocean.
4. Refer back to previous filmstrips and discuss the reasons why we should be concerned with maintaining the natural balance in the ocean.

Projects. Following are some suggested topics for special reports or research projects:
1. Research and report upon the creation of the St. Lawrence Seaway or the land drainage projects in the Netherlands.
2. Study the habitat and feeding habits of a threatened ocean species, such as the whale or the sea lion. What effects would the destruction of this species have upon other forms of ocean life?
3. Research and report upon the continental drift theory, or some similar theory of continental origin.

CHECKLIST 5-1   THE OCEANS: TOPICS FOR INDEPENDENT STUDY*

1. Bathyscapes
2. Bathysphere
3. Beebe, William
4. Cable Controlled Underwater Recovery Vehicle
5. "Calypso"
6. Cartography
7. Center for Advanced Marine Study
8. Joseph Conrad
9. Continental Drift
10. Continental Shelf
11. Coral
12. Cormorant
13. Cousteau, Jacques
14. Cousteau Society
15. Crabs
16. Crayfish
17. Crustaceans
18. Currents
19. Damselfish
20. Darwin, Charles
21. Decompression
22. Desalination of Sea Water
23. Diatoms
24. Dinoflagellates
25. Divers and Diving
26. Diving Bells
27. Diving Saucer
28. Dolphins
29. Ecosystems
30. Elements in Seawater
31. Endangered Species
32. Energy from the Sea
33. Environmental Protection Agency
34. Fins
35. Fish
36. Florida Aquanaut Research Expedition
37. Food Chain
38. Galapagos Islands
39. Glaciers
40. Great Barrier Reef
41. Gulf Stream
42. Haddock
43. Helium Diving
44. Heyerdahl, Thor
45. Hurricanes
46. Icebergs
47. Intergovernmental Oceanographic Commission
48. International Commission for the Prevention of Pollution of the Sea by Oil
49. International Commission of North American Fisheries
50. Kelp
51. "Kon Tiki"
52. Lagoons
53. Lobsters
54. Manatee
55. Manganese
56. Mariculture
57. Marine Sciences
58. Massachusetts Institute of Technology
59. Maury, Matthew Fontaine
60. Melville, Herman
61. Mollusks
62. Moon and Tides
63. National Oceanic and Atmospheric Administration
64. "Nautilus"
65. Nickel
66. Oceanographic Institute (Paris)
67. Oceans
68. Oysters
69. Parrotfish
70. Pearl Diving
71. Phosphorescence
72. Photography
73. Photosynthesis
74. Peccard, August
75. Peccard, Jacques
76. Plankton
77. Plate Tectonics
78. Pollution
79. Polyps
80. Porcupinefish
81. Porpoise
82. Shrimp
83. Skate
84. Snail
85. Spearfishing
86. Species
87. Sponges
88. Squid
89. Starfish
90. Sunfish
91. Swordfish
92. Symbiosis
93. Temperature
94. Tides
95. Topography
96. Tuna
97. Verne, Jules
98. Walrus
99. Water Spout
100. Waves
101. Whale
102. Wrecks

*Prepared by Corinne P. Clendening and Ruth Ann Davies.

RESOURCE LIST*

BOOKS

The Cousteau Almanac: An Inventory of Life on Our Water Planet (Doubleday, 1981)

First over the Oceans by Melinda Blau (Silver, 1978)

A Look at the Earth around Us: Oceans by the Editors of National Geographic (National Geographic, 1981)

The Mysterious Underseas World by Jan L. Cook (National Geographic, 1980)

The Ocean World of Jacques Cousteau, 20 vols. (Grolier, 1973)

One Hundred Two Questions and Answers about the Sea by Peter Limburg and James B. Sweeney (Messner, 1975)

Projects in Oceanography by S. Simon (Watts, 1972)

The Sea's Harvest: The Story of Aquaculture by Joseph E. Brown (Dodd, 1975)

Story of Oceanography by Robert Boyer (Harvey, 1975)

Underseas Frontiers: An Introduction to Oceanography by C. B. Colby (Coward, 1977)

Wonders of the Kelp Forest by Joseph E. Brown (Dodd, 1974)

FILMSTRIPS

The Cousteau Oceanography Series: The Water Planet (Disney—each set 5 filmstrips, 5 cassettes or 5 records, 1 teacher's guide). Set 1: *Return to the Sea, To Save a Living Sea, The Liquid Sky, A Sea of Motion, The Invisible Multitude.* Set 2: *Anatomy of an Ocean, The Infinite Variety, The Act of Life, Time and the Sea, The Survivors*

Exploring Sea and Space (National Geographic—5 filmstrips and cassettes). Titles: *World beneath the Sea, Riches from the Sea, Benefits from Space, Looking Ahead in Sea and Space*

The Life of Fishes (Disney—6 filmstrips, 6 cassettes, 1 teacher's guide). Titles: *The Shaping of Life, The Range of Life, The Undersea Ecosystems, Survival, The Roots of Intelligence, The Fragile Balance*

. . . Marine Science Careers (Society for Visual Education—3 filmstrips, 2 cassettes). Titles: *The Oceanographer, The Marine Laboratory Technician, The Marine Electronic and Mechanical Technician*

The Restless Sea (adapted from the Walt Disney motion picture) (Disney—5 filmstrips, 5 cassettes or 5 records, 1 teacher's guide). Titles: *Oceanography—An Overview, Tides, Wind and Waves, Mr. C. Waters, Surface and Deep Ocean Currents, Life in the Sea—An Unfolding Story*

Sea Life (National Geographic—5 filmstrips, 5 cassettes). Titles: *The Saltwater World, The Shell Builders, Curiosities of the Sea, Surface Breathers: The Mammals, The Octopus*

MOTION PICTURES

The Restless Sea (Disney)

20,000 Leagues under the Sea (Disney)

*Prepared by Corinne P. Clendening and Ruth Ann Davies.

Model 6

Revving Up for Junior High School

GOAL—PHASE I: To acquaint the sixth-grade students in the gifted program and their parents with the seventh-grade gifted program, its philosophy, curricular offerings, extracurricular program, program options.

SCHEDULE: Phase I begins early in the second semester of grade six.

OBJECTIVES

To orient students and their parents to the scope and challenge of the junior high school gifted program.

To enable students to make informed choices.

To acquaint students and their parents with the electives program.

To acquaint students and their parents with the extracurricular program.

To acquaint students and their parents with the intramural and varsity sports program.

To encourage students to assess their own interests, academic strengths, academic weaknesses, and career aspirations before making decisions as to which courses and which extracurricular activities to choose.

To provide opportunities for students and their parents to meet and converse with the junior high school guidance counselors, the coordinator and teachers of the gifted program, the student council president, and the school library staff.

AGENDA for GROUP CONFERENCES

I. Overview of the multiphased program Revving Up for Junior High School.

259

A. The purpose of the program is explained.
   1. To provide opportunity for students in the gifted program and their parents to be informed about the junior high school opportunities: program offerings, extracurricular activities, independent study options, and acceleration possibilities.
   2. To enable students, in concert with their parents, to make informed choices and wise decisions as to course selection, activity choices, and scheduling possibilities.
   3. To stress the necessity for students to assess their academic strengths and weaknesses honestly and objectively in relation to the demands and performance level required of honors and accelerated courses.
   4. To equate realistically the out-of-class preparation time required for successful achievement in honors and accelerated courses with total time available to the student for overall schedule of studies and extracurricular activities.
   5. To relate student choice of gifted program alternatives seriously with student's overall, lifetime personal goals.
B. The separate phases of this program are explained.
   1. Phase I: Introduction to and overview of the junior high school instructional program.
   2. Phase II: Summer study program.
   3. Phase III: Orientation conferences and workshop.

II. The elementary gifted program is the foundation on which the secondary gifted program is built.
   A. The identical philosophy, commitment to excellence, and concern for the optimum development of each student unifies the K–12 program.
   B. The program is designed to encourage high individual performance and offers a continuous invitation to each student to realize his or her full potential as a gifted and talented human being.

III. The secondary gifted program, in addition to its emphasis on academic achievement, emphasizes the following:
   A. Leadership skills development
   B. Divergent thinking ability
   C. Creative thinking ability
   D. Humor and wit
   E. Personal integrity
   F. Healthy curiosity and interest
   G. Maturity of judgment and decision making
   H. Aesthetic awareness and appreciation

IV. The quest for personal excellence is the hallmark of the gifted program, K–12.

QUEST FOR PERSONAL EXCELLENCE

It is mete and right to march to a different drumbeat just so long as you keep in tune with your fellow human beings and in step with your own best self.

For knowledge is not enough; knowledge plus skills is not enough; knowledge coupled with integrity and wisdom is not enough; knowledge joined with compassion is not enough.

Only when all five—knowledge, skills, integrity, wisdom, and compassion—are blended so that each supports the other do we have the kind of person worthy to be called *gifted.*

V. The junior high school principal and/or coordinator of the gifted program and/or guidance counselor explain the following:

   A. Regular academic course offerings—open to all seventh-grade students.

      1. English and literature
      2. Social studies
      3. Mathematics
      4. Science

   B. Honors courses—enrollment in these courses is limited to exceptionally capable students; they are characterized by independent or tutorial work, place the responsibility for student progress more on the student than on the teacher, and emphasize reading and self-instruction.

      1. Honors English
      2. Honors Literature
      3. Honors Social studies
      4. Honors Mathematics
      5. Honors Science

   C. Elective Courses.

      1. Art
      2. Band
      3. Chorus
      4. Dance/ballet
      5. Dramatics
      6. Electronics
      7. Graphic arts
      8. Homecoming
      9. Orchestra
     10. Photography
     11. School newspaper
     12. Television/radio
     13. Typing

   D. Accelerated Courses.

      1. Advanced mathematics: Algebra I, Algebra II, Geometry
      2. Advanced science: Botany, Zoology, Biology, Physics
      3. Foreign languages: French, German, Latin, Spanish, Russian
      4. Advanced social studies: World Cultures, American Government

   E. Mini-courses: courses that are abbreviated *in scope* but not abbreviated *in depth;* time allocation is usually not more than 45 days or one-half semester in length.

      1. The Black Experience (see Model 8)
      2. Creative Writing
      3. Greek and Roman Mythology
      4. Independent Study: Techniques, Procedures, Tools (see Model 7)
      5. The Oceans: A Key to Our Future (see Model 5)

   F. Independent study—two distinct types of independent study are independent study within the framework of honors courses and independent study separate and distinct from prescribed courses.

G. Extracurricular activities.
   1. Clubs, such as:

Chess	Science
Dramatics	Service
Journalism	Television Programming

   2. Sports such as:

Baseball	Jogging
Basketball	Skiing
Football	Soccer
Golf	Swimming
Hockey	Wrestling

H. Summer study—may be home-based, school-based, or a combination of both.
   1. Home-based study can be arranged with the coordinator of the junior high school gifted program and/or junior high school librarians.

   Students may borrow for home use print and nonprint media as well as the equipment required for the use of filmstrips, cassettes, and so on.

   Basic reading lists of recommended titles for honors courses are available for the students to follow in anticipation of the coming school year.

   Students with a special interest in any area are encouraged to schedule a conference with a teacher in that special area and discuss possible avenues of exploration, materials, and activities.

   2. School-based study is scheduled and conducted under the direction and guidance of a teacher or teachers. Typical summer courses are:

   BASIC: An Introduction to Computer Programming
   An Introduction to Biology
   An Introduction to Botany
   An Introduction to French
   An Introduction to German
   An Introduction to Latin
   An Introduction to Life on the Earth (BBC Program)
   An Introduction to Russian Literature
   An Introduction to Spanish
   An Introduction to Zoology
   A Writer's Workshop

STUDENTS COMPLETE TWO SURVEYS

1. *The Kuder E General Interest Survey* (Science Research Associates) is administered to the students in the gifted program. This survey is an effective means of identifying student interests. Knowledge of interests will facilitate student selection of appropriate educational courses and will aid in career decision making. The interest profiles obtained from the Kuder Survey will be shared with the individual student and his or her parents during the seventh-grade orientation conferences.
2. The Torrance Tests of Creative Thinking (Ginn) are administered to the students in the gifted program. These tests are used to determine the creative strength of the student in the areas of ideation fluency, flexibility, and originality. The creativity analysis results of the Torrance Tests will be shared with the student and his or her parents during the seventh-grade orientation conference.

GOAL—PHASE II: To provide opportunity for students in the gifted program to elect a summer study program of their own choice.

SCHEDULE: Phase II begins at the end of sixth grade and extends to the beginning of the seventh grade.

OBJECTIVES

To enable each student to select an at-home or at-school summer study program of special personal interest and challenge.

To encourage the student to select those learning experiences that he or she will personally enjoy.

To provide opportunity for the student to engage in a course of study or learning experience not available to him or her during the school day because of scheduling conflicts.

To provide opportunity for the student to strengthen areas of academic weakness and to sharpen thinking-learning-communicating skills preparatory to moving into the junior high school program.

TYPICAL HOME STUDY PROGRAMS

1. Reading List: Honors Literature—Introduction to Literature. Theme: Courage to Survive

    ### BOOKS: FICTION

    Avalanche by Arthur Roth (Scholastic, 1979; paper)

    Cay by Theodore Taylor (Doubleday, 1969; paper, Avon)

    Deathwatch by Robb White (Doubleday, 1972; paper, Dell)

    Frogmen by Robb White (Doubleday, 1973; paper, Dell)

    Frozen Fire by James Houston (Atheneum, 1977)

    Game of Truth by Edith Maxwell (Dodd, 1976)

    The Guns of Navarone by Alistair MacLean (Fawcett, 1977; paper)

    Julie of the Wolves by Jean Craighead George (Harper, Newbery Award, 1973)

    Kidnapped by Robert Louis Stevenson (Grosset, n.d.; paper, Penquin)

    Long Claws by James Houston (Atheneum, 1978)

    Lord of the Flies by William Golding (Coward, 1978)

    Mayday, Mayday by Hilary Milton (Watts, 1979)

    Robinson Crusoe: My Journals and Sketchbook by Robinson Crusoe (Harcourt, 1974)

    True Grit by Charles Portis (Simon & Schuster, 1968)

    Two for Survival by Arthur Roth (Scribner, 1976)

    ### BOOKS: NONFICTION

    Behind Enemy Lines: American Spies and Saboteurs of World War II by Milton J. Shapiro (Messner, 1978)

    The Commandos of World War II by Hodding Carter (Random, 1981; paper)

Guadalcanal General: The Story of A. A. Vandergrift by John Foster (Morrow, 1966)

A Handbook for Emergencies: Coming Out Alive by Anthony Greenbank (Doubleday, 1976)

Howl Like the Wolves: Growing Up in Nazi Germany by Max Von der Grun (Morrow, 1980)

John F. Kennedy and PT-109 by Richard Tregaskis (Random, 1962)

The Rage to Survive by Jacques Vignes (Morrow, 1976)

Ranger Battalion: American Rangers in World War II by Milton J. Shapiro (Messner, 1979)

Rescue: True Stories of Heroism by L. B. Taylor, Jr. (Watts, 1978)

Thirty Seconds Over Tokyo by Ted Lawson (Random, 1981; paper)

True Spy Stories by James B. Sweeney (Watts, 1981)

World War II Resistance Stories by Arthur Prager and Emily Prager (Watts, 1979)

SOUND FILMSTRIPS

The Cay (Pied Piper Productions—1 filmstrip, 2 cassettes or 2 records, 1 guide)

Deathwatch (Insight Media, dist. by Pied Piper Productions—1 filmstrip, 1 cassette, 1 guide)

Julie of the Wolves (Miller-Brody—2 filmstrips, 2 cassettes or 2 records)

Kidnapped (Disney—2 filmstrips, 2 cassettes or 2 records)

2. Write It Skillfully: The Basic Principles of Writing Correctly and Creatively

The purpose of this self-study program is:

To provide motivation for the improvement of writing skills.

To emphasize basic principles of writing in several genres.

To stress the methods of organizing materials before approaching an assignment.

To encourage student writing without pressure or fear of being graded on the product.

This study program is built around the Encyclopaedia Britannica sound filmstrip set *Write It Skillfully!* (6 filmstrips, 6 cassettes, 1 guide). The individual filmstrips are:

Write It Correctly: identifies common errors in grammar and punctuation and describes how they can be corrected.

Write It Clearly: shows the importance of organizing, sequencing, and presenting essential information in a concise, straightforward manner.

Write It to Entertain: stresses the significance of plot, setting, characterization, and dialogue in short story writing.

Write It to Delight: analyzes the differences between poetry and other genres.

Write It to Inform: traces the sequential process involved in nonfiction writing.

A junior high school English teacher is available for scheduled student conferences to discuss writing skills development and techniques.

3. Building Background Knowledge of the Computer. This is required of those who are to participate in the summer computer laboratory course *BASIC: An Introduction to Computer Programming.*

   Each student is required to read *Computers* by Linda O'Brien (Watts, 1978) and "Computer," a *World Book Encyclopedia* reprint (1982).

   Each student is required to build background knowledge by studying the information in the following filmstrips:

   Computer Awareness (Society for Visual Education—4 filmstrips, 4 cassettes, 24 skill sheets, 1 guide)

   > *What Computers Do*
   > *How Computers Work*
   > *Everyday Computers*
   > *Introduction to Programming*

   Introduction to Computers (Society for Visual Education—4 filmstrips, 4 cassettes, 24 skill worksheets; Apple and TRS Disks available)

   > *The Purpose of Computers*
   > *Hardware and Software*
   > *The Impact of Computers*
   > *Understanding Programming*

   Each student is required to the complete the summary guide Computer Background Knowledge Summary (see Learning Guide 6-1).

4. Exploring the Cosmos

   Carl Sagan, Cornell University astronomer, shares with the students his understanding of the universe in the following filmstrip programs (Films, Inc.—each 3 filmstrips, 3 cassettes)

   > *Cosmos:* Series A—*A Voyage through the Cosmos, Is There Life on Mars?, The Expanding Universe*
   > *Cosmos:* Series B—*Evolution: The Four Billion Year Legacy, The Origin of Life, The Search for Extraterrestrial Life*

GOAL—PHASE III: To provide an orientation program to minimize student feeling of apprehension and to facilitate, instead, student self-understanding and confidence.

OBJECTIVES

To provide opportunity for each student in the gifted program to:

Become acquainted with his or her faculty adviser.

Become acquainted with his or her student mentor.

Explore with the coordinator of the gifted program his or her profiles from the Kuder E General Interest Survey and the Torrance Tests of Creative Thinking.

Participate in a "Know Yourself" workshop.

Become acquainted with and form friendships with students in the regular school program as well as those in the gifted program.

ORIENTATION PROCEDURE

1. Prior to the opening of school, each student receives a letter from the junior high school principal or coordinator of the gifted program welcoming him or her to the junior high school. The letter also informs the student of the following:
   a. The name of his or her faculty adviser and the scheduled time and place for the first conference with the adviser.
   b. The name of his or her student mentor and the scheduled time and place for the first conference with the student mentor.
   c. The name of his or her homeroom teacher and the location of the homeroom.
   d. The student's schedule: subject, time, classroom number.
2. The student conference with the adviser provides opportunity for the student and his or her parents to ask questions, to discuss the Kuder Interest Survey and the Torrance Creative Thinking profiles, and to share concerns.
3. The "Know Yourself" workshop is conducted by a teaching team including the school psychologist, the coordinator of the gifted program, the guidance counselor, and several student representatives from the eighth- and ninth-grade gifted programs.
   a. The following concepts are introduced and discussed: What are the behavioral characteristics of superior students?

      Background information: In recent years a number of writers have called attention to the need for a wider range of criteria in judging gifted, talented, and creative young people. It is the considered opinion of the leaders in the field of educating the gifted that there are certain characteristics that indicate true giftedness.

      Joseph S. Renzulli, Bureau of Educational Research, University of Connecticut, and his research assistants have devised an instrument called "Scales for Rating the Behavioral Characteristics of Superior Students" (published by Creative Learning Press, Mansfield Center, CT), which is to be used by teachers for identifying students for inclusion in the gifted program.

      The nine sections of the rating scale are:

      > I: Learning Characteristics
      > II: Motivational Characteristics
      > III: Creativity Characteristics
      > IV: Leadership Characteristics
      > V: Artistic Characteristics
      > VI: Musical Characteristics
      > VII: Dramatics Characteristics
      > VIII: Communication Characteristics—Precision
      > IX: Communication Characteristics—Expressiveness

      In this workshop, the discussion will focus on the first four of these sections.

   b. The purpose of this workshop is to encourage each student to set *personal goals* and *personal behavioral standards* to be used as guides for his or her performance at school, at home, and in the community. Students are given instructions and directed to answer questions.

      Carefully read the characteristics listed under Part I and then rate yourself honestly under each question; compute your rating for section I.

Carefully read the characteristics listed under Part II and then rate yourself honestly under each question; compute your rating for section II.

Carefully read the characteristics listed under Part III and then rate yourself honestly under each question; compute your rating for section III.

Carefully read the characteristics listed under Part IV and then rate yourself honestly under each question; compute your rating for Section IV.

What have you learned about yourself?

What motivational characteristics do you need to strengthen?

What leadership characteristics do you need to strengthen?

c. The concept of being in competition with oneself is discussed.

d. The concept of self-actualization is discussed.

e. The concept of emotional maturity is discussed.

f. The concept of being a responsible person is discussed.

g. The concept of personal excellence is discussed.

4. In summation, the class views and discusses the filmstrip series *Feeling Good about Yourself: How to Build Self-Confidence* (Guidance Associates—4 filmstrips, 4 cassettes or 4 records).

LEARNING GUIDE 6-1 COMPUTER BACKGROUND KNOWLEDGE SUMMARY

Student _____ Date _____

1. Define the term *computer:*

2. What features does a computer share with a calculator?

3. How is the computer used in business and industry?

4. How is the computer used in government and law enforcement?

5. How is the computer used in engineering?

6. How is the computer used in science?

7. How is the computer used in education?

8. How is the computer used in the home?

9. What is a digital computer?

10. What is an analog computer?

11. What is a hybrid computer?

12. Define the following:

Bit—

Data base—

Hardware—

Microprocessor—

Network—

Program—

Software—

Terminal—

Model 7

Independent Study:
Techniques, Procedures, Tools
(Honors Mini-Course)

GRADE: 7

GOAL: To prepare seventh-grade students in the gifted program to undertake independent research projects with skill, competence, and enjoyment.

OBJECTIVES

To introduce the purpose of independent research.

To introduce students to the learning laboratory concept of *both* the junior and senior high school libraries.

To introduce students to the special reference collection in *both* the junior and senior high schools.

To introduce students to special microfilm and microfiche collections in *both* the junior and senior high school libraries.

To reinforce and extend students' knowledge of both the input and process phases of independent study.

To encourage students to begin and maintain their own style manual.

To motivate students to view research as a challenge rather than a threat.

INTRODUCTION

This course is scheduled at the beginning of seventh grade in order to equip students to be effective, efficient, and competent independent learners. The skills of independent learning are acquired; they are not inborn. There are basic learning skills that must be learned and scientifically practiced until they become a normal part of each student's functioning as an intelligent, competent, efficient learner. The purpose of this mini-course is to introduce, reinforce, and then extend the skills of thinking, learning, and communicating. To enable each student to become a *skillful* researcher-communicator is the basic goal of the secondary instructional program.

Student Orientation

I. Why spend nine weeks in a course on the techniques, procedure, and tools for independent study?
   A. Education on the secondary level is far more demanding, far more challenging, and far more complex than that previously experienced.
   B. The sound filmstrip set *Why Am I Studying This?* (Educational Enrichment Materials—each 1 filmstrip and 1 cassette) is presented and discussed. The individual titles in this series are:
      1. *Why Am I Studying English?*
      2. *Why Am I Studying Mathematics?*
      3. *Why Am I Studying Science?*
      4. *Why Am I Studying Social Studies?*
   C. School is *not* preparation for life; it *is* life; this concept is discussed.
      1. Evidence of being an educated person is not having a head full of facts; rather, it is being able to bring to bear on any problem-solving situation those facts, concepts, and ideas that are germane to the task at hand.
      2. Knowing how to locate information and how to acquire understanding through purposeful and appreciative use of print and nonprint carriers of information are the hallmarks of an educated person.
   D. Independent study is of two main types:
      1. Independent study within the framework of honors courses in English, foreign languages, literature, mathematics, science, social studies, and speech arts.
      2. Independent study separate and distinct from prescribed courses.
   E. Successful completion of this course is a prerequisite for any student electing honors courses or independent study separate from the regularly scheduled courses.

II. The school and public libraries are learning laboratories where the purposeful and scientific use of media provides the student with the means of becoming a participant in all that human beings have ever thought, questioned, dreamed, created, experienced, achieved, and valued.
   A. The school librarian is a teacher whose special subject is learning itself.
      1. The librarian is the key to the resources of the library.
      2. The librarian is an interpreter of media; a means of locating, organizing, interpreting, relating, synthesizing, and evaluating information.
      3. The librarian is a concerned counselor and guide to be consulted when one is searching for answers to personal problems or questing for advice, reassurance, or encouragement.
   B. Locating, interpreting, assimilating, and communicating information is both a science and an art.
      1. Locating information is a science.
      2. Using the right tools intelligently is a science.
      3. Following directions is a science.
      4. Following learning guides is a science.
      5. Organizing information is a science.
      6. Assimilating or digesting information is a science.

7. Evaluating information is a science.
8. Following a style manual is a science.
   a. A style manual is a guide to the accepted manner of preparing research reports or manuscripts.
   b. Each student will in this mini-course begin his or her own style manual and will continue to maintain and expand this manual each year.
   c. Using a style manual is a great time saver.
9. Communicating what you have learned is both a science and an art.
   a. Writing the report is a science because there are basic rules—grammar, composition, format—that must be followed.
   b. How you express your ideas can be as creative and as imaginative as you can make it—writing or speaking creatively with smooth and polished style is an art.

III. Study skills techniques are reinforced and extended through the class study of the following filmstrips (all Education Enrichment Media)
   A. *Developing Library Skills* (6 filmstrips, 6 cassettes, 12 spirit duplicating masters)

Understanding the Libary	*Locating Facts*
Locating Books	*Using Periodicals*
Doing Research	*Using Nonprint Material and Equipment*

   1. These filmstrips describe functions, sections, and services of school and public libraries and teach students how to use them.
   2. Clear, concise terminology moves each demonstration along a logical, stepwise sequence and zeroes in on research techniques; locating books; the Dewey decimal system; the card catalog; fact-finding; using almanacs, atlases, and periodicals; using vital nonprint resources such as recordings, cassettes, pictures, filmstrips, videotapes, microfilm, microfiche, and support equipment such as projectors, readers, and printers.
   B. *Study Skills* (8 filmstrips, 8 cassettes, 1 guide, 25 student workbooks)

Outlining	*Reference Material*
Summarizing	*Taking a Test*
Note-Taking	*Studying*
Writing a Paper	*How to Think Successfully*

   1. These filmstrips recommend specific techniques and procedures for students to follow to acquire successful study habits.
   2. Each filmstrip provides concrete directions for putting each principle into practice.
   3. The student workbook includes follow-up activities that provide dozens of opportunities for the student to use these newly acquired skills.

IV. The following special reference tools are introduced:
   A. Almanacs, Fact Books, Yearbooks
   1. *Facts on File: A Weekly Digest of World Events and Cumulative Index* (Facts on File, 1940 to date)
   2. *Hammond Almanac of a Million Facts, Records, Forecasts* (New American Library, 1979 to date)
   3. *Information Please Almanac* (Simon and Schuster, 1947 to date)

    4. *Reader's Digest Almanac and Yearbook* (Reader's Digest, 1966 to date)

    5. *Statesman's Year Book: Statistical and Historical Annual of the States of the World* (St. Martin's, 1864 to date)

    6. *Statistical Abstract of the United States* (Government Printing Office, 1878 to date)

    7. *United Nations Statistical Yearbook* (UNIPUB, 1949 to date)

    8. *World Almanac and Book of Facts* (Newspaper Enterprise Association, 1868 to date)

    9. *World Almanac Book of Who* (Prentice-Hall, 1980)

  B. Biographical Dictionaries and Indexes—General

    1. *Biography Index: A Cumulative Index to Biographical Material in Books and Magazines* (Wilson, 1946 to date)

    2. *Current Biography* (Wilson, 1940 to date)

    3. *Dictionary of American Biography,* 15 vols., 6 supps. (Scribner, 1935–1979)

    4. *Dictionary of National Biography,* 20 vols., 2nd to 7th supps. (Oxford, 1912–1971)

    5. *McGraw-Hill Encyclopedia of World Biography,* 12 vols. (McGraw, 1972)

    6. *Notable American Women, 1607–1950: A Biographical Dictionary,* 3 vols. (Harvard University Press, 1972)

    7. *Webster's American Biographies* (Merriam, 1979)

    8. *Webster's Biographical Dictionary* (Merriam, 1980)

    9. *Who's Who in America* (Marquis, 1899 to date)

    10. *Who's Who in the World* (Marquis, 1970 to date)

    11. *Who's Who of American Women* (Marquis, 1958 to date)

  C. Indexes to Newspapers, Periodicals, and Books

    1. *Essay and General Literature Index* (Wilson, 1900 to date)

    2. *General Science Index* (Wilson, 1978 to date)

    3. *Guide to Microforms in Print.* (Microform Review, 1961 to date)

    4. *Humanities Index* (Wilson, 1974 to date)

    5. *National Geographic Index,* 2 vols., 1 supp. (National Geographic, 1886–1981)

    6. *New York Times Index* (New York Times, 1851 to date)

    7. *Readers' Guide to Periodical Literature* (Wilson, 1900 to date)

    8. *Social Sciences Index* (Wilson, 1974 to date)

V. "How to Do Research," a *World Book Encyclopedia* reprint, is introduced as the basic style guide to be followed in the junior high school program* (see Learning Guide 7-1 at the end of this model).

  A. Each student receives a copy of this 33-page guide.

    1. The student places this guide in his or her own style manual.

    2. The student is encouraged to touch base with this guide when preparing any research assignment.

  B. The students are introduced to *The World Book Student Handbook* vols. I and II (Chicago: World Book–Childcraft International, 1981).

    1. *The World Book Student Handbook: Student Guide* contains the following units:

---

*The *World Book Encyclopedia* reprint "How to Do Research" (Chicago: World Book–Childcraft International, 1982) is available at the cost of 25¢ for up to 19 copies; 20 or more copies cost 20¢ each.

Unit 1: Getting the Most Out of School
Unit 2: A Guide to Classroom Skills
Unit 3: A Guide to Reading Skills
Unit 4: A Guide to Writing Skills
Unit 5: A Guide to Speaking Skills
Unit 6: A Guide to Vocabulary Skills
Unit 7: A Guide to Research Skills
Unit 8: A Guide to Study Skills
Unit 9: A Guide to School Activities
Unit 10: A Guide to Your Future

2. *The World Book Student Handbook: Information Finder* contains the following units:

Unit 1: Facts about Writing, Language, and Spelling
Unit 2: Basic Information about Mathematics
Unit 3: Basic Information from the Physical Sciences
Unit 4: Basic Information from the Earth Sciences
Unit 5: Basic Information from the Life Sciences
Unit 6: Places around the World
Unit 7: Important Dates in History
Unit 8: People Who Made History
Unit 9: Presidents and Prime Ministers
Unit 10: Highlights of Literature

3. Multiple copies of both volumes of *The World Book Student Handbook* are available in the school library and may be borrowed for home use.

VI. The students organize their loose-leaf, three-ring notebook style manuals. They include the following:
   A. Title page, which in addition to the title highlights the student's name, grade and homeroom, and home address.
   B. Section dividers labeled for the following:
      1. Assignments
      2. Checklists
      3. Learning Guides
      4. Reference Tools*
      5. Research Guides
      6. Research Papers
      7. Terminology
      8. Test-Taking Tips
      9. Thinking-Learning-Communicating Skills

VII. The function of the faculty mentor as consultant and guide is discussed.
   A. Independent study requires that the student be mature enough to use common sense and good judgment.
      1. Recognize own limitations.
      2. Respect the value of consulting with someone who knows a great deal more than the student does.
      3. Realize the value of sharing concerns, weighing options, avoiding pitfalls waiting for the novice, having the synergistic bonus of profiting from knowledge and experience of others.
   B. The courtesy of prescheduling a conference with a consultant or mentor is discussed (see Checklist 7-1 at the end of this model).

*File in this section the booklet *How to Use the Readers' Guide to Periodical Literature* (New York: Wilson). This excellent tool is available from the publisher in class-size lots at no charge to schools.

CHECKLIST 7-1   STUDENT REQUEST FOR CONFERENCE

Student _____ Grade _____ Homeroom _____

Date of Request _____

REQUEST FOR CONFERENCE WITH:

_____ Teacher

_____ Librarian

_____ Mentor

_____ Principal

PREFERABLE TIME OF CONFERENCE:

_____ Day   Period _____

REASON FOR CONFERENCE:

Examples:

    Earning a scouting merit badge in space exploration
    Planning an assembly program
    Interview for school newspaper

_____

_____

_____

_____

_____

_____

_____

_____

_____

_____

_____

LEARNING GUIDE 7-1   HOW TO DO RESEARCH*

"... you have been preparing reports of one kind or another ever since you first learned to write.... And you have been doing some kind of research all your life, too."

How to Do Research

You need help. That's why you're reading this article. You have to prepare a written or oral research report. If you have never had to do research before, you may not be sure how to begin or how to go about completing your assignment.

This article, "How to Do Research," shows you simply, clearly, step-by-step how to handle the problems you are likely to meet as you proceed with your research. It also shows you how to write a report and how to give an oral report. You will learn how to apply and improve the basic skills involved in:

1. Choosing a subject, and limiting that subject to a topic that you can handle comfortably but significantly;

2. Locating the information you need for your report (it's easy once you know where and how to find what you're looking for);

3. Using the library, reference books, and other sources of information;

4. Taking readable and usable notes;

5. Developing an outline for your report;

6. Organizing your notes and ideas;

7. And, finally, preparing your written or oral report.

You have your work cut out for you, but it's really not as big or as difficult a job as it sounds. Actually, you have been preparing reports of one kind or another ever since you first learned to write or give book reports. This is just a different kind of report. And you have been doing some kind of research all your life, too. If, for example, you like music, you certainly drop into your local music store to listen to and buy records and tapes. Probably, you also trade records and talk about music with your friends. You may also try to find out about the latest hits from radio, television, newspapers, and magazines.

In short, you have been doing original research that involves activities such as reading books and articles, interviewing people, forming or changing opinions, reaching conclusions, and expressing your opinions. In any research paper you prepare, you'll apply skills you've learned and used before. You'll simply use them in a different way to search for facts, ideas, and experiences—largely through reading, but also through audio-visual materials, personal interviews, and letters. Then you'll present a written or oral report. The style of a written research report is a little different (only a little) from the style used for other written assignments. It's a bit more formal, but it's easy to learn what to do and how to do it. The same is true of an oral research report.

Students often ask: "Why should I have to do a research report? Why should I have to learn these 'new' research skills? What's in it for me? Wouldn't I be just as successful and happy if I never did a research report?" These are good questions. Doing a research report is worth all the work you put into it. Here are some reasons why:

■ In school, you'll have to give a number of written or oral research reports. So, if you learn how to go about your research and how to prepare this kind of report properly, you'll find future assignments easier to handle.

■ If you *really* learn how to use a library, you will have mastered a skill that will be useful to you the rest of your life. No matter where you go or what you do, you'll need to know how to look for information and how to analyze and evaluate what you find.

■ In any business or profession, you'll be able to put to good use your ability to locate, collect, organize, and evaluate information and ideas. And you'll be able to present both written and oral reports in clear and convincing form.

■ Lastly, there is a special kind of feeling you get when you have completed a job you set out to do, even if it's been assigned to you. Step by step you follow the trail of research. You stick with it. You grow with it. Before you know it, you've written a small "book." You're an expert—maybe only a mini-expert, but still an expert. You know more about some aspect of a subject than most people do. You may even know more about it than your teacher.

Planning your work

When you go on a car trip, you need to plan. You set a schedule, get road maps, choose the best route, figure a budget, and so on. The same is true when you prepare a research report. You need to plan how to get from *here*—your assignment—to *there*—your finished report. But before you do anything, you have to know where you are going.

Check with your teacher to be sure you understand all of the requirements for the report. Is there a minimum or maximum word limit? When do you have to hand in the report? Must it be typed? Should it be in a binder? Do you have to hand in the final outline? Are quotations and facts to be credited in footnotes? Is there to be a bibliography? How many sources do you have to include in your bibliography? What style are you to use for the footnotes and bibliography? And, most important, what is the purpose of the assignment?

Once you have the answers to these and other questions, get to work right away. The longer you put off starting, the harder it will be. You'll find that an early start pays off—

LEARNING GUIDE 7-1 (cont.)

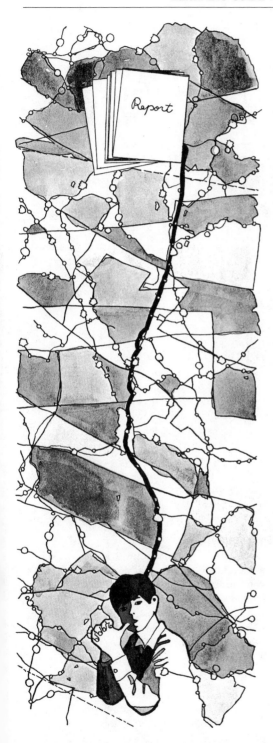

"You need to plan how to get from *here*—your assignment—to *there*—your finished report."

there won't be any last-minute panic. Writing a research report is not really difficult. You can get where you want to go if you (1) explore thoroughly, (2) make notes clearly and accurately, and (3) outline logically the material you want to cover.

Teachers usually expect a short report to be handed in a few days after the assignment. But a research report (which in written form may run to more than a thousand words) will be assigned early in the term, to be completed some weeks later. The more time your teacher gives you to do the work, the more will be expected of you in the way of ideas, research, and quality—and that means more planning. Here are the 10 basic steps involved in doing a research report:

1. Choose a subject and limit it to a specific topic.

2. Do some general background reading, jotting down the main ideas you think belong in a paper on your topic.

3. Organize your ideas in a logical sequence. This is your preliminary outline.

4. List all the sources you think you may be able to use for your report. This is your working bibliography.

5. Locate the sources listed in your working bibliography, and the others to which these will lead you.

6. Read carefully and take notes based on your sources.

7. Organize your notes and prepare the final outline.

8. Write, revise, and rewrite your report. If you are giving an oral report, practice speaking from notes.

9. Prepare the documentation (footnotes and bibliography) in final form.

10. Type (or write) a final copy to hand in. If you are giving an oral report, have a dress rehearsal.

Discouraged by the "Terrible Ten"? Don't be. You're on your way. The following sections will show you how to do each of these 10 steps.

LEARNING GUIDE **7-1** (cont.)

"...select a topic you can live with and work with."

Getting started

Step 1   Choosing a subject

The first thing to do is to choose a subject for your research. "But," you may say, "I don't have to worry about choosing a subject. Our teacher told us exactly what to write about." That's fine—but a word of warning anyway. Make sure you understand your assignment. If you aren't absolutely sure, *ask.* Even though you didn't choose the subject of your paper, you can make it yours. Set your mind to find it interesting. If you approach the work in the right spirit, half the job is done.

Suppose, however, you're encouraged to choose your own subject. Don't settle on the first idea that occurs to you. Examine a number of possible subjects. One way to do this is to look at the Reading and Study Guides included in the Index to WORLD BOOK, in this volume. These guides suggest many topics for study and investigation. Here are a few pointers to help you avoid some common dangers when choosing a subject for a research report.

■ *Choose a subject that interests you.* Maybe you already know a little about a particular subject and want to know more, or maybe a subject has some special meaning for you. You're going to spend time reading for this report;

make sure the subject is worth the time to you! Is it related to your hobby? To your life and experience? To your goals and ambitions? To your other courses? For a written report, you will usually be allowed to choose any subject that interests you, so long as it meets with your teacher's approval. But if you are going to give an oral report, you should also consider the interests of your audience—your fellow students. Try to select a subject that will interest as many of them as possible. That way you will have a better chance of holding their attention.

■ *Choose a subject you know something about.* If you are too ambitious and want to write on a subject that calls for information that is far beyond your ability to handle, you will become discouraged or find yourself parroting material you do not really understand. A good, honest research paper is one in which you deepen and extend what you already know. If you choose a subject totally unfamiliar to you, you'll probably write a bad paper.

■ *Choose a subject treated in available reference sources.* Find out what special reference books your school and community libraries offer in your subject. General reference sources, such as encyclopedias, give you a broad picture and many basic facts. But special reference works are limited to a particular subject field. Before

LEARNING GUIDE 7-1 (cont.)

you are through you will need a number of special works dealing only with your subject or, sometimes, with only a very small part of it. If your school or community library has nothing on your subject–either because it is too new or too highly specialized, or because the library is too limited–change the subject. Your librarian will be glad to help you find out what resources–books, audio-visual materials, and so on–are available.

■ *Limit your subject to a specific topic.* Learn to limit your research. Don't try to write the entire history of anything. As subjects for a report, "The American Revolution" and "The Space Program" are too broad. You'll go beyond your word limit before you have started. If the subject you choose is too vast in scope, your treatment will be of the "once-over-lightly" variety–and that's not a good research report. So define your subject, narrow it down to a *topic* you can cover within the limits of your report. Instead of "The American Revolution," perhaps it will be "Concord: The Shot Heard Round the World"; rather than "The Space Program," it may be "The First Moon Shot." These are topics on which you can focus, on which you can say something.

■ *Choose a topic that is not too elementary.* Some topics don't lend themselves to reading or

"The most useful beginning point for research is a reliable encyclopedia."

investigation or extended study because they're just too simple, or too temporary in interest, or too "thin." For example, "Stickball" or "Fashion Fads" might be fine subjects for short informal essays, but they do not have much intellectual content and you would run out of sources–and information–very fast if you chose them as subjects for a research paper.

■ *Choose a topic on which you have an open mind.* If you are going to take sides before you even begin the hunt for facts, you are defeating the purpose of research, which is to discover "truth." Your paper will lack balance. For example, do not decide in advance that all-protein diets are the best reducing diets, and then carefully select facts to prove your point. Instead, try investigating a subject such as "Safe Reducing Diets for Teen-agers," using reference sources on nutrition to achieve a balanced and accurate report.

■ *Know when to stop researching.* Your job is to find *enough* material for your report–not *all* the material that may be available. Don't try to make your report the last word on the subject. Hours spent searching for an obscure reference, a tantalizing but–in terms of your report–unimportant fact isn't getting on with the job. Form a clear idea as to the kinds of information you need for your purposes. When you have enough, stop researching and start organizing.

Now you are ready to select a topic you can live with and work with. Good hunting!

Step 2   Reading for background

Suppose you've chosen the topic, "Indians in Fact and Fiction." On a television program dealing with the life of the Indians in the United States today, you heard that many of us have false pictures of Indians that go back to Chingachgook and Magua, characters in James Fenimore Cooper's book *The Last of the Mohicans.* You have read the book. Do you simply start writing? *Definitely not!* Before writing a single sentence, get an overview of your topic. You have to see the topic in perspective before you can zero in on it. You have to get a broad, comprehensive look at the field of which it is a part.

First, consult your teacher and your librarian. But don't expect them to do your thinking for you. Prepare for the meeting by drawing up some questions. (Was Cooper the first American novelist to write about the Indians? Who is the best writer on Indians today?) The teacher or librarian may also have questions to ask *you*. Knowing the problems and dangers that lurk in a topic as broad as "Indians in Fact and Fiction," they may suggest that you limit your research to novels written during a specific period of time, to one or two writers, or even to one or two representative books. You may also be asked to examine your purpose. Do you want to find out something in particular? To make a definite point? Chances are they will also suggest that you begin by reading a number of articles in a good general encyclopedia, because getting started on a topic you know something about—but not very much—means doing general background reading.

The most useful beginning point for research is a reliable encyclopedia. An encyclopedia won't tell you everything you will need to know, but it's a wonderful place to start because it will give you a good overview of your topic and suggest related material. In addition, encyclopedia articles often include charts, diagrams, maps, photographs, and bibliographies. To make the best use of an encyclopedia, be sure to consult the index and to follow up cross-references. If you are using WORLD BOOK, you might also want to read How to Get the Most out of World Book in Volume A.

When you are skimming an encyclopedia article for background, what should you be reading for? Believe it or not, for *pleasure!* An encyclopedia article will turn up many aspects of your subject that you haven't thought of. This is where your exploration begins, and your research report is just that— exploration. The ideas and facts that you find in this first reading will prompt you to ask some of the "five W's": Who, What, Why, Where, and When. *Who* said or wrote it? *What* can you find to back it up? *Why* is it true (or false)? *Where* did it take place? *When* did it

happen? Usually you will also want to know *How* it happened.

As you read, write down the main ideas you *think* belong in a report on your topic. These ideas will form the basis for your attack on your subject. They will give you the main idea, or purpose, for your report. But every attack, no matter how clear its purpose, must have a battle plan. After you've read the encyclopedia articles (there are usually several related ones) on your topic, prepare your preliminary outline.

Step 3   The preliminary outline

If you express ideas clearly and logically, a reader or listener will understand and remember what you have said. Clear and logical expression requires organization—and organization means some kind of outlining. An outline is the backbone of a good oral or written report. It gives you, and your audience, the framework for what you want to say.

Everything starts with your decision about your main idea. This is called the *thesis*, or purpose, of your paper. Test your thesis by trying to state it in one clear sentence. Ask yourself: "What do I want to say? What am I going to cover? What are the important points to develop?" Write down each major idea. Don't be too concerned about order or completeness. This is a preliminary outline, to be used as a guide to the kinds of information to look for. Without it, you may wander from the point.

There are two standard types of outline, the *topic outline* and the *sentence outline*. The topic outline, which consists of words or phrases, is easier to do and allows you more freedom in writing or speaking. The sentence outline, made up of complete sentences, is closer to the final form of your report. Both outlines must (a) give the purpose of the paper, (b) show the relationship between the facts, and (c) develop a logical conclusion. The preliminary outline is usually a topic outline. Keep it simple, using only main topics and first-order subtopics.

LEARNING GUIDE 7-1 (cont.)

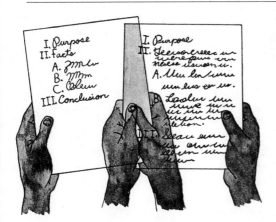

"...outlines must (a) give the purpose of the paper, (b) show the relationship between the facts, and (c) develop a logical conclusion."

As you go deeper into your research, you may want to change, or even discard, this outline, but you should have something with which to start. It will give form and direction to your thinking, reading, and writing. The process of going from a rough outline to a final outline can teach you many things that go beyond the problem of how to do a research report. You will be learning how to think. Between the first and the last outline, there may be many outlines. You will see how ideas grow and develop. You will change one of the main ideas to a minor subdivision. You will drop some ideas. You will add new ones. Outlining requires *thinking through* a subject, putting together the ideas that belong together.

The working bibliography

You are now ready to list sources to use in researching your topic. This list of sources is your working bibliography. A working bibliography gives you some idea as to the kind of research that has already been done on your topic. It will also help you to find out what material the library has on your topic. Remember, however, that this is a *working* bibliography. It will grow and change as your search for information leads you from one source to another. First, list any sources given in the encyclopedia articles you read. Many of the articles in WORLD BOOK, for example, have lists of books for further reading. Look, too, at the Reading and Study Guides in this volume of WORLD BOOK, for each guide lists a number of books for suggested reading and research, as well as other sources of information. Later, when you start your research proper, you will find still other sources in books, in magazine and newspaper indexes, and under appropriate headings in the card catalog and vertical file.

To prepare your working bibliography, get a supply of standard-size file cards (3 x 5 inches, 4 x 6, or 5 x 8), ruled or blank. Cards are easier to organize than a notebook, and when you are ready to write your report they can be arranged in any order. Also, those that are not used can be discarded without affecting your organization. At the same time, get two file

Typical bibliography card

Source number (to use on note card)

Author, title, and publication data (in style of final bibliography)

Call number of book

Library that has the book

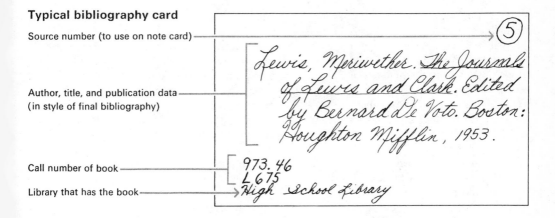

boxes, one to hold your bibliography cards and the other for the note cards you will soon be preparing.

When you locate a source of information—a book, article, pamphlet, record, tape, filmstrip, and so on—make a complete record of it on a bibliography card—in ink. List only one source on a card. For a book, each card should contain the full name of the author, the title (as it appears on the title page), and complete publication data (the place of publication, the name of the publisher, and the date of publication). For a magazine article, include the name of the author, the title of the article, the name of the magazine, the date (day or month) of publication, and the pages on which the article appears.

To avoid confusion later, the form of entry used on the bibliography card should be the same as that to be used in the final bibliography. Make out a bibliography card for every source you consult. If a source does not have what you want, draw a diagonal line through the card and file it. This way you will always have a complete record of the sources you consulted.

In addition, three other pieces of information will be useful. First, number each bibliography card in the upper right-hand corner. Use this number on your note card (in place of author and title) to identify the source of the note. It is a good idea to include, perhaps in the lower left-hand corner, the call number of the book and the library where you found it. Then, if for any reason you should need the material again, you can find it easily.

Researching your report

Step 5   Where to find information

The famous English writer Dr. Samuel Johnson once said, "Knowledge is of two kinds. We know a subject ourselves, or we know where we can find information on it." Now that you are ready to start doing the research for your report, you will have to learn your way around a library so that you can find the books and other sources of information that you will need. Teachers and librarians can give you some help, but you're going to have to learn to do most of the work yourself.

The card catalog. The place to start your search for source materials is the card catalog. The card catalog consists of one or more cabinets containing drawers of catalog cards. These cards, arranged alphabetically, are a record of every book (and often other material) in the library. For most books there is one card under the author's name, one under the title of the book, and one or more under the subject(s) of the book.

There are several ways to find material you want. If you don't know the author or title, as is likely, look under possible subject headings. But you have to use your imagination to think of subject headings. The fact that there are several subject cards for most books is a big help. Start by looking for specific rather than general headings—*water pollution* rather than *pollution; Lewis and Clark expedition* rather than *U.S. history*. Your reading in the encyclopedia should provide you with a number of possible subject headings, but if you can't find what you need, ask the librarian for help.

Catalog cards contain a wealth of information, and an experienced researcher can often tell from a card if a book will be of help. Shown on the opposite page is a typical set of cards distributed by the Library of Congress. The author card tells you that in this edition of *The Journals of Lewis and Clark* there are "lii" (52) pages of front matter preceding the text (an indication that there is a lengthy introduction). The brief quotation below the page information line tells you that this is condensed from the original journals, published some 50 years earlier. Depending upon your needs, this may or may not be important. Students of American history and literature will also find the editor's name informative, because De Voto is a recognized authority on the Western frontier.

Despite the fact that a catalog card tells you

The card catalog

The card catalog is the key to the books in a library. There are cards
entered under the name of the author, the title, one or more subjects,
and even the editor or a joint author. The call number indicates
where you will find the book on the shelf.

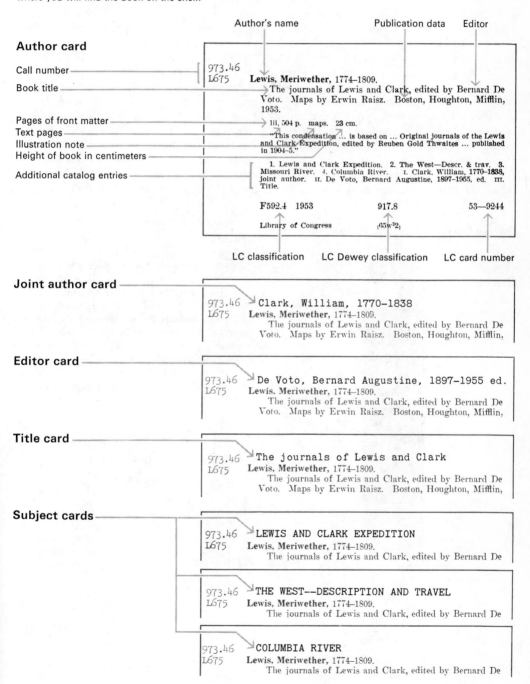

Author card

Author's name   Publication data   Editor

Call number
Book title

973.46
L675

Lewis, Meriwether, 1774–1809.
The journals of Lewis and Clark, edited by Bernard De
Voto. Maps by Erwin Raisz. Boston, Houghton, Mifflin,
1953.

Pages of front matter — lii, 504 p. maps. 23 cm.
Text pages
Illustration note — "This condensation ... is based on ... Original journals of the Lewis and Clark Expedition, edited by Reuben Gold Thwaites ... published in 1904–5."
Height of book in centimeters

Additional catalog entries —
1. Lewis and Clark Expedition. 2. The West—Descr. & trav. 3.
Missouri River. 4. Columbia River. I. Clark, William, 1770–1838,
joint author. II. De Voto, Bernard Augustine, 1897–1955, ed. III.
Title.

F592.4   1953   917.8   53—9244

Library of Congress   ᵣ65w³2ᵢ

LC classification   LC Dewey classification   LC card number

Joint author card

973.46
L675

Clark, William, 1770–1838
Lewis, Meriwether, 1774–1809.
The journals of Lewis and Clark, edited by Bernard De
Voto. Maps by Erwin Raisz. Boston, Houghton, Mifflin,

Editor card

973.46
L675

De Voto, Bernard Augustine, 1897–1955 ed.
Lewis, Meriwether, 1774–1809.
The journals of Lewis and Clark, edited by Bernard De
Voto. Maps by Erwin Raisz. Boston, Houghton, Mifflin,

Title card

973.46
L675

The journals of Lewis and Clark
Lewis, Meriwether, 1774–1809.
The journals of Lewis and Clark, edited by Bernard De
Voto. Maps by Erwin Raisz. Boston, Houghton, Mifflin,

Subject cards

973.46
L675

LEWIS AND CLARK EXPEDITION
Lewis, Meriwether, 1774–1809.
The journals of Lewis and Clark, edited by Bernard De

973.46
L675

THE WEST—DESCRIPTION AND TRAVEL
Lewis, Meriwether, 1774–1809.
The journals of Lewis and Clark, edited by Bernard De

973.46
L675

COLUMBIA RIVER
Lewis, Meriwether, 1774–1809.
The journals of Lewis and Clark, edited by Bernard De

LEARNING GUIDE 7-1 (cont.)

a great deal, you should look at the book itself. The call number in the upper left-hand corner of the card tells you where to find the book. Most libraries use the Dewey Decimal Classification System for nonfiction. (Fiction is arranged alphabetically by author on separate shelves.) The very largest libraries, however, use the Library of Congress Classification System (LC) to organize books by subject fields.

On the card illustrated there are two Dewey Decimal Classification numbers. One, centered near the bottom of the card, has been suggested by the Library of Congress. The other, in the card's upper left-hand corner, has been assigned as this library's call number. Both classifications are correct. This library, however, thought readers and researchers would prefer to have the book shelved with works on

history rather than with those on geography and travel. In most school and public libraries you will be able to go directly to the shelves, where you will find the books arranged in Dewey Decimal or LC order. In larger libraries, however, you will have to note the call number and other information on a slip of paper. An assistant will then get the book for you.

On the nonfiction shelves you will find all kinds of books to help you in your research. There will be histories of literature, journals, biographies, and thousands of other works. From a research point of view, these books are classed as either *primary* or *secondary* sources. A primary source is a firsthand account by someone who witnessed what is being written about, as in the case of a diary. An author using a primary source as the basis for a work

Dewey Decimal Classification

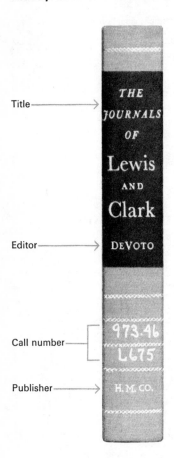

Title
Editor
Call number
Publisher

This numbering system, devised by Melvil Dewey in 1876, is a method for classifying books by subject so that books on related material are shelved together. There are 10 main classes, 000 to 900, each of which is divided into 10 subclasses or divisions (*e.g.,* 970). These are further divided into 10 sections (*e.g.,* 973). Continued decimal notation (*e.g.,* 973.4 and 973.46) permits ever-finer subdivisions. This number appears on each library book and determines the way the books are arranged in the library. By getting the number from an author, title, or subject card in the card catalog, you can quickly locate any book on the shelves.

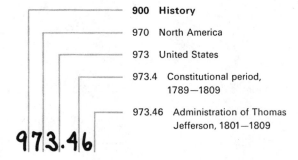

900   History

970   North America

973   United States

973.4   Constitutional period, 1789—1809

973.46   Administration of Thomas Jefferson, 1801—1809

LEARNING GUIDE 7-1 (cont.)

"Some reference books tell you *where to find* information
... and some *contain* information...."

creates a secondary source. *The Journals of Lewis and Clark*, for example, is a primary source, but the introduction is a secondary source.

Reference books. After examining the card catalog, and the arrangement of nonfiction works on the shelves, look for the reference section of the library. This will be a special area set aside for the guides and general reference works that are in constant use.

At this point, you might ask: What is a reference book? Generally speaking, a reference book is any book you consult for specific information rather than read straight through for pleasure. Strictly speaking, however, a reference book is a work arranged so as to make it easy to find information. This arrangement may be alphabetical, chronological, or on any other systematic basis. Encyclopedias, dictionaries, handbooks, and atlases are all works of this type. There are, however, many other books, such as *The Concise Cambridge History of English Literature*, that serve a reference function because they are comprehensive, reliable, and include indexes and other aids.

Some reference books tell you *where to find* information (indexes, bibliographies) and some *contain* information (encyclopedias, dictionaries, manuals). Both kinds may be classed as *general* (dealing with many subjects) or *special* (dealing

with only one subject). The list of selected reference books at the back of this volume suggests many other works that will be useful for different areas of research. There are, however, at least four reference works (in addition to the encyclopedia) with which you should be familiar. These are: (1) the dictionary, (2) yearbooks and almanacs, (3) *The Readers' Guide to Periodical Literature,* and (4) *The New York Times Index.*

Most people think of—and use—a dictionary as the authority for the spellings and meanings of words. But a good dictionary has a great deal more to offer. Look through the front pages of a dictionary to see for yourself how many different kinds of information it contains. And don't overlook the many special dictionaries of slang, of synonyms and antonyms, of rhyming words, and of abbreviations.

Yearbooks published as annual supplements to encyclopedias, and yearly almanacs, such as *The World Almanac and Book of Facts,* contain an astonishing amount of up-to-date information in many fields. These works carry facts and statistics on business, sports, entertainment, foreign countries, population, and summaries of developments in various fields during the year. They are extremely useful for information about current events.

If you need really up-to-the-minute informa-

"...you will have to learn your way around a library so that you can find the books and other sources of information that you will need."

tion on a current problem, such as pollution or drug abuse, two periodical indexes will give you the help you need. These are *The Readers' Guide to Periodical Literature* and *The New York Times Index*. These two publications can also be used to get contemporary views of events or issues of many years ago.

The Readers' Guide to Periodical Literature indexes more than a hundred of the most important general (nontechnical) magazines. It is issued regularly throughout the year, and cumulated at intervals until it becomes a complete annual volume. The list of periodicals indexed varies from volume to volume, so be sure to check the list included in the volume you are using. This reference tool is especially useful because it indexes magazine articles by author, title, and subject, uses catalog subject headings, and describes each entry.

The New York Times Index is an index to the news printed in *The New York Times*. It is used much like the *Readers' Guide*, although it is chiefly a subject listing. Brief synopses of many articles often make it possible to answer a ques-

tion without reference to the newspaper itself. By giving the date on which news was reported, this work also serves as a guide to most other newspapers. Many libraries keep *The New York Times* on microfilm to preserve space. Check with your librarian to find out what newspapers are kept, either on microfilm or in bound volumes.

Additional library resources. In addition to books, magazines, and newspapers, most libraries offer a number of other features and services. A great deal of the material any library collects consists of pamphlets and similar nonbook items of current and topical interest. Such material is kept in standard filing cabinets—called the *vertical file*—where it is arranged alphabetically by subject. A look in the vertical file will often turn up information that cannot be found in any other source. Films, filmstrips, records, and tapes are other potential sources of information offered by many libraries. When these cannot be loaned out, the library will provide facilities for their use. Check to find out how your library indexes

LEARNING GUIDE 7-1 (cont.)

these materials. Libraries may also be able to obtain books and other material from nearby libraries. If you really need material your library does not have, ask the librarian about getting it through an interlibrary loan.

Other sources of information. There are, of course, many ways to obtain information for your research report other than in your school or public library. Which ones you use will depend upon the subject you are researching. Many fields of research can be better handled in museums and art galleries, especially when these have libraries of their own or an education department through which you can obtain assistance. Trade and professional organizations, business groups, and government bureaus related to your field of research are other possible sources. People working in the field you are researching may also be able to help you. If they live in or near your community, you might be able to talk to them personally. If not, you will have to ask your questions by letter.

Step 6 **Using sources of information**

Judging reference sources. When using any reference work, there are a number of things to look for. Examine your sources with a critical eye. Know *what* you are using and *why*.

■ *Authority.* Who is the author? Does he or she have a particular point of view? Is the author a recognized expert in this field? Is there clear evidence (footnotes, appendixes, notes) of scholarship? If there is no individual author (and sometimes even if there is), who is the publisher? Does this company publish other works of this kind or in this field?

■ *Date of Publication.* If you are checking a periodical index, make sure you have the volume or issue you want. You won't, for example, find anything on *Sputnik I* in a magazine or newspaper published before October, 1957 (*Sputnik I* was launched on October 4, 1957), nor will you be likely to find a reference to the President's 1968 State of the Union message in a guide covering 1971 (it just isn't news anymore). If you are using a book, check the

copyright date on the back of the title page—the book won't have information on anything after that date. In some specialized fields, you will need the most recent works available.

■ *Edition.* Is this a first edition or a revised edition? (Information about the edition will appear on the title page or the copyright page.) If a work has gone through a number of revisions or editions, it is because there has been a demand for it—it has proved reliable and useful to others and should be of use to you.

■ *Arrangement.* How are the contents arranged? Is there a good index? Can you find what you want with a minimum of trouble?

■ *Treatment and Scope.* Is this a work meant for scholars or for the general public? Will it serve your purposes? Is the scope of the work clearly indicated (see the title page, preface, or introduction) so that you can tell if it *ought* to contain what you are looking for? What is not covered?

■ *Bibliography.* Does the author list the sources used? Does he or she provide a list of suggested readings that might be of help?

■ *Special Features.* Are there instructions telling you how to use the work? Is there a list of the abbreviations used? Look especially for limitations to the usefulness of the work.

Using a reference book. One of your reference sources is in front of you. First, check both the table of contents and the index. The table of contents cannot be used in the same way as the index, nor can it take the place of the index. The table of contents is usually just a list of the chapter titles, although it may tell what each chapter is about. The index, on the other hand, is an alphabetical list of the important topics in the book and gives the page or pages on which a fact or subject is treated. It also helps by telling you if what you want is in the book at all. To use an index well, you must look up your topic by the most specific word—the word which most clearly describes that topic. If you are searching for information about the Missouri River, look under "Missouri," not "river"; for President Thomas Jefferson, look under "Jefferson," not "President." Some indexes do have general entries for broad topics, so that you might find what you want under "river," or "president," but specific entries are more common. (See the Index to WORLD BOOK in this volume for examples of how topics are indexed.)

There are a number of kinds of indexes. The most common is a general index (names, titles, subjects). In some books, however, there may be several indexes: a title index, a subject index, an author index, and even (in collections of

"A personal interview may give you more material for your report than any other source."

poetry) a "first-line" index. When you are consulting an encyclopedia or set of books of several volumes, the general index (usually in the last volume) indicates the volume and the page.

Using the index, find the text pages you want and skim them quickly to see if they contain information you can use. To skim intelligently, read the headings (if any), the first or *topic sentence*, and the last or *summary sentence* of each paragraph. This method will help you to spot the main ideas. If the book (or magazine article) does not seem to have what you are looking for—even though you thought it might—discard it and move on to another possible source.

When you find a book that has what you need, read the text closely, take notes, and, of course, fill out a bibliography card. But don't put the book back on the shelf yet. While you have the book, look at the front and back matter. The *front matter*, or preliminary pages, includes such parts as a foreword, a preface, and an introduction. The *back matter* may consist of appendixes, notes, a glossary, and a bibliography.

Using other sources of information. You may be able to get information through letters and personal interviews. Letters to professional and business associations and to government agencies often produce specific facts and views that might otherwise be difficult to find. Such groups, however, vary considerably in their ability to answer requests for information and to assist with student projects. A courteous telephone call or letter will tell you if such help is possible.

If you do decide to write for information, keep your request within reasonable limits. The people to whom you will be writing are busy. Also, some time may go by before you get an answer. Don't put yourself in a position where everything depends upon help from an outside source. Be prepared to go ahead if you have not had a reply by a certain date. If you do get a reply, be sure to send a thank-you note.

People in your town may be first-rate sources of up-to-date information on your topic. A personal interview may give you more material for your report than any other source. It is smart to "exploit" local talent if you go about it in the right way. The same rules of courtesy

LEARNING GUIDE 7-1 (cont.)

and consideration apply to a request for information or an interview as to any other social situation. Perhaps the best procedure is to write a short note, introducing yourself. Explain your problem and specify the kind of information you need. Say that you would be grateful for any possible help. Make yourself available at any time convenient to the person to whom you are writing. Don't forget to include your telephone number and address.

You will spare yourself nervousness and your host valuable time if you come to the interview prepared. Know your subject and exactly what you want to find out. Prepare a few definite questions in advance, and write them out. Above all, pay attention to the answers to your questions. Be prepared to take notes. Ask permission to quote directly. If the person you are interviewing is willing, you may want to use a tape recorder. Whichever method of taking notes you use, make sure you quote accurately and that you have the necessary information (full name, position, and organization) for your footnotes and bibliography. Express your appreciation when you leave and write a thank-you note.

Taking notes. A good research report starts with good notes. Clear and accurate notes make for clear and accurate writing. After you skim a book or article you may find that it has information on your topic. If so, go back and read carefully, making notes about the most important points. There are many systems used for taking notes—which one you use is not important. But it is important that you use a system. Here are some tips on how to take notes.

Use cards, as you did for your working bibliography. Write in ink, on one side of a card only. If you must continue on the reverse side, write "OVER" at the bottom of the card. Keep a red pencil handy for underlining items you want to emphasize. Put only one item (fact, idea, quotation) on a card. Then you can arrange, alphabetize, shuffle, and combine your notes in any way you want. At the top right-hand corner of the card, write the number of the bibliography card to show the source of the information. Don't forget to include the page number(s) as part of the identification. You may need this information later for a footnote. At the top of the card, write in capital letters a short heading, called a "slug," showing the main head or subhead in your outline to which the note refers. If your note card is labeled in this way, you'll save time when you organize the cards and revise your preliminary outline before writing your first draft. Above all, take the time to write clearly and legibly. Be sure when the time comes to use the note—which may be days or weeks later—that you can read and understand what you wrote.

Write your note *after* you have digested what you have read, especially if it's on a controversial subject. Let the material register in your mind. Evaluate it. Should you use it? If you're just going to transfer sentences and paragraphs from sources to your notes, and then to your paper, you'll be working with your pen but not with your head. As you read, ask yourself such questions as these. Who is the author? How recent is this material? How reliable is the author? What makes the author an expert?

Typical note card

Slug (outline topic to which note refers) ───→ TREATMENT OF WOMEN ⑤

The Shoshone "treat their women but with little respect [sic], and compel them to perform every specus of drudgery.... the man dose [sic] little else except attend his horses [,] hunt [,] and fish."

Source number (from bibliography card) ───

Page reference (to use in footnote) ─── (Lewis) p. 208

How complete is the information? How much is fact? How much is opinion? What evidence is given for debatable statements?

When you write your note, it may be a summary, a paraphrase, a direct quotation, or any one of these combined with a personal comment. But don't use too many quotations. Notes in which you summarize, paraphrase, or comment on what you've read are more effective than quotations because they are *yours*, not someone else's. Use quotations when you need an expert witness for something you could not know, or when you want to hold someone accountable for a particular idea or statement. If you do quote, copy exactly, down to the last punctuation mark. Whatever else, *don't plagiarize*. You are plagiarizing if you copy someone else's words without putting them in quotation marks and giving the source.

Preparing your report

Step 7   The final outline

Now that you have examined the source materials, and have enough information in your notes to cover the topics you noted on your preliminary outline, it is time to review and organize. The first thing to do is to compare your statement of purpose with your notes.

Does the statement still make sense? Should you revise it because you now know more than when you started? Remember, the statement of purpose is the peg on which you are going to hang your report. Work to develop it. Get it right.

Read your notes carefully. Arrange and rearrange them. Can you still follow the general plan indicated by your preliminary outline?

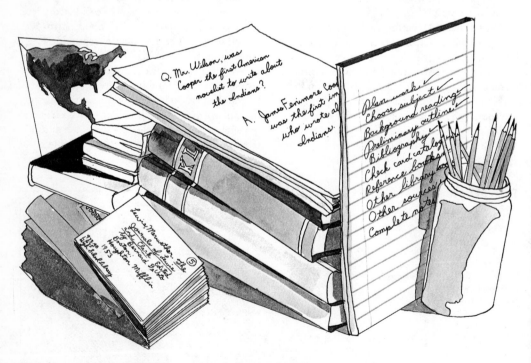

"If you have done a good job with your research, if your notes are complete and understandable, you've finished the most difficult part."

LEARNING GUIDE 7-1 (cont.)

Should you change one or more of the main topics? Should you revise or eliminate any of the slugs on the cards? Are there any notes that should be dropped because they do not further your statement of purpose? Are there any serious gaps still to be filled in? All of this will help you decide just how to present your material. Sometimes the material will almost organize itself. But usually you will have to decide how to organize it, based on your purpose.

There are a number of ways of presenting your report. You may, for example, decide to arrange the material in chronological order. Usually such an approach begins with the earliest material and proceeds to the most recent. But sometimes you can start with a recent event and then go back to show what had taken place earlier. Other approaches include comparison and contrast, cause and effect, and the arrangement of topics in order of increasing importance. Comparison and contrast can be especially effective when dealing with topics in literature and with social problems. A cause-and-effect approach is suited to many topics, and can be presented in either direction—that is, you can go from cause to effect or from effect to cause.

When you have your note cards arranged in what seems to be the most logical way, use them to build your final outline. Look first for the large, obvious divisions and use them for the main topics. The fewer main topics, the better. Three to five will usually do very nicely. A main topic should be broad enough to allow for full development of the idea it encompasses. When you have settled on the main topics, look to see how these can be subdivided. Remember, each subtopic must relate to the main topic of which it is a part, and that you cannot have fewer than two subtopics. If you have only one subtopic, it must be included in the main topic.

The final outline can be either a topic outline or a sentence outline, but it cannot be a combination of both. In either form, the heads must be expressed in parallel grammatical style. All topics of equal importance should be equally indented. Topics and subtopics are organized with Roman numerals, capital letters, Arabic numerals, and lower-case letters, in that order (*e.g.*, I, A, 1, a). If you need more subdivisions, first use Arabic numerals and then lower-case letters, enclosing both in parentheses. All numerals and letters not in parentheses are followed by periods. Here is the topic outline for this article:

  I. Introduction
 II. Planning your work
III. Getting started
    A. Step 1: Choosing a subject
    B. Step 2: Reading for background
    C. Step 3: The preliminary outline
    D. Step 4: The working bibliography
 IV. Researching your report
    A. Step 5: Finding sources of information
       1. The card catalog
       2. Reference books
       3. Additional library resources
       4. Other sources of information
    B. Step 6: Using sources of information
       1. Judging reference sources
       2. Using a reference book
       3. Using other sources of information
       4. Taking notes
  V. Preparing your report
    A. Step 7: The final outline
    B. Step 8: Writing and revising
    C. Step 9: Documenting your report
       1. Footnotes
       2. Bibliography
    D. Step 10: Preparing the final report
       1. The written report
       2. The oral report

Step 8   **Writing and revising**

With your final outline in front of you and your note cards assembled in proper order, you are ready to start your first (rough) draft. If you have done a good job with your research, if your notes are complete and understandable, you've finished the most difficult part. From here on, if you stick to the job, you'll have few real problems.

When writing the first draft, let your ideas pour out. Write from your notes, but try to avoid copying them word for word. Think about what they mean, the ideas they stand for. Concentrate on organization, on building from one idea to the next. What counts is getting your ideas down on paper in an orderly

"Concentrate on organization, on building from one idea to the next."

way. At the same time, plan now for footnotes and quotations.

Even if you are making an oral report, it is a good idea to draft a written version from which to prepare your speaker's cards. These cards should contain key words, ideas, and even full sentences. Write in ink, or type, on one side only, so that you can read the notes easily. Number the cards to assist in keeping them in order. Use red ink for underlining main heads and important subheads. Your speaking notes should follow the same principles of organization as a written report. Observe the same requirements in speaking that you do in writing: clear statements, logical development, proof by examples, definite references, and, of course, acknowledgment of sources. Communicate what you want to communicate.

Write or type this first draft on standard-size paper, $8\frac{1}{2}$ x 11 inches. For this rough draft, use double or even triple spacing, with wide margins, so as to leave room for additions and corrections. When you include a quotation, be sure

that you copy it exactly, word for word—and don't forget to put it in quotation marks. When a quotation is more than five lines long, it should be indented and single spaced—without quotation marks. If you omit part of a quotation, use an ellipsis (. . .) in place of the part left out. If you have to insert any words of your own in the quotation to make the meaning clear, these are enclosed in brackets ([]). If you need a footnote, write the number of the source (the number you put on the bibliography card) and the page referred to in the margin so that you can pick it up when you revise.

Are you surprised that you will have to write more than one draft, that you will have to rewrite at all? The famous American humorist, James Thurber, said that he rewrote his short story "The Secret Life of Walter Mitty" 15 times. Another famous writer, Margery Allingham, once explained why she rewrote her detective novels four times: first, to get down everything in her mind; second, to put in what she'd left out; third, to cut down words and cut out repetitions; fourth, to make it sound as if it had just been written. A research paper does not have the same requirements as a fine short story or a novel, but you do want to write clearly, logically, and correctly. Your teacher/reader will be even happier if you write simply and forcefully. None of these aims can be achieved in only one writing. You won't have to rewrite 15 times—or even 4—but you'll have to revise at least once.

Begin your revision by checking your organization. Is the introduction brief, interesting, and to the point? Does it make clear the thesis, the purpose, the main idea of the paper? Is the organization logical within each paragraph, and from one paragraph to the next? Are the ideas in proper order? Are they developed with examples and proof? Are they clearly expressed and effective? Does each idea build and expand on preceding ideas? You may find it necessary to change the order of some paragraphs, to transpose sentences or words, and even to insert new sections in order to make your points. Is the last paragraph the most forceful you can think of? Do the facts presented support your conclusions?

This done, review your work again, checking sentence structure, paragraphing, choice of

LEARNING GUIDE 7-1 (cont.)

words, and the mechanics of grammar. Here are some common mistakes to avoid:

1. Careless spelling
2. Run-on sentences and incomplete sentences
3. Sentences too long, not clear, or full of repetitions or unnecessary words
4. Inaccurate capitalization or abbreviation
5. Lack of agreement between subject and verb
6. Use of vague words and general expressions instead of concrete, specific, vivid language
7. Illogical paragraphing
8. Lack of connection between paragraphs
9. Incorrect use of quotation marks
10. Misuse of words

There are still other things to check for. Have you clearly indicated quoted material? Have you inserted footnotes to credit quoted sources, the ideas of others, and to support facts you could not possibly know? Have you copied names and dates exactly? Do your footnotes and bibliography follow the required form? Do you have enough sources in your bibliography, and are they sufficiently varied? Finally, be aware of your style, of *how* you write. This is a formal paper, and you should be objective. This does not, however, mean dull. Try to state your findings and conclusions in clear, straightforward, and simple terms.

Step 9   Documenting your report

One of the major differences between a research report and other papers based on your reading is the use of *documentation*. On every page of your report where you have used words, ideas, facts, or statistics that you've "borrowed," you must credit the source in a footnote. The source is then fully identified in the bibliography. This is documentation.

Footnotes. Not all teachers insist on footnotes, so be sure they are required before you include them. Footnotes serve a variety of pur-

poses. In addition to documenting sources, a footnote may also (1) explain a point more fully, (2) make an editorial comment, (3) add an interesting sidelight, (4) be a cross-reference to another part of the report, or (5) offer a difference of opinion. For an oral report you will want footnotes on any of your speaker's cards that have material needing documentation. You won't read these, but you may be called upon to give the source of a fact or quotation you worked into your speech.

There are a number of different forms used for footnotes. Use the form your teacher prefers. In general, footnotes are numbered consecutively, beginning with 1. Indicate a footnote by placing an Arabic numeral after the text material to be documented. This numeral should be raised a little above the line. At the bottom of the page, place the same numeral before the footnote, again slightly raised above the line. Type a line about $1\frac{1}{2}$ inches long between the text and the footnotes. Notice that a footnote contains only enough information to identify the source. It is not as complete as will be the entry in the bibliography. (The sample bibliographic entries show how these are handled.) This is one way you might footnote a quotation from a book:

```
In a confidential message to Congress
proposing an expedition to the Pacific
Ocean, President Jefferson stated
(regarding the Indians): ". . . I
trust and believe we are acting for
their greatest good. . . ."[1]
```

[1]Albert Fried, *The Essential Jefferson*, p. 429.

For a quotation from a magazine article, this is a standard form for a footnote:

```
Some of the greatest novels are not
entirely works of fiction. Ernest
Hemingway, for example, "constantly
used real people and situations in
his fiction."[2]
```

[2]Alfred Kazin, "Hemingway As His Own Fable," *Atlantic*, June 1964, p. 54.

Footnotes for material taken from letters or based on interviews follow the same style.

[1]Eleanor Nebit, personal letter.
[2]John Sanders, personal interview.

LEARNING GUIDE 7-1 (cont.)

If you refer to more than one letter from the same person, it will be necessary to include the date in order to distinguish between the references.

There are a number of ways to shorten additional references to a source previously cited. One way is the use of Latin abbreviations. Such terms as *ibid.*, *op. cit.*, and *loc. cit.* are not as mysterious as they might at first appear (see the glossary at the back of this volume). Some teachers prefer Latin abbreviations. Others may want you to use English terms or shortened entries.

Bibliography. You are now in the home stretch. After you finish your bibliography you will have all the basic work completed. Your bibliography is a list of all the sources—books, magazines, interviews, letters, audio-visual materials—that you used in preparing your report. Note that it is *not* a list of all the sources you consulted—only the ones you actually used. The bibliography documents your work. It tells the readers where you got your information and provides them with a list of material should they wish to read more on the topic.

If you have filled in your bibliography cards properly, preparing the final bibliography is easy. All you have to do is to arrange the cards alphabetically by author (or title) and copy the information. Most research report bibliographies are arranged in a single alphabetical listing. There may, however, be times when it is more helpful to the readers to separate your sources into categories—books and periodicals, primary sources and secondary sources, and so on.

There are various ways to list sources in a bibliography, so ask your teacher what style he or she wants you to follow. Here are some sample bibliographic entries for books, periodicals, and other sources:

"Botulism." The World Book Encyclopedia. 1980 ed. Vol. 2, p. 424.

Ford, Barbara. Animals That Use Tools. New York: Simon & Schuster, 1978.

Kleinfeld, Sonny. "The Handicapped: Hidden No Longer." Atlantic. December 1977, pp. 86–89.

Nebit, Eleanor. Director of Public Relations, Art Society, Chicago, Illinois. Personal letter, 28 August 1979.

Simply Metric. Film, 1976. 18½ min, sound, c, 16mm. Produced by FilmFair Communications.

Sullivan, Walter. "Solar Energy Held Still Decades Away." The New York Times, 1 February 1979. p. A7.

You should have a bibliography for an oral report, too. For your talk, your bibliography cards will do very nicely should you be called upon to cite a source in full. However, your teacher may want a written list of sources. Be sure to check beforehand to see if you have to turn in a bibliography.

Step 10   Preparing the final report

After you've set up your footnotes and bibliography in the required form, you are ready to type (or write carefully) the final copy of your report or prepare the final note cards for your oral presentation. Stop before you start. Let the first (or second or third) draft cool off in your desk drawer for a day or two before you come back to it. This is the time to go out and have some fun! Relax, enjoy yourself, and forget about your report for the time being. When you do come back to prepare the final copy, you'll be able to read what you've written with a more detached point of view.

When you do come back to your report, try to anticipate how it will be judged. Now is the time to ask yourself the hardest questions of all: "If this were somebody else's paper or talk, what would I think of it? Does this writer or speaker have something to say? Is it being said clearly? Is it convincing?" Also, what will your teacher be looking or listening for? How will your work be evaluated?

Here is a list of the things teachers usually keep in mind:

1. Does the writer (speaker) make the purpose clear and succeed in fulfilling that purpose?

2. Does the speaker look at and address the audience?

3. Does the speaker use complete sentences?

LEARNING GUIDE 7-1 (cont.)

Does he or she speak slowly and distinctly so that everyone can hear?

4. Are there any glaring errors in English usage?

5. Is the report typed or written carefully?

6. Is the report clear and interesting?

7. Are statements supported by facts and examples?

8. Are quotations used in moderation?

9. Are the sources used properly acknowledged in footnotes and in a bibliography?

10. What is *my* reaction to the report? How did the *class* react to the report?

The written report. After you feel that you have said what you wanted to say in the way you wanted to say it, you're ready to make the final copy. If you are going to turn in a handwritten report, use ruled paper, $8\frac{1}{2}$ x 11 inches, and write on one side only. If you are typing your report, observe the following rules (or any special ones your teacher may give you):

1. Use regular, white typing paper, $8\frac{1}{2}$ x 11 inches. Type on one side only.

2. The left-hand margin should be $1\frac{1}{2}$ inches and all other margins 1 inch, except for the table of contents and the chapter titles. These should be 2 inches from the top of the page.

3. Double space the text and between footnotes and bibliographic entries. Triple space between chapter titles and the first line of text, and between the last line of text and the footnotes. Single space footnotes, bibliographic entries, and any quotations that are indented rather than run-in with the text.

4. Indent the first line of each paragraph and the first line of each footnote five spaces. If a footnote has a second line, bring that line all the way out to the margin. In a bibliographic entry, indent the second and any following lines five spaces.

5. Underline the titles of books, magazines, newspapers, and plays. The titles of short stories, magazine articles, and poems should be enclosed in quotation marks.

6. Number all pages. Use small Roman numerals, centered at the bottom of each page, for the introductory pages, beginning with the table of contents (outline). Use Arabic numerals, centered at the top of the page, for all text pages except the opening page of a chapter. Here the page number should go at the bottom of the page.

7. The title page should contain the title of the report, your name, and the date. It often also includes the name of the school, the class, and the teacher's name. These parts should be arranged neatly, and in the sequence required by your teacher.

When the final copy is finished, go over it one more time to check for any errors you may have made in typing or writing. Then assemble the pages in the following order:

1. Blank page (for teacher's comments)

2. Title page

3. Table of contents (outline)

4. Text

5. Bibliography

6. Blank page

Finally, put your report in a folder or binder. And that is it. You are finished! Just don't forget the very last thing you have to do. Get the report in on time.

The oral report. Except for not having to type a final copy, the work done for an oral report is much the same as for a written report. What, then, is the difference between preparing a written research report and an oral report? In one word: practice. Organize your note cards and number them so that you can keep them in order. After you have your notes well organized, try them out at home in the privacy of your room. Stand straight, look up, speak up, speak slowly and clearly. Then do

LEARNING GUIDE 7-1 (cont.)

it again. And again. Don't memorize; just repeat the talk until you are completely at home with every part of your report.

During your practice sessions, work on (1) timing, (2) continuity, and (3) pronunciation and enunciation.If your talk is to run about 15 minutes, allow about 2 minutes for the introduction, 10 minutes for the body, and 2 minutes for the conclusion. The secret to achieving continuity is the logical organization of ideas, all closely linked together. Make sure the transition from one idea to the next is smooth, that one flows easily into the next. Don't be afraid to repeat yourself, just don't repeat unnecessarily. Use repetition for effect, to make a major point, or to hold the attention of your audience. Most important of all, make certain you know how to pronounce properly every word you intend to use. At the same time, work on your enunciation. Don't slur the final endings on words such as "interesting" and "happening." If you're really practical, you'll have a dress rehearsal. Deliver the talk before someone you trust, and ask for constructive advice.

When giving your talk, you may want to use various audio-visual aids—the chalkboard, a tape recorder, a record player, diagrams, charts, and so on. These should not be used to pad out your talk. They should make a real contribution by helping to present material in the best and most interesting way. Make sure you have all the materials in advance, that they're in working order, that you know how to make them work, and that you have provided time for using them in the overall plan of your talk. And don't forget to indicate on the proper note cards what aids you want to use and when.

The night before you are due to speak, go through your cards once more, but quickly, just to fix ideas in your mind. Then go to sleep and rest easy. Many students find the prospect of making an oral report terrifying. It needn't be. The group listening to you is in the same fix you are. Their turns will be coming, too. So talk *to* them, not *at* them. Get your eye off the crack in the ceiling and your mind off your teacher's marking book. Talk to your friends. You have prepared well and you will speak well.

"When giving your talk, you may want to use various audio-visual aids...."

Abraham H. Lass, the contributor of this article, is Principal of Abraham Lincoln High School, Brooklyn, N.Y. He is the author of Success in High School *and* How to Prepare for College, *and coauthor of* The Way to Write *and* The College Student's Handbook.

Glossary

A selected list of terms and abbreviations commonly encountered in research.

abr. Abridged; abridgment

added entry The heading above the author line on a catalog card. The card is filed by this entry.

annotation A brief description of the content of a book.

anon. Anonymous (author unknown)

appendix A section that follows the text, containing material relative to but not essential to the subject.

author number See Cutter number

bibliography A list of books or writings or sources. May be general, selective, on a particular subject, or have a common theme; often annotated.

bk., bks. Book(s)

c. or *ca.* *circa,* about. Refers to an approximate date (*e.g., c.* 1340).

call number The classification (Decimal) number (*q.v.*) and the Cutter number (*q.v.*). Used to request a book.

cf. Confer; compare one source with another

ch., chap., chaps. Chapter(s)

class number The number by which a book is identified in a classification system (*e.g.,* the Dewey Decimal Classification System or the Library of Congress Classification System). It indicates the subject matter of the book.

col., cols. Column(s)

continuation A work (*e.g., The World Almanac*) issued at regular intervals.

copr.; © **Copyright** The copyright notice usually consists of the symbol © (with or without the word copyright) and the year in which the book was copyrighted. May apply to the entire work or only a part. It generally appears on the verso of the title page.

corporate author An organized body (institution, government agency, or company) acting as author.

cross-reference A reference to another entry. A *see* reference is to the preferred entry, the one under which the material appears; a *see also* reference is to related material.

cumulate The contents of several volumes arranged into one volume.

Cutter number A number added to the subject classification. Preceded by one or more initials from the author's name, this number makes it possible to arrange books alphabetically by author within a subject. Sometimes called the author number. *See also* call number.

documentation Support for a statement, as in a footnote or bibliography.

e.g. exempli gratia, for example

ed., eds. Editor(s); edition(s)

ellipsis Three spaced periods used to indicate an omission. At the beginning of a sentence, may or may not be followed by a capital letter; at the end of a sentence, is preceded by a period.

enl. Enlarged (*e.g.,* enl. ed.)

et al. et alii, and others

et seq. et sequens, and following

etc. et cetera, and so forth

f., ff. And the following (*e.g.,* pp. 65 f.; pp. 64 ff.)

fig., figs. Figure(s)

front. Frontispiece

i.e. id est, that is

ibid. *ibidem,* the same. In a footnote, refers to the book cited in immediately preceding reference. Ibid. takes the place of the author's name, the title, and as much of the material in the preceding footnote as is identical. The page number may differ.

id. idem, the same. Used in place of the author's name in additional references within a single footnote.

il., illus. Illustrations, illustrator, illustrated

incunabula Books printed before 1501.

infra See below; to be mentioned later.

l., ll. Line(s)

LC Library of Congress

loc. cit. loco citato, in the place cited. In a footnote, refers to a passage already identified when there are intervening references to other sources.

main entry The catalog card that has full information about a book (the author card).

MS., MSS. Manuscript(s)

n., nn. Note(s)

N.B. *Nota bene,* note well; take notice

n.d. No date of publication or copyright given.

n.p. No place of publication given.

no., nos. Number(s)

op. cit. opere citato, in the work cited. In a footnote, refers to a previously identified work when a different part is cited and there are intervening references. Pages are included in the citation.

open entry A continuation (see above), shown on the catalog card by a hyphen after the date. The volumes the library has are usually listed.

p., pp. Page, pages

paraphrase A restatement conveying the general meaning of the original.

pass. passim, here and there; throughout the work (*e.g.,* pp. 60, 81, *et pass.*)

periodical Primarily a magazine, published at regular or irregular intervals.

pl., pls. Plate(s)

printing date The year the book is printed (usually appears on the title page). Not always the same as the copyright date.

pseud. Pseudonym, a name other than an author's real name; a pen name.

pt., pts. Part(s)

pub. Published, publication

q.v. quod vide, which see

recto Right-hand page of a book; the back of a verso page

rev. Revised, revision

scope extent of treatment, coverage

series title The collective title for a group of books.

sic So, thus, in this way. Used within brackets in a quotation to show that an error is in the original: "It was to [sic] late."

slug Heading on a note card indicating the topic.

sup., supp., suppl. Supplement

supra See above; previously mentioned

thesis The statement of purpose, the proposition to be explained or proved.

tr., trans. Translator, translation

v., vol., vols. Volume(s)

v. vide, see

verso Left-hand page of a book; the back of a recto page

viz. videlicet, namely. Introduces examples or lists.

vs. Versus, against

Selected Reference Books

The following list of general and special reference books will give you some idea of the variety of works available for research. In order to list as many books as possible, information is limited to titles and individual authors. Within each group, the books are listed alphabetically by title.

In the section on special reference works, the number in parentheses after a heading—Theater (792)—is the Dewey Decimal Classification for that group. Although some libraries may give different classifications to certain titles, this device will assist you in locating books in these subject fields.

The books listed below were selected from the many that exist under each subject heading. They represent some of the most inclusive sources of information on various subjects of interest to students from the junior high school through the college level. Students should find these books most useful in helping them accumulate the kind of information they need in order to write essays, term papers, reports, theses, and dissertations. The books listed below are available in most school and public libraries.

General reference books

Almanacs and yearbooks

Britannica Book of the Year, 1938-
Collier's Year Book, 1939-
The Encyclopedia Americana Annual, 1923-
Information Please Almanac, 1947-
Whitaker's Almanack
The World Almanac and Book of Facts, 1868-
The World Book Year Book, 1922-

Bibliographies

Books in Print, 1948-
Book Review Digest, 1905-
Cumulative Book Index, 1898-
Paperbound Books in Print, 1955-
The Reader's Adviser
Subject Guide to Books in Print, 1957-
Vertical File Index of Pamphlets, 1935-

Biography

Indexes
Biography Index, 1946-

International
Contemporary Authors, 1962-
Current Biography, 1940-
McGraw-Hill Encyclopedia of World Biography
The New Century Cyclopedia of Names
Webster's Biographical Dictionary

United States
Concise Dictionary of American Biography
National Cyclopedia of American Biography, 1892-
Who's Who in America, 1899-
Who's Who of American Women, 1958-
Who Was Who in America, 1897-1973
Who Was Who in America: Historical Volume, 1607-1896

Great Britain and Canada
The Canadian Who's Who, 1910-
Dictionary of Canadian Biography
Dictionary of National Biography
Who's Who, 1849-
Who Was Who, 1897-1960

"Curious fact" books

A Book About a Thousand Things, George Stimpson
Famous First Facts, Joseph N. Kane
Guinness Book of World Records

Encyclopedias, general

Collier's Encyclopedia
Compton's Encyclopedia and Fact-Index
Encyclopaedia Britannica
Encyclopedia Americana
Merit Students Encyclopedia
The World Book Encyclopedia

English-language dictionaries

General dictionaries
Funk & Wagnalls New Standard Dictionary of the English Language
Oxford English Dictionary
Webster's Seventh New Collegiate Dictionary
Webster's Third New International Dictionary of the English Language
The World Book Dictionary

Abbreviations
Abbreviations Dictionary, Ralph DeSola

Rhymes
The Poet's Manual and Rhyming Dictionary, Frances Stillman and Jane S. Whitfield

Slang
A Dictionary of Slang and Unconventional English, Eric Partridge

Synonyms and antonyms
Roget's International Thesaurus
Webster's New Dictionary of Synonyms

Periodicals and newspapers

Bibliographies
Ayer Directory of Publications, 1880-
Ulrich's International Periodicals Directory

Indexes
The New York Times Index, 1913-
Nineteenth Century Readers' Guide to Periodical Literature, 1890-99, 1900-22
Readers' Guide to Periodical Literature, 1900-

Research, library use, and writing

The ABC of Style: A Guide to Plain English, Rudolph Flesch
Basic Reference Sources, Louis Shores
The Elements of Style, William Strunk and E. B. White
How to Do Library Research, Robert B. Downs and Clara D. Keller
A Manual for Writers of Term Papers, Theses, and Dissertations, Kate L. Turabian
The Modern Researcher, Jacques Barzun and Henry F. Graff
The Research Handbook, Adrian A. Paradis
The Research Paper, Lucyle Hook and Mary V. Gaver
The Use of Books and Libraries, Raymond H. Shove and others
Using Books and Libraries, Ella V. Aldrich
Writer's Guide and Index to English, Porter G. Perrin

LEARNING GUIDE 7-1 (cont.)

Special reference books

The humanities: The meaning of man's life.

Architecture (720)
Everyman's Concise Encyclopaedia of Architecture, Martin S. Briggs
A History of Architecture on the Comparative Method, Sir Banister F. Fletcher

Art, general (700)
Art Index, 1929-
Art Through the Ages, Helen Gardner

Literature (800)
American Authors and Books, 1640 to the Present Day, William Burke and Will Howe
Brewer's Dictionary of Phrase and Fable, E. C. Brewer
British Authors Before 1800, Stanley J. Kunitz and Howard Haycraft, eds.
Cassell's Encyclopaedia of World Literature
The Concise Cambridge History of English Literature, George Sampson
Crowell's Handbook of Classical Literature, Lillian Feder
Cyclopedia of World Authors, Frank N. Magill, ed.
Familiar Quotations, John Bartlett
Granger's Index to Poetry
The New Century Handbook of English Literature, Clarence L. Barnhart and William D. Halsey, eds.
Play Index [1949-52; 1953-60; 1961-67; 1968-72]

Music (780)
Grove's Dictionary of Music and Musicians
The New Oxford History of Music

Mythology (290)
The Classic Myths in English Literature and in Art . . . ., Charles Mills Gayley
Mythology, Edith Hamilton
New Larousse Encyclopedia of Mythology

Philosophy (100)
Masterpieces of World Philosophy in Summary Form, Frank N. Magill, ed.
The Story of Philosophy, Will Durant

Theater (792)
Oxford Companion to the Theatre, Phyllis Hartnoll, ed.
A Pageant of the Theatre, Edmund Fuller
Shakespeare's Theatre, C. Walter Hodges

The sciences: Nature and the physical world.

General (500; 600)
American Men and Women of Science
Dictionary of Scientific Biography
McGraw-Hill Encyclopedia of Science and Technology
Van Nostrand's Scientific Encyclopedia
Words of Science and the History Behind Them, Isaac Asimov

Biology (574)
Compton's Dictionary of the Natural Sciences
The Dictionary of the Biological Sciences, Peter Gray
The Peterson Field Guides [series]

Engineering (620)
The American Heritage History of Flight, Arthur Gordon
The Evolution of the Machine, Ritchie Calder

Medicine (610)
Dorland's Illustrated Medical Dictionary
A History of Medicine, Brian Ingles

Oceanography (551.4)
The Encyclopedia of Oceanography, Rhodes W. Fairbridge
Exploring the Ocean World: A History of Oceanography, C. P. Idyll, ed.

Zoology (590)
Collegiate Dictionary of Zoology, Robert W. Pennak
The Larousse Encyclopedia of Animal Life
The Mammal Guide: Mammals of North America North of Mexico, Ralph S. Palmer

The social sciences: Man and society.

General (300)
International Encyclopedia of the Social Sciences
A Modern Dictionary of Sociology, George A. Theodorson and Achilles G. Theodorson

Anthropology (570)
Anthropology A to Z, Gerhard Heberer
The Origin of Races, Carleton Coon and E. E. Hunt, Jr., eds.

Customs and folklore (390)
Anniversaries and Holidays: A Calendar of Days and How to Observe Them, Mary Hazeltine
Funk & Wagnalls Standard Dictionary of Folklore, Mythology and Legend

Economics (330)
Economics: Ideas and Men, Fon W. Boardman
The Worldly Philosophers: The Lives, Times, and Ideas of the Great Economic Thinkers, Robert L. Heilbroner

Geography and travel (900-919)
Columbia-Lippincott Gazetteer of the World
Fodor's Modern Guides [series]
Goode's World Atlas
Larousse Encyclopedia of World Geography

History (900-909; 930-999)
Basic Documents in American History, Richard B. Morris
Dictionary of American History
Encyclopedia of American History
An Encyclopedia of World History, William L. Langer
The Gateway to History, Allan Nevins
History and Historians, Fon W. Boardman

Law (340)
Black's Law Dictionary, Henry Campbell Black
Charter of the United Nations: Commentary and Documents, Leland M. Goodrich, *et al.*

Statistics (310)
Historical Statistics of the United States, Colonial Times to 1957
The Statesman's Yearbook
Statistical Abstract of the United States
Statistical Yearbook [United Nations]

U. S. federal and state governments (353)
The Book of the States [yearbook]
Monthly Catalog of United States Government Publications, 1895-
United States Government Organization Manual
United States Government Publications, Ann Morris Boyd and Rae Elizabeth Rips

Model 8

The Black Experience
(Honors Mini-Course)

GRADES: 7–9

DESCRIPTION: An elective nine-week honors mini-course.

GOAL: To provide opportunity for students to reweave the tapestry of Afro-American history.

OBJECTIVES

To provide a panoramic view of the black people's struggle to be freed from the chains of slavery and racial discrimination.

To introduce students to the vital contributions made by black people in every walk of American life.

To enable students to perceive history as living drama.

To impress students with the fact that many kinds of people, including both black and whites, stand tall in the making of this nation.

To encourage students to identify and empathize with all human beings—regardless of color or creed—who have suffered or now suffer injustice, exploitation, and/or social indignities.

To challenge students to become *change agents* for a better world.

COURSE OUTLINE

I. Purpose: To provide a depth study of Afro-American history: the causes, the events, the people, the issues.

II. Schedule: Class, group, and individual student activities for this course are set forth in Handout 8-1, Schedule (see the end of this model).

301

III. Orientation
    A. Handout 8-2, Course Goal and Objectives (see the end of this model) is distributed and discussed.
    B. The basic orientation tool is the *World Book Encyclopedia* reprint "Black Americans: The Story of Black Americans—Yesterday and Today."* (Each student receives a copy of this reprint to use as a guide throughout the course.)
        1. The following topics are developed in the foregoing reprint:
           a. The African Heritage
           b. The Slave Trade
           c. Slavery in America: In Colonial Times; After the Revolutionary War; Growth of Slavery; Free Blacks
           d. Changing Status of Black Americans: Emancipation; After Reconstruction; Through the World Wars
           e. The Civil Rights Movement: The Legal Battle; The "Black Revolution"; Violence and Racial Tension
           f. Black Militancy: Unrest in the Cities; Black Power; The King Assassination; Student Militancy; The Black Panther Movement; Conflict among Blacks
           g. Black Americans Today: Political Gains; Unsolved Problems
        2. The following related topics present varied avenues for independent research:

POLITICAL FIGURES

Bond, Julian	Hastie, William H.
Bradley, Thomas	Hatcher, Richard G.
Brooke, Edward W.	Jordan, Barbara C.
Bruce, Blanche K.	Pinchback, P. B. S.
Chisholm, Shirley	Powell, Adam Clayton, Jr.
Coleman, William T., Jr.	Revels, Hiram R.
Duvalier, François	Stokes, Carl B.
Harris, Patricia R.	Young, Andrew J., Jr.

ATHLETES AND SPORTS LEADERS

Aaron, Henry	Louis, Joe
Abdul-Jabbar, Kareem	Mays, Willie
Ali, Muhammad	Owens, Jesse
Ashe, Arthur	Paige, Satchel
Baylor, Elgin	Pelé
Brown, Jim	Robertson, Oscar
Chamberlain, Wilt	Robinson, Frank
Foreman, George	Robinson, Jackie
Gibson, Althea	Robinson, Ray
Johnson, Jack	Russell, Bill

CIVIL RIGHTS LEADERS

Abernathy, Ralph D.	Farmer, James L.
Carmichael, Stokely	Gregory, Dick
Du Bois, W. E. B.	Hooks, Benjamin L.
Evers (brothers)	Jackson, Jesse L.

The World Book Encyclopedia reprint "Black Americans" (Chicago: World Book–Childcraft International, 1978) is available at the cost of 25¢ for up to 19 copies; 20 or more copies cost 20¢ each.

Jordan, Vernon E.
King, Martin Luther, Jr.
Luthuli, Albert John
McKissick, Floyd B.
Malcolm X
Meredith, James H.
Parks, Rosa Lee

Randolph, A. Philip
Rustin, Bayard
Terrell, Mary Church
Wells-Barnett, Ida Bell
White, Walter F.
Wilkins, Roy
Young, Whitney M., Jr.

EDUCATORS AND SCHOLARS

Bethune, Mary McLeod
Cary, Mary Ann Shadd
Clark, Kenneth Bancroft
Franklin, John Hope
Frazier, E. Franklin
Johnson, Charles S.
Locke, Alain L.

Mays, Benjamin E.
Moton, Robert R.
Nabrit, James M., Jr.
Quarles, Benjamin A.
Washington, Booker T.
Weaver, Robert C.
Woodson, Carter G.

JAZZ MUSICIANS AND SINGERS

Armstrong, Louis
Basie, Count
Coltrane, John W.
Davis, Miles
Ellington, Duke
Fitzgerald, Ella
Gillespie, Dizzy
Handy, W. C.
Hawkins, Coleman
Henderson, Fletcher

Hines, Earl
Holiday, Billie
Joplin, Scott
Lewis, John A.
Monk, Thelonious
Parker, Charlie
Smith, Bessie
Tatum, Art
Young, Lester W.

OTHER SINGERS AND ENTERTAINERS

Ailey, Alvin
Anderson, Marian
Belafonte, Harry
Berry, Chuck
Burleigh, Harry T.
Dunham, Katherine
Hayes, Roland
Horne, Lena
Jackson, Mahalia

Maynor, Dorothy
Mitchell, Arthur
Poitier, Sidney
Price, Leontyne
Robeson, Paul
Robinson, Bill
Waters, Ethel
Wonder, Stevie

MILITARY FIGURES

Attucks, Crispus
Christophe, Henri
Davis, Benjamin O., Jr.

Delany, Martin R.
Dessalines, Jean J.
Toussaint l'Ouverture

SCIENTISTS

Banneker, Benjamin
Carver, George W.
Drew, Charles R.

Julian, Percy L.
Lawless, Theodore K.
Williams, Daniel Hale

WRITERS

Baldwin, James A.
Bontemps, Arna
Brooks, Gwendolyn
Cleaver, Eldridge
Cullen, Countee
Dunbar, Paul L.

Ellison, Ralph
Giovanni, Nikki
Haley, Alex
Hamilton, Virginia
Hansberry, Lorraine
Harper, Frances E. W.

Hughes, Langston
Johnson, James W.
McKay, Claude

Taylor, Mildred
Wheatley, Phillis
Wright, Richard

OTHER BIOGRAPHIES

Allen, Richard
Beckwourth, James P.
Bland, James A.
Bunche, Ralph J.
Cuffe, Paul
Douglass, Frederick
Du Sable, Jean Baptiste P.
Estevanico
Forten, James
Garvey, Marcus
Hall, Prince
Healy, James A.
Henson, Matthew A.
Johnson, John H.
McCoy, Elijah

Marshall, Thurgood
Matzeliger, Jan E.
Muhammad, Elijah
Prosser, Gabriel
Rillieux, Norbert
Rowan, Carl T.
Russwurm, John B.
Smalls, Robert
Sullivan, Leon H.
Tanner, Henry O.
Truth, Sojourner
Tubman, Harriet
Turner, Nat
Vesey, Denmark
Walker, David

HISTORY

Abolitionist
Black Codes
Carpetbagger
Civil War
Emancipation Proclamation
Freedmen's Bureau
Grandfather Clause
Jim Crow

Ku Klux Klan
Lynching
Niagara Movement
Proslavery Movement
Reconstruction
Scalawag
Slavery
Underground Railroad

ORGANIZATIONS

Association for the Study of
  Afro-American Life and
  History
Black Panther Party
Congress of Racial Equality
National Association for the
  Advancement of
  Colored People
National Medical Association

Rosenwald Fund, Julius
Southern Christian Leadership Conference
Southern Education Foundation
Student Nonviolent Coordinating Committee
United Negro College Fund
Urban League

RELIGION

African Methodist Episcopal Church
African Methodist Epsicopal Zion Church
Black Muslims
National Baptist Convention of America

National Baptist Convention, U.S.A., Inc.
National Primitive Baptist Convention in the U.S.A.

OTHER RELATED ARTICLES

American Literature (The
  Harlem Renaissance;
  The Black Experience)
Black History Week
Blues

Brown v. Board of Education of Topeka
Civil Rights
Ethnic Group
Henry, John

Jazz	Races, Human
Meharry Medical College	Racism
Minority Group	Segregation
Opera (*Porgy and Bess*)	Sickle Cell Anemia
Painting (History, Mythology, and Social Expression)	Spingarn Medal
	Spiritual

C. The definition of black Americans as presented in the *World Book Encyclopedia* reprint "Black Americans" is the working definition for this course:

> Black Americans are Americans mostly or partly of African descent. The more than 22 million black Americans make up the largest minority group in the United States. Most of them belong to the African geographical race. This race includes groups of related peoples in Africa south of the Sahara. The African race also includes descendants of people who moved from those regions of Africa—either voluntarily or against their will.
>
> Americans of African descent generally use three terms to refer to themselves: Negro, black, and Afro-American.

D. Each student will be responsible for three separate in-depth research reports (see Handout 8-1 at end of model).
   1. A topic pertinent to the theme "A People Uprooted."
   2. A topic pertinent to the theme "Slavery 1800–1865."
   3. A topic pertinent to the theme "Quest for Equality."
E. Handout 8-3, Initial Bibliography (see the end of this model), is distributed and discussed.
   1. Students are encouraged to examine the basic reference titles.
   2. The card catalogs of the school library and the public library should be consulted for additional titles.
F. A particularly valuable research tool, *Great Black Americans as Reported in the New York Times,* is introduced and explained (see Handout 8-4 at the end of this model).
   1. This collection pays tribute to 41 noteworthy black men and women who have achieved "real distinction in a wide range of honorable endeavors."
   2. Each biography is accompanied by 40 or more microfiche citations.
G. Two biography analysis guides, Handout 8-5, Biography Reading Summary Report, and Handout 8-6, Biographee Profile (see the end of this model) are presented and explained.

IV. Independent research, the writing and presentation of project reports, and group discussion and interaction next take place according to the schedule of activities as set forth in Handout 8-1.

V. Culminating Activities.
   A. As a summary of this course and as a predictor for the future, the class discusses Alex Haley's *Roots* (see Handout 8-7 [at the end of this model] and Learning Guide 8-1).
      1. The four-part filmstrip version of the television series "Roots" (Films, Inc.—each 3 filmstrips, 3 cassettes, 1 guide) is the basis of a five-day class synthesis of what has been learned through this mini-

course; the study frames at the end of the four units encourage the students to rethink and reexperience Afro-American history.

   a. *Roots* 1: *The Making of a Slave*
   b. *Roots* 2: *Adjusting to Plantation Life*
   c. *Roots* 3: *Masters and Slaves*
   d. *Roots* 4: *Civil War and Emancipation*

  2. The class searches for answers to the following questions:

   a. The success of the TV series "Roots" was a major event in media history—over 130 million people watched some or all of the two-week long series. Why?
   b. Did the dramatic portrayal of the history of black Americans and their struggle for freedom and equality "reach home" with the viewers and make them relive and suffer with the black people?
   c. Has this mini-course had a like impact on you, the student?

  B. The class, using Handout 8-2 as a guide, evaluates the effectiveness of this course.

HANDOUT 8-1   SCHEDULE

From	To	Number of Days	Activities	Where
		4	Course Orientation	Classroom
		6	Independent Research Topic: A People Uprooted	Library
		5	Reports and Discussion Topic: A People Uprooted	Classroom
		1	Written Summary: What I Have Learned	Classroom
		1	Choosing Topics for Independent Research	Classroom
		6	Independent Research Topic: Slavery 1800–1865	Library
		5	Reports and Discussion Topic: Slavery 1800–1865	Classroom
		1	Written Summary: My Reaction to Slavery	Classroom
		1	Choosing Topics for Independent Research	Classroom
		8	Independent Research Topic: Quest for Equality	Library
		6	Reports and Discussion Topic: Quest for Equality	Classroom
		1	Written Summary: What of the Future?	Classroom
		45 days		

HANDOUT 8-2   COURSE GOAL AND OBJECTIVES

GOAL

To provide opportunity for the students to reweave the tapestry of Afro-American history.

OBJECTIVES

To provide a panoramic view of the black people's struggle to be freed from the chains of slavery and racial discrimination.

To introduce the students to the vital contributions made by black people in every walk of life.

To enable the students to perceive history as living drama.

To impress the students with the fact that many kinds of people, including both black and white Americans, stand tall in the making of this nation.

To encourage students to identify and empathize with all human beings—regardless of color or creed—who have suffered or now suffer injustice, exploitation, and/or social indignities.

To challenge students to become *change agents* for a better world.

HANDOUT 8-3   INITIAL BIBLIOGRAPHY

REFERENCE TOOLS

The American Legacy ed. by David C. Whitney. 3 vols. Chicago: Encyclopaedia Britannica, n.d..

Annals of America ed. by Mortimer J. Adler et al. 23 vols. Chicago: Encyclopaedia Britannica, 1976.

The Ebony Handbook ed. by Doris E. Saunders and the Editors of Ebony. Chicago: Johnson Publishing, 1974.

The Encyclopedia of Africa. New York: Watts, 1976.

Great Black Americans as Reported in The New York Times. Sanford, N.C.: Microfilming Corporation of America, 1981. (See Handout 8-4, this model.)

Harvard Encyclopedia of American Ethnic Groups ed. by Stephen Thernstrom. Cambridge, Mass.: Harvard University Press, 1980.

*In Black and White ed. by Mary Mace Spradling. 3rd ed. 2 vols. Detroit: Gale, 1980.

Makers of America ed. by Wayne Moquin. 10 vols. Chicago: Encyclopaedia Britannica, 1971.

The Negro Almanac: A Reference Work on the Afro-American ed. by Harry A. Ploski and Warren Marr. New York: Bellweather, 1976.

The Negro in America: A Bibliography comp. by Mary L. Fisher. Cambridge, Mass.: Harvard University Press, 1970.

The Negro in American History ed. by Mortimer J. Adler et al. 3 vols. Chicago: Encyclopaedia Britannica, 1972.

ADDITIONAL PRINTED RESOURCES

Amiri Baraka (LeRoi Jones) by Lloyd W. Brown. *Perspectives on Black America series.* Boston: Twayne, n.d..

Andrew Young: Man with a Mission by James Haskins. Garden City, N.Y.: Dial, 1974.

The Assassination of Martin Luther King, Jr. by Doris Faber and Howard Faber. New York: Watts, 1978.

The Autobiography of Miss Jane Pittman by Ernest J. Gaines. Garden City, N.Y.: Dial, 1971.

Big Star Fallen' Mama: Five Women in Black Music by Hettie Jones. New York: Viking, 1974.

The Black Experience in America by Norman Coombs. Immigrant Heritage of America series. Boston: Twayne, 1972.

---

*Unparalleled reference source to information about more than 15,000 black individuals and groups all over the world who have distinguished themselves in 180 fields of endeavor.

Black People Who Made the Old West by William L. Katz. New York: Harper, 1977.

Blacks in America: 1954–1979 by Florence Jackson. New York: Watts, 1980.

Broken Promises: The Strange History of the Fourteenth Amendment by Richard Seller. New York: Random, 1972.

Charles W. Chestnutt by Sylvia Lyons Render. Perspectives on Black America series. Boston: Twayne, n.d..

Claude McKay by James R. Giles. Perspectives on Black America series. Boston: Twayne, 1976.

Eight Black American Scientists by Robert C. Hayden. Reading, Mass.: Addison, 1972.

Equal! The Case of Integration vs. Jim Crow: The Fourteenth Amendment by Leonard A. Stevens. New York: Coward, 1975.

Famous American Negro Poets by Charlemae Rollins. New York: Dodd, 1965.

Famous Black Entertainers of Today by Raoul Abdul. New York: Dodd, 1974.

George S. Schuyler by Michael W. Peplow. Perspectives on Black America series. Boston: Twayne, n.d.

Great Black Americans by Ben Richardson and William A. Fahey. New York: Harper, 1976.

Gwendolyn Brooks by Harry B. Shaw. Perspectives on Black America series. Boston: Twayne, n.d.

Human Rights by Gerald S. Snyder. New York: Watts, 1980.

I Always Wanted to Be Someone by Althea Gibson. New York: Harper, 1958.

I Am the Darker Brother: An Anthology of Modern Poems by Negro Americans ed. by Arnold Adoff. New York: Macmillan, 1968. Also paper.

I Know Why the Caged Bird Sings by Maya Angelou. New York: Random, 1970.

I Speak for My Slave Sister: The Life of Abby Kelley Foster by Margaret H. Bacon. New York: Harper, 1974.

In Their Own Words: A History of the American Negro 1619–1865 by Milton Meltzer. New York: Crowell, 1964.

In Their Own Words: A History of the American Negro 1865–1916 by Milton Meltzer. New York: Crowell, 1965.

In Their Own Words: A History of the American Negro 1916–1966 by Milton Meltzer. New York: Crowell, 1967.

James Baldwin by Louis H. Prass. Perspectives on Black America series. Boston: Twayne, 1978.

Jazz by Langston Hughes. Rev. ed. New York: Watts, 1982.

Jean Toomer by Brian J. Benson and Mabel M. Dillars. Perspectives on Black America series. Boston: Twayne, n.d.

Langston Hughes by James A. Emanuel. Perspectives on Black America series. Boston: Twayne, 1967.

The Magic of Black Poetry ed. by Raoul Abdul. New York: Dodd, 1972.

Martin Luther King: Fighter for Freedom by Edward Preston. Garden City, N.Y.: Doubleday, 1970.

Melvin B. Tolson by Joy Flasch. Perspectives on Black America series. Boston: Twayne, n.d.

Movin' Up: Pop Gordy Tells His Story by Berry Gordy, Sr. New York: Harper, 1979.

Nat Turner by Judith B. Griffin. New York: Coward, 1970.

Nine Black American Doctors by Robert C. Hayden and Jacqueline Harris. Reading, Mass.: Addison, 1976.

One Hundred Years of Negro Freedom by Arna Bontemps. New York: Dodd, 1961. Paper.

Paul Cuffe and the African Promised Land by Mary C. Aiken. New York: Elsevier-Nelson, 1977.

Paul Laurence Dunbar by Peter Revell. Perspectives on Black America series. Boston: Twayne, n.d.

The Poetry of Black America: Anthology of the Twentieth Century ed. by Arnold Adoff. New York: Harper, 1973.

Quiz Book on Black America by Clarence Blake and Donald F. Martin. Boston: Houghton, 1976. Also paper.

Remembering Song: Encounters with the New Orleans Jazz Tradition by Frederick Turner. New York: Viking, 1982.

HANDOUT 8-3 (cont.)

Richard Wright by Robert Felgar. Perspectives on Black America series. Boston: Twayne, n.d.

The Riddle of Racism by Carl S. Hirsch. New York: Viking 1972.

The Road to Freedom by James McCague. Champaign, Ill.: Garrard, 1972.

The Story of Stevie Wonder by James Haskins. New York: Lothrop, 1976.

They Showed the Way: Early American Negro Leaders by Charlemae Rollins. New York: Harper, 1964.

This Life: The Autobiography of Sidney Poitier. New York: Knopf, 1980.

Time of Trial, Time of Hope by Milton Meltzer. Garden City, N.Y.: Doubleday, 1966.

A Time to Be Human by John H. Griffin. New York: Macmillan, 1977.

The Trouble They Seen: Black People Tell the Story of Reconstruction ed. by Dorothy Sterling. Garden City, N.Y.: Doubleday, 1966.

W. E. B. Du Bois by Jack Moore. Perspectives on Black America series. Boston: Twayne, n.d.

Willard Motley by Robert E. Fleming. Perspectives on Black America series. Boston: Twayne, 1978.

Young and Black in America by Rae P. Alexander. New York: Random, 1970.

Zora Neal Hurston by Lillie P. Howard. Perspectives on Black America series. Boston: Twayne, n.d.

FILMSTRIPS

Afro-American History Program (Encyclopaedia Britannica—25 captioned filmstrips)
   A People Uprooted (1500–1800)
      Africa: Historical Heritage
      Africa: Artistic Heritage
      The Slave Trade
      Slavery in Plantation Virginia
      Black People in the Revolution
      Benjamin Banneker, Man of Science
      Richard Allen, Man of God
   Chains of Slavery (1800–1865)
      Harriet Tubman
      Frederick Douglass
      Black People in the Free North, 1850
      Black People in the Slave South, 1850
      Nat Turner's Rebellion
      Black People in the Civil War
   Separate and Unequal (1865–1910)
      Booker T. Washington: National Leader
      Bishop Turner: Black Nationalist
      Black People in the North, 1900
      Black People in the South, 1877–1900
      The Black Codes
      "Separate But Equal"
   Quest for Equality
      W. E. B. Du Bois
      Harlem in the Twenties
      Watts in the Sixties
      The March on Washington, 1963
      Martin Luther King, Jr.
      "Separate" Is Unequal

Almos' a Man by Richard Wright (Coronet—2 filmstrips, 2 cassettes, 2 worksheet masters, 1 guide)

American Negro Pathfinders (BFA—6 captioned filmstrips)
   Dr. Ralph Bunche: Missionary of Peace
   Justice Thurgood Marshall: Mr. Civil Rights
   General Benjamin O. Davis, Jr.: American Guardian

HANDOUT 8-3 (cont.)

A. Philip Randolph: Elder Statesman
Dr. Mary McLeod Bethune: Courageous Educator
Martin Luther King, Jr.: Non-Violent Crusader

The Bingo Long Traveling All-Stars and Motor Kings (Spoken Arts—4 filmstrips, 4 cassettes, 8 duplicating masters, 1 guide)
   The Black League
   Doing Your Own Thing
   Teamwork against the Odds
   A New Era

The Scholastic Black Culture Program (Scholastic—5 kits)
   Black Art Kit (1 filmstrip, 1 cassette or 1 record)
   Black Dance Kit (1 filmstrip, 1 cassette or 1 record)
   Black Music Kit (2 filmstrips, 2 cassettes or 2 records)
   Black Poetry Kit (2 filmstrips, 2 cassettes or 2 records)
   Black Religion Kit (2 filmstrips, 2 cassettes or 2 records)

Black Folk Music in America (Society for Visual Education—4 filmstrips, 2 cassettes 4 guides)
   Songs of Slavery
   Black Songs of the Civil War
   Black Songs after the Civil War
   Black Songs of Modern Times

Black Leaders of Twentieth Century America (BFA—10 filmstrips, 5 cassettes)
   Charles Drew   *A. Phillip Randolph*
   Mary McLeod Bethune   *Percy Julian*
   Langston Hughes   *Edward Brooke*
   Martin Luther King, Jr.   *Lorraine Hansberry*
   Malcolm X   *Carl Stokes*

The Dream Awake (Spoken Arts—7 filmstrips, 7 cassettes, 1 guide, 33 study prints)
   Africa
   The Amistad, Crispus Attucks, Harriett Tubman and the Emancipation Proclamation
   The Black Cowboy
   The Black Quartet—Frederick Douglass, Booker T. Washington, W. E. B. Du Bois,
      Marcus Garvey
   The Martyrs—Bessie Smith, Martin Luther King, Jr., Malcolm X
   Resurrection City and the Children
   The Black Arts

I'd Give My Life for the Cause (Martin Luther King, Jr.) (Educational Enrichment Materials—1 filmstrip, 1 cassette)

Jazz Milestones (Educational Enrichment Materials—6 filmstrips, 6 cassettes, 1 guide)
   Storyville   *Swing*
   Chicago   *Bop*
   The Rent Party   *Soul Jazz*

Martin Luther King, Jr.: The Choice to Be Great (Disney—1 filmstrip, 1 cassette or 1 record, 1 guide)

Scott Joplin: King of Ragtime (Spoken Arts—4 filmstrips, 4 cassettes, 8 spirit duplicating masters, 1 guide)
   Born of the Sod and Soil
   An American Musical Genius
   Talent against the Odds
   The Measure of Success

Voyages of Self-Discovery: Unknown Worlds Close to Home (Images of Man series) (Scholastic—1 filmstrip, 1 cassette or 1 record; also 1 slide set, 1 cassette)

MOTION PICTURES

Paul Robeson: Tribute to an Artist (Films, Inc.)

Roy Wilkins—The Right to Dignity (National Audiovisual Center)

NATIONAL PUBLIC RADIO PROGRAMS

The Black Music Tradition (National Public Radio—10 programs, 30 min. each)
    West African Heritage
    Gospel and Spirituals
    Soul
    Blues: Country Meets City
    Rhythm and Blues
    Early Jazz
    The Jazz Vocalist
    Jazz People
    Black Music in Theatre and Film
    Black Influence in the Recording Industry
Literature of the Black Experience (National Public Radio—6 programs, 1 hr. each)
    W. E. B. Du Bois   *Alice Walker*
    Langston Hughes   *Amiri Baraka* (LeRoi Jones)
    Ralph Ellison   *Richard Wright*

HANDOUT 8-4   GREAT BLACK AMERICANS AS REPORTED IN *THE NEW YORK TIMES**

CONTENTS

Introduction

Keys to Great Black Americans

The Black Americans

Note: The 41 Black Americans are identified here by numbers, as shown, and by name both here and on the fiches.

1. Muhammad Ali
2. Marian Anderson
3. Arthur Ashe
4. Imamu Amiri Baraka (LeRoi Jones)
5. Julian Bond
6. Thomas Bradley
7. Ralph J. Bunche
8. George Washington Carver
9. Shirley Chisholm
10. Kenneth B. Clark
11. W. E. B. Du Bois
12. Duke Ellington
13. Ralph W. Ellison
14. Charles Evers
15. Althea Gibson and Wilma Rudolph
16. Kenneth Gibson
17. Alex Haley
18. Patricia Roberts Harris
19. Jesse Jackson
20. Mahalia Jackson
21. Maynard H. Jackson
22. James Earl Jones
23. Barbara Jordan
24. Vernon Jordan Jr.
25. Martin Luther King Jr.
26. Joe Louis
27. Thurgood Marshall
28. Jesse Owens
29. Leontyne Price
30. A. Philip Randolph
31. Charles Rangel
32. Paul Robeson
33. Jackie Robinson
34. Bayard Rustin
35. Booker T. Washington
36. Roy Wilkins
37. Richard Wright
38. Andrew Young
39. Coleman Young
40. Whitney Young Jr.

INTRODUCTION

"The great marvel of our times is that so many Negroes have been able to surmount the fearful obstacles of our melancholy history in this land and to achieve real distinction in a wide range of honorable endeavors."—Roy Wilkins, executive secretary, National Association for the Advancement of Colored People.

*From Microfilming Corporation of America, Sanford, NC.

HANDOUT 8-4 (cont.)

This collection of Great Black Americans pays tribute to 41 men and women who have "surmounted the fearful obstacles" Mr. Wilkins mentions. For most of them, success was achieved in the merciless glare of the public eye. All of them earned their advancement in a highly competitive society, one that presented much greater challenges to black aspirants than to ascendant whites.

These 41 persons nevertheless have reached national and some even international stature. To do this required courage of a high order—courage, persistence, and in many cases great gifts. Without the courage of these persons, it is worth noting, great gifts would have been muted, perhaps lost in the world.

It would be naive to believe these success stories were accomplished only by tenacious bravery. Of course there was "help along the way," friends, patrons, and mentors in the white power structure who gave support; there were opportunities seized, natural gifts nourished, and of course the indispensable, luck.

The larger-than-life talents of Paul Robeson, the charismatic leadership of Martin Luther King, Jr., and the greatly respected diplomatic skills of Ralph Bunche are exceptional by any criteria. These "greats" are obviously at home in our list. But what of less-well-known achievers, such as Maynard Jackson, Mayor of Atlanta, or psychologist Kenneth B. Clark? A black who has been elected head of the South's largest city, Mr. Jackson represents a phenomenon in the United States, a concatenation of successes and personal qualities that demand respectful acknowledgement. Dr. Kenneth Clark has achieved substantial professional success in a demanding calling and solid community status (New York City) in an era of great stress. Clearly persons like these did not have greatness thrust upon them, as accidents of fortune, but, as Shakespeare said, they "achieved greatness," by making good on their chances, using their gifts tirelessly, and braving sometimes formidable animosity.

The variety of callings represented in the collection is impressive. In the fields of politics, law, and government there are twelve leaders selected for this program; in music, four names that evoke immediate recognition; in sports, seven headliners (and not one a basketball player!); in literature, science, and the arts, ten famous names; and in civil rights and public affairs, eight persons who can claim place in the ranks of great dissenters.

The collection is not intended to be definitive in any way. It is a selection, and by the nature of the data base used it represents coverage of these persons only by the *New York Times*. But it is a suggestion of the richness and diversity of talent, of the courage, and of the irrepressible spirit that are found in the black population of the United States.

KEYS TO GREAT BLACK AMERICANS

THE MICROFICHES

The Great Black Americans microfiches are designed to facilitate student use of the program. . . . Across the top of the fiche is the header, showing the subject's name and number in this program. In the first row of images on the fiche are full pages of the *New York Times* containing certain articles relating to [the black American]. The rows of frames below the full pages contain additional articles, reviews, illustrations, and letters to the editor arranged in chronological order.

HANDOUT 8-5 BIOGRAPHY READING SUMMARY REPORT

Student _____ Date _____

Biography read _____

Author _____

Title _____

Publisher _____ Copyright date _____

1. Please check the appropriate category:
   _____ Individual biography
   _____ Collective biography
   _____ Autobiography
   _____ Biographical novel

2. Comment on the style and literary quality of the book you have read.

3. In what field or fields has the biographee made a contribution?

4. Critically evaluate the biographee's
      character:

      personality:

      sense of values:

      contribution to society:

5. To what extent could you share the biographee's problems, disappointments, achievements, aspirations, and goals?

HANDOUT 8-6　BIOGRAPHEE PROFILE

Biographee _____

		Rating Scale	
Common sense	0	5	10
Compassion	0	5	10
Courage	0	5	10
Creativity	0	5	10
Curiosity	0	5	10
Dedication to ideals	0	5	10
Determination	0	5	10
Drive	0	5	10
Emotional stability	0	5	10
Empathy	0	5	10
Foresight	0	5	10
Generosity	0	5	10
Giftedness	0	5	10
Honesty	0	5	10
Idealism	0	5	10
Imagination	0	5	10
Integrity	0	5	10
Introspection	0	5	10
Inventiveness	0	5	10
Love of God	0	5	10
Patriotism	0	5	10
Purpose	0	5	10
Rationality	0	5	10
Respect for law	0	5	10
Self-criticism	0	5	10
Self-discipline	0	5	10
Self-lessness	0	5	10
Sense of humor	0	5	10
Sense of justice	0	5	10
Sense of values	0	5	10
Sensitivity	0	5	10
Sobriety	0	5	10
Social consciousness	0	5	10
Stick-to-itiveness	0	5	10

HANDOUT 8-7 ALEX HALEY*

In 1977 television history was made when, over a period of five days, 130 million Americans viewed the adaptation of the book *Roots,* by Alex Haley. Haley's work, the story of one family's experience, from enslavement in Africa to emancipation in the United States, won immediate fame for its author and brought about a far-reaching reappraisal of blacks and black families in American history.

Haley became a professional writer at the age of 37, after 20 years of service as a cook in the U.S. Coast Guard. He contributed articles to magazines, taught English and writing, and in 1964, wrote the *Autobiography of Malcolm X,* an achievement which brought him little recognition.

Roots emerged from Haley's efforts to explore his own family's history. After years of research into slave records, property titles, auction proceedings and countless other documents, Haley produced a chronicle of several generations, in which he continually presented two often-forgotten realities to his readers: the brutality of slavery and the cohesion of black families.

For many blacks, *Roots* was an occasion for pride that they, like every other group in the United States, had come to this country with a culture and tradition. Some resented the television adaptation's stereotyped depiction of characters of both races. For whites seeing slavery through the eyes of a black family, *Roots* was a revelation and a cause for reflection. No other single work on race relations in America had gained such immediate and widespread popularity, and Haley received a special National Book Award as well as a Pulitzer Prize.

With this popularity came controversy. After the television version of *Roots* was shown, an English journalist challenged the historical authenticity of many situations presented in the book, and requested that Haley rebut these charges. At the same time, two American authors sued Haley, charging that he had copied parts of their books, both of which had dealt earlier with the same subject matter as *Roots.* One of these cases was dismissed, but Haley settled the other out of court for a sum thought to be hundreds of thousands of dollars.

In 1979, *Roots: The Next Generation,* the same black family's history from Reconstruction to the present, was aired to a television audience of 110 million people. This production, featuring several noted actors, was considered more serious than the earlier *Roots* by critics and audiences, and again gave rise to extensive reflection on the role of the black family in the formation of American society.

COMPREHENSION QUESTIONS

1. What were some of Haley's main methods of research in his quest for his family's history? (1976, N 23, 40:1/11C).
2. What reporter first challenged the historical authenticity of *Roots?* (1977, Ap 10, 1:5/3).
3. Who was the Gambian villager who told Haley the history of the Kinte clan? (1977, Ap 10, 1:5/3).
4. According to Haley, how were the false images blacks suffer from formed? (1977, My 30, 5:4/24D).
5. Which two authors accused Haley of copying material from their books? (1978, D 15, 1:5/27B).

DISCUSSION QUESTIONS

1. Why do you think the history of the black family was neglected for so long before the 1970s?
2. Is television the proper forum for the examination of the serious historical issues in *Roots?* Discuss.
3. How do you account for the popularity of *Roots?*

Great Black Americans as Reported in the New York Times (Sanford, N.C.: Microfilming Corporation of America, 1981), pp. 43–44.

HANDOUT 8-7 (cont.)

4. Do you believe Haley intended *Roots* to give blacks a sense of belonging to American society or of being separate from it?
5. How can *Roots* provide other ethnic groups with opportunities to look into their own cultures?

PROJECTS AND ACTIVITIES*

1. Read *The Autobiography of Malcolm X*. In a report, relate the major themes of this book to those of *Roots*.
2. After reading *Roots,* discuss whether this book has more value as a symbol, as Haley called it, or as a work of history.
3. Try to see the television adaptation of *Roots*. To what extent are characters of both races stereotyped? Explain to your class how these stereotypes might detract from the work's importance.
4. Write a genealogical autobiography.
5. See *Roots: The Next Generation* when it is next shown on television. Do you share the opinion of critics and some audiences that this presentation had more of an appeal than *Roots*? Write a short paragraph explaining . . .

FICHE INDEX (MARCH 1, 1964–MARCH 8, 1979)

1. In 'Uncle Tom' Are Our Guilt and Hope (illus.), 1964, Mr 1, VI, 23:1/8
2. Wolper Co. Is Sued On Topless Scene, 1976, My 27, 71:4/9B
3. A Saga of Slavery That Made the Actors Weep (illus.), 1976, Je 27, II, 1:6/9C
4. *Roots;* A Review (illus.), 1976, S 26, VII, 1:1/10B
5. Corroborating Evidence; Review of *Roots,* 1976, O 14, 35:2/11B
6. Success of Search for 'Roots' Leaves Alex Haley Surprised (illus.), 1976, N 23, 40:1/11C
7. ABC Will Show *Roots* in January, 1976, N 25, 59:1/12A
8. Brotherhood (letters to editor), (illus.), 1976, N 28, VII, 48:4/12B
9. TV Weekend, 1977, Ja 21, III, 21:1/12C
10. 'Haley Shows Us the Truth of Our Conjoined Histories' (illus.), 1977, Ja 23, II, 27:1/13A
11. *Roots* (advertisement) (illus.), 1977, Ja 23, IV, 28:1/1
12. ABC's *Roots* Garners a Top Nielsen Rating, 1977, Ja 26, III, 20:2/13B
13. *Roots* Getting a Grip on People Everywhere (illus.), 1977, Ja 28, II, 1:1/2
14. The Black Ghosts of History (edit.), 1977, F 2, 22:1/14B
15. 80 Million Saw *Roots* Sunday, Setting Record, 1977, F 2, II, 16:1/14C
16. Waiting to Meet Author of *Roots* (illus.), 1977, F 3, 8:3/15B
17. ABC Plans a *Roots* Sequel in Fall, 1977, F 5, 42:5/15C
18. *Roots:* The Poignant Saga, The Vital Blow to White Prejudices (letters to editor), 1977, F 8, 30:3/16A
19. *Roots* Success in South Seen as Sign of Change, 1977, F 10, 18:1/16B
20. Adoption Records: Buried Roots, 1977, F 25, 22:4/17A
21. *Roots,* Unique in Its Time, 1977, F 27, VII, 39:1/17B
22. Senate Honors *Roots* Author, 1977, Mr 15, 20:1/17C
23. *Roots* Has Widespread and Inspiring Influence, 1977, Mr 19, 46:1/18
24. Some Points of *Roots* Questioned; Haley Stands by Book as a Symbol, 1977, Ap 10, 1:5/3
25. Howe Gets History Book Award (illus.), 1977, Ap 12, 40:2/20A
26. Kunta Kinte's Village in Gambia Takes *Roots* Author to Its Heart (illus.), 1977 Ap 14, 1:5/4
27. Fact, Faction or Symbol? (illus.), 1977, Ap 15, 26:1/21A
28. Haley Visit Captivates Village Where *Roots* Began (illus.), 1977, Ap 18, 1:4/21B
29. Haley Gets Special Pulitzer Prize; Lufkin, Tex., News Takes a Medal, 1977, Ap 19, 1:1/5
30. Haley, Assailing Critic, Says *Roots* Is Sound, 1977, Ap 19, 3:1/22B
31. Novelist's Suit Charges *Roots* Copied Parts of Her 1966 Book, 1977, Ap 23, 1:1/6

*See also Learning Guide 8-1.

32. Alex Haley Denies Allegation That Parts of *Roots* Were Copied from Novel Written by Mississippi Teacher, 1977, Ap 24, 4:1/23A
33. *Roots:* About Accuracy of Detail and Historical Truth (letter to editor), 1977, Ap 25, 30:4/23B
34. Bantam Will Redistribute Books in *Roots* Dispute, 1977, Ap 26, 49:6/23C
35. Notes on People, 1977, Ap 28, III, 2:4/24A
36. Notes on People, 1977, My 20, II, 5:2/24B
37. *Roots* Grew Out of His *African,* Courlander Charges in Haley Suit, 1977, My 24, 32:2/24C
38. Alex Haley Honored at His 'Roots'—Hamilton College, 1977, My 30, 5:4/24D
39. *Roots:* Criticism Awaiting a Rebuttal (letter to editor), 1977, S 25, IV, 14:4/25A
40. TV: *Roots: One Year Later* Examines Impact of 8-Day Special, 1978, Ja 23, III, 21:2/25B
41. Jones Is Signed to Play Alex Haley, 1978, Jl 13, III, 22:1/25C
42. Federal Judge Rejects Claim That Alex Haley Copied Material, 1978, S 22, 45:1/26A
43. Suit Says *Roots* Copied from Novel (illus.), 1978, N 9, III, 21:1/26B
44. Haley Testifies He Wrote All Major Parts of *Roots,* 1978, N 28, III, 7:1/27A
45. *Roots* Plagiarism Suit Is Settled (illus.), 1978, D 15 1:5/27B
46. TV Sequel to *Roots:* Inevitable Question, 1979, F 15, III, 15:5/27C
47. Strong *Roots* Continues Black Odyssey, 1979, F 16, III, 1:5/28A
48. Let's Uproot TV's Image of Blacks, 1979, F 18, II, 35:1/7
49. *Roots II* Draws Well, But Not Like the Original, 1979, F 21, II, 18:5/28B
50. TV: End of *Roots II* Delineates 60's, 1979, F 25, 46:1/29A
51. 110 Million Saw *Roots II,* 1979, F 28, III, 22:3/29B
52. *Roots II* Strikes Personal Chords, 1979, Mr 8, III, 18:5/29C

LEARNING GUIDE **8-1**   ROOTS: ALEX HALEY'S ODYSSEY

1. Who is Alex Haley?
   SOURCES:
   Contemporary Authors: The Bio-Bibliographical Guide to Current Authors and Their Works (Gale, 1962 to date)
   Current Biography (Wilson, 1940 to date)
   Great Black Americans as Reported in The New York Times (Microfilming Corporation of America, 1981)
   Readers' Guide to Periodical Literature (Wilson, 1900 to date)
2. How did Alex Haley become interested in his family origins and how did he finally find the particular village in Africa from which his great-great-great-great grandfather was captured and sold into slavery in 1766?
   SOURCE:
   Alex Haley's Family Tree (Films, Inc.—1 filmstrip, 1 cassette, 1 guide)
3. How did Alex Haley's great-great-great-great grandfather, Kunta Kinte, become a slave?
   SOURCE:
   Roots 1: The Making of a Slave (Films, Inc.—3 filmstrips, 3 cassettes, 1 guide)
4. How did the slave masters attempt to eradicate the slaves' African identity?
   SOURCE:
   Roots 2: Adjusting to Plantation Life (Films, Inc.—3 filmstrips, 3 cassettes, 1 guide)
5. What forms of mental cruelty did the slaves suffer?
   SOURCES:
   The Peculiar Institution by Kenneth Stampp (Random, 1964; paper)
   Roots 3: Masters and Slaves (Films Inc.—3 filmstrips, 3 cassettes, 1 guide)

LEARNING GUIDE 8-1 (cont.)

6. Why were the hopes raised by the Civil War destroyed by the events of Reconstruction?
   SOURCES:

   Equal! The Case of Integration vs. Jim Crow: The Fourteenth Amendment by Leonard A. Stevens (Coward, 1975)

   Gone with the Wind by Margaret Mitchell (Macmillan, 1936)

   Roots 4: Civil War and Reconstruction (Films, Inc.)

7. Read the "Declaration of Interdependence" written by the historian-philosopher Will Durant. Is this declaration a fitting conclusion to your study of *Roots*?

DECLARATION OF INTERDEPENDENCE*

Human progress having reached a high level through respect for the liberty and dignity of men, it has become desirable to reaffirm these evident truths:

   That differences of race, color and creed are natural, and that diverse groups, institutions, and ideas are stimulating factors in the development of men;

   That to promote harmony in diversity is a responsible task of religion and statesmanship;

   That since no individual can express the whole truth, it is essential to treat with understanding and good will those whose views differ from our own;

   That by the testimony of history intolerance is the door to violence, brutality, and dictatorship; and

   That the realization of human interdependence and solidarity is the best guard of civilization.

Therefore, we solemnly resolve, and invite everyone to join in united action.

   To uphold and promote human fellowship through mutual consideration and respect;

   To champion human dignity and decency, and to safeguard those without distinction of race or color or creed;

   To strive in concert with others to discourage all animosities arising from these differences, and to unite all groups in the fair play of civilized life.

   Rooted in freedom, children of the same Divine Father, sharing everywhere a common human blood, we declare again that all men are brothers, and that mutual tolerance is the price of liberty.

*Will Durant and Ariel Durant, *Will and Ariel Durant: A Dual Autobiography*. Copyright © 1977 (New York: Simon & Schuster, 1977), p. 237. Reprinted by permission of Simon & Schuster, a Division of Gulf & Western Corporation.

Model 9

Experiencing Literature (Honors Program, 7–12)

INTRODUCTION

The secondary honors literature program continues the literature study program begun in the elementary grades. The goal of the secondary program coincides with that of the elementary: to provide an enrichment-acceleration program that affords the gifted student myriad opportunities to "experience" the best of the literary greats—past and present—with perception, appreciation, challenge, and delight.

The objectives of the secondary program also continue those outlined in Model 1, Experiencing Literature: A Continuous-Progress Literature Study Program, K–6. The purpose of the literature study program is to enable gifted students to:

Build in-depth knowledge of literature by sampling widely from and savoring deeply the best in the world of quality literature.

Form a wide acquaintanceship and build lasting friendship with authors and illustrators who have won literary acclaim.

Perceive the messages of literature as well as its themes, styles, and patterns of character, setting, and plot.

Explore with openness of mind all types and kinds of quality literature.

Realize that insight into human nature is a valued dividend accrued from reading.

Appreciate that the appeal of quality literature is timeless and universal.

View and value school and public libraries as one's own literary treasure trove.

Develop a lifelong, insatiable desire to read for information, recreation, and pleasure.

Appreciate that reading literature is both thought and emotion provoking, and, as such, can be the springboard for adventurous thinking.

Use the reading of literature as an impetus for personal experimentation with creative writing.

Become alive to the power and beauty of language and literature.

Honors Program

Enrollment in the Experiencing Literature program is limited to exceptionally able students. Responsibility for student progress is placed more on the student than on the teacher; independent study is a vital part of each course, grades 7–12. Emphasis is placed on reading literature and on interpreting and interacting with what is read; creative interpretation, both written and spoken, is emphasized. (See Bibliography: Basic Teacher Reference Books for Literature at the end of this model.)

Course Content

The Ginn Literature Series is the basic anthology series used for this course. It is a complete literature program for grades 7–12. The six volumes in the series share a common structural organization:*

Eight units of selections and instruction per text

Eight unit introductions

Eight unit reviews

Handbook and index of literary terms

Glossary

Index by literature types and authors and titles

The instruction in each of the six texts focuses on the following major areas of literary study:

Discussion: Levels and Ranges of Questions—questions of fact about the selection: *literal comprehension;* questions that require an *inference* from the selection; questions that require students to make *generalizations* preceded or followed by evidence to support the general statement; questions that require *application of ideas* to students' everyday lives.

Writer's craft: Questions related to a study of literary terms and concepts.

Composition: Assignments directly related to selections in the following modes: summary, expository, argumentative, descriptive, narrative.

Vocabulary: Instruction and exercises designed to enhance vocabulary development and related directly to selection content.

Author biographies: Postselection biographies in the grade 7–10 texts and preselection, biographies in the *American Literature* and *English Literature* texts.

A content analysis for each of the six texts in this excellent series follows (see Example 9-1, Literature Series).

*From Robert A. Bennett and others, *Teacher's Handbook for Types of Literature* (Lexington, Mass.: Ginn, 1981), pp. viii–xii.

EXAMPLE 9-1 LITERATURE SERIES*

INTRODUCTION TO LITERATURE, GRADE 7

1 Courage†

The Most Dangerous Game, *Richard Connell*
Courage, *Dudley Randall*
Mary McLeod Bethune, *Dorothy Nathan*
The Courage That My Mother Had, *Edna St. Vincent Millay*
David and Goliath, *Bible (I Samuel: 17)*
Hope, *Emily Dickinson*
First Crossing of the Atlantic, *Samuel Eliot Morison*
How Whirlwind Saved Her Cub, *Dorothy Johnson*
To James, *Frank Horne*
I'll Give You Law, *Molly Picon*

2 Determination

The Pacing Goose, *Jessamyn West*
Mother to Son, *Langston Hughes*
Top Man, *James Ramsay Ullman*
Lucinda Matlock, *Edgar Lee Masters*
My Furthest-Back Person—"The African," *Alex Haley*
Rural Dumpheap, *Melville Cane*
Fable for When There's No Way Out, *May Swenson*
The Microscope, *Maxine Kumin*
The Small Miracle, *Paul Gallico*

3 Plot and Character

The Sea Devil, *Arthur Gordon*
Good-by, Grandma, *Ray Bradbury*
Through the Tunnel, *Doris Lessing*
The Inspiration of Mr. Budd, *Dorothy Sayers*
The Street of the Three Crosses, *Josephina Niggli*
The Strangers That Came to Town, *Ambrose Flack*
The Apprentice, *Dorothy Canfield Fisher*
Last Cover, *Paul Annixter*

4 The Art of Storytelling

The Telltale Heart, *Edgar Allan Poe*
Charles, *Shirley Jackson*
Raymond's Run, *Toni Cade Bambara*
A Letter to God, *Gregorio Lopez y Fuentes* (translated by *Donald A. Yates*)
Weep No More, My Lady, *James Street*
The Celebrated Jumping Frog of Calaveras County, *Mark Twain*
The Gift of the Magi, *O. Henry*
Rip Van Winkle, *Washington Irving*

5 Drama

The Pen of My Aunt, *Josephine Tey*
Grandpa and the Statue, *Arthur Miller*
Flight into Danger, *Arthur Hailey*

---

*From *Introduction to Literature, Exploring Literature, Understanding Literature, Types of Literature, American Literature, English Literature* of the Ginn Literature Series by Robert A. Bennett and others. Copyright © 1981 by Ginn and Company (Xerox Corporation). Used with permission.

†See Model 6, Revving Up for Junior High School; *Typical Home Study Program*, Reading List 1—Courage to Survive.

EXAMPLE 9-1 (cont.)

---

6 Poems

NARRATIVE POEMS

The Cremation of Sam McGee, *Robert Service*
Elizabeth Blackwell, *Eve Merriam*
How They Brought the Good News from Ghent to Aix, *Robert Browning*
The Princess of Pure Delight, *Ira Gershwin*
Lord Randal, *Anonymous*
Bonny Barbara Allan, *Anonymous*
Robin Hood and Alan-a-Dale, *Anonymous*
Get Up and Bar the Door, *Anonymous*

DESCRIPTIVE POEMS

Values in Life

Mama Is a Sunrise, *Evelyn Tooley Hunt*
A Red, Red Rose, *Robert Burns*
Abou Ben Adhem, *Leigh Hunt*
Direction, *Alonzo Lopez*
"I'll tell you how the sun rose," *Emily Dickinson*

The Human Experience

"The days and months do not last long," *Pai Ta-Shun*
Aztec Poem, *Anonymous*
"Blow, blow, thou winter wind," *William Shakespeare*
"O when I was in love with you," *A. E. Housman*
The First Snowfall, *James Russell Lowell*

Nature

September, *Helen Hunt Jackson*
Daffodils, *May Swenson*
Rain, *Frank Marshall Davis*
"A trout leaps high," *Onitsura*
Hokku Poems, *Richard Wright*

Patriotism

My Native Land, *Sir Walter Scott*
My Land Is Fair for Any Eyes to See, *Jesse Stuart*
Song of the Settlers, *Jessamyn West*
I, Too, *Langston Hughes*
The Star-Spangled Banner, *Francis Scott Key*

HUMOROUS POEMS

Sara Cynthia Sylvia Stout Would Not Take the Garbage Out, *Shel Silverstein*
The Porcupine, *Ogden Nash*

Limericks

"A puppy whose hair was so flowing," *Oliver Herford*
"There was an old man of Nantucket," Princeton Tiger
"Pa followed the pair to Pawtucket," Chicago Tribune
"A decrepit old gas man named Peter," *Anonymous*
Achilles Deatheridge, *Edgar Lee Masters*
Ode to a Violin, *Luis Omar Salinas*

7 Myths, Fables, and Folktales

MYTHS

Greek Myths

Prometheus and Pandora, *Thomas Bulfinch*
Phaëthon, Son of Apollo, *Olivia E. Coolidge*

EXAMPLE 9-1 (cont.)

Pygmalion and Galatea, *Miriam Cox*
Hercules, *Edith Hamilton*

Norse Myths

The Building of the Wall, *Padraic Colum*
Baldur the Beautiful, *Olivia E. Coolidge*

Native American Myths

The Cheyenne Account of How the World Was Made, *Mary Little Bear Inkanish*
The Seven Stars, *John Stands in Timber and Margot Liberty*

FABLES

Fables by Aesop

The Lion and the Mouse
The Milkmaid and Her Pail
The Jay and the Peacocks
The Fox and the Crow
The Hare and the Tortoise

A Modern Fable

The Tortoise and the Hare, *James Thurber*

FOLKTALES

African Folktales

Anansi Owns All Tales That Are Told, *Ashanti*
The Third Gift, *Jan Carew*

Mexican Folktales

The Three Counsels, *Riley Aiken*
Popocateptl and Ixtlaccihuatl, *Juliet Piggott*

Japanese Folktales

Urashima, *Miriam Cox*
Three Strong Women, *Claus Stamm*

8 THE NOVEL
Winter Thunder, *Mari Sandoz*

EXPLORING LITERATURE, GRADE 8

1 ENCOUNTERS
Leiningen versus the Ants, *Carl Stephenson*
from I Know Why the Caged Bird Sings, *Maya Angelou*
A Blessing, *James Wright*
Rattlesnake Hunt, *Marjorie Kinnan Rawlings*
The Black Stallion and the Red Mare, *Gladys Francis Lewis*
Highway: Michigan, *Theodore Roethke*
Battle of the Depths, *Paul Annixter*

2 SCENES FROM AMERICA
A Song of Greatness, *Traditional Chippewa*
Paul Revere's Ride, *Henry Wadsworth Longfellow*
Prairie Winter, *Rose Wilder Lane*
Thomas Jefferson 1743–1826, *Rosemary and Stephen Vincent Benét*
The Other Pioneers, *Robert Félix Salazar*
A Wild Strain, *Paul Horgan*
Johnny Appleseed: A Pioneer Hero, *W. D. Haley*
Paul Bunyan of the North Woods, *Carl Sandburg*

EXAMPLE 9-1 (cont.)

from Pioneers in Protest, *Lerone Bennett, Jr.*
Nancy Hanks, *Rosemary and Stephen Vincent Benét*
O Captain! My Captain!, *Walt Whitman*
On the Death of a President, *Ann Stanford*
A Measure of Freedom, *Jade Snow Wong*
in the inner city, *Lucille Clifton*
Sunset: St. Louis, *Sara Teasdale*
Midwest Town, *Ruth DeLong Peterson*
Stephen's First Week, *Eva Knox Evans*
New Mexican Mountain, *Robinson Jeffers*
Zuni Prayer, *Traditional*
I Have a Dream . . . , *Martin Luther King, Jr.*
Shirley Chisholm: College Years, *Shirley Chisholm*
How I Learned to Speak, *Helen Keller*

3 PLOT

The Redheaded League, *Sir Arthur Conan Doyle*
The Long Way Around, *Jean McCord*
All Summer in a Day, *Ray Bradbury*
Stranger on the Night Train, *Mary Hocking*
The Ransom of Red Chief, *O. Henry*
Without Words, *Elliott Merrick*
All You've Ever Wanted, *Joan Aiken*
The Problem of Cell 13, *Jacques Futrelle*

4 CHARACTERIZATION

Say It with Flowers, *Toshio Mori*
The No-Talent Kid, *Kurt Vonnegut, Jr.*
The Torn Invitation, *Norman Katkov*
Pecos Bill Invents Modern Cowpunching, *James Cloyd Bowman*
The Legend of Sleepy Hollow, *Washington Irving*
Going to Run All Night, *Harry Sylvester*
The Revolt of "Mother," *Mary E. Wilkins Freeman*

5 PLAYS

The Ugly Duckling, *A. A. Milne*
Twelve Angry Men, *Reginald Rose*

6 POETRY

To Look at Any Thing, *John Moffitt*

NARRATIVE POETRY

The Highwayman, *Alfred Noyes*
The Charge of the Light Brigade, *Alfred, Lord Tennyson*
The Glove and the Lions, *Leigh Hunt*
aesop revisited by archy, *Don Marquis*
Casey at the Bat, *Ernest Lawrence Thayer*

DESCRIPTIVE POETRY

Absolutes, *Gustave Keyser*
Desert Noon, *Elizabeth Coatsworth*
Song of the Truck, *Doris Frankel*
Crossing, *Philip Booth*
Sea Lullaby, *Elinor Wylie*
Silver, *Walter de la Mare*
Tree, *Lenore Marshall*
The Double Play, *Robert Wallace*
Fog, *Carl Sandburg*

EXAMPLE 9-1 (cont.)

Song of the Sky Loom, *Tewa Indian*
American Gothic, *Samuel Allen*
Catalogue, *Rosalie Moore*
Sea Fever, *John Masefield*

CONCERN FOR OTHERS
The Sleeper, *Edward Field*
Time to Talk, *Robert Frost*
if you have had your midnights, *Mari Evans*
An Easy Decision, *Kenneth Patchen*
Those Winter Sundays, *Robert Hayden*
The Twenty-third Psalm, *Bible*

VIEWPOINTS
Taught Me Purple, *Evelyn Tooley Hunt*
Dream Variation, *Langston Hughes*
A Psalm of Life, *Henry Wadsworth Longfellow*
Death at Suppertime, *Phyllis McGinley*
The Immigrant Experience, *Richard Olivas*
To Kate, Skating Better Than Her Date, *David Daiches*
The Choice, *Dorothy Parker*

PORTRAITS OF YOUTH AND AGE
Carriers of the Dream Wheel, *N. Scott Momaday*
Aunt Sue's Stories, *Langston Hughes*
My Grandmother Would Rock Quietly and Hum, *Leonard Adame*
pinones, *Leroy V. Quintana*
A Spring Night, *Robert Beloof*
Fifteen, *William Stafford*
Advice to a Girl, *Sara Teasdale*

7 NONFICTION NARRATIVE
Roberto Clemente—A Bittersweet Memoir, *Jerry Izenburg*
The Life and Death of a Western Gladiator, *Charles G. Finney*
from A Peculiar Treasure, *Edna Ferber*
Four Years in a Shed, *Eve Curie*
from Lame Deer: Seeker of Visions, *John Fire/Lame Deer*
Battle by the Breadfruit Tree, *Theodore J. Waldeck*
That Legendary Ride, *Duke Kahanamoku*

8 THE NOVEL
The Call of the Wild, *Jack London*

UNDERSTANDING LITERATURE, GRADE 9

1 REFLECTIONS

Flowers for Algernon, *Daniel Keyes*
Mirror, *John Updike*
"I'm Nobody! Who Are You?" *Emily Dickinson*
conceptuality, *Mari Evans*
Side 32, *Victor Hernandez Cruz*
I Have Bowed Before the Sun, *Anna Lee Walters*
Your World, *Georgia Douglas Johnson*
Fear Not the Night's Darkness, *Tina Morris*
Marigolds, *Eugenia Collier*
The Road Not Taken, *Robert Frost*
Ride a Wild Horse, *Hannah Kahn*
Muddy Road, *Anonymous*
A Mother in Mannville, *Marjorie Kinnan Rawlings*

EXAMPLE 9-1 (cont.)

Locked In, *Ingemar Gustafson*
Plain, *Miller Williams*
Ambivalence, *Mark Greenspan*
Fool's Paradise, *Isaac Bashevis Singer*

2 MODERN DRAMA

Trifles, *Susan Glaspell*
The Miracle Worker, *William Gibson*

3 SHORT STORIES

The Lady, or the Tiger, *Frank R. Stockton*
The Open Window, *Saki*
The New Mirror, *Ann Petry*
Love Is a Fallacy, *Max Shulman*
The Monkey's Paw, *W. W. Jacobs*
The Cask of Amontillado, *Edgar Allan Poe*
You Need To Go Upstairs, *Rumer Godden*
Conquistador, *Prudencio de Pareda*
The Rocket Man, *Ray Bradbury*
A Visit of Charity, *Eudora Welty*
Blues Ain't No Mockin Bird, *Toni Cade Bambara*

4 POETRY: LANGUAGE AND IMAGE

Crystal Moment, *Robert P. Tristram Coffin*

FIGURATIVE LANGUAGE

Fable, *Ralph Waldo Emerson*
Prayers of Steel, *Carl Sandburg*
Poetry Is A Tressel, *Nikki Giovanni*
Lyric 17, *José Garcia Villa*
Metrical Feet, *Samuel T. Coleridge*
Night Clouds, *Amy Lowell*

IMAGES

The Open Door, *Elizabeth Coatsworth*
400-Meter Freestyle, *Maxine W. Kumin*
Tenement Room: Chicago, *Frank Marshall Davis*
Fueled, *Marcie Hans*
"Apparently with no surprise," *Emily Dickinson*
Tropics in New York, *Claude McKay*
Cavalry Crossing a Ford, *Walt Whitman*
"O what is that sound," *W. H. Auden*
Moco Limping, *David Nava Monreal*
Pigeon Woman, *May Swenson*
"My Mama moved among the days," *Lucille Clifton*
The Bishop of Atlanta: Ray Charles, *H. Julian Bond*
Your Laughter, *Pablo Neruda*
"in Just-" *e. e. cummings*
from Pippa Passes, *Robert Browning*

5 EPIC LITERATURE

The Iliad, *Homer* (translated by I. A. Richards)
Miniver Cheevy, *Edward Arlington Robinson*
from Morturi Salutamus, *Henry Wadsworth Longfellow*
The Battle of the Ants, *Henry David Thoreau*

EXAMPLE 9-1 (cont.)

6 POETRY: LANGUAGE AND SOUND

RHYTHM AND SOUND
The Raven, *Edgar Allan Poe*
Once by the Pacific, *Robert Frost*
Runagate Runagate, *Robert Hayden*
Drum, *Langston Hughes*
Gamboling on the Gumbo, *Walt Kelly*
Onomatopoeia, *Eve Merriam*
The Word Plum, *Helen Chasin*
The Cataract of Lodore, *Robert Southey*
Jamaica Market, *Agnes Maxwell-Hall*

LIGHT VERSE
Pediatric Reflection, *Ogden Nash*
Reflection on Babies, *Ogden Nash*
The Parent, *Ogden Nash*
The Latest Latin Dance Craze, *Victor Hernandez Cruz*
One Perfect Rose, *Dorothy Parker*
I'll Take the High Road Commission, *Ogden Nash*
To a Captious Critic, *Paul Lawrence Dunbar*

7 NONFICTION

The Unicorn in the Garden, *James Thurber*
from Platero and I, *Juan Ramón Jiménez*
from These Were the Sioux, *Mari Sandoz*
Mijbil, *Gavin Maxwell*
from The Lady and the Sharks, *Eugenie Clark*
Flood, *Annie Dillard*
A Madness of Nature, *Franklin Russell*
Shakespeare's London, *Marchette Chute*

8 SHAKESPEAREAN DRAMA

Romeo and Juliet, *William Shakespeare*

TYPES OF LITERATURE, GRADE 10

1 THE SHORT STORY

The Sniper, *Liam O'Flaherty*
Safe and Soundproof, *Joan Aiken*
The Sentimentality of William Tavener, *Willa Cather*
Chee's Daughter, *Juanita Platero and Siyowin Miller*
The Necklace, *Guy de Maupassant*
By the Waters of Babylon, *Stephen Vincent Benét*
The Waltz, *Dorothy Parker*
The Third Level, *Jack Finney*
Management, *Margaret Lamb*
The Cop and the Anthem, *O. Henry*
Harrison Bergeron, *Kurt Vonnegut, Jr.*
The Man without a Country, *Edward Everett Hale*
The Street of the Cañon, *Josephina Niggli*
The Crop, *Flannery O'Connor*

2 MODERN DRAMA

The Old Lady Shows Her Medals, *J. M. Barrie*
The Diary of Anne Frank, *Frances Goodrich and Albert Hackett*

EXAMPLE **9-1 (cont.)**

3 LYRIC POETRY

kidnap poem, *Nikki Giovanni*
The Secret, *Denise Levertov*
Unfolding Bud, *Naoshi Koriyama*
Exeunt, *Richard Wilbur*
Water Picture, *May Swenson*
Three Jet Planes, *May Swenson*
Moonlight Night: Carmel, *Langston Hughes*
"The Sky is low," *Emily Dickinson*
"I like to see it lap the Miles," *Emily Dickinson*
dandelions, *Deborah Austin*
The night is darkening round me, *Emily Brontë*
Cargoes, *John Masefield*
Time, You Old Gypsy Man, *Ralph Hodgson*
Limited, *Carl Sandburg*
The Coach of Life, *Alexander Pushkin*
Southern Mansion, *Arna Bontemps*
Four Preludes on Playthings of the Wind, *Carl Sandburg*
The Fish, *Elizabeth Bishop*
Their Lonely Betters, *W. H. Auden*
Auto Wreck, *Karl Shapiro*
The Umpire, *Walker Gibson*
When I Heard the Learn'd Astronomer, *Walt Whitman*
The Fawn, *Edna St. Vincent Millay*
The Gray Squirrel, *Humbert Wolfe*
the lesson of the moth, *Don Marquis*
Mending Wall, *Robert Frost*
A Fence, *Carl Sandburg*
Lemon, *Rita Mendoza*
Two-Part Pear Able, *May Swenson*
Yet Do I Marvel, *Countee Cullen*

THEME

from Ecclesiastes, *Bible*
Eleven, *Archibald MacLeish*
Peter at Fourteen, *Constance Carrier*
"Out, Out—" *Robert Frost*
I Followed a Path, *Patricia Parker*
To Be of Use, *Marge Piercy*
When I Think About Myself, *Maya Angelou*
Here—Hold My Hand, *Mari Evans*
Where Have You Gone, *Mari Evans*
Finis, *Waring Cuney*
Housecleaning, *Nikki Giovanni*
For My People, *Margaret Walker*
Sonnet 43, *Elizabeth Barrett Browning*
Sonnet 60, *William Shakespeare*
Dulce et Decorum Est, *Wilfred Owen*
There Will Come Soft Rains, *Sara Teasdale*

4 NARRATIVE POETRY

The Puritan's Ballad, *Elinor Wylie*
Death of the Hired Man, *Robert Frost*
Gareth and Lynette, *Alfred, Lord Tennyson*

EXAMPLE 9-1 (cont.)

5 BIOGRAPHY AND AUTOBIOGRAPHY

BIOGRAPHY
Harriet Tubman: The Moses of Her People, *Langston Hughes*
Lincoln Speaks at Gettysburg, *Carl Sandburg*
I Will Lift Up Mine Eyes, *Shirley Graham*
The Campers at Kitty Hawk, *John Dos Passos*

AUTOBIOGRAPHY
from Barrio Boy, *Ernesto Galarza*
from Agatha Christie: An Autobiography, *Agatha Christie*
A Christmas Memory, *Truman Capote*
from Alone, *Richard E. Byrd*

6 SHAKESPEAREAN DRAMA

adapted from An Introduction to Shakespeare, *Marchette Chute*
The Tragedy of Julius Caesar, *William Shakespeare*

7 THE ESSAY

DESCRIPTIVE ESSAY
Morocco, *Anaïs Nin*
The Lobstering Man, *Robert P. Tristram Coffin*
The Marginal World, *Rachel Carson*

NARRATIVE ESSAY
Scent of Apples, *Bienvenido N. Santos*
The Dog That Bit People, *James Thurber*
A Dissertation upon Roast Pig, *Charles Lamb*
Untying the Knot, *Annie Dillard*
The Cliché Expert Reveals Himself in His True Colors, *Frank Sullivan*
My Dungeon Shook, *James Baldwin*

8 THE NOVEL
The Pearl, *John Steinbeck*

AMERICAN LITERATURE, GRADE 11

1 MAJOR THEMES IN AMERICAN LITERATURE

SENSE OF PLACE
The Gift Outright, *Robert Frost*
Where Mountain Lion Lay Down With Deer, *Leslie Marmon Silko*
from A Discourse of the Plantation of the Southern Colony in Virginia, *George Percy*
from Roughing It, *Samuel Langhorne Clemens*
from Of Time and the River, *Thomas Wolfe*
from A Walker in the City, *Alfred Kazin*
Southbound on the Freeway, *May Swenson*
i yearn, *Ricardo Sánchez*
Iowa Farmer, *Margaret Walker*

THE INDIVIDUAL
I Hear America Singing, *Walt Whitman*
Of Individualism in Democratic Countries, *Alexis de Tocqueville*
"The Soul selects her own Society," *Emily Dickinson*
A Delicate Balance, *José Armas*
The Bride Comes to Yellow Sky, *Stephen Crane*
Lost Sister, *Cathy Song*
The Creative Dilemma, *James Baldwin*
On Being a Granddaughter, *Margaret Mead*

EXAMPLE 9-1 (cont.)

THE AMERICAN DREAM

America the Beautiful, *Katharine Lee Bates*
from The Law of the Great Peace, *Iroquois Confederacy*
The Mayflower Compact, *William Bradford*
The Declaration of Independence, *Thomas Jefferson*
Lenox Avenue Mural, *Langston Hughes*
Winter Dreams, *F. Scott Fitzgerald*
from I Know Why the Caged Bird Sings, *Maya Angelou*
I Have a Dream, *Martin Luther King, Jr.*
A Vision Beyond Time and Place, *N. Scott Momaday*

2 A NEW LAND

Night Chant/Blessing Way, *Navaho*
Now I Am Left, *Algonkin*
from The History of Plymouth Plantation, *William Bradford*
from A History of the Dividing Line, *William Byrd*
Speech to the General Court, *John Winthrop*
To My Dear and Loving Husband, *Anne Bradstreet*
The Author to Her Book, *Anne Bradstreet*
Captivity Narrative, *Mary Rowlandson*
Huswifery, *Edward Taylor*
Meditation Six, *Edward Taylor*
from Sinners in the Hands of an Angry God, *Jonathan Edwards*

3 A NEW NATION

The Sale of the Hessians, *Benjamin Franklin*
from Poor Richard's Almanac, *Benjamin Franklin*
Speech in the Virginia Convention, *Patrick Henry*
from The American Crisis, *Thomas Paine*
To the Right Honourable William, Earl of Dartmouth, *Phillis Wheatley*
Letter to Her Husband, *Abigail Adams*
from Notes on the State of Virginia, *Thomas Jefferson*
Letter to Thomas Jefferson, *Benjamin Banneker*
This In an American, *Hector St. John de Crèvecoeur*

4 A NEW LITERATURE

Rip Van Winkle, *Washington Irving*
Thanatopsis, *William Cullen Bryant*
from Self Reliance, *Ralph Waldo Emerson*
Concord Hymn, *Ralph Waldo Emerson*
Brahma, *Ralph Waldo Emerson*
Young Goodman Brown, *Nathaniel Hawthorne*
My Lost Youth, *Henry Wadsworth Longfellow*
The Tide Rises, the Tide Falls, *Henry Wadsworth Longfellow*
Declaration of Sentiments, *Elizabeth Cady Stanton*
Ain't I a Woman?, *Sojourner Truth*
The Pit and the Pendulum, *Edgar Allan Poe*
To Helen, *Edgar Allan Poe*
Sonnet—To Science, *Edgar Allan Poe*
The City in the Sea, *Edgar Allan Poe*
Where I Lived and What I Lived For, *Henry David Thoreau*
from Narrative of the Life of Frederick Douglass, *Frederick Douglass*
Bury Me in a Free Land, *Frances E. W. Harper*
Bartleby the Scrivener, *Herman Melville*

EXAMPLE 9-1 (cont.)

5 A NEW MATURITY

Gettysburg Address, *Abraham Lincoln*
The Death of President Lincoln, *Elizabeth Keckley*
A Noiseless Patient Spider, *Walt Whitman*
One's-Self I Sing, *Walt Whitman*
There Was a Child Went Forth, *Walt Whitman*
"Success is counted sweetest," *Emily Dickinson*
"Because I could not stop for Death," *Emily Dickinson*
"After great pain, a formal feeling comes," *Emily Dickinson*
The Invalid's Story, *Samuel Langhorne Clemens*
Let Me Be a Free Man, *Chief Joseph*
Four Meetings, *Henry James*
A Church Mouse, *Mary E. Wilkins Freeman*
Sympathy, *Paul Laurence Dunbar*
Of the Meaning of Progress, *W. E. B. DuBois*
from The Storm and Other Stories, *Kate Chopin*

6 TWENTIETH CENTURY: THE MODERN WORLD

PROSE

A Wagner Matinée, *Willa Cather*
from Dust Tracks on a Road, *Zora Neale Hurston*
The Secret Life of Walter Mitty, *James Thurber*
The Bear, *William Faulkner*
Big Two Hearted River: Part II, *Ernest Hemingway*
The Chrysanthemums, *John Steinbeck*
The Man Who Saw the Flood, *Richard Wright*
The Jilting of Granny Weatherall, *Katherine Anne Porter*
Freedom—July, 1940, *E. B. White*

POETRY

Richard Cory, *Edwin Arlington Robinson*
Patterns, *Amy Lowell*
Chicago, *Carl Sandburg*
"The people will live on," *Carl Sandburg*
Departmental, *Robert Frost*
Birches, *Robert Frost*
Stopping By Woods on a Snowy Evening, *Robert Frost*
Spring and All: I, *William Carlos Williams*
"Pity me not because the light of day," *Edna St. Vincent Millay*
"I(a," *e. e. cummings*
"maggie and milly and molly and may," *e. e. cummings*
"!" *e. e. cummings*
From the Dark Tower, *Countee Cullen*
America, *Claude McKay*
Song of the Son, *Jean Toomer*
Musician, *Louise Bogan*
Manhole Covers, *Karl Shapiro*
Song, *H. D.*
What Are Years?, *Marianne Moore*
Silence, *Marianne Moore*
At the Fishhouses, *Elizabeth Bishop*
A Black Man Talks of Reaping, *Arna Bontemps*

7 MODERN AMERICAN DRAMA

Our Town, *Thornton Wilder*

EXAMPLE 9-1 (cont.)

8 TWENTIETH CENTURY: OUR TIME

PROSE

    The Prison, *Bernard Malamud*
    The Life You Save May Be Your Own, *Flannery O'Connor*
    Did You Ever Dream Lucky? *Ralph Ellison*
    The Notebook, *Norman Mailer*
    Breach of Promise, *Jessamyn West*
    I Stand Here Ironing, *Tillie Olsen*
    from The Plum Plum Pickers, *Raymond Barrio*
    Man and Daughter in the Cold, *John Updike*
    from The Bluest Eye, *Toni Morrison*
    A Father-to-Be, *Saul Bellow*
    Seeing, *Annie Dillard*
    Dead Boy, *John Crowe Ransom*
    Thirteen Ways of Looking at a Blackbird, *Wallace Stevens*
    The Horse Chestnut Tree, *Richard Eberhart*
    The Waking, *Theodore Roethke*
    Involved, *A. R. Ammons*
    truth, *Gwendolyn Brooks*
    "Life for my child is simple, and is good," *Gwendolyn Brooks*
    The Beautiful Changes, *Richard Wilbur*
    Frederick Douglass, *Robert Hayden*
    Astronauts, *Robert Hayden*
    Garden of My Childhood, *Kuangchi C. Chang*
    Ghost of a Chance, *Adrienne Rich*
    Preface to a Twenty Volume Suicide Note, *Amiri Baraka*
    Summer Remembered, *Isabella Gardner*
    I Am a Black Woman, *Mari Evans*
    Water, *Robert Lowell*
    Mushrooms, *Sylvia Plath*
    Gold Glade, *Robert Penn Warren*
    Alone/December/Night, *Victor Hernandez Cruz*
    Courage, *Anne Sexton*
    New Face, *Alice Walker*
    Dreaming America, *Joyce Carol Oates*
    Dream of Rebirth, *Roberta Hill*

ENGLISH LITERATURE, GRADE 12

1 THE MIDDLE AGES—TO 1500

THE ENGLISH LANGUAGE AND ITS BEGINNINGS

THE LANGUAGE: OLD ENGLISH

OLD ENGLISH LITERATURE

    from Beowulf, Anonymous translated by *J. Duncan Spaeth*
    from Ecclesiastical History of the English People, *Saint Bede*
    Pangur Bán, Anonymous translated by *Robin Flower*
    Anglo-Saxon Riddles, Anonymous translated by *Burton Raffel*

THE LANGUAGE: MIDDLE ENGLISH

MIDDLE ENGLISH LITERATURE: THE POPULAR TRADITION

    The Ballad

    Edward, Anonymous
    Sir Patrick Spence, Anonymous
    Johnie Armstrong, Anonymous
    Get Up and Bar the Door, Anonymous

EXAMPLE 9-1 (cont.)

The Drama

Noah's Flood, Anonymous

MIDDLE ENGLISH LITERATURE: THE COURTLY TRADITION

from Le Morte D'Arthur, *Sir Thomas Mallory*

MIDDLE ENGLISH LITERATURE: THE EMERGING WRITER

from Prologue to The Canterbury Tales, *Geoffrey Chaucer* translated by *Nevill Coghill*
The Pardoner's Tale, *Geoffrey Chaucer* translated by *Nevill Coghill*
The Nun's Priest's Tale, *Geoffrey Chaucer* translated by *Nevill Coghill*

2 THE RENAISSANCE 1485–1660

THE LANGUAGE

THE TIMES

THE LITERATURE OF THE RENAISSANCE

The English Bible: the Book

Psalm 8
from The Book of Job

Songs and Sonnets: The Nature of Love and the Love of Nature

Sonnet, *Sir Philip Sidney*
Description of Spring, *Henry Howard, Earl of Surrey*
Song *from* Twelfth Night, *William Shakespeare*
Song *from* Cymbeline, *William Shakespeare*
Sonnets 18, 29, 55, 73, 116, *William Shakespeare*
Song, *John Donne*
On My First Son, *Ben Jonson*
To Celia, *Ben Jonson*
To the Virgins, to Make Much of Time, *Robert Herrick*
To Lucasta, Going To the Wars, *Richard Lovelace*

The World of Dreams

from The Faerie Queene, *Edmund Spenser*

The World of Affairs

from The New Atlantis, *Francis Bacon*
Of Studies, *Francis Bacon*

The Religious Lyric: Meditation and Vision

Death, Be Not Proud, *John Donne*
from Meditation XVII, *John Donne*
The Church Windows, *George Herbert*
Easter Wings, *George Herbert*
Virtue, *George Herbert*
The Retreat, *Henry Vaughan*

The Limits of Knowledge and the Scope of Wisdom

On His Having Arrived at the Age of Twenty-three, *John Milton*
To the Lord General Cromwell, *John Milton*
On His Blindness, *John Milton*
from Areopagitica, *John Milton*
from Paradise Lost, *John Milton*

3 THE RENAISSANCE DRAMA

Darkness and Living Light

EXAMPLE 9-1 (cont.)

Shakespeare, the Man
The Elizabethan Stage
About The Tragedy of Macbeth
The Tragedy of Macbeth, *William Shakespeare*

4 THE ENLIGHTENMENT 1660–1780

THE LANGUAGE

THE TIMES

THE LITERATURE OF THE ENLIGHTENMENT

Images of Order

from The Pilgrim's Progress, *John Bunyan*
Song for St. Cecilia's Day, *John Dryden*
from Essay on Man, *Alexander Pope*
from Essay on Criticism, *Alexander Pope*

The Study of Humankind: The Innocent Observer

The Spectator Club, *Richard Steele*
A Young Lady of Fashion, *Joseph Addison*
from The Rape of the Lock, *Alexander Pope*

The Study of Humankind: The Triumph of Satire

from Gulliver's Travels, *Jonathan Swift*
A Modest Proposal, *Jonathan Swift*

The Power of Common Sense

from Preface to Shakespeare, *Samuel Johnson*
from The Life of Samuel Johnson, *James Boswell*
from Letter: "The Gentry," *Earl of Chesterfield*

Far from the Madding Crowd

Elegy Written in a Country Churchyard, *Thomas Gray*

The Enlightenment: The Development of the English Novel

from Pride and Prejudice, *Jane Austen*

5 THE ROMANTIC PERIOD 1780–1830

THE LANGUAGE

THE TIMES

THE LITERATURE OF THE ROMANTIC PERIOD

Uncommon Songs of Common People

Sweet Afton, *Robert Burns*
For A' That, *Robert Burns*
To a Louse, *Robert Burns*
O, Wert Thou in the Cauld Blast, *Robert Burns*
John Anderson My Jo, *Robert Burns*
The Lamb, *William Blake*
On Another's Sorrow, *William Blake*
A Poison Tree, *William Blake*
The Tiger, *William Blake*

People Speaking to People

from A Vindication of the Rights of Woman, *Mary Wollstonecraft*
from The Prelude, *William Wordsworth*

EXAMPLE 9-1 (cont.)

Composed upon Westminster Bridge, *William Wordsworth*
London, 1802, *William Wordsworth*
It Is a Beauteous Evening, *William Wordsworth*
The World Is Too Much with Us, *William Wordsworth*
The Solitary Reaper, *William Wordsworth*
Frost at Midnight, *Samuel Taylor Coleridge*
Dream Children, *Charles Lamb*

International Heroes

Lochinvar, *Sir Walter Scott*
Proud Maisie, *Sir Walter Scott*
from Childe Harold's Pilgrimage, *Lord Byron*
from Don Juan, *Lord Byron*
She Walks in Beauty, *Lord Byron*

Unacknowledged Legislators

To a Skylark, *Percy Bysshe Shelley*
Ode to the West Wind, *Percy Bysshe Shelley*
Ozymandias, *Percy Bysshe Shelley*
On First Looking into Chapman's Homer, *John Keats*
To Autumn, *John Keats*
Ode on a Grecian Urn, *John Keats*
Ode to a Nightingale, *John Keats*

The Romantic Period: The Development of the English Novel

from Jane Eyre, *Charlotte Brontë*

6 THE VICTORIAN PERIOD 1830–1914

THE LANGUAGE

THE TIMES

THE LITERATURE OF THE VICTORIAN PERIOD

Doubt and Faith

Ulysses, *Alfred, Lord Tennyson*
from In Memoriam A. H. H., *Alfred, Lord Tennyson*
Crossing the Bar, *Alfred, Lord Tennyson*
No Coward Soul Is Mine, *Emily Brontë*
The Night Wind, *Emily Brontë*
Isolation, *Matthew Arnold*
Dover Beach, *Matthew Arnold*
Say Not the Struggle Naught Availeth, *Arthur Hugh Clough*

The Nature of the Individual

My Last Duchess, *Robert Browning*
Home Thoughts, from Abroad, *Robert Browning*
Home Thoughts, from the Sea, *Robert Browning*
Prospice, *Robert Browning*
Sonnets 14, 28, 43, *Elizabeth Barrett Browning*
Lost Days, *Dante Gabriel Rossetti*
Shut Out, *Christina Rossetti*
Invictus, *William Ernest Henley*

Old Themes and New Voices

Lucifer in Starlight, *George Meredith*
A Mad Tea Party, *Lewis Carroll*

EXAMPLE 9-1 (cont.)

Jabberwocky, *Lewis Carroll*
Spring, *Gerard Manley Hopkins*
God's Grandeur, *Gerard Manley Hopkins*
Spring and Fall, *Gerard Manley Hopkins*
Recessional, *Rudyard Kipling*
The Ballad of the East and West, *Rudyard Kipling*
Loveliest of Trees, *A. E. Housman*
To an Athlete Dying Young, *A. E. Housman*
On Wenlock Edge, *A. E. Housman*
When I Was One-and-Twenty, *A. E. Housman*
The Darkling Thrush, *Thomas Hardy*
In Time of "The Breaking of Nations," *Thomas Hardy*
Channel Firing, *Thomas Hardy*

The Victorian Period: The Development of the English Novel

from Great Expectations, *Charles Dickens*

7 THE TWENTIETH CENTURY: NEW PERSPECTIVES 1914–1945

THE LANGUAGE

THE TIMES

THE LITERATURE OF THE TWENTIETH CENTURY, 1914–1945

The Need for Renewal

The Machine Stops, *E. M. Forster*
Preludes, *T. S. Eliot*
Journey of the Magi, *T. S. Eliot*
The Lake Isle of Innisfree, *W. B. Yeats*
The Old Men Admiring Themselves in the Water, *W. B. Yeats*
Sailing to Byzantium, *W. B. Yeats*

Human Beings and Inhuman Society

The Rocking-Horse Winner, *D. H. Lawrence*
The English Are So Nice, *D. H. Lawrence*
Shakespeare's Sister, *Virginia Woolf*
The Unknown Citizen, *W. H. Auden*

War and Peace

The Soldier, *Rupert Brooke*
Strange Meeting, *Wilfred Owen*
As the Team's Head-Brass, *Edward Thomas*
Naming the Parts, *Henry Reed*
Watching Post, *C. Day Lewis*
The Burning of the Leaves, *Laurence Binyon*
London, 1940: After the Raid, *Elizabeth Bowen*
The Demon Lover, *Elizabeth Bowen*

The Adventure of Growth

Fern Hill, *Dylan Thomas*
"What I expected," *Stephen Spender*
Norfolk, *Sir John Betjeman*
Original Sin on the Sussex Coast, *Sir John Betjeman*
Departure in the Dark, *C. Day Lewis*
Musée des Beaux Arts, *W. H. Auden*
Piano, *D. H. Lawrence*
The Truisms, *Louis MacNeice*
from A Portrait of the Artist as a Young Man, *James Joyce*

EXAMPLE **9-1** (cont.)

The Twentieth Century, 1914–1945: The Development of the English Novel

from To the Lighthouse, *Virginia Woolf*

8 THE TWENTIETH CENTURY: TIME OF TRIAL 1945–

THE LANGUAGE

THE TIMES

THE LITERATURE OF THE TWENTIETH CENTURY, 1945–

Displaced Persons and Lost Connections

In Memory of W. B. Yeats, *W. H. Auden*
Elegy for J. F. K., *W. H. Auden*
Politics and the English Language, *George Orwell*
The Whitsun Weddings, *Philip Larkin*
Mr. Bleaney, *Philip Larkin*
Not in the Guide-Books, *Elizabeth Jennings*
New Worlds, *Elizabeth Jennings*
The Lost Symbols, *Elizabeth Jennings*
The Horses, *Ted Hughes*
Hawk Roosting, *Ted Hughes*
Not Waving But Drowning, *Stevie Smith*
Pretty, *Stevie Smith*
The Bright Field, *Derek Walcott*
B. Wordsworth, *V. S. Naipaul*
Disembarking at Quebec, *Margaret Atwood*
Further Arrivals, *Margaret Atwood*
First Neighbors, *Margaret Atwood*
The Planters, *Margaret Atwood*

The Comedy of Despair

from A Man of the People, *Chinua Achebe*
A Separate Peace

The Twentieth Century, 1945–: The Development of the English Novel

from The Golden Notebook, *Doris Lessing*

EPILOGUE
from Tradition and the Individual Talent, *T. S. Eliot*

ENRICHMENT-ACCELERATION ACTIVITIES

The teacher of the honors literature program values the anthology as a guide, a frame of reference, and a plan for basic literary skills development. The anthology in the hands of a creative teacher becomes an introduction to the study of literature, a means of orientation, *and* an enticement to further exploration.

The success of an enrichment-acceleration literature program depends in large measure on the ready availability and accessibility of appropriate support media when the use of the media is timely to the literary unit, theme, or work being studied. Therefore, close cooperation between the school librarian and the teacher is mandatory. The following four guidelines will facilitate building library support programs of depth, breadth, relevance, and challenge.

1. Provide opportunity for students to read the entire literary work if only a selection from that work has been highlighted in the literature anthology, as in the examples below.

> In grade 7, after reading the selection *My Furthest-Back Person—"The African"* by Alex Haley, students should read *Roots* by Haley (Doubleday, 1976). (See Learning Guide 8-1, *Roots: Alex Haley's Odyssey*, in Model 8 for additional support media.)
>
> In grade 8, after reading a selection from *I Know Why the Caged Bird Sings*, students should read the entire autobiography by Maya Angelou (Random, 1970).
>
> In grade 9, after reading from *The Iliad*, students should read the entire epic poem by Homer (Doubleday, 1975).
>
> In grade 10, after reading the selection from *Agatha Christie: An Autobiography*, students read the entire autobiography (Ballantine, 1978).
>
> In grade 11, after reading the selection from *Poor Richard's Almanac* by Benjamin Franklin, students should read the entire work (McKay, 1976).
>
> In grade 12, after reading the selection from *Pride and Prejudice* by Jane Austen, students should read the entire work (Dutton, 1976).

2. Provide opportunity for students to become acquainted with writers as human beings as well as literary figures, as in the examples below.

> In grade 7, after reading the short story *The Telltale Heart* by Edgar Allan Poe, students should become acquainted with Poe as a human being by reading *Edgar Allan Poe: Visitor from the Night of Time* by Philip Stern (Harper, 1973) and by viewing the sound filmstrip *Edgar Allan Poe* (Encyclopaedia Britannica).
>
> In grade 8, after reading the excerpt from the novel *The Call of the Wild* by Jack London, students should become acquainted with London as a human being by reading *Jack London* by Earle Labor (Twayne, 1974) and by viewing the sound filmstrip *Jack London: A Life of Adventure* (Guidance Associates).
>
> In grade 9, after reading *The Iliad* by Homer, students should become acquainted with Homer as a human being by reading *Homer* by Andre Michalopoulos (Twayne, 1966) and by viewing the sound filmstrip set *Homer's Mythology: Tracing a Tradition* (Guidance Associates).
>
> In grade 10, after reading *The Pearl* by John Steinbeck, students should become acquainted with Steinbeck as a human being by reading *John Steinbeck: Nature and Myth* by Peter Lisca (Harper, 1978) and by viewing the sound filmstrip *John Steinbeck* (Encyclopaedia Britannica).
>
> In grade 11, after reading, "Where I Lived and What I Lived For" by Henry David Thoreau, students should become acquainted with Thoreau as a human being by reading *Henry David Thoreau: A Man for Our Time* by James Daugherty (Viking, 1967), by viewing the sound filmstrip *Henry David Thoreau* (Encyclopaedia Britannica) and the motion picture *Talking with Thoreau* (Encyclopaedia Britannica).
>
> In grade 12, after reading the selection *Shakespeare, the Man,* students should become acquainted with Shakespeare as a human being by reading *Shakespeare of London* by Marchette Chute (Dutton, 1950) and by viewing the sound filmstrip *Shakespeare, The Man* (Educational Enrichment Materials) and the motion picture *Shakespeare of Stratford and London* (National Geographic).

3. Provide opportunity for students to read other literary works by an author highlighted in the anthology, as in the examples below.

> In grade 7, after reading a selection by Alex Haley, students should learn of other Haley books and articles, such as: *Autobiography of Malcolm X* by Malcolm X and Alex Haley (Ballantine, 1976) and "Sea Islanders, Strong-willed Survivors Face Their Uncertain Future Together," in *Smithsonian*, October 1982, pp. 88–97.

In grade 8, after reading a selection by Maya Angelou, students should learn of other Angelou writings, such as (all Random House): *Gather Together in My Name* (1974), *Just Give Me a Cool Drink of Water* (1971), *Oh Pray My Wings Are Going to Fit Me Well* (1975), and *Singin' and Swingin' and Gettin' Merry Like Christmas* (1976).

In grade 9, after reading a selection by Isaac Bashevis Singer, students should learn of other Singer writings, such as (all Farrar): *A Day of Pleasure: Stories of a Boy Growing Up in Warsaw* (1969), *Gimpel the Fool and Other Stories* (1959), and *The Spinoza of Market Street* (1961).

In grade 10, after reading a selection by Agatha Christie, students should learn that Christie was a prolific writer (68 novels, more than 150 short stories, and 17 plays) and should read some of her famous detective stories, such as: *Death on the Nile* (Dodd, 1969), *Destination Unknown* (Dodd, 1978), *Hercule Poirot's Christmas* (Dodd, 1974), *Murder of Roger Ackroyd* (Garland, 1976), *Murder on the Orient Express* (Dodd, 1978), *The Mysterious Affair at Styles* (Dodd, 1975), and *Why Didn't They Ask Evans?* (Dodd, n.d.).

In grade 11, after reading *Our Town* by Thornton Wilder, students should read other Wilder works (both Harper): *Bridge of San Luis Rey* (1967) and *Three Plays: Our Town, Skin of Our Teeth, Matchmaker* (1957).

In grade 12, after reading a selection by Charles Dickens, students should read other Dickens works in addition to *Great Expectations,* such as *Adventures of Oliver Twist* (Oxford, n.d.), *Bleak House* (Houghton, 1956), *Christmas Carol* (Lippincott, 1952), *David Copperfield* (Macmillan, 1962), *Mystery of Edwin Drood* (Oxford, 1972), and *Tale of Two Cities* (Macmillan, 1962).

4. Provide opportunity for the students to build in-depth knowledge of the various literary genres and/or themes highlighted in the anthology, as in the examples below.

In grade 7, after reading Greek myths, students should delve deeply into the subject and explore widely using both print and nonprint media (see Bibliography for Independent Study: Greek Mythology at the end of this model).

In grade 8, after reading narrative, descriptive, and thematic poetry, students should delve deeply into the subject and explore poetry by using both print and nonprint media (see Bibliography for Independent Study: Poetry at the end of this model).

In grade 9, after reading about "Search for Identity," students as a class should explore this theme using the following sound filmstrip sets: *Am I Worth While? Identity and Self-Image* (Guidance Associates), *The Search for Self in Literature* (Guidance Associates), *The "I" in Identity* (Encyclopaedia Britannica).

In grade 10, after reading short stories, students should delve deeply into the subject and explore widely using both print and nonprint media (see Bibliography for Independent Study: Short Story at the end of this model).

In grade 11, after reading about the theme "Contemporary American Writers Speak to Young People about Concerns of Our Own Times," students should delve deeply into the subject and explore widely essays and articles dealing with contemporary concerns, using the following indexes to identify essays and articles of both interest and substance: *Essay and General Literature Index* (Wilson), *General Science Index* (Wilson), *Humanities Index* (Wilson), *Readers' Guide to Periodical Literature* (Wilson), *Social Sciences Index* (Wilson), and *Vital Speeches of the Day* (City News).

In grade 12, after reading about "Renaissance Drama," students should have the opportunity to make an in-depth study of Shakespeare and his dramatic works. Such a study requires resources beyond the holdings of the senior high school library. A bibliography of media available in the public library should be made available to the students to facilitate their search for information on Shakespeare, the dramatist (see Bibliography for Independent Study: Shakespeare Lives! at the end of this model).

Parental Permission for Student to Read

An honors literature study program offers the student opportunities to read quality literature—classic and contemporary—of a serious and challenging nature. Prior to a student's being enrolled in an honors literature course, the parents should be requested to give their consent in writing for the student to read on an *advanced, mature* level.

BIBLIOGRAPHY: BASIC TEACHER REFERENCE BOOKS FOR LITERATURE

Anatomy of Wonder: A Critical Guide to Science Fiction ed. by Neil Barron. 2nd ed. New York: Bowker, 1981.

Banned Books by Anne Lyon Haight, rev. and enl. by Chandler B. Grannis. 4th ed. New York: Bowker, 1978.

Black Literature for High School Students by Barbara Dodds Stanford and Karima Amin. Champaign, Ill.: National Council of Teachers of English, 1978.

Creative Dramatics Handbook ed. by Harriet W. Ehrlich. Champaign, Ill.: National Council of Teachers of English, 1974.

Fantasy in Literature by John Aquino. Developments in Classroom Instruction series. Washington, D.C.: National Education Association, n.d.

Fantasy Literature: A Core Collection and Reference Guide by Marshall B. Tymn, Kenneth J. Zahorski, and Robert H. Boyer. New York: Bowker, 1979.

Films and Filmstrips for Language Arts: An Annotated Bibliography. Champaign, Ill.: National Council of Teachers of English, 1981.

Guide to Play Selection: A Selective Bibliography for Production and Study of Modern Plays ed. by Joseph Mersand. Champaign, Ill.: National Council of Teachers of English, 1975.

Guide to Post-Classical Works of Art, Literature, and Music Based on Myths of the Greeks and Romans by Ron Smith. Champaign, Ill.: National Council of Teachers of English, 1976.

Guide to World Literature ed. by Warren Carrier and Kenneth Oliver. Champaign, Ill.: National Council of Teachers of English, 1980.

Horror Literature: A Core Collection and Reference Guide by Marshall B. Tymn. New York: Bowker, 1981.

Ideas for Teaching English in the Junior High and Middle School ed. by Candy Carter and Zora M. Rashkis. Champaign, Ill.: National Council of Teachers of English, 1980.

Literature as Exploration by Louise M. Rosenblatt. 3rd ed. Champaign, Ill.: National Council of Teachers of English, 1976.

Living with Adolescent Literature ed. by Donald R. Gallo. Champaign, Ill.: National Council of Teachers of English, 1980.

Mythologies of the World: A Guide to Sources by Ron Smith. Champaign, Ill.: National Council of Teachers of English, 1981.

Paperbound Books for Young People: From Kindergarten through Grade 12. 2nd. ed. New York: Bowker, 1980.

Poetry: Reading, Writing, and Analyzing It ed. by Donald Gallo. Champaign, Ill.: National Council of Teachers of English, 1979.

Reading and Literature: American Achievement in Perspective by Alan C. Purvis. Champaign, Ill.: National Council of Teachers of English, 1979.

Science Fiction as Literature by John Aquino. Developments in Classroom Instruction series. Washington, D.C.: National Education Association, 1976.

Teaching English and the Humanities through Thematic Units by John H. Bushman and Sandra Jones. Champaign, Ill.: National Council of Teachers of English, 1979.

Teaching Fiction: Short Stories and Novels ed. by Kenneth Donelson. Champaign, Ill.: National Council of Teachers of English, 1974.

Teaching Shakespeare ed. by James E. Davis. Champaign, Ill.: National Council of Teachers of English, 1978.

Teaching the Art of Literature by Bruce E. Miller. Champaign, Ill.: National Council of Teachers of English, 1980.

Teaching the Gifted and Talented in the English Classroom by William W. West. Champaign, Ill.: National Council of Teachers of English, 1980.

Thematic Units in Teaching English and the Humanities ed. by Sylvia Spann and Mary Beth Culp. Champaign, Ill.: National Council of Teachers of English, 1975. First supp., 1977; Second supp., 1980; Third supp., 1980.

TEACHER AND STUDENT REFERENCE BOOKS

American Writers ed. by Leonard Unger. 6 vols. and supp. 1. New York: Scribner, 1974–1979.

Author Biographies Master Index. 2 vols. Detroit: Gale, 1978.

Contemporary Authors. Detroit: Gale, 1962 to date.

British Writers ed. by Ian Scott-Kilvert. 7 vols. New York: Scribner, 1979–1981.

Dictionary of Literary Biography. Detroit: Gale, 1978 to date.

European Authors, 1000–1900: A Biographical Dictionary of European Literature ed. by Stanley Kunitz and Vineta Colby. New York: Wilson, 1967.

Good Reading: A Guide for Serious Readers ed. by J. Sherwood Weber. 21st ed. New York: Bowker, 1978.

Great American Writers/One as Reported in The New York Times Sanford, N.C.: Microfilming Corporation of America, 1980.

Great American Writers/Two as Reported in The New York Times. Sanford, N.C.: Microfilming Corporation of America, 1981.

Great American Writers/Three as Reported in The New York Times. (Sanford, N.C.: Microfilming Corporation of America, 1982.

Great Books of the Western World ed. by Robert M. Hutchins and Mortimer Adler. 54 vols. Chicago: Encyclopaedia Britannica, 1952.

The Reader's Advisor: A Layman's Guide to Literature ed. by Sarah L. Prakken. 12th ed. 3 vols. New York: Bowker, 1977.

Science Fiction Writers: Critical Studies of the Major Authors from the Early Nineteenth Century to the Present Day ed. by E. F. Bleiler. New York: Scribner, 1982.

Twayne's English Authors Series Boston: G. K. Hall, 1964 to date.

Twayne's United States Authors Series. Boston: G. K. Hall, 1964 to date.

Twayne's World Authors Series. Boston: G. K. Hall, 1966 to date.

Twentieth Century Authors: A Biographical Dictionary of Modern Literature. New York: Wilson, 1942. Supp. 1955.

World Authors: 1950–1970 ed. by John Wakeman. New York: Wilson, 1975.

World Authors: 1970–1975 ed. by John Wakeman. New York: Wilson, 1979.

BIBLIOGRAPHY FOR INDEPENDENT STUDY: GREEK MYTHOLOGY

PRINT MEDIA

Art Tells a Story: Greek and Roman Myths by Penelope Proddow. New York: Doubleday, 1979.

Bullfinch's Mythology by Thomas Bullfinch. 2nd rev. ed. New York: Crowell, 1970.

Classic Myths in English Literature and Art by Charles M. Gayley. Rev. ed. New York: Wiley, 1939.

Crowell's Handbook of Classical Mythology by Edward Tripp. New York: Crowell, 1970.

Funk and Wagnalls Standard Dictionary of Folklore, Mythology, and Legend ed. by Maria Leach. New York: Funk and Wagnalls, 1972.

Gods and Mortals in Classical Mythology by Michael Grant and John Hazel. Springfield, Mass.: Merriam, 1973.

Golden Fleece and the Heroes Who Lived before Achilles by Padriac Colum. New York: Macmillan, 1962.

Greek Gods and Heroes by Robert Graves. New York: Dutton, n.d.

Greek Myths by Olivia Coolidge. Boston: Houghton, 1949.

Greek Way by Edith Hamilton. New York: Norton, 1948.

Heroes of Greece and Troy by Robert Graves. New York: Walck, 1961.

Larousse World Mythology by Pierre Grimal. New York: Putnam, 1968.

Mythologies of the World: A Concise Encyclopedia ed. by Max S. Shapiro. New York: Doubleday, 1979.

Mythology by Edith Hamilton. New York: Little, 1942.

New Century Handbook of Greek Mythology and Legend ed. by Catherine B. Avery. Englewood Cliffs, N.J.: Prentice-Hall, 1972.

New Larousse Encyclopedia of Mythology ed. by Felix Guirand. Rev. ed. New York: Putnam, 1969.

A Treasury of Edith Hamilton ed. by Doris F. Reid. New York: Norton, 1969.

Trojan War by Olivia Coolidge. Boston: Houghton, 1952.

Words from the Myths by Isaac Asimov. Boston: Houghton, 1961.

NONPRINT MEDIA: FILMSTRIPS

Greek and Roman Mythology (Encyclopaedia Britannica—6 filmstrips, 6 cassettes). Titles: *Poseidon and Athena; Psyche and Eros; Pyramus and Thisbe; Jason and the Golden Fleece; Theseus, Hero of Athens; Daedalus and Icarus.*

Greek Mythology (Coronet—6 filmstrips, 6 cassettes). Titles: *Why We Study It; Origin of the Gods; The Olympic Gods,* Parts I and II; *Lesser Gods and Spirits; Legendary Heroes.*

Heroes of the Greek Myths (Spoken Arts—4 filmstrips, 4 cassettes, 1 guide). Titles: *Hercules and the Golden Apple, The Golden Fleece, Hector and Achilles, The Cyclop's Cave.*

Heroines and Goddesses of the Greek Myths (Spoken Arts—4 filmstrips, 4 cassettes, 8 duplicating masters, 1 guide). Titles: *Atalanta, Athene and Arachne, Demeter and Persephone, Pandora.*

Monsters of the Greek Myths (Spoken Arts—4 filmstrips, 4 cassettes, 8 duplicating masters, 1 guide). Titles: *The Chimaera, The Gorgon's Head, The Minotaur, The Dragon's Teeth.*

Mythology: Gods and Goddesses (Guidance Associates—2 filmstrips, 2 cassettes or 2 records, 1 guide).

Mythology Is Alive and Well (Guidance Associates—2 filmstrips, 2 cassettes or 2 records, 1 guide).

NONPRINT MEDIA: MOTION PICTURES

Note: Motion pictures, as well as other nonprint media, should be available for individual student viewing.)

The Greek Myths Parts I and II (Encyclopaedia Britannica).

BIBLIOGRAPHY FOR INDEPENDENT STUDY: POETRY

PRINT MEDIA: ANTHOLOGIES, GUIDES, AND HANDBOOKS

Contemporary American Poetry by A. Poulin, Jr. Boston: Houghton, 1975.

The Dark Tower: 19th Century Narrative Poetry ed. by Dairine Coffey. Great Neck, N.Y.: Core Collection, 1979.

The New Poets: American and British Poetry since World War II by M. L. Rosenthal. New York: Oxford, 1967.

The Oxford Book of American Light Verse. New York: Oxford, 1979.

The Oxford Book of American Verse. New York: Oxford, 1950.

The Oxford Book of Ballads. New York: Oxford, 1973.

The Oxford Book of Light Verse. New York: Oxford, 1979.

The Oxford Book of Modern Verse. New York: Oxford, 1936.

The Oxford Book of Nineteenth-Century English Verse. New York: Oxford, 1964.

The Oxford Book of Twentieth-Century English Verse. New York: Oxford, 1973.

Poetry Handbook by Babette Deutsch. 4th ed. New York: Funk and Wagnalls, 1974.

The Poetry of Black America: Anthology of the Twentieth Century ed. by Arnold Adoff. New York: Macmillan, 1969.

Reflections on a Gift of Watermelon Pickle and Other Modern Verse ed. by Stephen Dunning et al. New York: Lothrop, 1966.

Settling America: The Ethnic Expression of Fourteen Contemporary Poets ed. by David Kherdian. New York: Macmillan, 1974.

Some Haystacks Don't Even Have Any Needle: And Other Complete Modern Poems ed. by Stephen Dunning et al. New York: Lothrop, 1969.

Understanding Poetry by Cleanth Brooks and Robert Penn Warren. New York: Holt, 1976.

Western Wind: An Introduction to Poetry by John Frederick Nims. New York: Random, 1974.

The World Split Open: Four Centuries of Women Poets in England and America ed. by Louise Bernikow. Random, 1974.

NONPRINT MEDIA: FILMSTRIPS

America! The Poetry of a Nation (Guidance Associates—2 filmstrips, 2 cassettes or 2 records, 1 guide)

Carl Sandburg (Encyclopaedia Britannica—1 filmstrip, 1 cassette)

e. e. cummings (Encyclopaedia Britannica—1 filmstrip, 1 cassette)

Edgar Allan Poe (Encyclopaedia Britannica—1 filmstrip, 1 cassette)

Henry Wadsworth Longfellow (Encyclopaedia Britannica—1 filmstrip, 1 cassette)

Marianne Moore (Encyclopaedia Britannica—1 filmstrip, 1 cassette)

Langston Hughes (Encyclopaedia Britannica—1 filmstrip, 1 cassette)

Poetry (Guidance Associates—3 filmstrips, 3 cassettes or 3 records, 1 guide)

Poetry Classics (Educational Enrichment Materials—each set 4 filmstrips, 4 cassettes). Set I: *Paul Revere's Ride* (Longfellow), *The Pied Piper of Hamelin* (Browning), *The Raven* (Poe), *The Walrus and The Carpenter: The Gardener's Song* (Carroll). Set V: *Lyrics from the Plays of Shakespeare* (Shakespeare), *Two Romantic Views of Scotland* (Burns and Scott), *Walt Whitman: A Poet's Journey, Daffodils* (Wordsworth).

Robert Frost, (Encyclopaedia Britannica—1 filmstrip, 1 cassette)

Spoon River Anthology: Selected Poems (Coronet—2 filmstrips, 2 cassettes)

BIBLIOGRAPHY FOR INDEPENDENT STUDY: SHORT STORY

Good Reading: A Guide for Serious Readers ed. by J. Sherwood Weber, 21st ed. (New York: Bowker, 1978), is a standard guide used in college and public libraries since 1932. It is particularly useful for advanced placement and independent study courses in high school. This standard guide will serve as an introduction to your independent study of the short story. (Note that this annotated bibliography differs from most standard listings in that it contains author birth/death dates as well as other data in an unusual form.) Read the introductory essay "The Short Story" by Arthur Zeiger in *Good Reading*, pp. 125–126; then select from the recommended titles those anthologies and works by individual authors you wish to explore.

ANTHOLOGIES

There are countless good paperbound (P) and hardcover (H) anthologies of short stories old and new. Listed below are a few representative titles.

44 Irish Short Stories (1955). An excellent anthology edited by Devin Garrity: from Yeats and Joyce to O'Connor, O'Faolain, and McLaverty. H—Devin.

French Stories and Tales (1954). Representative collection from Balzac and Flaubert to Gide. P—WSP.

Great American Short Stories (1959). From Poe to the 1950s. P—Dell.

Great English Short Stories (1959). A representative collection. P—Dell.

Great German Short Novels and Stories (1952). Fifteen stories and short novels, including Goethe's *Sorrows of Young Werther* and Mann's *Death in Venice*. H—Modern Lib.

Great Russian Short Stories (1959). A stimulating and representative collection. P—Dell.

Great Spanish Short Stories (1959). Another good assortment. P—Dell.

INDIVIDUAL AUTHORS

Aleichem, Sholom (Shalom Rabinowitz). 1859–1916. *Stories and Satires*. The "Jewish Mark Twain," Aleichem writes with understanding, compassion, and love about the Yiddish-speaking Jews of Eastern Europe.

Babel, Isaac. 1894–1938. *Collected Stories* (1955). Stories of civil war and of Russian life before and after the Revolution by a Russian master believed to have died in a concentration camp. P—NAL.

Barth, John. b. 1930. *Lost in the Funhouse* (1968). Witty, technically adroit, occasionally overingenious but immensely enjoyable nevertheless. H—Doubleday; P—Bantam, G&D.

Barthelme, Donald. b. 1933. *Unspeakable Practices, Unnatural Acts* (1968). Brilliant, often surreal fragments by a satirist who is also an extraordinary stylist: perfect sentences, words that "twitter, bong, flash and glow signals of exquisite distress." H—FS&G: P—PB.

Benét, Stephen Vincent. 1898–1943. *Selected Works* (1960). Colorful, romantic stories dealing mostly with America's past. H—HR&W.

Bierce, Ambrose. 1842–1914. *In the Midst of Life* (1898). Sardonic sketches of soldiers and civilians in the terrifying world of our Civil War and after. P–NAL.

Bradbury, Ray. b. 1920. *The Golden Apples of the Sun* (1953). One of several first-rate collections of tales of fantasy and science fiction by a master of the genre. H—Greenwood; P—Bantam.

Caldwell, Erskine. b. 1903. *Complete Stories* (1953). Tales of ribald humor, social protest, and tragedy. H—Little.

Capote, Truman. b. 1924. *The Grass Harp and A Tree of Night and Other Stories* (1950). Nebulous, haunting stories. P—NAL.

Cheever, John. b. 1912. *The Enormous Room* (1953), *The Housebreaker of Shady Hill* (1958), and *The Brigadier and the Golf Widow* (1964). Wry commentaries on individual and societal manners in contemporary American metropolis, suburbia, and exurbia. o.p.

Chekhov, Anton. 1860–1904. *Short Stories*. Carefully wrought, skeptical commentaries on Russian life and character. Chekhov's indirect, implicational narrative technique has profoundly influenced 20th-century fiction.

Colette (Sidonie Gabrielle Colette). 1873–1954. *My Mother's House* (1953). Reminiscences of childhood by one of the most celebrated French writers of this century. P—FS&G.

Conrad, Joseph. 1857–1924. *Stories*. The master of the sea story is equally the master of the psychological tale. Incisive probings into the dark places of the human psyche.

Coover, Robert. b. 1932. *Pricksongs and Descants* (1969). Biblical episodes, myths, and fairy tales transmuted by psychological realism into startling and intriguing modern stories. P—NAL.

Coppard, A. E. 1878–1957. *Collected Tales* (1948). The major work of a British master, ranging from naturalism to fantasy to symbolism. H—Bks for Libs.

Crane, Stephen. 1871–1900. *Stories*. Narratives by a pioneer of realism in America.

De la Mare, Walter. 1873–1956. *Stories*. Fascinated by the "twilight side of life," de la Mare created stories and tales of an unforgettable world of fantasy, dreams, and the supernatural.

Dinesen, Isak (Baronesse Karen Blixen). 1885–1962. *Seven Gothic Tales* (1934). Jewel-like, richly embroidered tales of a romantic past peopled by cavaliers, maidens, and ghosts. P—Random.

Farrell, James T. b. 1904. *Stories*. Stories of 20th-century urban America by the author of *Studs Lonigan*. H—Vanguard.

Faulkner, William. 1897–1962. *Stories*. Richly varied short fiction ranging in time from the early settling of Mississippi to post–World War II days, by a master of form, subtlety, symbolism, and psychological insight. H—Modern Lib, Random.

Fitzgerald, F. Scott. 1896–1940. *Stories* (1951). Gay and tragic stories by the spokesman for the Jazz Age. H & P—Scribner.

Forster, E. M. 1879–1970. *The Celestial Omnibus* (1911). Graceful, witty, delightful exercises in fantasy. P—Random.

Gass, William. b. 1924. *In the Heart of the Heart of the Country* (1968). Diverse and remarkable "experimental" stories—ranging from a dispassionate recording of correlatives of pain to the earthy interior monologue of a "latter-day Molly Bloom." H—Har-Row; P—PB.

Gogol, Nicolai V. 1809–1952. *The Overcoat and Other Tales of Good and Evil* (1957). Seven stories, all enormously important in the development of modern fiction: grotesques, moralities, acute psychological revelations, biting satires. H—Norton.

Hawthorne, Nathaniel. 1804–1864. *Stories and Tales.* Deeply symbolic and carefully wrought studies of sin and retribution and romantic tales of colonial New England, by a master who helped establish the form as a serious literary type.

Hemingway, Ernest. 1899–1961. *Short Stories.* Various collections of the short fiction by one of the most significant, influential, and controversial writers of our time. H & P—Scribner.

Henry, O. (William Sydney Porter). 1862–1910. *Short Stories.* Ingenious, swiftly paced, skillfully plotted trick- or surprise-ending stories by a most widely read and imitated practitioner.

Irving, Washington. 1783–1859. *Sketch Book* (1820). Warmly colored, romanticized sketches, tales, and essays, such as "Rip Van Winkle" and "Legend of Sleepy Hollow." H—Dodd, Dutton; P—NAL.

Jackson, Shirley. 1919–1965. *The Lottery* (1949). Terrifying and macabre vignettes of the tensions underlying contemporary life. P—Popular Lib.

James, Henry. 1843–1916. *Short Stories.* Intricate analyses of conflicting personalities and their psychological and emotional reactions by a consummate craftsman.

Joyce, James. 1882–1941. *Dubliners* (1914). Joyce sought his material in the lives of insignificant people in "dear, dirty Dublin." Rich in insight, subtly symbolic, essentially simple in structure, *Dubliners* is a towering landmark in the evolution of the short story. H—Modern Lib, Viking Pr; P—Viking Pr.

Kafka, Franz. 1883–1924. *Selected Short Stories.* Strikingly existentialist commentaries on the meaninglessness of modern life presented in terms of grotesque imagery and surrealistic symbols. P—Modern Lib.

Kipling, Rudyard. 1865–1936. *Stories.* One of the last of the great romantics ranges from the hill towns of India to the jungles of Mowgli, Kaa, and Rikki-Tikki-Tavi.

Lardner, Ring. 1885–1933. *Best Short Stories.* Satirical tales—sometimes humorous, often bitter—debunking hypocrisy in American life. P—Scribner.

Lawrence, D. H. 1885–1930. *Complete Short Stories* (1961). Lawrence's "religion of the blood" animates these vigorous and provocative stories of confrontations between man and woman, child and adult. P—Viking Pr 3 vols.

London, Jack. 1876–1919. *Stories.* Narratives of violence, action, and atmosphere, set from the Far North to the South Seas.

Malamud, Bernard. b. 1914. *The Magic Barrel* (1958) and *Idiots First* (1963). Ironic, highly individualistic stories of American Jews at home and abroad, tempered by nostalgia for the Jewish past. H—FS&G: P—FS&G, PB.

Mann, Thomas. 1875–1955. *Stories of Three Decades.* Masterly, lengthy short stories on themes ranging from the adolescent to the artist. H—Knopf.

Mansfield, Katherine. 1888–1923. *Stories.* Penetrating character studies in the Chekhov manner, and impressionistic portraits of situations. H—Collins-World, Knopf; P—Random.

Maugham, W. Somerset. 1874–1965. *Complete Short Stories.* Dramatic accounts by a popular raconteur, mostly dealing with strange people in faraway places. P—WSP 4 vols.

Maupassant, Guy de. 1850–1893. *Stories.* Realistic impressions of French life, deftly constructed and brilliantly ironic.

Melville, Herman. 1819–1891. *Stories.* Impressive provocative tales.

Mishima, Yukio. 1925–1970. *Death in Midsummer and Other Stories* (1966). Frequently sensational but riveting tales by the Japanese writer who has made the deepest impress on the West. P—New Directions.

O'Connor, Flannery. 1925–1964. *A Good Man Is Hard to Find* (1955) and *Everything That Rises Must Converge* (1965). Artistry, social awareness, the grotesque, and the need for faith characterize these stories of the contemporary South. First title: H—HarBraceJ; P—Doubleday. Second title: H & P—FS&G.

O'Connor, Frank. 1903–1966. *Stories*. (1952). Humor, insight, and satire mark these representative stories by a leading Irish writer. H—Knopf.

O'Faolain, Sean. b. 1900. *Short Stories* (1961). Effective narratives about contemporary Ireland. P—Little.

O'Hara, John. 1905–1970. *Short Stories*. Social satire of individual and societal absurdities. P—Popular Lib.

Poe, Edgar Allan. 1809–1849. *Tales*. Memorable stories of atmosphere, horror, and ratiocination by a founder and master of short fiction.

Porter, Katherine Anne. b. 1894. *Stories*. Beautifully wrought and subtle narratives of varied moods, themes, and settings. H—HarBraceJ; P—NAL.

Pritchett, V. S. b. 1900. *The Sailor, Sense of Humor, and Other Stories* (1956). Mostly about the double lives of middle-class Britishers tormented by changing social forces. o.p.

Purdy, James. b. 1923. *Color of Darkness* (1957) and *Children Is All* (1962). Misfits trapped in a purgatory of the unloved, the unwanted, and the alienated, by an outstanding "black humorist." P—New Directions.

Roth, Philip. b. 1933. *Goodbye, Columbus, and Five Short Stories* (1959). Roth writes with irony and understanding about the American Jew in a variety of settings ranging from army training camp to big city. H—Modern Lib.

Saki (H. H. Munro). 1870–1916. *The Best of Saki* (1961). Sophisticated treatment of affectations of English society; short-short stories of fantasy and surprise with an undercurrent of serious commentary. P—Viking Pr.

Salinger, J. D. b. 1919. *Nine Stories* (1953). Perceptive depiction of problems of children and child-like adults, narrated with warmth, understanding, and sympathy. H—Little; P—Bantam.

Saroyan, William. b. 1908. *My Name Is Aram* (1940). Fresh and exuberant stories of a young Armenian in Fresno, California. H—HarBraceJ; P—Dell.

Singer, Isaac Bashevis. b. 1904. *Gimpel the Fool & Other Stories* (1957) and *The Spinoza of Market Street* (1961). Marvelous stories, rooted deep in folk memory, intensely real even when the theme is supernatural. First title: H—FS&G. Second title: H—FS&G; P—Avon.

Stafford, Jean. b. 1915. *Collected Stories*. (1966). Disturbing depictions of neuroses in contemporary American life enlivened by occasional humorous stories of "bad" characters in Colorado. H & P—FS&G.

Steinbeck, John. b. 1902–1968. *The Long Valley* (1938). Powerful short fiction about the American West. P—Bantam, Viking Pr.

Thomas, Dylan. 1914–1953. *Adventures in the Skin Trade* (1955). Includes individualistic short stories and sketches, employing melodrama, fantasy, humor, and surrealism. P—NAL, New Directions.

Thurber, James. 1894–1961. *The Thurber Carnival* (1945). Selections from an American humorist, one of the best of our time, whose warmth and insight are tempered by a gratifying malice. H—Har-Row, Modern Lib; P—Dell, Har-Row.

Turgenev, Ivan. 1818–1883. *Sketches from a Hunter's Album* (1852). Enormously influential and absorbing stories in which plot evolves from character, naturally and convincingly. P—Penguin.

Twain, Mark (Samuel L. Clemens). 1835–1910. *Stories*. Collections of the shorter works of America's greatest humorist.

Updike, John. b. 1932. *Pigeon Feathers and Other Stories* (1962), *The Music School* (1966), and *Museums and Women* (1972). The often engaging stories of a talented and prolific writer, sometimes a bit slick but always crafted, intelligent, and genuinely perceptive. H—Knopf; P—Fawcett World.

Verga, Giovanni. 1840–1922. *She Wolf and Other Stories*. Highly skillful reconstructions of Sicilian life in the 1860s. P—U of Cal Pr.

Welty, Eudora. *Stories*. Sensitive, masterly worked tales about contemporary Mississippi. H—HarBraceJ, Modern Lib; P—HarBraceJ.

Wodehouse, P. G. 1881–1976. *Most of P. G. Wodehouse* (1969). A generous sampling of the hilarious effects achieved by intricate plotting and soufflé dialogue. Psmith, Jeeves, Bertie Wooster, and Mr. Mulliner are maybe stock characters but surely enduring ones. H & P—S&S.

Wolfe, Thomas. 1900–1938. *The Hills Beyond* (1941). Semiautobiographical stories reminiscent of his loose novels but more carefully and economically written. H—Har-Row; P—NAL.

Wright, Richard. 1908–1960. *Uncle Tom's Children* (1938) and *Eight Men* (1961). Relentlessly honest, moving accounts of the black experience in a hostile white world. First title: H & P—Har-Row. Second title: P—Pyramid Pubns.

SHORT STORY ANALYSIS

Using the Correlation Chart I as a model, design your own analysis form (see p. 348). Use the analysis form to summarize the various short stories you have read.

FILM ADAPTATIONS

The American Short Story Filmstrip Collection offers nine excellent adaptations of the award-winning film series first screened on Public Broadcasting Service (PBS) (Coronet—each 2 filmstrips, 2 cassettes, 4 reproducible masters, 1 guide):
Parker Adderson, Philosopher
The Blue Hotel
The Jolly Corner
I'm a Fool
Bernice Bobs Her Hair
Soldier's Home
Almos' a Man
The Displaced Person
The Music School

Use the American Short Story Filmstrip Program Correlation Chart II as an index to the contents of the nine short stories listed above (see p. 349).

BIBLIOGRAPHY FOR INDEPENDENT STUDY: SHAKESPEARE LIVES!*

CHARACTERS

Burton, Philip. [r 822.33 G9] *The Sole Voice: Character Portraits from Shakespeare*. Dial Press, N.Y., 1970.

Coe, Charles Norton. [822.33 G39] *Shakespeare's Villains*. Bookman Associates, N.Y., 1957.

Jameson, Anna Brownell. [r 822.33 Ga] *Shakespeare's Heroines: Characteristics of Women, Moral, Poetical, and Historical*. Dent, London, 1904.

Jones, Ernest. [circ. 822.33 S8993] [r 822.33 S896] *Hamlet and Oedipus*. Doubleday, N.Y., 1949.

Rosenberg, Marvin. [PR 2819 .R65] *The Masks of King Lear*. University of California Pr., Berkeley, 1972.

Wilson, John Dover. [822.33 G31] *The Fortunes of Falstaff*. Cambridge University Pr., Cambridge, 1964.

Wilson, John Dover. [822.33 S8993a2] *What Happens in Hamlet*. Cambridge University Pr., Cambridge, 1970.

CONCORDANCES, ENCYCLOPEDIAS, HANDBOOKS AND BIBLIOGRAPHIES

Alden, Raymond MacDonald. [r 822.33 D9995] *A Shakespeare Handbook*. F.S. Crofts & Co., N.Y., 1932. This particular handbook is concerned with the 19 plays usually studied

*This bibliography was prepared and distributed by the Carnegie Library of Pittsburgh, a free public library maintained by the City of Pittsburgh and County of Allegheny, with supplemental appropriations from the State of Pennsylvania. The bracketed numbers throughout indicate call numbers of the Carnegie Library, which will facilitate student access to materials. Students should become aware that call numbers are not interchangeable from one library to another.

CORRELATION CHART I*

Title	Author	Historical Period	Region/ Community	Alienation (Individual vs. Group)	Death	Adolescent Rite of Passage	Midlife Crisis	War/ Aftermath	Prejudice	Irony	Cultural Change	Violence

*Adapted from Coronet K–12 Catalog, 1982 (Chicago: Coronet), p. 31.

CORRELATION CHART II: AMERICAN SHORT STORY FILMSTRIP PROGRAM*

Title	Author	Historical Period	Region/ Community	Alienation (Individual vs. Group)	Death	Adolescent Rite of Passage	Midlife Crisis	War/ Aftermath	Prejudice	Irony	Cultural Change	Violence
Parker Adderson, Philosopher	Ambrose Bierce	Civil War	Rural South		•		•	•				•
The Blue Hotel	Stephen Crane	1880's	Nebraska Frontier Town	•					•	•		•
The Jolly Corner	Henry James	1900's	New York City	•			•				•	
I'm a Fool	Sherwood Anderson	1919	Small Town Ohio			•						
Bernice Bobs Her Hair	F. Scott Fitzgerald	1920's	Midwest Suburban			•				•		
Soldier's Home	Ernest Hemingway	Post WWI	Midwest Small Town	•		•		•				
Almos' a Man	Richard Wright	Depression	Rural South	•		•			•			•
The Displaced Person	Flannery O'Connor	Late 1940's	Rural Georgia						•	•		•
The Music School	John Updike	Early 1960's	Affluent Suburb				•				•	

*Coronet K–12 Catalog, 1982 (Chicago: Coronet), p. 31.

in high school and college, "and by other mature, but not learned readers." Alden, late professor of English at Stanford University, divides his studies into linguistic understanding of Shakespeare's English and historical sources of these plays.

Bartlett, John. [rq PR 2892 .B34 1953x] *A Complete Concordance or Verbal Index to Words, Phrases and Passages in the Dramatic Works of Shakespeare with a Supplementary Concordance to the Poems.* Macmillan, London, 1953.

Evans, Gareth L. [PR 2894 .E83x] *The Shakespeare Companion.* Scribners, N.Y., 1978.

Halliday, Frank Ernest. [822.33 HZ2] *A Shakespeare Companion 1564–1964.* Schocken Books, N.Y., 1964. Another copy is available in the Reference Department.

Jaggard, William. [r 822.33 A5] *Shakespeare Bibliography: A Dictionary of Every Known Issue of the Writings of Our National Poet and of Recorded Opinion Thereon in the English Language, with Historical Introduction.* Stratford-on-Avon, Shakespeare Pr., 1911.

O'Connor, Evangeline M.J. [PR 2892 .044] *Who's Who and What's What in Shakespeare.* Avenel Books, N.Y., 1978.

Smith, Gordon Ross. [rq Z 8811 .S64] *A Classified Shakespeare Bibliography.* 1936–1958. Pennsylvania State University Press, University Park, 1963.

Spevack, Marvin. [rq PR 2892 .S6] *A Complete and Systematic Concordance to the Works of Shakespeare.* Hildesheim, Georg Olms, 1968–70, 6 v.

Wells, Stanley W. [r Z 8811 .W44] *Shakespeare: Select Bibliographical Guides* ed. by Stanley Wells. Oxford University Pr., London, 1973.

EDITIONS

Bartlett, Henrietta C. [r 822.33 A13] *Mr. William Shakespeare: Original and Early Editions of His Quartos and Folios, His Source Books and Those Containing Contemporary Notices.* Yale University Pr., New Haven, 1922.

Bartlett, Henrietta C., and Alfred W. Pollard. [qr 822.33 A18] *A Census of Shakespeare's Plays in Quarto, 1594–1709,* rev. and extended. Yale University Pr., New Haven, 1939.

Evans, Gwynne Blakemore, ed. [r PR 2754 .E9 1974b] *The Riverside Shakespeare.* Houghton Mifflin, Boston, 1974. Collected works of Shakespeare with "re-edited text, generally modern in spelling and punctuation."

Furness, Horace Howard, ed. [qr 822.33 J] *New Variorum Edition of Shakespeare.* Lippincott, N.Y., 1880–1944, 27 v.

Kozlenko, William, ed. [PR 2851 .K6] *Disputed Plays of William Shakespeare.* Hawthorn Books, N.Y., 1974. An anthology of plays possibly written by Shakespeare.

Martin, Michael Rheta, and Richard C. Harriet. [r PR 2898 .M39] *The Concise Encyclopedic Guide to Shakespeare.* Horizon Pr., N.Y., 1971.

Rowse, A.L. [rq PR 2754 .R67] *The Annotated Shakespeare.* Crown, N.Y., 1978, 3 v.

Shakespeare, William. [PR 2754 .R67] *The Complete Works of Shakespeare.* Hardin Craig, ed. Scott, Foresman & Co., Glenview, Ill., 1973.

Shakespeare, William. [PR 2848 .A2 B6 1978x] *Shakespeare's Sonnets,* edited with analytic commentary by Stephen Booth. Yale University Pr., New Haven, Conn., 1977.

LANGUAGE AND VERSIFICATION

Ellis, Alexander John. [r 421.5 E53] *On Early English Pronunciation with Especial Reference to Shakespeare and Chaucer* . . . Asher & Trubner, London, 1869–89, 5 v. in 3.

Gordon, George Stuart. [r 420.6 S67 no. 29] *Shakespeare's English.* Clarendon Pr., Oxford, 1928.

Ness, Frederick William. [r 822.33 HA 5] *The Use of Rhyme in Shakespeare's Plays.* Oxford University Pr., London, 1941.

SHAKESPEAREAN TIMES

Akrigg, G.P.V. [942.06 A31] *Jacobean Pageant or the Court of King James I.* Harvard University Pr., Cambridge, Mass., 1962.

Brown, Ivor. [822.33 HN 24] *Shakespeare and His World.* Henry Z. Walck, N.Y., 1964.

Brown, Ivor. [822.33 HN 20] *Shakespeare in His Time.* Nelson, Edinburgh, 1960.

Halliday, F.E. [822.33 HN 21] *Shakespeare in His Age.* Thomas Yoseloff, N.Y., 1956.

Rowse, A.L. [DA 356 .R65 1978] *The England of Elizabeth: The Structure of Society.* University of Wisconsin Pr., Madison, 1950. Reprinted 1978.

Shakespeare's England: An Account of the Life and Manners of His Age. 2 v. [822.33 HN 12] Clarendon Press, Oxford, 1916.

Smith, Lacey Baldwin. [q 940.5 S65a] *The Horizon Book of the Elizabethan World.* American Heritage Publishing Co., N.Y., 1967.

Tillyard, E.M.W. [820.9 T46] *The Elizabethan World Picture.* Macmillan, N.Y., 1944.

Wilson, John Dover. [822.33 HN 19a] *Life in Shakespeare's England, a Book of Elizabethan Prose.* Barnes & Noble, N.Y., 1969.

THE AUTHORSHIP CONTROVERSY

Gibson, H.N. [822.33 AB 29] *The Shakespeare Claimants: A Critical Survey of the Four Principal Theories Concerning the Authorship of the Shakespeare Plays.* Barnes & Noble, N.Y., 1962.

Grebanier, Bernard. [822.33 EA 2] *The Great Shakespeare Forgery.* W.W. Norton, N.Y., 1965.

Hoffman, Calvin. [822.33 AB 20a] *The Murder of the Man Who Was 'Shakespeare.'* Grosset & Dunlap. N.Y., 1960. "This is the book which proves almost beyond a shadow of a doubt that Christopher Marlowe is the author of the plays and poems attributed to the actor-businessman named William Shakespeare"—from the preface.

Sweet, George Elliott. [PR 2947 .E6 S9 1963] *Shake-speare, the Mystery.* Neville Spearman, London, 1963.

Wadsworth, Frank W. [822.33 AB 24] *The Poacher from Stratford; a Partial Account of the Controversy Over the Authorship of Shakespeare's Plays.* University of California Pr., Berkeley, 1958.

THE ELIZABETHAN STAGE

Bradbrook, Muriel C. *The Living Monument: Shakespeare and the Theatre of His Time.* Cambridge University Pr., London, 1976.

Chambers, E.K. [792 C35e] *The Elizabethan Stage.* Oxford University Pr., London, 1950.

Gurr, Andrew. [792 .0942 G97] *The Shakespearean Stage: 1574–1642.* Cambridge University Pr., Cambridge, 1970.

Harbage, Alfred. [822.33 HL 18] *Shakespeare's Audience.* Columbia University Pr., N.Y., 1941.

Harrison, G.B. [822.09 H29] *Elizabethan Plays and Players.* Routledge & Sons, London, 1940.

Hodges, C. Walter. [792 H664a] *The Globe Restored.* Coward-McCann, N.Y., 1968.

Holmes, Martin R. [PR 2995 .H56 1972x] *Shakespeare and His Players.* Scribners, N.Y., 1972.

Hotson, Leslie. [792 H82s] *Shakespeare's Wooden O: A Study of Theatres in Shakespeare's Day.* Rupert Hart-Davis, London, 1959.

Lawrence, William J. [792 L42pr2] *Pre-Restoration Stage Studies.* Benjamin Blom, N.Y., 1967.

Lawrence, William J. [792 L42t2] *Those Nut-cracking Elizabethans: Studies of the Early Theatre and Drama.* Haskell House, N.Y., 1969.

Salgado, Gamini, ed. [PR 3091 .E95] *Eyewitnesses of Shakespeare: First Hand Accounts of Performances, 1590–1890.* Barnes & Noble, N.Y., 1975.

Sprague, Arthur Colby. [822.33 HL19] *Shakespeare and the Actors: The Stage Business in His Plays (1660–1905).* Harvard University Pr., Cambridge, Mass., 1945.

Styan, J.L. [822.33 HL 40] *Shakespeare's Stagecraft.* Cambridge University Pr., Cambridge, Mass., 1967.

Thorndike, Ashley H. [792 T39] *Shakespeare's Theater.* Macmillan, N.Y., 1962.

Whanslaw, H.W. [792 W59] *The Bankside Stage Book.* Wells Gardner, Darton & Co., London, 1924. ". . . for those who would like to have a practical model of a Tudor playhouse in which they can produce in miniature their Shakespeare, Jonson. . . ."

BIOGRAPHY

Burgess, Anthony. [PR 2894 B79 1972] *Shakespeare.* Penguin Books, Baltimore, 1972. Shakespeare for Everyman; beautifully and profusely illustrated.

Chute, Marchette. [822.33 B45] *Shakespeare of London.* Dutton, N.Y., 1949. The introduction to Shakespeare for two generations of school children.

Fido, Martin. [q PR 2894 .F45 1978bx] *Shakespeare*. Hammond, Inc., Maplewood, N.J., 1978.

Fraser, Antonia. [DA 391 .F7 1975x] *King James IV of Scotland, I of England*. Knopf, N.Y., 1975.

Fraser, Antonia, ed. [DA 28.1 .L58 1975bx] *The Lives of the Kings and Queens of England*. Knopf, N.Y., 1975.

Fraser, Antonia. [92 M439fr] *Mary Queen of Scots*. Delacorte, N.Y., 1969.

Gardner, John C. [PR 1905 .G3] *The Life and Times of Chaucer*. Knopf, N.Y., 1977.

Greenblatt, Stephen. [PR 2335 .G7] *Sir Walter Raleigh: The Renaissance Man and His Roles*. Yale University Pr., New Haven, Conn., 1973.

Jenkins, Elizabeth. [92 E485j] *Elizabeth the Great*. Coward-McCann, N.Y., 1959.

Lacey, Robert. [DA 86.22 .R2 L3 1974x] *Sir Walter Raleigh*. Atheneum, N.Y., 1974.

Murry, John Middleton. [822.33 D9998a] *Shakespeare*. Jonathan Cape, London, 1936.

Neale, John E. [92 E485m3] *Queen Elizabeth I*. Jonathan Cape, London, 1958.

Quennell, Peter. [822.33 B54] *Shakespeare, A Biography*. World Publishing Co., Cleveland, Ohio, 1963.

Ross Williamson, Hugh. [PR 2673 .R66 1973] *Kind Kit: An Informal Biography of Christopher Marlowe*. St. Martin's Press. N.Y., 1972.

Rowse, A.L. [q PR 2894 .R66 1977b] *Shakespeare the Elizabethan*. G.P. Putnam's Sons, N.Y., 1977. Easy reading; profusely illustrated.

Rowse, A.L. [PR 2894 .R6x] *Shakespeare the Man*. Harper & Row, N.Y., 1973. It is in this volume that Rowse reveals the identity of the Dark Lady of the Sonnets. Interesting and very readable.

Rowse, A.L. [822.33 B53] *William Shakespeare*. Harper & Row, N.Y., 1963.

Schoenbaum, Samuel. [PR 2894 .S33 1977] *William Shakespeare, a Compact Documentary Life*. Oxford University Pr., N.Y., 1977.

Smith, Lacey Baldwin. [DA 355 .S59] *Elizabeth Tudor: Portrait of a Queen*. Little, Brown & Co., Boston, 1975.

Van Doren, Mark. [822.33 D103] *Shakespeare*. Holt, N.Y., 1939.

Williams, Neville. [DA 355 .W4816 1972] *All the Queens Men: Elizabeth I and Her Courtiers*. Macmillan, N.Y., 1972.

Williams, Neville. [92 E485ws] *Elizabeth the First, Queen of England*. Dutton, N.Y., 1968.

Williams, Neville. [92 H4516w] *Henry VIII and His Court*. Macmillan, N.Y., 1971.

CRITICISM AND INTERPRETATION, SERIALS

Boas, Frederick Samuel. *Aspects of Classical Legend and History in Shakespeare*. Milford, London, 1943. Proceedings of the British Academy.

Bradley, A.C. [822.33 D13] *Shakespearean Tragedy*. Macmillan, London, 1960.

Bromley, John C. [PR 2982 .B7] *The Shakespearean Kings: A Study in Political Drama*. Colorado Associated University Pr., Boulder, Colo., 1971.

Campbell, Lily B. [PR 2983 .C3 1973x] *Shakespeare's Tragic Heroes: Slaves of Passion*. Peter Smith, Gloucester, Mass., 1973.

Chambers, E.K. [822.33 D88] *William Shakespeare: A Study of Facts and Problems*. 2 vols. Clarendon Press, Oxford, 1930.

Coles, Blanche. [822.33 G38] *Shakespeare's Four Giants: Hamlet, Macbeth, Othello and King Lear*. Richard R. Smith, Rindge, N.H., 1957.

Faber, Melvin D. [r 822.33 HC10] *The Design Within: Psychoanalytical Approaches to Shakespeare*. Science House, N.Y., 1970.

Granville-Barker, Harley. [PR 2976 .G668 1974] *More Prefaces to Shakespeare*. Princeton University Pr., Princeton, 1974.

Granville-Barker, Harley. [822.33 D81a] *Preface to Shakespeare*. 2 vols., Batsford, London, 1961; 1964. Also available in Reference Department.

Granville-Barker, Harley, and G.B. Harrison. [822.33 D998] *A Companion to Shakespeare Studies*. Cambridge University Pr., Cambridge, 1934.

Hankins, John Erskine. [PR 2072 .H35 1967x] *Shakespeare's Derived Imagery*. Octagon Books, N.Y., 1967.

Harrison, G.B. [822.33 D135] *Shakespeare's Tragedies*. Oxford University Pr., N.Y., 1956.

Keeton, George Williams. [r 822.33 HC9] *Shakespeare's Legal and Political Background*. Pitman, London, 1967.

Knight, G. Wilson. [822.33 D111a] *The Crown of Life; Essays in Interpretation of Shake-speare's Final Plays.* Methuen, London, 1961.

Knight, G. Wilson. [822.33 D96a2] *The Imperial Theme: Further Interpretations of Shake-speare's Tragedies Including the Roman Plays.* Methuen, London, 1961.

Knight, G. Wilson. [822.33 Y87] *The Mutual Flame: On Shakespeare's Sonnets and "The Phoenix and the Turtle."* Methuen, London, 1955.

Knight, G. Wilson. [822.33 D90ac] *The Wheel of Fire: Interpretations of Shakespearean Tragedy.* Methuen, London, 1965.

Kott, Jan. [822.33 D194] *Shakespeare, Our Contemporary.* Doubleday, N.Y., 1964.

Lawrence, William W. [822.33 D89a] *Shakespeare's Problem Comedies.* Frederick Ungar, N.Y., 1960.

Moulton, Richard Green. [r 822.33 HJ] *Moral System of Shakespeare.* Macmillan, N.Y., 1907.

Muir, Kenneth, and Samuel Schoenbaum. *A New Companion to Shakespeare Studies.* Cambridge University Pr., Cambridge, 1971.

Partridge, Eric. [r 822.33 HJ3] *Shakespeare's Bawdy: A Literary and Psychological Essay and a Comprehensive Glossary.* Dutton, N.Y., 1948.

Payne, Pierre Stephen Robert. [PR 2894 .P35 1980] *By Me, William Shakespeare,* Everest House, N.Y., 1980.

Rossiter, A.P. [822.33 D171] *Angel with Horns, and Other Shakespeare Lectures.* Theatre Arts Books, N.Y., 1961.

Schoenbaum, Samuel. [PR 2894 .S3] *Shakespeare's Lives.* Oxford University Pr., N.Y., 1970. Scholarly, impressive; a classic.

Shakespeare Association. [r 822.33 HP2] London, 1917–1938 (Papers, no. 1–4, 6–22).

Shakespeare Studies. [r 822.33 HP3] [822.33 HP] v. 1 (1965)–date.

Shakespeare Survey. [r 822.33 D27] [822.33 D119] v. 1 (1948)–date.

Siegel, Paul N., ed. [822.33 D190] *His Infinite Variety: Major Shakespearean Criticism since Johnson.* Lippincott, Philadelphia, 1964.

Spencer, Theodore. [822.33 D108] *Shakespeare and the Nature of Man.* Macmillan, N.Y., 1961.

Stephenson, Henry T. [r 822.33 D22] *The Study of Shakespeare.* Holt, N.Y., 1915.

Tillyard, E.M.W. [822.33 D116] *Shakespeare's Problem Plays.* University of Toronto Pr., Toronto, 1964.

Westfall, Alfred Van Rensselaer. [r 822.33 D26] *American Shakespearean Criticism, 1607–1865.* Wilson, N.Y., 1939.

Wordsworth, Charles. [r 822.33 F4] *Shakespeare's Knowledge and Use of the Bible.* Smith, Elder & Co., London, 1880.

SHAKESPEARE IN SCIENCE AND TECHNOLOGY

Butterfield, Herbert. [r 509 B98a2] *Origins of Modern Science: 1300–1800.* Rev. ed. Macmillan, N.Y., 1957.

Ellacombe, Henry N. [r 822.33 H41] *Plant-Lore and Garden-Craft of Shakespeare.* Edward Arnold, London, 1896.

Field, Benjamin Rush. [r 822.33 HC8] *Medical Thoughts of Shakespeare.* Easton, Pa., Andrews & Clifton, 1885.

Gerard, John. [qr 580 G31] *Gerard's Herball.* Houghton, 1928. Gerard and Shakespeare were neighbors during the time Shakespeare wrote many of his finest plays.

Grigson, Geoffrey. [QK 306 .G792 1975bx] *The Englishman's Flora.* Paladin, St. Albans, England, 1975. Illustrated with woodcuts from sixteenth-century herbals. Houghton, N.Y., 1928.

Hall, A.R. [509 H16] *The Scientific Revolution, 1500–1800; The Formation of the Modern Scientific Attitude.* Longmans, N.Y., 1954.

Lorwin, Madge. [r TX 737 .L57] *Dining with William Shakespeare.* Atheneum, N.Y., 1976.

Pledge, H.T. *Science since 1500: A Short History of Mathematics, Physics, Chemistry, Biology.* Peter Smith, Gloucester, Mass., 1969.

Rohde, Eleanour Sinclair. [580.9 R62a] *The Old English Herbals.* Dover, N.Y., 1971. Discusses Gerard's herbal.

Seager, Herbert West. [r 822.33 HH6] *Natural History in Shakespeare's Time.* AMS Pr., N.Y., 1971.

Talbot, Charles Hughes. [r 610 .942 T15] *Medicine in Medieval England.* Oldbourne, London, 1967.
Trow-Smith, Robert. [630 .942 T77] *English Husbandry from the Earliest Times to the Present Day.* Farber, London, 1951.

BOOKS FOR CHILDREN

Brown, Ivor. [j 822.33 HN1] *Shakespeare and His World.* Walck, N.Y., 1964.
Buckman, Irene. [J 822.33 H30] *Twenty Tales from Shakespeare.* Methuen, London, 1963.
Buckman, Irene. [j PR 2877 .B8] *Twenty Tales from Shakespeare.* Random House, N.Y., 1965. Includes photographs from stage productions.
Chute, Marchette. [j 822.33 H29] *Stories from Shakespeare.* World Publishing Co., Cleveland, Ohio, 1956. Another copy of this book may be found in the Popular Library.
Cullum, Albert. [j PR 2877 .C8] *Shake Hands with Shakespeare.* Citation Press, N.Y., 1968. Producing Shakespeare in elementary grades.
Hodges, Cyril W. [j 822.33 HL1] *Shakespeare's Theatre.* Coward-McCann, N.Y., 1964.
Lamb, Charles, and Mary Lamb. [j 822.33 H1a] *Tales from Shakespeare.* Several editions, publishers and years.
Serraillier, Ian. [j 822.33 H31] *The Enchanted Island; Stories from Shakespeare.* Walck, N.Y., 1964.
Shakespeare, William. [j 822.33 L] *Constellation: A Shakespeare Anthology.* Edited by Margaret Hodges. Farrar, Straus and Giroux, N.Y., 1968.
Shakespeare, William. [j 822.33 Y13] *Seeds of Time.* Selections from Shakespeare. Atheneum, N.Y., 1963.
Shakespeare, William. [j 822.33 Y12] *Songs from Shakespeare.* A.S. Barnes, N.Y., 1961.
Updike, John. [j 822.33 P76] *Bottom's Dream.* Knopf, N.Y., 1969. Adapted from *A Midsummer Night's Dream* with music by Felix Mendelssohn.
White, Anne Terry. [j 822.33 B5] *Will Shakespeare and the Globe Theater.* Random House, N.Y., 1955.

MUSIC-ART

ART BOOKS

The Boydell Shakespeare Prints. B. Blom, N.Y., 1968. The Boydell Shakespeare Gallery (1789–1805) in England exhibited paintings based on Shakespeare's works only. This volume contains reproductions of engraved prints after those paintings.
Kelly, Francis Michael. [r 391 L72a] *Shakespearean Costume for Stage and Screen.* A. and C. Black, London, 1938.
Linthicum, Marie Channing. [391 L72a] *Costume in the Drama of Shakespeare and His Contemporaries.* Russell and Russell, N.Y., 1963.
Smith, Irwin. [725.82 S64] *Shakespeare's Globe Playhouse: A Modern Reconstruction in Text and Scale Drawings.* Scribner, N.Y., 1956.

SLIDES

A Day at the Globe Theater.
The Globe Theater: Its Design and Construction.
The Life of Shakespeare: Shakespeare's London.
The Life of Shakespeare: The Stratford Years and Shakespeare's London.

MUSIC RECORDINGS

Arne, Thomas. [AL 3394LP] *Songs to Shakespeare Plays.*
Britten, Benjamin. [AL 3832LP] *A Midsummer Night's Dream* (opera).
Dances of Shakespeare's Time. [AL 1020LP].
Giannini, Vittorio. [AL 5398LP] *The Taming of the Shrew* (opera).
Liszt, Franz. [AL 9583LP] *Hamlet* (symphonic poem).
MacDowell, Edward. [AL 4226LP] *Hamlet and Ophelia Op. 22.* (symphonic poem).
Music of Shakespeare's Time. [AL 7144LP].
Paine, John Knowles. [AL 4226LP] *The Tempest* (symphonic poem).
Porter, Cole. [AL 824LP] *Kiss Me, Kate.* A musical comedy about a divorced husband-and-wife acting team who are reunited for a production of Shakespeare's *Taming of the Shrew.*

Prokofiev, Serge. [AL 6439LP/AL 7354LP] *Romeo and Juliet* (ballet).

Rodgers, Richard. [AL 5892LP] *The Boys from Syracuse.* Shakespeare's *Comedy of Errors* transformed into a musical comedy.

Songs of Shakespeare's Time. [AL 6963LP].

Strauss, Richard. [AL 58LP] *Macbeth* (symphonic poem).

Verdi, Giuseppe. [AL 9234LP/AL 8286LP] [AL 2051LP/AL 354LP] *Macbeth* (opera).

Walton, William. [AL 8921LP] *Troilus and Cressida* (opera).

MUSIC BOOKS AND SCORES

Arne, Thomas. [qM 784 A74sn] *Nine Shakespeare Songs.* Chappell, London, 1963.

Edwards, Edward, ed. [qM 784.8 E31] *Book of Shakespeare's Songs, with Musical Settings by Various Composers.* G. Schirmer, N.Y., 1903.

Elson, Louis. [822.33 HGa] *Shakespeare in Music.* AMS Press, N.Y., 1971.

Greenhill, James. [rML 80 .S5 G8 1974] *A List of All the Songs and Passages in Shakespeare Which Have Been Set to Music.* Reprint of 1884 edition. Folcroft Library Edition, Folcroft, Pa., 1974.

Hartnoll, Phyllis. [780.9 H33] *Shakespeare in Music.* St. Martin's Pr., N.Y., c1964.

Kines, Tom. [M 784.8 K262s] *Songs from Shakespeare's Plays, and Popular Songs of Shakespeare's Time.* Oak Publications, N.Y., 1964.

Long, John H. [822.33 HG9 and r 822.33 HG7] *Shakespeare's Use of Music.* 3 volumes. University of Florida Pr., Gainesville, 1955–1971.

Vincent, Charles John. [qM 784.8 V34f2] *Fifty Shakespeare Songs.* C.H. Ditson & Co., N.Y., 1906.

MISCELLANEOUS

Bentley, Nicolas. [PR 2877 .B4 1972b] *Nicolas Bentley's Tales from Shakespeare.* Simon & Schuster, N.Y., 1972.

Deutsch, Babette. [822.33 H30] *The Reader's Shakespeare.* Julian Messner, N.Y., 1976. An invitation to the enjoyment of the great plays; suitable for all ages.

Finkelstein, Sidney W. [PR 3017 .F5] *Who Needs Shakespeare?* International Publishers, N.Y., 1973. A good introduction for the general reader.

Greenwood, Sir Granville George. [r 822.33 AB3] *Shakespeare's Handwriting.* Lane, London, 1920.

Hazlitt, William C. [r 822.33 F] *Shakespeare Jest Books.* Reprints of the early and very rare jest books supposed to have been used by Shakespeare. Sotheran and Co., London, 1881.

Hazlitt, William C. [r 822.33 F3] *Shakespeare's Library.* A collection of the plays, romances, novels, poems and histories employed by Shakespeare in the composition of his works. Reeves & Turner, London, 1875, 6 v.

Jorgens, Jack J. [PR 3093 .J6] *Shakespeare on Film.* Indiana University Press, Bloomington, 1977.

Lanier, Emilia. [PR 2296 .L27 S2 1979] *The Poems of Shakespeare's Dark Lady;* introduction by A.L. Rowse. Clarkson N. Potter, Inc., N.Y., 1978.

Shakespeare, William. [r 822.33 B6] *(Facsimile of His Will).* Century, 1927.

Thornbury, George Walter. [r 822.33 HN10] *Shakespeare's England; or Sketches of Our Social History in the Reign of Elizabeth.* Longman, London, 1856, 2 v.

Webster, Margaret. [822.33 D107a] *Shakespeare without Tears.* World Pub. Co., Cleveland, 1955.

The Reference Department has facsimiles of the following first quartos:

As You Like It (1623)
Coriolanus (1623)
Hamlet (1603)
King Henry IV (1598)
King Henry V (1600)
King John (1591)
King Lear (1608)
King Richard II (1597)
King Richard III (1597)
Love's Labor Lost (1598)

Merchant of Venice (1600)
Merry Wives of Windsor (1602)
Midsummer Night's Dream (1600)
Much Ado about Nothing (1600)
Othello (1622)
Pericles (1609)
Romeo and Juliet (1597)
Sonnets (1609)
Taming of the Shrew (1594)
Titus Andronicus (1594)
Troilus and Cressida (1609)

The Reference Department has facsimiles of the following Shakespeare First Folios: *Dramatic Works* (1623); *Comedies Histories Tragedies* (1623) (1632) (1664) (1685).

Recorded versions of all of Shakespeare's plays are available in the Popular Library.

Model 10

Becoming Acquainted with James A. Michener (Honors American Literature)

GRADES: 11 or 12.

DURATION: 45 Days.

GOAL: To provide an in-depth study of James Michener as writer, citizen of the world, and advocate for the brotherhood of the human race.

OBJECTIVES

To introduce the students to the science and the art of literary criticism.

To introduce the students to the process of writing themes about literature.

To employ the Michener novel *Hawaii* as a means of building understanding and appreciation of the literary stature, style, and power of James Michener.

INTRODUCTION

This program exemplifies a teacher-designed learning experience, bringing greater scope and challenge to an honors course in American literature. Mention of James Michener is omitted in the text anthology, *American Literature* (Columbus, Ohio: Ginn, 1981), even though Michener is recognized as one of the most widely read and highly acclaimed contemporary writers and was awarded the Medal of Freedom by President Ford in 1977.

The novel *Hawaii* (New York: Random, 1959) is the common-reading experience to be read, pondered, discussed, and enjoyed in this unit. *James A. Michener* by A. Grove Day, 2nd ed., Twayne's United States Authors Series (Boston: G. K. Hall, 1977) is also a required common reading experience. This concise, clearly written, authoritative, critical study of Michener not only serves as a lively introduction to Michener the writer and Michener the man, but is an outstanding example of literary criticism.

STUDENT ORIENTATION

I. The goal of this unit is to provide an in-depth study of James Michener, as writer, citizen of the world, and advocate for the brotherhood of the human race.
  A. Michener is a world-acclaimed writer, a respected journalist, and a fearless advocate of the rights of all peoples.
  B. Michener's writings embrace both fiction and nonfiction titles, numbering 21 major works; all are in print, many in both hardback and paperback.

II. The objectives of this unit are:
  A. To introduce the student to the science and the art of literary criticism, a basic requirement for performing well on the college boards.
  B. To introduce the students to the process of writing themes about literature, a basic requirement for performing well on the college boards.
  C. To have the students read, ponder, analyze, and *enjoy* Michener's monumental novel *Hawaii*.

III. Unit requirements (see Handout 10-1):
  A. Thirty-five days will be devoted to reading, discussing, and reacting to the novel *Hawaii*.
  B. Three days will be devoted to reviewing the process of writing themes about literature; two themes are required.
  C. Seven days will be devoted to closure activities, including:
    1. Seeing the motion picture *Hawaii* (United Artists, 1966); comparing and contrasting the motion picture with the novel.
    2. Students reading to the class their summarizing themes; class interaction will be a vital part of the summarizing activities.

IV. *James A. Michener* by A. Grove Day is a superlative example of literary criticism.
  A. The following parts of the book are required reading:
    1. About the Author
    2. Preface
    3. Chronology
    4. Chapter 1. Citizen of the World
    5. Chapter 2. Start in the South Pacific
    6. Chapter 6. Passages to the Fiftieth State
    7. Chapter 9. Area of Assessment
    8. Selected Bibliography
  B. The first required theme will be on the topic "My Assessment of James Michener" (see Handout 10-1).
    1. Preparatory to drafting your theme on the assessment of Michener, read and reread Chapter 9 from *James A. Michener*.
    2. Carefully consider the following quotes:

> Michener in his author stance is closer to the soapbox than to the laboratory of the social scientist. He is highly moral and confessedly optimistic, and is committed to a faith in progress and the rational improvability of man. His characters are often chosen or molded to enact his theme, but seldom does he offer for our admiration a "hairy

ape" with strong back and weak mind, or a Strindbergian neurotic, or an alcoholic, dope-riddled, epicene antihero, or a flabby victim of "circumstance" or "society" in a world he never even tried to make. Michener is frank to the point of horrifying some of his otherwise adoring readers, but frankness is expected nowadays in any novel that does not wish to be damned as Victorian.

And perhaps he is most of all the contemporary reporter, in fiction as well as fact—one of the noble, articulate band of rovers that keep showing our generation what we are really like. . . . So long as modern Americans need to know who they are, so long will Michener's books be read.*

V. Review of the process of writing themes stresses the following:[†]
   A. Definition—to be a theme a piece of writing must have a *central idea* as its core.
      1. Everything in the theme should be directly related to this central theme.
      2. "A theme should be a brief 'mind's full,' not an exhaustive treatment."
   B. Principles guiding the writing of a theme:
      1. The theme should cover the topic
      2. The central idea should govern the theme's development
      3. Every part of the theme must contribute to the understanding of the central idea
   C. Resist the temptation to be a narrator rather than an interpreter
   D. Use accurate and forceful language
   E. Keep all detail relevant to the topic

VI. Preparatory to reading *Hawaii,* the students discuss the hierarchy of first reading, then comprehending, and finally appreciating what is read.
   A. In the Preface to *James A. Michener,* Grove Day states:

   > Although I have a high opinion of James A. Michener's contribution to our literature, I am less concerned with booming the Michener shares on some sort of literary stock exchange than with trying to help his many readers discover his ideas and appreciate the richness of many other qualities of his work. As a writer and professor myself, I am as involved as anyone with the glaring fact that too many people read but do not comprehend—and that many who comprehend do not appreciate.[‡]

   B. The reading of such a voluminous novel as *Hawaii* with both comprehension and insightful appreciation is an assignment worthy of the collegiate level; it will demand concentrated effort and careful note taking, as well as being caught up in the story itself.

VII. Upon completing the reading of *Hawaii,* the following culminating-closure activities are engaged in:
   A. The students write and then share with the class a theme on the topic, "My Favorite Character in the Novel, *Hawaii.*"

*A. Grove Day, *James A. Michener,* 2nd ed., p. 165. Copyright © 1977 by Twayne Publishers, Inc., and reprinted with the permission of Twayne Publishers, a Division of G.K. Hall & Co., Boston.
[†]Adapted from Edgar V. Roberts, *Writing Themes about Literature,* brief ed. (Englewood Cliffs, N.J.: Prentice-Hall, 1982), pp. 8–34.
[‡]Day, *James A. Michener,* preface.

B. The class views the motion picture, *Hawaii* (United Artists) and discusses the following:
   1. Was the motion picture an accurate interpretation of the novel?
   2. Were the characters convincing?
   3. Which medium gave the greater emotional impact, the novel or the motion picture?
   4. If you had been writing a review of the motion picture *Hawaii* for the *The New York Times,* what would you have said?
C. Students summarize their understanding and appreciation of Michener by writing on the topic, "My Appraisal of James Michener, the Writer and the Man."

HANDOUT 10-1 SCHEDULE

From	To	Number of Days	Activities
		3	Orientation to the unit *Becoming Acquainted with James A. Michener;* reviewing the process of writing themes about literature; introduction of *James A. Michener* by A. Grove Day; the assigned readings are to be completed in one week
		3	From the novel *Hawaii* read Part I, "From the Boundless Deep," and Part II, "From the Sun Swept Lagoon," pp. 1–118
		8	Read Part III, "From the Farm of Bitterness," pp. 121–369
		1	Theme 1, "My Assessment of James Michener," is due; Class discusses the assessments of James A. Michener
		8	Read Part IV, "From the Starving Village," pp. 373–598
		8	Read Part V, "From the Inland Sea," pp. 601–803
		7	Read Part VI, "The Golden Men," pp. 807–937
		2	Theme 2, "My Favorite Character in *Hawaii,"* is due; the motion picture *Hawaii* is presented
		5	Individual students read their "Favorite Character" themes Class summarizes the assessments of James A. Michener
		45 days	

Model 11

Exploring World Cultures
(Honors Social Studies)

GRADES: 8–10.

DURATION: One year (two semesters).

GOAL: To provide an opportunity for students to build an understanding and appreciation of those elements essential for perceptive exploration of any given culture.

INTRODUCTION

This program is based on the course of study presented in the annotated edition of *Exploring World Cultures* by Esko E. Newhill and Umberto La Paglia (Lexington, Mass.: Ginn, 1981), pp. T-1–T-32. The course as outlined in the Teacher's Introductory Manual is an exceptionally well-organized and well-developed teaching-learning program. The teacher of an honors course in world cultures will find eight units of study, completely outlined and developed. Each unit is developed under the headings Purposes, Learning Objectives, Skill Development, Reading for Understanding, and Testing Your Values. Reproduced here are the purposes of each of the eight units.

UNIT ONE: THE MIDDLE EAST (CHAPTERS 4–9)

To understand how size, geographical features, and climate have influenced the development of the Middle East.

To examine major trends, peoples, and events in the Middle East's history.

To analyze how religion and tradition shaped Muslim society.

To examine the Middle East's economic development from agriculture to modern technology.

To understand the varied political systems of the Middle East.

To examine the cultural contributions of Islamic civilization.

To evaluate the Middle East's current status and involvement in world affairs.

UNIT TWO: AFRICA (CHAPTERS 10–15)

To understand how varied climates, geographical features, and size have influenced Africa's development.

To examine trends, events, and ideas that shaped African history.

To analyze African social patterns.

To contrast rural and urban economies in Africa.

To analyze African political development before and since movements for independence.

To examine African cultural contributions.

To evaluate Africa's present role and status in world affairs.

UNIT THREE: INDIA (CHAPTERS 16–21)

To understand how size, climatic features, and natural geographic frontiers have influenced India's development.

To examine major trends, individuals, and events in Indian history.

To examine the caste system and its relation to the Hindu religion.

To compare and contrast the traditional Indian village subsistence economy with modern attempts to industrialize.

To analyze India's three historic government patterns: monarchy, colonialism, and independence.

To examine India's contributions to world religion and art.

To evaluate India's current status and role in world affairs.

UNIT FOUR: CHINA (CHAPTERS 22–27)

To understand how size, climate, and natural geographical barriers have shaped China's development.

To examine major events and individuals in Chinese history.

To compare and contrast social structure, religion, and values before and since the establishment of the People's Republic.

To analyze how Communist policies have altered China's agricultural economy.

To contrast traditional and Communist political structures.

To identify China's contributions to world culture.

To understand China's role and status in the contemporary world.

UNIT FIVE: JAPAN (CHAPTERS 28–33)

To understand how an island structure and limited resources molded Japanese development.

To examine the evolution of Japanese history, including contributions of key individuals and events.

To contrast traditional and modern Japanese society, culture, and religion.

To examine how World War II transformed Japan's economy.

To compare Japanese imperial monarchy with modern parliamentary government.

To analyze Japan's contributions to the arts.

To understand Japan's status and role in the modern world.

UNIT SIX: SOUTHEAST ASIA (CHAPTERS 34–39)

To understand how vastness and geographic variety have shaped Southeast Asia's development.

To examine how China, India, and Europe have influenced Southeast Asia's history.

To analyze Southeast Asia's ethnic and social diversity.

To understand Southeast Asia's key economic realities: underdevelopment and subsistence agriculture.

To analyze Southeast Asia's varied attempts to attain government organization and political stability.

To examine Southeast Asia's contributions to world culture.

To evaluate Southeast Asia's current role and status in world affairs.

UNIT SEVEN: THE SOVIET UNION (CHAPTERS 40–45)

To understand how size, climate, and lack of natural frontiers have influenced Russia's development.

To examine major trends, individuals, and events in Russian history.

To compare and contrast tsarist and Communist social patterns.

To examine Russian economic evolution from serfdom to collectivization.

To analyze and compare tsarist and Communist political structures.

To examine Russian contributions to the arts and sciences.

To evaluate the Soviet Union's current status and involvement in world affairs.

UNIT EIGHT: LATIN AMERICA (CHAPTERS 46–51)

To understand how size, climate, and varied geography have influenced Latin America's development.

To examine major trends, individuals, and events that shaped Latin America's history.

To evaluate the role of racial and religious patterns in the development of Latin America's society.

To compare and contrast traditional agriculture with modern industrial and agricultural systems.

To analyze the varied political systems of Latin America.

To examine Latin America's contributions to world culture.

To understand Latin America's contemporary role and status in world affairs.

Complementing the noteworthy print and nonprint media listed in the basic text, one additional sound filmstrip set, *How to Study Cultures: A Unit of Study* (United Learning), provides invaluable assistance in orienting students to basic elements in the study of any particular culture. The Teacher's Guide to this set follows.*

HOW TO STUDY CULTURES: A UNIT OF STUDY

CONTENTS

General Description of the Program

Unit Objectives

Materials in the Unit

Instructional Notes

Suggested Instructional Procedures

    Lesson One: Culture: The Way People Live

---

*This Teacher's Guide (1979) is reproduced with permission of the producer, United Learning (Niles, Ill.). *Note:* The tapes, filmstrips, and other media included in this program are the exclusive property of United Learning. Copying or duplication of these materials in any form requires written permission from United Learning.

GENERAL DESCRIPTION OF THE PROGRAM

This unit of study is designed to give secondary grade level students a perspective on how to study any culture. The unit aims at helping students identify the basic elements of culture. The students are asked to select a culture for an in-depth study. They will conduct meaningful research using Culture Study Guides which center on the following topics: environment, subsistence activities, technology, values and beliefs, forms of communication, social organization and culture change.

The core content of this unit of study is presented in eight sound filmstrips. Detailed Suggested Instructional Procedures accompany each sound filmstrip, and the teacher is provided with instructional activities that are related to the content of the sound filmstrips. Depending upon your instructional schedule, you may wish to devote from three to five class periods on each of the eight lessons in this unit of study.

UNIT OBJECTIVES

After viewing the sound filmstrips and participating in the lesson activities, the students should be able to achieve the objectives stated below.

Identify the basic elements of any culture.

Define the term "culture."

Explain the influence that environment has on a culture.

Discuss procedures and techniques anthropologists use in studying a culture.

Conduct in-depth research on a culture of their choice.

Explain that cultures have developed different levels of technology and that members of a culture use technology and social organizations to adapt to their environment.

Discuss how values and beliefs affect human behavior.

Describe various forms and purposes of communication.

Identify various kin and non-kin groups that exist within a culture.

Explain that change takes place in every culture and that members of a culture must adjust to changing conditions.

MATERIALS IN THE UNIT

SOUND FILMSTRIPS

This unit contains eight full-color sound filmstrips. Each tape cassette has an audible tone on one side for manual advance and an inaudible 50HZ signal on the reverse side for use on automatic-advance projectors. The filmstrip titles and their specific themes are:

1. *Cultures: The Way People Live.* Culture is defined as the total way of life of any given society. All cultures must attend to satisfying the basic needs of their members.
2. *How Anthropologists Study Cultures—A Case Study.* The research techniques and procedures of Professor Oswald Werner, anthropologist at Northwestern University, are examined. Dr. Werner is studying the Navajo culture in Monument Valley, Arizona.
3. *How Environment Affects Culture.* All cultures must adapt to their environments and use the resources in the most effective manner. To a certain extent, environment determines how members of a culture meet their basic needs.
4. *How Cultures Meet Economic Needs and Wants.* Members of a culture use technology to help meet their basic needs. Various types of economies have emerged in different cultures including: hunter-gathering, herding, agriculture, industrial, and mixtures of the aforementioned.
5. *Beliefs and Values Shape Human Behavior.* Members of a culture must learn the beliefs and values of the culture in which they are growing up. These beliefs and values will strongly influence the way they think and behave.
6. *Communication Forms in Culture.* Members of a culture communicate through language, art, music, and artifacts. This communication helps bond together the members of the culture.
7. *How Cultures Are Organized.* Members of a culture belong to a variety of kin and non-kin groups. An individual may belong to an extended family as well as a nuclear family and may belong to religious, political, occupational, and recreational groups.
8. *How Cultures Change.* All cultures change. Some change more rapidly than others. Change occurs as a result of discovery, invention, diffusion, and education.

TEACHER'S GUIDE

This book contains Suggested Instructional Procedures for each of the eight lessons that comprise this unit of study.

SPIRIT MASTERS

Listening Activities, Study Guides, and a Unit Evaluation have been prepared on spirit masters. You will be advised as to when to use the various spirit masters in the Suggested Instructional Procedures that accompany each lesson.

INSTRUCTIONAL NOTES

It is suggested that you preview each sound filmstrip and read the related Suggested Instructional Procedures before involving your students in the lesson activities. In this way you will become familiar with the instructional materials available to you and will be better prepared to adapt the various elements of the program to the needs of your class.

It is not essential that you present each lesson in numerical order. You may wish to rearrange the lessons in an order that better fits your approach to the study of culture.

It is suggested that the sound filmstrip presentations take place before the entire class and under your direction. The lesson activities grow out of the content of the sound filmstrips. Therefore, the presentations should be a common experience for all students. We urge that you take a strong leadership role in the presentation of this unit of study.

As you review the instructional program outlined in the Guide, you may find it necessary to make some changes, deletions, or additions, to fit the specific needs of your students. We encourage you to do so, for only by tailoring this program to your students' needs will they obtain the maximum instructional benefits afforded by the materials.

PICTURE NOTES

The photographs within this series represent a collection of slides from all over the world obtained through several years of travel by photographers, anthropologists and others.

Because of their uniqueness, we recommend that you pay special attention to the picture comments and incorporate this valuable collection into your study of world cultures as well as using it as a resource for other areas of study.

UNIT FOLDER

Instruct each student to begin a Cultures Folder. All notes, listening activities, study guides, writing projects and the unit evaluation may be stored in it.

LESSON I: CULTURE: THE WAY PEOPLE LIVE*

  I. Teacher Preparation
  Filmstrip Summary: Culture: The Way People Live
  This filmstrip defines culture as the total way of life of any given society. Everyone is born into a culture, but no one is born with a culture. Culture is acquired by learning. Family, friends, teachers, etc., help individuals learn the ways of the culture. The process of learning the ways of one's culture is called acculturation.

  Members of every culture must work out ways to deal with their environments and to satisfy their basic needs for food, clothing, and shelter. Human beings have developed tools and technological systems to help them cope with their environment.

  Cultures develop world views which serve as explanations of how the world began and predictions of how it will end, what is beautiful and what is ugly, what is good and what is bad.

 II. Student Preparation
  Materials needed: Pencil or pen, paper, a folder.

III. Student Objectives
  After viewing the sound filmstrip and participating in the lesson activities, the students should be able to:
  1. Define the term "culture."
  2. Explain that since culture is learned it can be changed.
  3. Explain that all cultures must devise ways to satisfy basic human needs.
  4. Compare various cultures in terms of how they satisfy their basic needs for food, clothing, and shelter.

*Viewing Time: 14:02, Frames: 73

5. Explain that cultures may be studied in a systematic manner by examining various aspects of culture: subsistence activities, level of technological development, social organization, communication, and world view.

IV. Introducing the Lesson
1. Explain that in this sound filmstrip the students will learn a method for studying culture.
2. Ask the students to write a definition of culture on a piece of paper prior to seeing the sound filmstrip. After the sound filmstrip presentation, ask them to compare their definition with the one stated in the filmstrip.

V. Filmstrip Presentation
1. Introduce this sound filmstrip by telling the students that they should listen for a definition of culture and begin to think about developing categories within which all cultures could be studied.
2. Present the sound filmstrip.

VI. Follow-up Activities
1. *Discussion.* Discuss what the term culture means. Help students understand that culture is the "total way of life of any given society."
2. *Project.* Ask each student to get a "Cultures Folder." They can buy it or make it out of construction paper. In it they should keep all important papers such as notes, listening activities, and research guides.
3. *Lecture.* Tell students that it is wise to develop a method for studying any culture. A systematic method for examining any culture is to establish categories within which research can be conducted. Categories which will be used in this program are: subsistence activities, level of technological development, social organization, forms of communication, culture change, and world view. These are basic elements of any culture.
4. *Discussion.* Discuss the following statements: "Everyone is born into a culture, but no one is born with a culture"; "Culture is learned"; "Since culture is learned, it can be changed."
5. *Defining and Discussing.* Define "basic human needs" as the needs for food, clothing and shelter. Discuss why it is true that environment helps determine ways cultures satisfy basic human needs.
6. *Cultural Comparisons.* Ask the students to compare various cultures in terms of ways they satisfy their basic needs.

Example	Eskimos	19th Century Bedouins	18th Century Great Plains Indians	Contemporary U.S.A.
Food				
Clothing				
Shelter				

7. *Defining Terms*. Ask the students to define the following terms: extended family, nuclear family, tribe, and clan. Then ask, what do they have in common? (They are all social groupings.) Ask if they can think of other social groupings in our society.

LESSON II: HOW ANTHROPOLOGISTS STUDY CULTURE—A CASE STUDY*

I. Teacher Preparation
Duplicate Spirit Master 1

Filmstrip Summary: How Anthropologists Study Culture—A Case Study.

In this sound filmstrip, the students will see anthropologist Oswald Werner at work in the field as he endeavors to prepare a Navajo folk-medical encyclopedia. He and his staff are working with people of the Navajo tribe who live in the Monument Valley area of Arizona. Werner is preparing the encyclopedia in order to preserve knowledge of old methods used by Navajos when practicing medicine. This sound filmstrip shows what a field study is like and how modern anthropologists gather and organize information about cultures they study.

II. Student Preparation
Materials needed: Pencil or pen, paper.

III. Student Objectives
After viewing the sound filmstrip and participating in the lesson activities, the students should be able to:
1. Explain methods used by modern anthropologists to gather and organize information about other cultures.
2. Explain the purpose of Professor Werner's field study.
3. Discuss the meaning of the terms "key trait" and "basic element."

IV. Introducing the Lesson
Tell the students that in this filmstrip they will learn about Dr. Oswald Werner and his associates' research among the Navajos of the Monument Valley area of Arizona. Ask your students to listen carefully for the purpose of Werner's study.

V. Filmstrip Presentation
1. Distribute the Listening Activity, Spirit Master 1. Ask your students to complete the Listening Activity as the sound filmstrip progresses (if lighting permits) or immediately following the filmstrip presentation.
2. Present the sound filmstrip.

VI. Follow-up Activities
1. *Listening Activity*. Use the Listening Activity to discuss the content of the sound filmstrip. Ask your students to file this Listening Activity in their Cultures Folders.
2. *Discussion:* How would you like the lifestyle of an anthropologist? Explain your answer.

*Viewing Time: 12:35, Frames: 69.

LESSON III: HOW ENVIRONMENT AFFECTS CULTURE*

I. Teacher Preparation

Duplicate Spirit Masters 2 and 3

Materials: Students will need mural-size lengths of butcher paper.

Filmstrip Summary: How Environment Affects Culture

This sound filmstrip explains that an environment can influence the way people live in terms of the kinds of subsistence activities they carry on and the level of technological development they have achieved. All cultures must adapt to the environment in which they live by using the resources in their environment to their advantage. Human beings can live in about any earthly environment but life is easier in some environments than in others.

II. Student Preparation

Materials needed: Pencil or pen, art supplies to draw and color.

III. Student Objectives

After viewing the sound filmstrip and participating in the lesson activities, the students should be able to:

1. Give examples of ways in which environment affects culture.
2. Discuss what the phrase "adaptation to an environment" means.
3. Select a culture upon which to do an in-depth study.
4. Describe the environmental conditions of the culture they have selected for their in-depth studies.
5. Describe how members of their selected culture satisfy their basic needs for food, clothing, and shelter.
6. Tell how some cultural groups use religious practices to control or change environmental factors.
7. Tell how people use technology to control or change elements in their environment.

IV. Introducing the Lesson

1. Prior to showing the sound filmstrip, discuss the following concepts with your students:
   a. A culture must adapt to the environment in which it lives.
   b. The environment influences how a culture develops and at what rate it develops.

V. Filmstrip Presentation

1. Explain to your students that this sound filmstrip deals with the influence of environment upon culture.
2. Present the sound filmstrip.

VI. Follow-up Activities

1. *Art Project.* Divide your students into small groups of four to six. Give each group a long length of white butcher paper. Ask each group to select a different environment. Tell them to prepare a topographical sketch with a settlement of people in the picture. The scene should show the basic climatic and topographic features of the environment and it should show how the people in the settlement have used the resources available in the environment to meet their basic human needs

*Viewing Time: 13:50, Frames: 75.

for food, clothing, and shelter. Instruct the students to show seasonal variations.

2. *Discussion.* Does adaptation to an environment mean fitting in or exploiting the environment to the benefit of the people who live there?

3. *Discussion.* How does technology (tools and knowledge of how to use them) help people adapt to and even control their environment? What are some examples?

4. *Discussion.* How do some cultures use religious beliefs and practices to aid them in their adaptation to their environment?

5. *In-depth Study.* Ask each of your students to select a culture for an in-depth study.

   Explain to your students that a major portion of this unit will involve an in-depth study of a culture of their choice. You may want the students to work in small groups of two to three.

   One basic purpose of this unit is to help students learn *how* to study another culture. Culture Study Guides are provided in this unit to aid students in their research. These study guides will help students focus their research around various categories such as environment, subsistence activities, technology, social organization, world view, and communication.

   Distribute the Culture Study Guide sheets, Spirit Masters 2 and 3, and give your students time to conduct research to answer the questions on the two spirit masters. Assist them as needed.

   Once your students have completed work on their study guides, ask them to place them in their Cultures Folders.

LESSON IV: HOW CULTURES MEET ECONOMIC NEEDS AND WANTS*

  I. Teacher Preparation
     Duplicate Spirit Masters 4 and 5
     Filmstrip Summary: How Cultures Meet Economic Needs and Wants
     Cultures develop technologies to adapt to their environment. Some cultures develop simple technologies while others develop extremely complex technologies. Cultures use technology to help provide food, clothing, shelter, and other necessities.

     Cultures around the world have also developed a variety of economic systems to meet their needs and wants. Some economies are: hunter-gatherer, herding, simple and mechanized agriculture, and modern industrial.

 II. Student Preparation
     Materials needed: Pencil or pen, paper.

III. Student Objectives
     After viewing the sound filmstrip and participating in the lesson activities, the students should be able to:
     1. Describe the level of technology developed in the culture they are studying in-depth.

*Viewing Time: 12:10, Frames: 71

2. Describe the type of economy that exists in the culture they are studying in-depth.
3. Define the term "technology."
4. Name the major economic systems mentioned in the sound filmstrip and describe the major characteristics of each.
5. Explain why cultures develop technologies.

IV. Introducing the Lesson
Explain that this sound filmstrip tells about how cultures all over the world have developed technologies and economic systems to help meet their needs for food, clothing, shelter, and other necessities.

V. Filmstrip Presentation
1. Distribute the Listening Activity, Spirit Master 4, and ask your students to complete it during or immediately following the sound filmstrip presentation.
2. Present the sound filmstrip.

VI. Follow-up Activities
1. *Listening Activity*. Go over the Listening Activity with your students. Use this activity to discuss the basic content of the sound filmstrip. Ask your students to file this activity sheet in their Cultures Folders.
2. *Defining and Discussing*. Ask your students to define the term *technology*. They may have to use a dictionary. Help them understand that all cultures have developed technologies. (*Definition:* A collection of tools and machines and a knowledge of how to use them. The sum of ways in which a group of people provide themselves with goods and services.) Members of a culture use technology to get at the resources in their environment and to use them to provide food, clothing, shelter, and other necessities.
3. *Discussion.*
   a. What would life be like without the knowledge of how to use fire? This question could be used as the basis for a creative writing assignment.
   b. Of the major economic systems mentioned in the sound filmstrip (hunter-gatherer, herding, simple and mechanized agricultural and modern industrial), how would you describe the level of technology that has developed in each? You may want to ask your students to rank order the economies in terms of complexity.
4. *Culture Study Guide.* Distribute the Culture Study Guide, Spirit Master 5, and ask each student to complete it for the culture he/she is studying in-depth. Assist your students as needed. When completed, the Culture Study Guide should be placed in the student's Cultures Folder.

LESSON V: BELIEFS AND VALUES SHAPE
HUMAN BEHAVIOR*
I. Teacher Preparation
Duplicate Spirit Master 6
Filmstrip Summary: Beliefs and Values Shape Human Behavior

*Viewing Time: 11:35, Frames: 73.

This sound filmstrip illustrates how beliefs and values serve as guides to human behavior. People all over the world have developed religious belief systems to help explain why things are the way they are and to answer the question: What is the purpose of life? Members of a culture share beliefs and values and pass them on from generation to generation. These beliefs and values vary from culture to culture.

II. Student Preparation
Materials needed: Pencil or pen, paper.

III. Student Objectives
After viewing the sound filmstrip and participating in the lesson activities, the students should be able to:
1. Define the terms "belief" and "value."
2. Discuss how beliefs and values affect the way people behave.
3. Make a list of beliefs and values they hold and tell how they influence their behavior.
4. Describe how people acquire values and beliefs.
5. Describe some of the major beliefs and values held by members of the various cultures students are studying in-depth.

IV. Introducing the Lesson
1. Ask your students to develop definitions for the terms beliefs and values. Write the definitions which your students develop on the chalkboard.
2. Help students understand that beliefs are convictions that certain things are true and that people value certain material goods, relationships, procedures, etc., because they are of worth and are precious to them.
3. For more technical definitions of the terms belief and value, see Louis E. Raths' *Values and Teaching** or other texts prepared by Raths, Simon and Kirchenbaum on the subject of values clarification.
4. Discuss with the students that members of all cultures develop beliefs and values and that these serve as guides to human behavior. Stress that as people develop lifestyles in a variety of environments, certain things are treated as true, right, desirable, or worthy. These values and beliefs become general guides to human behavior and they are passed on from generation to generation.

V. Filmstrip Presentation
1. Explain that this sound filmstrip shows how people all over the world develop beliefs and values and that beliefs and values serve as guides to human behavior.
2. Present the sound filmstrip.

VI. Follow-up Activities
1. *Discussion.* How do beliefs and values affect the way people behave? Give examples.
2. *Discussion.* Ask your students to explain how individuals acquire values. You may wish to point out, as does Louis E. Raths in *Values and Teaching,* that values are:

*Raths, L. E., Harmin, M., and Simon, S. B., *Values and Teaching.* Columbus, OH: Charles E. Merrill, pp. 28–29.

  a. Chosen freely
  b. Chosen from among alternatives
  c. Chosen after thoughtful consideration of consequences of each alternative
  d. Prized and cherished
  e. Publicly affirmed
  f. Acted upon
  g. Consistently acted upon

3. *Chalk Talk.* Members of a culture share certain values. To illustrate this point, place the chart below on the chalkboard.

We Value:

Material Objects	Relationships	Techniques/ Procedures	States of Being

Ask the students to name things under each category which members of our culture agree have value.

Discuss how selected items listed influence individual behavior in our culture.

4. *Oral Report.* Ask your students to bring in pictures from magazines showing what members of our culture value. Each student can show his/her pictures to the rest of the class and explain why they feel the particular thing shown is valued and how that value affects the way people behave.

5. *Discussion.* Why might differing values and beliefs cause conflict between members of various generations living within the same culture? Give examples based on personal experiences.

6. *Defining Terms.* Ask your students to define each of the following terms: animism, totism, polytheism, and monotheism.

7. *Discussion.* Discuss this statement from the filmstrip: "Whether animistic, totemistic, polytheistic, or monotheistic, each religion gives us a way to communicate with the Power or powers we believe lie beyond ourselves . . . and to influence them."

8. *Discussion.* Why do you suppose people have an urge to explain how the world began and why do they try to figure out why things are the way they are?

9. *Creative Expression.*
  a. Make a totem pole or draw a picture of a totem pole.
  b. Write a creation story for the culture you are studying in-depth.
  c. Make a mural showing a creation story.

10. *Research.* Ask your students to find stories of creation from various cultures. Have them summarize the stories and present them to the class in an oral report form.

11. *Values Clarification.* This is an opportune time to help students clarify their values. Raths has many interesting activities in *Values and Teaching.*

12. *Culture Study Guide*. Distribute the Culture Study Guide, Spirit Master 6, for this sound filmstrip. Assist the students as needed. Once the students have completed this exercise, ask them to file the Study Guides in their Cultures folders.

Lesson VI: Communication Forms in Culture*

1. Teacher Preparation
Duplicate Spirit Masters 7 and 8
Filmstrip Summary: Communication Forms in Culture
In this sound filmstrip, students will learn that language is our primary method of communication and it may create a bond between members of a culture. Human beings also use artistic expression (visual, performing and literary arts) to communicate. In cultures with highly developed technologies, people use mass communication systems to communicate with millions of people at the same time.

II. Student Preparation
Materials needed: Pencil or pen, paper.

III. Student Objectives
After viewing the sound filmstrip and participating in the lesson activities, the students should be able to:
1. Define the term "communication."
2. Name three forms of communication.
3. Describe the forms of communication present in the culture that they are studying in-depth.
4. Describe the technology that has developed in our culture to aid in communication between members of our culture.
5. Convey a mood or feeling through art or poetry.
6. Describe ways that language can be a bond between members of the same culture, and ways it can create a communication barrier between members of different cultures.

IV. Introducing the Lesson
1. Tell your students that this lesson concerns itself with various forms of communication in cultures.
2. Ask your students if they can think of different forms of communication.
3. Ask your students to define the term "communication." Help them understand that communication involves individuals sending and receiving messages.

V. Filmstrip Presentation
1. Tell the students that in this sound filmstrip they will learn about three forms of communication and how common language tends to bond members of a culture together.
2. Distribute the Listening Activity and ask your students to complete it during or immediately following the sound filmstrip presentation.
3. Present the sound filmstrip.

*Viewing Time: 13:10, Frames: 79.

VI. Follow-up Activities

1. *Listening Activity.* Go over the Listening Activity with the students using it to summarize the basic content of the sound filmstrip. This activity sheet should be placed in the student's Cultures Folder.

2. *Discussion.* How would you describe the technology that has developed in our culture to aid in communication between members of our culture?

3. *Projects.* Ask your students to draw a picture or write a poem which conveys a feeling or mood.

4. *Report.* Ask your students to conduct research and prepare a report on any of the following topics:

> Printing Press   Television
> Telegraph   Radio
> Telephone

Tell the students to describe in their reports how any one of the above items was invented and how the one they selected improved communication in our culture. You may also want them to describe the systems of communication that have developed around each invention.

5. *Discussion.* Why do you suppose written language occurs most often in societies where record keeping is important?

6. *Oral Reports.* Ask your students to bring in pieces of art or pictures of pieces of art. Ask the students to do oral reports on the message they feel the artist is trying to convey in the art.

7. *Listening to Records.* Bring records to class and ask the students to listen to them to discover the message the composer is trying to get across to the listener. You may wish to bring in some of the classics (Mozart, Debussy, Beethoven, etc.) or the work of more contemporary artists.

8. *Culture Study Guide.* Distribute the Culture Study Guide for this lesson, Spirit Master 8. Assist the students as needed. Once your students have completed this exercise, ask them to file it in their Cultures Folders.

LESSON VII: HOW CULTURES ARE ORGANIZED*

I. Teacher Preparation

Duplicate Spirit Masters 9, 10 and 11

Filmstrip Summary: How Cultures Are Organized

One means by which cultures adapt to their environment is through social organizations. There are two types of social groups: kin and non-kin. The family, nuclear or extended, is a kin group which serves basic social and economic functions for its members. Examples of non-kin groupings are groups organized around religious beliefs, recreational interests, political convictions, and occupational interests and goals. In all of these groupings individuals have status and perform roles.

II. Student Preparation

Materials needed: Pencil or pen, paper.

*Viewing Time: 14:05, Frames: 72.

III. Student Objectives

After viewing the sound filmstrip and participating in the lesson activities, the students should be able to:

1. Diagram a family.
2. Define the terms: status, role, nuclear family, extended family, monogamy, polyandry, polygyny, patrilineal descent and matrilineal descent.
3. Describe the social organization that exists in the cultures they are studying in-depth.
4. Name kin and non-kin groupings that exist in cultures.

IV. Introducing the Lesson

1. Explain to your students that cultures develop a social organization to help individuals meet social, emotional, and economic needs. Social groupings may be organized along kin or non-kin lines.
2. Ask your students to name kin and non-kin groupings that exist in our society and instruct them to explain how each group named helps individuals meet their needs.

V. Filmstrip Presentation

1. Distribute the Listening Activity that accompanies this sound filmstrip.
2. Present the sound filmstrip.

VI. Follow-up Activities

1. *Listening Activity.* Go over the Listening Activity with your students. Use this activity to summarize the basic content of the sound filmstrip. Ask your students to place the Listening Activity in their Cultures Folders.
2. *Defining Terms.* Ask your students to use dictionaries to define the terms "nuclear family" and "extended family."
3. *Family Diagrams.* Distribute Spirit Master 10, *Diagramming Your Family.* Read the directions aloud to your class and answer any questions the students may have prior to permitting them to begin. You may wish to diagram your own family on the chalkboard using the given symbols as an example. This spirit master should be placed in the students' Cultures Folders.
4. *Discussion.*
   a. How do you feel about monogamy vs. polyandry and polygyny? Why do you feel the way you do? Do you think you might feel differently if you lived in a culture that did not practice monogamy?
   b. Name some non-kin groupings that exist in our culture. What are their purposes? How does one become a member?
5. *Defining Terms.* Ask your students to use dictionaries to define the terms "status" and "role."

   Status: Each person may have more than one status depending upon his/her personal prestige in the group within which he/she functions. Status refers to personal prestige (esteem) in one's family, among co-workers, in the community, among friends, or in the public at large.

   Role: The conduct expected in each status is called a role. Parents play one role, for example, while children play another.

6. *Culture Study Guide.* Distribute Spirit Master 11, the Culture Study Guide for this lesson. Assist the students as needed. Once the students have completed this exercise, ask them to file it in their Cultures Folders.

LESSON VIII: HOW CULTURES CHANGE*

I. Teacher Preparation
Duplicate Spirit Masters 12–17
Filmstrip Summary: How Cultures Change
In this final filmstrip of the series, the students will learn that all cultures change over time. They will learn that cultures change as a result of discoveries and inventions as well as through contact with other cultures. Certain factors such as tradition, habit, and varying values and beliefs may deter changes or slow the rate of change. Change may cause conflict between members of a culture when one group has a vested interest in the ways of the past and another group wishes to change for the future.

II. Student Preparation
Materials needed: Pencil or pen, paper.

III. Student Objectives
After viewing the sound filmstrip and participating in the lesson activities, the students should be able to:
1. Explain that all cultures change.
2. Name some causes that bring about cultural change.
3. Name some factors that cause resistance to change and that may slow down the rate of change.
4. Describe changes in the culture that they are studying in-depth.
5. Make comparisons between the cultures they are studying in-depth and the culture in which they live.
6. Describe how change may cause conflict between members of the same culture.

IV. Introducing the Lesson
1. Explain that in this lesson the students will learn that all cultures change. They will learn about factors that bring about change, and they will learn about factors that cause resistance to change which may result in a slowing of the rate of change.

V. Filmstrip Presentation
1. Distribute the Listening Activity, Master 12, for this lesson. Ask the students to complete it during or immediately following the sound filmstrip presentation.
2. Present the sound filmstrip.

VI. Follow-up Activities
1. *Listening Activity.* Go over the Listening Activity with your students. Use this activity to summarize the content of the sound filmstrip. Ask your students to place the Listening Activity in their Cultures Folders.
2. *Defining and Discussing.* Ask your students to define the term "ethno-

*Viewing Time: 13:43, Frames: 63.

centrism." Discuss: How might ethnocentrism act as a deterrent to change?

3. *Discussion:*
   a. How might improving the literacy rate among members of a culture help bring about change within the culture?
   b. Can you think of technological innovations that have taken place in our culture which have brought about changes in the way people live, communicate, travel, and in what they value?
   c. Why do you suppose that oil production has had little effect on the traditional religious values held by the Islamic population of the Middle East?
   d. Why is it that culture change may cause conflict between members of the same culture?

4. *Chalk Talk.* Place the name of an item on the chalkboard.

   Examples: internal combustion engine, telephone, telegraph, airplane, snowmobile, Freon, typewriter, cotton gin, computer, penicillin, etc.

   Ask your students to brainstorm about changes that have occurred in our culture as a result of the presence of these items in our culture. Suggest that the students think of other material things that have resulted from the introduction of these items into our culture as well as changes in attitudes, values, and beliefs held by members of our culture. Use the chalkboard to record student responses.

5. *Essay.* You may wish to ask your students to write essays on how our culture has changed as a result of contact with members of other cultures.

6. *Projecting.* What changes might come about in our culture as a result of the energy crisis? This question may be a good subject for a mural or essay.

7. *Culture Study Guide.* Distribute Spirit Master 13, the Culture Study Guide for this lesson. Once your students have completed the Study Guide, ask them to place it in their Cultures Folders. Assist them with their research as needed.

8. *Chalk Talk.* Not all changes have the same impact on people's lives as do other changes. Ask your students to think of changes that occurred in their community and then ask them to fill in a chart like the one below. Have the students consider how the changes affected their lives. Place the chart on the chalkboard.

What Technological Change Occurred? _____

Areas of One's Life	Changed Greatly	Changed Slightly	Did Not Change
Job/School			
Daily Routine			
Values			
Other			

The chart may be completed for other people familiar to the students.

9. *Comparison Chart.* Distribute the Comparison Chart, Spirit Masters 14–16. Encourage your students to complete the entire chart if possible. Tell them to use as few words as possible when completing the various categories. Assist your students as needed in detecting similarities and differences between our culture and the one they have been studying in-depth. This chart should be filed in the students' Cultures Folders.

VII. Unit Test

Distribute the Unit Test and use it to assess student progress based on this unit of study.

VIII. Cultures Folder Evaluation

Collect the Cultures Folders that the students have prepared during this unit of study. Evaluate them in terms of neatness, orderliness, quality of notes, and whether required materials have been filed in the folder for the duration of the unit.

Model 12

Message and Meaning (Honors Course in Communication)

GRADES: 8–10.

DURATION: One year to two semesters.

GOAL: To provide the opportunity for the students to understand, to appreciate, and to practice the science and the art of effective oral and written communication; to speak and to write with skill and confidence.

INTRODUCTION

This program is based in part on the course of study presented in the *Teacher's Guide for Communicating Message and Meaning* by Gail Witt. The Contents* of the guide follows.

A Note from the Author
Introduction to the Guide
Course Outlines
Section 1: Establishing a Foundation
    1. Verbal Messages
    2. Nonverbal Messages
    3. Vocal Messages
    4. Listening for Meaning in Messages
Section 2: Personally Speaking
    5. Interpersonal Communication
    6. Interviews
    7. Introductions and Directions
Section 3: Interacting with Others
    8. Informal Talk: Conversation
    9. Group Discussion
    10. Debate

*Gail Witt, *Teacher's Guide for Communicating Message and Meaning* (Lexington, Mass.: Ginn, 1982), p. iii. Copyright © 1982 by Ginn and Company (Xerox Corporation). Used with permission.

Section 4: Public Speaking
   11. Purposes and Types of Public Speaking
   12. Finding Suitable Topics
   13. Researching and Structuring Speeches
   14. Techniques of Delivery
   15. Analyzing and Responding
Section 5: Speaking Out
   16. Oral Interpretation
   17. Group Interpretation
Section 6: Speaking Theatrically
   18. Informal Theater
   19. Acting
   20. Producing Plays
Appendix
   Parliamentary Procedure
   International Phonetic Alphabet

The emphasis in *Communicating Message and Meaning* is on oral communication. Content for *what* is being communicated is of equal importance with *how* ideas and information are being communicated. Therefore, the teacher of gifted students will highlight the techniques and sources of locating information, processing information, and communicating information as a foundation for effective speaking. In this course, there is a dual emphasis on writing and speaking with power.

So comprehensive and flexible is the basic textbook, *Communicating Message and Meaning,* that alternative curriculum organization patterns are offered for teacher consideration in the *Teacher's Guide* (pp. vii–xii). These alternative patterns are outlined below.

ALTERNATIVE CURRICULUM ORGANIZATION

From teacher to teacher and school district to school district, emphasis in a speech course differs. Although no book can be everything to everyone, this book certainly provides a vast choice of information which can be taught in a semester's course, a year's course, or even a two-year course.

SEMESTER COURSES

The following outlines give alternative methods of organizing semester courses—each with a different emphasis. The information within each outline is sequential; however, the four different outlines are not sequential. They are intended to stand as independent units of study.

I. INTRODUCTION TO SPEECH

Chapters	Time Line (Weeks)
A. Verbal Messages	2
B. Nonverbal Messages	1
C. Vocal Messages	
D. International Phonetic Alphabet (supplemental unit)	2
E. Listening for Meaning in Messages	2
F. Interpersonal Communication	2
G. Informal Talk: Conversation	1

H. Debate	2
I. Purposes and Types of Public Speaking	1
J. Researching and Structuring Speeches	2
K. Techniques of Delivery	2
L. Analyzing and Responding	1
Total	18 weeks

II. SPEAKING AS A PERFORMING ART

Chapters	Time Line (Weeks)
A. Verbal Messages	2
B. Nonverbal Messages	2
C. Vocal Messages	
D. International Phonetic Alphabet (supplemental unit)	2
E. Listening for Meaning in Messages	2
F. Interpersonal Communication	2
G. Interviews	2
H. Introductions and Directions	1
I. Informal Talk: Conversation	2
J. Group Discussion	3
Total	18 weeks

K. Oral Interpretation	4
L. Group Interpretation	3
M. Informal Theater	4
N. Acting	5
O. Producing Plays	2
Total	18 weeks

III. GENERAL INTRODUCTORY SPEECH

Chapters	Time Line (Weeks)
A. Verbal Messages	2
B. Nonverbal	2
C. Vocal Messages	1
D. Listening for Meaning in Messages	2
E. Interpersonal Communication	2
F. Interviews	1
G. Informal Talk: Conversation	2
H. Group Discussion	2
I. Debate	2
J. Purposes and Types of Public Speaking	2
Total	18 weeks

K. Finding Suitable Topics	2
L. Researching and Structuring Speeches	3
M. Techniques of Delivery	2
N. Analyzing and Responding	1
O. Oral Interpretation	2
P. Group Interpretation	2
Q. Informal Theater	2
R. Acting	3
S. Producing Plays	1
Total	18 weeks

Two-Year Course

The following outline develops a two-year, sequential introduction to all aspects of oral communication. While the chapters are the same, it is assumed that the teacher will utilize all of the activities, resources, and suggestions in the text and the teacher's guide for expanding each chapter to its fullest. This outline also allows ample time for repeated practice of each concept presented.

I. INTRODUCTION TO ORAL COMMUNICATION: 1ST YEAR

Chapters		Time Line (Weeks)
A. Verbal Messages		3
B. Nonverbal Messages		3
C. Vocal Messages		3
D. International Phonetic Alphabet (supplemental unit)		1
E. Listening for Meaning in Messages		4
F. Interpersonal Communication		4
	Total	18 weeks
G. Interviews		2
H. Introductions and Directions		2
I. Informal Talk: Conversation		4
J. Group Discussion		3
K. Debate		5
L. Parliamentary Procedure (supplemental unit)		2
	Total	18 weeks

II. INTRODUCTION TO ORAL COMMUNICATION: 2ND YEAR

Chapters		Time Line (Weeks)
A. Review parts A, B, C, and E from 1st year		2
B. Review part F from 1st year		1
C. Purposes and Types of Public Speaking		3
D. Finding Suitable Topics		2
E. Researching and Structuring Speeches		3
F. Techniques of Delivery		3
G. Analyzing and Responding		2
H. Practice a Variety of Speeches		2
	Total	18 weeks
I. Oral Interpretation		4
J. Group Interpretation		3
K. Informal Theater		4
L. Acting		4
M. Producing Plays		3
	Total	18 weeks

With parts K, L, and M, a teacher may want to have the students work, step-by-step, toward actually producing a play. If this is the case, the time line should be adjusted as follows:

	Weeks
I. Oral Interpretation	3
J. Group Interpretation	2
K. Informal Theater	4
L. Acting	3
M. Producing Plays	3
N. Class Play	3
Total	18 weeks

If the decision is made to produce a play, consideration should be given to children's theater. It is ideal for beginning drama students for the following reasons.

1. The dialogue and plot are simple.
2. The motivation is generally very good.
3. The sets, props, and costumes can be provided easily and inexpensively.
4. The audience, usually the children at a nearby elementary school, are a responsive and appreciative group.

Each chapter in the basic text follows a similar format. After the introduction of new information, students use the information immediately in the section "Thinking It Over." Review questions appear at the end of the chapter in the section "Learning by Doing." In the *Teacher's Guide,* a wealth of activities is developed including supporting charts, guides, and checklists (see Examples 12-1 to 12-8).

EXAMPLE 12-1   ADDITIONAL ACTIVITIES I*

1. Have the students observe a televised discussion group, such as "Meet the Press." They should evaluate one participant in terms of his or her qualifications and responsibilities. You may want to have them use a critique form to evaluate the performance.
2. Have the students evaluate the moderator of the same televised group in terms of his or her qualifications and responsibilities. What type of leader was the moderator?
3. Based on the students' own experiences, they should list the qualities and attitudes that help make certain individuals strong or weak members of a discussion group.
4. Ask a community leader to speak to the class on the importance of discussion and debate.
5. Have students select a topic and decide which type of discussion would best suit that problem and explain why.
6. Have a class discussion on the differences between discussion, conversation, and speech-making.
7. Below is a critique form you might want to have your students use.

*From Gail Witt, *Teacher's Guide for Communicating Message and Meaning* (Lexington, Mass.: Ginn, 1982), pp. 91–92.

EXAMPLE 12-1 (cont.)

GROUP DISCUSSION CRITIQUE

Question _____

Rating Scale: 1: poor   2: fair   3: adequate   4: good   5: excellent

PARTICIPANTS	1	2	3	4	5	6	7	8
Knowledge of the problem								
Logic in reasoning								
Skill in following "pattern"								
Willingness to promote discussion								
Cooperation in thinking and contributing								
Speaking skills								
Totals								

THE LEADER

Skill in stating the problem	Skill in clarifying, summarizing, and pointing up
Skill in stimulating the discussion without dominating	Skill in handling the various kinds of conflicts
Skill in guiding the pattern of reflective thinking	Skill in stimulating a cooperative spirit
Skill in encouraging the inclusion of all points of view	Skill in controlling the pace to all members and the time limit

Group Grade _____

Participants' Grades

1. _____ 2. _____ 3. _____ 4. _____ 5. _____ 6. _____ 7. _____ 8. _____

EXAMPLE 12-2   AUDIENCE ANALYSIS*

Based on the next speech you give in class, write an analysis of your audience. You should indicate what you know about class members and how you will try to adapt this information to your presentation. Indicate all factors that you think will be helpful in your preparation. (Answers will vary. Ask for a written analysis of the audience and a list of what factors will be considered in preparing the speech.)

After presenting your speech to the class, write two to three paragraphs which describe at least two individuals in your audience. Indicate what they did during your speech. Were their reactions predictable? Why or why not? (Reactions will vary. Suggest that your students discuss verbal, vocal, and nonverbal responses and other types of feedback.)

AUDIENCE INFORMATION SURVEY

Instructions: This information survey is intended to gather information about members of this audience to assist future speakers. Please do not identify yourself by name since the

*From Gail Witt, *Teacher's Guide for Communicating Message and Meaning* (Lexington, Mass.: Ginn, 1982), p. 150.

EXAMPLE 12-2 (cont.)

information will be tabulated and reported without reference to specific individuals. Circle the answers that best represent your current status.

1. Age group: 12–14; 15–17; 18–20
2. Sex: male; female
3. I currently live in: a city; a suburb; a small town; a rural area
4. I belong to the following school organizations: band or orchestra; choir or glee club; art club; student council; pep club or booster club; debate team; drama club or Thespians; a school service club; newspaper staff; yearbook staff; Future Farmers of America; Future Homemakers of America; National Honor Society; basketball team; football team; golf team; soccer team; volleyball team; wrestling team; swim team; other
5. I have lived in this area for: 0–1 year; 2–4 years; 5–7 years; 8–10 years; 11–13 years; 14–16 years; all my life
6. My main pastimes and interests are (check as many as apply): reading; writing; painting; drawing; woodworking; metal working; pottery or ceramics; car repair/restoration; hunting; fishing; boating; athletics; dancing; cooking or baking; camping; sewing; knitting; sculpture; electronics or computers; travel; foreign languages; animals; hiking; jogging; horticulture; macramé; singing; playing a musical instrument; other
7. If you now have a part-time job, indicate the approximate number of hours you work each week at the job: 4–6; 7–9; 10–12; 13–15; 16–18; 19–21; 22–25; 26 or more
8. What grade are you in? 9th; 10th; 11th; 12th
9. When you graduate from high school, what do you intend to do? go to a 4–year college; go to a 2–year college; go to a vocational school; get a job

EXAMPLE 12-3 ADDITIONAL ACTIVITIES II*

1. Throughout this unit, have your students keep a file of the critiques that you and their classmates have given them. About halfway through the unit, they should compose an outline that summarizes the critiques by highlighting their outstanding strengths and weaknesses. Periodically these outlines should be updated. In this way, students will see if they are making any progress toward improving their weaknesses.
2. . . . Have students develop a post-speech analysis questionnaire and a shift-of-opinion ballot. Discuss these post-speech analysis instruments in class.
3. Using the Audience Analysis and Adaptation Sheet, have students give a speech, conduct a post-speech analysis, and present the speech a second time, making any necessary adaptations.
4. Following the Audience Analysis and Adaptation Sheet are other critique sheets you might want to have your students use as various types of speeches are presented.

(Example 12-3 cont. on next page)

*From Gail Witt, *Teacher's Guide for Communicating Message and Meaning* (Lexington, Mass.: Ginn, 1982), p. 151.

EXAMPLE 12-3 (cont.)

AUDIENCE ANALYSIS AND ADAPTATION SHEET

Name _____ Date _____

Topic _____

Rating Scale: 1: inadequate   2: poor   3: fair   4: good   5: excellent

	Speech 1	Speech 2
Approach	_____	_____
Poise	_____	_____
Eye contact	_____	_____
Adaptation of physical delivery	_____	_____
Adaptation of vocal delivery	_____	_____
Adaptation of language	_____	_____
Adaptation of content	_____	_____
Adaptation of organization	_____	_____

Grade _____

Comments:

EXAMPLE 12-4   INTRODUCTORY SPEECH*

Name _____ Date _____

Topic _____

Rating Scale: 1: inadequate   2: poor   3: fair   4: good   5: excellent

Choice of subject	_____
Creativity of introduction	_____
Interesting content	_____
Amount of detail	_____
Adequate content in terms of time limit	_____
Basic organization	_____
Freedom from notes	_____
Confidence	_____

*From Gail Witt, *Teacher's Guide for Communicating Message and Meaning* (Lexington, Mass.: Ginn, 1982), p. 152.

EXAMPLE 12-4 (cont.)

Volume   _____

Articulation   _____

Posture   _____

Gestures   _____

Eye contact   _____

Vocal emphasis   _____

Grade _____

Comments:

EXAMPLE 12-5 DEMONSTRATION SPEECH*

Name _____ Date _____

Topic _____

Rating Scale: 1: inadequate   2: poor   3: fair   4: good   5: excellent

Analysis of audience in choice of topic   _____

Approach   _____

Poise   _____

Handling of visual aids   _____

Eye contact   _____

Use of gestures   _____

Volume   _____

Rate   _____

Pause   _____

Articulation   _____

Introduction   _____

Use of supporting material   _____

Conclusion   _____

Grade _____

Comments:

*From Gail Witt, *Teacher's Guide for Communicating Message and Meaning* (Lexington, Mass.: Ginn, 1982), p. 153.

EXAMPLE 12-6 INFORMATIVE SPEECH*

Name _____ Date _____

Topic _____

Rating Scale: 1: inadequate   2: poor   3: fair   4: good   5: excellent

Approach to platform   _____

Poise and confidence   _____

Eye contact   _____

Volume   _____

Rate   _____

Posture   _____

Gestures   _____

Vocal emphasis   _____

Introduction:

    Attention getter   _____

    Statement of purpose   _____

    Preview of main points   _____

Body:

    Clear identification of main points   _____

    Adequate use of supporting material   _____

    Clear transitions   _____

Conclusion:

    Summary of main points   _____

    Reminder of purpose   _____

    Final statement   _____

Grade _____

Comments:

*From Gail Witt, *Teacher's Guide for Communicating Message and Meaning* (Lexington, Mass.: Ginn, 1982), p. 154.

EXAMPLE **12-7** PERSUASIVE SPEECH*

Name _____ Date _____

Topic _____

Rating Scale: 1: inadequate   2: poor   3: fair   4: good   5: excellent

Attention getter   _____

Clarity of thesis   _____

Clarity of organizational pattern   _____

Transitions   _____

Conclusion   _____

Use of logical (logos) appeals   _____

Use of emotional (pathos) appeals   _____

Variety of supporting material   _____

Persuasive nature of speech   _____

Memorization   _____

Vocal variety   _____

Volume   _____

Eye contact   _____

Gestures   _____

Posture   _____

Grade _____

Comments:

EXAMPLE **12-8** CONTROVERSIAL SPEECH†

Name _____ Date _____

Topic _____

Rating Scale: 1: inadequate   2: poor   3: fair   4: good   5: excellent

Clear statement of stand on issue   _____

Reasons for stand on issue   _____

*From Gail Witt, *Teacher's Guide for Communicating Message and Meaning* (Lexington, Mass.: Ginn, 1982), p. 155.
†Ibid., p. 156.

EXAMPLE 12-8 (cont.)

Supporting material for reasons (reasons, examples,
statistics, quotes, facts)   _____

Clear organization   _____

Eye contact   _____

Variety in vocal inflection   _____

Poise and confidence   _____

Grade _____

Comments:

HANDBOOKS

In addition to the textbook, *Communicating Message and Meaning,* several basic handbooks are used. *Don't Talk . . . Communicate* by the Department of the Navy (Washington, D.C.: Government Printing Office, 1980) provides an excellent introduction to the science of purposeful and effective communication. The *Contents** of this handbook follows:

PART I
    Preface
  1. Speaking of Communication
  2. Presentation Preliminaries
  3. Audience Analysis
  4. Selecting Your Material
  5. Writing Your Presentation
  6. Considering Visual Aids
  7. The Three R's: Rehearse, Rehearse, Rehearse
  8. Critique and Finishing Touches
  9. Staging the Presentation
10. Delivering the Presentation

PART II
    Designing Communications Graphics
    Conclusion

Throughout this course, a basic text is *Writing with Power: Techniques for Mastering the Writing Process* by Peter Elbow. This handbook, which is used in a number of college freshman English courses, provides practical step-by-step guidance in how to write effectively. The Contents[†] of this excellent writing guide follows.

---

*From U.S. Department of the Navy, *Don't Talk . . . Communicate* (Washington, D.C.: Government Printing Office, 1980), p. 3.

[†]From Peter Elbow, *Writing with Power: Techniques for Mastering the Writing Process* (New York: Oxford, 1981), pp. x–xi. Copyright © 1981 by Oxford University Press, Inc. Reprinted by permission.

I. SOME ESSENTIALS
   Introduction: A Map of the Book
   1. An Approach to Writing
   2. Freewriting
   3. Sharing
   4. The Direct Writing Process for Getting Words on Paper
   5. Quick Revising
   6. The Dangerous Method: Trying To Write It Right the First Time
II. MORE WAYS OF GETTING WORDS ON PAPER
   Introduction
   7. The Open-ended Writing Process
   8. The Loop Writing Process
   9. Metaphors for Priming the Pump
   10. Working on Writing While Not Thinking about Writing
   11. Poetry as No Big Deal
III. MORE WAYS TO REVISE
   Introduction
   12. Thorough Revising
   13. Revising with Feedback
   14. Cut-and-Paste Revising and the Collage
   15. The Last Step: Getting Rid of Mistakes in Grammar
   16. Nausea
IV. AUDIENCE
   Introduction
   17. Other People
   18. Audience as Focusing Force
   19. Three Tricky Relationships to an Audience
   20. Writing for Teachers
V. FEEDBACK
   Introduction
   21. Criterion-Based Feedback and Reader-Based Feedback
   22. A Catalogue of Criterion-Based Questions
   23. A Catalogue of Reader-Based Questions
   24. Options for Getting Feedback
VI. POWER IN WRITING
   Introduction
   25. Writing and Voice
   26. How To Get Power through Voice
   27. Breathing Experience into Words
   28. Breathing Experience into Expository Writing
   29. Writing and Magic

At the conclusion of most of the chapters in *Writing with Power,* the author presents a short summary of basic elements or a section of advice. These summary sections are invaluable and make an excellent source of writing guidelines for inclusion in the student's notebook for the course.

Complete as the textbook *Communicating Message and Meaning* is, the creative teacher will find additional enrichment-acceleration experiences to introduce. For example, a unit on journalism as a career would be appropriate and well worth teacher and student exploration. Such a unit might highlight the following topics:

1. Kinds of journalism.
   a. Broadcast journalism: television (see Example 12-9 at end of this model), radio.
   b. Newspaper journalism: features, "straight" news, specialized news, editorials.

HANDOUT 12-1   A STATEMENT OF PRINCIPLES*

PREAMBLE

The First Amendment, protecting freedom of expression from abridgment by any law, guarantees to the people through their press a constitutional right, and thereby places on newspaper people a particular responsibility.

Thus journalism demands of its practitioners not only industry and knowledge but also the pursuit of a standard of integrity proportionate to the journalist's singular obligation.

To this end the American Society of Newspaper Editors sets forth this Statement of Principles as a standard encouraging the highest ethical and professional performance.

ARTICLE I—RESPONSIBILITY

The primary purpose of gathering and distributing news and opinion is to serve the general welfare by informing the people and enabling them to make judgments on the issues of the time. Newspapermen and women who abuse the power of their professional role for selfish motives or unworthy purposes are faithless to that public trust.

The American press was made free not just to inform or just to serve as a forum for debate but also to bring an independent scrutiny to bear on the forces of power in the society, including the conduct of official power at all levels of government.

ARTICLE II—FREEDOM OF THE PRESS

Freedom of the press belongs to the people. It must be defended against encroachment or assault from any quarter, public or private.

Journalists must be constantly alert to see that the public's business is conducted in public. They must be vigilant against all who would exploit the press for selfish purposes.

ARTICLE III—INDEPENDENCE

Journalists must avoid impropriety and the appearance of impropriety as well as any conflict of interest or the appearance of conflict. They should neither accept anything nor pursue any activity that might compromise or seem to compromise their integrity.

ARTICLE IV—TRUTH AND ACCURACY

Good faith with the reader is the foundation of good journalism. Every effort must be made to assure that the news content is accurate, free from bias and in context, and that all sides are presented fairly. Editorials, analytical articles and commentary should be held to the same standards of accuracy with respect to facts as news reports.

Significant errors of fact, as well as errors of omission, should be corrected promptly and prominently.

ARTICLE V—IMPARTIALITY

To be impartial does not require the press to be unquestioning or to refrain from editorial expression. Sound practice, however, demands a clear distinction for the reader between news reports and opinion. Articles that contain opinion or personal interpretation should be clearly identified.

ARTICLE VI—FAIR PLAY

Journalists should respect the rights of people involved in the news, observe the common standards of decency and stand accountable to the public for the fairness and accuracy of their news reports.

Persons publicly accused should be given the earliest opportunity to respond.

Pledges of confidentiality to news sources must be honored at all costs, and therefore should not be given lightly. Unless there is clear and pressing need to maintain confidences, sources of information should be identified.

These principles are intended to preserve, protect and strengthen the bond of trust and respect between American journalists and the American people, a bond that is essential to sustain the grant of freedom entrusted to both by the nation's founders.

*American Society of Newspaper Editors, adopted Oct. 23, 1975.

2. Statement of Principles of journalism (see Handout 12-1).
3. Creative Code of the American Association of Advertising Agencies (see Handout 12-2).
4. Jobs of disc jockey and radio announcer: *Into Radio* (Random—1 filmstrip, 1 cassette).
5. A Day in the Life of the *Los Angeles Times: Newspaper Story* (Encyclopaedia Britannica—motion picture).
6. Edwin Newman Explains Print and Broadcast Journalism: *What Is Journalism?* (Guidance Associates—2 filmstrips, 2 cassettes).
7. The Operation and Function of a Newspaper: *Your Newspaper* (Coronet—6 filmstrips, 6 cassettes).
8. Who Puts the News on Television?: *TV News: Behind the Scenes* (Encyclopaedia Britannica—motion picture); *Whe Puts the News on Television?* (Random—1 filmstrip, 1 cassette, 1 book); *Making the News: A Prime Time School Television Curriculum Project* (see Example 12-9 at the end of this model).

Two valuable sources of contemporary radio programs dealing with issues and concerns of today should be highlighted in this unit. They are the Cambridge Forum, which offers approximately 300 cassette tapes of Forum discussion programs, and National Public Radio, which offers approximately 800 cassette tapes of radio programs dealing with contemporary issues. These radio program tapes are of value not only for their content but for their offering students models to study for the techniques and approaches to informational radio programming.

HANDOUT 12-2 CREATIVE CODE OF THE AMERICAN ASSOCIATION OF ADVERTISING AGENCIES*

We, the members of the American Association of Advertising Agencies, in addition to supporting and obeying the laws and legal regulations pertaining to advertising, undertake to extend and broaden the application of high ethical standards. Specifically, we will not knowingly produce advertising which contains:

a. False or misleading statements or exaggerations, visual or verbal.

b. Testimonials which do not reflect the real choice of a competent witness.

c. Price claims which are misleading.

d. Comparisons which unfairly disparage a competitive product or service.

e. Claims insufficiently supported, or which distort the true meaning of practicable application of statements made by professional or scientific authority.

f. Statements, suggestions or pictures offensive to public decency.

*American Association of Advertising Agencies.

EXAMPLE 12-9   MAKING THE NEWS: A PTST CURRICULUM PROJECT*

We live in a society in which individuals are frequently called upon to express their opinions on a variety of complex issues that will determine the quality of their lives. A continuous input of accurate information is essential if these decisions are to be informed and responsible. Much of the public now relies on televised broadcasts as their major source of news about the world around them.

In the face of this growing reliance on television for information, it is crucial that students and teachers explore the critical decisions involved in news broadcasts. *Making the News: A PTST Curriculum Project* is divided into five sections. The first four will explore television news in its major formats: the evening news, the documentary, the interview, and the television magazine. A final section, "Outside Considerations," will examine other factors relating to television news production such as Federal Communications Commission (FCC) regulations. The focus in each section will be on the critical decisions that are involved, and often dictated by each format.

Each format will be examined from the perspective of the following critical decisions: (1) the selection of the issue or event to be included in each program, (2) the structure of the story, (3) the depth and length, and (4) the perspective and objectivity maintained in the coverage.

CLASSROOM APPLICATION

CONTENT

The sections focusing on specific news formats each contain an introduction and a teaching framework based on the four critical production decisions. The discussion of each critical decision involves questions for consideration, background information, and suggested student projects and activities. Teachers may develop separate lessons around the materials provided for each critical decision or may choose to discuss each news format in broader terms.

While the background material is intended as reference for teachers, it also may be duplicated for student use. (The guide may be reproduced as any black line master.) The questions *For consideration* are intended to raise critical concerns about TV news production and to direct attention to specific aspects of news production. Use the questions as a starting point for class discussion. A listing of print and nonprint resources is included for further research.

MECHANICS

Use *Making the News* during a concentrated period or throughout the school year. Television viewing provides the framework for the curriculum project and the catalyst for class discussion. Use the sample TV viewing logs [the end of this Example] to focus students' viewing toward consideration of particular issues. For example, when discussing story selection, students may log each of the major stories reported on the three network newscasts in a given evening. Using the log, students come to class prepared to analyze and discuss the programs. Viewing assignments should be made early in the week so students can record information throughout the week. Assignments should be flexible to accommodate those students who may not be able to see a particular newscast or program. Teachers may wish to send home a letter informing parents that television viewing is a homework assignment.

The curriculum project may be used in a variety of classroom settings. Social studies teachers might focus on current events. How are issues of public importance treated by television news? English and journalism teachers may use the unit as a vehicle for news-writing activities, comparative analysis of language used on TV newscasts and in newspapers, or exercises in connotation and denotation of words. Media teachers may involve students in production experiences which demonstrate the time constraints involved in news production. Discussions may highlight the ways in which audiovisual techniques affect the content and style of newscasts.

*Reprinted with permission by Prime Time School Television, 40 E. Huron Street, Chicago, IL 60611.

EXAMPLE 12-9 (cont.)

ACKNOWLEDGMENT

Prime Time School Television has long recognized the importance of providing a unit of study focusing on televised news. Since television news is part of many students' daily experience, it is of particular importance to explore the nature of the newscasts and their impact on students' perceptions of the world.

We are most grateful to ABC for not only recognizing the need for such materials, but also for providing the financial and staff resources which made this unit possible. The invaluable insights and experiences, shared generously by the staff and executives of ABC News, under the direction of its President, Roone Arledge, provide a unique perspective on the production of the news. While ABC news programs are used as models, students and teachers will compare reporting among networks and local newscasts vis-a-vis print journalism as they use the curriculum project.

THE NETWORK EVENING NEWS

Because the evening news is the single most important news format in television, it is essential that students and teachers examine it critically and formulate some viewing guidelines to help them evaluate both the content and the presentation of the news. Av Westin, Executive Producer of *World News Tonight,** calls the evening news an illustrated headline service that gives an overview of the major events of the day. Some critics have claimed that a headline service is inadequate in that it provides only superficial coverage of the news. This section will examine this question, as well as issues such as objectivity of coverage, the reasons for a story's inclusion, and the depth and length of the reporting.

One portion of the evening news section is entitled "A Day in the Newsroom: The Process." Here the students will be given a behind-the-scenes look at the people, and job responsibilities, involved in the production of one day's newscast. This section illustrates the tremendous time constraints affecting the production of the evening news.

SELECTION OF TOPICS. FOR CONSIDERATION:

Are the events and issues covered on a given day the most important? Are certain areas or issues neglected or consistently under-reported? How large a factor is the visual appeal in the selection of a story? How does this compare to newspapers?

"News is a combination of two things: what is important and what is interesting. What is important is what the audience should hear about, what will affect them directly. What is interesting is what the audience wants to hear about, whether or not it will have any particular direct or important effect on their lives. Sometimes the two coincide, sometimes they don't." (Mike Stein, Editorial Producer, *World News Tonight.*)

By conventional journalistic standards, the importance and interest of a story would be the primary considerations in its selection. However, because the same network news is transmitted to disparate communities across the United States, the question of importance and interest necessarily takes on a broader focus. What is important to the audience in New York may not be of interest or importance to viewers in Idaho.

There are also some unwritten guidelines that facilitate the judging of a story's "newsworthiness." By convention, certain subjects are regularly covered on the network newscasts. Whether these stories merit daily coverage has been a topic of some discussion by television critics.

Events that affect the nation as a whole, such as foreign policy decisions or energy shortages, are certainly both important and of interest to most viewers. Generally, the federal government, particularly the President, is considered newsworthy on any given day. Correspondents regularly cover the White House, Congress, and House and Senate hearings.

The stories that have been singled out for their substantive importance must still conform to criteria dictated by television as a medium. Television is a visual medium. "Physiologically, the eye takes precedence over the ear. What one sees, one retains the most.

*As this project went to press, PTST learned that Av Westin had been promoted to Vice-President of Program Development for ABC News.

EXAMPLE 12-9 (cont.)

Combining the visual with the audio reinforces the impact of the message. . . . How we use pictures is important to the success of how well we transmit information. . . . If the picture and narration fight, confusion results. The best reportage is reduced to 'oatmeal' and the best pictures to 'wallpaper.' " (Av Westin, Executive Producer, *World News Tonight.*) Film and tape footage present the source of action or conflict and provide immediacy. Given two stories of equal substantive importance, the one with the more dramatic visuals is almost always given preference. After all, the aura of "you are there" is what makes television news unique.

Occasionally, production concerns also play a role in dictating the selection of a news story. Time is needed, after the footage is shot, for the tape or film to be edited and matched with a narrative for the evening broadcast. In some situations, getting the tape or film out of a country may be extremely difficult. Transmitting the tape involves special considerations: cost and availability of satellite time, existence of telephone cables for transmission; affiliates' equipment capabilities to edit and "feed" tapes to the network.

Finally, producers establish selection criteria. Av Westin starts with some basic assumptions. "I believe the audience at dinner time wants to know the answers to three very important questions: Is the world safe? Are my hometown and my home safe? If my family is safe, then what happened in the past 24 hours to make them better off or to amuse them? . . . I think television news *is* an illustrated headline service which can function best when it is regarded by its viewers as an important yet fast adjunct to the newspapers."

ACTIVITIES

1. Discuss: What is news? Who do you think decides which events are newsworthy? Should the news inform? Entertain?

2. How do time constraints affect story selection for the evening news?

3. Using several morning newspapers and current news magazines, select the stories for a mock evening newscast. Focus on criteria for story selection and order. Consider the amount of time you wish to give to national, international, and local events. Will you have special features, sports coverage, editorials? Divide the 22-minute newscast among your reports. The class should work in small groups and compare their outlines, focusing on the stories they selected as well as their reasons for excluding others. (Note: "A Day in the Newsroom: The Process" is a good resource for this activity.)

STRUCTURE. FOR CONSIDERATION:

How does the order of the news stories affect the viewer? Do we watch "anchor personalities" because we like them or do we watch a network or local newscast for its excellence in news coverage? What has become of commentary TV, the equivalent of the newspaper editorial?

There is an established order in the structure of the evening newscasts. Like the stories on the front page of a newspaper, the lead stories of a TV newscast are most important. Traditionally, news stories are grouped thematically: Presidential news will be grouped together, as well as foreign, political, and economic news.

The format of the newscast is also highly structured. The anchor person acts as the cement of the broadcasts, pulling together reports from the field correspondents, providing the transitions, and delivering the "tell" stories. The best anchor person also lends the news an air of paternal order, having established a rapport with a large number of viewers. These anchor persons can play an important part in viewer selection of one network over another.

ACTIVITIES

1. List each story reported in a newscast. Note if the report had accompanying videotape or film or if the report was accompanied by a graphic. Which reports were more interesting? In what order were the reports presented?

2. Watch the *MacNeil/Lehrer Report* (PBS). The 30-minute program is devoted to the coverage of one particular topic. Compare this format to the format of ABC, CBS, and NBC national news. What are the advantages and disadvantages of each format?

3. Analyze the form of the news "story." Is it a narrative containing a lead, a conflict, and a conclusion? Compare to the structure of a newspaper story.

EXAMPLE 12-9 (cont.)

4. Compare ABC's trio of anchors with the structure at CBS and NBC. What are the pros and cons of the different structures?

DEPTH AND LENGTH. FOR CONSIDERATION:

Compare the depth of coverage in newspapers to TV. Do you think one-half hour is an adequate length of time in which to cover the day's news? How might an hour-long news program provide more in-depth coverage? Would people watch?

The evening network news broadcasts are 30 minutes long. After the time allocated to commercials is subtracted, approximately 22 minutes remain to report the news of the day. It is often stated that if these 22 minutes were converted into print, they would be roughly equivalent to two columns on the front page of the *New York Times*. To make a fair comparison between television newscasts and newspapers, one must take into consideration the total TV news output of a network: documentaries, interviews, special events, magazine formats, and the evening news. Additionally, Producer Av Westin says, "One must take into consideration the fact that 'space' on television is equal to time. When one runs an interview with a crying survivor, the emotion conveyed and the impact of the tears are far greater when seen on television than when reported in print. What takes only one line of print space could easily take 45 seconds or a minute of air time. So, the often-repeated statement that 22 minutes of air time is the equivalent to two columns of the *New York Times* is simply mixing apples and oranges."

Typically, a broadcast will consist of six or seven taped "hard news" stories, each one or two minutes in duration; intermixed with the "hard news" are perhaps one or two slightly longer feature stories or continuing special series reports. The verbal reports or "tells," which make up about six minutes of each program, run from 15 to 30 seconds. These reports introduce and punctuate taped stories and summarize stories that do not lend themselves to visual treatment or more in-depth coverage.

The lack of depth in the coverage of the evening network news is a central point of criticism and, paradoxically, results from its main attraction. It is the immediacy and fast pacing of the television newsclips that captivate the viewer. However, it is often difficult to maintain the pacing and also convey complex or subtle ideas. The public has come to expect compact outlines, in film form, of an event. Usually the coverage is given a narrative structure, complete with conflict and resolution, to make it easier to follow.

ACTIVITIES

1. Brainstorm: What are the differences between print and nonprint news? List pros and cons of each.

2. A news story must tell who, what, where, when, why, and how. Watch an evening newscast and list several events reported. Does each answer the necessary questions? Compare the facts in the news report to those in the newspaper. What details were added in the newspaper? How did the accompanying video portion give more details about the event?

3. The average news story is one to two minutes in length. Select three current events in your community and write a one- or two-minute newsclip. Students should research the topic, interview resource people, and prepare copy. The class should compare different students' treatment of the same event. Did the clip answer the questions who, what, where, when, why, and how? Expand the project by producing graphics (posters, photographs, slides); audiotapes; or videotapes to accompany the newsclip. Discuss the facts that were included in each newsclip and those that were omitted. Did the graphics enhance audience understanding of the issue?

OBJECTIVITY. FOR CONSIDERATION:

Should reporters always be objective in their coverage of stories? Why? Can a correspondent's language influence the viewer's opinion? Do network news programs demonstrate a geographical bias toward Washington and New York?

"I don't think it's any of our business what the moral, political, social, or economic effect of our reporting is. I say let's get on with the job of reporting the news—and let the chips fall where they may." (Walter Cronkite, CBS News, *Saturday Review*, December 12, 1970.)

EXAMPLE 12-9 (cont.)

Traditionally, the evening newscaster has been seen as a straight reporter of the news, informing the public about the events of the day. Any analysis or commentary is clearly delineated from straight reporting.

Frank Reynolds, ABC News, maintains the role of the newscaster is not to influence or sway the public but to give the public information about issues which will affect them. In discussing the debate over ratification of the SALT II Treaty, Reynolds states that "the coverage of the SALT debate is going to be one of our most challenging responsibilities. . . . Our job is not to influence the Senate, not to defeat or ratify the SALT treaty, but just to provide a better informed electorate."

The "Fairness Doctrine" governs the overall objectivity of news presentations. Fairness is regulated by libel laws and FCC rules. Generally stated, both sides of an issue must be given equal air time. (See "Outside Considerations" for more detail.)

ACTIVITIES

1. What is the relationship between news broadcasts and public opinion? Do the mass media shape public opinion or reinforce and reflect existing opinion?

2. Loaded words: Objectivity is fundamental in presenting the news. Word choice is of particular importance. Write five news headlines and experiment by replacing the nouns and verbs with words that have different connotations. For example: "Students Protest Draft" can become "Hippies Storm Pentagon." Compare television news broadcasts in terms of "loaded" words.

3. Obtain a copy of former Vice-President Spiro T. Agnew's speech in Des Moines, Iowa, on November 13, 1969 (*New York Times,* November 14, 1969) in which Agnew discussed the power of the news media. Discuss the power and responsibility involved in TV news production. Do you agree or disagree with Agnew? Consult Walter Lippmann's *Public Opinion* (NY: New York Free Press, 1965) for a general discussion of the journalist's responsibility.

4. Examine several news reports for objectivity. Are representatives from both sides of the issue included?

5. "A candidate uses everything just to entice us [TV broadcasters] into giving him a few minutes. . . . If they [the candidates] speak all day, they may reach 15,000 people. But, if they get just two minutes on the evening news, they get 60 million. They hop all over the state, just so we'll hop with them. . . . The politicians still manipulate us. We all know that." (Harry Reasoner, *Chicago Sun-Times,* June 10, 1976.) How much coverage of political events is there on network and local newscasts? What is a press conference? What is a press release? How do TV and newspaper reporters find out about a candidate's activity? Secure press releases from local campaign offices. (See *Boys on the Bus* by Timothy Crouse, NY: Random House, 1973, which documents media coverage of the 1972 Presidential election.)

GENERAL ACTIVITIES

1. TV viewing logs should be used as students watch the evening news. See [the end of this Example] for samples and instructions.

2. Discuss: Do you watch the news? How often? Do you read newspapers or news magazines? In what ways do you learn about world, national, state, and local events?

3. Discuss: Do economic considerations affect the content and airing of television news broadcasts? What role do ratings play in determining news format and content? (Note: These questions are applicable in discussions related to the four news formats.)

4. Av Westin, *World News Tonight* Executive Producer, used the following exercise with news reporters across the country. It works as well with students: Select a national news story and write it as a local story. Focus on the local impact of the event, considering the broad implications of the story.

5. What historic events have you witnessed on the news? How did the news coverage affect your perceptions of the event? Interview parents, relatives, and friends regarding significant news reports which they can recollect.

6. Invite representatives from local television stations to class to share their experiences, or visit a local TV station to watch news production.

7. Research changes in TV news beginning with Edward R. Murrow.

EXAMPLE **12-9 (cont.)**

8. Students with a particular interest in science and electronics might research the workings of television transmission via satellite; telephone cables; and the sending of scripts by "rapidfax" and video editing.

9. Discuss a particular issue, such as busing and school desegregation. In *Remote Control* (Ballantine Books, 1978, p. 91), Frank Mankiewicz and Joel Swerdlow maintain that ". . . unless there is violence, or the threat of it, busing is rarely covered on television." Do you agree or disagree? Consider television's orientation toward action and drama, rather than "talking heads."

10. Research costs for 20-second, 30-second, and one-minute commercials during local news, network news, prime time entertainment programs, and sports events such as the Superbowl. Compute the approximate cost of the commercial per home.

11. Why might the affiliates be reluctant to expand network news to 60 minutes? Would profits be a consideration? Do the advertisers pay the local affiliate or the network for a commercial? Refer to Edward Jay Epstein's *News from Nowhere: Television and the News.* (See "Resources.")

12. What types of products are advertised during the network shows? Local news? What assumptions about the audiences are being made by the advertisers?

13. Discuss: Do news broadcasts give the people what they want to see or what they need to know?

14. Compare local news broadcasts in terms of tone, style of reporting, emphasis on commentators' personalities, features, and amount of hard news. Contrast network news with local news. What is the tone of each broadcast?

15. News consultants, who are experts in market research and television technology, have been criticized for bringing show-business values to news. Read Ron Powers' *The Newscasters* (see "Resources") and the August 6, 1979, issue of *Broadcasting Magazine,* which focuses on "Local TV Journalism in 1979: Rising to Meet the Expectations." Discuss the pros and cons of news consultants.

16. Develop a questionnaire to survey people in your community and school regarding their opinions about evening newscasts. Questions about changes people would like to see in the news should be included. Publish the results in the school newspaper (or contact the local television station).

A DAY IN THE NEWSROOM: THE PROCESS

Every day, decisions are made about the content and the presentation of the evening news. This section gives a minute-by-minute look at the people who produce the news and the decisions they must make as they work toward the 6:00 PM deadline.

The coverage of a particular day's events actually begins at the Assignment Desk on the day preceding the broadcast. It is here that the correspondent, producer, and camera-crew assignments are made. There are several sources on which the Assignment Desk relies to make its decisions. A "futures" file is kept on potential stories, often months before they break. For example, coverage of the SALT talks might be planned long before the talks begin. The Assignment Desk also relies on AP, UPI, and Reuters wire services for information about breaking news events and on correspondents and bureaus for reports on scheduled events such as White House activities, press conferences, and Senate hearings.

At ABC, the *World News Tonight* senior producers maintain close contact with the Assignment Desk around the clock. A final check on the next day's arrangements is made late the night before. Everyday the Assignment Desk prepares a report called "Troop Movements," describing which crews are positioned where in anticipation of the next day's news events. Each morning the Assignment Desk also prepares a "situationer," giving a status report on the location of the staff and a summary of the events being covered. The "situationer" is continually altered during the course of the day.

At approximately 9:00 AM the senior news staff arrives in the newsroom and begins the process of "reading-in." This consists of going through the overnight dispatches and cables from correspondents and bureaus around the world. Wires and cables from UPI, AP, and the Reuters News Service are also read to keep abreast of overnight develop-ments and breaking stories. It is during this period of the morning that the daily "situa-

EXAMPLE 12-9 (cont.)

tioner" is issued, detailing where stories are breaking and who will be covering the day's stories.

At 10:00 AM representatives from *World News Tonight, Good Morning America,* Special Events, and other relevant divisions of ABC News gather for the morning conference. ABC News Bureaus from all around the country are linked in a joint conference call. The purpose of this open conference is to advise everyone throughout the network as to who is covering what events and to accept suggestions or amendments.

While the executive producer can direct the allocation of his news gathering resources from New York, he relies, in large part, on the news judgment of the correspondents, producers, and cameramen in the field. As Av Westin puts it: "The pictures taken by the cameraman to illustrate the story are fixed in film. The accompanying narration by the correspondent is, for all practical purposes, unchangeably contained on the audiotape or on the sound track. What the cameraman, producer, and correspondent include or omit in the field determines whether that story is complete enough to be broadcast."

At 10:30 AM the senior producers and editors gather again to read wires, speak to correspondents, and continue the process of determining the lineup of news stories for the evening broadcast. During this period the producers are continually on the phone with correspondents and field producers trying to get a feeling for the importance and interest of each story. The 22 minutes allotted for the newscast is now tentatively divided into segments of varying lengths.

Much of this time before lunch is also spent selecting the most important or "lead" story. Sometimes the lead is not a single story but a combination of related items which, together, are the most important element of the day. For example, the lead might consist of a number of facts relating to the Mideast from Jerusalem, Cairo, and Washington.

The evening news is divided into segments with commercials serving as the demarcation lines. The lead story of each segment is important because it sets a theme or tone for that segment. An effort is made, as much as possible, to establish connections between stories, thereby giving each section of the newscast continuity.

Between 10:30 and 12:00 all the Bureaus have reported in, the wires have been read, the available film and videotape is mostly known, and the field producers have given evaluations of their stories.

Sometime between 12:00 and 1:00, the senior staff will propose the first story lineup. This lineup will start to determine what stories will be on the evening news and approximately how long each story will be. Decisions about the visual aspects of the newscasts are made as discussion of graphics and the editing of film and videotape continues.

In addition, mechanical problems in either transmitting or transporting a story to the control room in New York must be ironed out. For example, satellite time must be ordered for a transmit from a foreign correspondent, but satellites are not always available; it may not be possible to transmit material from Cambodia on a Thursday via satellite because the "bird" is tied up by an Australian sporting event. Or, problems might arise in an airline schedule that is carrying film for the 6:00 PM newscast. All these factors are considered and, hopefully, solved with a comfortable time margin to spare.

During the afternoon, the lineup is revised to reflect the most current news developments and a new lineup is issued. A late-breaking story, like the DC-10 crash at Chicago's O'Hare Field, may bump a previously planned story off that night's news "menu." On a typical day, the lineup may go through four or five revisions before the final selection process is completed. The importance of the lineup cannot be overestimated: "A lineup tells the staff what stories are scheduled for broadcast; where stories will originate; what priorities should be set for processing and editing; what long lines (telephone lines) need to be ordered; what graphics need to be ordered and produced; what shipping arrangements should be preserved or altered; what script needs to be written and how the narrative should be contracted; what commercials are scheduled for broadcast; and finally, what order and for how long stories are expected to run." (Av Westin.)

From 3:00 to 6:00 PM scripts from Washington, Chicago, and London are sent to ABC New York to be analyzed and edited. Correspondents' scripts from all over the world are sent in to New York for the same purpose. It is here that the producers and film editors use their critical judgment in matching the visuals to the narration. "The senior producers

EXAMPLE 12-9 (cont.)

decide if the story has been adequately covered and they also estimate how long the report should run. In most cases, correspondents deliberately overwrite their scripts giving the producers at home the option of editing it down: selecting which portions of interviews are to be used and which elements in the narration are to be kept and which discarded. Sometimes during the afternoon the anchormen will submit their copy to a senior editor or producer for approval." (Av Westin.)

Videotape and film are sent in to New York for editing during this period. The pieces must be cut down to specific lengths, as every second of the broadcast must be timed and accounted for. The difficult part of the editing task is to maximize the visual portion of a tape while maintaining a logical continuity with the correspondent's narration. If the visual images and the narration aren't coordinated, the viewer's attention is split. The producers and editors are all working toward the 6:00 PM deadline.

At 6:00 PM *World News Tonight* goes on the air, directed from a control room in New York for the first feed before transmission to the stations. ABC News feeds out *World News Tonight* at three times: 6:00 PM, 6:30 PM, and 7:00 PM. This is done to offer the affiliates the option of when to air *World News Tonight* vis-a-vis their own local news.

The 22 minutes of news that is aired represents 24 hours of planning, writing, filming, and editing. The stories in the evening broadcast are the survivors of the day-long elimination process of reports and events from all around the world.

THE DOCUMENTARY

More than any other format, the documentary has the potential to effect social change. It provides an in-depth film report on a particular issue or state of affairs documenting real people in real situations. Most documentaries explore issues that are, in general, to complex for the shorter news formats to cover. It is their depth and thoughtfulness that gives documentaries powerful impact. For example, the CBS documentary *The Selling of the Pentagon* involved investigation of the military-industrial complex that led to congressional investigations of the defense industry and cost overruns on military terms.

SELECTION OF TOPIC. FOR CONSIDERATION:
Why would a story be particularly suited to the documentary format? What are the goals of a good documentary? Are topics selected for their mass appeal or because of their social significance?

Obviously, the topic of a documentary must have enough substance to merit an in-depth analysis. Pam Hill, Executive Producer of Documentaries at ABC, looks at issues that are "of some importance to the American public, issues that are in the news and merit the kind of special attention and money that we commit, and issues to which we feel we can bring, in an hour, a particular relevance and depth."

While documentaries often focus on topics similar to those covered on the evening news broadcasts, they also afford the freedom to explore more unconventional subjects such as social trends. For example, ABC produced a documentary called *Men Under Siege: Life with the Modern Woman* on the changing role of men in today's society. This is certainly a more delicate and subtle subject than the traditional hard news documentary, yet it is a subject that is of great importance and interest to a large segment of the nation.

ACTIVITIES
1. Ask students to prepare a list of subjects they would like to see as documentaries. Discuss: What makes a good subject? What are the goals of your documentary? How do you want the audience to react? What knowledge do you wish to impart? How can these objectives best be achieved? Consider people to be interviewed, facts to be compiled.

2. Divide the class into groups to produce documentaries using videotape, audiotape, and photographs or slides or Super 8 film. Present the completed subjects to the class, in the school media center, or at an assembly.

3. Evaluate the selection and treatment of a topic on a current documentary. Did the topic warrant the added depth of a documentary treatment? Is the topic one currently in the news or one of recurring social concern?

EXAMPLE 12-9 (cont.)

STRUCTURE. FOR CONSIDERATION:

Must a documentary reach a conclusion to be an effective piece of journalism? Is there a large enough audience for documentaries to justify a regular time slot during prime time viewing hours?

There is no one formula for a documentary. In fact, the structure is often dictated by the subject matter. For example, an investigative piece such as ABC's Arson: Fire for Hire requires a narrator because there is so much complex information that must be communicated to the viewers. On the other hand, issues that are revealed emotionally such as youth violence and restlessness are often best conveyed through primary sources.

A conventional form for network documentaries does exist but the parameters of the documentary structure have been expanded. Pam Hill describes the classic documentary, at its best, as "a lucid exposition, using authorities from the field to buttress the information, and a carefully honed narration by an identifiable on-camera person who leads the viewer through by the hand." When well done, the classic documentary is a powerful piece of journalism. However, it is not necessary for a documentary to adhere rigidly to the expository essay model to be successful.

Many topics are too subtle and undefined for there to be a clear right or wrong. It is the norm for a documentary to present the viewer with different aspects of an issue without making an assertion or drawing a conclusion. There may be departures from the conventional structure, however, opening up new subject areas for documentaries. For example, changing sex roles in America is a worthy subject for a documentary, but it might be better handled by going directly to those affected and letting them tell their own stories without the use of statistics, experts, and on-camera narration. While a thematic focus is still required, the camera can be used to simply record different viewpoints, and the audience can draw their own conclusions.

Where to place documentary programming in the network schedule is a continuing dilemma for network executives since, traditionally, nonfiction has not fared as well in the national ratings as entertainment programming. Unfortunately, the programming structure of the networks has had an adverse effect on the success of documentaries. Frequently they have been victims of the ratings competition among the networks. Fearing a poor showing in the ratings, documentaries are often scheduled in "throw-away" time slots, in competition with shows like the Oscar presentations. In addition, documentaries are not scheduled with any consistency. This irregular scheduling prevents documentaries from gaining a faithful following of viewers. Recently, however, documentaries have been getting more support at some of the networks.

ACTIVITY

Select several subjects of current interest and controversy such as nuclear waste disposal, changing sex roles, or teenage alcoholism. Divide the class into groups to develop possible documentary structures. Students should consider various approaches such as expository essays, interviews, narration, etc., as they were going to produce the documentary. Follow-up discussion should focus on which structures are most effective, appropriate for the topic, and fair.

DEPTH AND LENGTH. FOR CONSIDERATION:

What type of subjects warrant the expanded treatment of a documentary?

The documentary borrows many of the visual techniques of feature film. It is the marriage of good filmmaking with good writing and solid reporting that gives a documentary depth. Since film is transitory, the images must make a strong impression for the few seconds they are on the screen. Editing, camera angles, animation, or compression of time can all be utilized to communicate a point of view or an atmosphere to the viewer. The viewer must not be lulled into thinking that visual techniques are a supplement to a documentary's narrative. In the well-made documentary, the visuals and the narrative are equal partners, one incomplete without the other, in developing a theme.

While there is no established time limit, one hour is the standard length of most documentaries.

ACTIVITIES

1. Assign documentaries for home viewing and/or rent outstanding TV documentaries such as *The Selling of the Pentagon* (CBS), *The Police Tapes* (ABC), or *Harvest of Shame* (CBS). (Distributors are listed in "Resources.")

· **EXAMPLE 12-9 (cont.)**

2. Discuss: What is the purpose of the documentary? Does it expose a problem or present solutions to existing problems? Does the documentary present one viewpoint or does it show opposing views? Who are the authorities? What other experts might have been consulted?

OBJECTIVITY. FOR CONSIDERATION:
What is the distinction between "fairness" and "objectivity"?
Strong investigative journalism often results in documentaries with distinct conclusions. This does not mean that documentaries are unfair. A conscientious journalist will usually represent the contrasting viewpoints surrounding an issue in order that the subject under study be put in perspective for the audience. Richard Gerdau, a documentary producer at ABC, comments on objectivity: "If you've been fair in getting to a conclusion, and if the audience is aware of the way you've gotten there, then it is appropriate to draw a conclusion . . . especially if you are doing an investigative piece on arson or murder or police corruption, for example, where you can demonstrate a legitimate wrong, something illegal or something immoral. However, if the topic is an issue like abortion, a tremendous amount of objectivity is required because there are no clear right and wrong answers."

ACTIVITIES
1. Analyze a TV documentary. Is it objective? What is the main point? How does the producer prove the point or expose the subject? Are various sides of the issue explored? What conclusions are reached? Do you agree with them? How might camera shots, narration, music, or interviews have been used to reach a different conclusion?
2. Consider the impact of the audiovisual techniques on the content and purpose of the documentary. How do different camera movements and shots affect the viewer? What shots are included to support the point of view of the documentary? What role does editing play in the development of a point of view?
3. Listen carefully to the narration of the documentary. If there were no narration, what would a given scene mean to you? Clip photos from magazines and write two opposing narrations for the same picture.

GENERAL ACTIVITY
The documentary has the power to effect social change. Trace the political and social effects of a particularly powerful documentary such as CBS's *The Selling of the Pentagon,* which aired on February 23, 1971, using magazine and newspaper articles of the times.

THE INTERVIEW
The interview format attempts to offer a candid, revealing look at newsmakers. Interview shows are live and unrehearsed. This means that if interviewers ask penetrating questions, viewers will be able to witness a public figure being tested without the benefit of prepared statements or a controlled environment. The panelist format, with a guest facing several correspondents, creates an adversarial tension that fosters insightful questions and commentary.

News interview broadcasts such as ABC's *Issues and Answers* invite guests to be interviewed by correspondents from the network or by a panel of journalists. In another form of interview, a guest is interviewed by an individual correspondent.

SELECTION OF TOPIC. FOR CONSIDERATION:
Why are so many of the guests politicians? Is the purpose of the interview show to "make" news through some controversial disclosure or to provide the public with information about important events affecting the country?
On all of the panel interview shows, the guests are usually members of the U.S. government or heads of state from around the world, although an occasional guest from the social sciences or arts will be invited. The one-to-one interviews are more eclectic in their selection of guests. Bill Moyers on PBS, for example, might interview anyone from a theologian to a modern artist.

While the choice of the guest on a particular Sunday morning is the network's, a guest can use one of the interview shows as a means of catching the public eye. Nevertheless, there is a genuine competition among the network interview shows, ABC's *Issues and*

EXAMPLE 12-9 (cont.)

Answers, NBC's *Meet the Press* and CBS's *Face the Nation* to schedule the current "hot newsmaker." The purpose of these interviews is not only to enlighten the public on the guest's political views, but also to grant insights into the true nature of the individual.

ACTIVITIES

1. Whenever possible, use the TV listings to determine the guests on interview programs. Call local stations for guest information. Divide the class into groups to research each guest. Students should use TV newscasts, newspaper and news magazine accounts as a starting point to prepare five questions for their assigned guest. Compile each group's list of questions and distribute them before the Sunday broadcast. In class, discuss each guest: why he or she may have been selected; the individual's background; the current issues with which the individual is involved; and students' questions. As students watch their assigned program, they should compare their questions with those asked by the panel of journalists. Follow-up discussions should focus on the types of questions posed by the journalists, as well as the information students learned about their respective guests. Also, ask the class to analyze the performance of both the panelists and guest.

2. During a given week, use newspapers, news magazines, and TV newscasts to identify public figures you would like to see interviewed. Write one paragraph explaining your reasons for choosing this person. Were any people selected by the class interviewed on television?

STRUCTURE. FOR CONSIDERATION:

Does the structure allow for an exchange of ideas or is the subject interrogated? The interview program is not as visual as the other formats. What are the pros and cons of this? Compare the different interview formats: the panel interview vs. the dual questioners on Issues and Answers *and either of these formats to a one-to-one interview. How does the format affect the excitement and content of the interview?*

The physical layout of the studios for the weekly interview programs has a great impact on the mood of the program. In both *Face the Nation* and *Meet the Press* the isolated guest faces a panel of journalists who take turns asking questions. While the interviews are by no means interrogation sessions, the temptation to view the panel and the guest as adversaries is almost irresistible. The guest may appear to be on trial, questioned by prosecuting reporters trying to force a self-incriminating statement or, at least, a newsworthy comment. There is rarely an opportunity for the guest to enter into a dialectical discussion with a journalist, or even to get off the defensive, since he or she is continually being questioned. In contrast, ABC's *Issues and Answers* format, with two interviewers seated next to the guest, is less formal in format.

It is easier for an Interviewer to develop and work toward an interview strategy when he/she is interacting with a guest on a one-to-one basis. An interviewer like Barbara Walters or Bill Moyers strives to establish a rapport with the guest and build a certain rhythm and pace to the interview. By altering the rhythm at the right moment, a correspondent like Walters can obtain answers and admissions from normally taciturn subjects.

ACTIVITIES

1. Contrast the adversary format of the interview programs with interviews found in newspapers and news magazines. Compare the substance of the interviewee's statements and your impressions of the individual. Analyze the remarks. What are the advantages or disadvantages of the TV interview program?

2. Who are the correspondents or journalists on a given program? What types of interview techniques do they employ? What is the structure of the interview? Discuss the amount of research necessary for an effective interview.

DEPTH AND LENGTH. FOR CONSIDERATION:

Does the live interview format provide a more accurate picture because there is less opportunity for manipulation either by the guest or by the media? Do correspondents' questions cover a wide variety of topics, or are particular subjects explored in detail? Might a single interviewer have a better chance of investigating an issue in depth?

The panel news programs potentially allow an in-depth evaluation of the guest. As

EXAMPLE 12-9 (cont.)

Peggy Whedon, Producer of ABC's *Issues and Answers,* puts it, "A live interview allows the viewer a chance to see the way the leaders of the world think and how they arrive at their decisions." This has the potential to provide a more accurate picture than reading an editorial or someone's interpretation. While the journalists may not have the opportunity to put all their questions to the guest (the programs are 30 minutes long), the viewer usually is granted a critical, unrehearsed look at the guest for virtually the whole program.

The degree that the public facade of the guest is penetrated depends entirely on the incisiveness of the journalists and the candor of the guest. The crucial factor in a good interview is the journalist's ability to ask probing questions and follow-ups to obtain other than routine responses. However, when a number of panelists are involved, it is difficult for any one journalist to establish a rapport with the guest. On the other hand, the panelists can build on each other's questions, and the sum of their queries can be enlightening.

ACTIVITIES

1. Select a particular news event involving a public figure frequently seen on the news, for example, President Carter, President Anwar Sadat, Senator Edward Kennedy. Watch TV news reports and newspaper accounts of the event to understand the issues and to determine the individual's positions and involvement. Prepare 10 questions as the basis for an interview with the public figure. Teachers may wish to ask students to research thoroughly the issues and role play the interviews.

2. What makes a good interview? Brainstorm a list of criteria and develop guidelines for conducting interviews. Focus on the importance of research and preparation. Develop a variety of questioning techniques to elicit more than a yes/no answer. Divide the class into small groups to conduct five-to-10-minute interviews with a local community leader, faculty member, student council officer, etc., about issues of local concern. Students might begin by listening to correspondents on the interview programs as well as to special reports by Barbara Walters, Mike Wallace, Bill Moyers, and Tom Brokaw, noting the various types of questions asked and the ways in which the interviews build on the subjects' responses. Students should work in pairs interviewing each other to practice asking questions and developing listening skills. Finally, each group of students should select the person they wish to interview, research the subject, and prepare questions. Questions should be reviewed before the actual interview. Audiotape the interviews for classroom review and critique.

OBJECTIVITY. FOR CONSIDERATION:

What special perspectives about the "newsmakers" do TV interview programs give the viewer? Is the view consistent with the way the person is presented in newspapers and other TV formats?

In one sense, the interview show is the most objective news format on the air. It is the only format in which politicians and officials are regularly broadcast live to the public. There is no editing, no interpretation, and no use of "show-business" technique. The audience is left to formulate its own opinion of the guest.

Occasionally, the adversary relationship between the panel and the guest becomes too pronounced. Obviously, this inhibits an objective interview. However, the panels are usually coolly and fairly moderated.

On the one-to-one level, the interviewing style of the correspondent dictates the tone of the interview. Some interviewers take an amicable approach. Others openly grill their guests. But regardless of the interviewer's style, the most revealing interviews often are the result of pointed questions.

ACTIVITIES

1. Do you get as accurate a picture of a newsmaker on the other news formats as on the live interview shows? What are the differences? Compare TV coverage to print. Clip articles from newspapers and news magazines to further analyze the different media presentations.

2. Discuss the ways in which the interview programs provide for an objective view of the guest newsmaker.

EXAMPLE 12-9 (cont.)

GENERAL ACTIVITY

Ask students to complete the following TV viewing log while watching the network interview programs.

Guests	Interviewers	Questions Asked
1.	1.	1.
2.	2.	2.
	3.	3.
		4.
		5.

DISCUSS:

1. Were topics discussed on the program subsequently reported in newspapers or on TV news? Did the program generate news?

2. Find articles in which views opposing those expressed by the guests are detailed. Compare the statements.

3. How might the topics discussed on the program affect life in your community?

THE TELEVISION MAGAZINE

The television magazine borrows a little from the print and a little from the newscast format, puts on the serious face of the documentary, and flirts with light human interest.

The production decisions of the different television magazines, *60 Minutes, 20/20,* and *Prime Time Sunday,* are influenced by the overall philosophy about the role that the TV magazine should play in society. There appear to be two basic approaches to television magazine reporting: it can serve to uncover corruption, in the tradition of muckraking journalism, and act as a social force. And, the magazine can present interesting features and social phenomena, usually of a "soft news" nature, to the viewer. While most magazines blend features with more serious pieces, each magazine has a distinctive and consistent style in its coverage of serious stories.

SELECTION OF TOPIC. FOR CONSIDERATION:

Are the topics selected intended to expose areas of controversy? How large an impact do TV magazine stories have on society? Do magazine programs treat news stories as drama?

In a *Parade Magazine* interview, Marion Goldin, one of the producers of CBS's *60 Minutes,* defined a good TV magazine story as "a micro that tells the macro—a small story, easy to get at—but which has a scope larger than itself. It has victims and culprits and drama without distortion. I don't like dull movies, and I don't like dull TV."

Unlike the evening news, the magazine has no journalistic obligation to report the stories of the day as they break. The individual stories are also not as lengthy or as detailed as most documentaries. As news, they must contain substance, but they must also have enough of the "man bites dog" element to attract and hold an audience. It is, in a sense, news as drama.

ACTIVITY

Divide the class into small groups to propose topics for a TV magazine. Each group should present its ideas to the class. Discuss interest; length; timeliness; action; fame of people involved; economic, social, and political relevance as criteria in selection.

STRUCTURE. FOR CONSIDERATION:

How does the structure of the TV magazine compare to the evening news in terms of depth, length, and pacing?

The structure of television magazines is often compared to "classic" print magazines. There is a similar blending of eye-catching visuals with print that can be either breezily informative or insistently revealing. One of the most appealing aspects of the magazine format is that it offers this potpourri of news stories and journalistic styles.

EXAMPLE 12-9 (cont.)

ACTIVITY

Examine the structure of each segment of the program. How is it organized? How is it different from a report about the same event on the evening news? In a documentary?

DEPTH AND LENGTH. FOR CONSIDERATION:

Is depth sacrificed in order to maintain viewer interest?

The television magazine, because it is loosely defined, is flexible as to the air time allowed for each story within the entire program's prescribed length. However, a balance must be reached between journalistic depth and maintaining the pace and variety of the program, which is true of any televised news presentation. Since television magazines are designed to appeal to the viewer with a variety of interests, there are inherent restrictions on the amount of time devoted to any one story.

ACTIVITY

Organize a debate about one of the subjects on *20/20, Prime Time Sunday,* or *60 Minutes.* Stress the depth of research involved in investigative reporting and the need to understand and present both sides of an issue.

OBJECTIVITY. FOR CONSIDERATION:

Are investigative pieces objective in their approach? Are the events and interviews presented in the piece intended to lead the viewer to a predetermined conclusion?

Occasionally, magazine stories will be recounted in the form of a dramatic expose. The reporter plays out the popular fantasy of calling some magnate or crook onto the carpet, forcing him to admit to wrongdoing through interrogation. Al Ittleson, Executive Producer of ABC's news magazine, *20/20,* comments: "The viewers can get a dramatic, moving, insightful piece of information. However, I'm not sure that they are getting all the information that they should. But they do get a good piece of television. It is one of the dangers, but it is also one of the reasons why people watch TV."

Critics have claimed that, occasionally, the dramatic machinery will be set into motion over issues that are not really that electrifying. This serves both to manufacture controversies and to bias the viewer. The audience can get so caught up in the momentum of the narrative that they lose their own critical sense of objectivity.

Then, too, the reporters have become so well-known that their personalities, real or perceived, intrude into the reporting. For example, America has witnessed Mike Wallace successfully grill and expose so many people that, as soon as he appears on the screen, viewers may tend to side with him and assume that his subject is, in some way, guilty.

ACTIVITY

Discuss the pros and cons of muckracking TV journalism. Are the investigative journalists watchdogs or sensationalists? What are the societal benefits of this type of journalism? Consider the interview techniques. What types of questions are asked? Are subjects "set-up"? What audiovisual techniques are used to strengthen the interview?

OUTSIDE CONSIDERATIONS

There are fundamental considerations that influence the policies and the shape of news programs. Analysis of televised news would be incomplete without an examination of Federal Communications Commission (FCC) regulations, particularly the Fairness Doctrine, and recent court decisions that have had an impact on all forms of journalism.

FCC REGULATIONS AND THE FAIRNESS DOCTRINE. FOR CONSIDERATION:

Do the networks have a responsibility to the public? If so, do they adequately fulfill that responsibility? Do newspapers have a similar responsibility?

Since 1928, the federal government has regulated access to television airwaves. Licenses were granted by the FCC to individual stations to broadcast on specific frequencies. Neither stations nor networks own the airwaves. They are subject to government regulations and are regarded as holding a public trust.

As licensees, not owners, the networks are subject to government regulation. By contrast, owners of newspapers have private rights and are not subject to federal regulatory interference. Not surprisingly, the networks want the same freedom granted the print

EXAMPLE 12-9 (cont.)

journalists. As George Watson, Washington Bureau Chief for ABC, puts it: "From a First Amendment perspective, I favor the deregulation of broadcasting. I do not believe that the Fairness Doctrine insures balance or fairness. I'm very wary of an interposing government determining what is fair and not fair. If you like the decisions in one era, you may discover you don't like them in another. If the FCC has been, by and large, benign in its regulation of broadcasting, we had a whiff of what might happen in the Nixon era, and it could happen again."

On the other hand, proponents of the Fairness Doctrine have argued that it is needed in order to assure full realization of First Amendment rights. Nicholas Johnson, former FCC Commissioner, has said that "the Fairness Doctrine is, of course, designed and administered in ways which seek to serve this need." Another Fairness Advocate, Professor Jerome Barron, argued in the *Harvard Law Review* that the public right to access to television is necessary if we are to breathe life into First Amendment rights.

While the FCC is prohibited by the Communications Act from any type of direct censorship, it has influenced the presentation of the news through the Fairness Doctrine. The basic principle behind the Fairness Doctrine was stated in the Commission's 1949 Report on Editorializing: "It is the right of the public to be informed, rather than any right on the part of the government, any broadcast licensee, or any individual member of the public to broadcast his own particular views on any matter which is the foundation stone of the American system of broadcasting." Should a station decide to air one side of a certain issue that it deems to be of "public importance," it must then grant time for the opposing side to state its viewpoint.

ACTIVITIES

1. What is the Federal Communications Commission? What are its responsibilities? How are members selected? Who are the current Commissioners?

2. Is the periodic licensing renewal process for television stations a good idea? What are the alternatives?

3. According to the "Fair and Equal Time Provision," Section 315 of the Federal Communications Act of 1934, broadcasters who grant free time to one candidate must grant equal time to all others. How does network and local news coverage reflect this provision? Pay particular attention to Presidential campaign coverage.

THE NEWS AND FIRST AMENDMENT RIGHTS. FOR CONSIDERATION:

Why is an understanding of the workings of a free press important to us? Are there subjects which should not be covered on television newscasts? Are there appropriate limits on the First Amendment? Is it absolute?

The free flow of information is vital to a democratic society. Much of the public relies on the media to keep informed and so help to insure responsible participation in the process of self-government. When the freedom of the press is abridged, the loss of individual freedoms may follow.

To many journalists in this country, the time between 1978 and 1979 will be thought of as the year they saw the privileges of a free press steadily slip away. A series of Supreme Court decisions may have seriously restricted the type of stories that journalists will be willing to investigate in the future. Police now have the right to confiscate, under certain circumstances, a reporter's confidential notes; government investigators may have access to phone records; and police are permitted, under the law, to carry out surprise search and seizure raids of newspaper and television offices. These decisions may inhibit journalists from investigating controversial stories, especially ones concerning government. A reporter's ability to obtain information is also affected. News organizations fear that if sources know that they no longer have any guarantee that their identities will be kept confidential, many will refuse to talk.

The *Herbert vs. Lando* case is one of these recent decisions. It involved an episode of the CBS television magazine *60 Minutes*. *60 Minutes'* journalists were investigating Army Lieutenant Colonel Anthony Herbert's claim that he was removed from his position in the Army for reporting U.S. atrocities in Vietnam to his superiors. Herbert sued the producer, Barry Lando; journalist Mike Wallace; CBS; and *Atlantic Monthly* magazine (which printed

EXAMPLE 12-9 (cont.)

Lando's version of his investigation of Herbert); claiming that they made him look like a liar in front of the nation.

During the pretrial sessions, Barry Lando answered questions about who he had interviewed and what he had learned, but he refused to explain why he chose to believe certain sources over others and why he edited out certain segments of the interview and aired others. CBS appealed a lower court ruling that forced Lando to explain his editorial decisions, and in 1977, it won a temporary victory when the Circuit Court of Appeals ruled that it was "an absolute privilege to refuse to answer any questions about editorial thoughts or conversations." However, in April 1979, the Supreme Court reversed the decision and ruled in favor of Herbert.

ACTIVITIES

1. How are your personal rights related to freedom of the press? For example, what is the status of the individual's rights in societies where there is no freedom of the press?

2. Consider: Your high school newspaper editor wants to print an article evaluating teachers in your high school. The school board refuses to allow the article to be printed. Discuss: What options does the editor have? What are the limits of a free press?

TV VIEWING LOG ACTIVITIES—EVENING NEWS

The viewing logs are used to record information from newscasts. The same log may be focused to compare national network newscasts, to compare local newscasts, or to contrast national and local newscasts. Students may be divided into groups to direct their viewing toward a particular news program. Class discussion should highlight the comparisons among broadcasts, as well as comparisons between print and TV news. Using the information logged from the newscasts, discuss the following questions as the class studies the evening news.

1. What was the order of the stories? What was the "lead"? Do you feel it was the most important story of the day?

2. How much time was devoted to local, national, world events?

3. What are the implications of each story for your community?

4. Compare coverage of the same event by different networks. Who was interviewed? Describe the accompanying videotape. Was there live coverage? Was the reporting objective?

5. How much time is devoted to hard news? To features? To special series reports?

6. Compare newscasters in terms of style, tone, expression.

(See the TV viewing logs on pp. 412 and 413.)

RESOURCES

PRINT—BOOKS

Arlen, Michael. *The Living Room War.* New York: Viking Press, 1969.

Brown, Les, *Television: The Business Behind the Box.* New York: Harcourt, Brace, Jovanovich, 1971.

Cater, Douglass, et al. *Television as a Social Force: New Approaches to TV Criticism.* New York: Praeger, 1975.

Cirino, Robert. *Power to Persuade: Mass Media and the News.* New York: Bantam, 1967.

Diamond, Edwin. *The Tin Kazoo.* Cambridge: The MIT Press, 1975.

Efron, Edith. *The News Twisters.* Los Angeles: Nash Publ., 1971.

Epstein, Edward Jay. *News from Nowhere: Television and the News.* New York: Random House, 1973.

Fang, Irvine E. *Television/Radio News Workbook.* New York: Hastings House, 1974.

Gans, Herbert J. *Deciding What's News: A Study of CBS Evening News, NBC Nightly News, Newsweek and Time.* New York: Pantheon Books, 1979.

Johnson, Nicholas. *How To Talk Back to Your TV Set.* New York: Bantam, June 1970.

Kosinski, Jerzy. *Being There.* New York: Harcourt, Brace, Jovanovich, 1971.

TV VIEWING LOG—EVENING NEWS

Directions: List each story reported on the evening news and check the appropriate columns.

Network:

Circle One: National   Local

Time	Story	International	National	Local	Politics	Economics	Arts	Sports	Features	Other
2 min.	Carter Health Plan		✓		✓	✓				
1 min.										
30 sec.	Kennedy Objections		✓		✓	✓				
5 min.	John Wayne's Death: Obit and Comments	✓	✓	✓			✓			
1 min.										
20 sec.	Nicaragua Evacuation	✓			✓					
20 sec.	Hijack	✓	✓		✓	✓				
25 sec.	DC-10	✓	✓							

This viewing log may be used with individual stories reported on the evening news, documentaries, magazine, or interview programs. Use the log to discuss the specific stories in detail and to analyze the critical production decisions involved.

TV VIEWING LOG

Directions: This log may be used in connection with each of the four news formats. Write the news event in the center box and consider implications of the event and critical decisions involved in production of the story.

Discuss local, national, international implications of the event.

NATIONAL - FUTURE OF NASA
INTERNATIONAL - WHAT IF IT FELL ON OTHER COUNTRIES?
LOCAL - WHAT LOCAL PRECAUTIONS ARE BEING TAKEN?

IMPLICATIONS

POSSIBLE CATASTROPHE IF SKYLAB FELL IN HEAVILY POPULATED AREA
WHOLE WORLD WAS AFFECTED

Is treatment of the subject fair? Were all sides of the issue/event fairly represented?

NASA SCIENTISTS INTERVIEWED TO ANSWER CRITICS. OUTSIDE SCIENTISTS WERE INTERVIEWED.

OBJECTIVITY

NEWS STORY: SKYLAB IS FALLING.

NEWS SOURCE: 20/20 TV MAGAZINE

NEWS STORY—BRIEF DESCRIPTION

Why was the story included in the news?

SELECTION

Why was the event covered on this news format? How did visuals enhance the copy?

Was the subject treated in sufficient detail? Were you able to understand the report?

FILM SIMULATION OF SKYLAB ORBIT AND PROBABLE PATH OF RE-ENTRY WERE SHOWN.

SKYLAB WAS FALLING BECAUSE OF A COMBINATION OF THINGS, GRAVITY, SUN SPOTS, MISCALCULATIONS AMONG THEM.

STRUCTURE

DEPTH AND LENGTH

413

EXAMPLE 12-9 (cont.)

Mander, Jerry. *Four Arguments for the Elimination of TV.* New York: Wm. Morrow and Company, 1978.

Mankiewicz, Frank, and Joel Swerdlow. *Remote Control: Television and the Manipulation of American Life.* New York: Ballantine Books, 1978.

Powers, Ron. *The Newscasters.* New York: St. Martin's Press, 1977.

Riley, David J. *Freedom of Dilemma: Critical Readings in the Mass Media.* Glenview, Ill.: Scott, Foresman and Company, 1971.

Schiller, Herbert I. *The Mind Managers.* Boston: Beacon Press, 1974.

Skornia, Harry J. *Television and the News: A Critical Appraisal.* Palo Alto, Calif.: Pacific Books, 1968.

PRINT—BOOKS ESPECIALLY FOR STUDENTS

Heintz, Ann Christine, Lawrence M. Reuter, and Elizabeth Conley. *Mass Media.* Chicago: Loyola University Press, 1972.

Littell, Joseph F. *Coping with the Mass Media.* Evanston, Ill.: McDougal, Littell and Company, 1972.

Rissover, Fredric, and David C. Birch. *Mass Media and the Popular Arts.* New York: McGraw Hill, 1971.

Schrank, Jeffrey. *TV Action Book.* Evanston, Ill.: McDougal, Littell and Company, 1974.

Valdes, Joan, and Jeanne Crow. *The Media Works.* Dayton, Ohio: Plfaum/Standard, 1973.

PRINT—ARTICLES

Arlen, Michael J. "The Air," *New Yorker,* November, 1978.

Cronkite, Walter. "What It's Like to Broadcast News," *Saturday Review,* December 12, 1970.

Furlong, William Barry. "Manipulating the News," *TV Guide.* June 11 and 18, 1977.

"The Hottest TV News Controversies" (interview), *TV Guide,* January 13, 1979.

McMillan, Penelope. "Some of TV's Best Interviewers," *TV Guide,* August 13, 1977.

Massing, Michael, Joel Kotkin, and Patricia Ohmans. "It's News to You—Special Interests behind the Scenes," *New Times,* October 2, 1978.

Mitgang, Herbert. "Are Current Court Decisions Scaring Off Media?" *TV Guide,* June 9, 1979.

Pressman, Gabe. "Happy News? No! It's Time for the Real Stuff," Address to New York Publicity Club.

Sevareid, Eric. "What's Right with Sight and Sound Journalism," *Saturday Review,* October 2, 1976.

"TV News of the Future—As Seen by Network Chiefs," *U.S. News and World Report,* November 20, 1978.

PRINT—JOURNALS OR COLUMNS OF INTEREST

Broadcasting Magazine; Broadcasting Yearbook; Columbia Journalism Review; Communication; Journal of Broadcasting; Journal of Communication; Local TV/Radio Critics; *New Yorker,* Television Section, see especially Michael Arlen's articles; *New York Times,* Television Section, see especially John O'Connor's articles; *Television News Index and Abstracts; Television Quarterly; TV Guide; Variety*

NONPRINT—FILMS

"The Television Newsman," Pyramid Color 12 min., Rental $30.

"The Electric Flag," Pyramid Color 12 min., Rental $15.

"Televisionland," Pyramid Color 12 min., Rental $20.

"The Making of a Live TV Show," Pyramid Color 24 min., Rental $30.

NONPRINT—FILMSTRIP

"Mass Media: Impact on a Nation." Guidance Associates Filmstrip.

NONPRINT—NETWORK DOCUMENTARIES: DISTRIBUTORS

ABC: Donna Sessa, Multimedia Div., ABC Pictures Int'l., Inc., 1330 Avenue of the Americas, New York, NY 10019.

EXAMPLE 12-9 (cont.)

CBS: Dolores Sura, CBS, 51 West 52nd Street, New York, NY 10019.

NBC: Films, Incorporated, 1144 Wilmette Avenue, Wilmette, IL 60091.

PBS: The Public Television Library, Video Program Services, 476 L'Enfant Plaza, S.W., Washington, DC 20024.

PRINT—INTERVIEW PROGRAMS (TRANSCRIPTS)

Issues and Answers, Transcript Bureau, 1201 Connecticut Avenue, Washington, DC 20036 (25c/self-addressed envelope).

Meet the Press, Kelly Press, P.O. Box 8648, Washington, DC 20011 (50c/self-addressed envelope).

Face the Nation, CBS News/Washington Office, 2020 "M" Street, N.W., Washington, DC 20036 (no charge, self-addressed envelope).

MacNeil Lehrer Report, WNET, P.O. Box 345, New York, NY 10019 ($1/self-addressed envelope).

NONPRINT—RECOMMENDED PROGRAMS TO WATCH

EVENING NEWS

ABC World News Tonight; CBS Evening News; NBC Nightly News; PBS MacNeil/Lehrer Report; Local, network, and independent broadcasts

INTERVIEW

ABC Issues and Answers; CBS Face the Nation; NBC Meet the Press; PBS Bill Moyer's Journal; PBS John Calloway Interviews; Barbara Walters' Specials

DOCUMENTARY

ABC News Closeup; CBS Reports; NBC Documentaries; also watch for the National Geographic Society or Jacques Cousteau type documentaries.

MAGAZINE

ABC 20/20; CBS 60 Minutes; NBC Prime Time Sunday; PBS Bill Moyer's Journal

OTHER PROGRAMS OF INTEREST

ABC Good Morning America; CBS Morning News; CBS Universe; NBC The Today Show; PBS The Advocates; PBS Washington Week in Review; PBS Wall Street Week; TV News: Free or Controlled? Check fall listings for this one-half hour special.

Model 13

The Decade of the 1970s
(Seminar or Independent Study)

GRADES: 11 or 12.

DURATION: 45 Days.

GOAL: To provide opportunity for the students to explore and examine America's immediate past as a prologue to the immediate future.

INTRODUCTION

This seminar is divided into four main parts: Orientation, Independent Research, Student Research Presentations, and Group Summation (see Handout 13-1, Schedule, for time allotted each part).

ORIENTATION

An introduction to the course is provided by the seminar participants' viewing, analyzing, and discussing the six-part sound filmstrip set *American Decades: The 1970s* (see Handout 13-2). The six areas emphasized in this sound filmstrip set are:

1. Popular Culture
2. United States Politics: People and Issues
3. The United States and the World
4. Science in the Seventies
5. Women: Progress and Change
6. Newsmakers: People and Events

Procedure: Following the viewing of each sound filmstrip, the seminar participants receive a handout that includes Discussion Guide and Projects (see Handouts 13-3 to 13-8). The discussion is not limited to the questions posed on the handout. A free exchange of ideas among the seminar participants is encouraged. Likewise, the Projects are but suggestions offered for student consideration. Participants are responsible for undertaking a serious and demanding research project of special interest to the student him- or herself. A period of 4 weeks or 20 days is devoted to the student's working in the school library on his or her research project. There are no classes held during this four-week period.

INDEPENDENT RESEARCH

The teacher of the seminar and the librarians serve as mentors to the students; conferences are scheduled when and as requested by individual students.

The librarians orient the students to basic research tools especially useful in researching the decade of the 1970 (see Handout 13-9).

Students are instructed to use, as their style guide, *Research Papers: A Guided Writing Experience for Senior High School Students* by Richard Corbin and Jonathan Corbin, 2nd rev. ed. (Rochester, N.Y.: New York State English Council, 1978; dist. by the National Council of Teachers of English, Urbana, Ill.).

Students are informed that a senior year seminar, Advanced Research: The Techniques and Tools of Scholarship, would be an invaluable learning experience for those wishing to go on to college.

Students work independently, completing their research and their typewritten reports. The requirement for the research report is that it be typed, double spaced, and no less than four and not more than six pages, exclusive of the bibliography. Each research paper is to be submitted, with appropriate cover sheet, in a folder or theme binder.

STUDENT RESEARCH PRESENTATIONS

Prior to each presentation the presenter will distribute to the seminar participants an outline of his or her presentation, appropriate abstracts or support statements, and a bibliography (see as examples Handouts 13-9, 13-10, and 13-11).

GROUP SUMMATION

Group summation may be oral or written. The following two essay questions may serve as examples of the type of essay questions asked on Advanced Placement American History Tests:

1. What does the following statement mean?
   "By the end of the 1970's, Americans began to realize that their options were limited in a changing world and that sheer power no longer was a guarantee that the country would always get its way." Give examples to support your answer.*
2. *The Pentagon Papers* was a 40-volume study, commissioned by Secretary of Defense Robert McNamara, covering American involvement in Southeast Asia from World War II to mid-1968. The documents were not officially released by the Nixon Administration, but the *New York Times* began publishing them on June 13, 1971. Two days later, the *New York*

American Decades: The 1970s Teacher's Guide (Niles, Ill.: United Learning).

Times was restrained by court order from further publishing of the Pentagon Papers. This action was the first such restraint in the name of "national security" in the history of the United States. The *New York Times* appealed to the Supreme Court, and the restraint was lifted on June 30, 1971, in a 6-to-3 ruling. If you had been a Supreme Court justice hearing this appeal by the *New York Times,* how would you have voted? Explain in detail the legal basis for your decision.

HANDOUT 13-1 SCHEDULE

From	To	Number of Days	Activities	Where
		12	Orientation	Classroom
		20	Independent Research	Library
			Written Research Report Due	
		10	Student Research Presentation	Classroom
		3	Group Summation	Classroom
		45		

HANDOUT 13-2 TEACHER'S GUIDE—AMERICAN DECADES: THE 1970s (1970–1979)*

1. *Popular Culture* tells about various trends and fads that dominated popular culture during the 1970s. During the decade, Americans were fascinated with television watching, movie-going, self-improvement, sports and sports heroes, and electronic gadgets.

2. *United States Politics: People and Issues* describes political issues that faced Americans and their leaders during the 1970s, such as the termination of American involvement in the Vietnam War, the Watergate scandal, the Arab oil embargo, American hostages held captive in Iran, and an inflationary economy. Americans celebrated their country's 200th birthday during the 1970s, but also learned that their country's power and resources were limited. Issues facing the Nixon, Ford, and Carter Administrations are examined.

3. *The United States and the World* describes domestic and foreign events that affected the lives of Americans, such as the presidential elections of 1972 and 1976, the withdrawal of American troops from Vietnam, the Watergate scandal, the changing relationship between the People's Republic of China and the United States, the 1973 Arab oil embargo, the Panama Canal Treaty, the Camp David Middle East Peace Accords, and the seizing of the American Embassy in Iran.

4. *Science in the Seventies* describes some major American scientific advances in space, energy, and medicine that occured during the 1970s, such as the explorations of the moon, Mars, Jupiter, and Saturn, the building of the Alaskan pipeline, and the development of solar and nuclear technology, ultrasound and the CAT scanner.

5. *Women: Progress and Change* highlights some of the major accomplishments of the women's movement in the 1970s, as well as women who achieved high acclaim in the fields of medicine, science, sports, entertainment, and business. Over a million women entered the work force during the decade and many rose to prominent positions. The concepts of "men's jobs" and "women's jobs" became outdated, but women's salaries still lagged behind those of men. By the end of the decade, the Equal Rights Amendment still had not been passed by enough state legislatures to become part of the United States Constitution.

6. *Newsmakers: People and Events* chronicles the major news stories of the 1970s. News events as diverse as anti-war protests, cult murders and violence, presidential elections and scandals, sports triumphs, and social and legal controversies are described.

*This United Learning program consists of 6 filmstrips, 6 cassettes, and a teacher's guide with scripts, visual descriptions, discussion questions, and unit test.

HANDOUT 13-3   DISCUSSION GUIDE FOR POPULAR CULTURE

1. What do you think the phrase "The Me Decade" means?
2. Why do you think that the quest for self-improvement and self-enlightenment dominated the culture of the 1970s?
3. Why do you think Americans spend so many hours watching television?
4. Why do you believe "The Deer Hunter" and "Apocalypse Now" were popular movies of the '70s?
5. What were some other popular movies of the '70s? Why do you think Americans were fascinated with movies such as "Star Wars," "Saturday Night Fever" and "Manhattan"?
6. What types of music were popular during the 1970s?
7. What sports dominated the 1970s, from the standpoint of both spectator and participant appeal?
8. What were some electronic technologies and innovations of the 1970s?
9. What were some fads of the 1970s?
10. The filmstrip speaks of the death of Elvis Presley during the 1970s, and refers to him as "perhaps the greatest legend the (music) industry had ever known." Can you think of other "legends" that died during the 1970s, such as John Wayne and Hubert Humphrey?

PROJECTS

1. Conduct research and prepare reports on the following religious movements during the 1970s:
    The Hare Krishnas
    Jim Jones and the People's Temple
    The Unification Church
2. Prepare a catalog of clothing fashions and hair styles popular during the 1970s, by cutting and pasting pictures from magazines and catalogs published during the decade.
3. Choose a "Popular Culture Category" below and write a report on its impact on the culture of the '70s, as well as the famous people associated with it.

    Television: "All in the Family," "Saturday Night Live," etc.; Carroll O'Connor, Walter Cronkite, Howard Cosell, etc.

    Sports: Football, baseball, raquetball, tennis, jogging, etc; O.J. Simpson, Hank Aaron, Terry Bradshaw, Bjorn Borg, Billie-Jean King, Chris Evert-Lloyd, Muhammed Ali, etc.

    Theatre/Dance: Mikhail Baryshnikov, "A Chorus Line," etc.

    Films/Movies: "The Deer Hunter," "Apocalypse Now," "The Godfather," "Saturday Night Fever," "Julia," etc.; George C. Scott, Jane Fonda, John Travolta, Woody Allen, etc.

    Music: Disco, Rock and Roll, New Wave, etc.; The Rolling Stones, Donna Summer, The Bee Gees, Linda Ronstadt, Elvis Presley, etc.

HANDOUT 13-4 DISCUSSION GUIDE FOR U.S. POLITICS: PEOPLE AND ISSUES

1. Do you believe the United States should have become involved in the Vietnam War? Why or why not?
2. When America is involved in a war, do you believe American citizens have the right to protest that involvement?
3. How did the Arab oil embargo of 1973 show Americans that they had to limit the amount of energy they used?
4. What is inflation and how does it affect the buying power of the American dollar?
5. Do you think President Nixon should have resigned? Why or why not?
6. Do you believe President Ford should have pardoned Richard Nixon?
7. The sound filmstrip states, "As Carter took office, the mood of the American people seemed to rise above the shadow of Watergate." Why do you think this was so?
8. Do you believe President Carter should have granted amnesty to Vietnam War draft dodgers? Why or why not? Why do you think he did so?
9. The sound filmstrip states that, "By the end of the 1970s, Americans began to realize that their options were limited in a changing world and that sheer power no longer was a guarantee that the country would always get its way." What do you think this statement means? Give examples to support your answer.

PROJECTS

1. Conduct research and prepare reports on any of the following topics:

   The United States involvement in the Vietnam War
   The Protest Movement against American involvement in Vietnam
   The Student Protest at Kent State University
   The Watergate Scandal
   The Arab Oil Embargo of 1973
   The Presidential Elections of 1972 and 1976
   The Equal Rights Amendment
   Causes and Effects of Inflation on the American Economy
   The Bicentennial Celebration
   The Camp David Middle East Peace Accords
   The Seizing of American hostages at the American Embassy in Tehran, Iran
   The Soviet Union's invasion of Afghanistan
   The 1980 American boycott of the Moscow Olympic Games

2. Prepare a biography on prominent political figures of the 1970s, such as:

Richard Nixon	Jimmy Carter
Spiro Agnew	Ronald Reagan
Gerald Ford	Edward Kennedy
John Dean	John Anderson

3. Prepare a timeline showing major political events that occurred during the 1970s.
4. Find political cartoons from magazines published during the '70s depicting famous politicians of the decade, such as those listed above. What is the cartoonist saying about the character and the times?

HANDOUT 13-5   DISCUSSION GUIDE FOR THE UNITED STATES AND THE WORLD

1. What are some reasons why many Americans were against their country's involvement in the Vietnam War?
2. How might an oil shortage affect the lifestyles of Americans?
3. Why did Arab oil suppliers place an embargo on oil being shipped to the United States in 1973?
4. Why did Richard Nixon resign as President of the United States?
5. How did Gerald Ford become the only President of the United States who was not elected by the people to serve in that capacity?
6. Why do you suppose a change in U.S./China relations was advantageous to both the People's Republic of China and the United States?
7. Why did the United States give control of the Panama Canal to Panama?
8. How did Pres. Carter help develop the Camp David Middle East Peace Accords?
9. Do you believe President Carter should have permitted the Shah of Iran to enter the United States for medical treatment? Why or why not?

PROJECTS

1. Conduct research and prepare reports on any of the following topics:
   American involvement in the Vietnam War
   The 1973 Arab Oil Embargo
   The resignation of Richard M. Nixon as President of the United States
   President Nixon's trip to the People's Republic of China
   The Presidential Elections of 1972 and 1976
   U.S./China relations
   The Carter Administration's Energy Program
   The history of the Panama Canal and America's involvement in the Canal Zone
   The Camp David Middle East Peace Accords
   The seizing of American hostages at the American Embassy in Tehran, Iran
2. Prepare reports on how the following people influenced and/or changed United States relations with the rest of the world:
   Richard Nixon   Gerald Ford
   Henry Kissinger   Jimmy Carter
3. Prepare a timeline showing major breakthroughs and/or setbacks of the foreign policies under the Nixon, Ford and Carter Administrations.
4. Find political cartoons from magazines published during the 1970s depicting the United States relationships with the other countries of the world. What is the cartoonist saying about the characters and the times?

HANDOUT 13-6   DISCUSSION GUIDE FOR SCIENCE IN THE SEVENTIES

1. What were the major accomplishments in space exploration during the 1970s?
2. By 1979, only three planets had not been visited by unmanned spacecraft from Earth. Which three planets were they?
3. What are Black Holes?
4. What are some challenges facing American scientists in the area of Energy?
5. Why is solar energy considered "free" and "renewable"?
6. What happened at Three Mile Island in 1979, and how did it alter American thinking about using nuclear energy?
7. What is gasohol?
8. How does burning coal damage the environment?
9. What was the purpose of "Earth Day"?
10. What were some major breakthroughs in the area of medicine during the 1970s?
11. What is a quark?

PROJECTS

Conduct research and prepare reports on any of the following topics:
Apollo 13 Space Mission to the Moon   Skylab
American/Russian rendezvous in space   Viking Space Missions to Mars

HANDOUT 13-6 (cont.)

Voyager Mission to Jupiter
Pioneer 11 Mission to Saturn
Black Holes in Space
The North Slope (Alaska) Oil Reserves
The Alaska Pipeline
Using Solar Energy
The Carter Energy Program
The Accident at Three Mile Island
Nuclear Power Plants

Creating Energy through the Fusion
  Process
Processing Shale Rock for Oil
Making Gasohol
Earth Day, April 22, 1970
The CAT Scanner
Ultrasound
Gene Splitting
Quarks

HANDOUT 13-7   DISCUSSION GUIDE FOR WOMEN: PROGRESS AND CHANGE

1. What does the statement, "For women, the 1970s was a decade of beginnings" mean?
2. Why do you think men with whom women worked were often surprised and sometimes resentful to find out how well women could perform in what were considered "macho" jobs?
3. What happened to the gap between men's and women's salaries during the 1970s?
4. Why do you think women were generally paid less than men during the 1970s?
5. How did day care centers help women with small children who wanted or needed to work?
6. Approximately how many women per year entered the work force during the 1970s?
7. How did the fact that women worked outside the home change many aspects of the husband/wife relationship?
8. How did the concept of "male" jobs and "female" jobs change during the 1970s? Give examples.
9. Why do you suppose The Equal Rights Amendment had not been ratified by the required number of states as the decade ended?
10. What were two contrasting views on abortion held by women during the 1970s?

PROJECTS

1. Conduct research and prepare reports on any of the following topics:
   The Equal Rights Amendment
   How Day Care Centers Helped Working Mothers
   Women in Business and Industry
   Women in Science and Medicine
   Women in Traditionally Male Jobs
   Men in Traditionally Female Jobs
   Incomes of Working Women as Compared to Men
   Women in News Broadcasting
   Women in Entertainment
   Women in Sports; Women in Politics; Women in Music
   Women's Contrasting Views on Abortion
2. Prepare reports on the following women's contributions to their professions and to the women's movement during the 1970s (add to the list as desired):

Dixie Lee Ray	Gloria Steinem	Ellen Stewart
Nancy Kassebaum	Brigadier General	Jane Fonda
Bella Abzug	Jeanne M. Holm	Mary Tyler Moore
Patricia Harris	Leslie Stahl	Kathleen Nolan
Jane Byrne	Barbara Walters	Billie Jean King
Diane Feinstein	Jane Cahill Pfeiffer	Chris Evert
Margaret Hance	Sara Caldwell	Tracy Austin
Rosalynn Carter	Linda Ronstadt	Martina Navratilova
Betty Ford	Alberta Hunter	Nancy Lopez
Pat Nixon	Nancy and Ann Wilson	Nancy Lieberman
Lady Bird Johnson		

HANDOUT 13-8   DISCUSSION GUIDE FOR NEWSMAKERS: PEOPLE AND EVENTS

1. Why can the 1970s be described as a time of "testing, turbulence and transition"?
2. What happened in 1972 that tipped off the Watergate Scandal? Do you believe that the "bugging" of a political party by another political party is wrong? Why or why not?
3. Why did Vice President Spiro Agnew resign in 1973?
4. Why did President Nixon resign in 1974?
5. How did Gerald Ford become President of the United States?
6. Why did Bert Lance resign in 1977?
7. Why do you think it's possible that religious leader Jim Jones could persuade over 900 of his followers to commit suicide?
8. Discuss the controversies surrounding major issues of the 70s, such as abortion, gay rights, capital punishment, etc.

PROJECTS

1. Conduct research and prepare reports on any of the following topics:
   The Bicentennial Celebration
   The May Day Anti-War March in 1971
   Massacre at My Lai, Vietnam
   Daniel Ellsberg and the Pentagon Papers
   The Charles Manson "Family"
   The 1971 California Earthquake
   The Watergate Scandal
   Jim Jones and the mass suicide in Guyana
   Palestinian acts of terror at the 1972 Munich Olympic Games
   American/Russian Rendezvous in space
   The Camp David Middle East Peace Accords
   Rescue of the *Mayaguez*
   The conviction of Dr. Kenneth Edelin
   The Viking Space launch to Mars
   Son of Sam Murders
2. Prepare a biography on any of the following people:

Daniel Ellsberg	Muhammed Ali
George McGovern	Howard Hughes
George Wallace	Elvis Presley
Patty Hearst	Pope John Paul II
Alexander Solzhenitsyn	Mother Theresa

3. Prepare a timeline showing major news events of the 1970s.

HANDOUT 13-9   INDEPENDENT RESEARCH: BASIC REFERENCE TOOLS

Note: *Before a title indicates that it is available *only* in a public library and is *not* available in a school library.

* *Applied Science and Technology Index.* New York: Wilson, 1958 to date. Monthly, annual.
* *Art Index.* New York: Wilson, 1929 to date. Quarterly, annual.

Biography Index. New York: Wilson, 1946 to date. Quarterly, annual.

Biological and Agricultural Index. New York: Wilson, 1964 to date. Monthly, annual.

The Book of American Rankings: Social, Economic and Political Rankings. New York: Facts on File, 1979.

Book Review Digest. New York: Wilson, 1905 to date. Monthly, annual.

Cambridge Forum Broadcast Tapes Checklist. Latest issue. Cambridge, Mass.: Cambridge Forum. Annual.

* *Congressional Record.* Washington, D.C.: Government Printing Office, 1873 to date. Daily, annual.

Conservation Yearbook. U.S. Department of the Interior. Washington, D.C.: Government Printing Office, 1964 to date. Annual.

CQ Almanac. Congressional Quarterly Service. Washington, D.C.: Congressional Quarterly. 1945 to date. Annual.

Current Biography. New York: Wilson, 1940 to date. Monthly, annual.

Editorial Research Reports. Congressional Quarterly Service. Washington, D.C.: Congressional Quarterly. 1956 to date. Monthly, semiannual.

* *Editorials on File.* New York: Facts on File, 1970 to date.

The Encyclopedia of American Facts and Dates. 7th rev. ed., ed. by Gordon Carruth. New York: Crowell, 1979.

The Encyclopedia of Jazz in the Seventies by Leonard G. Feather and Ira Gitler. New York: Horizon Press, 1976.

Essay and General Literature Index. New York: Wilson, 1900 to date. Monthly, annual.

Facts on File Yearbook. New York: Facts on File, 1940 to date.

General Science Index. New York: Wilson, 1978 to date. Monthly, annual.

Great Black Americans as Reported in The New York Times. Sanford, N.C.: Microfilming Corporation of America, 1981. Program guide and microfiche.

Great Events/One as Reported in The New York Times. Sanford, N.C.: Microfilming Corporation of America, 1978. Program guide and microfiche.

Great Events/Two as Reported in The New York Times. Sanford, N.C.: Microfilming Corporation of America, 1980. Program guide and microfiche.

Great Events/Three as Reported in The New York Times. Sanford, N.C.: Microfilming Corporation of America, 1981. Program guide and microfiche.

Great Events/Four as Reported in The New York Times. Sanford, N.C.: Microfilming Corporation of America, 1982. Program guide and microfiche.

Great Personalities/One as Reported in The New York Times. Sanford, N.C.: Microfilming Corporation of America, 1979. Program guide and microfiche.

Great Personalities/Two as Reported in The New York Times. Sanford, N.C.: Microfilming Corporation of America, 1981. Program guide and microfiche.

Great Personalities/Three as Reported in The New York Times. Sanford: N.C.: Microfilming Corporation of America, 1981. Program guide and microfiche.

Great Personalities/Four as Reported in The New York Times. Sanford, N.C.: Microfilming Corporation of America, 1982. Program guide and microfiche.

Great Presidential Campaigns as Reported in The New York Times. Sanford, N.C.: Microfilming Corporation of America, n.d. Program guide and microfiche.

Great Scientific Adventures/One as Reported in The New York Times. Sanford, N.C.: Microfilming Corporation of America, 1981. Program guide and microfiche.

Great Scientific Adventures/Two as Reported in The New York Times. Sanford, N.C.: Microfilming Corporation of America, 1982. Program guide and microfiche.

Great Sports Stories as Reported in The New York Times. Sanford, N.C.: Microfilming Corporation of America, 1981.

Great Supreme Court Decisions as Reported in The New York Times. Sanford, N.C.: Microfilming Corporation of America, 1981. Program guide and microfiche.

Humanities Index. New York: Wilson, 1974 to date.

McGraw-Hill Yearbook of Science and Technology. New York: McGraw, 1966 to date. Annual.

National Public Radio Cassette Catalogue. Latest issue. Washington, D.C.: National Public Radio. Annual.

The New York Times Index. New York: The New York Times, 1913 to date. Semimonthly, annual.

The New York Times School Microfilm Collection Guide. Sanford, N.C.: Microfilming Corporation of America, 1851 to date. Annual.

Play Index. New York: Wilson, 1949 to date. Irregular.

Reader's Guide to Periodical Literature. New York: Wilson, 1900 to date. Semimonthly, annual.

Representative American Speeches. New York: Wilson, 1967 to date. Annual.

Science Year: The World Book Science Annual. Chicago: World Book–Childcraft International, 1965 to date. Annual.

Scientific American Cumulative Index, 1948–1978. New York: Scientific America, 1979.

Social Sciences Index. New York: Wilson, 1974 to date. Quarterly, annual.

Statistical Abstract of the United States. Bureau of the Census. Washington, D.C.: Government Printing Office, 1878 to date. Annual.

UNESCO Statistical Yearbook. New York: UNIPUB, 1952 to date. Annual.

United Nations Statistical Yearbook. New York: UNIPUB, 1949 to date. Annual.

Vital Speeches of the Day. Southold, N.Y.: City News, 1934 to date. Semimonthly, annual.

World Book Yearbook. Chicago: World Book–Childcraft International. Annual.

Yearbook of Science and the Future. Chicago: Encyclopaedia Britannica, 1968 to date. Annual.

HANDOUT 13-10 WATERGATE REVISITED

PART I: STUDENT RESEARCH PRESENTATION

I. The Watergate Affair
    A. Background events
        1. Pentagon Papers
        2. Watergate break-in
    B. Watergate cover-up
    C. Congress investigates
        1. Ervin Committee hearings
        2. Discovery of the tapes of president's conversations
    D. Special prosecuting force appointed
II. President Nixon's involvement
    A. Denied prior knowledge of Watergate cover-up
    B. Dismissed Ehrlichman and Haldeman
    C. "The Saturday Night Massacre"
    D. House Judiciary favors impeachment
    E. Resigned
    F. Pardoned by President Ford
III. Watergate in retrospect
    A. Memoirs of participants
        1. John Dean
        2. John Ehrlichman
        3. H. R. Haldeman
        4. Leon Jaworski
        5. Richard Nixon
    B. Appraisal a decade later
        1. "The Legacy of Watergate," *Newsweek*, June 14, 1982, pp. 36–40
        2. *Watergate: Ten Years After*, National Public Radio Broadcast, NPR Journal series (1 cassette)
        3. "Where Are They Now," *Newsweek*, June 14, 1982, pp. 42–45
        4. Henry Kissinger, "Years of Upheaval: Watergate," *Time*, March 8, 1982, pp. 42–61

PART II: CHRONOLOGY*

Date	Event
May 28, 1972	Democratic National Committee Headquarters at Watergate is broken into, electronic surveillance equipment installed.
June 17, 1972	Five men are arrested at Democratic National Committee Headquarters while attempting to repair electronic equipment.
June 28, 1972	G. Gordon Liddy, counsel to FCRP, is fired when he fails to cooperate with FBI agents investigating the Watergate break-in.
July 1, 1972	John Mitchell resigns as CRP Chairman.
July 14, 1972	Hugh Sloan resigns as FCRP Treasurer.
July 31 to August 10, 1972	Press reports suggest that money for Watergate break-in came from CRP funds given by Liddy to one of the arrested men.
August 16, 1972	CRP Chairman Clark MacGregor acknowledges that Liddy spent CRP funds for security program.

Watergate Special Prosecution Force: Final Report (Washington, D.C.: Government Printing Office, 1977), pp. 43–63.

HANDOUT 13-10 (cont.)

August 30, 1972	The President announces that Dean has conducted and completed an investigation into the Watergate affair. Claims that no one in the White House or employed by the administration was involved.
September 15, 1972	Bernard Barker, Virgilio Gonzalez, E. Howard Hunt, G. Gordon Liddy, Eugenio Martinez, James W. McCord, Jr., and Frank Sturgis are indicted for their parts in the June 17, 1972, break-in at Democratic National Committee Headquarters.
September 17 to October 25, 1972	Press reports suggest that CRP maintained a secret cash fund controlled by Mitchell, Stans, Magruder, Kalmbach and Haldeman, which was used to finance the Watergate break-in and other sensitive political projects.
October 26, 1972	MacGregor acknowledges existence of special cash fund, but denies it was used for sabotage against Democrats.
January 8, 1973	Watergate break-in trial begins.
January 11, 1973	Hunt pleads guilty to charges in break-in indictment.
January 15, 1973	Barker, Sturgis, Martinez and Gonzalez plead guilty to charges in break-in indictment.
January 15 to January 22, 1973	Press reports suggest that Watergate defendants were being paid by unnamed sources—possibly CRP—and that they were promised money and clemency to plead guilty.
January 30, 1973	Liddy and McCord are convicted on all counts of break-in indictment.
February 7, 1973	Senate unanimously passes S. 60, a resolution creating the Select Committee on Presidential Campaign Activities.
March 19, 1973	McCord writes to Judge Sirica alleging that perjury was committed at trial and that defendants were pressured to remain silent.
March 23, 1973	Judge Sirica issues provisional sentences for Watergate break-in defendants, except McCord; makes McCord's letter public.
April 5, 1973	L. Patrick Gray's nomination to become Direction of the FBI is withdrawn.
	Judge W. Matt Byrne reports a personal meeting with Ehrlichman, where Ehrlichman suggested a possible future assignment for Byrne.
April 17, 1973	The President announces White House staff will appear before the Senate Select Committee, and that there have been major new developments in the Watergate investigation, that real progress has been made toward finding the truth.
April 19, 1973	Attorney General Richard Kleindienst removes himself from Watergate case. Henry Petersen

HANDOUT 13-10 (cont.)

	assumes responsibility for conduct of Watergate investigation.
April 23, 1973	White House issues a statement denying that the President had any prior knowledge of Watergate affair.
April 27, 1973	Gray resigns as acting director of the FBI.
	Washington Post reports Gray destroyed documents in Howard Hunt's files after a discussion with Ehrlichman and Dean.
	Judge Byrne reads memo at Ellsberg/Russo trial describing Hunt and Liddy break-in of Dr. Fielding's office.
	Hugh Sloan is accused of submitting false documents to the General Accounting Office. GAO cites CRP and Maurice Stans for four campaign expenditure violations.
April 30, 1973	Haldeman, Ehrlichman, Dean and Kleindienst resign. The President nominates Elliot Richardson to become new Attorney General.
May 4, 1973	George A. Hearing is indicted on two counts of fabricating and distributing illegal campaign literature (18 U.S.C. 612). Pleaded guilty May 11; sentenced to a one-year prison term on June 15.
May 7, 1973	A spokesman for the President denies that there were any offers of clemency to anyone connected with the Watergate affair.
	Richardson announces that he will appoint a special prosecutor.
May 9, 1973	Egil Krogh resigns; claims full responsibility for the Fielding break-in.
May 9 to May 22, 1973	Richardson confirmation hearings are held before the Senate Judiciary Committee.
May 10, 1973	Mitchell, Stans, Robert Vesco and Harry Sears are indicted for attempting to impede an SEC investigation of Vesco.
May 11, 1973	Judge Byrne dismisses all criminal charges against Ellsberg and Russo in Pentagon Papers case.
May 17, 1973	Senate Select Committee begins public hearings.
May 21, 1973	Richardson announces nomination of Archibald Cox as Special Prosecutor.
May 23, 1973	Richardson is confirmed by Senate to become new Attorney General.
May 25, 1973	Richardson is sworn in as Attorney General. Cox is sworn in as Special Prosecutor.
June 12, 1973	Court orders use immunity for Dean and Magruder.
June 25, 1973	Dean tells Senate Select Committee that the President knew of the cover-up as early as September 1972.
June 27, 1973	Dean submits "enemies list" memorandum of August 16, 1971, to Senate Select Committee.

HANDOUT 13-10 (cont.)

	Fred LaRue pleads guilty to an information charging one-count violation of 18 U.S.C. 371, conspiracy to obstruct justice.
June 30, 1973	Earl Silbert, Seymour Glanzer and Donald Campbell, Assistant U.S. Attorneys for the District of Columbia, withdraw from the Watergate investigation.
July 7, 1973	The President informs the Senate Select Committee that he will not personally appear before the Committee and that he will not grant the Committee access to presidential files.
July 16, 1973	Herbert Kalmbach, in testimony before the Senate Select Committee, claims that John Ehrlichman approved cash payments to the burglars who broke into Watergate.
	Alexander Butterfield informs the Senate Select Committee of the presidential taping system.
July 20, 1973	Liddy refuses to take an oath as a witness before the House Armed Services Subcommittee during a Watergate-related investigation.
July 23, 1973	Senate Select Committee issues subpoenas for White House tapes and documents.
	Special Prosecutor Cox issues grand jury subpoena for tapes and documents needed for investigation into the Watergate cover-up.
July 24, 1973	Ehrlichman tells the Senate Select Committee that break-in at Fielding's office was legal, and that it was undertaken for national security purposes.
July 25, 1973	The President informs Judge Sirica of his decision to refuse to comply with the Special Prosecutor's subpoena.
July 31, 1973	The *Washington Post* reports that the President did not sign the deed giving his papers to the National Archives, that the deed was not delivered until April 1 of 1970 (nine months after the effective date of the 1969 law prohibiting tax deductions for such gifts) and that the deed was never accepted by the Archives as a formal written document.
August 9, 1973	Senate Select Committee files suit against the President for failure to comply with their subpoena.
August 13, 1973	Grand Jury II is empaneled to investigate campaign contributions, political espionage, plumbers and ITT.
August 16, 1973	Magruder pleads guilty to one-count violation of 18 U.S.C. 371, conspiracy to unlawfully intercept wire and oral communications, to obstruct justice and to defraud the United States.
August 29, 1973	Judge Sirica enforces grand jury subpoena to

HANDOUT 13-10 (cont.)

	the President for nine presidential conversations.
September 11, 1973	Oral arguments are heard before the U.S. Court of Appeals concerning refusal of the President to comply with the Special Prosecutor's subpoena.
October 1, 1973	Donald Segretti pleads guilty to three counts of violating 18 U.S.C. 612, distributing illegal campaign literature.
October 11, 1973	Krogh is indicted on two counts of violating 18 U.S.C. 1623, making a false declaration before a grand jury.
October 12, 1973	U.S. Court of Appeals orders the President to produce subpoenaed tapes.
October 17, 1973	Minnesota Mining and Manufacturing pleads guilty to a violation of 18 U.S.C. 610, illegal campaign contributions; fined $3,000.
	Harry Heltzer of Minnesota Mining and Manufacturing pleads guilty to a non-willful violation of 18 U.S.C. 610, illegal campaign contributions; fined $500.
	American Airlines pleads guilty to a violation of 18 U.S.C. 610, illegal campaign contributions; fined $5,000.
	Goodyear Tire & Rubber Company pleads guilty to a non-willful violation of 18 U.S.C. 610; fined $5,000.
	Russell DeYoung of Goodyear Tire and Rubber pleads guilty to a non-willful violation of 18 U.S.C. 610; fined $1,000.
October 19, 1973	The President offers the Stennis tapes compromise. Orders Special Prosecutor Cox to seek no further litigation.
	Dean pleads guilty to an information charging a one-count violation of 18 U.S.C. 371, conspiracy to obstruct justice.
	Dwayne O. Andreas, Chairman of the Board, and First Interoceanic Corporation plead not guilty to four counts of non-willful violations of 18 U.S.C. 610. Both were acquitted on July 12, 1974.
October 20, 1973	Special Prosecutor Cox holds a press conference where he explains his refusal to comply with the President's order.
	The President orders that the Special Prosecutor be fired. Richardson resigns in protest and Ruckelshaus is fired. Acting Attorney General Bork fires Special Prosecutor Cox. Special Prosecution Force is transferred to the Department of Justice, Criminal Division.
October 23, 1973	The President informs Judge Sirica that he will comply with grand jury subpoena.
October 31, 1973	J. Fred Buzhardt, Special Counsel to the President, informs the Court that two of the subpoenaed tapes do not exist.

HANDOUT 13-10 (cont.)

November 1, 1973	Acting Attorney General Bork announces the selection of Leon Jaworski to succeed Archibald Cox as Special Prosecutor.
November 2, 1973	Watergate Special Prosecution Force is re-established by an order of the Acting Attorney General.
November 5, 1973	Leon Jaworski is sworn in as the new Special Prosecutor. Segretti is sentenced to serve six months in prison.
November 7, 1973	Senate passes S.R. 194, affirming the authority of the Select Committee to subpoena and sue the President.
November 9, 1973	Final Watergate break-in sentences are handed down.
November 12, 1973	Braniff Airways pleads guilty to a violation of 18 U.S.C. 610, illegal campaign contributions; fined $5,000.
November 13, 1973	Harding L. Lawrence of Braniff pleads guilty to a non-willful violation of 18 U.S.C. 610; fined $1,000.
	Gulf Oil Corporation pleads guilty to a violation of 18 U.S.C. 610; fined $5,000.
	Claude C. Wild, Jr., of Gulf Oil, pleads guilty to a violation of 18 U.S.C. 610; fined $1,000.
	Ashland Petroleum Gabon, Inc., pleads guilty to a violation of 18 U.S.C. 610; fined $5,000.
	Orin Atkins of Ashland Petroleum pleads no contest to charges of non-willful violations of 18 U.S.C. 610; fined $1,000.
November 21, 1973	Buzhardt informs Judge Sirica of an 18½-minute gap on the tape of a June 20, 1972, conversation between the President and Haldeman.
	Judge Sirica appoints a panel of scientific experts to examine tapes of presidential conversations handed over in compliance with the July 23rd grand jury subpoena.
November 29, 1973	Dwight Chapin is indicted on four counts of violating 18 U.S.C. 1623, making false declarations before a grand jury.
November 30, 1973	Krogh pleads guilty to an information charging one-count violation of 18 U.S.C. 241, conspiracy to violate civil rights.
	Judge Sirica holds hearings, *in camera,* concerning executive privilege claims on three of the subpoenaed tapes.
December 4, 1973	Phillips Petroleum Company pleads guilty to a violation of 18 U.S.C. 610, illegal campaign contributions; fined $5,000.
	William W. Keeler, of Phillips Petroleum, pleads guilty to a non-willful violation of 18 U.S.C. 610; fined $1,000.
December 6, 1973	Brief for the U.S. in conviction appeal of G. Gordon Liddy is filed (DNC break-in).

HANDOUT 13-10 (cont.)

December 19, 1973	Carnation Company pleads guilty to a violation of 18 U.S.C. 610; fined $5,000.
	H. Everett Olson, of the Carnation Company, pleads guilty to a non-willful violation of 18 U.S.C. 610; fined $1,000.
January 7, 1974	Grand Jury III is empaneled to investigate matters similar to those investigations carried out by Grand Jury II.
January 21, 1974	Herbert Porter is charged with a one-count violation of 18 U.S.C. 1001, making false statements to agents of the FBI.
January 24, 1974	Krogh is sentenced to a prison term of two to six years, all but six months suspended. October 11 indictment is dismissed.
January 28, 1974	Porter pleads guilty to January 21 information.
February 6, 1974	House of Representatives authorizes House Judiciary Committee to investigate if grounds exist to impeach the President.
February 25, 1974	Herbert W. Kalmbach pleads guilty to a one-count violation of the Federal Corrupt Practices Act, and one count of promising Federal employment as a reward for political activity. He is sentenced to serve 6–18 months and fined $10,000 for the first count, six months for the second. Sentences are to run concurrently.
March 1, 1974	Watergate cover-up indictment: Colson, Ehrlichman, Haldeman, Mardian, Mitchell, Parkinson, and Strachan are charged with offenses stemming from events following the break-in at the Democratic National Headquarters on June 17, 1972.
March 4, 1974	Briefs for the U.S. in conviction appeals of McCord and Hunt are filed.
March 6, 1974	Hearing is held before Judge Sirica on transfer of grand jury materials to the House Judiciary Committee.
March 7, 1974	Fielding break-in indictment: Barker, Colson, DeDiego, Ehrlichman, Liddy, Martinez are charged with offenses stemming from the September 3–4, 1971, break-in at the Los Angeles office of Dr. Fielding.
	Diamond International Corporation pleads guilty to a violation of 18 U.S.C. 610; fined $5,000.
	Ray Dubrowin, of Diamond International, pleads guilty to a non-willful violation of 18 U.S.C. 610; fined $1,000.
March 15, 1974	Special Prosecutor Jaworski issues subpoena for specified documents for use in grand jury.
March 18, 1974	Judge Sirica announces decision to permit transfer of grand jury material to the House Judiciary Committee.
March 20, 1974	Haldeman and Strachan file petition for writ of

	mandamus with U.S. Court of Appeals concerning transfer of grand jury material.
March 21, 1974	U.S. Court of Appeals hears Haldeman and Strachan petition. Denied later in the day.
March 26, 1974	Grand jury materials are transferred to the House Judiciary Committee.
March 29, 1974	President complies with the Special Prosecutor's March 15 subpoena.
April 1, 1974	Brief for the U.S. in conviction appeals of Barker, Martinez, Sturgis, and Gonzalez is filed.
April 3, 1974	Howard E. Reinecke indicted on three counts of perjury.
April 5, 1974	Chapin found guilty on two of three counts.
	American Ship Building is charged with one count of conspiracy and one count of illegal campaign contributions, 18 U.S.C. 610.
	George M. Steinbrenner, III, President of American Ship Building, is charged with one count of conspiracy, five counts of willful violation of 18 U.S.C. 610, two counts of aiding and abetting an individual to make a false statement to agents of the FBI in violation of 18 U.S.C. Sections 2 and 1001, four counts of obstruction of justice in violation of 18 U.S.C. 1503 and two counts of obstruction of a criminal investigation, 18 U.S.C. 1510.
	John H. Melcher, Jr., Vice-president of American Ship Building, pleads guilty to a charge of being an accessory after the fact to an illegal campaign contribution; fined $2,500.
	Porter is sentenced to a minimum of 5 months and a maximum of 15 months in prison, all but 30 days suspended. Served April 22 to May 17.
April 16, 1974	Special Prosecutor issues a trial subpoena for 64 White House taped conversations.
April 28, 1974	Mitchell and Stans are acquitted on all charges in Vesco trial.
April 30, 1974	President submits transcripts of recorded conversations to House Judiciary Committee.
May 1, 1974	Thomas V. Jones, President of Northrop Corp., pleads guilty to a one-count charge of willfully aiding and abetting a firm to commit a violation of a statute prohibiting campaign contributions by Government contractor, 18 U.S.C. 611; fined $5,000.
	Northrop Corporation pleads guilty to violations of 18 U.S.C. 611; fined $5,000.
	James Allen, of Northrop, pleads guilty to non-willful violations of 18 U.S.C. 610; fined $1,000.
May 3, 1974	Panel of experts appointed by Judge Sirica

HANDOUT 13-10 (cont.)

	issues a report on their examination of White House tapes.
May 6, 1974	Lehigh Valley Cooperative Farmers pleads guilty to a violation of 18 U.S.C. 610; fined $5,000.
May 15, 1974	Chapin is sentenced to serve 10 to 30 months.
May 16, 1974	Kleindienst pleads guilty to a violation of 2 U.S.C. 192, refusal to answer pertinent questions before a Senate Committee. Later sentenced to serve 30 days, and fined $100. Sentence is suspended.
May 17, 1974	Richard Allison, of Lehigh Valley Cooperative Farmers, pleads guilty to a non-willful violation of 18 U.S.C. 610; fined $10,000. Sentence is suspended.
May 20, 1974	Judge Sirica enforces Special Prosecutor's trial subpoena of April 16.
May 21, 1974	Magruder is sentenced to a prison term of ten months to four years.
May 22, 1974	DeDiego indictment is dismissed in Fielding break-in case.
May 28, 1974	Francis X. Carroll pleads guilty to non-willful violations in Lehigh Valley contributions case, 18 U.S.C. sections 2 and 610.
May 31, 1974	Supreme Court grants writs of certiorari on enforcement of tapes subpoena.
	Chief Judge George Hart grants an extension to Grand Jury I. Expiration date set at December 4, 1974.
June 3, 1974	Charles Colson pleads guilty to an information charging one count of obstruction of justice. Previous indictments are dismissed.
June 7, 1974	Court of Appeals denies petition for writ of mandamus to recuse Judge Sirica.
June 14, 1974	Court of Appeals hears oral arguments in the appeals of Liddy, Barker, Martinez, Sturgis, McCord, Hunt, and Gonzalez.
June 21, 1974	Colson is sentenced to serve one to three years in prison and is fined $5,000.
June 24, 1974	National By-Products, Inc., pleads guilty to a violation of 18 U.S.C. 610; fined $1,000.
June 26, 1974	Fielding break-in trial begins.
June 27–28, 1974	James St. Clair appears before the House Judiciary Committee to present a defense for the President.
July 8, 1974	Supreme Court hears oral arguments in *U.S. v. Nixon*.
July 12, 1974	Jury returns guilty verdict against Ehrlichman, Martinez, Liddy and Barker in Fielding break-in trial.
July 23, 1974	David Parr pleads guilty to a one-count charge of conspiracy to make an illegal cam-

HANDOUT **13-10 (cont.)**

	paign contribution. He is later sentenced to four months in prison and fined $10,000.
July 24, 1974	Supreme Court unanimously upholds Special Prosecutor's tapes subpoena for Watergate trial.
July 25, 1974	Supreme Court denies petition for writ of certiorari to review ruling concerning recusal of Judge Sirica.
July 27, 1974	Jury finds Reinecke guilty on one count of perjury. House Judiciary Committee adopts Article I of impeachment resolution charging the President with obstruction of justice.
July 29, 1974	John Connally is indicted on two counts of accepting an illegal payment, one count of conspiracy to commit perjury and obstruct justice, and two counts of making a false declaration before a grand jury.
	Jake Jacobsen is indicted on one count of making an illegal payment to a public official.
	House Judiciary Committee adopts Article II of impeachment resolution charging the President with misuse of powers, violating his oath of office.
July 30, 1974	House Judiciary Committee adopts Article III of impeachment resolution charging the President with failure to comply with House subpoenas.
July 31, 1974	Sentences are handed down in Fielding break-in case.
	Harold S. Nelson pleads guilty to charges of conspiracy to make an illegal payment to a Government official, and to make illegal campaign contributions.
August 1, 1974	Associated Milk Producers, Inc., pleads guilty to one count of violating 18 U.S.C. 371, and five counts of violating 18 U.S.C. 610; fined $35,000 (campaign contributions).
August 2, 1974	Dean is sentenced to serve a prison term of one to four years.
August 7, 1974	Jacobsen pleads guilty to July 29 indictment.
August 9, 1974	Richard Nixon resigns from office.
August 12, 1974	Norman Sherman pleads guilty in a dairy contributions matter to non-willful violation of 18 U.S.C. 610, sections 2 and 610.
	John Valentine pleads guilty in a dairy contributions matter to non-willful violation of 18 U.S.C. 610, sections 2 and 610.
August 14, 1974	U.S. Court of Appeals denies Haldeman petition for writ of mandamus concerning validity of grand jury.
August 15, 1974	Members of the Special Prosecution Force meet with White House Counsel to discuss status of Nixon materials.

HANDOUT 13-10 (cont.)

August 22, 1974	U.S. Court of Appeals suggests a three to four week continuance for *Mitchell et al.* trial.
August 23, 1974	American Ship Building Company pleads guilty to April 5 indictment.
	George M. Steinbrenner, III, pleads guilty to one count from the April 5 indictment that charged a violation of 18 U.S.C. 371 conspiracy and an information charging one count of violating 18 U.S.C. sections 3 and 610.
August 30, 1974	Steinbrenner is fined $15,000; American Ship Building fined $20,000.
September 2, 1974	Supreme Court denies Ehrlichman's application for stay of trial.
September 8, 1974	President Ford pardons Richard Nixon.
	President Ford announces the agreement between Sampson and Nixon giving Nixon ownership and control over access to Nixon Administration papers.
September 9, 1974	Brief for the U.S. in the conviction appeal of Dwight Chapin is filed.
September 17, 1974	LBC&W, Inc., pleads guilty to one count of non-willful violation of 18 U.S.C. 610; fined $2,000.
	William Lyles, Sr., of LBC&W, pleads guilty to two counts of non-willful violation of 18 U.S.C. 610; fined $2,000.
September 20, 1974	U.S. Court of Appeals denies Strachan's petition for a writ of mandamus.
	U.S. Court of Appeals denies Mitchell and Ehrlichman petitions for writs of prohibition and/or mandamus seeking indefinite postponement of the trial.
September 28, 1974	Senate Select Committee completes its work.
September 30, 1974	Strachan's case is severed from *Mitchell et al.* trial.
October 1, 1974	Watergate cover-up trial begins.
October 8, 1974	Greyhound Corporation pleads guilty to a violation of 18 U.S.C. 610; fined $5,000.
October 12, 1974	Leon Jaworski announces his resignation as Special Prosecutor, effective October 25.
October 17, 1974	Richard Nixon asks the Court to enforce September 7 Nixon-Sampson agreement.
October 23, 1974	Time Oil Corporation pleads guilty to two counts of violating 18 U.S.C. 610; fined $5,000.
	Raymond Abendroth, of Time Oil, pleads guilty to two counts of non-willful violation of 18 U.S.C. 610; fined $2,000.
October 26, 1974	Henry S. Ruth, Jr., is sworn in as the third Special Prosecutor.
November 8, 1974	Edward L. Morgan pleads guilty to one count of conspiracy to impair, impede, defeat and obstruct the proper and lawful governmental

	functions of the IRS. He is sentenced, on December 19, to serve two years in prison, all but four months suspended.
November 9, 1974	Special Prosecutor Ruth, Mr. Buchen, counsel to the President, Mr. Sampson of General Services, and Mr. Knight, of the Secret Service, sign an agreement that permits the Special Prosecutor to gain access to Nixon Administration tapes and documents pertaining to his investigations.
November 11, 1974	Supreme Court denies Haldeman petition for writ of certiorari to review denial of mandamus relating to grand jury extension.
November 15, 1974	Jack Gleason pleads guilty to an information charging a one-count violation of the Federal Corrupt Practices Act. Sentence is suspended.
December 3, 1974	Charles N. Huseman of HMS Electric Corp. pleads guilty to a non-willful violation of 18 U.S.C. 610; fined $1,000.
December 6, 1974	Liddy files petition for writ of certiorari in break-in conviction.
December 10, 1974	Tim Babcock pleads guilty to a charge of a one-count violation of making a contribution in the name of another person. Sentenced later to four months in prison.
December 11, 1974	Harry S. Dent, Jr., pleads guilty to a one-count charge of violating the Federal Corrupt Practices Act. He is sentenced to one month unsupervised probation.
December 12, 1974	Court of Appeals affirms the convictions of Liddy and McCord in Watergate break-in.
December 13, 1974	DKI for '74 pleads guilty to violations of failing to report receipt of contributions and failure to report names, addresses, occupations and principal places of business of persons making contributions. Sentence is suspended.
December 19, 1974	President Ford signs S. 4016 into law—the Presidential Recordings and Materials Preservation Act.
	Stuart H. Russell is indicted on one count conspiracy to violate 18 U.S.C. 610, two counts of aiding and abetting a willful violation of 18 U.S.C. 610 (campaign contributions).
December 23, 1974	Jack Chestnut is indicted on one count of willful violation of 18 U.S.C. 610, aiding and abetting an illegal campaign contribution.
December 29, 1974	Watergate cover-up case goes to the jury.
December 30, 1974	Ashland Oil, Inc., pleads guilty to five counts of violating 18 U.S.C. 610; fined $25,000.
January 1, 1975	Jury convicts all but Parkinson in cover-up trial.
January 8, 1975	Dean, Magruder and Kalmbach are released from prison; sentences are reduced to time served.

HANDOUT 13-10 (cont.)

January 13, 1975	U.S. files memorandum in opposition to Liddy's petition for certiorari.
January 27, 1975	Liddy petition for certiorari is denied.
January 28, 1975	Ratrie, Robbins and Schweitzer, Inc., pleads guilty to violations of 18 U.S.C. 610; fined $2,500.
	Harry Ratrie and Augustus Robbins, III, of RR&S, plead guilty to non-willful violations of 18 U.S.C. 610; sentences suspended.
February 7, 1975	Court of Appeals hears oral arguments in Chapin appeal.
February 10, 1975	McCord files petition for writ of certiorari in break-in conviction.
February 12, 1975	Grand Jury II expires.
February 19, 1975	Frank DeMarco and Ralph Newman are indicted for conspiracy to defraud the U.S. and the IRS in connection with the donation of the pre-presidential papers of Richard Nixon.
February 21, 1975	Sentences handed down in cover-up trial.
February 25, 1975	Court of Appeals affirms convictions of Barker, Martinez, Sturgis, Gonzalez and Hunt in Watergate break-in.
March 4, 1975	Brief for the U.S. to reinstate DeDiego indictment is filed.
March 10, 1975	At the request of the Special Prosecutor, charges against Strachan are dropped.
March 12, 1975	Maurice Stans pleads guilty to three counts, violation of the reporting sections of the Federal Election Campaign Act of 1971, 2 U.S.C., Section 434(a) and (b), 441; and two counts violation of 18 U.S.C. 610, accepting an illegal campaign contribution.
March 14, 1975	LaRue is sentenced to serve six months in prison.
March 19, 1975	DeMarco and Newman file a motion to have their case transferred.
March 31, 1975	Brief for the U.S. in the conviction appeal of Howard Reinecke is filed.
April 2, 1975	Trial of John Connally begins.
April 16, 1975	Court of Appeals reinstates DeDiego indictment.
April 17, 1975	Connally is acquitted on two counts.
April 18, 1975	Court dismisses remaining three counts against Connally on motion of the Special Prosecutor.
April 21, 1975	McCord petition for writ of certiorari is denied.
April 23, 1975	Morgan is released from prison.
May 2, 1975	Brief for the U.S. in the conviction appeal of Ehrlichman, Barker, Martinez, and Liddy is filed (Fielding break-in).
May 5, 1975	Babcock files appeal of sentence on his guilty plea.

May 6, 1975	U.S. files petition for a writ of mandamus in DeMarco-Newman case.
May 8, 1975	Jury in New York City finds Chestnut guilty.
May 14, 1975	Stans is fined $5,000.
May 19, 1975	Judge Gesell dismisses charges against De-Diego at the request of the Special Prosecutor.
May 29, 1975	McCord is released from prison.
June 6, 1975	Court of Appeals hears oral arguments in Reinecke appeal.
June 11, 1975	Wendell Wyatt pleads guilty to a misdemeanor violation of the reporting provisions of the Federal Election Campaign Act of 1971.
June 18, 1975	Court of Appeals hears oral arguments in Ehrlichman appeal (Fielding break-in).
June 23–25, 1975	Richard M. Nixon gives sworn testimony in matters under investigation by the Special Prosecutor.
June 26, 1975	Chestnut is sentenced to serve four months in prison and is fined $5,000.
July 3, 1975	Grand Jury III expires.
July 11, 1975	Russell convicted on all three counts in San Antonio, Texas.
July 14, 1975	Court of Appeals affirms Chapin conviction.
July 18, 1975	Wendell Wyatt is fined $750.
September 11, 1975	Judge Ferguson grants dismissal of two charges against Frank DeMarco.
September 18, 1975	DeMarco trial begins in Los Angeles.
October 1, 1975	Armand Hammer pleads guilty to three counts of violating 2 U.S.C. 440; making a contribution in the name of another person.
October 9, 1975	Judge Ferguson dismisses the remaining charges against Frank DeMarco, and discharges the case.
October 15, 1975	Brief for the United States is filed in the Watergate cover-up appeal.
October 16, 1975	Report of WSPF is released to the public.
October 16, 1975	Henry S. Ruth, Jr., resigns as Special Prosecutor.
October 17, 1975	Charles F. C. Ruff is sworn in as Special Prosecutor.
October 28, 1975	Newman trial begins in Chicago.
November 12, 1975	Jury convicts Newman on all charges.
December 8, 1975	United States Court of Appeals for the District of Columbia reverses conviction of Howard E. Reinecke.
	Court of Appeals for the Fifth Circuit reverses a lower court ruling and sustains the motion to dismiss an indictment against Jake Jacobsen.
December 14, 1975	Judge Jones withdraws Armand Hammer's October 1 guilty plea, and enters a plea of not guilty for the defendant.

HANDOUT **13-10 (cont.)**

December 22, 1975	Judge Gesell reduces Chapin's sentence of from ten to thirty months, to six to eighteen months.
January 6, 1976	Court of Appeals hears oral arguments in Watergate cover-up appeals.
	Ralph Newman is fined $10,000.
January 29, 1976	James R. Jones pleads guilty to violating reporting provision of the Federal Election Campaign Act.
February 10, 1976	Court of Appeals affirms lower court sentence of Tim Babcock.
February 13, 1976	Court of Appeals affirms lower court denial of sentence reduction for G. Gordon Liddy.
March 4, 1976	Armand Hammer re-enters his guilty plea in Los Angeles.
March 8, 1976	Court of Appeals affirms lower court conviction of Jack Chestnut.
March 12, 1976	WSPF indicts Claude C. Wild, Jr., on two counts of making illegal campaign contributions.
March 16, 1976	James R. Jones is fined $200.
March 23, 1976	Armand Hammer is fined $3,000 and placed on probation for one year.
May 17, 1976	Court of Appeals rules on Fielding break-in case; affirms convictions of Ehrlichman and Liddy and reverses convictions of Barker and Martinez.
June 4, 1976	WSPF indicts William C. Viglia on making false statements to a grand jury.
	Judge Hart vacates prison sentence and fines Tim Babcock $1,000.
June 24, 1976	Judge Waddy dismisses the second count of the Wild indictment.
July 2, 1976	Viglia pleads guilty to June 4 indictment.
July 26, 1976	Trial of Claude Wild begins.
July 27, 1976	Wild is acquitted.
August 3, 1976	Viglia is sentenced to serve one year in prison.
August 5, 1976	Court of Appeals for the Fifth Circuit vacates judgment and dismisses indictment against Stuart Russell.
August 20, 1976	Judge Hart places Jake Jacobsen on probation for two years.
September 23, 1976	W. Marvin Watson pleads guilty to being an accessory after the fact to Armand Hammer's illegal campaign contributions; he is fined $500.
October 12, 1976	Court of Appeals rules on Watergate cover-up case; affirms lower court convictions of Haldeman, Ehrlichman and Mitchell; Mardian's conviction is reversed and his case is remanded for re-trial.

HANDOUT **13-10** (cont.)

October 14, 1976	WSPF releases statement on Ford investigation.
November 10, 1976	Indictments against Barker and Martinez are dismissed.
November 18, 1976	Viglia is released from prison; sentence is reduced to time served.
January 7, 1977	Indictment against Mardian is dismissed.
January 21, 1977	Court of Appeals rules in *U.S.* v. *Wild;* reverses decision of lower court and reinstates second count of the indictment.
February 22, 1977	Supreme Court denies Ehrlichman petition for certiorari in Fielding break-in.
March 30, 1977	Court of Appeals affirms ruling of lower court in *U.S.* v. *DeMarco.*
May 16, 1977	Supreme Court denies Wild petition for certiorari.
May 23, 1977	Supreme Court denies petitions for certiorari in Watergate cover-up appeal.

PART III: BIBLIOGRAPHY

Blind Ambition: The White House Years by John Dean. New York: Simon & Schuster, 1976.
The Company by John Ehrlichman. New York: Simon & Schuster, 1976.
The End of Power by H. R. Haldeman. New York: Times Books, 1978.
"The Legacy of Watergate," *Newsweek,* June 14, 1982, pp. 36–40.
Memoirs by Richard Nixon. New York: Grosset, 1978.
*The New York Times School Microfilm Collection Guide: Period 13, Richard Nixon and
    Watergate, 1973–1974.* Sanford, N.C.: Microfilming Corporation of America, 1979.
The Right and the Power: The Prosecution of Watergate by Leon Jaworski. New York:
    Reader's Digest Books, dist. by Crowell, 1976.
Watergate Special Prosecution Force: Final Report. Washington, D.C.: Government Printing Office, 1977.
"Where Are They Now," *Newsweek,* June 14, 1982, pp. 42–45.
"Years of Upheaval: Watergate" by Henry Kissinger, *Time,* March 8, 1982, pp. 42–61.

HANDOUT **13-11**   JONESTOWN: A CASE STUDY OF MASS SUICIDE*

PART I: STUDENT RESEARCH PRESENTATION

I. Introduction: On November 18, 1978, the following events took place:
  A. Congressman Leo Ryan, three American newspaper reporters, and a cult member were shot on the order of cult leader Jim Jones.
  B. Jim Jones, head of the People's Temple of Disciples of Christ cult, ordered members of the church to commit suicide by drinking fruit juice mixed with cyanide.
    1. The vast majority of the 911 members voluntarily drank the poisoned fruit juice.
    2. Among them were 260 children.
    3. Members who refused were either forced to drink the poison or injected with the poison.
II. Who was Jim Jones?
  A. Jim Jones was a preacher in San Francisco.
    1. Founded the People's Temple of Disciples of Christ.

*Great Event Three as reported in the *New York Times* (Sanford, N.C.: Microfilming Corp.
of America, 1981), pp. 81–82.

HANDOUT 13-11 (cont.)

     2. Became a political activist in California.
     3. Combined religion and politics.
     4. Preached the brotherhood of man, socialism, and obedience to Jones as the representative of Christ.
  B. He established Jonestown in Guyana as a socialist-religious community.
     1. Members voluntarily left the United States and migrated to Jonestown.
     2. Members voluntarily gave to Jones their money and possessions.
III. Jones's power was absolute.
  A. Exuded great charm, warmth.
  B. As a preacher, was dramatic and inspiring.
  C. Gave the members of the community a feeling of security and love.
  D. Vast majority were convinced of his loving concern for each one of them; they trusted him and obeyed him without question.
  E. Those who became disenchanted and wanted to leave were prevented from doing so; some were threatened with death if they openly expressed dissatisfaction.
  F. Rumors that some were being held prisoner and that many were being criminally exploited reached the attention of California Congressman Leo Ryan.
     1. He went to Jonestown to investigate.
     2. He was returning to the United States with evidence he had gathered as well as with members who wanted to return to the United States—to be rescued from the cult.
  G. Jim Jones ordered the entire group killed as they were about to board the plane.
  H. Realizing that he had no other alternative but to take his own life to avoid prosecution, he ordered all the members to join him in his suicide.
     1. Eyewitness accounts of those few who successfully hid in the jungle tell of the happenings.
     2. Hundreds of hours of tapes, including the entire suicide tragedy, were found by U.S. authorities and were made available to newspapers and other reporters. There can be no question of what was said and what was done—it is beyond doubt.
IV. Jonestown in retrospect.
  A. Psychologists and psychiatrists offer the following explanations:
     1. Many people want security and will give up their freedom for security.
     2. Many people want identity with a cause and will sacrifice willingly for that cause.
     3. Many people are spellbound by oratory and personal charm; they cannot see below the surface of the *real* person who is exploiting them; Jones left a personal bank account of $10,000,000.
  B. Suicide is a many-faceted phenomenon in human history.
     1. Psychiatrists identify three main kinds of suicide:
       altruistic, egoistic, and anomic.
     2. In what way is suicide an outgrowth of group rather than individual impulse?
  C. One commentator suggested that the news media are reluctant to publicize religious issues and disputes, and, therefore, had not exposed Jim Jones for the fraud he was. The question remains, would anyone have believed that what happened at Jonestown was within the realm of possibility?

PART II: BIBLIOGRAPHY

Great Events/Three as Reported in The New York Times. Sanford, N.C.: Microfilming Corporation of America, 1981, pp. 81–82. Program guide and 48 microfiche.
The New York Times School Microfilm Collection: Subject Index 1979. Sanford, N.C.: Microfilming Corporation of America, 1981.
Suicide by Emile Durkheim. New York: Free Press, 1951. Also paper.
Suicide: The Hidden Epidemic by Margaret O. Hyde and Elizabeth H. Forsyth. New York: Watts, 1978.

HANDOUT 13-11 (cont.)

AUDIO PRINT MODULE

Father Cares: The Last of Jonestown (National Public Radio—2 parts, 90 min. each; 2 cassettes, 1 Teaching Guide).* Part 1: *Father Cares: The Last of Jonestown*—a dramatic documentary based on James Reston, Jr.'s book *Our Father Who Art in Hell,* which is based on the tapes found in Jonestown and released to Reston under the Freedom of Information Act. Part 2: *National Call-In and Panel Discussion.*

*The teacher's guide to the Audio Print Module *Father Cares: The Last of Jonestown* (Washington, D.C.: National Public Radio), is a 16-page booklet "designed to augment the material in the audio portion of the module." In addition to providing summaries of both programs, it offers a chronology of Jim Jones' life and the events of Jonestown as well as questions and topics for discussion and research. Also a series of short essays explores the issues surrounding Jim Jones and the People's Temple and contains background information on the people and events in Guyana.

Model 14

Advanced Placement
American History

GRADES: 11 or 12.
DURATION: One year (two semesters).

PURPOSE

The Advanced Placement Program in American History is designed to provide
students with the analytic skills and factual knowledge necessary to deal critically with the problems and materials in American history. The program prepares students for intermediate and advanced college courses by making demands on them equivalent to those of full-year introductory college courses.
Students should learn to assess historical materials—their relevance to a given
interpretative problem, their reliability, and their importance—and to weigh
the evidence and interpretations presented in historical scholarship. An Advanced Placement American History course should thus develop the skills necessary to arrive at conclusions on the basis of an informed judgment and to
present reasons and evidence clearly and persuasively in essay format.[*]

INTRODUCTION

A History of the United States by Daniel J. Boorstin and Brooks Mather Kelley
(Lexington, Mass.: Ginn, 1981) has been selected as the basic textbook[†] because of its scholarly but readable text, student appeal, skill integration, and
direct involvement of the learner in the interpretation of history. The textbook
has an attractive format, is copiously illustrated, and is organized for easy
retrieval of pertinent information.

[*]*Advanced Placement Course Description: History* (New York: College Entrance Examination
Board, 1981), p. 1.
[†]This text is the authors' selection; the College Board does not recommend specific texts for any
Advanced Placement course.

The *Teacher's Guide* to the textbook (Ginn, 1981) is a teaching tool second to none in the entire field of American history study. This 320-page guide is in reality a total course of study, including:

1. Instructional objectives for each of the 35 textbook chapters, stressing both cognitive and affective domains.
2. Teaching suggestions for each of the 35 textbook chapters, providing a wealth of instructional procedures, techniques, strategies, and activities.
3. Up-to-date, comprehensive, and relevant bibliographies for each of the 12 major units.
4. Fifty handouts are included, each of which—whether a chronology, statistical summary, historical document, or graphic—brings greater impact to student awareness and involvement in America's history.
5. Twelve unit tests in addition to a final test.

Throughout this course a collateral reference source, *Documentary Sources of Western Civilization* by Eric Rothschild (Sanford, N.C.: Microfilming Corporation of America, 1977), is required reading. This reference set is a comprehensive collection of primary source material in American history in microform. These materials include rare historical texts available only from such research facilities as the Library of Congress, Yale University Library, the New York Public Library, and Columbia University Libraries; government documents and other materials drawn from the collections of the National Archives; oral histories from Columbia University's outstanding Oral History Research Collection; and newspapers from England and the United States. This set is more comprehensive and provides more "raw" materials than any other primary source collection in print. Moreover, it is a *total program* for the study and interpretation of history.

The primary source selections in microform are accompanied by curriculum support materials, guides, and indexes. All material is organized chronologically and by 18 major universal themes:

1. Communication and Transportation
2. Dissent: Reform or Revolution
3. Education and the Values of Society
4. Exploring the Unknown
5. The Farmer and the Worker
6. Law, Judicial Systems, and the Values of Society
7. Lawlessness, Corruption, and Violence
8. Politics, Leaders, and Heroic Myths
9. Minorities, Immigrants, and Slaves
10. Poverty and the Response to It
11. Religion and the Values of Society
12. Science, Medicine, Technology, and the Environment
13. Sports and Leisure Time
14. Urbanization and Industrialization
15. Utopia
16. War and Peace
17. Women
18. The Young

Documentary Sources of Western Civilization is an excellent resource for preparing students for the Advanced Placement exam in American History, especially for the essay and document-based questions. The Advanced Placement exam requires that students demonstrate skill in historical analysis, broad knowledge of trends and events, and the ability to define and formulate judgments of historical data and the relationships of individuals, groups, and ideas in the process of history.

STUDENT ORIENTATION

    I. Students are introduced to the Advanced Placement Program.
        A. Each student receives a copy of the booklet *Advanced Placement Course Description: History.**
        B. The following sections are read and discussed:
            1. The Program
            2. The Course Descriptions
            3. The Examinations
            4. The Reading
            5. The Grades
            6. The Student and College
            7. American History: Purpose, Students, College Course, Advanced Placement Course, The Examination

    II. Students are introduced to the basic text, *A History of the United States.*
        A. The authors of this textbook are noted scholars, historians, and writers.
            1. Daniel J. Boorstin, Pulitzer Prize–winning historian, educator, and author, was appointed Librarian of Congress in 1975. He had previously been director of the National Museum of History and Technology, prior to which he was professor of history at the University of Chicago for 25 years. Dr. Boorstin received his undergraduate degree from Harvard University and his doctorate from Yale. As a Rhodes Scholar he attended Oxford and earned two law degrees, then practiced law for a time in London. As a writer, Dr. Boorstin has received wide acclaim. His trilogy, *The Americans* (New York: Random), received the following awards: the first volume, *The Colonial Experience* (1958), won the Bancroft Prize; the second volume, *The National Experience* (1965), received the Parkman Prize; and the third, *The Democratic Experience* (1973), was awarded the Pulitzer Prize for History and the Dexter Prize. (Boorstin's trilogy is required reading—see Handout 14-1 at the end of this model, the Schedule).
            2. Brooks Mather Kelley is a research affiliate in history at Yale University. He was University Archivist and Curator of Historical Manuscripts at Yale, has taught American history at the Illinois Institute of Technology, and has been visiting professor at Brown University. Dr. Kelley received his undergraduate degree from Yale University and his M.A. and Ph.D. from the University of Chicago. His publications include *Yale: A History and New Haven Heritage . . .* and numerous articles and book reviews.

B. The Prologue sets forth the underlying theme of the course of study as well as the textbook (see Handout 14-2 at the end of this model).

C. The headnotes of each chapter are invaluable thought-generators and thought-directors worthy of being read and pondered.

D. The section and chapter reviews are invaluable resources for self-evaluation: read and respond to each question. If you can answer correctly, move on to the next section or chapter. If you cannot, restudy the section or chapter. Preparation for adequate performance on the collegiate level begins with the student's assuming responsibility for his or her own intellectual discipline and growth.

III. Students are introduced to the reference set *Documentary Sources of Western Civilization.*

A. Each student receives the brochure *Documentary Sources of Western Civilization,* supplied free of charge by the publisher. The following descriptors are highlighted:

1. Description of the program
   a. Master Guide—3 volumes
   b. Subject Index
   c. Topic Books—18 separate books
2. Documents—1,000 landmark documents. Bibliographic information included under each
3. Available on 21 reels of microfilm or on 1,150 105 × 148 mm microfiche. The advisability of using a microfilm reader-projector or a microfiche reader-projector in the classroom to share the original documents with the class is demonstrated.*

B. Sample questions from the Advanced Placement Examination in American History, which are based on interpreting historical documents, are examined and discussed.

IV. Students are introduced to the *Harvard Guide to American History* by Frank Freidel and Richard K. Showman, rev. ed., 2 vols. (Cambridge, Mass.: Belknap Press of Harvard University Press, 1974).

A. The *Harvard Guide* is a standard bibliography of the most valuable works about American history; covers all phases and periods of American history (see Handout 14-3 at the end of this model).

B. This is a *selective* bibliography; the editors have selected the best from the available materials.

V. Students are introduced to the Library of Congress, the Presidential Libraries, and the British Library.

A. Each student receives a copy of the booklet *The Library of Congress: Services to the Nation* (Washington, D.C.: Library of Congress, 1981). The following facts are highlighted:

1. Collections of the Library of Congress include almost 80 million items covering virtually every subject in formats that vary from papyrus to microform.
2. Materials are acquired at the rate of 10 items a minute.

---

*Questions about any phase of this program, including the various types and sources of microform equipment, should be directed to the attention of Howard F. McGinn, Jr., Microfilming Corporation of America, 1620 Hawkins Ave., Box 10, Sanford, N.C. 27330; telephone 800-334-7501.

3. The library has 532 miles of shelves, 20 million books and pamphlets in 60 languages, more than 35 million manuscripts, a 6-million piece music collection, and 10 million photographs and fine prints.

4. For those not able to visit the library, special services are available. Through the interlibrary loan program, materials from the Library of Congress are sent on request to academic, public, or special libraries. The library's National Referral Center is a free service that directs persons who have reference questions to organizations likely to provide the answer; it employs a subject-indexed, computerized file of information for about 13,000 organizations.

5. The staff offers assistance in locating source materials in libraries in the United States and throughout the world.

6. For information, contact by letter or by telephone The Information Office, Library of Congress, Washington, D.C. 20540.

B. Students are introduced to the Presidential Libraries as research depositories. The following facts are highlighted:

1. There are seven Presidential Libraries and one Presidential Museum in the United States.

2. These libraries offer primary source materials such as presidential papers, letters, speeches, and drafts of important documents.

3. Each of the Presidential Libraries is open to the public; each provides on request descriptive booklets detailing the special collections and memorabilia available in the particular library (see Handout 14-4 at the end of this model).

C. Students are introduced to the British Library. The following facts are highlighted:

1. The British Library was established in July 1973 under Act of Parliament; the nucleus for the British Library was the reference library of the British Museum, which had been established in 1757—just in time to house contemporary British accounts of the American Revolution.

2. The British Library is one of the finest research libraries in the world.

3. Books in the reference collection number 10 million.

4. The Official Publications Library houses the largest collection in Europe of official papers of all periods and all countries.

5. The Newspaper Library contains newspapers published after 1800 from all countries and also British provincial papers published before 1800—a rich resource for Colonial American newspapers and journals.

6. All departments of the Reference Division maintain information services; electrostatic copies of most material are made available on request.

7. Photographs, microfilm, and enlargements of microfilm can be supplied of any material; the Newspaper Library supplies free of charge a catalog, *Microfilms of Newspapers and Journals for Sale.*

8. Questions concerning procedure to follow in obtaining materials, advice, information, etc., can be sent directly to the British Information Service.

9. The address of the Reference Division of the British Library is Great Russell Street, London WC1B 3DG, England.

VI. Students are reminded to use the *Student's Guide for Writing College Papers* by Kate L. Turabian, 3rd ed. (Chicago: University of Chicago Press, n.d.) as their style manual and guide for writing research papers.

VII. Students discuss the view of historic continuity as expressed by the philosopher-scholar Moses Hadas:

> View history as "a continuous texture, rolling endlessly off a loom, with colors and patterns growing sometimes richer and more vivid, sometimes fading to drabness, sometimes recalling older patterns, sometimes developing new. What is expected of the humanities is that they familiarize us with antecedent stretches of the work, so that we have a basis for evaluating and perhaps shaping new patterns."*

A. Boorstin's trilogy, *The Americans,* unrolls for the reader the tapestry of our history.

B. The first volume of this work, *The Americans: The Colonial Experience,* is to be read at the conclusion of Unit 1: The Making of Americans as a summary of America's colonial experience.

C. The second volume, *The Americans: The National Experience,* is to be read at the conclusion of Units 2, 3, and 4.

D. The third volume, *The Americans: The Democratic Experience,* is to be read at the conclusion of Units 5–12.

Culminating-Closure Experiences

In 1981, the editors of *Time, Fortune, Money, Life, Discover, People,* and *Sports Illustrated* published special reports on the theme "American Renewal." Each magazine treated a different set of issues; each offered suggestions and recommendations about what could and should be done. All told, there were 23 articles, published as a separate magazine-type book entitled *American Renewal.*[†] The contents of this publication are:

"Introductory Essay" by Henry Grunwald, Editor-in-Chief, Time Inc.

TIME

"To Reform the System." Needed: major changes in government—but not constitutional surgery.

"To Rebuild the Image." Needed: a consistent foreign policy—and muscle.

"To Revive Responsibility." Needed: individual awareness of a new sense of nationhood.

FORTUNE

"How to Regain Our Competitive Edge." A fitness program for industry will require a major shift in the way we use our resources.

"A Tax Strategy to Renew the Economy." First, effective incentives to divert more dollars from spending to savings. Second, depreciation reforms to encourage productive business investment.

---

*Moses Hadas, *Old Wine, New Bottles: A Humanist Teacher at Work* (New York: Simon & Schuster, 1962), p. 16.

[†]Copies of this reprint are available at the cost of $1.50 each. Bulk orders are available: 1–10 copies, $1.50 each; 11–50 copies, $1.25 each; 51–250, $1 each. Send name and address with payment to American Renewal, Time Inc., Box 11011, Chicago, IL 60611.

"The Right Way to Strive for Equality." The commendable push to end discrimination has taken some unexpected and costly turns. Better balance will bring better results.

MONEY

"Fighting Inflation: The Price and the Payoff." Here's what each of us will have to give up in order to bring down those spiraling numbers.

"Your Stake in Boosting Investment." Consuming less and saving more now will bring on a business expansion that benefits everybody.

"A Balance Sheet of Assets." For all its flaws, the United States has unique and sometimes undervalued strengths.

LIFE

"A Call for Quality Education." With discipline and a demand for results, we must recommit our schools to excellence.

"Marshall High Shapes Up." In a Chicago inner-city school, discipline and imagination bring heartening success.

"Cheers for the Tutoring Team." Arizona students help out their classmates.

DISCOVER

"Time to Halt the Retreat from Space." A renewed program would broaden the frontiers of technology, as well as of the mind and spirit.

"Making Science Work." Some prescriptions for the future.

"Energy: Battle for Survival." U.S. policy should encourage development and use of the promising alternatives to oil.

PEOPLE

"Caring." What can one person do? Eight citizens have found the rewards of volunteering by working in their own communities.

"Adapting." As the modern family is redefined, a Pittsburgh steelworker and his young daughter survive the trials of single parenthood.

"Sharing." How can traditional families survive? The Brophys of Colorado fight to stay together on the land.

"Thinking." A panel of experts offers a prognosis for that endangered domestic species: the family.

SPORTS ILLUSTRATED

If the lessons of sport—discipline, competitiveness, teamwork—are to have value in society at large, if indeed the path to the boardroom leads through the locker room, we had better change our priorities.

2. Students receive copies of *American Renewal* six weeks prior to the semester review.
    A. Students are requested to carefully consider the 23 articles; to choose a minimum of two to present to the class.
    B. The presentation during the review session should be limited to three to five minutes to allow for class interaction.
    C. Students are encouraged to offer alternative suggestions for American renewal.
3. As a summation, the students read and discuss *Epilogue: The Mysterious Future* (see Handout 14-5 at the end of this model).

HANDOUT 14-1 SCHEDULE

From	To	Number of Days	Activities
		3	Orientation to the Course of Study and to the Advanced Placement American History Program
		10	Unit 1: The Making of Americans
		1	Unit 1: Review
		14	Unit 2: Forming a New Nation
		1	Unit 2: Review
		14	Unit 3: E Pluribus Unum: One Made from Many
		1	Unit 3: Review
		14	Unit 4: A Nation Growing and Dividing
		1	Unit 4: Review
		14	Unit 5: The Rocky Road to Union
		1	Unit 5: Review
		14	Unit 6: The New Industrial Age
		1	Unit 6: Review
		1	Semester Review
First Semester		90 days	
		12	Unit 7: Democratic Reforms and World Power
		1	Unit 7: Review
		12	Unit 8: From Boom to Bust
		1	Unit 8: Review
		14	Unit 9: Depression at Home and Aggression Abroad
		1	Unit 9: Review
		2	Preparation for Advanced Placement American History Test
		14	Unit 10: Postwar Problems
		1	Unit 10: Review
		14	Unit 11: Turbulent Times
		1	Unit 11: Review
		14	Unit 12: The United States Looks Ahead
		1	Unit 12: Review
		2	Course Review
Second Semester		90 days	

HANDOUT 14-2 PROLOGUE*

American history is the story of a magic transformation. How did people from everywhere join the American family? How did men and women from a tired Old World, where people thought they knew what to expect, become wide-eyed explorers of a New World?

Our history is the story of these millions in search of what it means to be an American.

*Daniel J. Boorstin and Brooks Mather Kelley, *A History of the United States*. Copyright © 1981 by Ginn and Company (Xerox Corporation). Used with permission (Lexington, Mass.: Ginn, 1981), p. 1.

HANDOUT 14-2 (cont.)

In the Old World people knew quite definitely whether they were English, French, or Spanish. But here it took time for them to discover that they really were Americans.

What does it mean to be an American? To answer that question we must shake hands with our earlier selves and try to become acquainted. We must discover what puzzled and interested and troubled earlier Americans.

What has been especially American about our ways of living and earning a living? Our ways of making war and making peace? Our ways of thinking and hoping and fearing, of worshiping God and fighting the Devil? Our ways of traveling and politicking, of importing people, of building houses and cities? These are some of the questions we try to answer in this book.

Discovering America is a way of discovering ourselves. This is a book about us.

HANDOUT 14-3 *HARVARD GUIDE TO AMERICAN HISTORY:* CONTENTS ANALYSIS*

VOLUME I

PART ONE: RESEARCH METHODS AND MATERIALS

1. Research, Writing, and Publication
2. Care and Editing of Manuscripts
3. Materials of History
4. Aids to Historical Research
5. Printed Public Documents
6. Unpublished Primary Sources
7. Microform Materials
8. Printed Historical Works

PART TWO: BIOGRAPHIES AND PERSONAL RECORDS

9. Travels and Description
10. Biographies and Writings

PART THREE: COMPREHENSIVE AND AREA HISTORIES

11. Introduction to American History
12. Regional, State, and Local Histories
13. Westward Expansion and the Frontier

PART FOUR: HISTORIES OF SPECIAL SUBJECTS

14. Physical Environment
15. Government
16. Law
17. Politics
18. Economic History
19. Demography and Social Structure
20. Immigration and Ethnicity
21. Social Ills and Reform
22. Social Manners and Customs
23. Education
24. Religion
25. Intellectual History
26. Literature
27. Communication
28. The Arts
29. Pure and Applied Sciences

Harvard Guide to American History, ed. by Frank Freidel and Richard K. Showman, rev. ed., 2 vols. (Cambridge, Mass.: Belknap Press of Harvard University Press, 1974).

HANDOUT 14-3 (cont.)

VOLUME II

Part Five: America to 1789

30. Colonial Period to 1789
31. Age of Discovery
32. Non-English Settlements in America
33. Rise of Anglo-America
34. Development of the Colonies, 1688–1763
35. British Empire and Colonial Policy, 1660–1763
36. Revolutionary Era, 1763–1789
37. Histories of Special Subjects

Part Six: United States, 1789–1860

38. United States, 1789–1860
39. Federalist Era, 1789–1801
40. Republican Supremacy, 1801–1817
41. New Nationalism, 1817–1829
42. Jacksonian Democracy, 1829–1841
43. Manifest Destiny
44. Old South, Slavery, and Abolitionism
45. Making of the Civil War

Part Seven: Civil War and Reconstruction

46. Civil War, 1860–1865
47. Era of Reconstruction, 1865–1877

Part Eight: Rise of Industry and Empire

48. The Gilded Age, 1877–1900
49. American Empire, 1898–1933

Part Nine: Twentieth Century

50. United States in the Twentieth Century
51. Progressive Era
52. The Twenties
53. Depression, Hoover Administration, and New Deal
54. World War II, 1941–1945
55. Domestic Issues since 1945
56. Foreign Relations since 1945

HANDOUT 14-4   PRESIDENTIAL LIBRARIES AND MUSEUMS

Herbert Hoover Presidential Library and Museum, West Branch, IA 52358
Franklin D. Roosevelt Library and Museum, Albany Post Road, Hyde Park, NY 12538
Harry S. Truman Library, Independence, MO 64050
Dwight D. Eisenhower Library, Abilene, KS 67410
John F. Kennedy Library, Columbia Point, Boston, MA 02125
Lyndon B. Johnson Library and Museum, 2313 Red River, Austin, TX 78705
Gerald R. Ford Library, 1000 Beal Avenue, Ann Arbor, MI 48109
Gerald R. Ford Museum, 303 Pearl Street N.W., Grand Rapids, MI 49504

HANDOUT **14-5**   EPILOGUE: THE MYSTERIOUS FUTURE*

When we look back on the story of America, we feel very wise. In some ways we really are even wiser than William Bradford or Benjamin Franklin or George Washington or Abraham Lincoln.

We know what they did not know. What for us is history, for them, would have been prophecy. For we know how it turned out. They had to guess.

We can see how right it was for the Pilgrims to risk the long voyage across the wild ocean. We see how lucky it was that the thirteen little colonies somehow united for independence. We can see how much better the American Revolution would have been fought with a stronger, more unified Continental Army.

We can see how futile were all the "compromises" on slavery before the Civil War. We can see, too, the Civil War toll in blood and hate. We can see that while the Civil War abolished slavery and saved the Union, it cost more than 600,000 lives and created new hates that would not quickly die.

From American history we can learn that the future is always full of surprising secrets. This New World has been such an exciting place because it has been so new. The great achievements of America are mostly things that never before seemed possible.

Which signers of the Declaration of Independence in 1776 could have imagined that their feeble little confederation, in two centuries, would be the world's greatest democracy—a continent-nation of more than 200 million people, the refuge of the world, the strongest nation on earth?

Of those 55 men in Philadelphia struggling in the hot summer of 1787 to agree on how to prevent the colonies from falling apart—how many would have believed that their work would become the longest-lived written constitution in history?

Who would have imagined that a nation of immigrants, the most miscellaneous people on earth, would someday be the most powerful? Or that men and women from the Western Hemisphere, from all over Europe, from Africa and Asia—of many races and religions and traditions—would adopt one language, and become loyal builders of one new nation?

Who would have guessed that out of the American wilderness (still only half explored in 1850) so soon would come men to explore the moon, and then to send marvelously complicated machines into space to photograph and study the planets of our solar system? Or that modern science, which brings us from the whole universe the boundless vistas of the radio-telescope, would discover strange new kinds of knowledge, and keep us ever faithful to the motto, "Toward the Unknown!"

These were some of the happy surprises. But there were others not quite so happy, and to the founders of our nation just as secret.

Who would have guessed that, within less than 200 years, a trackless half-mapped continent could be crisscrossed by superhighways, defaced by billboards and tin cans? Who would have guessed that Americans would perfect horseless carriages to go a hundred miles an hour—and yet be stuck in traffic jams where they could not even move as fast as a walking horse? Or that ten times as many would be killed by these horseless carriages every year as were killed in all the battles of the American Revolution?

Who would have imagined that the fresh air of a New World would begin to be smoke-filled? Or that the sparkling waters of lakes and rivers would become so darkened and dirtied by factory sewage that even the fish found them unlivable and the birds no longer enjoyed their shores?

Who would have believed that the wonderful American silences—once broken by Indian chants or the songs of birds or the call of the coyote—would be shattered by the roar of speeding jets, lumbering trucks, and ear-jarring motocycles? Who would have believed that a continent, once frightening by its emptiness, would now terrify people by crowding them together?

Who would have believed that a nation of nations, created by peoples of all races from everywhere, which had suffered through a bloody war for union and for freedom, would see new forms of racism?

HANDOUT 14-5 (cont.)

Who would have believed that a nation designed to be a refuge for all people from the violence of the Old World could ever be plagued by reckless violence within?

Who would have foreseen that a nation rich in natural resources—in coal, oil, uranium, natural gas, and flowing water—would fear that it might be crippled by a lack of enough energy to run its cars and factories and to warm its houses?

But Americans have always faced hard problems. We, even more than other people, love the adventure of the unexpected. Ours has always been a story of dealing with the unknown, a story of movement and discovery—to America, within America, from America. The future is just as much a mystery story as it ever was.

Americans have been planters in this faraway land, builders of cities in the wilderness, Go-Getters. Americans—makers of something out of nothing—have delivered a new way of life to far corners of the world.

If the future is a mystery story, then, that does not frighten Americans. For we Americans have always lived in the world's greatest treasure house of the unexpected.

Model 15

Data Processing:
An Introductory Course

GRADES: 11 or 12.

DURATION: One year (Two semesters).*

GOAL: To introduce the students to the world of computers—how they work, their myriad uses, their evolution, hardware and software, information-processing systems, and programming in BASIC.

OBJECTIVES

To provide a general orientation to the computer—what it is, what it does, what it cannot do, and how it operates.

To provide insight into the social and economic impact of computers today and in the future.

To provide information about computer occupations.

To provide at the senior high school level computer programming experience so that students will better be able to judge whether to pursue data processing at the collegiate level.

INTRODUCTION

The search for an introductory data processing course that was both "basic" and highly "teachable"—written in a clear, understandable style; with contents organized in a manageable, step-by-step sequence; and offering a total program of uniform excellence—had ended for the authors of this book in disap-

*The course as outlined in *Data Processing: An Introduction with BASIC* by Donald D. Spencer, 2nd ed. (Columbus, Ohio: Merrill, 1982) is designed for use in an introductory course on the collegiate level of one semester's length. It is recommended that a total of two semesters be devoted to this course when it is being offered to a class. If this program is used as a programmed text for independent study, the one semester may well be appropriate.

pointment until *Data Processing: An Introduction with BASIC* by Donald D. Spencer came to hand.

Besides the basic text, this very teachable program includes (also by Spencer and published by Merrill, 1982) *Instructor's Professional Resource Guide* and *Student Guide*.

The basic text is divided into four parts, which contain 23 chapters. The chapters are divided into short topics (see Example 15-1, Data Processing Contents, at the end of this model). Interpersed throughout each chapter are review questions to help the student evaluate and reinforce his or her grasp of the basic concepts.

The *Instructor's Professional Resource Guide* could well serve as a model of pedagogical course design. It offers the teacher study guides, test banks, transparency masters, chapter notes, and teaching aids and suggestions.

The *Student Guide* is designed to help the student "recognize, study, review and remember the important ideas, terms, concepts and techniques" outlined in the text.

The author stresses the point that "no mathematical or data processing background is required or assumed; no specific computer make or model is featured. The book may be used without access to a computer" (preface, p. viii).

An enrichment learning experience worthy of the students' time is the introduction of *The New York Times Information Service's Data Bank*. The service makes available on request a comprehensive booklet entitled *The Information Bank*. This booklet explains in detail the following:

1. The Information Bank Concept
2. The Information Bank Database
3. Information Bank Abstracts
4. How the Information Bank Is Used
5. The Information Bank System
6. Increasing Research Productivity
7. Applications and Results: Case Studies

EXAMPLE 15-1   DATA PROCESSING CONTENTS*

1. *Welcome to the World of Computers*	Review Questions
A Computerized World	Telling the Computer What to Do
Why Study about Computers?	Computer Occupations
Computers for Many Purposes	Computer Trends
Review Questions	Review Questions
How the Computer Works	Summary
Basic Components of a Computer System	Key Terms
PART ONE: APPLICATIONS AND HISTORY	
2. *What Computers Can Do*	Computers in Education
Impact on Society	Review Questions
Review Questions	Computers in Transportation
Computers in Business and Finance	Review Questions
Review Questions	Computers and Crime
Computers in Medicine	Computers for Control

*Donald D. Spencer, *Data Processing: An Introduction with BASIC*, 2nd ed. (Columbus, Ohio: (Merrill, 1982).

EXAMPLE 15-1 (cont.)

EXAMPLE 15-1 (cont.)

EXAMPLE 15-1 (cont.)

Directory of Major Publishers, Producers, and Distributors

AMS Press, Inc.
56 E. 13 St.
New York, NY 10003

Abingdon Press
201 Eighth Ave. S.
Nashville, TN 37202

Harry N. Abrams, Inc.
110 E. 59 St.
New York, NY 10022

Addison-Wesley Publishing Co., Inc.
Jacob Way
Reading, MA 01867

Advanced Placement College Board
(see The College Board)

Airmont Publishing Co., Inc.
(Distributed by Associated Booksellers)

Allyn and Bacon, Inc.
470 Atlantic Ave.
Boston, MA 02210

American Association of Advertising
  Agencies
666 Third Ave., 13 fl.
New York, NY 10017

American Automobile Association
8111 Gatehouse Rd.
Falls Church, VA 22042

American Broadcasting Co.
1330 Ave. of the Americas
New York, NY 10019

American Elsevier Publishers
2 Park Ave.
New York, NY 10016

American Fisheries Society
5410 Grosvenor Lane
Bethesda, MD 20014

American Heritage Press
1221 Ave. of the Americas
New York, NY 10036

American Library Association
50 E. Huron St.
Chicago, IL 60611

American Pageant
Produced by Media Systems
Consultants for the Perfection Form Co.
Logan, Iowa 51546

American Society of Newspaper Editors
Box 551
1350 Sullivan Trail
Easton, PA 18042

Appleton-Century Crofts
(see Prentice-Hall, Inc.)

Archway Paperbacks
630 Fifth Ave.
New York, NY 10020

Associated Booksellers
147 McKinley Ave.
Bridgeport, CT 06606

Association Sterling Films
(see Sterling Educational Films)

Astor-Honor, Inc.
270 Madison Ave.
New York, NY 10016

Atheneum Publishers
122 E. 42 St.
New York, NY 10017

Avon Books
959 Eighth Ave.
New York, NY 10019

BFA Educational Media
Bailey Film Associates
Box 1795
2211 Michigan Ave.
Santa Monica, CA 90406

Ballantine Books
Division of Random House
201 E. 50 St.
New York, NY 10022

Bantam Books, Inc.
666 Fifth Ave.
New York, NY 10019

Barnes & Noble, Inc.
10 E. 53 St.
New York, NY 10022

Beacon Press
25 Beacon St.
Boston, MA 02108

Belknap Press
(see Harvard University Press)

Bellwether Publishing Co.
167 E. 67 St.
New York, NY 10021

Benziger, Bruce & Glencoe, Inc.
866 Third Ave.
New York, NY 10022

Bobbs-Merrill Co.
4300 W. 62 St.
Indianapolis, IN 46206

Bookman
(see Twayne Publishers)

R. R. Bowker Co.
1180 Ave. of the Americas
New York, NY 10036

Boy Scouts of America
North Brunswick, NJ 08902

Bradbury Press
2 Overhill Rd.
Scarsdale, NY 10583

George Braziller, Inc.
One Park Ave.
New York, NY 10016

British Library Reference Division
Great Russell St.
London WC1B 3DG

Bureau of Indian Affairs
Department of the Interior
C St. between 18 & 19
Washington, DC 20240

Cambridge Forum
3 Church St.
Cambridge, MA 02138

Cambridge University Press
32 E. 57 St.
New York, NY 10022

Capitol Records
1750 N. Vine St.
Hollywood, CA 90028

Center for Southern Folklore
Box 40105
Memphis, TN 38104

Childcraft Educational Corp.
(see World Book—Childcraft International, Inc.)

Children's Book Council
67 Irving Pl.
New York, NY 10003

Childrens Press, Inc.
1224 W. Van Buren St.
Chicago, IL 60607

Child's World
1556 Weatherstone Lane
Elgin, IL 60120

Citadel Press
120 Enterprise Ave.
Secaucus, NJ 07094

Citation Press
(see Scholastic Book Services)

City News
163 Dreiser
New York, NY

Clarion Books
(see Houghton Mifflin Co.)

Charles Clark, Inc.
168 Express Drive, South
Brentwood, NY 11717

The College Board
888 Seventh Avenue
New York, NY 10019

Collier Macmillan, Inc.
866 Third Ave.
New York, NY 10022

Collins & World
2080 W. 117 St.
Cleveland, OH 44111

Columbia Broadcasting Co.
51 W. 52 St.
New York, NY 10019

Columbia University Press
562 W. 113 St.
New York, NY 10025

Congressional Information Service
7101 Wisconsin Ave.
Washington, DC 20014

Congressional Quarterly
1414 22 St., N.W.
Washington, DC 20037

CORE Collection Books
11 Middle Neck Rd.
Great Neck, NY 11021

Coronet Instructional Media
65 E. South Water St.
Chicago, IL 60601

Costeau Society, Inc.
777 Third Ave.
New York, NY 10017

Council for Exceptional Children
1920 Association Dr.
Reston, VA 22091

Coward, McCann & Geoghegan, Inc.
200 Madison Ave.
New York, NY 10016

Creative Education
(see Creative Educational Society, Inc.)

Creative Educational Society, Inc.
123 S. Broad St.
Mankato, MN 56001

Creative Learning Press, Inc.
Box 320
Mansfield Center, CT 06250

Crestwood House, Inc.
Box 3427
Highway 66 South
Mankato, MN 56001

Criterion Books, Inc.
666 Fifth Ave.
New York, NY 10019

Thomas Y. Crowell Co.
666 Fifth Ave.
New York, NY 10003

Crown Publishers, Inc.
One Park Ave.
New York, NY 10016

D.O.K. Publishers
71 Radcliffe Rd.
Buffalo, NY 14214

Delacorte Press
(see Dell Publishing Co.)

Dell Publishing Co.
One Dag Hammarskjold Pl.
New York, NY 10017

Dial Press
One Dag Hammarskjold Pl.
New York, NY 10017

Dillon Press, Inc.
500 S. Third St.
Minneapolis, MN 55415

Disney Educational Media, Inc.
500 S. Buena Vista St.
Burbank, CA 91521

Disney Studios
(see Disney Educational Media, Inc.)

Dodd, Mead & Co.
79 Madison Ave.
New York, NY 10016

Doubleday & Co., Inc.
245 Park Ave.
New York, NY 10017

Dover Publications, Inc.
180 Varick St.
New York, NY 10014

E. P. Dutton & Co., Inc.
201 Park Ave.
New York, NY 10003

Educational Dimensions Group
Box 126
Stamford, CT 06904

Educational Enrichment Materials
110 S. Bedford Rd.
Mt. Kisco, NY 10549

Elsevier-Nelson
(see American Elsevier Publishers)

Encyclopaedia Britannica Educational
    Corp.
425 N. Michigan Ave.
Chicago, IL 60611

M. Evans & Co., Inc.
216 E. 49 St.
New York, NY 10017

Evans-Dutton
(see M. Evans & Co., Inc.)

Everest House Publishers
1133 Ave. of the Americas
New York, NY 10036

Eye Gate Media
146-01 Archer Ave.
Jamaica, NY 11435

Face the Nation
Transcript Dept.
CBS News/Washington Office
2020 M St., N.W.
Washington, DC 20036

Facts on File, Inc.
119 W. 57 St.
New York, NY 10019

Farrar Books
Box 2029
Roosevelt Field Station
Garden City, NY 11530

Fawcett Books
1515 Broadway
New York, NY 10036

Fideler Co.
31 Ottawa Ave.
Grand Rapids, MI 49503

Field Enterprises Educational Corp.
510 Merchandise Mart Pl.
Chicago, IL 60654

Films, Inc.
1144 Wilmette Ave.
Wilmette, IL 60091

Folcroft Library Editions
Box 182
Folcroft, PA 19032

Folkways Records
43 W. 61 St.
New York, NY 10023

Follett Library Book Company
4506 Northwest Highway (Route 14 &
  31)
Crystal Lake, IL 60014

Follett Publishing Co.
1010 W. Washington Blvd.
Chicago, IL 60607

Forest Service
U.S. Department of Agriculture
14 & Independence, S.W.
Washington, DC 20250

Four Winds Press
(see Scholastic Book Services)

Free Press
(see Macmillan, Inc.)

Funk & Wagnalls Co.
(Distributed by Thomas Y. Crowell Co.)

Gale Research Co.
Book Tower
Detroit, MI 48226

Gambit
27 North Main St.
Meeting House Green
Ipswich, MA 01938

Garrard Publishing Co.
Champaign, IL 61820

Ginn & Co.
Editorial Offices: 191 Spring St.
Lexington, MA 02173
Order Dept.: Box 2649
1250 Fairwood Ave.
Columbus, OH 43216

Girl Scouts of the U.S.A.
830 Third Ave.
New York, NY 10022

Glencoe Press, Inc.
(see Benziger, Bruce & Glencoe, Inc.)

Golden Press
(see Western Publishing Co., Inc.)

Government Printing Office
(see Superintendent of Documents)

William Greaves Productions, Inc.
254 W. 54 St.
New York, NY 10019

Greenwillow
105 Madison Ave.
New York, NY 10016

Greenwood Press, Inc.
51 Riverside Ave.
Westport, CT 06880

Grolier, Inc.
575 Lexington Ave.
New York, NY 10022

Grosset & Dunlap
51 Madison Ave.
New York, NY 10010

Guidance Associates
757 Third Ave.
New York, NY 10017

E. M. Hale & Co.
1201 S. Hastings Way
Eau Claire, WI 54701

G. K. Hall & Co.
70 Lincoln St.
Boston, MA 02111

Hamish Hamilton
Box 57
North Pomfret, VT 05053

Hammond, Inc.
515 Valley St.
Maplewood, NJ 07040

Harcourt Brace Jovanovich, Inc.
757 Third Ave.
New York, NY 10017

Harmony Books
One Park Ave.
New York, NY 10016

Harmony/Crown
One Park Ave.
New York, NY 10016

Harper & Row Publishers, Inc.
10 E. 53 St.
New York, NY 10022

Harvard University Press
79 Garden St.
Cambridge, MA 02138

Harvey House, Inc.
(see E. M. Hale & Co.)

Haskell House Publishers, Inc.
Box FF
Blythebourne Station
Brooklyn, NY 11219

Hastings House Publishers, Inc.
10 E. 40 St.
New York, NY 10016

Hawthorn Books, Inc.
260 Madison Ave.
New York, NY 10016

Heritage Press
170 Franklin St.
Buffalo, NY 14202

Larry Hill
(see Lawrence Hill & Co., Inc.)

Lawrence Hill & Co., Inc.
520 Riverside Ave.
Westport, CT 06880

Hill & Wang, Inc.
19 Union Sq.
New York, NY 10003

Holiday House, Inc.
18 E. 53 St.
New York, NY 10022

Holt, Rinehart & Winston, Inc.
383 Madison Ave.
New York, NY 10017

Horizon Press Publishers
156 Fifth Ave.
New York, NY 10010

Houghton Mifflin Co.
2 Park St.
Boston, MA 02107

Indiana University Press
Tenth & Morton Sts.
Bloomington, IN 47401

International Publishers
381 Park Ave. S.
Suite 1301
New York, NY 10016

Issues & Answers TV Program
Transcript Bureau
1201 Connecticut Ave.
Washington, DC 20036

Johnson Publishing Co., Inc.
820 S. Michigan Ave.
Chicago, IL 60605

Alfred A. Knopf, Inc.
201 E. 50 St.
New York, NY 10022

Kurzweil Computer Products
33 Cambridge Pkwy.
Cambridge, MA 02142

Larousse & Co., Inc.
572 Fifth Ave.
New York, NY 10036

Christopher Lee Productions
2321 W. Houghton Lake Dr.
Houghton Lake, MI 48629

Lerner Publications Co.
Box 130
Sturgis, MI 49091

Library of Congress
Info. Office
Washington, DC 20540

Library Products
Box 130
Sturgis, MI 49091

Life
(see Time-Life Books)

J. B. Lippincott Co.
E. Washington Sq.
Philadelphia, PA 19105

Listening Library, Inc.
One Park Ave.
Old Greenwich, CT 06870

Little, Brown & Co.
34 Beacon St.
Boston, MA 02106

Live Oak Media
Box 116
Somers, NY 10589

Longman, Inc.
72 Fifth Ave.
New York, NY 10011

Lothrop, Lee & Shepard Co.
105 Madison Ave.
New York, NY 10016

Loyola University Press
3441 N. Ashland Ave.
Chicago, IL 60611

M.I.T. Press
28 Carleton St.
Cambridge, MA 02142

McDougal, Littell & Co.
Box 1667
Evanston, IL 60204

McElderry-Atheneum Co.
(see Atheneum Publishers)

McGraw-Hill Book Co.
1221 Ave. of the Americas
New York, NY 10036

David McKay Co., Inc.
750 Third Ave.
New York, NY 10017

Macmillan Educational Corp.
(see Macmillan, Inc.)

Macmillan, Inc.
866 Third Ave.
New York, NY 10022

Macneil/Lehrer Report TV Program
Transcripts Dept.
WNET
Box 345
New York, NY 10019

Julia MacRae, Franklin Watts, Inc.
387 Park Ave. S.
New York, NY 10016

Marquis-Who's Who Books
200 E. Ohio St.
Chicago, IL 60611

Media Basics
(Distributed by Charles Clark, Inc.)

Meet the Press TV Program
Transcripts Dept.
Kelly Press
Box 8648
Washington, DC 20011

Mentor Books
(see New American Library)

G. & C. Merriam Co.
47 Federal St.
Box 281
Springfield. MA 01101

Merriam Webster
(see G. & C. Merriam Co.)

Julian Messner, Inc.
One W. 39 St.
New York, NY 10018

Methuen, Inc.
733 Third Ave.
New York, NY 10017

Metropolitan Museum of Art
255 Gracie Sta.
New York, NY 10161

Microfilming Corporation of America
1620 Hawkins Ave.
Sanford, NC 27330

Microform Review, Inc.
Box 405
Saugatuck Sta.
Westport, CT 06880

Miller-Brody Productions, Inc.
(see Random House, Inc.)

Mook & Blanchard
Box 1295
La Puente, CA 91749

William Morrow & Co., Inc.
105 Madison Ave.
New York, NY 10016

Music Sales Corp.
33 W. 60 St.
New York, NY 10023

NAL
(see New American Library)

NASA Publications
National Aeronautics & Space Adminis-
tration
Washington, DC 20546

Nash Publishing Co.
(see E. P. Dutton & Co., Inc.)

National Audiovisual Center
Washington, DC 20409

National Audubon Society
950 Third Ave.
New York, NY 10022

National Broadcasting Co.
30 Rockefeller Center
New York, NY 10020

National Council of Teachers of English
1111 Kenyon Rd.
Urbana, IL 61801

National Education Association
1201 16 St., N.W.
Washington, DC 20036

National Gallery of Art
Constitution Ave. at Sixth St., N.W.
Washington, DC 20560

National Geographic Society
17 and M Sts., N.W.
Washington, DC 20036

National Park Service
Dept. of the Interior
Washington, DC 20240 ·

National Public Radio
2025 M St., N.W.
Washington, DC 20036

National Wildlife Federation
8925 Leesburg Pike
Vienna, DC 22180

New American Library
1301 Ave. of the Americas
New York, NY 10019

New York Times Co.
Book Div.
330 Madison Ave.
New York, NY 10017

New York Times Information Service,
Inc.
Mount Pleasant Office Park
1719 Route 10
Parsippany, NJ 07054

Newspaper Enterprise Assn.
200 Park Ave.
New York, NY 10166

W. W. Norton & Co., Inc.
500 Fifth Ave.
New York, NY 10036

Oak Publications
(see Music Sales Corp.)

Oceanic Society
Box 36
Uxbridge, MA 01569

Oxford University Press
200 Madison Ave.
New York, NY 10016

Pacific Books
Box 558
Palo Alto, CA 94302

Pantheon Books
201 E. 50 St.
New York, NY 10022

Parents Magazine Press
52 Vanderbilt Ave.
New York, NY 10017

Parnassus Press
4080 Halleck St.
Emeryville, CA 94608

Pendulum Press, Inc.
Academic Bldg., Saw Mill Rd.
West Haven, CT 06516

Penguin Books, Inc.
625 Madison Ave.
New York, NY 10022

Pennsylvania State University Press
215 Wagner Bldg.
University Park, PA 16802

Perfection Form
1000 N. Second Ave.
Logan, IA 51546

PET Library, Ltd.
Division of Sternco Industries, Inc.
50 Cooper Sq.
New York, NY 10003

Pflaum Publishing Co.
2285 Arbor Blvd.
Dayton, OH 45402

Phi Delta Kappa Educational Foundation
Eighth & Union, Box 789
Bloomington, IN 47401

Philomel Books
51 Madison Ave.
New York, NY 10010

Pied Piper Productions
Box 320
Verdugo City, CA 91046

Pinetree Media, Ltd.
Box 909, Falls Sta.
Niagara Falls, NY 14303

Platt & Munk Publishers
1055 Bronx River Ave.
Bronx, NY 10472

Plays, Inc.
8 Arlington St.
Boston, MA 02116

Praeger Publishers
111 Fifth Ave.
New York, NY 10003

Prentice-Hall, Inc.
301 Sylvan Ave.
Englewood Cliffs, NJ 07632

Prime Time School Television
40 E. Huron
Chicago, IL 60611

Public Broadcasting Service
475 L'Enfant Plaza, S.W.
Washington, DC 20024

Puffin Books
(see Penguin Books, Inc.)

G. P. Putnam's Sons
200 Madison Ave.
New York, NY 10016

Pyramid Press Publishing Co.
1686 Marshall St.
Benwood, WV 26031

Pyramid Publications, Inc.
9 Garden St.
Moonachie, NJ 07074

Quadrangle
The New York Times
10 E. 53 St.
New York, NY 10022

Rand McNally & Co.
Box 7600
Chicago, IL 60680

Random House, Inc.
201 E. 50 St.
New York, NY 10022

Reader's Digest Press
10 E. 53 St.
New York, NY 10022

Reader's Digest Services, Inc.
Educational Div.
Pleasantville, NY 10570

Rinehart Publishing Co.
(see Holt, Rinehart, & Winston, Inc.)

Ronald Press Co.
79 Madison Ave.
New York, NY 10016

Russell & Russell Publishers
122 E. 42 St.
New York, NY 10017

SVE
(see Society for Visual Education, Inc.)

St. Martin's Press, Inc.
175 Fifth Ave.
New York, NY 10010

Schirmer Books
866 Third Ave.
New York, NY 10022

Schloat Productions
(see Sunburst Communications, Inc.)

Schocken Books, Inc.
200 Madison Ave.
New York, NY 10016

Scholastic Book Services
906 Sylvan Ave.
Englewood Cliffs, NJ 07632

Schwann Record Catalogs
535 Boylston St.
Boston, MA 02116

Science Research Associates
155 N. Wacker Dr.
Chicago, IL 60606

Scientific American
415 Madison Ave.
New York, NY 10017

Scott, Foresman & Co.
1900 E. Lake Ave.
Glenview, IL 60025

Scott Publishing Co.
10102 F St.
Omaha, NE 68127

Scott Publishing Co.
3 E. 57 St.
New York, NY 10022

Charles Scribner's Sons
597 Fifth Ave.
New York, NY 10020

Seabury Press, Inc.
815 Second Ave.
New York, NY 10017

Sears Roebuck & Co.
925 Hohman Ave.
Chicago, IL 60607

Silver Burdett Co.
250 James St.
Morristown, NJ 07960

Simon & Schuster, Inc.
1230 Ave. of the Americas
New York, NY 10020

Peter Smith Publisher
6 Lexington Ave.
Gloucester, MA 01930

Smithsonian Institution Press
Rm. 2280
Arts & Industries Bldg.
Washington, DC 20013

Society for Visual Education, Inc.
1345 Diversey Pkwy.
Chicago, IL 60614

Spoken Arts, Inc.
310 North Ave.
New Rochelle, NY 10801

Sterling Educational Films
241 E. 34 St.
New York, NY 10016

Sterling Publishing Co.
419 Park Ave.
New York, NY 10016

Sunburst Communications, Inc.
39 Washington Ave.
Pleasantville, NY 10570

Superintendent of Documents
U.S. Government Printing Office
Washington, DC 20402

Teaching Resources Films, Inc.
Station Plaza
Bedford Hills, NY 10507

Time-Life Books
Division of Time, Inc.
Alexandria, VA 22314

Time-Life, Silver Burdett Inc.
(see Time-Life Books)

Times Books
3 Park Ave.
New York, NY 10016

Troll Associates
320 Rte. 17
Mahwah, NJ 07430

Tudor Publishing Co.
31 W. 46 St.
New York, NY 10036

Charles E. Tuttle Co., Inc.
28 S. Main St.
Rutland, VT 05701

Twayne Publishers
Div. of G. K. Hall & Co.
70 Lincoln St.
Boston, MA 02111

Frederick Ungar Publishing Co., Inc.
250 Park Ave. S.
New York, NY 10003

UNIPUB
Xerox Publishing Co.
1180 Ave. of the Americas
New York, NY 10036

United Artists
729 Seventh Ave.
New York, NY 10019

United Learning
6633 Howard St.
Niles, IL 60648

United Nations
Office of Public Information
New York, NY 10017

U.S. Dept. of Agriculture, Forest Service
14th St. and Independence Ave., S.W.
Washington, DC 20250

U.S. Dept. of Labor
200 Constitution Ave., N.W.
Washington, DC 20210

U.S. Government Printing Office
(see Superintendent of Documents)

U.S. Office of Gifted & Talented
Donahue Bldg., Rm. 3538
Sixth & D Sts., S.W.
Washington, DC 20202

U.S. Postal Service
Stamp Information Service
Box 764
Washington, DC 20036

University of California Press
2223 Fulton St.
Berkeley, CA 94720

University of Toronto Press
33 E. Tupper St.
Buffalo, NY 14203

University of Utah Press
Bldg. 513
Salt Lake City, UT 84112

University of Wisconsin Press
114 N. Murray St.
Madison, WI 53715

Upstart Library Promotionals
Box 976
Hagerstown, MD 21740

D. Van Nostrand Co.
450 W. 33 St.
New York, NY 10001

Vanguard Press, Inc.
424 Madison Ave.
New York, NY 10017

Viking Press
625 Madison Ave.
New York, NY 10022

Henry Z. Walck, Inc.
750 Third Ave.
New York, NY 10017

Walker & Co.
720 Fifth Ave.
New York, NY 10019

Walt Disney
(see Disney Educational Media, Inc.)

Frederick Warne & Co.
2 Park Ave.
New York, NY 10016

Franklin Watts, Inc.
730 Fifth Ave.
New York, NY 10019

Western Publishing Co., Inc.
150 Parish Dr.
Wayne, NJ 07470

Westminster Press
Rm. 905
Witherspoon Bldg.
Philadelphia, PA 19107

Weston Woods Studios
Weston, CT 06883

James T. White Co.
1700 State Highway 3
Clifton, NJ 07013

Albert Whitman & Co.
560 W. Lake St.
Chicago, IL 60606

John Wiley & Sons, Inc.
605 Third Ave.
New York, NY 10016

H. W. Wilson
950 University Ave.
Bronx, NY 10452

Windmill/Simon & Schuster
(see Simon & Schuster, Inc.)

Winston Publishers
(see Holt, Rinehart & Winston, Inc.)

World Book—Childcraft International,
  Inc.
Box 3565
Merchandise Mart Plaza
Chicago, IL 60654

World Book Encyclopedia, Inc.
510 Merchandise Mart Plaza
Chicago, IL 60654

World Publishing Co., Inc.
2080 W. 117 St.
Cleveland, OH 44111

Yale University Press
302 Temple St.
New Haven, CT 06520

Index